ALONG
THE
LINES OF . . . .

ACKNOWLEDGEMENTS

The publishers and editors are grateful for the efforts of the following individuals in making this anthology possible:

Stephen Docherty, John Jackson, Natasha Jackson,
Peter Jones and Joanne Sydenham,

ALONG THE LINES OF....

An Anthology
of verse from the
younger generation

Vanessa Sydenham
Editor

Steve Sydenham
Publisher and Managing Editor

Copyright © 2002 Poetry In Print
as a compilation

Individual copyright to poems
belong to the poet

Cover design and artwork
by Amanda Ross
Prontaprint, Paignton

All rights reserved
No part of this book may be
reproduced in any way without
express permission of the publisher
in writing

ISBN 0-9542332-0-4

Published by
Poetry In Print
PO Box 141
Paignton
TQ3 1YY

Printed in Scotland
by Bell & Bain Ltd., Glasgow

INTRODUCTION

Welcome to our fourth anthology of verse specifically for children and young adults. This came about as a direct result of a competition open to schools and we sincerely thank teachers and parents for their enthusiasm and for helping to make the competition and the anthology such a success.

Congratulations to the winners of the competition and to all of our young contributors, well done, a superb effort by all concerned. Most of the poems that appear within these pages are from young poets whose work is appearing in print for the first time and for many we are sure it will not be the last.

The competition was open to all ages and abilities and for some of the contributors an extraordinary effort was required simply to submit an entry. To these children in particular the excitement of seeing their work published means so much and we sincerely hope this will help to encourage them to write even more in the future. The comments made by their teachers and parents has been most rewarding to all concerned at Poetry In Print.

Theories of what a poem should be are only of minor importance here. It is more important that the student has taken the time to write something, perhaps loosely poetic, but interesting and often unique. The editors have truly enjoyed putting this anthology together. The poems are written with such honesty and openness, coupled with a lively imagination and expression that can only come from young minds.

We wish all of our young contributors much success for the future and hope all of their dreams and aspirations come true and we thank them very sincerely for their efforts.

CONTENTS

Introduction	v
Contest winners	vi
The poems	7
Biographies of poets	338
Index of poets	357

Prizewinners
Open Poetry Competition for Schools

15-18 Years

1st: **Katy Harrison** / Tring, Herts **(Tring School)**

2nd: **Zoë Nicolaides** / Ash, Surrey **(Ash Manor School)**

3rd: **Katherine Barron** (Ash Manor School)   **Stephen Humphrey** (Tring School)
Carly Llewellyn (Baines School)   **Lauryn Riley** (Ash Manor School)
Rosie Woodworth (Ripon Grammar School)

11-14 Years

1st: **Elishia Chave** / Ashburton, Devon **(South Dartmoor Community College)**

2nd: **Natalie Reynolds** / Carshalton Beeches, Surrey **(Wallington High School)**

3rd: **Anna Blunt** (Mayflower High)   **Robert Burton** (Borden Grammar)
Rebecca Hodgson (Bingley Grammar)   **Sally Langford** (Bideford College)
Katie Upton (Bideford College)

8-11 Years

1st: **Jade Gambrill** / Whitstable, Kent **(Swalecliffe County Primary)**

2nd: **Stephanie Butler** / Hatton, Warks. **(Abbotsford School)**

3rd: **Dominic Allan** (Epping Junior)   **James Flynn** (Northbourne Primary)
Jessica Hocking (Stowford Primary)   **Nathan Skelley** (Stowford Primary)
Luke Tarmey (Abbotsford School)

7 Years & under

1st: **Jake White** / Thackley, W. Yorks. **(Wellington Primary School)**

2nd: **Sophia Landon** / Salisbury, Wilts **(Wyndham Park Infants School)**

3rd: **Rebecca Beresford** (Harpur Hill Primary)   **Stephen Hall** (Theydon Bois Primary)
Shenton Morgan (Roselands Infants)   **Katherine Reggler** (Mells First)
Kirsty Wright (St Peter's Primary)

**Congratulations to the Runners-up
and to <u>ALL</u> entrants for such a magnificent effort - Well Done**

First Prize Winners

Time vs Time

To Yesterday,

Babyhood and above, I have been protected from things and thoughts which may have affected,
The ageing and progression of my day-to-day thinking, to save my mind from twisting and sinking.

Violence and sadness were all kept at bay to stop my reasoning from starting to sway,
How could you guess and how could you know that one day I would have those feelings on show.

Alcohol will corrupt and drugs will bring pain, but your holy path leads back to the same.
You despise your government, yet you pay your bills; distortions dismissed because they don't come as pills.

Inside the music of our many mixed cultures are the messages we crave, like meat to the vultures.
All you can decode are the swear words you are hearing, when really it's the heavy issues you are truly fearing.

Your religion and politics are out-dated drugs, challengers and visionaries are what you label 'thugs'.
Despite our many differences, can't we be together? Instead of every tie, we have to cut and sever.

Now I stand before you, I dare you to accept, seeing from my eyes is just another step.
Be brave enough to bridge the gap and allow yourself to see: that all I have become is somebody known as me.

Signed, Tomorrow

Katy Harrison (Age 17)

Second Chances

You hide under a cloak of white,
That represents purity and kindness,
When underneath is a hollow shell
Full of horrors, evil and nothingness

You don't understand affection and love,
But grief and devistation you believe to be
The answer to the trouble caused by you,
Is a lie to seal it that can't be seen.

Truth has never passed your lips,
Only false hopes and false dreams,
You fool people in desperate times
There is no hope for you or so it seems

Do you believe in second chances
For even the cruelest of souls
Even for those who have broken hearts,
For theirs is as black as coal.

Forgiveness is an action for many
For many whose souls really are pure
So find the right rainbow with its pot of gold
And maybe one day your heart may be cured.

Elishia Chave (Age 13)

First Prize Winners

The Boy

Everyone is having fun,
In the picturesque, setting sun,
But one boy is out of sight,
Looking like a ghost in the eve of the night

The tear drops fall heavy and dry,
As he wanders under the blue night sky,
The wind slaps his frozen cheek,
But there alone, it's cold and bleak.

His hands and feet are frozen bare,
Not even a hat covered his uncut hair,
As the place is covered with white snow,
He's a loner without, anywhere to go,

His bony limbs drag on the ground,
The breath from his lips not making a sound,
In amongst the huge city streets,
He turns away in shame, by all he meets.

Jade Gambrill (Age 10)

5, 4, 3, 2, 1

Blast off, it's gone, it's off to space,
America tries to win the race,
People stare, jaws drop in wonder,
Fire thrusts and engines thunder.

Tension rising, pinned in seat,
Wondering if our Maker we'll meet,
Thoughts of loved ones fill our minds,
All unsure of what we'll find.

We gaze in wonder through the glass,
An ocean of stars as we zoom past,
We've travelled far from Earth to space,
We're nearly there, we've won the race.

"Houston, Houston, we're ready to land,
Prepare for wonder, we're on the sand,"
People cheer, then silence came,
Neil Armstrong with his words of fame.

"One small step for man,
And one giant leap for mankind."

Jake White (Age 7)

Second Prize Winners

The Argument

Your words hit me like thunder,
The look you stare freezes me.
We flicker,
Like a candle.
In a chilling,
Wind swept room.
One will win; one will fail to defeat.
So much said, feelings shred.

You stop.
The bitter taste,
I feel shattered, forty winks
Suddenly I think, I've heard you.
So much said feelings shred.
A tear, a cold sour tear,
Tumbles, tumbles down.

Zoe Nicolaides (Age 15)

The Enchanted Blanket

The magic of autumn reveals itself,
In a shower of colour from the trees,
The papery leaves drift to the ground,
Answering the forest floor's pleas,
For a patchwork winter blanket,
With a patch of chocolate leather,
And another of saffron velvet,
To protect it from the bitter weather,
The harsh wind caresses the fabric,
Though it's wrinkled and frail like an old woman's hand,
As it passes it whispers sweet nothings to its lover,
The earthy ground no longer bland,
This natural beauty remains unspoilt,
Until children run through the leaves to hear them crunch,
Enthralled they trample through again and again,
Listening excitedly to hear them scrunch,
Every year the towering giants surrender their leaves,
As they sink to their final resting place,
They dwindle and spiral sauntering lazily,
Drifting unhurried to the end of the race.

Natalie Reynolds (Age 13)

Second Prize Winners

Beach

Stretched out sleepily in the shade,
On a day when the sun is as fierce
As a massive giant overpowering the earth
I'm feeling really hot and sticky
And my face is as red as a ripe red chilli.
The sea looks like a gentle, lapping pet dog,
As I head towards it for a well deserved swim;
But the burning sand covers my feet
Like a small child cuddled up on a cold winter's night.
Making me run as fast as a cheetah sprinting to catch it's prey.
I'm so glad to reach the water.
I splash about like an otter entering the water for the first time.
The tiny waves welcome me
Like my dog when I have been away for a long time,
And I feel as happy and content as I have ever felt.

Stephanie Butler (Age 11)

Dragon Dance

A Chinese dragon is in the street
And dancing on its Chinese feet
Its bulging eyes are shining bright
They are shining in the night
Its claws are sharp
Its tail is thin
It's ready to dance the New Year in.
It has a veil over its head
And all the smoke is puffing red
Its scales are blue, green and red
But the colour is changing instead
Pink, purple, yellow and green,
This is the poem you have seen.

Sophia Landon (Age 7)

Third Prize Winners

Judgement Day

A glazed bead tumbles onto a sacred, scarlet floor,
Joining in matrimony with the sickening descent of blood.
As I stare at you, friend.
Gnarled, desperate claws caress the eternal names,
Rewarded only by stone, like memories they are eroded, scratched.
That steamy earth did launch a thousand decrepit souls beyond the taunt of any bullet.
As I stare at you, friend.
Autumn harvest reaped our glory.
As seedlings we were led to believe our right was to grow,
To stand tall and sacrifice our blossoms to the sun.
The sun did shine with rejection that day.
Through the deafening silence you were laid to rest.
My roots clung to the soil; their continuous strength caused rotting within.
This agonising sting and the insanity, repulsive, wretched, vindictive, insanity!
As I stare at you, friend.
Gouging great pits of remorse, that constant hollow, raw asking.
The vision cloudy, like fond Christmas's of past.
I bring my hideous precipice before you.
Praying your world of tranquillity and devotion can arouse some sympathy for those awaiting their harvest.
As I leave you, friend.

Katherine Barron (Age 15)

The Sanctuary

Heavenward it reaches, climbing up out of the choking tide
Of weeds, tall grass, and forgotten names.
Sonorous chimes call the believer from across the gravestones to prayer.

A monument to grandeur, and to the faith of men.
Smooth flat stone with gleaming flint work with shimmering stained glass
To create a resplendent Gothic prison.

Its hostages are not human. They are dark confessions of the soul.
They are sorrowful goodbyes, the hurts and tears and woes,
And secrets of the past.

Up, upwards they rise, high into forgotten rafters.
High up where no human hears they wail ever on;
The turbulent verse of the gargoyles.

So far from men. So far from God.

Strung up within the rafters, high above his alter grand,
Is suspended the crucified keeper of these dark shadows,
Presiding with pained pity and anger.

Their time cannot be served. Yet where shall be our sanctuary
When the stone is smashed, the rafters ripped open,
And demons roam the earth once more?

Stephen Humphrey (Age 17)

Third Prize Winners

A Flight Of Mourning

A white dove glides across the shattered battlefields
Shot down as though the campaign was its own
It fell
The purest of all
Plummets into the burning black of mankind
The blemished corpse is soiled
Smothered, allowed to suffocate in depravity

Missiles collide with the enemy mound
Illuminating the veiled night sky
Beyond the continuous pit of despair
Which has become our haven

The final raid
A propelling charge of immortality
Ensures weakened casualties remain
Posted amid the profligacy of earlier bombardment

Dawn emerges wounded and torn
The will of survival dispatching the power of greed
Leaving the ghostly silence of Earth's own hell

Lauryn Riley (Age 15)

A Possible Happiness

The sound of the rain on my window
The flutter of birds in the trees
The passing of a beautiful rainbow
All stir happy feelings for me.
The sight of fun filled children
And a couple or two in love
Coloured butterflies riding the wind
Knowing Angels watch from above.
A feeling of everlasting friendship
The loyalty of cat and dog
Watching favourite celebrity on TV
Helping children cheer themselves up.
Knowing that sometime I'll be wanted
That there will be someone for me
And meanwhile I'll watch the stars twinkle
And let that smile just be. . .

Carly Llewellyn (Age 18)

To Dream Only

For all the flowers of the earth we're but a single Rose
empowered by blood filled petals as upon us they enclose

For all the beautiful creatures that pursue this land
we stand only small in the black dirty sand

Inside this hidden life we look out through the rusted jail bars
but our eyes are blinded by shiny black and we may only dream of those . . . stars?

Looking through the steam filled glass the colour strikes your face
the writhing mood fills the darkness at a slow encurling pace

Its beauty brings kindness to a poor man's eyes
but it's blunt and cruel and so painfully wise

Surrounded by darkness into this beauty we're born
but this can only be fake as we conceal the truth. One single thorn.

Rosie Woodworth (Age 15)

Third Prize Winners

To All Who Seek To Judge Me

You people say you know me, you're phoney, say you care,
But all you every think of is the way I cut my hair.
You tell me what to do and say and the way that I should feel,
You tell me what is right and wrong; my hurt I must conceal.
I try so hard to please you but you always ask for more,
You want me to be perfect; when I'm not, you close the door.
You judge me for me family, for the things I like to do,
You treat me like I'm worthless, but you haven't got a clue.
You tell me what's important, you never understand
That maybe things that matter aren't the things you touch by hand.
You talk to me of things you've never even done,
How wonderful your life is, all the lies you've spun.
I know that I don't matter, I mean nothing to you,
You hear but you don't listen, you claim but have no proof.
Maybe I'm not good enough for you or for your world,
You push me down and tread upon the fire I have burned.
For once I wish you'd see me, push all that aside,
See what really matters, see through to what's inside.
Just once, I wish you'd do that, accept the things I do,
Then you can forget me, but I'll remember you.

Sally Langford (Age 14)

Fear

When I meet him
He embraces me
Suffocatingly.
I can't breathe.
When He lets go,
He leaves me wet with sweat.
His claw like fingers trap mine.
They cover my eyes.
I can't see.
It is pitch black.
His coming scares me.
I don't know what will happen next.
I lose control.
I will upset Him,
If I scream.
I stay still.
I remain silent
Until He lets go
When I next meet him,
He will overpower me again.

Anna Blunt (Age 12)

Care

Sitting on a cold unwelcoming stair,
Her face drawn with heavy lines of care,
The grey, depressed sky reflecting her mood,
Her empty stomach yearning for a morsel of food,
She could no longer go on, she had tried her best,
Weeping for the love she was forced to lay to rest.

Her long, lank hair falling about her pale face,
She felt alone in every hectic place,
A glistening tear plots its course down her cheek,
Exposing an emotion, unable to speak,
So she remains upon the lonely stair,
Her face contorted with lines of heavy care.

Rebecca Hodgson (Age 14)

Third Prize Winners

A Perfect Day

The silky, soft silhouette slept silently in the sun,
Its long lazy day had only just begun,
Curled up like a summer's bud, full of promise and delight,
Dreaming of the mysteries that happen in the night.

Slowly it reveals itself, yawning, stretching every limb,
Engrossed in exercise to keep it very trim.
Slowly sauntering with an elegant glide, wandering along,
A silent hunter amongst the bustling throng.

Carefully, the creeping cat crawls amongst the leafy trees,
Keeping a beady eye on the birds and bees.
In a flash, the predator pounces and picks off its prey:
A delicious end to another perfect day.

Katie Upton (Age 12)

Alone

I'm all alone no-one to turn to,
Broken in two no-one to care for.
Frightened to go to sleep in case I die,
All alone, no food, no drink.

Alone at night in a doorway,
Leaning on concrete, cold and dry.
Only a miracle can save me,
No-one to care for me,
Everybody just walks by and by and by.

James Flynn (Age 11)

Storm

The wild storm rages like an angry giant.
Dominant, dynamic lightning shoots through the air, like fiery weapons.
It's thunderous voice rants and roars furiously, like a murderer in rehab.
It's icy bitter hold grips the house as tightly as a python gripping a helpless baby.
The rain beats furiously against the windows like a load of cement being hurled from the sky.
Inside the fire greets us like Satan picking us up to go to Hell
And we feel like children camping out by the fire, flaming furiously.

Luke Tarmey (Age 10)

The Great White Shark

This scavenging beast lurks in the depths of the ocean,
Searching, forever searching for carcasses of past kills
Then it notices,
A shadow moving overhead.
The shadow was of an adult elephant seal.
The shark moves, only slowly at first.
The further up it goes, the faster it gets,
Then it strikes once, twice, thrice.
The seal was killed instantly by the massive jaws.
The shark then tore away at the flesh.
When it had its fill it left,
The carcass began to drift away,
The blood trail attracting other sharks,
There will be none left for another day.

Robert Burton (Age 12)

Third Prize Winners

Monsters In My Room

I had a dream
It seemed so real, while I lay in my bed,
Shrieking, wailing monster things
Were running through my head
Some were big and some were small
And some had weird faces
They made a noise and screamed a lot
And went to funny places
From out of my head into my room
The monsters start to play
They only ever come at night
And never through the day
They hide behind the chest of drawers
And jump up on the table
I'd like to go and join them too
If only I was able
But every time I've tried to go
And join the monster fun
They disappear to where they're from
And monster fun is done

Dominic Allan (Age 9)

Noises In The Night

In the night
I hear an owl hoot
And a dog bark
And sometimes
I hear the trees branches rustling
And the wind blows gently
To get me to sleep

Kirsty Wright (Age 5)

Inside My Head

Inside my head
I'm under the sea
There's lots of dolphins that can carry me
There's whales and sharks
Starfish and octopus'
And lots more
It's blue and yellow
With bits of it green
That's the sea the sand
And of course the seaweed

Rebecca Beresford (Age 7)

Sunrise

The sun's glass is full
Brightness overflows,
Shadows awake,
From down below.

The cold thief is gone,
Summer's painter is back,
Drawing on earth's features,
Until night comes back.

The animals come out,
Venturing for food,
The stomping of a bear,
Says it's in a mood.

Ghosts drop down to earth,
Frightened of the light,
Tourists come to see,
The beautiful sight.

The leaves light up,
And the birds sing a song,
The day has just begun,
But it won't last for long.

Nathan Skelley (Age 9)

Third Prize Winners

Around The World

Rice noodles put together
Chinese cook in a wok in all kinds of weather.
Spicy foods Tandoori dishes
These are the Indian wishes.
Italians like pasta shapes,
French drink wine made out of grapes.

People wear saris to keep cool
Others just trunks for a swimming pool
Eskimos wear a big thick woolly jacket
So the polar bears make a big racket
Some men from Sudan paint their bodies with mud
Then slip and lose their blood.

African bushmen build huts with grass
Americans have lots of silver and brass.
In cities people live in big flats
With roof gardens on top they like wearing hats
In china some houses are floating boats
Its much too hot to wear their coats.

Everywhere is different as you can see
Each individual likes how they can be

Stephen Hall (Age 7)

The Dandelion's Clock

It ticks and tocks all day long,
with colour and splendour,
for everyone,
looking like a golden song.

It ticks and tocks all day long,
shines and combs its golden locks,
and then when winter comes,
it huddles down upon the ground.

It ticks and tocks all day long,
but then one very nice day,
it flies quite away,
but then it lands,
with a silken gland,
to grow again.

Katherine Reggler (Age 7)

A Message In A Bottle

It stayed there no one to read it,
In a hole in the sand,
Surrounded by the sea if you touched it with your hand,
The wind blows some air along the rocky sea,
No one will open my bottle,
It's locked with a key.

It's surrounded by the sand, palm trees too,
Bananas grow there, they really, really do.
It sails away beside a ship,
It's just having a little dip.
And now it's gone sailing away,
Until it comes back another day.

Jessica Hocking (Age 8)

Who Has Seen The Wind?

Who has seen the wind?
Neither you or I
But when the branches sway and crack
The wind is whirling by.

Who has seen the wind?
Neither I or you
But when the trees go falling down,
The wind is zooming through.

Shenton Morgan (Age 7)

The Blank Page

Words come before me,
But they slip through my fingers,
If only I could grab them,
Write them down.
Ideas run past,
I try to chase them,
But they're out of my reach.
Anyway what would I write?

Phrases, metaphors,
Similes and verbs,
Trapped in a whirlwind,
With no one to help,
No hand to reach out.

Words, what are they really?
Nothing, just letters put together.
Why am I even here?
I don't want to write.

Time is up. It's over. Done!
Looking down at the blank page,
What am I to do?

Alice Appleyard (Age 11)

Last Day At School

Last day at school
Children have new friends
Coats are old and too small
There are shoes to mend

Last day at school
We get boring jobs to do
Need to tidy classroom
Need to get old work down
We need a broom

Last day at school
We see old wallpaper up on the wall
Nothing had been changed
Nothing was there at all
People were playing ball

Last day at school
We see old carpet on the ground
The teacher turns the lights out
We all put chairs up
The teacher shouts

Judd Aris (Age 7)

Cats

It's a killer prowling its territory,
Crawling slowly like wind to grass
The ground is their trampoline,
Jumping miles in the air
It's like a tightrope walker walking a fence,

Running endlessly back and forth,
Dashing, whizzing and jumping
Its eyes are schizophrenic,
Skipping from cute to evil
Its eyes are torches
Shining bright light through the darkness.

They are Gods of Egypt,
Praised by all living things
They are a touch of Heaven,
They are immortal.

Philip Abbott-Garner (Age 12)

Green Poem

A crocodile swimming in the river
A football pitch very noisy
Trees swaying in the breeze
Stems are rising in the garden
Painting with some green paint
Reading with a book
Sailing in a boat

Laura Apps (Age 8)

At Winter's Door

At winter's door
Strong winds begin,
As snow comes in

People outside wrapped up warm,
Robins singing sweetly
At winter's door

People scrapping frozen cars,
Leaves from bare trees float softly to the ground,
At winter's door

In the house decorations are around,
At winter's door
At winter's door

Kate Adams (Age 11)

My Mummy And Daddy

They are always there for me,
They pick me up when I hurt my knee.

They keep me away from danger,
They never let me talk to strangers.

They buy me lots of new things,
They buy me jewellery like necklaces and rings.

They take me to lots of places like the park,
They once took me to see a shark.

Me and my Mum cook sweet things like buns,
When I go out with my Dad I have lots of fun.

They are my parents and they're the best,
They're better than the rest.

We will never be apart
They will always be in my heart.

I love my Mum, I love my Dad,
They're my parents, that's why I'm so glad.

Ifrah Asmat (Age 10)

Our Class Cat

He scratches his nose when it snows,
When it snows he scratches his toes
He will give you scratches and patches,
He has freezing toes when it snows

Lauren Akers (Age 7)

My New Hamster

Black ones, white ones,
Sandy and patchy ones.
Some are sleepy, some are lively.
But that one looked at me
With a twitchy nose and twinkly eyes

That's the one!
I carry her home in a cardboard box.
Scuffling, sniffing, nose and paws,
Poking through the air holes.
Home to the cage I have prepared.

Climbing up the side, falling off the top.
My acrobatic hamster
Runs down the tunnel, gets in the wheel,
Gnaws at the nuts,
Then curls up to sleep in a bed of fluff.

Philippa Ainsworth (Age 10)

Monster Madness

Meat chomper growled,
Jaw snapper howled.

Bone cruncher snarled,
Vain pincher ate a child.

Nail nibbler cried,
Cloth chewer wanted to hide.

Brain bubbler burped,
Skin scavenger jerked.

Feet smeller let out gas,
Tummy tumbler was a lass.

Rubbish rumbler jumped,
Leg burper thumped.

You know what, they all
Live under my bed!

Gabrielle Atkinson (Age 10)

Untitled

I'm slowly walking
Through a blur of colour,
And as I ponder,
I see it fall.
I'm falling down slowly
    Down,
    Down,
    Down,
   Going
  Going,
Gone.

Richard Astill (Age 8)

The Love Of Night

The night goes on
In rain or snow
It will return to dawn
It goes but it will never disappear in your heart
It stays forever

As I'm listening
The moon is glistening
Going around earth in a prayer

The Stars are twinkling bright
All through the night
Like a dragon fly in the sky
It never dies for there it lies.

Dakota Acock (Age 9)

The Bears On Picnic Day

Paddington thought it was at the station,
Yogi Bear was playing with Jason,
Brown Bear was practicing his equations,
So they all missed the picnic.

Bruno went to the bank to get some money,
Pooh got stuck in a pot of honey,
Old Bear stopped to stroke a bunny,
So they all missed the picnic.

If you go down to the woods today,
Don't be surprised to hear someone say,
Wasn't it quiet at the picnic today,
For today's the day the bears forgot their picnic.

Elizabeth Antell (Age 9)

Winter

Blankets of snow carpet the earth,
Icicles drip from the top of the oak trees,
Leaves dance with joy,
Others throw white, frozen snowballs.

Trees fidget with excitement
Damp flowers shiver,
Icy rivers moan with angry wind,
Cows graze on sparkling wet fields.

Sun struggles through clouds,
It sends a powerful ray of heat upon the earth.

Luke Anderson (Age 11)

Colourful Oak Trees

Colourful oak trees
Noisy Traffic
Colourful oak trees
Angry crocodile
Colourful oak trees
Splodgy paint
Colourful oak trees

Reese Almond (Age 7)

Animal Poem

Near the trees a lion waited
Across the trees Zebras ran
On the horizon the moon went down
Over the shells the universe watched
Below the sea the fish jumped
Between the sea a dolphin wailed
Within the horizon a shark charged
On the trees a monkey watched
Within an hour animals gather.

Mubeen Akhtar (Age 10)

The Old Oak Tree

As the tree stands and reaches the sky,
He feels like he is very high,
Everyone looks at him
Then gives him a sudden grin.

As he watches people go by,
He can't walk so he starts to cry,
As I sit and watch the tree
He likes looking at me.

As he sits and stares
His leaves fall off and turn him bare,
Some people just look at him
It makes him look very dim.

I like the tree
And he likes me
I hope he can invite
Me to tea.

Teresa Ager (Age 9)

Neighbours

My neighbours are the ones from hell!
Believe me I know them well,
They wake up at nine a.m.
And play loud music all weekend.
They play in the garden with a ball,
And kick it over the garden wall.
They get on our nerves all of the time,
If you think I'm moaning,
You should hear them whine
They drive round the corner to the pub,
They whack the wall like wild thugs.
They go to bed really late,
They make their guests wait and wait.
If you want to hear some more,
Come round and knock on their door!!!

Lauren Avis (Age 12)

The Silent Ark

I cling to my owner's leg, not knowing what to expect.
He tugs at my lead and I faithfully follow, not knowing what to expect.
He leads me through the iron gates, my claws tapping the glossy floor.
All the time he is reassuring me, telling me it's okay.

But it's not okay I'm being led to the silent ark yet I do not know what to expect.
The air is full of death and cries as I pass each door,
I know I am farther into death and there is no turning back
As I am led to join the others on the silent ark.

We join a line with other owners and their companions,
All awaiting to board the silent ark, with no return ticket at our paws.
They wait patiently not knowing what to expect, blind to the truth.
The silent ark is waiting and I am one of the crew.

And my time has come to board the silent ark, the captain rushed and bothered.
I am disconnected from my lifeline and dragged towards my doom,
The captain takes my scruff and plunges the needle deep.
I slowly drift away and now ready to join the silent ark.

As my life has ended and I am now no longer needed.
My body is tossed among the others and we are boarded onto the silent ark.
My life journey has ended but my journey on the silent ark
Has only just begun.

Amie Alberio (Age 14)

Ebony The Attentive Dog

Ebony's an attentive dog, he's called the idol cop -
For he's the master cop who'll catch any bad crop.
He's hell for the criminals heaven for the law.
For when a crimes discovered - "Ebony upholds the law"

Ebony, Ebony, there's not one like Ebony.
He's stuck to every country law, he sticks to all the felony.
He'll sort out all the criminals with his deadly paw.
For when a crime's discovered - "Ebony upholds the law."

Rory Abel (Age 11)

I Like My Teachers

I like my teachers,
They are very kind,
But I don't understand them,
They boggle up my mind!

I like my teachers,
They teach me at their school,
I find it annoying when we are in a middle of a sum,
Then we have to go to the hall.

If we forget our P.E. kit,
The teachers make us write out lines
But I don't understand them,
They boggle up my mind

Robynne Armstrong (Age 8)

So Solid Trees

Branches dance on dance floor
Dropping leaves while they rap
Leaves lightly fall to the DJ's attack

Wind singing with the leaves
Jumping to great beats
While trees sit back in their seats

Leaves hit the floor with splits
With rhymes coming out of lips
While crowd gather they become great hits

Jay Alexander (Age 11)

Queen Elizabeth II

It all happened in a marvellous dream:

I walked down the royal hall of Buckingham Palace,
The walls covered in portraits of the Royal Family,
The long ceiling painted fresh, pure white, like snow,
Chandeliers covered in golden diamonds,
The windows layered in silky curtains.

I opened a huge pine door,
Inside there were shelves choked with real china ornaments,
A wooden fire glowing on the shiny wooden floor,
In the corner of the room there was a small wooden staircase,
I lightly put my trainers on one of the stairs, it made a small creak.

I started walking up the staircase,
When I got up there I found myself in Queen Elizabeth's bedroom,
The room was huge, more chandeliers were hanging from the ceiling,
In a chair near the window I could see the Queen sipping a cup of tea,
I walked closer, the Queen's corgis were next to her, their fat bellies spread out on the floor.

The bedroom had a huge bed with pure gold curtain rails,
The covers were covered in crochet patterns,
All of a sudden, I woke up, it had all been a dream.

Jessica Axten (Age 11)

The Huge Grey Giants

The huge grey giants
Standing still as time goes by
How long have they been standing there?
They sink beneath the murky sky
They are still there upon the hill
The huge grey giants will never fall
As the sinking sun disappears
They cast a shadow upon the hill

Connor Allen (Age 8)

The Dolphin

Moving through the turquoise waters,
The dolphin swims,
Gliding, gracefully.
Tranquil and calm.
Skin silky and sleek.
Unforgettable to touch.
An intelligent creature,
Peaceful, a friend.
The dolphins chatter,
Shrill and high.
Splashing, twirling
Leaping in the air.
An amazing experience.

The dolphin.

Samantha Abel (Age 14)

My Dog Bels

Bels is happy, cheerful and kind.
She likes to break flowerpots.
She likes to dig holes sniffing for rabbits
When she quietly sniffs the rabbits
"Here girl," my mum calls.
Then she rushes inside to see me.
She jumps up playfully on me and I say
"I love you Bels. I love you so."
She is the best dog in the world and she will always be.

Victoria Axon (Age 6)

Francis Drake

When Francis Drake was very young, he went to sea and lost his tongue,
The crew all made him scrub the deck, he said to himself oh what the heck!

One day the cat flew over board, oh Francis Drake he was so broad,
He quickly jumped to save the cat, and landed in the Captain's hat!

The crew made him Captain in that day, and that was in the month of May,
They finally reached the Spanish shore, and quickly cried we want some more!

They hopped out of the big fat ship, they fell and broke one arm one hip,
The Spanish said you'll never win, your muscles are the size of a pin!

A battle broke out between the two, they could only hide inside the loo,
When the battle was over phew at last, Francis Drake looked back to the past!

As fast as he could he sailed back home, the Queen gave him a fancy dome,
Drake went away for a well earned rest, but still be carries on his massive quest!

The reason Drake is famous today, is because he decided that one day,
He would sail around the world on a ship, he was the first Englishman to do that trip!

Joanne Atkins (Age 10)

My Horse

Small and white
Ears pricked up high
A warming sight
Clip clop hooves
Swishing tail
Fields so green
Hills so high
A love so rare
A friend for life

Laura Allen (Age 8)

That's Odd!

The trees are multi coloured
The flowers are made of plastic
The bees go woof and the dogs go buzz
People are made of paper and paper is made of flesh
The rivers flow out chocolate and chocolate is made of water
Everything is odd and all a big blunder
Everyone's hair is green
And every can of paint is made out of lightning and thunder
And as I said before
It's just a very big blunder!

Laura-Jayne Ashman (Age 12)

Green Is . . .

Green is peace living in our hearts
if we were all green there'd be no more wars

Green is a calm, quiet colour
like grass swaying in the breeze

Green is a tree standing very still

Green is grass gleaming in the sun
or shining with dew drops

Green is seaweed on the sea bed

Molly Allen (Age 9)

Goodnight

Hear the sound of crickets collecting their tickets
The moon collecting noon
And the smell of the wet pond
Which the wet dog was very fond of
And the cows bow
And I hear a call like a bouncing ball
And when the sun comes up to play
All the animals run away
And the dew drops
Are like wet shops
And now we have to stop
Like a pouncy cop

Hollie Allison (Age 8)

The Sky

The sky has the sound of nothing,
It's a birds race track
A blue blanket that covers us when we're day dreaming,
Opposite of the under world
Inky black night sky
Swimming pool blue day sky.
It has magnificent wild life
God's heavenly kingdom,
Changes from blue to grey
Winter grey, summer blue,
Beautiful cold and peaceful atmosphere
With fabulous views.
Some bits are clean some bits are polluted.
And huge buildings scrape the ceiling of the earth.

Thomas Anders (Age 10)

Baa!

If you can survive Foot and Mouth,
Or maybe even help others,
If you can pretend you're thin and not look fat,
And be loathed and not care better,
Be great and resist the sheepdog,
Yet not get bitten,
Or be bitten and not bite back,
And yet not have a big fleece nor a large leg,

If you can keep your fleece when all about you,
Are having theirs clipped and blaming it on you,
If you can sit there and look idle,
When all others are itching with excitement,
If you can eat grass all day,
And not go hungry,
Yours is the paddock and everything that's in it,
And - what's more - you'll be a sheep, my lamb!

Ben Abrams (Age 11)

Fifty Years

Fifty years is so long
It's probably really shocking and happy
Forever she might smile
To be happy all through her life
You would be happy if you were the Queen

You will never like another Queen more than Queen the second
Everybody thinks the Queen is special
At the Golden Jubilee it's very special
Really special Queen
She's special in every way

Melissa Amphlett (Age 8)

My Pussy Cat

I love my little pussy cat,
Its fleece is white as snow
It has black spots like ink
And a little, little nose!
I love my little pussy cat
It follows me around the house,
Then in the garden,
Then she sleeps on my lap,
And makes not a sound

Natalie Adams (Age 10)

I Like . . .

I like cats,
I like dogs,
But I don't like rats,
And I don't like frogs.

I like pans,
I like eggs,
But I don't like fans,
And I don't like pegs.

I like toys,
I like stars,
But I don't like boys,
And I don't like cars.

I like pens,
I like shops,
But I don't like hens,
And I don't like lolly pops.

Katie Armento (Age 10)

Snow Is . . .

Icing on a cake
Candy floss
A dish of ice-cream
A giant freezer
A sparkly blanket
An enormous cloud
A sea of white
A plump white cushion
A water slide
A danger zone
White chocolate
Whipped cream

Grace Andrews (Age 12)

Sir Francis Drake

When Francis Drake sailed the world, across the sea all rocky and curled,
He named his ship the Golden Hind, and left his poor old Country behind.

Two ships were burnt for warmth and heat, one turned round they thought they were beat,
One ship sank with all its crew, for the boat and the crew their trip was through.

Sir Drake sailed back to Plymouth, where he was met by jolly old Queen Elizabeth,
And the Queen was also very keen, to ask the chap where he'd been.

The Queen asked Francis to invade Cadiz, so Francis though this would be a whizz,
When Francis got to the mighty city, he burnt it down and said what a pity.

Sir Francis Drake took a holiday, and decided to go very far away,
But the Queen a new Spanish fleet, and suddenly thought she wanted them beat.

Sir Francis was knighted, they called him the Great, and went up to Queen Elizabeth's gate,
The royal food in which he ate, the Queen said Francis you are the great.

Harvey Ahern (Age 10)

Woof!

A dog leaping around like a dolphin,
Brown fur with splodges of black drippy paint,
Waggy tail like a mouth smiling at you,
Bright, round, smooth collar shiny blue.

Sharp ears like the nib of a pen,
Nose all slippery, sloppy and soaking wet,
Long bumpy tongue like a snake,
Never asleep, always wide awake.

Rebecca Atcheler (Age 9)

Endangered Pandas

A Panda is a lovely thing,
Black and white and grey,
A Panda is a lovely thing,
Eating bamboo all day.

The China forests are full of Bamboo,
And that's what the Pandas like to chew
So when you cut down all the trees,
Think, because there soon may only be three.

Emily Adams (Age 9)

The Storm

A storm is like a king, not paid any taxes.
He wants to get revenge on those who do not pay.
If something is stopping him from getting to the village
His thunder soldiers get it out of the way.

He has a heart of stone,
And a breath of ice.
His hair seems to move,
As if it were full of mice.

However he floods the land with tears,
So he can't be all bad.
Because he doesn't touch the village,
The people are really glad

Graham Ashton (Age 11)

Beach Time Fun

Sand sinks
Sea winks
Curvy waves
Make little caves
This is beach time fun.

Children cry
Men pry
Waves lap
Women nap
This is beach time fun.

Sarah Anderson (Age 13)

Carbohydrate

C auliflowers are green and yellow also shaped like a flower.
A pples are crunchy and munchy.
R adish's are white and mix it with salad.
B ananas are yellow, curved and sweet.
O lives are lovely to oil.
H erbs are used for flavouring food.
Y oghurts come in different flavours like strawberry and apricot.
D ates are purple and sticky
R aspberries are red and sometimes sweet or sour.
A rtichoke is a plant with flower made as a veg.
T omatoes are red and have juicy stuff inside.
E ggs come in different kinds like scrambled egg.

Shahnaz Ali (Age 8)

Purple

Purple is the colour of the plums on my tree
Purple is the wine that a child is not allowed to drink
Purple are the grapes on a grape branch
Anger makes your face go purple when you're in a mood
Purple is the colour of my favourite leaves on the floor
Purple is the colour of my purple pencil
Purple is my favourite colour
Purple is the sky when it is a lovely day
Purple is the tail of a toucan

Bryony Allen (Age 8)

Friends!

My friends are really cool,
I don't know what to do.
But they always give me a headache,
By shouting and screaming down my ear!

My friends are really cool,
I don't know what to do.
But when I'm really stuck,
They really help me out!

Sarah Appleton (Age 11)

Happiness

Happiness is pink,
It smells like red roses,
Happiness tastes like honey,
It sounds like a kitten purring,
It feels like rabbits fur,
Happiness lives in a little cottage
Full of beautiful flowers

Henna Altaf (Age 10)

Yellow

Working in a literacy book
Hot sun
Working in a literacy book
Happy day
Working in a literacy book
Blond hair
Working in a literacy book
Sour lemons
Working in a literacy book

Jamie Austin (Age 8)

On The Sea Bed

Sharks slip by slyly,
Gnawing on an animal,
Fish go by in shoals,
Without a care in the world
The sea is larger than life

Luke Ashworth (Age 11)

Whirlwinds

Whirlwinds are fierce, whirlwinds are fast.
They search through the city,
But don't look to stop.
Souls are lost,
Belongings destroyed.
People have to move
It changes
Their lives
But soon it
Moves on
And eventually
Dies!

Gary Askew (Age 14)

An Island Of Memories

An Island of memories
Is a camera which film develops instantly,
A story you can read again and again.
It is a camera always on record.
A TV programme you can watch whenever you want
And all this is locked away,
Largely inside your head.

Jeni Allen (Age 12)

Wild Horse

He's a wild horse, no fence can keep him in
He wanders as free as waves upon the sand
The world is his oyster
He's the master of this land.
He's a wild horse, nobody controls him
He's never there when I want to ride
But if I go to the moors and call him
He's instantly by my side.
He's a wild horse, a free spirit
Bucked me off a thousand times
A lonely horse, a crazy horse
But I don't care, he's mine.
He's a wild horse, a lonely horse
Together we died in 1824
Victims of a fire
Still we roam the moor.

Amber Allen (Age 13)

The Shark

Sam the shark
Swims past a shipwreck
Sam saw a ship above his head
He swam up and . . . . .
SNAP!!!
All the men started screaming
One man named Striker
Got eaten!! by Sam.
After that, Sam got caught in a net
The boat that had caught him was called the 'Sea Shell'
Sam was surprised
Sam struggled so hard that he pulled . . . .
All the men in.
Finally he got out and he was so angry
That he ate all of the men in the water.

James Anderson (Age 8)

Happiness

Happiness is a big bright rose,
It smells like a fresh flower.
Happiness tastes like fresh strawberries,
It sounds like birds singing and tweeting.
Happiness feels like an open bright pink rose,
It lives in a light pink village.

Naeem Ahmed (Age 10)

Ten Posh Pandas

Ten Posh pandas eating pie with perfume,
Nine polite pandas dancing in pyjamas,
Eight powerless pandas panicking at playtime,
Seven passionate pandas patching up their pillows
Six pop pandas pointed at their pocket money
Five police pandas playing in the pond,
Four podgy pandas plastered up the playground
Three pandas with pacemakers
Two pasty pandas paddling in the pool
One popping panda performing with her pal

Aliena Archer (Age 11)

If I Had Wings

If I had wings
I would taste the icy moon
As smooth as silk

William Austin (Age 8)

How To Make A Teacher Mad

Crush a class of kicking boys,
Boil with a pinch of gastly girls,
And stir with a wet playtime.

Leave for two minutes then gradually knead,
Wait for a moment and then add pencil flickings,
As the water turns death.

As the mixture goes bad increase the concoction with,
Visious doodles and a hint of bad language,
When the mix goes evil.

As you get ready to cook chop up ruler fight evenly,
Then put it in the oven bad children mark 5 and serve,
Viola an angry teacher.

Peter Arrow (Age 9)

Raindrops

Pit a pat a raindrops falling down on me,
Pit a pat a raindrops don't hit that tree,
Pit a pat a raindrops making everything soggy,
Pit a pat a raindrops you wet my doggy

Pit a pat a raindrops getting granny wet,
Pit a pat a raindrops hitting the vet,
Pit a pat a raindrops playing in the mud,
Pit a pat a raindrops isn't this fun!

Jessie Anderson (Age 11)

My Poem

Out, out brief candle!
Lifes but a walking shadow, if poor player,
That struts and frets his hour upon the stage,
And then he is heard no more.
It is all a tale told by an idiot, full of sounds and fury,
Signifying nothing.

Tom Alison (Age 9)

Untitled

I'm walking down the street and who do I meet
Rosey Severs, Rosey Severs
I saw Rosey Severs walking with beavers
Rosey Severs, Rosey Severs

John Amissah (Age 10)

The River

High up in the mountains, dripping ice begins to melt,
Shivering streams, clatter over shining rocks beneath,
With quickening speed the streams dash at full pelt,
Burbling, swirling with sounds like chattering teeth.
Gullies formed, the stream becomes an eager young river,
Straight down it flows crashing over the rocks,
And then, slowly meandering like a slithering snake, around the banks.
Past the silent shepherds looking after their flocks.

Michael Antona (Age 10)

Rainbow Boy

There was a boy of many colours
From head to toes, moods and others
His skin of a chocolate brown
You could see he was blue when he frowned
His hair was of jet black
Red was anger which he did lack
His eyes were a hazelnut brown
This boy and his colours were a rainbow around town.

Katrina Adams (Age 13)

What Makes The Teacher Angry

Carefully drain out a bowl of calling out boys,
Tenderly boil a handful of ruler fights,
Spread a spoonful of arguing girls and
Carefully melt a pinch of boys flicking paper.

Add a drop of girls writing on the walls,
Cut a touch of scruffy homework,
Shake a dash of swearing boys,
To finish off a awful wet play.

Lucy Adams (Age 10)

The Tiger Poem

The tiger has feet like lions feet
The tiger has whiskers like spikey arrows
The tiger has a tail like a piece of rope
The tiger has claws like somebody's nails
The tiger has eyes like human's eyes
The tiger has feet like lions feet

Ross Ayling (Age 9)

The Tree

When I go past my house,
I see a big brown, golden tree,
Leaves drop, like when a bird swoops,
Animals climb the tree,
It's bushy, it's green and it gives oxygen,
I love this tree,
I don't want it to run out,
It's electrical, its old,
It's probably older than Father Christmas,
I don't want it to go.

Martin Barnard (Age 12)

Sharks

I think sharks are rather dangerous
Their teeth are very dangerous
They're quiet killers
They do not have a miller
Their teeth are two sets of danger
Their prey are like dolphins and whales
They spin like a gigantic screw driver
Their only mode is killer mode
They drive like mad
And no-one seems to like them much

Jacob Bolt (Age 7)

Images Of India

Flies land on me,
When I flick them off they bounce back like boomerangs.
The heat is unbearable
And my pale skin is sticky with sweat.

Surrounded by Farmland,
I smell cow dung and the sweetness of grass.
Spice and Incense
Cling to my clothes like cobwebs.

Noises of animals flood my ears,
Goats being herded from field to field,
Cockroaches scuttling across the floor
Mice climbing up walls.

I breath in dusty air,
The grit fills my lungs
My mouth goes dry
And I taste salty sweat.

Around me
Dogs prowl the streets searching for food.
Ragged beggars follow me tugging on my western clothes
Their eyes pleading for money.

Karina Bual (Age 14)

What Is Blue?

Blue is the colour of the deep blue sky,
That swoops across the other clouds.
Blue is the colour of blackberry pie
That your mum always says eat up eat up,
Blue is the colour of the teachers pen,
That she always writes with,
Blue is the colour of some detective men,
That are very very merry,
Blue is the colour of a floating ferry.

Jonathan Burns (Age 7)

There's A Bat In The Kitchen

There's a bat in the kitchen,
What are we going to do?
Pick it up and flush it down the loo.
Or could we sell it to the zoo?

There's a bat in the classroom,
What are we going to do?
We could put it in the darkroom
But what about the cloakroom?

There's a bat in the playground,
What are we going to do?
It's giving us the runaround
What shall we do?

Katie Beresford (Age 11)

Last Day At School

Last day at school
Children play toys or games
Children check lost property
Because clothes don't have names

Last day at school
Children empty trays
Children feeling excited
Children playing maze

Last day at school
Teacher tidying classroom
Children really happy
Teacher cleaning with broom

Last day at school
Teacher cleans walls
Children collect lunch boxes
Down the curtain goes
The children say bye bye

Ryan Bass (Age 7)

My Family And Me

Daddy's Big
I am small
James is naughty
Lindsay's tall

Mum works hard
Sally's neat
Luke shouts out loud
But Jordan has smelly feet!

Grandpa's grumpy
Nana's pretty
That's my family
Oh what a pity!

Jasmine Barker (Age 6)

The Halls Of Silence

```
HE    LL       I N
THE HALL
       HA     IL
THE HALL  OF
    E  A        S E
T     ALL      SI  N
                I  N
THE HALL  OF
    E  A  S       E
       ALLS O    IL
T       ALLS    I  N
                I  N
THE HALL  OF
    E  A  S      E
THE HALLS OF SILENCE
```

Nate Barker (Age 14)

A Unicorn Recipe

1. Get a pot of stars
2. A little bit of mars
3. A diamond for an eye
4. A ray of sunlight for its tail
5. Some daisy chains for its mane
6. And some white feathers for the fur
7. Some broken glass for teeth
8. Some disco music to make it dance
9. A sharp thorn for the horn
10. Some golden sun for the hooves

Lily Bennett (Age 8)

The Queen

The Queen has been our Queen for fifty years
She is kind and gentle
She goes all round the world and gets a lot of cheers
She always wears a beautiful smile
And will wipe away your tears
So come on let's celebrate
Our Queen's Golden Jubilee Year

Radhika Bali (Age 7)

What Is?

What is red? A strawberry is red
Growing in the fields.

What is orange? An apricot is orange
Swinging in the trees.

What is yellow? A dandelion is yellow.
Swaying in the fields.

What is green? Grass is green
Blowing in the wind.

What is blue? A starfish is blue
Drifting in the sea.

What is indigo? A kingfisher's head is indigo
Swooping down to catch a fish.

What is violet? The braised down sky is violet.
On a cold winter's day.

Melissa Bellamy (Age 7)

What Is Magic?

What is magic?
Is it sparks that fly?
Or someone who's nosy,
And rather sly?

Who is magic?
Is it Sabrina the witch?
Or Harry Potter,
Or a tramp in a ditch?

I wish I was magic,
Maybe I am,
I wonder if I can shoot sparks,
Maybe I can!

I know what magic is,
It's all in your heart,
The way you treat people,
That's the only part.

Charlotte Bignell (Age 9)

Losing Someone

She sits, waiting desperately for news
In the relatives room of casualty.
Then the doctor walks in
And she knows from the look on her face,
She knows what she is about to hear:
We are very sorry; he died a few minutes ago.
And she goes numb, she can't move.
She regains control and whispers:
"Can I see him?"
Then she is walking towards the room
Where she knows the love of her life is lying cold and still.
She walks in, kisses his cold lips and touches his lifeless hand.
An unbearable sense of loss washes over her and she breaks down.
And then she is running away from it all
Running to find a hole to crawl into and hide until everything is all right again
But deep down she knows that she is wrong and nothing will ever
Be all right again.

Elizabeth Brent (Age 13)

My Mum . . . .

My mum kisses me goodnight.
She tucks me up all tight.
She turns off the light.
It is no longer bright.
My mum wakes me up.
She puts my milk in a cup.
She makes daddy's dinner,
And puts on Frank Skinner.

Ciara Brundell (Age 7)

Chinese Dragon

A dragon is dancing down the lane,
With breathing fire and golden flames
And with scaly green skin,
It is a beautiful Chinese dragon
With beautiful skin
And marvellous scaly skin,
With flames of red
While people are making a din,
A wonderful sight to see.

Chloe Burke (Age 6)

Dentist

Walking to the **DENTIST**
Waiting for my name
Feeling nervous
Suddenly I am called!
Walk in - sit down.
Chair hummed
Gerring worried.

Mum *murmuring*.

I hear the drill
there it was.
Gulping every second.
I woke up.
I got up
I went downstairs.
A DREAM

Sophie Boddy (Age 10)

Storms

What is thunder?
A giant's drum wildly beating.
Why does it rain?
It's the clouds losing weight.
What is lighting?
A snake's electric tongue.
What is wind?
A giant Hoover switched to blow.
What are hailstones?
The sky falling in.
What is a storm?
A giant throwing away his troubles.
Why are storms destructive?
Because someone's banished them to a dark hole.
Where do storms go?
Back to the dark hole of evil.

Amy Brunsdon (Age 11)

Sea Poems

One by one, one by one,
Spiky jellyfish eating buns in the sun.

Two by two, two by two,
Washing wind blows the sparkling crew.

Three by three, three by three,
Soft, stripy seahorses in the sea.

Four by four, four by four,
Fish are jumping in the sea and more.

Five by five, five by five,
Sparkling, scaly fish are ready to dive.

Six by six, six by six,
Sparkling jellyfish doing their tricks.

Seven by seven, seven by seven,
Six glittering fish, 5 more makes eleven!

Eight by eight, eight by eight,
Seven jellyfish eat their bait.

Nine by nine, nine by nine,
Jumping jellyfish in a line.

Ten by ten, ten by ten,
By the end of the day.....they were men!

Alex Bailey (Age 7)

My Uncle

My Uncle is wicked and cool
He thinks the bath is a swimming pool.
My Uncle is wicked and cool,
But he really, really is a fool.

My Uncle went to Disneyland
Where he nearly broke someone's hand!
My Uncle went to Disneyland.
Where he ate all the beach sand.

My Uncle is as stupid as can be.
He broke our front door key.
My Uncle is as stupid as can be,
Because he nearly drove over me.

My Uncle is a pheasant,
Because every year he buys us a bird as a present.
My Uncle is a pheasant,
Because he leaves bird prints in presents he's sent.

My Uncle has a pet.
He makes me take it to the vet.
My Uncle has a pet.
He makes me clean it when it's dirty and wet.

Rebecca Butler (Age 9)

Night

The moon drops its purse and twinkling 5p's come tumbling down,
Into the trees standing proud in the mist which hangs like a gown,
I hear the owls hooting, they sound like a person blowing a horn,
A skunk raids a dustbin but all he can find is a bag of popcorn,
I finished my journey the sun starts to rise and the sky turns red,
The owl and the skunk and other night creatures are going to bed.

Kimberley Betts (Age 10)

Zebra

His colour is like stripey parallel lines
And feels soft and comfortable

His ears are like mice ears,
His eyes are like horse's eyes.

The tail looks like an elephant tail
His tongue is like a human tongue.

Do you like Zebra?

Aron Berry (Age 9)

Peace Poem

What happened in the USA
Was a terrible thing to see.
I wish all races in the world
Could live in harmony.

All those innocent lives cut short,
Their loved ones left behind.
Why can't people on this Earth
Be gentle loving and kind.

The cruelty in this world must stop
We all must work for peace.
No more innocent lives should be lost
This terrorism has to cease.

Victoria Binnington-Barrett (Age 12)

The People In My Life

If my teacher were an alcoholic drink,
She'd be Bucks Fizz,
Strongly flavoured and fizzy like fireworks.
Every time I open it,
She would give me the warmth to smile.

If my brother were a building,
He'd be Buckingham Palace,
To show everyone how brilliant he is.
He'd be like the Queen,
Famous, proud, posh and royal.

If my postman were a pet,
He'd be a rabbit,
Always hopping around the town
Like a kangaroo, fast and agile,
Delivering mail to houses.

Angela Band (Age 11)

The Dark Is . . .

An endless echo,
Your child's nightmare,
Someone's chamber of fear,
Their space ships destiny,
A long lost forest,
A storm on a gloomy day
Your pens splodge of leaking ink,
An ugly looking monster,
A bed for glittering stars,
A never ending eerie darkness,
A resting place for martians,
A pitch black island,
A disaster waiting to happen,
A life long world of melted chocolate.

Gregory Beaven (Age 9)

The Man Who Wasn't There

A man walked down the cobbly road
No breath came from his mouth
He whistled an old but loud tune.
He was an unknown man
He didn't have fine robes
But a small purple tunic
He didn't want money or fine gold
But he stopped as the sun rose
And slowly disappeared.
As he faded he shouted
He was gone from dusk 'til dawn
He called to the nearest rose field
I am no man to pity
For I am the unknown
      MAN!

Rebecca Baxter (Age 12)

The Sahara To Me

Every fine sand grain,
Gives you no pain,
Squishy and soft,
Like hay in a loft,
Dunes so yellow,
Comfortable and mellow,
That's the Sahara to me.

Every camel so grumpy,
Riding them is so bumpy,
Their big, fat lumps,
Like long road humps,
They lollup along,
Gurgling a song,
That's the camels to me.

Kate Barton (Age 14)

The Promise Of Summer

The cool wind rustles in the whispering leaves
The blossom drifts off the spring trees,
The glistening dew falls crisp and cold
The rising sun glows warmly gold,
The tiny fruits will ripen again,
The fluffy clouds mean sun not rain,
The children play in sparkling streams,
The world of magic summer dreams.

Mimi Bygrave (Age 9)

Robins

Robins, robins, robins
Cuddly and cute
Their big red breasts
Shine on the snowy rooftops
They dance as the icy snowflakes
Come falling down
And the misty cold air covers the robins' world
As winter comes.

Christopher Brazier (Age 9)

Sir Francis Drake

Francis Drake sailed the world, across the seas jewelled and pearled,
He called his ship the "Golden Hind", took his ships and men behind.

One ship sank with all its crew, one ship turned, their trip was through,
Two were burnt for warmth and heat, he carried on, he wasn't beat.

Drake sailed back to lovely Plymouth, and was met by Queen Elizabeth,
And the Queen was very keen, to ask the fellow where he'd been.

He was asked to invade Cadiz, to fight and fight to make it his,
They blew up the Spanish castle, and gave the town a bit of hassle.

Poor old Drake had a rest, then came a letter at his chest,
To open the letter he was keen, "come very quickly" signed the Queen.

There he was with ships and men, to drive the foes back to their den,
There he was, he succeeded, to go back home, the Spanish pleaded.

The Spanish didn't sink a ship, for Francis that was just a trip,
The royal food, Francis ate, he was named Sir Francis the Great!

Mitchell Bennellick (Age 10)

Inside My Head

Inside my head
There's a place
Full of candied castles
And seas of sweets
Minstrel mice
Hiding under chocolate logs
Jelly frogs swimming in a pool
Of caramel creme.

Jack Beswick (Age 8)

Eagle

I can fly in the sky,
no one messes with I.
I am braver than you may think,
maybe I want to go home,
maybe I don't.
It is my choice!
NOT YOURS!!

Rebekah Barker (Age 11)

I'm A Diplodicus

Hocus pocus
Plodding through the swamp
Chomp, chomp, chomp
I'm a Diplodice
Stomp, stomp, stomp.

Grass for breakfast
I could eat a tree
Chomp, chomp, chomp
Grass for tea
Stomp, stomp, stomp.

Hocus, pocus, rocus
I'm a Diplodicus
Chomp, chomp, chomp
Running through the swamp
Stomp, stomp, stomp.

Louise Brough (Age 8)

The Queen Mother

Q ueen's are very rich like the wonderful Queen Mother,
U p in Scotland she was born.
E veryone treats her like a Grandmother.
E ven though she is dead she still means a lot to us,
N obody has ever said they don't like the Queen Mother.

M eeting people and making friends is what she did.
O pening new hospitals and helping the poor is what she liked,
T hinking about the Queen I think she is a star in everyone's eyes,
H ating anything at all isn't her thing,
E ven in the last stage of her life she made people happy,
R emembering the Queen is the best!!!!

Yasmin Begum (Age 10)

The Disaster

Life was fine,
Not much money, not much food,
But life was still fine,
We would live it as it came,
An Indian motto.

Working in class,
My friend was with the teacher,
The earth rumbled, everyone ran,
Two stayed here with me,
And didn't run from
The disaster.

It was madness, the roof fell in,
On the teacher's desk where she was no more,
I heard screaming and footsteps running,
And the earth rumbled once more.

I looked
Rubble around me,
Rubble above me,
I heard a scream,
Mine.

Rebecca Bishop (Age 11)

The Storm

Crash! The tree collapsed as lightning struck,
The waves of the sea smacked the rocks,
Thunder deafened the sailors after the strike of the clock,
Everyone knew-the storm had begun.

Rain was like stones falling down from the sky,
Wind was like the wail of the baby that cried,
Thunder was like the roar of a lion with pride,
Everyone knew-the storm had begun.

Lightning had finished and was replaced with the sun,
Rain was quieter to the patter of feet,
Wind became the sweat of the burning heat,
Everyone knew-the storm had ended.

Indra Balaratnam (Age 11)

Why?

Why does the moon orbit the earth?
How did gravity get its name?
Why do people not fall off the earth?
Why do people get the blame?
Is there life on the moon?
Why don't people have pet baboons?
Why doesn't the moon create its own light?
Why is the sun ever so bright?

Thomas Bird (Age 11)

Leisure

What is this life if full of care,
I've plenty time to stand and stare

Time to have a kick or two,
Playing football is what I like to do.

Time to go to my guitar lessons,
Next it's my math sessions.

Time to watch Bradford play,
Are they going to lose. No way!

Time to watch Bradford play on the muddy pitch,
The goalie Gary is very titch.

A good life I've got, its full of care,
I'm pleased I've got time to stop and stare.

Elliot Bedford (Age 9)

My Favourite Things

My favourite things are:

Scruffy dogs
and slimy frogs

Small snakes
and big cakes

Quick mice
and well done rice

Small moth eating bats
and stinky rats

A little baby hen
and my own name Ben

A very well known fox
and my brother's box

My Nan's Golden Retriever
and my very own beaver.

Benjamin Brown (Age 10)

Rain

Muddy puddles in the rain
Pitter-patter-pitter-patter-plop!

We're running in this weather
Pitter-patter-pitter-patter-plop!

It is raining in the streets
Pitter-patter-pitter-patter-plop!

Harry Betts (Age 7)

Foot And Mouth

Foot and mouth in Cumbria all farmers watch with dread,
Could this outbreak spell disaster? They'll know in the weeks ahead.
Those old enough to remember the 1960's the misery and the strife,
Will always be haunted by the changes to their life.

The men in white coats arrive and tell us our future clear,
They'll give us compensation but all we know is fear.
No entry signs litter the land on gates no longer used,
Footpaths closed, get off my land, keep out, all right of way refused.

The smell of burning rides the wind and catches in the throat,
The farmer in his empty field shrugged deeper in his coat.
Was it only weeks ago the future looked so bright?
Now death and ruin stalk the fields like a thief in the night.

No livestock left to graze the field where once proud champions ruled,
All gone in days to ditch and pyre and a lesser lonely world.

Katie Buncombe (Age 12)

Guess What I Am

I am furry and cuddly
I sleep in the daytime
I have a cage
As small as a rabbit

Hannah Beavis (Age 7)

Autumn

Dead leaves lying still
Wanting to blow home somewhere
Never stopping still

Frankie Bent (Age 8)

My Quiet Place

My quiet place is my bedroom
I like my toys to play with
It is comfy in my bedroom
I can run *OUT* of my bedroom

Jack Bearne (Age 6)

What Is Yellow

Yellow is a ball,
that bounces high
Yellow is a sunflower,
that touches the sky
Yellow is a sweet,
that tastes like lemon
Yellow is a sun,
that blazes in the sky
Yellow is hair,
that shines on a princess' head
Yellow is corn,
that grows in a field
Yellow is paint,
that you do art with
Yellow is a wall,
that makes your room look colourful
I like yellow
It makes me feel bright

Chloe Bullock (Age 7)

The Martian

Flying to earth
From the sun
Slamming down on your bum
Despicable body
Weird eyes
He really likes apple pies

Broken ship
What to do
Questions, questions, then someone shouted boo
Oh look
It's his dad
He reminded his family of an Irish lad

He mended his ship
Now to travel home
He knocked over a gigantic gnome
Back at home
On the sun
Clutching the steering wheel made his hands go numb

Michael Baxendale (Age 11)

Our Playground

The bell goes for play, and we all run out
The football game is about to start,
First kick of the ball with a kick and a rush.
But important to is the ability to pass.

When one boy falls he falls on the grass,
So fresh, so clean the smell of the grass.
He lingers for a moment enjoying the grass.
But then he gets up and begins to pass.

Each boy that falls they smell the grass.
They love the smell of new mown grass.
So much so that they forget to pass.
But then the whistle goes and it's time to go in.
Until the next playtime
Let the game begin.

Ben Brooks (Age 10)

Tickles

Tickles are made from within the haunted house,
Only from the sound of a jelly mouse.
Tickles are made from the scab of a fish,
Only with the blood from a dirty dish
Tickles are made from laughter and fun,
Only with the hand that bangs a drum.
Tickles are made to make you smile,
If they don't go and run a mile.

Scott Bradshaw (Age 11)

Summer Time

Flowers bloom,
There is no gloom,
Everyone is happy,
Smiles are everywhere,
Everyone takes their share,
Everyone is kind,
The sun is shining,
No-one is whining.

Jade Bransom (Age 9)

Goblin Market

Croaked every elf
When they spied her glaring
Squirling, skatering, smirking
Hopping, skipping, sprinting
Chucking and puffing
Sneering, snorting, snooping
Smirking and gloating
Stopping and going
Full of airs and laughter
Pulling cheeky faces
Good and evil
Monkey like and ape like
Lizard and snake like
Slug paced in a hurry
Tiger roaring and lion growling
Dodging, prodding, falling
Squealing like a squirrel
Swinging like a monkey
Charging like an ape

Siân Bowen (Age 10)

Change

The Summer
still tans
burning and browning
with wondrous colours
as it did last year.

The Autumn
still falls
blowing and changing
as it did last year.

The Winter
still freezes
whitening and glossing
as it did last year.

The Spring
still blossoms
with daffodils and lilies
as it did last year.

Melissa Brady (Age 9)

Night Storm

The heavy dark cushion is dragged across the sky smothering aaaaal heaven's candles in its path.
This everlasting blanket is broken only by the flash of a plunging dagger releasing air to the people below.
The banging of the mallet on the heavy sky extracts a cool shower to purify the air.
The last match is struck and then the lamps are lit.
The night is cool and clear and out the stars do peer.

Emma Bowe (Age 13)

My Big Brother

My big brother is a pain
He drives me insane
He plays in my wheelchair
He steals my teddy bear
He takes my toys
He makes lots of noise
But I don't care
He can be fair
I love my brother
I wouldn't have any other

Emma Brown (Age 8)

The Eagle

Feathers on his neck
Feathers on his head
His feathers as soft as a pillow
He flies soft and swift
He swoops across the sky
He glides through the sky
He hunts for his prey
Or tracks down his prey
He soars across the sky
Swoops for his prey
Beak as sharp as scissors
And nails as sharp as knives
Eyes as red as flames

Loui Branch (Age 9)

The Snail

It slithers silently and slowly from a-b,
Never stops just keeps on going.
And the heavy burden on his back is his home,
That he carries like a rucksack,
Nobody likes the snail; they sprinkle their white powder
Of death around the pest making him melt like
Chocolate in sunlight.
Behind the creature he leaves a trail of the silver glint of a ten pence
Piece catching the light.
Where he lives, a small jungle, very neat and
Well proportioned.
Usually stays in the shade under a green oval umbrella,
Never moves just stays.
But with one quick stamp the creature's gone,
A yellow yoke on the floor, spread out like butter over toast.

James Bulpin (Age 12)

A New Beginning

At the crack of dawn,
The light creeps through
The fluffy white clouds,
Which look like woolly sheep.

The flowers open up,
A sea of golden daffodils,
The bright new green grass,
Like a puddle of bright green paint.

The eggs that crack,
The birds that sing,
Listen to their joyful songs,
Like the night time lullaby.

The wake up call from the cockerel,
The mooing from the cow,
Are the signs of a new day,
A new begining of a new day,
A new begining of a sunny happy day.

Chris Byrom (Age 11)

My Quiet Place

My quiet place is my dream
I like my dream because it's magic
It is fun
I jump out of my dream

Daniel Beaumont (Age 7)

You're As Useless

You're as useless
As a bird without wings
As a choir that doesn't sing
As a pen without ink
As a pig that's not pink

You're as useless
As a dog without a tail
As a letter box without mail
As a shop without sweets
As a car without seats

You're as useless
As a wedding without a ring
As a monkey that doesn't swing
As a bag without straps
As an audience without a clap.

Vicki-Lea Bell (Age 11)

My Pets

My dog, my dog.
The tongue that lolls,
The warm hot breath,
The wagging tail,
The black wet nose,

My dog, my dog.
My cat, my cat.

The long whiskers,
The sleek tail,
The padded paws,
The pink small nose,

My cat, my cat.
My bird, my bird.

The hard beak,
The smooth feathers,
The tiny claws,
The squeaky voice,

My bird, my bird.

MY PETS, MY PETS!

Danielle Barford (Age 11)

The Elements

Tornadoes whisk,
Hurricanes blow,
Twirling twisters,
Cyclones circumnavigate the globe.

Flaming volcanoes erupt,
The flames of the world,
Burning bright,
Fireballs flying through the air.

Thundering waterfalls,
Marching rain soldiers,
Destroying flushing floods,
Slowly sliding streams.

Earth shakes
Buildings tumbling down,
Nowhere to hide,
Rocks falling.

Tim Bunting (Age 12)

The Easter Pansy
(please read from the bottom and from left to right)

flowers.
of Easter
princess
is the pretty
The royal purple pansy
beautiful and as soft as velvet.
pansy
delicate, dainty, delightful
it became a
at last
and
I waited
and
but I waited
seed
pansy
brown
an old
planted a pansy seed
I

Jennie Batten (Age 9)

Poor Car

This dutch toy car was somebody's racing car,
It has been stolen by a toy army man because of its smashed window,
When blown back as fast as a cheetah,
Sitting by the junkyard waiting to be crushed.

Joshua Albright (Age 9)

Hedgehog

I have a see-through hedgehog,
It's nearly all glass,
Except for its whiskers and eyes.

It's lost some of its spikes,
It's over ninety years old,
It came from my Great Grandad.

My little hedgehog must have missed him,
When he went to fight,
In World War II

He passed it on to my Nanna,
The little hedgehog was with her for a very long time,
Before he came to me.

James Beaumont (Age 10)

A Conversation With The Queen

"Do you like you crown jewels?" I asked
"Sometimes" she said.
"Do you like your corgis?" I asked
"Sometimes" she said.
"Do you like your palace?" I asked
"Sometimes" she said.
"Are your grandchildren naughty?" I asked
"Sometimes" she said.
"Do you like being the queen?" I asked
"Sometimes" she said.
"Do you like to have servants?" I asked
"Sometimes" she said.
"Do you like to do Kung Fu?"
"Yes as a matter of fact I jolly well do"

Harry Bullough (Age 11)

Beautiful Night Time

The hawk circles the rabbits
Rustling is heard from squabbling squirrels
Fighting for the chestnuts
As the timid mice look on.

The night settles down,
Everything falls asleep
The sun sets low
In to a slumber long and deep.

Abigail Burrell (Age 9)

My Sister Alice

If my sister were a tree,
She'd be a chestnut tree,
Big and young,
Flowing like a feather in the wind,
I like to sit under her so she'll protect me,
From the sun's rays and all the kind of weather.

Harriet Baggaley (Age 11)

The Cupboard Under the Stairs

The cupboard under the stairs is dark and gloomy.
Under the stairs it's not very roomy,
They say a monster, ten feet tall,
Lives in that dungeon in the hall.

That monster, under the stairs,
Is ugly and covered in hairs.
I wish one day he'd go away,
And never come again to play,
At the cupboard, under the stairs.

Roly Bagnall (Age 10)

Spring's Here

Spring time is my favourite of the year
Lambs leap,
Bunny rabbits hop,
Chicks cheep,
Sun shines,
Flowers bloom,
Trees blossom,
Clouds disappear,
Children run, laugh and play
And I love it!

Holly Brook (Age 8)

Ocean Waves

The sea lies
Sparkling, glittering, gently stroking golden shores,
Shapeless fingers hugging tight the sun-warmed sands,
Long and slow.
Over and over it rises and falls,
Wearing with pride its white adornments.

The sea roars,
Its placid surface shattered by crashing waves
Over and over it rises and falls,
Bearing smugly its towering foaming crown
It gnaws and snaps with frothing jaws,
As over and over it rises and falls,

As it calms,
The monarchy is returned to its regal posture,
Softly swaying in the breeze, to and fro,
While around it, time drifts along,
Autumn leaves on the wind,
As over and over, waves rise and fall.
Waves rise and fall

Florence Bawden (Age 12)

Thoughts Of A Young QueenQueen

Crowned a Queen against a backdrop of shame,
At sixteen years I must carry the family name.
No tears allowed
For my brother who died,
A smile on my face
Though I'm weeping inside.

I think of my age,
All that I'd planned to do.
It seems so far away now
From this life, so new.

A girl in the crowd,
A bit younger than me,
Is carefree and laughing
It's painful to see.

My maid smiles from my side, she understands.
Under my cloak we quickly squeeze hands.
I face my future,
And expect the worse.

Emma-Louise Burgess (Age 16)

A Boy's Head

Inside my head there is a gigantic
tap shoe, tippy, tapping away.

Inside my head there is a super fast,
blue sports car shooting past at 150 mph.

Inside my head there is a black and
white dog bounding in a park.

Inside my head there is a football,
a red and white strip and Michael Owen scoring a goal!

My spaceship, that is shown in Star Wars: Episode III
lurks in the deepest, darkest corners of my head.

Inside my head are riches, mansions,
swimming pools, a millionaire is just around the corner.

Daniel Batty (Age 10)

Days Of The Week

I like Monday because it is a fun day
I like Tuesday because it is a choose day
I like Wednesday because it is Ben's day
I don't like Thursday because it is the worst day
I like Friday because it is MY DAY.

Tiffany Bowmer (Age 7)

The Outsider

The small runny nosed boy
Waits in a corner
For the next boy to mock or tease him,

The small runny nosed boy
Never smiles
Never talks
He just sits there fiddling with a box,

The small runny nosed boy
Has no friends or a pet
Except for the tadpole he keeps in a jar,

The small runny nosed boy
Never ventures far
He just mopes around the side of the playground,

The small runny nosed boy
Never gets a card
On Christmas or Birthdays
He just gets hit hard,

The small runny nosed boy
Hides in a secret place
It's the only place of his own.

Simon Bird (Age 11)

What Is Black?

Black is a dog
That barks at you
Black is the dark
That goes in your shoe
Black is a hole
That can be deep
Black is a rat
That no-one would keep
Black is space
That has no air
Black is the colour
Of a big ugly bear
Black is a monster
That is very grim
Black is some hair
That needs a trim

Ben Bowles (Age 7)

A Spring Tart

A spoon full of colour,
A whisk of green grass,
Leaves falling down on the grass.

Pink blossom blooming
Red roses growing
Mix steadily
Leave to cool
Frogs jumping in a pool.

Victoria Bates (Age 9)

Goblin Market

Giggled every elf
When they saw him peeping
Came towards him wobbling
Leaping, hobbling, slithering
Growling and hissing
Gobbling, groaning, gawking
Laughing and chuckling
Sliding and pouncing
Full of laughter and anger
Pulling scary faces
Posh and evil
Tiger-like and snake-like
Monkey and gorilla like
Cheetah paced
Tiger voiced and hissing
Running faster all the time
Hissing like snakes
Creeping like tigers
Slithering like snakes

Ashley Bailey (Age 11)

The Paradise Bird

Rainforest, Rainforest dark as night
Tall tree's blocking out the light
Suddenly a flash of rainbow colours,
The bird of paradise is taking flight!

Like a rainbow against the green
Reflecting like gems, across a stream
Paradise bird, paradise bird, bird of every colour
Makes the Rainforest brighter than any other.

Oh paradise bird, oh paradise what would,
We do, without the beautiful colours of
    YOU!

Sian Byrne (Age 9)

The Wind

The wind whispers in the trees,
Batters the windows,
Visciously blows and slams doors.
The old tree groans as the wind whooshes past
In a tirade of leaves and twigs.
Everyone takes cover.
The wind goes alone.,
Drain pipes rattle
The wind blows an icy breath down our necks.
It makes us shiver, shake and quiver.
We cannot see the wind at all
Not even at night.
Because the wind whispers alone.

Poppy Barlow Griffin (Age 9)

Swimming

S wimming is the best
W here ever I go I remind my Mum swimming.
I t makes me really excited
M y Mum says should we go swimming
M aryah and my mates go and swim
I n the deep end
N othing is better than swimming
G oing to swimming is nice.

Sameena Bibi (Age 9)

Too Late To Wish

You should have wished upon a star my lord
But the lonely days have come

You should have wished upon a star my lord
But now the darkness has begun

You should have wished upon a star my lord
But the enemy has taken over the law

You should have wished upon a star my lord
But now the pain hurts more and more

You should have wished upon a star my lord
But we have no more men left to fight

You should have wished upon a star my lord
But now it's just you and me fighting the cold night

You should have wished upon a star my lord
But the lonely days have come

You should have wished upon a star my lord
But now our time is done

Harriet Berney (Age 11)

My Dog
(Dedicated to 'Tizzy')

Big brown eyes,
Staring up at me,
Begging for the leftovers,
From my tea.
Velvety ears,
And a big wet nose,
A warm wet tongue,
For licking my toes.
Rolling in the mud,
Getting messy paws.
Leaving muddy footprints,
When she comes indoors
My dog cheers me up,
When I'm feeling sad.
She's the best friend,
I've ever had.

Stephanie Buttle (Age 12)

Friendship

A friend is someone who is always there,
And someone who will always care,
A person needed in your life,
To be there for you and share your troubles.

A good friend would never lie,
She should always be there by your side,
A decent friend would never ignore you,
Always include you, even if they bore you.

A friend is someone who will give you support,
And always give a second thought,
Never go off and leave you alone,
Always walk with you while you're walking home.

Ulia Blower (Age 14)

Amulet

Inside the jaguar's jagged, teeth, the leafy mountains,
Inside the leafy mountains, the jaguar's silky paws,
Inside the jaguar's silky paws, the streaming, soggy river,
Inside the streaming, soggy river, the jaguar's sleek body,
Inside the jaguar's sleek body, the stuffy, steamy air,
Inside the stuffy, steamy air, the jaguar's razor, sharp claws,
Inside the jaguar's razor, sharp claws, the antelope's blood,
Inside the antelope's blood, the midnight sky,
Inside the midnight sky, the jaguar's stony eyes,
Inside the jaguar's stony eyes, the burning sun,
Inside the burning sun, the jaguar's stealthy tail,
Inside the jaguar's stealthy tail, the gentle, warm breeze,
Inside the gentle, warm breeze, the jaguar's jagged teeth.

Lauren Beckley (Age 11)

Yarnbury Moor

Walking round Yarnbury Moor,
Watching rabbits hopping joyfully
Nibbling grass as they go,
Little fluffy tails bobbing in and out of view.

Walking round Yarnbury Moor,
Trees swaying gently in the wind
Holding birds, brown, grey and black,
Chirruping chicks waiting hungrily for their tea.

In the past of Yarnbury Moor,
Hunters waiting ready to pounce,
Like a cat, killing a mouse,
Rabbit pie cooked and ready to eat.

Walking round Yarnbury Moor,
Lambs calling out for their mothers,
Mothers calling back to their lambs
Running to be reunited with them.

Rosanna Booth (Age 10)

The Sea Is . . . .

A giants blood,
A nightmare of blue,
A bottomless pit,
A never ending horror,
A dim death trap,
Below lie creatures to fear,
A foaming serpent waiting in the deep,
The end of the world lies at its
       FEET
  Cold
    Deep
      Vast

Robert Barham (Age 10)

Chinese New Year

Flags flap flap,
Dancers tap, tap,
Dragons slap, slap.

People imagine
A real dragon.
People imagine a fiery dragon.

Flags flap, flap,
Dancers tap, tap,
Dragons slap, slap.
People clap, clap.

Jack Binge (Age 8)

Summer Poem

When summer comes,
The nights are light,
We get to stay up,
And fly our kite.

We see leaves on trees,
And flowers on plants,
We see loads of insects,
Especially ants.

We play out in the sun,
With slides and swings,
We sit on our sun chairs,
While the birds sing.

Get your shorts and skirts on,
And maybe sandals too,
Get your sun hats on,
Beside the sea that's blue.

Jessica Barton (Age 9)

Autumn Leaves

Rustling leaves
Over the trees
Making rustling noises.

Rustling woo rustling woo
Over the trees over the blue.
Over the sky and over their lives.
Rustling woo rustling woo
Over the trees over the blue.
Over the sky and over their lives.

Pink spots blue hairr
Over all different kinds of people.

Rustling woo rustling woo
Over the trees over the blue.
Over the sky and over their lives.
Rustling woo rustling woo
Over the trees over the blue.
Over the sky and over their lives.
With peace which ends well.

Emma Boyce (Age 9)

Falling

Blackness
Nothing.
Brightness: Light, noises . . .
Voices, voices, dying away,
They're gone.
The eternal flames
Scorching my head . . .
A flurry of fire.
I'm fine, I'm fine, really, I am.
Confusion smothers my thoughts,
Like a heavy fog,
Spiralling towards
My mind.
A river of lava,
Flooding my head
With pain,
And mystification.
I'm scared,
I'm really scared,
Someone help me,
But there's no-one,
In this vast black hole of
Unconsciousness.

Victoria Ball (Age 11)

Tessa The Dog

My dog is black and brown and has white spots.
She sleeps in her cosy bed next to the phone on the table.
She is still a puppy but I love her very much.
I think she is wonderful with lots of white spots.
My dog is the very best
And I love her so much.
She catches the ball in the garden.
She sleeps ever so quietly.

Robyn Buisson (Age 7)

Chinese Dragon

The Chinese Dragon
Has a waving tail
With sharp claws
Its bulging eyes
Are blazing red
With golden scale
While smoke is puffing
From its head.

Lucy Burt (Age 6)

The Sea Is An Army Of Soldiers

The sea is an army attacking the land,
Its soldiers are hurtling stones and sand.
They catapult pebbles and march in waves
And persistently charge as if they are brave.

Their uniform colour is seaweed green
So they can creep up on the enemy without being seen.
They wear white hats, which gleam and shine
And they polish them at night, which takes a long time.

They go out all night and every single day;
They've never even stopped to go out to play.
The army of soldiers survive all weather,
They are invincible they live forever!

Kate Bolton (Age 10)

The Hill Fort

On a dark night the villagers gather,
To the safety the hill fort offers,
The moon and sea sit and watch,
As the villagers gather.

As the hill fort gates shut tight,
The fear grows,
Voices grow louder as danger nears,
As the villagers gather.

Rain burns as fire rises,
As the hill fort is engulfed the flames burn,
For days long gone,
As the villagers gather.

Josh Brimson (Age 11)

Ten Little Children

Ten little children, standing in a line,
One fell over, then there were nine.

Nine little children, sitting on a gate,
One fell off backwards, then there were eight.

Eight little children, chomping on some melon,
One felt sick, then there were seven.

Seven little children, picking up some sticks,
One scratched himself badly, then there were six.

Six little children, playing near a hive,
A bee came out, then there were five.

Five little children, walking round a store,
The store closed early, then there were four.

Four little children, went into the sea,
One got washed out, then there were three.

Three little children, trying to solve a clue,
He nearly got blown up, then there were two.

Two little children, laying under the sun,
One got sun-burnt, then there were one.

One little child, stood on his own,
He ran away, then there were none.

Amy Brown (Age 9)

Diary Of A Pal
(First World War)

I wish this measly war was over,
I miss my farm's fields of sweet white clover.
The only things I have from my home
Are a photograph and an old fir cone.

Sometimes we do nothing but fight,
This war is really a terrible blight.
When the deadly gas bombs zoom over,
All our men rush to try and take cover.

I really hate this thing called my bed,
All the mud round it is stained a dark red.
I have only one tattered blanket to go over me,
There are dirty wooden boards as far as I can see.

Why does the war have to go this way?
My best mate died the other day.
He got a bullet through his head,
A sniper saw him and shot him dead.

All the food we get is dried,
The packets are only five inches wide.
We only get alcohol when we can find it,
And if we do, we have to hide it in our kit.

Katharine Bagnall (Age 11)

Colours

Red is the disappearing sun at sunset.
Blue is the clear swimming pool.
Pink is the beautiful blossom that grows in Spring.
Green is the wavy grass.
Grey is the enormous elephant.

Ben Bradford (Age 6)

Red

I really love the colour red
Because it's the colour of my Ted.

Georgia Binfield (Age 5)

When I Gazed Into The Future

When I gazed into the future, I saw the world turning a deeper shade of red.
When I gazed into the future, I saw hundreds of people with cancer but none of them were dead.

When I gazed into the future, I saw that global warming never happened and it was just a dream.
When I gazed into the future, I saw pink and purple leaves floating down the stream.

When I gazed into the future, I heard the sound of a mysterious bird yellow, blue and green.
When I gazed into the future, I heard no sound of a sparrow, they were nowhere to be seen.

When I gazed into the future, I smelt the smell of fresh bread with orange and tangerine.
When I gazed into the future, I smelt the strong aroma of coffee but not brown aquamarine.

When I gazed into the future, I was amazed with what I saw,
No more hunger, disease, thirst and of course no more war!

Ellen Baker (Age 10)

Sir Francis Drake

There was a boy, Francis Drake, he sailed a sea and one lake
He went on a very short trip, one day he almost got a dip.

He sailed the Spanish Panama, the ship smelt of a bad banana
He really was magnific, he sailed America and the Pacific.

Drake left England behind and sailed with the Golden Hind
Elizabeth loved the things he stole, especially the Spanish gold.

He sailed to San Francisco, it was England he missed though
He sailed with pearls the seas were curled and the sun was shining.

"Around the world I've been, an amazing sight I've seen",
He fought with his sword and threw Spaniards overboard.

He was on a holiday at then end of sunny May
When a note came to say the, the Spanish are at the bay.

So in the end he won and had so much fun,
Now we still remember and celebrate in December.

Emma Louise Brown (Age 9)

Fifty Years

J oyful
U nique
B eautiful
I ncredible
L oving
E xtraordinary
E xciting

P assionate
A rtistic
R ewarded
T alented
Y ou

Amelia Baker (Age 9)

Celebration and Thanksgiving

My sister is carrying the message
In the Jubilee Baton
A special message that will go
All the way round the country
A flashing light beeps
With every breath the runner takes
When it gets back to the Queen
She will take the letter out
And read it and celebrate.

Matthew Brown (Age 8)

Children Playing

Children playing in the square
Oh how I wish I was there
But unfortunately it cannot be
As I'm not allowed to play with thee

From my window I see the square
As everybody turns to stare,
Oh how I wish I was there
Down there in the square

Lauren Baring (Age 12)

My Winter Wonderland

Soft white snow above the worms,
It's so cold the worms will squirm.
The snow is so cold.
My Grans not too old.
To be welcome in my Winter wonderland.

Snowball fights, who will win?
My brother has a sly grin.
My sister would cheat,
I'm dead meat.
Fighting in my Winter wonderland.

Making angels in the grass
I would fall on my...burn
We all would walk hand in hand
Walking in my Winter wonderland.

Yvonne Bamgboye (Age 10)

In The Sea

I'm swimming at the seaside
I'm swimming in the sea
I have a fin, some gills and spiky teeth
I have a twisted jaw
My tail is big and strong
And 15 metres long
I'm white and grey
I'm looking for some food
I see my friend Great White Fin
Follow me I said to him

What am I?

A little Great White Shark.

Matthew Bolton (Age 8)

Scorching Summer

Summer is the best time of year,
When the grass is green and the sky is clear.
We also have so much fun
Playing about in the scorching sun.

The sun sizzles like a frying pan,
Making you need a very good fan.
Summer makes you sweaty and hot,
That's why we end up drinking a lot.

Swimming pools also come in handy,
Or maybe go down to the beach where it is nice and sandy.
It's so hot I get a drink from the tap
But that isn't much help so I put on my cap.

Robert Beattie (Age 10)

I Put On My Radio

I put on my radio,
And it said a cheetah escaped from the zoo.
Then I heard a noise,
It was the cheetah drinking out of the loo.
I looked out in the front garden,
I stared at the house,
All of a sudden,
It turned into a mouse.
Mum came out and had to shout,
I went to the front room I saw a log.
All of a sudden,
It turned into a dog.
I looked at the tree,
All of a sudden,
It turned into a bee.
Then I ran outside and climbed up a tree.

Ashley Baxendale (Age 9)

The Door

Go and open the door,
Maybe your friends are waiting for you,
Or a glamorous beach just to yourself.

Go and open the door,
Maybe a mysterious old man is riding a crazy cat,
Or a spider eating mankind.

Go and open the door,
Maybe a dry dog is swimming in crystal clear water,
Or a dog inside a mirror magic world.

Go and open the door,
A dog is walking on its own,
Or a grim door leading to a smaller broken door
Going to a peaceful place in the middle of nowhere.

Lilian Brenton (Age 9)

Harry Potter Poem

Harry, Hermoine and Ron,
Went to see President Ding Dong,
Ron fell in a three foot well,
Hermoine said so long,
Dumbledore came marching
No-one noticed he brought a cart in,
Snape laughed and said "tara!"
McGonagal came in and said Sarah's not in,
Ron got out of the well then he fell alone,
He just started singing a song!

Rebecca Boweren (Age 9)

Isn't It Amazing

Isn't it amazing,
how stars shine so bright.
Not in the morning,
only at night.

Look up at the sun shine,
look up at the light.
Best to look up quickly,
because it's nearly night.

A little busy bee,
working all day long.
Never knows what time to stop,
because his clock is always wrong.

Umut Bektas (Age 8)

Woodland

The Spring
Awakening
Creatures are being born
Blossoms are in the trees again
New life

Summer
Lots of creatures
Trees are in full blossom
Squirrels are scampering in the trees
Hot sun

Autumn
Leaves are brown
Grey clouds are in the sky
Preparation for hibernation
Disappearing sun

Winter
Trees are stripped bare
Blanket of snow on the ground
The animals are all asleep
Year end

Michael Buckley (Age 10)

My Hobby

Quietly I run,
Secretly I hide,
Quickly I scramble up your wall.

Lock your doors
And your windows too;
Put your valuables away.

I may come creeping,
I may come stealing,
I will come for your things.

So don't go to sleep,
And stay up all night,
With your gun and your guard dog.

But I will still come,
Quick and like a gust of wind,
To take your possessions away.

Laura Bowden (Age 13)

If You Want To See A Tiger

If you want to see a Tiger
You must creep down the gloomy,
Deserted, Jungley forest, I know a tiger
Who's living down there:- he's creepy
He's a fierce, he's a scary, he's a wild!

Yes, if you really want to see a Tiger,
You must creep down the gloomy deserted jungley forest!

Go to the deserted forest and say:
"Stripey Tiger!
Stripey Tiger!
Stripey Tigerrrrrrrrrr!"

And up he'll come-
Don't stick around!
Run for your life!

Natasha Brady (Age 8)

Exams

Exams are scary,
They give me the quivers,
I get so cold my skins like ice,
The silence is deadly.

Getting worried feeling sick,
Lots to do not donw eyt,
Ah he's finished must get on,
It's playtime,
I'm finished now but more to come yet.

Shaun Brook (Age 10)

My Recipe For An Angry Teacher

First weigh out a little drop of
Cheeky boys having ruler fights,
Next mix a big pinch of giggling girls
Plaiting each others hair with fighting boys.
After that bake the giggling girls plaiting each others hair
And cheeky boys having a ruler fight,
Wait for the ink splodges
Finally serve a bag of boasting boys.

Elliott Ball (Age 10)

Haunted Island

On a haunted island far away
Where the mummies sleep
And the spiders creep,
Where the ghosts go wwwoooooo
And the monsters rrrrooooaarrr,
Children scream, but want far more!
Where vampires suck,
Where werewolves are out of luck,
You're sure to be in for a fright,
So don't expect a dreamy night.
When you're in this island of scares,
You're really having a night of nightmares!

Louis Budd (Age 10)

Inside My Head

Inside my head is a beach.
There's people everywhere in the sea.
There's people looking at the sun.
And I am making sand castles.
There's Mums, Dads and children playing games in the sand.

Inside my head there's a fairy castle.
With pictures on the walls and floor.
Fairies gave me food and drinks.
There are thousands of teddy bears.
I took ten of them home with me.

Rose Bennett (Age 8)

Weather

What is thunder?
A hammer crashing onto a nail.

What is fog?
Darkness not knowing where you are.

What is a hurricane?
A terrifying whirl pool sucking up anything in its path.

What are clouds?
Fur balls being coughed up by a cat.

What is hail?
An avalanche of jagged icy rocks cascading down a steep mountain.

Finlay Barnham (Age 11)

Fred The Fire

Fred likes to burn his naked way,
He has an evil disappearing friend
And his name is Ghastly Smoke.
With one flash of smoke Fred appears,
Nothing can defeat the powerful Fred
Fred's powerful enemy is Blue Water.
So it is bye bye to Ghastly Smoke and Fred the Fire.

Laura Bird (Age 11)

Love

You can buy cheese, you can buy lamb,
You can buy apple, you can buy ham,
You can buy ale and beer and wine,
You can buy chives and garlic and thyme,
You can buy chocolate and all things sweet,
You can buy anything to eat.
You can buy butter and lard and stork,
You can buy mutton and beef and pork,
You can buy partridge and pheasant and dove,
But the one thing you cannot buy is

LOVE

Amy Bolton (Age 9)

Playtime

At playtime we skip
At playtime we race
At playtime we go all over the place
At playtime we hop
At playtime the bell makes us stop with a bump

Hollie Burt (Age 9)

Yellow Poem

Beautiful buttercups
Blowing in the breeze
Crushed bananas
Beautiful buttercups
Blowing in the breeze
Juicy lemons
Beautiful buttercups
Blowing in the breeze

Jessica Busby (Age 8)

It Has To Be The Blackest

I am walking along the streets
The lamps are still not bright,
I start to go on the path,
The lights are still not on,
I turn the corner and still no light,
I walk back home
Back to number 1
And there is still no light.

Hannah Baldwin (Age 9)

Dark

When it's dark feel a fright,
When curtains sway,
I hate the howl of the wind,
And the little creatures noises,
That sound so pleasant in the day,
Sound so awful in the night,
When the wind starts to rise,
And the rain starts to fall.

Lauren Baker (Age 10)

?!

Should you meet a herd of zebras
And you cannot tell the hebras
Of the zebras from the shebras -
Watch which way each zebra pebras.

Maia T. Bainbridge (Age 11)

Our Little Star!

I've always had a big brother, I've never seen or heard of before.
But I know he's always been there, for me and for you.
He shows us our way home, he's our little star.
You might not always know it, but it's somewhere in your heart;
That our little Ben is always there.
We will never forget our little star, there's always room in our heart.
I believe that a phoenix can rise again, and so can Ben.
Some part of our life has to be bad, and Ben being gone is bad.
All we have to do is think of the good bits,
Come on mom and dad, he had a happy life.
Nobody knows why he left, maybe to give his life to me and Jack;
Whatever the reason he will always be there.
The five of us, although there seems as if there's only four.
But mom and dad, life isn't all that bad,
Because you got to hold your little boy; as well as having me and Jack.
One more thing mom and dad, the brightest star in the sky belongs to Ben,.
And you know why? Because he had you as parents;
The best thing that has ever happened!

Anna Brookes (Age 11)

Me, Me And Me

Footie   - Player
Hair   - Geller
Bike   - Rider
Ball   - Kicker
Try   - Scorer
Ball   - Shooter
Netball   - Hater
Dog   - Owner
Friend   - Maker
Pet   - Lover
Pheasant - Shooter
Go-kart   - Racer
Meat   - Eater
Great   - Swimmer
TV   - Watcher

This is me.

Henry Barron (Age 11)

The Magic Box

I will put in the box,
My first birthday card,
The splish and the splash of a dolphin,
Or my mum's first five merit sticker.

I will put in the box
The light of the sun, twinkle of a star
Or the whistling of a bluebird.

My box is like a treasure chest stacked high
With precious gold.

I will bury my box in a Sandy beach
And maybe one day someone will find my box and treasure it forever.

Marie Bannister (Age 9)

Deep In Space

Deep in space,
Without your mates,
You'll find some aliens,
Talking to Rumanians
You'll be surprised.
The aliens will rise
Your body will dry
You'll cry.
So deep in space
Without your mates.

Juwaria Bibi (Age 9)

Ten Things Found In A Castle Window Ledge

A piece of sticky chewing gum stuck to the bar
Two very long hairs about to tumble off the edge
A gone off packet of crunchy crisps
And six swishing cobwebs

Annabel Beilby (Age 7)

The Tiger

Tiger tiger with stripes so bright,
They even show up in the night,
When you pounce the forest shivers,
And when you roar the sun hides.

Nicole Ball (Age 5)

Remote Control

You press a button
And the TV changes channel
I can't believe it's just a black panel

Stephanie Boorer (Age 10)

Weather

What is thunder?
An angry elephant stampeding through an overgrown jungle.

What gives snow its sparkle?
Tiny crystals trapped in the beautiful white wool sheared from sheep.

How high does the rainbow go?
As high as the Imaginations of Man.

What is the taste of fog?
A vanilla lolly swirling round and round in your mouth.

What is the sound of hailstones falling?
Golf balls rebounding over green hills.

Hannah Bayfield (Age 11)

The Storm

The black noisy clouds are rushing across the evil sky.
It is always moving like a herd of bulls in a field,
It is as noisy as a band and it is clashing like cymbals
Whenever there is a jolt of lightning it clashes down to earth
The storm is a horrendous house it frightens me every time.

Kieran Bunce (Age 9)

Spring Changes

The daffodils grow up and up,
Trees grow blossom,
Squirrels try to find their hoard of nuts,
The birds come back,
A caterpillar can turn itself into a chrysalis that turns into a butterfly,
And what was once a baby turned into me!

Tom Boroughs (Age 6)

Music In The Last Fifty Years

Frank Sinatra flew to New York, New York,
He saw Cliff Richard who was on his Summer Holiday.
Cliff was dancing with Elvis who was wearing his Blue Suede Shoes.
A few weeks later whilst eating fish and chips in Liverpool
Elvis came across the Beatles who were needing some serious Help
About what happened Yesterday,
But poor Elvis was distracted by his Hound dog.
Abba walked down to Waterloo Station to watch
Flash on television with Queen.
When they got there Queen were chatting away to
Madonna about the Material Girl.
The Spice Girls met up with Hear-say to tell them
How to Spice Up Your Life,
And this is where it comes to an end.
Hear'say have nobody to talk to.

Kaneesha Bose (Age 10)

The Universe

Comets fly past in space
Supernovas explode here
Space is truly immense

Jonathan Biggin (Age 14)

Toaster

Fire breathing, fire breathing
Burning all the toast,
Fire breathing, fire breathing
Popping out the toast.

Fergus Barnham (Age 9)

Stonehenge

Some stones rest upon each other
One stone looks up to God
God was watching, watching,
Watching the stones,
Stones stones climbing away
Small bits breaking off
The stones look up to the clouds and sky
One stone looks like it is falling
The sun makes shadows on the stones
And the moon makes the stones glow

Adam Bishop (Age 7)

A Mouse's Journey

Mice, mice in town
scattering around
very, very quietly,
squeaking like mad,
looking for another place to eat,
very quietly creeps into the cat's flap,
making sure he doesn't get eaten himself,
for there is a cat in the house,
trotting to the cupboard,
as silent as a fish,
looking for the cheese.
There I go
walking home
as silent as me.
Like a mouse.

Joseph Brook Kent (Age 8)

Staffordshire

Seasons rolling all into one,
Fishing, swimming, having fun.
Horseback riding over hills and dales,
Exploring the land 'til the sunlight fails.
Birds singing so peaceful here,
Hope I'll come again next year.

Emma Brunning (Age 12)

Going To Sleep

In my bedroom all is quiet,
Except the slamming door,
When the cars roar by,
Wind rushes through my door,
Then my eyes slowly close,
My brain switches off.
Then the silence of morning opens.

Katie Baldwin (Age 9)

Orange Is . . .

Orange is like a tiger
Running in the wind
Strong and wonderful
Like the sun
Orange is a beam of light
Shining in the sky
Orange is a joyful and happy colour
It's bright and pretty
Orange is a pretty flower
Gleaming around the world.

Stephanie Brooks (Age 9)

My Best Friend

My best friend
He's a lot shorter than me
My best friend
We play football together
He's better than me
He always wears sporty clothes.
Adidas trousers, a Nike jumper.
He always wears trainers,
He used to play for a team.
Browny coloured hair, freckles
And a nice smile.
His eyes
I think they're brown.
That's Charlie,
My best friend.

Aaron Bentley (Age 15)

The Queen

I like the queen
She's not mean
Also rich
Does she stitch?
What does she do?
Does she like the colour blue?

Emily Brierley (Age 10)

Inside My Head

Inside my head
There's a spooky house
Full of scary skeletons
With wiggling bones
Mysterious mummies walking
With their arms outstretched

Lee Bentley (Age 8)

The Forest's Story

I remember when life was good
When my flowers were bright and tall,
My trees would stand up-right and proud,
And my berries were always ripe

Clear as a diamond my water flew by
Without a care in the world
And the fish danced around,
I liked the way the birds felt welcome
To come and hide away

The lady-birds would settle
And sleep on my green leaves
The squirrels would play and steal my nuts
Life was always fun!

But now nothing is the same
My brambles have gone
The animals have run to safety
The flowers have been removed

All is left is my memory of fun and life!
But I still have one question
Why . . . . . .?

Ellis Brennan (Age 11)

Love

Love is red,
It is shaped like a red heart.
Love tastes like thick chocolate,
Which has been sent from your secret admirer.
It feels like a furry loveable teddy.
It smells like roses,
That have just been cut.

Maria Bhatti (Age 9)

Dolphin, Dolphin

Dolphin, Dolphin swimming free
All around the deep blue sea,
Up out of the water you fly
Like a bird in the sky.

Grey and graceful through the air
Then back down without care,
With blow hole spurring on your head
Then its back down to the sea bed.

You look at me with mouth all laughing
Then off you go darting, darting,
I've seen Dolphins in a captive pool
But it's great to see you in a school.

Now you have gone out to sea
All that's left is memory.

Ashleigh Brindle (Age 8)

I Made A Funny Wish!!!

I made a funny wish,
that was to be a fish,
one day it came true,
I came out spotty and blue.
Don't laugh imagine if it was you.
A flapping fin instead of an arm,
I went mad, mum said keep calm.
Then I saw a shark,
I didn't know what to do,
I swam away,
wouldn't you?
He chased me near the beaches,
he chased me around the rocks,
he chased me in the Mediterranean,
he chased me like a fox.
Now this is true,
the adventure never ended,
you wouldn't of liked that to have been you?

Lucy Barrett (Age 8)

My Friend Carina

I've got a friend called Carina
She has a braid in all the time
She's got gold glasses
She's got blondy, browny hair.
She's got green eyes
And she is a cheeky monkey.
She is the best at RM Maths in the class
She has got a cousin called Sophie
And she calls her dopey
She has got a sister called Kayleigh
Carina is my best friend.

Melissa Barker (Age 8)

Hope And Despair

Hope is a shimmering blue
It smells of lily flowers
It tastes like honey and sugar
It sounds like a flickering fuzz
She feels delicate and silky.
She lives deep in our hearts

Despair is a putrid green
It smells of burning flesh
It tastes of sickly sweetness
Despair sounds like drumming feet
It feels as hot as fire
Despair lives in the centre of the sun.

Imogen Buller (Age 10)

Frog Explanation

Some people see me as an ugly frog,
Which will soon be turned into a prince.
You might think I was a puppet,
From a show you used to watch.
You could have heard a joke about me,
And laughed and not realised how it made me feel.

But I am real.
As I leap in my pond,
You might catch me in a jar,
And take me in your home.
You giggle at my slimy skin,
And scream and shout if you see me.
But I am a swimmer, swimming in my pond.

All I want is for you to see how I really am,
Not think of me as some ludicrous toy.
Don't eat my legs for your dinner.
I just want a pond to live in,
Where I'm out of danger.
Please give me love.

Leoni Belsman (Age 10)

Traveller

T ourist, travelling the world.
R oaming everywhere all over.
A dventurer moving from place to place.
V oyager sea to sea coast to coast.
E xplorer finding different things.
L onely on your own.
L eader of your own gang.
E ndless journey never stopping.
R owdy in the car all the time.

Laura Boxall (Age 10)

The Fire

Animals, animals leaping high,
They all don't know why,
High and low and everywhere,
They're jumping, speeding and leaping.

Fire, Fire spitting out all its flames,
There's smoke in the air spinning round and round,
Fires shooting up to the sky,
Fires shooting up very high,
Speeding across the ground really fast.
How was it made? Please tell me now.

Hunters hunters running for their lives,
That we're going to kill with their knives
Sprinting, jumping 1, 2, 3,
For all they've done their time will come

Hannah Bates (Age 8)

What Is . . . A Tree?

In Spring it is a little cygnet,
growing proper feathers

In Summer it is a great green giant,
reaching up to the sky

In Fall it is a withering rose,
dropping it's petals one by one

In Winter it is an unsuccessful scarecrow,
calling to the birds

But to me a tree is the ghost,
that casts the shadows on my wall.

Claire Bryant (Age11)

The Dark

The dark is black and gloomy
A bat's day time
A hedgehog's heaven
An owl's restaurant
A star's playtime

The dark is a mother's relaxation
People's sleep, a driver's hell
A fox's hunting time
The night

The dark is an ant's camouflage
A farmer's nightmare
A time for dreams
A club's money maker.

Katie Bennett (Age 9)

My Dream

I can't stop shaking
And I can't move at all,
Hiding behind the twigs and branches
Thinking I'm going to fall.

I'm getting very scared
I think I should get down,
But if I wake the lions
They'll scare me with their frown.

I've only woke the lions up
I think I'm going to scream,
But in the end I shouldn't be scared
Because it's just a dream.

Joseph Brough (Age 9)

My Bedroom

My dad walks in to my bedroom and says it's a tip
My mum says I give her too much lip

In comes my brother and joins us as well
And shouts "This looks like hell"
"Phwaar what's that smell".

We hunt high and we hunt low
But the smell it does not go

We look in the cupboard and under the bed
It smells to me as if something is dead

I look behind the chair,
To see what is there,
I look by my feet,
To see a mouldy old sweet

I have found the smell
I can go and tell
My friends can come round
To see what I have found

Jessica Beazer (Age 11)

I Like Exercising

I like exercising
I like skipping
I like swimming
I like jogging

I like to stretch in the morning
I like to eat healthy food.
To keep my heart beating
So I will be fit all the time.

Sarah Binns (Age 8)

Finding A Dead Snail

Shivering through your bones
When you feel a slimy snail,
Crushed in a puddle is its shell
Followed by a trail.

I pick up the snail's body
It's wet and covered in salt,
The feelers look all shiny
And smell of mouldy malt.

I handle the crushed shell
It's hard like broken lead
I take it home to mum
The poor old snail is dead.

Ellen Bates (Age 9)

Ten Little Children

Ten little children playing with a mine
One blew up then there were nine

Nine little children walking through a gate
One hit the fence then there were eight

Eight little children walking through heaven
One fell down then there were seven

Seven little children playing with bricks
One got squashed then there were six

Six little children having a dive
One fell off the board then there were five

Five little children knocking on a door
One hit the bricks then there were four

Four little children hanging on a tree
One fell down then there were three

Three little children sitting on the loo
One fell in then there were two

Two little children looking at the sun
One turned blind then there was one

One little child his name was John
He fell over then there were none

Alexander Bateson (Age 8)

Spiders Spiders

Spiders are scary
And ever so hairy
Because they do not shave!

Charlie Barker (Age 8)

Thunder And Lightning

T he thunder is loud
H ere is the big BANG
U nder the covers you go
N o! Thunder!
D o not hurt me
E xciting boom
R ain rushing

L ong flash
I t's exciting
G o lightning
H ere's lightning
T he fast light
N o way please stop
I 'm scared
N umber of seconds
G o away, lightning

Jamie Clements (Age 9)

Chocolate

Imagine a world made of chocolate,
A mixture of white, dark and milk,
You could pick a piece of a tree, you could eat anything you liked.
Imagine a house of chocolate,
When you eat it, It melts in your mouth,
You cannot resist it,
Tasting the creamy chocolate,
When the sun shines the world would melt
But what will happen,
Who knows??
I'm made of chocolate, I can eat myself,
I can nibble away
All day, every day,
Till guess what?
Till I'm all gone.

Beth Bird (Age 9)

Winter

Winter is when the landscape is white,
It is when all the birds take flight,
When Father Christmas comes at night,
And when the cold seems to bite,
It is when rain falls from a great height,
When in the street begins a snow fight,
And when the celebrity turns on the Oxford Street lights,
All of this is winter for me, what else could all of it be?

Nicola Britton (Age 12)

Farmyard

The farm door creaked as the farmer slurped his spaghetti
The cat screamed as the door shut
The farmer's wife yelled as she sizzled the sausages
The pigs snorted as the kids gave them food
The mice squeaked as they ran for food
The drinks popped as the farmer put it in the glasses
The wind howled in the night sky

Daysheen Bhogal (Age 9)

The Future

When I gaze into the future, I saw robots, money,
Lots of things but never Pooh's honey.
When I gaze into the future, I saw space ships,
Aliens, all over Mars, and oranges with no pips.
When I gaze into the future, I saw cars with no wheels,
Same with bikes and strangely enough shoes with no heels.

Tom Bennett (Age 11)

Night Time

The owls are hooting,
Sweeping, shooting,
Through the starlit sky.

The cats are yowling,
Screeching, howling,
Breaking the silence of the night.

The rats are squealing,
Fidgeting, feeling
For scraps left in the kitchen.

The floor boards are creaking
The boiler pipes squeaking
Echoing through the quiet house

The birds are chirping,
Flying and sweeping
Through the sunlit sky.

Hannah Burns (Age 11)

Nothing To Do?

Nothing to do?
Nothing to do?
Smear the phone in sticky glue.
Turn the telly upside down!
Throw your sister down the town.
Saw the table into half,
Tell the teacher not to laugh!
Put some nails in dad's cap,
Then go off and have a nap.

Heather Barral (Age 8)

The Crab

Red crab
Big snapping claws
Crawling on bumpy rocks
Red crab shutting tight on its prey
It kills

George Blower (Age 9)

Cactus

The cactus is so prickly,
And spikes grow back so quickly,
If I had to conclude,
That it had an attitude,
It would probably be quite fickly.

Edward Bullinger (Age 12)

Fish

Beneath the sea,
they swim around
and communicate without a sound.

In the water so very clear,
speaking words that no-one can hear.
they seem to know when danger's near,
and that's their sign to disappear.

When the seagulls come for lunch,
gathering in flocks,
the fish get scared and hide away underneath the rocks.

Amy Bradshaw (Age 10)

The Storm

Hurricanes blow, phone wires whistle,
Wind is as sharp as a thorn covered thistle.

Children play, despite the damp,
Cub Scouts work on the winter camp.

Rain pours, down to the ground,
As it falls, it makes a dripping sound.

Sun comes out, from behind the clouds,
Children laugh, being very loud.

Josh Bolding (Age 8)

What Makes The Teacher Angry

Add a hint of spitting boys and knead till smooth and flat for 5 to 10 mins
Pour a class of shouting children and add a dollop of swearing boys to give it a kick.

Gently roll and sprinkle a dash of giggling girls to spice it up.
Drizzle some girls playing with their Barbies and lay it on a bed of bullies.
Gently tip a ruler fight and whisk till golden brown.

Also add a pinch of cheeky girls for the finishing touch.
Then serve to make a teacher angry.

William Bayton (Age 10)

Hamster

Fluffy
With small blue eyes
Sleeping in its soft bed.
Running in its pink Hamster ball
All night.

Emma Barrett (Age 8)

What Makes A Potion

The juice from a star,
The heal from a medicine,
The death of a drug,
What makes a potion?
The teachers ungetroundable attitude,
The shine on a church bells ring,
The perfectness of a circle,
What makes a potion?
The colour from a felt pen nib,
The deadliness of a snake,
The left thumb nail of a spider,
What makes a potion?

Sam Brown (Age 12)

If I Ruled The School

If I ruled the school
It would be cool
We would have a massive swimming pool
We would have a party in the hall

Dolphins are swimming
Mobiles are ringing
Schools out lets shout

Late in early out
Lets change this school
Lets make it cool.

Jessica Adams and Bryony Baldwin (Age 12)

Silver Moon

Mars shines red and glittery,
A heart which has just been broken.
Trees stand alone like evil hearted phantoms,
Still waiting for people to pass.

The moon is round,
A mouth gobbbling up glittering sweets in the sky.

His silver refelction mirrored in every puddle.

Hannah Bardsley (Age 9)

Friends

He is always there when I'm sad
to cheer me up and make me glad.
He stands by me through thick and thin,
I try to do the same to him.
We play football and lots of games,
we never call each other names.
With him I don't pretend,
because he will always be my friend.

Jack Bradshaw (Age 8)

Babies

Babies dribble,
Blow raspberries,
Babbies tumble,
Babies sleep all day.
I like babies because they are clever.
Babies make me laugh.
I like babies because I can play with them.

Katie Beech (Age 16)

Water

The first time I see water in the sea
I am wearing swimming clothes,
There are fish swimming,
The water is transparent,
Now I am going to swim with the fish,
I am jumping in,
I am wet and water is down me,
Jelly fish and crabs,
I get sand in my toes,
The waves are lifting me up and putting me down,
There is a shark!
I swim to my mum

Jack Butcher (Age 9)

Seasons

In the summer I like to swim
In the winter I stay in
In the autumn I play in the leaves
And in the spring I climb the trees

When I swim I splash about
When I'm in I scream and shout
When I'm playing in the leaves
I jump about, shout and scream
And when I climb up in the trees
I sit and eat my ice-cream.

Clarissa Baker (Age 8)

1 2 3 4 5

When I was 1 I was a baby

When I was 2 I was a baby as well

When I was 3 I was a baby again

When I was 4 I was big

And now I'm 5 I'm here!

Alex Blackford (Age 5)

Stonehenge

The huge rocks standing tall,
Great stones remaining high
Silence falling all around,
The wind bouncing off the rocks,
The great stones standing as time goes by
Huge rocks as silver as the moon
Rock lying still lying as time goes by

Fraser Browning (Age 8)

The Canine Rhyme

The labrador has gleaming, glittering eyes like a moonlit city at night.
He has slender, slim legs like a model on a catwalk.
The soft, padded paws run speedily down the street.
His whining noise begging for more.
His beautiful fluffy ears are as soft as feathers.
He glides around the room chasing a ball.
This playful pup leaps and knocks you down to your knees.
You laugh as he licks your face with a rough, slobbery tongue.
You can tell he likes it here.

Rebecca Button (Age 10)

Why?

Why do clouds float across the sky?
Why do living creatures, live and die?

Why don't we float around in the air?
Why do things happen that aren't really fair?

Why do birds have a nest?
Why do we stop to have a rest?

Why does light come on when we flick a switch?
Why does water run through a ditch?

Why do trees come up from the ground?
Why does the world spin around and around?

Harriet Brundle (Age 10)

Nature Living

A heavy cart rambles
Snow melting
Deep in the hill mist.

Flutters a butterfly,
With a leaf stuck in his mouth.
A crow is crowing.

The puppy sleeps
Under the willow.
And from the grass creeps a ladybird.

Rachel Boyall (Age 8)

T.V.

T.V. in the living room,
T.V. in the garden,
T.V. when you're really tired,
T.V. when you're bored.
Hey! This episodes new please don't turn it off.
I prefer a video
T.V.'s big and small
Kids watch in the morning,
Teenagers in the afternoon
And adults in the evening
T.V. blaring loud at night
T.V. in the day,
Can you cope?
Does it drive you crazy,
Or does it drive you mad?

Andrew Britton (Age 9)

Heard It In The Playground

Heard it in the playground
Miss he's eating a sweet
Don't you mean eaten a sweet.
Heard it in the playground
You love Tarzan.
Heard it in the playground
Good tackle Ross.

Heard it in the playground
Miss, Miss he thinks he's a black belt haiya!
Heard it in the playground
Pear brain, gorilla breath.

Heard it in the playground
Telling of you.

James Blandamer (Age 9)

Inside The Cat

Inside the cat's teeth, a snow capped mountain,
Inside the snow capped mountain, the cat's fur,
Inside the cat's fur, long green grass,
Inside the long green grass, the cat's whiskers,
Inside the cat's whiskers, a strong statue,
Inside the strong statue, the cat's claw,
Inside the cat's claw, the mouses squeak,
Inside the mouses squeak, a deafened sound,
Inside the deafened sound, the cat's purr,
Inside the cat's purr, a trickling waterfall,
Inside the trickling waterfall, the cat's wet nose,
Inside the cat's wet nose, a pointed hill,
Inside the pointed hill, the cat's teeth.

Jack Bishop (Age 10)

The Sea Is...

A deep blue hole
A freezing blanket.
A living soup.
A mysterious fog
A blue monster waiting to pulll you under.
Deadly water
A wet playground full of ships
A marky pudd.
A deep bearth
A frothedge.
The sea is.

Dennis Burfoot (Age 9)

Motorcross

Motorcross is really great fun,
Over the jumps and around the track,
Together me and my Dad go fast,
Oh no I've fallen off again,
Come over here and give me a hand,
Rain's on it's way, we need to get going,
Only two laps to go, to catch the leader
Second place now, I need to go faster,
Sorry Dad, took you on the last corner,
The Finish.

Harry Brookes (Age 9)

Nature

Nature is a beautiful thing
Flowers grow to the sound of spring
The sky is blue and the grass is green
The birds are beautiful to be seen
Animals have homes in the trees
We get our sweet honey from the bees
Nature also includes us all
The fat, the thin, the tall, the small.

Chelsea Buckingham (Age 11)

The Sea Is . . .

A lion pouncing for its prey,
An endless dark lake blowing in the wind,
A bottomless well,
An octopus leaking blue blood,
A grey, misty phantom,
A never-ending corridor of a haunted house,
A deathtrap,
    black,
        deep,
            evil.

Rosie Bowler (Age 9)

Going To Space

I'm going to space:
"I'm going to space"
Moon and stars.
Yellow and bright
In a rocket I may go?
On to a big hot place.
No i can not go on this one hot and yellow.
On to mars, off I go!
An alien on mars I am dead or I am in bed!

Laura Black (Age 8)

What Is Yellow?

Yellow is the sunset
That means it's going to be dark.
Yellow is the colour of a duck
That walks in the park.
Yellow is a school pencil
That's what you write with when you do maths.
Yellow is a beautiful daffodil
That grows on the path.

Georgina Boxall (Age 6)

Winter

Winter is the time of year,
When all the snow has appeared,
Trees are icy, grey and old,
Wrap up warm it will be cold.
The grass is covered in a blanket of white,
The animals hibernate day and night.
The trees are stripped of all their leaves,
Everyone feels the winter breeze.
The snow falls like a shooting star,
As the three kings travel from afar.

Lauren Bean (Age 11)

The Recipe For An Angry Teacher

First of all mix up a bowl of 3 mucky children stupidly messing about
Six non-eaten lunches and 65 shameful excuses
When it's turned into liquid add exactly a pinch of bad language
And some unworthy behaviour to give it a kick.

Dollop all the friends falling out you have into another bowl
And sprinkle a few rubbers being thrown on top.
Mix both bowls together, bake until red and . . . Eureka!!!
An angry teacher.

Benjamin Beagley (Age 10)

What Makes A Teacher Angry!

Pour a gang of paper aeroplane throwing boys into a
Jugful of unbelievably wrong spellings.
Whisk in a large handful of wriggling girls
Trying to be good but not succeeding
And then combine with pencil flicking and blind pulling.
Divide the fierce ruler fights with a bowlful of doodling work.
Now boil it up with the teacher's sweat for an hour
Then for the finishing touch sprinkle a shouting boy on the top
And WALLA the cake is finished.

Thomas Bates (Age 9)

Glasses!

Glasses are terrible, glasses are bad
Glasses are a punishment for being really bad.
You put those dreaded things on and you turn to the mirror,
And see those dreaded things on your nose,
And then you start to shiver,
You run down stairs and say "Dad, Dad",
These glasses on my nose look really really bad.
I begged and begged and begged again.
Until the day was through,
And after that I went to bed.
Wahoo, wahoo, wahoo.

Matthew Bate (Age 11)

A Girl At the Beach

There was a girl at the beach
She was eating a big peach
When she dropped it in the sand
'Twas like a very different land
When the land began to sink
'Twas like a hidden rock going pink
When the sand went yellow again
'Twas like a sparkling golden pen
When the golden pen ran out
'Twas like a snake trying to shout
When the snake ran out of breath
'Twas like a person who's been touched by death

Jemma Bowes (Age 11)

My Mum

My mum is a big comfy chair.
She takes me to the summer fair.
I love my Mum such a lot,
Sometimes she calls me a little tot.
My Mum is fun all the time,
We make up some funny rhymes.
She bought me some rabbits.
I said "Sorry" for my habits
Oh I love, I love my Mum.

Mica Budd (Age 8)

Trees In Winter

In winter the trees look black
They have lost their leaves
Their branches are bare
And the twigs look like fingers
Pointing to the sky.

When the sun shines through
When branches you can see
The shadows on the ground
Making dainty patterns

Bethany Chismon (Age 6)

Midnight Party!

The light has gone,
So come along,
And have a midnight party.
I've got some snacks and movies to see,
So let's watch jaws,
Whoopee!
I'm scared to death,
Turn it off now.
The midnight party has ended!

Jade Bolton (Age 11)

My Home

I live by the seaside with a green on the side
Through my window I can see houses,
Through my brother's I can see the sea,
With flowers in my neighbours garden it brightens up the place,
I walk the dogs who make me laugh
They run and jump and have the cutest faces.

Katie Birch (Age 10)

Forest In Moonlight

Trees stretch in their sleep, under a blanket of snow,
And stars wink in the twilight as if they know,
I'm not meant to be here, that I should be in bed,
With badgers below and owls hooting ahead.
Foxes glow red, as warm as a fire,
And trees bend upwards as if their desire,
Was to catch the moon in its misty sky,
As bats in their darkness flutter by
The blueness is fading, dawn is near,
The sky, so heavy, is becoming clear,
My eye-lids are closing, my legs growing weak,
As I fall in the silver, so sleek and so deep.

Elizabeth Bardsley (Age 10)

Dogs!

I don't like dogs,
They have big sharp claws,
They're fierce and scary,
They have big sharp teeth to bite you in half!
They have big tall hairy legs,
That can run for miles and miles,
I don't like dogs,
They chase you until you are out of breath,
They can smell you even when you are not there

    I don't like Dogs!

Emma Bellamy (Age 9)

The A.J.B.

Yo! The A.J.B. tha place to be
Shout out if you want to be me.
Time to rock and roll
If you think you're a Barbie doll!
It is time to rock and roll if you're an A.J.B.!

Aaron Barton (Age 8)

Imagination

I magination is a dream
M aking a dream world for you
A llowing you in charge all around
G leaming with joy
I n a world of your own
N ice people only in your world
A place called paradise
T all and grand you stand
I magining another world
O n another planet
N otice your imagination sent you somewhere else again.

Laura Boxall (Age 11)

Lunch Time

It's time for lunch
That's after brunch

I wash my hands in the sink
And after, have a little drink

In school dinners they have some meat
And pretty much to eat

But at first we say our prayers
Sometimes we haven't enough chairs

We always make a lot of noise
It's mostly all the boys.

Mayumi Blackmoor (Age 8)

Planet

The sun is sizzling silently,
While mercury works metallic magic.
Venus is very valuable
And the Earth is extraordinary
Mars is a monster of metal.
Jupiter is a jungle of jewels.
Saturn is a spectacular sensation
And Uranus is unbeatable
Neptune is the king of the night
Pluto is a prince and a purple sight.

Kerrie Black (Age 11)

Tiger

Tiger, tiger in the forest
Crouching low to catch your prey
Your big green eyes
Watch as you wait

Tom Burrows (Age 5)

Smoking

Smoking kills, it's not right,
People hold the butt, they hold it tight,
Then it goes into the mouth,
Ready to light, not in the house,
Every time you're about to light,
Your lungs just cannot fight,
Smoking isn't a joke,
You will sometimes even choke,
So when you think "that looks nice",
For your own safety, consider twice.

Laura Creese (Age 13)

I'll Fly Through Heaven

I'll fly through heaven on Angels wings,
And hear the radiant voices sing.

I'll sit on a white cloud and watch the sea,
And meet the angel who watched over me.

I'll look down on you with all my love,
And enter your soul from heaven above.

I'll meet God but not the Devil,
Whites the flow and reds the rebel.

I'll go to heaven but not to hell,
And be reborn on Earth to tell,

Of my journeys in the heavens,
Not to sit on cloud 9 but on cloud 7.

I'm dreaming all this in my head,
But hopefully it'll happen when I'm dead.

Sarah Clements (Age 12)

My Dog

I have a little dog
His name is Robbie Rob
And he's barking so much
We can't let him out
When he goes in the garden
It makes the neighbours shout
He runs to the back door pricking up his ears
He chases all the birds
He really is quite fierce

Abigail Cross (Age 6)

Kamikaze

He will die tonight,
Strapped inside his vehicle.
Honoured by his fate.

Sam Cloake (Age 11)

Black

Black is a night
That tries to kill you
Black is a dog
That quite needs the loo
Black is a storm
That makes a loud sound
Black is a shadow
That covers the ground.

Heni Ciechanowicz (Age 7)

Used To Be

You used to be my S.A.Ts paper,
We would never fail.
You used to be my guidance map,
We'd travel up and down dale.
You used to be my joke book,
With a funny joke to tell.
Although we had our arguments, you would never yell.
You used to be my guardian angel, looking over me.
Together we were Ying and Yang,
A true friend you used to be.

You used to be my Holy Book,
Helping me live life to the full.
You used to be my magnet,
You would push although I'd pull.
You used to be my sunshine, sending out your rays.
Playing, talking, shopping, walking,
That's how we used to spend our days.
You were like a favourite toy, we'd play every day.
That's how you used to be,
Until you passed away.

Leah Cowan (Age 12)

The Chinese Dragon

The Chinese dragon is looking good
While stepping over piles of wood,
Blowing fire is its desire,
Cracker strings go bang
And cymbals clang
And fireworks fill the sky,
The colour of lanterns glow.

Joseph Corley (Age 6)

Birds

Flying through the air
In a lovely breeze
Wings flapping gently,
Through the breezy air.

Andrew Costin (Age 7)

In The Jungle

There's a jungle in India
And in the jungle there's some trees
And between the trees there's a swamp
And in the swamp there's a crocodile
And in the crocodile there's an arm
Along comes a boy and puts his hand in the water and
SNAP!!
His arm fell off.

Henry Baker (Age 9)

Maryling & Christian

There was a girl called Maryling, who had a boyfriend who was very charming,
Everyone thought they were slaughtered but really drowned in the Tamiami water.

Her charming boyfriend was called Christian who was the son of a Mexican,
Everyone thought they were slaughtered but really drowned in the Tamiami water.

The loving birds left a note, that they personally wrote,
Everyone thought they were slaughtered but really drowned in the Tamiami water.

They jumped into the raging stream, so that they could see the heavens gleam,
Everyone thought they were slaughtered but really drowned in the Tamiami water.

Their parents looked all around, until eventually they were found,
Everyone thought they were slaughtered but really drowned in the Tamiami water.

They're all alone, who were quietly at their home,
Everyone thought they were slaughtered but really drowned in the Tamiami water.

David Craig (Age 11)

Rivers

Fast flowing,
Water going,
Bending, whirling,
Swishing, curling,
Fish swimming,
Birds skimming,
People fishing,
Forever wishing,
They could be
Completely free,
Like the river
Seemed to be.

Vicky Currigan (Age 14)

Love Is . . .

Love is seeing my furry, fluffy dog sleeping in her warm bed.
Love is looking at my brightly coloured room on a Saturday morning.
Love is the sound of the twittering birds singing on a bright, shiny Saturday.
Love is hearing my mum saying she loves me so much.
Love is the smell of pretty, red flowers growing nicely.
Love is the smell of perfume on me.
Love is touching my warm baby brother when I see him.
Love is the feel of my white rabbit.
Love is the taste of apple pie in the dark of the night.
Love is taste of hot chocolate in the morning.
Love is when all the world is being happy and joyful.

Lois Curley (Age 7)

Subjects

English pen,
Maths protractor,
Science goggles,
P.E. Trainers,
Geography atlas,
R.E. Bible,
History timeline,
Music triangle,
German dictionary,
French vocab book,
Technology apron,
I.T. keyboard,
Art paintbrush,
Heavy bag!

Linzi Cureton (Age 12)

The Leopard's Eye

Inside the leopards's eye, the spinning planet.
Inside the spinning planet, the leopard's spots.
Inside the leopard's spots, a jungle of thriving plants.
Inside the jungle of thriving plants, the leopard's whiskers
Inside the leopard's whiskers, the guiding arrows.
Inside the guiding arrows, the leopard's teeth.
Inside the leopards teeth, the zebra's stripes.
Inside the zebra's stripes, the disastrous death.
Inside the disastrous death, the leopard's claws.
Inside the leopard's claws, the compass facing north.
Inside the compass facing north, the leopard's fur.
Inside the leopard's fur, a silk coat.
Inside the coat of silk, the leopard's eye.

Natalie Collingwood (Age 11)

Please Mr Harvey

Please Mr Harvey
This boy called Jack
Keeps using my rubber
And is poking my back.

Just go and ignore him
Just get on with your work
Or go and sit somewhere else then
But don't be a jerk.

Please Mr Harvey
This boy called Jack
Keeps calling me names
And is eating a snack.

Just move away from him
Just go and tell him off
Don't bother me
Or that's another point off.

Jordan Cartwright (Age 9)

The Spell Of Life

The soul from a river,
The shine from the sky,
A HEAD.

The mass of the world,
The depth of the sea,
A BODY.

The tickle of a spider,
The riggleness from a worm,
THE ARMS.

The ice from hell,
The goodness of a witch,
THE LEGS.

The shine from heaven,
The light of the world,
THE SPELL OF LIFE.

Leon Carter (Age 12)

Last Day At School

Last day at school
We empty our trays
Take pictures home
We look forward to the summer holidays

Last day at school
We collect our p.e. bags
Clean the walls
With dirty rags

Last day at school
We stack our chairs
Tidy up the classroom
Change the clothes that I wear

Last day at school
We shut the door
Say bye bye
And clean the floor

Hannah Conway (Age 7)

Rulers Of The Skies

Blazing fiercely
He's God of the day,
Reigning from dawn
'Til light fades away.

A flickering ball
Of raging white light,
Scorching the eyes
From morning 'til night.

Yet when the sun fades
The Moon she awakes,
Her pale gleam mirrored in pools
Glittering silver in lakes.

She bathes all the land
In her soft glowing light,
Calm and serene
Goddess of the night.

Melanie Clegg (Age 13)

Tonight At Noon

Tonight at noon Vinnie Jones will go through a whole movie without killing anyone
Hitler will declare peace, love and serenity throughout the world
Tonight at noon Bill Gates will look at something and not say, "I can make a dollar out of that!"
Tonight at noon George Bush will not squint at the camera
Anthony Worrell-Thompson will not add six bottles of Vodka to his "Homemade Pizza"
Anne Widdecombe will wear Spandex shorts and nothing else to Parliament
Ainsley Harriot will not smile for a year
Brighton & Hove Albion will battle it out with Dover United for the Premiership
Tonight at noon I didn't do it.

Nathaniel Clark (Age 11)

Gazed

When I gazed into the future, I saw the world turning a darker shade of blue.
When I gazed into the future, we were extinct and dinasours ruled the earth again.
When I gazed into the future, I saw millions of people in the desert,
Dying of hunger and dehydration.
When I gazed into the future, I saw animals ruling the world as humans turned out to be slaves.
When I gazed into the future, I saw clouds packed full of acid rain
After the sun had set and the acid rain would start again,
When I gazed into the future, I saw schools getting demolished and kids ruling the earth.
When I gazed into the future, I saw America still at war with Afghanistan,
Even though it wasn't a big war.
When I gazed into the future, I saw Diseases, illnesses any type of cancer never existed.
When I gazed into the future, people never died.
When I gazed into the future, I saw that bullies never existed,
And never would and war never existed.
When I gazed into the future, the world was at peace at last.

Gemma Coombs (Age 11)

The Reader

You blink. A shudder in your face
Only for a split second then,
Back to the story.

Muscles tense,
A feeling of worry comes across,
Then safety arrives,
But not for you...
For someone else,
Are they real?

You turn the page
A short break,
Showing the distinction
Between fantasy and reality.
There you are in silence,
Watching letters, black marks across the page.
You are drawn back in.

But for how much longer?

Jake Clayton (Age 12)

Trees In Winter

As we wandered through the woods
the trees looked rather bare.
The sky was dark behind them
but we didn't seem to care.
The branches bending in the breeze
overlapping other trees.
It was a cold December evening,
the moon was shining bright,
our shadows reflecting on the bark,
it gave us such a fright.
Then the snow began to fall
and every tree looked white.
It layed on twigs and branches
it made a pretty sight.
As we came to the end of the woods
we looked back at the trees.
In a few months time,
the buds will form.
It will look a different scene.

Ben Chapman (Age 10)

What Happened At Midnight

I woke up at midnight
And heard the window creaking
The wind whistling
And footsteps coming down the corridor
I ducked down under my covers and squealed.
I peeped over my covers and saw it,
A quivering light,
In a bright red smoke it disappeared

Virginia Coates (Age 9)

Heavy Rain On Our Village

Rain smashes on the dustbin lids.
Streams start to flow down the road.
The cows stay under the trees.
When cars hit the puddles
It splashes like waterfalls.
Cars go home and get warm by the fire.
Children run home.
Blackbirds fly to their nests.

Daniel Coverdale (Age 8)

How To Conquer The Breeze

Mild as a mouse,
When it whistles it is like your ancestors speaking to you;
It has been to the immense height of the mountains,
And then back to me.

It has soared through the ferny forests,
And wriggled through the tightest gaps,
It's the gentlest thing on earth,
It's always there for me.

It has smelt the freshest of fruit,
Which it carries on its travels from place to place, look down at the deep blue sea,
It has felt the blistering heat and the icy cold,
And it is always looking after me.

It has glanced at the most enormous animals,
It sends ripples across the calm water,
Whipped up from the meandering river;
It always relaxes me.

It has toothcombed every inch of the earth,
It has scoured every part of our body,
As soothing as a tender lullaby,
And that's what comforts me.

Nathan Cherrington (Age 10)

Grapes

When I take a bunch of grapes,
And pick them off one by one,
I can already taste,
The sweetness in my mouth,
As soon as I put it on my tongue,
And seal my lips like a door,
It bursts open like a balloon,
And the sweetness of the juice
Makes my tongue fizz.

Jordan Clague (Age 9)

The Fire

The flames burning red and hot,
Flickering flames dazzling in the eyes of the animals,
The terrifying flames,

Deer racing the boiling flames,
Deer racing like planes.

Hunters racing the dazzling flames,
Hunters racing like the wind.

Nick Cressey (Age 9)

Travel

Fly to Spain,
I can't wait.
There's my shoes
With my case
Here's my dad
Start the car.
There comes mum
Let's go far.

Luke Crocker (Age 10)

The Day The Inspectors Came

The day the inspectors came,
I didn't feel ashamed,
I thought my work was really good,
Then I went in the classroom and there he stood.

A big tall man with a greyish beard.
Stared at the class and looked very weird,
He gazed all around child by child,
Then came over to me in a very posh style.

Very good work very good indeed,
Then he rushed off to Micheala in a very posh speed.

Ashleigh Clark (Age 10)

Power Cut

A dreadful storm blew up in the night
It rattled the windows and gave me a fright!

I pulled the covers up over my head
And held on tight to my favourite ted.

Mum got up at half past three
She went down stairs and made cups of tea.

Soon after that the lights went out
"Mum come quick" I heard myself shout.

"I don't like it mum everything's gone black"
"What's happened mum are we under attack!"

Don't worry she said there'll be light again soon
I'll bring you a candle to lighten your room.

Callum Cummings (Age 8)

Tiger

Tiger lay there in the sun,
Baking like a cooking bun.
He likes to eat Rave birds,
Ripping out the guts-that hurts!
Still he lays there, strong and stiff,
Wake him and you're dead, biff, biff.
He can roar very loud,
Because of this he's proud.
To wake up is what he forgot,
And now he's starting to rot.

Ben Coveney (Age 9)

The Golden Coach

When the queen comes past in the coach of gold,
The crowd all cheer-what a sight to behold.

Six fine horses pulled the coach so proud,
All the people watching curtsied and bowed.

Fifty years since her coronation,
She's won the hearts of all her nation.

Flags are flying in every town and
The queen is wearing her beautiful crown.

At Westminster Abbey the coach pulls in
Out steps the queen with a royal wave and grin.

Onlookers clap and shout out with glee,
Today is the Queen's Golden Jubilee.

Hannah Clare (Age 9)

The Lion And It's Prey

It starts in a clearing,
Where the lion crouches down.
His ears suddenly prick up,
His eyes gleam in the sun.
The lion looks and sees a heard of Zebra's.
The lion listens and hears hooves of Zebra's.
Unseen he prowls in the long, green grass,
He pounces and leaps up high into the sky.
And lands on one Zebra,
He rolls off and starts a wild chase.
faster and faster the lion goes,
And in the end,
The lion has fresh flesh for his tea,
But don't be saddened that the lion got the upper hand,
For in the jungle,
Survival is the law of the land.

Charlotte Clark (Age 9)

Lonely

First a frosty snowflake,
Shimmering and shining,
Then another world,
Everything is white,
No sound, no people, no friends,
Dark black sky,
Shining silver moon,
I'm crushed by a giant snowflake,
No one to help me,
The frosted leaves capture me,
I cry but no one answers,
The dust grows,
But still the silver moon glistens,
The fear of the wind,
It whistles day and night,
I'll close my eyes and hope to get away.

Leanne Creasey (Age 10)

Star

I am a star, a star of nature
I am a star, a pop star of the future
I am in the spot, in the spotlight of night
To show the world, I am beautiful and bright.

I am a star, that belongs to a fairy
I am a star, that is not at all scary
I shine my brightest through the night
And by daybreak, I'm out of sight.

I am a star, that is made of gas
I am a star, that sparkles over your Earth
That can shoot over the biggest mass,
Your Earth, to signal Christ's birth.

James Cowburn (Age 11)

My Disco

At my disco I had much fun
I watched my friends run and run.
Chloe, Anna and Tim were there,
Georgina gave me a teddy bear.
Then it was time for the party food
We all gathered round in a hungry mood.
Jack grabbed a slice of birthday cake
And he just said it was a big mistake.
After tea we danced some more
And then some mums arrived at the door.
The kids went off in a single file
With a party bag and great big smile.
My mum swept up the barn floor
And then we left and locked the door.
That night I went straight to bed
With the music still echoing in my head.

Emily Clink (Age 9)

Darkness

Darkness makes it scary
Darkness makes us scared
I don't really like it
Someone might of glared

The stars glow in the darkness
And the moon's like a giant ball
Shiny lights in the darkness
I can see the glittery wall

Sophie Cole (Age 8)

The Bird

The bird
I am thinking of
Is big blue and white.
It's as white as a ghost
That shimmers in the night.
It's wings are a bright blue.
It's tail is white,
As white as
A clean tissue.

Anna Christoforou (Age 9)

Rain Poem

It's raining run to the car
Pitter patter pitter patter
My damp clothes stick to me
Pitter patter pitter patter
The rain makes music
Pitter patter pitter patter

Liam Cozens (Age 6)

Last Day At School

Last day at school,
We all empty our trays,
Everyone collects their art books,
Everyone goes home and plays.

Everyone takes their p.e. bags home,
They might grow out of their kit,
They get dressed in their p.e. clothes,
They run to get fit.

Children say goodbye to their teachers,
When children grow up an age
They meet their new teacher
And they start a new page

Alexander Chalstrey (Age 6)

Silver Is.....

Silver is as shiny as ice,
It blows up like the sun.
Silver is really cool,
It glitters like diamonds in the sky.
Silver gleams inside a crackling shell.
Silver is foil on the floor,
All crumpled and tattered.

Joseph Cozens (Age 9)

Poetry In Motion

I'm me, no-one else,
I'm just me, I'm just myself.
I'm extreme and I don't care,
About what I do, but you wouldn't dare.
Fear is only a four letter word,
And to do all this, you mustn't be scared,
To jump from a ladder and fail,
And go through a table, yet live to tell the tale.
Although you may think I'm wild,

Extreme is not a mood, it's a lifestyle.

Amy-Lou Cookson (Age 13)

Shooting Stars

I saw lots of shooting stars
Shoot across the sky in colours
They shoot around the planets and under the sun
They can be gold, a bright yellow
I saw one really small and one really big
I saw one high going up to the sky

Chelsie Charlton (Age 7)

Do You

Do you look at the world and see the laughter,
Or can you only see the tears?

Do you look at the world and feel love,
Or can you only focus on hate?

Do you look at the Third World and see the hope,
Or can you only see their despair?

Do you look at each day as a new beginning,
Or do you wish it would end?

When you look at a person do you see who they truly are,
Or can you only see who you think they are?

When you look at a wasteland do you see its potential,
Or can you only see destruction?

When you look at your life do you see the possible future,
Or can you only dwell on the past?

Do you look at everything and try to see the good,
Or can you only see the bad?

Well then,
Maybe you should look a little further.
You might be surprised by what you find.

Crysta Campbell (Age 16)

Dodi & Dad

We love Dodi and Dad,
Even though they are both quite mad.
Daddy's just a fool and Dodi likes to droole.
But without them we would be very cruel.

Ellie Collyer (Age 8)

Why?

Why is the sun ever so bright?
How does it give us the light?
Why don't the stars sleep at night?
Why don't they come out in broad daylight?
Why do animals have long curly tails?
Why do humans have ten funny toes?
How is glass transparent and wood opaque?
How do clouds float in the sky?
Why does gravity push us to earth?
How does electricity run through a circuit?
How is electricity very, very dangerous?
Why does rain drip on our heads?
Why do humans shoot animals dead?
How does the moon have a misty mood?
Why is friction a stopping force?
Why don't we fall off the face of the earth?
How does sound travel to ears?
How do we feel things, soft and hard?

Emma Cave (Age 11)

The Land Of Nowhere And Beyond

Somewhere, far, far away,
Near a place known to us as Sleepville,
Is the land of Nowhere.

Nowhere doesn't mean much,
That is to you, me and most people
But to a few its home.

Most of us visit Nowhere,
It's where our dreams seem real,
Our realities dead.

We visit without realising,
One minute discussing land shapes,
Next talking to your hero.

You could be at school,
Watching T.V. or talking,
You don't know when it will happen.

You don't know,
You just aren't ready; it's not time,
But it will still get you.

Lauren Caley (Age 11)

Apples

My apples look as good as the sun
They feel as good as sunflowers
My apples smell as good as plums
My apples taste as good as gold
I love apples

Millie Cox (Age 7)

The Centurion And the Unicorn

In a land of mythical creatures
The Centurian liked to shout
"I am better than everyone
I am the best about".
Until one day there was a call
About a beautiful sight
There was a galloping Unicorn
That killed with all its might
"I am the king of all the land
I will challenge you
Unicorns are best left alone
Three o'clock this afternoon"
So they battled all the night
And woke up at dawn
The unicorn charged at him
And remembered it was Christmas morn

Matthew Chaney-Williams (Age 10)

Birds

A bird is a flying thing,
That really loves to dance and sing.

Cheep Cheep churp churp,
At least they don't say burp burp.

Birds come and go saying meep meeps
And loud beep beeps.

They come in flocks,
If they talk to a hen they get chicket pox.

They roost and rest
But they can be a jolly big pest.

Birds are nice when they sing
But when they peck it really really does hurt and sting.

They fly and they make a wind
When they pass you by.

The sky is high and they like to fly
But somewhere along the line they have to die.

Robert Collins (Age 11)

Bullying

What's the point of bullying, it only brings pain,
Whether you show it or lock it in your brain
Get hit in the face or have your neck wrung
It could be a person or it could be a gang
Others are scared and will often not help
Even if you scream, you cry or you yelp
People encircling you, striking your shins,
Pushed to the floor or pushed over bins
Pain is like a rocket it builds up inside
Aggression like a knife piercing your side

Robert Cramer (Age 13)

Platonic Love

Through periods of stormy weather
You are the one who makes things better.
I smile when we are together,
I'm nothing when we are apart.
Through your endless devotion
I feel sublime emotion.

Together we will fight for our dreams
No matter how hopeless, no matter how far.
Nothing or anybody will ever rise above
Our ceaseless platonic love.

Mark Caney (Age 18)

I Will Put In My Stocking

I will put in my stocking
A bang from a cracker
The smell of a Christmas tree
The flash from a Christmas light
The scent of a Christmas turkey

I will put in my stocking
The excitement of waking up
The tearing of wrapping paper
The excitement of children opening presents!
The crash of children jumping down the stairs

I will put in my stocking
The joy of seeing my family,
The excitment of putting decorations up,
The joy of putting carrots above the fire
The mysterious arrival of Santa

My stocking is made of
The joy of throwing snowballs
The sizzling of the fire
The surprise of sledging
The coldness as the snow goes down your boots

Harry Croft (Age 10)

Flowers

Flowers have petals
With beautiful colours
Long green leaves come
From the ground.

Penny Cox (Age 5)

Stonehenge

The stones are appearing
From the dark misty shadows
Circling a large rock
Look up to the heavens
The colour of the moon
The stones are rough, hard
The stone crumbles to the ground.

Alice Cook (Age 7)

Pink

Pink is my favourite colour
I see it in my house
Lots of things are coloured pink
But not my little mouse

James Cook (Age 6)

Up In The Heavens

They are so elegant, ghostly and transparent.
Up in the heavens.

Their floating wings, sweet melody sings.
Up in the heavens.

They have a pure heart. God wishes to impart
Up in the heavens.

Lovely soft skin, free from sin,
Up in the heavens.

They watch over us, in our beds, with shining halos above their heads,
Up in the heavens.

"Alleluia!" they say, every Christmas day,
Up in the heavens.

"Glory to God." they shout with delight, at the end of a Christmas night,
Up in the heavens.

Ghostly figures they seem to be,
But no way, no way! not to me.

Zoe Charge (Age 11)

A Nonsense Poem

I like to dance, I like to sing but I lost my fairy wings,
I like to sing, I like to dance but especially when I'm in France,
I like to sing, I like to dance but everyone laughs.

Laura Coote (Age 8)

The Storm

The storm is very rough and the storm is very tough
As it crashes against the rocks with the locks close by.
The ships might go clash and they might go smash
And in the day the water will reflect the ships,
So the lighthouse has to protect the ships in the nights storm.
So don't be frightened when the sea is lightened
By the lighthouse in the nights storm.

Andrew Cass (Age 9)

Green Poem

I like fresh cut grass swaying flowers.
Long spiky green grass bouncy frogs.
Happy sun flowers swaying slowly on the grass green.
I like fresh cut grass long spiky green grass.
I like fresh cut grass happy sun flowers
Swaying slowly on the grass.

Kimberley Candler (Age 8)

The Icicle

The cold icicle
all alone in
the sun
melting
melting
going
going
gone

The cold icicle
like a chill
down the
spine
the
bleak
glitter
going

Tess Chisholm (Age 9)

Tiger

Snappy pussy cat
Zooming and fierce
Excellent swimmer
Silky and colourful
Smiley teeth
Gigantic and a great hunter

Nicola Cockburn (Age 8)

The Smell Collector

A stranger called this morning
Dressed all in black and grey
Put every smell into a bag
And carried them away

They milky tea
The rustled up toast
The dirty dog
The salt of the coast

They tangy marmite
The stench of cheese
My baby sisters nappy
The honey of the bees

The sweetness of the pickle
The aroma of my socks
The smell of my new carpet
The smell of the fish docks

A stranger called this morning
He didn't leave his name
Left us only scentless
Life will never be the same

Callum Crawford (Age 10)

If You Were A Snail

What would it be like if you were a snail?
Would you be happy or sad?
Would you paint your shell inside,
Have a sofa and maybe a T.V.?
Would you believe there is a God,
Prayer to him and ask for help?
Would you go to snail school,
And learn a snail language?
Would you have snail friends,
And even a snail boyfriend?
What would you feel if I,
Just came and step on you?
But no, I wouldn't do that!
'Treat others how you want to be treated back'
That is true even with snails.
You never know, they could grow,
And we would be the small ones!

Katherine Cooper (Age 13)

Reading

Some people say reading is bad
Some people say reading is good
But I love reading

Sometimes I read to my little cousins
Sometimes I read to my parents
Sometimes I read to myself
Sometimes I read in front of the class
I like to read when I am relaxed
I am one of those people
Who likes reading

Some people say reading is bad
Some people say reading is good
But I love reading

Aaron Cattermole (Age 12)

The River

The river is a child, a youth, a juvenile
A growing child on a long journey, a trip, a route
Stumbling over stones as toddlers do
Singing a song out of tune

The river is growing now, getting bigger and more mature
Starting to get rougher now, gruff and hoarse
Leaping over rocks like a child jumping gracefully
Hitting the sides like one kid hitting another

The river is older now, aged and elderly
Ready to end, break off and close
Into the sea it goes
And now it is part of a bigger family

Rochelle Christian (Age 11)

Shall I Compare Thee To A Starry Night?

Shall I compare thee to a starry night?
Thou art more lovely and magnificent,
A starry night is just a pretty sight,
But you also have splendour and brilliance.
Shall I compare thee to the break of day?
Thou art more warm and inviting,
The dawn signifies the start of one day,
You signify when my heart first did sing.
Shall I compare thee to a winter's morn?
Thou art more fresh and rejuvenating,
A winter's morn holds pure snow and white lawns,
But the key to my heart only you can bring.
There is nothing I can compare thee to fairly,
For this world holds nothing so wonderful as thee.

Komal Chadha (Age 13)

Who's There

The mist was lurking low
No place left to go
The dampness on the forest floor
It certainly wasn't there before
A cry from behind a tree
Are they calling out to me?
A gust of wind goes zooming past
I'm getting scared, "Who's there", I ask.
Another call from in a tree
Am I meant to hear their plea
A strange shadow goes drifting by.
"Just leave me alone, I heard your cry".
The branches start to move around
I shiver and tumble to the ground.

Eve Carson (Age 11)

The Owl

A hunter out on night duty,
Perching on his tree branch,
Eyes searching for his prey.
He hears a sound and stares at the rustling grass.
The feathers on his back start to tingle.
His eyes light up like flames.
This could be it!!
His talons stretch with excitement.
He waits for the right time,
Then attacks and grabs.
Success!
He flies into the dark midnight sky.

Emelia Cheese (Age 11)

I Found Lightning

I found a piece of lightning
In my garage.
It must of fell out of the sky,
I looked at it closely
I found a little tear.

I tried to pick it up
But the glow and shine got to me
And found my hand burnt to a tree,
I put it down
I tried to give it something to eat.

I tried to give it a new light bulb
Not like the one in this country
I gave it him
But he had a shock and ran,
He wanted to go back home.

I put it outside and threw it in the air.
But suddenly came back on my head
And that he told me he will now take me to his life.

Matthew Corcoran (Age 11)

Write a Poem The Teacher Said!

Write a poem the teacher said
So Sally went home and went to bed.
In the morning she remembered her task
Ideas she needed so she started to ask.
Her brothers, her sisters, her mum, her dad
She wrote them down on a silver pad
She conjured a poem from these ideas.
And returned to school without any fears.
The teacher said it was the best in the class
And she put it up in a frame of brass.
Everyone admired the work of art
And Sally was rewarded with a cherry tart.

Alice Cheeseman (Age 10)

Bob The Brachiosauras

A bossy banana neck Brachiosauras called Bob
Bends binoculars and bangs banjos with bark
He burps and burps until he is bombed
He's as big as a bus.
He can make bugs flea.
He begs for bubble-gum soda and begins to behave
He's a big, brown, boomerang, no . . . .
HE'S A BEAST!!!!!!

Cameron Crees (Age 8)

Sir Francis Drake

When Francis Drake was nearly 10
He went to sea with brainy men
And on his 27th trip
He became captain of the ship.

Then he landed in very mad Spain
To drink lots of champagne.
So the Spaniards tried to steal his goods
But Drake drove them into the woods.

Then to an island he would go
To warm up and make lots of dough
Then to the Pacific they sailed on
And one turned over they were gone.

Then he landed in good Plymouth
To see the great Queen Elizabeth
Then they celebrated a big feast
For Sir Francis Drake was not defeated

Lawrence Coles (Age 9)

What is White

White is a clean brand new rubber
White is a cold refreshing ice-cream
White is a sparkling white ruler
White is a bright white beam

White is a singing dove
White is a falling snowflake
White is the beautiful daises
White is the icing of a cake

White is the scrap piece of paper
White is the teacher's board
White is the rattle of a skeleton
White is the colour of sea cord

Jade Cooper (Age 8)

Inside My Head

Inside my head
There is a place
Where no human beings
Have ever set foot.
Full of beautiful glitter
And wonderful colours
Only I hold the key
For its tiny door.
A place for me,
No-one else.

Rhiannon Chown (Age 7)

The Dirt Monster

There was a little boy called Jim,
Who danced inside the rubbish bins.
He danced and pranced and rolled about,
Until his little eyes popped out.

When Jim came home his mother said,
"Go and have a bath," her face was bright red,
Silly Jim would always reply,
"Have a bath? I'd rather die."

One day he was dancing in the bins,
When Jim's fingers turned into baked bean tins,
Jim's eyes turned into garden peas,
And his hair turned into little bits of children's teas.

His nose turned into brussel sprouts,
And his tiny feet turned into trouts,
" I wish I"d washed," poor Jim cried,
"I wish you had too," his brain replied.

So never ever be like Jim,
And dance inside the rubbish bins,
Always wash and always dry,
Or you'll become a dirt MONSTER!

Hannah Cerasale (Age 11)

Sunset

Bright beams of light cover the lake,
The sun stares a shooting ray of fire through rocks,
Bolts of burning fire strike the stepped carvings,
Reflections quiet against the ripples,
Sunlit shadows run into the darkness,
Clouds sweat in the burning barrier of fire,
Sunset, sunset, sunset.

Jamie Cooper (Age 10)

The Waterfall

Crashing down the mountain side,
Creeping across into valleys,
It's me, the waterfall, sparkling and light blue.
Water clinging onto me,
Insects using me as a violent waterslide.
Turning into waves at the bottom,
It's me, the waterfall.
I am like a sideways river,
Lakes changing into a river, then into me.
Lily pads trickling down me
Like a raindrop on a window.
It's me the waterfall.
Now my life has horribly changed,
Factories are surrounding me,
Like soldiers ready for battle
I am wondering now
If my life will ever change back?

Victoria Crozier (Age 8)

Leisure

What is this life if full of care,
I've plenty time to stop and stare.

Time to rest my guitar upon my knee,
I practice my guitar in spare class 3.

Time to go and roller blade,
Sometimes you may need first aid.

Time to go and play in my room,
We sometimes take a glimpse at the moon.

Time to go to karate in the big hall,
All of us have a special call.

Time to go off to school,
Some of the people are really cruel.

Time to just stay at home,
And watch a programme about a cyclone.

A good life I've got, its full of care,
I'm pleased I've got time to stop and stare.

Scott Craig (Age 10)

Honey

H oney is yummy
O ranges are tasty
N uts in your tummy
E ggs round and boiled
Y ogurt scrummy

Becky Cackett (Age 8)

The Bean

Faraway, somewhere unknown to me,
I wait,
At first, life-less,
Feeding on water that surrounds me.

Then my legs sprout,
Spreading out for miles,
Slithering through the soil,
Deathly.

Then the rest of me,
Twisting up through morning dew,
Waking up to the world beyond me,
Tiredly.

But, grown by night,
Standing tallest in all meadow,
Ruling the tiny crowded Earth,
I am an unexpected guest.

Lisa Cooke (Age 11)

Seasons Of The Year

When Winter comes,
It's freezing cold and bitter,
The wind sways and swishes swiftly.
White spiders from the glorious heaven dance through the sky.

Near Spring the snow starts melting,
Flowers bloom,
Birds start to sing,
And animals are born.

When Summer arrives,
There are bright skies,
The heat is scorching,
And rays from the sun shoot and sparkle.

Autumn's here at last,
The weather is bitter,
The flowers close up,
And the sun disappears.

Zoe Chui (Age 9)

The Yeti Returns

The Yeti is a coming quickly go and hide
The Yeti is making the path be slippery and people slide
He lives so far away
People never see the light of day
The Yeti only eats humans
Chomp ahhhh my arm came off

Peter Caporn (Age 9)

Frog's Lament

You look at me and see a prince being trapped,
Needing a kiss to be rescued.
But my bright bobbly eyes and webbed feet,
Stop you from being my princess.

I can't attract you with my graceful leaps,
My bright green skin, nor my permanent smile.
My pogo stick jumps and long red tongue
Don't manage to impress you.

You think I have no heart or feelings,
Making fun of my bumpy skin,
I can hurt and cry inside, so yes, I do have some feelings.

All I want is a kind man's pond,
A bit of love instead of screams.
Not to be taken as a Frenchman's dinner,
And to be treated with a bit of dignity.

Emily Canfor-Dumas (Age 10)

The Wind

The wind dances in
The midnight air.
It dances and prances
Among the stars
As though it does not care.

Then it changes by dashing
And diving between trees
But in the morning
You wake to feel
The midsummer breeze

Then the day blows
Over to night
The wind howls like a wolf
It stands on the cliff top
Against the moon shining so bright

Yet again it is morning
But the wind moves on
A little more and a little more
Until it has gone.

Alice Clarke (Age 10)

Dog

A ball wrecker
A fast flier
A meat eater
A fleabag scratcher
A stick fetcher
A bone chewer
A barking hound
A people scarer
A hole digger
A brilliant listener

Alex Cook (Age 11)

A Birthday Cake

Yum! yum!
For my tum
Just looking at the cake
I get the cream on my thumb
And I stick it in my mouth.

I like it being my birthday
Birthday! Birthday! Birthday!
And maybe earthday
No way thank you.

I like cake
Cake! Cake! Cake!
And I also like to swim in a lake
But I think I will stick to cake.

Sophie Louise Canty (Age 9)

The Falls

Standing still, silent, watching the shimmering ripples
As the beating sun shines down on the peaceful river.

The roaring falls crash down on the river
As the sound runs down and through the valley.

It is hard to believe that this relaxing, peaceful, calm place
Would have been a noisy, smelly, oily place
Full of hardworking workmen and women.

I look across the beautiful green countryside
I hear animals and feel peaceful, I smell the countryside air.

Natasha Cahil (Age 10)

Ice-cream

Strawberry, chocolate, mint and chip
All very cold on my lip,
Vanilla as well in one big bowl,
Getting ready to gulp it whole.
Gooey lovely chocolate sauce,
Eat it for your second course.

Ashley Cradock (Age 10)

What Is A . . . . . Moon?

The moon is a blue topaz ring sitting there waiting to be tried on.
It is a sparkling colossal gem shining over us.
It is a gorgeous crystal dolphin lying on a dark table.
It is a splat of wet Tipp-ex on the wrong word.
It is a glistening milk bottle top catching the suns rays.
It is a dazzling coin in the morning sun.
It is a juicy lolly pop now going into my mouth.
It is a smiling face staring down at our every move.

Chantelle Church (Age 11)

The Turtle

His shell is a rock,
His head is a pebble.

His body is the colour of the summers grass,
He glides through the sea as a bird in the sky.

When he's in his shell he looks like a pie,
His tail is a tie.

His flippers move slow,
As he walks very low.

He's a very happy turtle with a very happy life.

Bethan Clark (Age 9)

Dogs

Dogs barking in the night,
Scrowching and howling although light.
Big Rotweiler messy but cute,
Always tries to look its best in a suit.
Spotty Dalmation in its white and black coat,
Watches the telly and hovers the remote.
Kennels and big teeth for bones.
Dogs they never play alone.
Sausage dog, tiny, long and fat,
Always sleep on your mat.
Dogs sleep,
Dogs weep,
Dogs, they just don't stop.

Coral Collison (Age 9)

Abracadabra

Abracadabra swim in a bog
Turn into a slippery frog.
Abracadabra burn and squirm
Turn into a wiggly worm.

Ben Carter (Age 11)

When I Was One

When I was one I sucked my thumb,
When I was two I went to the zoo,
When I was three I went to nursery,
When I was four I walked through the door,
When I was five I used a knife,
When I was six I did some tricks,
When I was seven I went to Devon,
When I was eight I stayed up late,
And now I'm nine everything's fine.

Nicholas Clarke (Age 9)

Dentist

The clock ticking, tick, tock, tick, tock,
Cars passing vrumm, vrumm.
The Dentist breathing
Door slamming behind me -
People screaming ahh, ouch, ooh
The sound of the drill grinding trega, trega.
The feelings of the chair, going down and down
And the butterflies in your tummy
The sound of the chair going up, mmmm.
His scary voice **"take a seat"**
He says it every time
A very low voice.

Samantha Cheeseman (Age 10)

Mice

Mice, they're soundless and swift
As fast as a car scuttling at a race
They are calm-squeakers
Mini - movers
As though they can scamper,
And not be heard.

Mice, their fur is as soft as silk,
As soft as a fluffy cloud in the sky
They are smooth - touchers
Warm - feelers
As though they can be touched
And not be felt

Mice, their homes are as black as night,
As black as a cave in the mountain side
They are cold - seekers
Wind - keepers
As though they can freeze,
And never be seen.

Lisa Daymond (Age 11)

The Lightning

The lightning is a mean dragon, evil brave and nasty
He crushes trees with his smashing claws
Burning houses with powerful crashing flames
The dark claws it bares on its arms
Crush and "crush, crush, crush, crush"!
The red glaring eyes burn
Damaging the white clouds

And with its swooping wings it zaps down
And scaring the souls out of the people
He guards the precious treasure
Shaking his dangerous tail
And crashing down the sky

Its jaws smashing around
Zooming through the sky
Flashing in the air
Blindingly he darted down
Striking the helpless ground
He zaps and zaps and zaps

Stephen Canning (Age 9)

The Sea

My gifted hands are everywhere
Creeping o'er the sand
My hunger never satisfied
From tasting crumbling land.

Winds and waves give me strength
To storm and do my best
Only the shining sun can tame
And make me take my rest.

Connor Crabb (Age 11)

The Fear Of Ghosts

I heard a voice and looked around
I saw a ghost and screamed aloud
I went to sleep the other night
And wakened up in such a fright
The ghost was white and creepy
Also tired and sleepy
I see its shadow every night
And it always gives me such a fright
So ghosts are my worst fear
And always will be 'till next year.

Bethany Croft (Age 10)

Robin Hood

Robin Hood and Merry Men
They like hurting other men
One day they came home,
And guess who's on the telephone,
Say Ma-ri-on

When they go into the forest,
They all remain modest,
Prince John tries to hurt them,
But he ended up as tall as a plant stem
Thanks to Ro-b-in

Luke Close (Age 9)

Night

When I walk out into the starry sky
I feel the breeze on my cheek
I imagine the moon as a ten pence coin spilling
Its fair share of pennies to the ground
The trees wrestling for its fair share
The leaves rustling under my feet
The sky black as a bottle of ink
The stars go on for ever

Jacob Carver (Age 10)

Sir Frances Drake

When Francis Drake was ten and a half
He was so very very daft
He really did shock the crew
Because he quickly learnt what to do.

Drake very nearly joined the navy
To show his great deal of bravery
Then the cat fell off the ship
Sir Francis jumped in for a dip.

The spanish he fought and fought
But he went back to Plymouth port
Then one night he had a feast
And he thought of a Spanish fleet

He named his ship the Golden Hind
And he left some of the crew behind
He got back at nine o'clock
And he caught Chicken Pox

Simon Cox (Age 10)

Football

Football, football is the best
Better than all the rest.
Football, football see them score
Mum reckons footballs a bore.
Football, football hear them cheer
Opponent fans start to jeer.
Football, football in my sleep
When they lose it makes me weep
Football, football is my dream
Will I ever make the team?

Mark Conium (Age 10)

Cats

Cats jump,
Cats pounce,
Cats are soft,
Cats are friendly,
Cats are sly,
Cats move quickly,
Cats lie down,
Cats are eating,
Cats are drinking,
Cats are smooth,
Cats are lively,
Cats leap,
Catching mice, catching rabbits,
Cats, cats, cats.

Saskia Cooper (Age 8)

The Queen

I had a dream that I was invited to London Palace
Now London Palace is a grand place
The great hall was first
It has glass ornaments that nan and grandad would die for!
It has a grandfather clock and a grand wooden staircase.
Then we went to the throne room
Well of course it had the throne, which maids were cleaning
The Queen said "Fifty years I've been on the throne"
Now I thought that was nifty!
Just then I met the Queen's husband Prince Phillip
"Meet you at the horse show" he said
And then he was off.
Well in that time I saw he was wearing very fine clothes.
It was soon after that I was at London Tower
There were lots and lots of jewels
And finally I was at the top
I saw a very shiny gold crown.
It had diamonds on it and then . . . . . nothing.

Sam Cupit (Age 9)

The Penguin

As he waddles across the ice
Like a man on stilts,
He slaps his flippers against his hips
And when he gets to the slippery slope,
He jumps on his belly and tries to cope
With the snow.

He dives off the edge of the iceberg,
Landing in the deep sea,
He swims around chasing his tail,
But gets distracted by a small fish.
Finally, he caught it, ate it -
It tasted delish!

Jade Coleman (Age 11)

An Easter Poem

Easter and eggs the words make a pair
But of the man who lived long ago do we care
Born in a stable on a cold winter's night
He came onto earth to give the world light
When we take the egg out of the box
Do we think of the man hung on a cross
He said "Lord forgive them they know not what they have done"
But he rose again and peace was to come
So in these times of trouble and strife
Think of the man who gave his life
The man who lived so long ago
Who was taunted and teased and put on show
But he forgave us all and let us live
So that we might learn one day to give
Think of the sight seen by Mary Magdalene
As you tuck into your chocolate once again

Stephanie Corfield (Age 8)

Weather

What is hail?
The hail is heaven and hell having a battle.

What is snow?
The snow is God's corn flakes para gliding down to earth.

What is rain?
The rain is Zeus trying out a new experiment.

What is frost?
The frost is God's kettle crying out for help.

What is the sun?
It is an orange getting stuck in a spider web.

Jahy Chima (Age 11)

Romans

The roman army marching down the road so straight,
To kill their running bait,
Swords, shields and armour clanking in the battle,
When villagers in the village trying to catch cattle,
Gladiators killing and showing their strength,
Slaves building a road with such length,
The Romans famous for power,
Their food must have been sour,
They invaded and had such a big kingdom,
Claudius chose slaves at random,
A slave sharpened a soldier's spear,
Romans food are deer,
I heard a Roman rumour,
A man killed a puma.

Thomas Clark (Age 9)

Earth

The earth awakes from its deep sleep
The flowers come to dance in the windy and rainy showers
The trees tingle in the lovely cool breeze
The rain trickles to the ground and forms small puddles
The wind whistles and blows a soothing tune
The sun goes down and sleeps when the day goes dark
The stars come out and twinkle when day becomes night
The moon floats to the top of the sky at night and throws down a beam of moonlight to earth
And that's when everything sleeps

Ben Collins (Age 11)

Under The Sea

Under the sea,
Under the sea,
Come and look under the sea with me.

Over the waves dolphins dive,
Beneath the waves crabs are alive.

From the great big whale,
And friendly seals,
To fish we eat and
The slithering eels.

When it's rough the ships might sink,
But Olly the octopus will give,
Them a wink.

Under the sea,
Under sea,
This is really the place to be.

Megan Cunningham (Age 9)

Questions

What is life?
What is death?
What will make me take my last breath?

What is love?
What is pain?
What are these confusions in my brain?

What is crime?
What is punishment?
Why does bending the rules give me nourishment?

What is war?
What is peace?
Will the fighting ever cease?

What is the start?
What is the end?
Will these cracks in my life ever mend?

Matthew Claxton (Age 16)

Then Feel Sorry For Me

If you dread going to school
Then feel sorry for me,
To start the day with double maths followed by double English,
Then to top it off a test at the end of the day
Then feel sorry for me.

If you have an absolute mad house
Then feel sorry for me,
My brother don't shut up
My sisters in another world
And my Mum, well we'll skip that one,
If you have an absolute mad house
Then feel sorry for me.

The problems we face at 11 years old,
I'm busy feeling *SORRY FOR ME!*

Nikki Cove (Age 11)

Abandoned

I am out alone on the street,
Not a pretty sight for you to meet.
I love my mum, I love my dad,
I wish I was home, not sad.
I love my parents.
I send them bottles of wine trying to get them back
But the answer is always NO!
I walked away but my mum came out
Begging me to come back.
So I am no longer
ABANDONED

Rachel Clifton (Age 8)

Ice Cold

Big jackets, scarfs and hats
Frozen leaves that crackle and snap.

Ice cold weather all around
The grass is frozen on the ground.

Snowball fights are always fun,
So avoid being hit make sure you run!

Build a snowman big and round
When the sun shines watch him melt to the ground.

Ice cold weather can give you a chill
Eat hot food to stop you being ill.

Charlie Connolly (Age 10)

My Cake Grandma

My cake Grandma,
Loves to see my face,
She's bouncy like a sponge,
Her hair sits comfortably on her head
Just like the icing.

Every time I see her,
Fairy cakes wait,
Soft butter filling,
Holding the delicate wings,
Securely in their place.

Samantha Cooper (Age 11)

Seasons

Spring is when all the flowers grow
And all the lawns need a mow.

Summer some have a splash
At the seaside we must dash.

Autumn with the falling leaves,
The harvest and buzzing bees.

Winter snow and frost is here
Christmas comes with it's good cheer.

Robert Cornwell (Age 9)

Peacocks

Colourful peacocks are always around
Strutting up and sometimes down.
Interesting food peacocks eat,
I don't think they eat meat.

Even though they have colourful wings,
They strut around their pens,
Showing off to other things,
Like cows, pigs or hens.

There are peacocks all over the earth,
Wonderful peacocks they are,
I don't know what they are worth,
I think they are worth more than a car.

Peacocks are very pretty,
So no-one would know,
That they are not witty,
Definitely not so.

Annabel Debenham (Age 8)

Fire

Fire is like . . . . .
A tiger pouncing on its prey,
A fierce shark grinding its jaw together,
A brightly coloured sheet,
A hot pepper spicy enough to burn your throat
A monster crashing down wood,
A never-ending death trap,
There's no turning back,
Once you go in you can't go out,
Watching you as you do to bed,
Death in your heart,
Fierce,
Demons eyes,
Watching, waiting to drop you dead.

Nina Christie (Age 9)

Apples

When I bite into a juicy red apple.
My tongue goes mad!
It feels like I could have another
Then another
It feels like my mouth has gone tangly.
It feels like I could chew it forever.
The taste makes me laugh.
It tickles my throat
Like my dad does.

Toby Crouch (Age 8)

Hamsters

Nibble! nibble! merry and bright,
I watched the hamsters play at night,
I got it out it BIT my thumb,
My hamster thought it looked really YUM!!!
I didn't like him very much,
But now I like him just as such.

Amy Cook (Age 10)

Autumn

It's Autumn time again,
Down comes the rain.
Days are getting shorter
Because years in the last quarter.
The weather is getting colder,
Especially if you're older.

Kerry Crocker (Age 8)

Sea

The sea is . . . .
A watery grave
A crashing hell
A giant's bath
A big blue shark waiting for you to enter its jaw
A blue sheet of velvet
A clapping audience
A spilled bottle of blue paint
A monster putting his arms out to get you
A wet blue heaven
Wet blue and roaring

Michael Cook (Age 9)

My Little Brother

As he jumps up and down he screams and shouts.
Then he falls over, looks at me, grins and shouts bad girl!
As if to say I made him fall!!
He stomps off and sits with his arms folded.
The house is peaceful for about five minutes,
Then he starts again, screaming and shouting.
It's none other than my little brother Jack.

Amber Coombes (Age 12)

My Holiday

H aving lots of fun at Castle Acre Priory and Ford.
O n the 1.0.W crabbing of the rocks cockling on the sand.
L ying in bed don't have to go to school and watch T.V.
I n the sea having fun swimming and splashing.
D igging on the sand making sand castles.
A good day at Oasis swimming
Y es what a shame back to school.

Robert Clarke (Age 11)

Feeling

When I feel lonley
I am as lonely as a dying flower.
When I feel happy
I am as happy as a rainbow.
When I feel angry
I am as angry as a shark.
When I feel sad
I am as sad as a grey cloud.

Samson Chung (Age 6)

Wanted

Wanted! Queen!
Must love corgis and horses
Essential: must own golden crown and coloured jewels
Important to have ruled for more than 49 years
Needs a good, firm handshake
Doesn't mind wearing silly hats
Must have beaming smile and
Love children, old people and everyone
(Has to try to like the Prime Minister)
First name must be Elizabeth

WARNING: DO NOT REPLY IF YOU ARE NOT THE QUEEN!

Laura Cartmell (Age 10)

Happiness

Happiness is yellow
As bright as the sun.
It smells like a rose,
And it tastes like a chocolate cake.

It sounds like bells ringing,
It feels soft and smooth
And it lives in a
Person's heart.

Saba Choudhry (Age 9)

The Daffodil

As the sun shines down
I grow and grow,
As the wind whips up
I wave to and fro,
I greet passers by with my yellow face,
My golden trumpet saluting the every day rat race,
As April approaches I wither and die
And wait another year before I appear.

Emma Cove (Age 8)

Tiger

Save de tigers
From de poachers
Save de tigers
From de builders
Beware of de tigers
If you hurt de tigers
The tigers will hurt you.

Scott Carter (Age 11)

Noises In The Night

I hear the trees are blowing,
Downstairs the lights are glowing,
I hear the pitter patter of the rain,
But I'm in bed, I won't complain.
The birds are singing a joyful tune,
In the bright light of the moon.
The sun has gone to bed and now I think I'll join him,
I'll listen to the sounds of night and see you in the morning.

Daisy Cooke (Age 9)

Where I Live

I live by the seaside,
I love the sand.
I take my brothers paddling,
Mum holds them by the hand.
The sand feels nice between my toes;
The boats are bobbing on the sea.
All different colours,
They look like a picture to me.

Alice Cook (Age 10)

Night Time

I walked down the path, feeling that I wasn't alone,
The owl's eerie hooting echoes around the snaggling trees,
Reaching for the silver moon,
Spilling its metallic blood over the wet, misty carpet of green.
The witches evil cackle, seizes my body with fear,
The weeds come to life as the gentle breeze swipes over their frail bodies,
Which twist and turn as they arise from their deep and murky sleep

Alfie Chapman (Age 9)

Yellow Birthday

Happy birthday to Jamie
And butter chips
Happy Birthday to Jamie
And baking sun
Happy birthday to Jamie
And yellow flowers
Happy birthday to Jamie

Dean Cossey (Age 8)

My Special Treasure

A watch is a golden treasure
A magic time machine
It's old, it's tatty, but it will always be new to me.

It's a pearl, it's a jewel
But anyway I think it rules
It was my granddads
And I hope it will be my grandson's grandson's grandsons.

A watch is a golden treasure
A magic time machine.

Reece Cheasman (Age 11)

The Sky

Flashing lightening fills the dark sky
Whizzing helicopters chop the air
Rumbling thunder creates a deafening noise
Shooting stars shoot past at 100 mph
A starry night twinkles brightly
Giant jumbo jets cruise along the sky
Leaving a white vapour trail on the horizon
Slowly moving satelite circles the earth
A pot of gold at the end of the colourful rainbow
Flying birds sweep into their nests
Fluffy clouds slowly moving as the earth turns on its axis
A shining moon peeps round the cloud
Fiery colours used for sunrise and sunset

Joshua Cook (Age 9)

Creation Poems

Cows and animals are in the meadows,
Roar, the lions were made king of the jungle,
Everyone would be glad to meet him,
Also he made light and darkness,
The sea and sun, so we could survive,
It is the world that God created,
On the world he planted plants, space and humans,
No-one else could make such a beautiful thing,
Such a lovely thing that God made for us.

Thomas Capewell (Age 10)

The Biglewop

In the dark muddy swamp next to the shop
Lives the Biglewop!
He has razor sharp teeth and is very fat
Because he always eats cats
So all you cats better watch out!
Or he could be eating you.

Ryan Curtis (Age 6)

Letter In A Bottle

In the early days on a rowing ship
I looked in the blue green sea
There was something green
Something shining at me
It could be a fish
Or, was it me
I thought and thought
What could it be
A letter in a bottle
It must be.

Lindsay Coles (Age 8)

Fire

My fingers hot and glowing,
Dancing while I destroy,
Houses, homes and belongings,
Crumbling in my path.

I only slaughter my enemies,
Because they're always in the way,
Starting me, then putting me out,
Water, my only fear.

Lana Crabb (Age 11)

Blue Is . . . .

Blue is calm and peaceful
Like a rainbow sparkling in the sky
Blue is the shimmering rain
Falling from the sky
Blue is happy, joyful times
Like Christmas with the Christmas tree
Blue is shining tears
Falling from people's eyes
Blue is a cold colour
Which washes bad dreams away

Emily Clarke (Age 8)

Tiger

Its skin is like a fluffy coat
Its eyes are like marbles
Its head is like a fluff ball
Its jaws are like a ball of spikes
Its tail is like a rope

Eoghan Connolly (Age 9)

Maryling & Christian

I had my whole life ahead of me, I sacrificed that life to be with thee.
I love my dear and sweet Christian, I know in my heart that he's the one.

My parents wanted us to be apart, they travelled fast much like a dart.
It was all a big and heavy con, I know in my heart that he's the one.

Our suicide notes were left at home, I told them to never feel alone.
We're in the canal and we are gone, I know in my heart that he's the one.

On my grave it said "Maryling Flores, we will miss her and she will be adored.
An education she had, a career she had none", I know in my heart that he's the one.

On his grave it said "Christian Davilan, he loved sports especially javelin.
His life in this world is now done", I know in my heart that he's the one.

I know we're missed but it's alright, now we're together day and night.
Our parents mourn for their daughter and son, I know in my heart that he's the one.

Lucy Davies (Age 11)

Mountains

Mountains are dusty and cloudy and hard
They have hard rocks on the mountains
Mountains are brown
Because they are so dusty and cloudy
That is why it is so brown

Brandon Connor (Age 7)

Exams Exams

Exams are the thing on my mind
It makes me feel cold inside
It makes me shiver when I quiver
I even feel like tearing up the paper
I always lose marks when I try to attempt
I always dreamed that would happen.

Stacey Cooney (Age 9)

Glad Tidings From SeahousesBoat

As Glad Tidings pulls in for us,
I take one last look at the harbour,
The water still and smooth like glass,
We clamber on our floating bus.

As we slowly leave the harbour mouth,
The water gets rough and choppy,
Water spraying over the passengers,
We head off to the south.

Now we're far out at sea,
The water like boiling jam,
Spitting and bubbling in a pan,
The engine humming like a bee.

We reach our destination,
Calm and gentle once again,
But we still have the journey back
Through all the exhilaration.

Mark Dickie (Age 13)

Honey The Honeybee

Honey the honeybee
Sips her tea,
She drinks Earl Grey
But only in May,
She sits on a throne
Made out of a bone,
Covered in silk that's red
Which she uses for her bed,
Wearing a crown
That matches her gown,
Her business makes lots of money,
Through making pots of honey.
Once upon a blue moon
She saw it glisten in her spoon,
All her wishes soon came true
She wished that she could be like Boo,
She then wished that she could be queen
'But make sure I'm not that mean'
This is how she ended up,
Drinking tea from a cup!

Caroline Drewitt (Age 11)

Fruit

Bananas are like crescent moons.
They are very tasty and tall.
First they are green and then turn yellow.
They're like soft, yellow cheese.
They're like girls wearing yellow dresses.
They are soft to eat yum! yum!
They are squidgy like peaches.

Apples are like full moons in the sky.
You can eat them with the skin on.
They are very hard but juicy and sweet.
Some can be different colours like yellow and red and green.

Grapes are like small green apples.
They are very juicy, like apples.
They're smooth like some other fruit.

Vanessa Douglas (Age 7)

Sunshine

Spring
Flowers daffodils
rabbits, chicks and plants
blossom, corn, warm, hot, boiling
summer sun, games, fun
drinks, cola
summer

Victoria Cox (Age 8)

Space

The sun and stars shine bright,
They shine 24/7, day and night.
They are really really far away,
I will go there for a holiday one day.

There are planets and moons near them too,
They were given names, I don't know by who.
There are also bright and quick shooting stars,
They look quite new, but they are really far.

Space men go to the moon every day,
Soon little kids will go there to play.
There will also be trips to Saturn and Mars,
And people will drive there in hover cars.

The sun is bright, big and gold,
Pluto is the opposite, small and cold.
So one day I will live on the sun,
I will sunbathe there and have lots of fun.

Max Dela Fuente (Age 14)

The Rocket

To the moon in a rocket.
Oh no I forget to lock it!
Where's the key?
It's in my pocket.
Oh no I dropped it!

Robyn Cattermole (Age 8)

Colours

Yellow is the shining sun.
Red is the juicy apple.
Blue is the beautiful sea.
Orange is the lovely orange.
Green is the colour of the grass
Black is the colour of the slimy mud.

Georgia Crandon (Age 6)

The Tiger

Tiger in the forest
Hunters nearby
Roar roar bang! bang!

Jake Davies (Age 5)

Inside My Head

Inside my head there's a treasure chest,
Filled with pictures, visions, galore!
And in a dream I scatter them,
And sort them on the floor.

Inside my head there's a countryside
With cows and sheep on greens;
Their babies prance about the fields,
And spirits ride the breeze.

Inside my head there's an ocean,
Its turtle patterns gleam,
The dolphin babes play happily,
Whilst whales dive to dream

Inside my head there's a cottage,
Where all my friends greet me,
And as I walk the gravel path,
I hum to the bees.

Inside my head there's a paradise;
No war, no death, no doom.
If the people share some love today,
We'll all be home soon.

Katie Davis (Age 12)

Late Again

Late again Michael?
What's the excuse this time?
Not my fault sir!
Who's fault is it then?
Spider sir!
Spider who?
The little one, it tried to bite me sir!
You missed R.E.?
I know it's very upsetting!
What about yesterday Michael?
What about yesterday sir!
You missed P.E.?
Oh that was the house it broke
What house?
My house it collapsed down!
Where do you sleep now?
Grandma's sir!
Will you have an excuse tomorrow?
No sir, I mean yes sir!

Michael De La Warr (Age 9)

Elephants

Elephants are gentle,
Lovely and kind.
Every infant is sweet,
Pretty and playful,
Hates mice,
And loves food,
Never meaning,
To hurt anyone.

Graham Davison (Age 9)

Fashion!

Fashion Fashion
is the fashion
skinny little bags
and tight skirts

All with hangers
hanging on the shelf
people picking them up
and trying them on

Fashion Fashion
is the fashion
big great flairs
and polo neck jumpers
with security tags on them
and people taking them home
after taking them off the shelf

Fashion Fashion
is the fashion

Jessica Down (Age 12)

The Magic Box

I will put in my box
A special family photo
A pretty painting from my favourite artist
A piece of my great great great granma's hair.

I will put in my box
My budgie that I've had since I was a baby
My favourite bit of my favourite dress
My funny book that my mum always reads to me

I will put in my box
A person sitting in a tree
A bird sitting in a chair
Somebody writing on fluff

It's hot in my box
It's got hearts on the lid
It's made out of feathers
And it's got worms for the hinges

Rose Dennis (Age 9)

Warning Poem

Come on Harrison,
I'll show you how to defeat the enemy.
You go on to the field,
Hoping to be victorious.
Everyone on your team needs to fight,
Together you have to be strong
And quick at seizing any opportunity.
Every five metres gained brings you closer to victory.
No-one should forget tactics
Because alone is a big disadvantage.
Harrison, the rugby pitch is a battlefield.

Matthew Dishman (Age 14)

Old Fashion To New

From mini skirts to bootleg trousers,
Crop tops to big long blouses,
Small, sweet sandals,
To knee high boots.
That's what the change in fashion's about.
From long white gowns, to tight mini dresses,
An old woolly cardi to the new short skirts.
Petite soft pumps to big fluffy slippers.
The old tweed suit to the smart suit and tie.
That's what the change in fashion's about.
Red lipsticks to the shimmering gloss.
Powder blue eyeshadow to the eye cream and sparkle,
Little pearl drops to big silver hoops.
A string of pearls to the glittering cross.
That's what the change in fashions about!

Laura Dickinson (Age 11)

The Monsters Of Eppomee

Over the rainbow, east of nowhere, lies the land of Eppomee.
Where Snufflepips skimper in the sun and the Shonray sarashes in the sea.

Deep amidst the brittlesnipe, the Taragnarath does lie in wait.
Pity the fool who dare go near him.
Pity the fool once it's too late.

In the glubmud schloomping, sliding, lingers the jarnashing Chanderon.
With outstretched claws this sly thief snatches.
(You know not what you love until it is gone.)

A thousand leagues under a spleshpool, lying in peace, is the Serananurn.
A water melody slowly lures you under the waves.
You'll never return.

Way up high in the Jo-bo trees the Chittermonger higiggles and sways.
Though harmless he is, he laughs and provokes
And will follow you round for many a day.

But I have this to say: The most dangerous of all is the man-eating Grabbite - he is ten feet tall.
He looms in the shadows in his own cave.
To go near him you're stupid or extremely brave.

But do not fear my child, these monsters are not here.
You see, over the rainbow, east of nowhere
Lies the land of Eppomee . . . .

Chloe Dungate (Age 12)

Bonfire Night

See the rockets
Taking off.
See the flames
Flying in the air.
See the Catherine Wheels
Go round and round
What a lovely sight.
See everything going together
What a wonderful night.

Peter Doyle (Age 6)

Cars

Cars are fast
Cars are slow
Don't get in the way
Or they will blow
So let's go
Zooming down the M25

Paul Dunbar (Age 15)

The Wild Cat

I am a wild cat
good and FREE
here me pppuuurrr
like the sea.

Rough and tough
like a whirling twister.
I pounce on my
PREY my prey is
DEAD! DEAD! DEAD!!!

Kayleigh Deol (Age 12)

Wolves

I think wolves are rather nice.
Their calls are loud
Their babies are proud
They are like a cloud
Their tails are pale
You know they're there
Standing like a pair
But I think wolves are nice.

Kieran Drann (Age 6)

Survival

I'm walking in black
And going through a tunnel
The rats squeak on by
Without a care in the world
I have one care, surviving.

Joe Deeks (Age 11)

The Cat And The Dog

Hey diddle diddle
The cat did a piddle
All over the kitchen mat,
The dog he laughed
To see such fun
And piddled all over
The cat.

Katie Dawes (Age 8)

What Where And Why

What is water?
  - A blanket on the river bed.

Why do trees have branches?
  - So they can wave at people as they walk by.

What are hailstones?
  - Soapflakes spitted out of a huge washing machine.

Where does the sea come from?
  - A huge tap on the earth.

What is the Ozone layer?
  - A sunhat protecting the earth.

Why does the clock have a face?
  - So it can see the time.

What is the future?
  - An everlasting space of time
    An everlasting space of time
    An everlasting space of time . . . .

Rebecca Dance (Age 11)

Fish

F is for fish, good-looking fish,
I can always make a tasty dish,
S tripy fish are so much fun,
H ave they been tasty as a bun!!!

Fatima Desai (Age 9)

Season Haiku

Spring
Spring is here again.
Crocuses smelling sweetly.
Birds sing daintily.

Summer
Summer is with us.
Beaches all packed with people.
Wonderful sunshine.

Autumn
Autumn leaves fall down.
Leaves go crunch under my feet.
Blackberries are ripe.

Winter
Winter snow drifts down.
Snowdrops in the garden bloom.
Frost is all around

Olivia Duff (Age 10)

I Like Rain

Drip drop I hear rain,
Pitter patter pitter patter plop plop plop!
Out we go, out we go,
Pitter patter pitter patter plop plop plop!
Splish splash we love rain,
Pitter patter pitter patter plop plop plop!

Alex Dixon (Age 7)

Planet Power

The solar-system is our space
It is the place of the human race.
The sun is a huge, fiery ball,
And compared to that, even Jupiter seems small.
Mercury is the closest to the sun
But it's so hot, it wouldn't be fun to visit Mercury's cratered face.
Venus also floats in space
It's the hottest planet of them all it's a gassy, cloudy, boiling ball.
Earth is the next one away
Where humans thrive and work and play, where plants and animals live their day.
Mars is the red cratered ball
The pinky sky is so pretty and all, the red planet the people call it.
Jupiter's the biggest one
It's gassy liquids have always spun, rocky surface, there is none
Saturn is the prettiest planet
It's icy rings circle around it, it's 18 moons circle it in orbit.
Uranus, the green, cold, sphere
Is very far away from here, it's several rings faint, not clear.
Neptune's winds and storms rage round
It was very, very recently found, it has no visible ground.
Pluto is the furthest away
It has a very, very short day it's cratered surface makes it like the moon in a way.

Charlotte Daniel (Age 10)

I Wonder

I wonder if the Queen ever cries?
If she's ever been deeply upset?
If someone has called her names?
No never!!

I wonder if the Queen is ever horrible?
If she has hurt anyone's feelings?
If she strops if she doesn't get her way?
No never!!

I wonder if the Queen is greedy?
If she demands money?
If she is never satisfied with all her fame and wealth?
No never!!

I wonder if she never listens?
If she listens to no plan but her own?
If she dismisses everyone else's ideas before she even hears them
No never!!

I expect the Queen is kind and thoughtful and always speaks her mind,
Thinks of others before herself.
But sometimes she can probably be a bit stroppy, a bit sad, a bit greedy,
No never!?

Jenni Duncumb (Age 10)

Homework

I don't like my homework,
Although it makes me think.
If I'm not in the mood,
I'll stuff it down the sink.

Sometimes my homework is actually fun,
But if its maths I'll have to run.
I could be playing outside in the sun.
But I'm here writing a poem (I like this one).

My mum has some rules,
That must be kept to.
No TV or playing,
Until homework is through

The point of my homework,
Is hard to see.
It's meant to help me,
With my GCSE's.

We make up excuses when it's not done,
"My dog ate it" is the best one.
All in all, it's a bit of a chore
I'm so glad we don't get much more.

Maddy Doyle (Age 10)

If

If I were Cal
I'd say
Give me my pal!

If I were Ben
I'd say
Give me that hen!

Cal Davies (Age 6)

Spring

'Tis a time of new,
On the leaves is no dew,
The mist is a rise,
Spring is our prize.

The flowers are here,
So's the fox and the deer,
New life is around,
Spring has been found.

Margot Douglas (Age 11)

Dolphins

I'm a dolphin having a ball,
In the big gloomy hall,
I thought I might just do a bit of bopping
To the OJ rapping.

Kelly Daniels (Age 10)

Nightmare Hall

A creaky door
A wonky floor
A screech comes from down the hall
A trip, A fall
A footstep in the hall
A shock A scream
A nightmare A dream
Darkness and gloom
Shadows loom
Cobwebs and coffins objects dropping
I run
I hide
I think I've died!
The clock strikes one I think the ghosts have gone

Amy Dive (Age 12)

Me!!

This how a life is meant to start,
The birth of someone is a very fine art.
The sperm is on its way and in tact,
It reaches the egg and I slowly begin to hatch.
I suddenly grow, am I a boy or girl?
In nine months or before you'll probably know.

As my features grow and I will eventually see vision,
Certain parts of my body multiply, this doesn't include division.
I am made up of different genes,
They are from two different people, or so it seems.
Now I have just one month to go,
I want it to be over, but it's deliberately going slow.
I am not able to speak,
So I open my eyes like small cylinders and have my first peak.
I know my life is not in my own hands, for at least the next fourteen years.
My throat begins to dry out and I get swollen glands.
You are only given just the one chance
And if you blow it your whole life flashes before your eyes, within one glance.
Of all the things I can be this is . . . . me!

Suzanne Drew (Age 14)

Happiness

Happiness is when you wake and there is a big breakfast waiting for you.
Happiness is when you are getting ready for school, but you hear it is closed down.
Happiness is when the bell rings at 3.20.
Happiness is when you get to go to the movie premiere for Harry Potter.
Happiness is when your dad comes and gives you a puppy.
Happiness is when you open your Christmas presents.
Happiness is being around your friends.
Happiness is when you have everything you ever wanted.

Hannah Divito (Age 10)

How To Make A Teacher Mad

Crunch a spoonful of careless mistakes
Weigh out a small bowlful of fighting boys
Add a drop of whining girls to give it some sound
Roughly mix in a sprinkle of calling out
Bake for 20 minutes
Then leave to cool for half an hour.

Bryony Davison (Age 10)

What Is A Dagger?

A dagger is a blade of pure steel,
A shining spike of silver paper,
A needle stained with blood.
When used, slashes with ease
Fitted in your hand.
And another clashes against its smooth edge.

Harry Dearsly (Age 10)

My Hamster

My hamster is fat,
So fat it doesn't fit into its wheel
It eats a bowl of food a day,
Nearly bigger than itself
It likes cornflakes, sunflower seeds
And crust from toast.

Richard Driver (Age 9)

Ravanelli Poem

One and a two and a three
Ravanelli, he plays football on the telly,
When he scores he shows his belly.
Aaah Ravanelli.

Joshua Davidson (Age 9)

Christmas Time

The first day of advent is finally here,
Which means that Christmas day is getting very near.
Icicles are hanging on rooftops and on trees,
All the water outside is beginning to freeze.
People are building snowmen from the crispy white snow,
Covering all the pathways which people used to know.
All the ponds are frozen, and have turned to ice,
Watching the children skate is really very nice.
Everyone's excited now because it's Christmas Eve,
Santa will come and visit tonight but then he has to leave.
In the middle of the night, we hear a bang on the floor,
It's Santa as he leaves us presents galore.
Finally it's morning we can see if Santa has been,
We rush downstairs and shout "hooray yes he's been"
We rip open all our presents and find lots of things inside,
Chocolates, toys and dolls and a new bike outside.
We're sad that Christmas is over and can't wait until next year,
Santa will come again if we're well behaved all year.

Hannah Drinkwater (Age 13)

Red

Red is the colour of the vampires blood on his dripping teeth.
Red is the colour of my mum's lips.
Red is the colour of my rosy cheeks.
Red is the colour of my handwriting pen.
Red is the colour of a postbox waiting to be emptied.
Red is the colour of a strawberry waiting to be eaten.

Jordan Dyer (Age 9)

Why

Why does the moon glow with the light?
Why does it stay up all night?

Why can't we land on the sun?
Jump about and have lots of fun?

Why isn't there life on Mars?
Why isn't it made of chocolate bars?

Why is space black and not bright?
Colourful with lots of light?

Why are stars so far away?
Why do we move so much every day?

Why is the sun hot with fire?
Why are there so many stars, I admire?

Why are the planets in one big line?
Why is it dark for all this time?

Why can't I go into space right now?
Why do all these things happen, how?

Oliver Denton (Age 11)

A Remarkable Adventure

I was at my desk with notes,
Two pages full.
When a poisonous snake
Thought they were dull.

The snake came creeping
Through the door.
Thinking it was quite funny
To see what I saw.

A pack of cheetahs were practicing
Cheating. They were quite sneaky,
Because when they played a game
Of chess the cheetahs won.

They thought it was great.
But then I
Showed them! And
They went home crying.

A zebra was stripping
his stripes
Replaced by red stripes
And switched off the lights.

Zak Davies (Age 8)

Can They Really Build Brains

Books are weird things wouldn't you say.
You can get good books
Like math books and other educational books.
Then again you can get exciting books,
Adventure books, fairy tale books and even scary books.
Also you can get calming books
Like aromatherapy books, yoga books and
Believe it or not
You can even get calming poems like "High Society".
Me, I prefer scary books
As they send a neck prickling chill up my spine.
Books!
Can they really build brains?

Deborah-Louise Drewitt (Age 12)

The Fire

Animals leaping hunters weeping
Blazing red fire
As they tread on twigs in the fire,
Animals howling
When they're prowling
Lots of noises going on
Lots of people leaping along,
Antelopes and deer
Hunters with spears,
Everyone's terrified,
It's a terrifying sight to see.

Jessica Dixon (Age 7)

Suffering

The elegant creature lay still on the path,
Not a wave rippled through its body.
It lay so still, not moving a muscle.
There was no-one around to help it,
It started to wheeze as it tried to breathe.
The sky opened and water started to drip out
The creature slowly moved its tongue and let the rain fall on it
The beautiful animal started to twitch
It tried with all its strength to pull its self up but failed
Many times it has tried and many has it failed.
But one day it will, one day it will rise.

Emily De Smet (Age 13)

Rainy Poem

Dripper dropper plop
Muddy puddles splash in the rain
Dripper dropper plop
Running gutters in the rain
Dripper dropper plop
Skipping in the rain
Dripper dropper plop.

Hannah Dawson (Age 6)

'Me'

I wish I looked different to how I do

As for the popular girls, they don't know
what I'm going through

For they are pretty and I am not

I just wish all the teasing would stop

I've had advice from the teachers who say
that I have perfectly normal features

But the problem is they don't understand. . .

At the moment, nobody can

Emily Davies (Age 11)

Spring ABC...

Animals	Blossom
Chicks	Daffodils
Easter	Flowers
Grow	Hedge
Insects	Just
Kicking	Loam
More	New life
Opening	Primroses
Quiet	Rabbits
Sunshine	Tulips
Under	Very
Wet	eXtra
Yellow	Zig zagging birds.

Bethan Dean (Age 8)

Sir Francis Drake

When Francis Drake sailed round the world, he went very far, the sea was curled,
His ship was named the 'Golden Hind', he set off with his ships in line.

One ship had sank with all its crew, so Francis Drake just sailed through,
Two ships got burnt, they were not beat, those ships had burnt for warmth and heat.

Sir Francis Drake sailed back to Plymouth, he then got met by Queen Elizabeth,
And Elizabeth was very keen, to see where Francis Drake had been.

The Queen asked Drake to invade Cadiz, so Francis Drake said OK to Liz,
Off Francis sailed to Spanish lands, he destroyed Cadiz with his own two hands.

Drake sat back and had a rest, soon a letter was at his chest,
He opened his letter, the colour was green, "Come quickly, Francis!" signed the Queen.

Drake was ready with men and ships, he'd gone to break those Spaniards hips,
Francis made it, he came through, the Spaniards ships sunk, so did their crew.

The Spaniards were angry, they had a hate, for Francis Drake while he just ate,
The Queen made Francis become a knight, Sir Francis The Great, he's always right!

Charlie Dowzell (Age 9)

Space

A is for astronauts exploring space
B is for black holes stopping the race
C is for comets with trailing tails
D is for danger losing your trail
E is for earth the planet we live on
F is for fuel like petrol and hydrogen
G is for galaxies which glint in the dark
H is for Hercules made out of stars
J is for Jupiter the liquid ball
L is for Lunar Module which is very tall

Adam Dyster (Age 8)

Space

Why do planets turn?
Why doesn't the sun go out?
Why don't stars fall out of the sky?
How do rockets begin to fly?
Where do black holes go to?
Are there aliens on other planets?
Why don't planets collide?
Why do some planets have more than one moon?
Have people really seen UFO's?
How many galaxies are there?
Why is the sun so hot?
How did the universe begin?
How are stars made?
Has anyone been to Pluto?
When will the universe end?

Andrew Douglass (Age 10)

College

Some little girls at primary school,
Think that college will be really cool,
But let me tell you now my friend,
The horror of college will never end,
When you travel there each day,
You'll pull your hair out on the way,
The teachers that are there will shout,
Up your ear hole, in and out,
You'll always be late for Geometry class,
And be caught by the monitor, without a pass,
Whilst in the Library, say one word,
And be stomped out by a student herd,
Children who look forward to college, few,
End up in University too!

Charlotte Debenham (Age 11)

The Devil's Snare

Three cackling witches flying astray,
Boiling and burning potions night and day,
To the Devil's house which is known as hell,
With bones and ashes in the Devil's cell.

One Demon which has a magician at its heels,
With vampires and bats,
Along with slugs and big rats,
Then a gigantic gold bell starts to peel.

Last but not least the slimy Devil's snare,
Wraps its vines around you,
And its big bulgy eyes start to stare!

Shane Donnelly (Age 11)

Autumn Fun

Autumn is fun, autumn is fun
Autumn is fun for everyone

Playing conkers, jumping in leaves
Eating sweet corn, collecting leaves

Autumn is fun, autumn is fun
Autumn is fun for everyone

Golden leaves fall on the ground
As they fall they twirl around

Autumn is lovely, autumn is great
All the other seasons can wait

Autumn is fun, autumn is fun
Autumn is fun for everyone

Calum Edser (Age 10)

The Ghost Train

The carriages rattle across the floor,
As we go through the spooky door.

This is the scream that comes from the train,
When we see the skull that has no brain!

The ghost waves his hands and floats about,
In the train we scream and shout!

The heart beat pounds from under the track,
We want to escape but there's no turning back.

We have had a terrible fright,
But through the door we see the light.

William Drummee (Age 9)

A Fruity Poem

What is green?
An apple is green.
Juicy and crunchy and green.

What is yellow?
A banana is yellow
The banana is moon shaped and yellow.

Hannah Dodd (Age 5)

The Night

The night is a black blanket
Night gets killed by the sun
When it's daylight
Night puts people to sleep
The night has lots of pets like
Bats, foxes and owls
The night has lots of children
Called stars
The night keeps us from harm.

Alisha Downing (Age 11)

Cakes

C akes are crumbly cakes are ice
   some with chocolate some with spice

A pple, raisin, chocolate chip
   I want every little bit.

K itchen, cooking, stirring, mixing,
   creaming, beating, icing, fixing.

E verybody eats them, nibbles them,
   licks them, gobbles them, picks at
   them and eats the cherry on the top.

S mall cakes big cakes thin cakes
   fat cakes. The uncooked mixture
   is lovely, but they're better when baked.

Eleanor De Maria (Age 8)

Heard It In Our Playground

Give me my ball back
Pass it to me come on grumpy
Shut your big mouth I'm telling of you
What did I do
You threw me down the loo at half past two
No I never
Yes you did
Liar liar your bum's on fire
Your hair's sticking up like a telephone wire
It is not
I'm not speaking to you grump
I'm telling of you again
Sooooo
Kiss chase
Teacher teacher he called me fatty
Sooooo

Megan Davis (Age 8)

The Cup final

I remember,
Walking on the pitch at Witton Albion
Pitch ready for an exhibition
And getting changed into the spanking new kit
Then warming up on the rock hard pitch

I remember,
Walking up the tunnel
The deafening noise
I spotted my mum and dad straight away
My legs started shaking and I was wondering
If I would be able to kick the ball

Matthew Davies (Age 12)

The Simpsons

Bart, Lisa, Maggie too
I like them what about you
Homer, Homer, is the dad
He drives Marge totally mad
Bart is being really cool
Whilst Homer is acting a fool
Maggie sucks her red dummy
While Homer fills his fat tummy
Lisa plays the saxophone
Whilst the dog chews his bone
Homer, Homer stuffs his face
While Bart is being a disgrace
Simpsons, Simpsons are the best
Better, better than the rest

Sam Deacon (Age 10)

Disappointment

Disappointment is when you lose out on something
Disappointment is when a house deal falls through
Disappointment is when I go to school
Disappointment is when you can't go clubbing
Disappointment is when you can't find a girlfriend
Disappointment is when your mum and dad shout at you
Disappointment is when mum goes shopping and doesn't buy anything you wanted
Disappointment is when there is nothing on TV
Disappointment is when there's nothing to do
Disappointment is when the heating breakes down and you're cold.

Thomas Davies (Age 10)

Somerset Shore

I shall go back to the Somerset shore, back to the place of fun.
I will lay with my cousins and along the sunny sand run.
The sea spray spitting in our faces and wind tearing at my skin,
And the occasional whimper from Thomas about seeing a shark's fin.

I shall go back to the Somerset shore, where the tide is its own,
And the never-ending stretch of blue, where I love to roam.

Lorna J. Dewey (Age 10)

All About Me!

I am a girl,
Who wants to twirl,
Loves to swirl.
You would not like it when I am cross.
You'll then see who is boss
So now you know all about me!
I'll now invite you to tea.

Hava Desai (Age 9)

The Zebra

Zak the zebra
Zipped across
The zebra
Crossing

Zak Davies (Age 4)

Charlie Cat

Charlie Cat can be a . . . .
Cat that can be crazy
Can also be a composing cat
Can't be a compelling cat
Charlie conducts cat bands
He is a male cat that's black
Charlie can be a spy cat.

James Dowds (Age 8)

The Dragon

I sit there, staring at the flames in the fireplace,
And I imagine it as a dragon spitting fire across the room.
It's great wings flapping, breaking, roaring as it gets bigger,
The horns on his head seem as if they are sending me to my doom.

The roars of the dragon were getting louder,
As he destroys a big city, he gets bigger, mightier
With a crash everything falls,
Just leaving the beast alone in the dark wilderness.

When the dragon is alone,
He starts to get weak
It is put down,
In one enormous creak.

Elliot Doyle (Age 12)

Snow Is . . .

A thick white blanket
Icing on a cake
As fluffy as candy floss
Fat white clouds floating in the air
A plump, white cushion
A dish of vanilla ice-cream
A bowl of whipped cream
A child's toy for winter
Mounds of dough
A surface of marzipan,
Crunchy, white
Millions of sparkling, white diamonds

Emily Dignum (Age 12)

You're My Pumpkin Tilly

You've got curlier hair than anyone
And you've got the brightest cheeks like a cherry
I taught you how to walk and talk
And say my name easily.
Sometimes you're bad sometimes good,
Sometimes you're even sad!
But most of all you're my pumpkin.
Your lips shimmer in the sunshine
They turn ruby red.
And you come out with amazing things you get from your head
And finally the day ends and you drop and fall to sleep on your head.

John Dean (Age 10)

Playtime

Playtime starts out fun
With your friends you play
Skipping if you're a girl, football if you're a boy
Girl or boy you can play the rest like,
Running, cats cradle.
You play games like french skipping
You can go on the climbing frame
You can even play basket ball.
Then when you're bored you can exercise
When the bell rings you have to stop.
When the whistle goes you have to be quiet.
Then your teacher comes
We go in the classroom
To learn lots of things to do with school
Like maths and library

Charlotte Dubois (Age 8)

Weather

What is the touch of the summer breeze?
The gentle caress of a lover's hand.

What is the sharp clatter of hail?
The hateful lash of a vicious tongue.

What is the sound of a snowflake falling?
The silent wing beats of a tiny dove.

What is the cold sting of a sudden rain?
The venomous flick of an adder's tongue.

What is the calmness of an autumn day?
The forgotten sensation of serene loneliness.

Rhiannon D'Averc (Age 11)

Seasons

Winter is the coldest season
With ice like my cold fingers
The snow falls, so I go out to play
And Christmas with carol singers
A crib is where Jesus lay

Spring is the warm season
With the sun just starting to appear
It's not too cold and it's not too hot
And summer is very near
I like this season a lot

Summer is the hottest season
With the sun blazing through the trees
Time to go on holiday
The flowers are full of bees
The butterflies say, "Move out of my way"

Autumn is the wettest season
With rain like a bucket of water being poured over a bug
All the rusty, brown leaves fall to the ground
The rain sinks into the earth like pulling your bath plug
The rain now makes a trickling sound

Lauren Devonshire (Age 11)

I Am A Little Mouse

I am a little mouse
And I live in a little house
Underneath the floorboards

I eat lots of cheese
And it makes me very pleased
Underneath the floorboards.

A cat came by
And winked his eye.
Underneath the floorboards.

He looked very fat
As he sat on the mat
Underneath the floorboards.

When the cat sprung I started to run
Underneath the floorboards.

I wasn't going to stay
So I had to get away
Underneath the floorboards.

Megan Edwards (Age 10)

The People Next Door

The people next door,
They only have one floor,
They are old and tired.

They always admire me,
They try to do things I do.

They try to follow me,
And I turned around and said BOOO!

They ran off home,
And locked themselves in the loo.

OH NO what did I do?

Alicia Day (Age 11)

Sun Up

A gas filled ball.
A flaming sphere.
Yellow as the desert.

A sunburning horror.
A dangerous journey.
Hot like the core.

A spaceship destroyer.
A hot day maker.
The centre of our life.

A light to us.
A need to plants.
How long will it last?

Stephen de Mora (Age 9)

Thoughts

Sticky as toffee
As fine as thread,
Dew drops racing around,
Like thoughts in your head.

Like a horoscope going round and round,
Then it finally touches the ground,
Gazing at this unusual sight,
Thinking you're dreaming in the inky night.

As quick as a cheetah,
As slow as sand,
Like a black bird,
But with no sound.

Olivia Danis (Age 11)

Summer Days

Haiku

Playing with my friends
Having late night barbecues
Enjoying the sun.

On the field running
Playing football on the grass
My sweat trickles down.

On the cycle path
Pedaling at my top speed
Braking at the turn.

My dog and me play
Batting the ball on the green
This is my summer.

Liam Emery (Age 12)

Crow

Black as night,
Feathers sleek as silk,
Enemy of Farmer,
He is quick and cunning.
The one who doesn't fall
For cheap tricks.
Cackling, cackling
At the dumb Farmer
Hearing him curse Crow
For the seeds he stole.
In flight, he is free,
Roaming his territory
And becoming one
With the vast sky.

Lisa Downing (Age 13)

Gold Is . . . .

Gold is sparkling treasure
it belongs on a king's head
Gold is an inspiring colour
it makes me jump with excitement
Gold is a bright star in the sky
it looks beautiful from far away
Gold gleams with delight
it's more beautiful than words can say
Gold is a jewel on a ring
it shines like the sun
Gold is the colour of the sun
it's like a palace in the sky.

Roan Davies (Age 9)

The Fascinating Part Of Spring

It's spring, it's spring the colours have come alive again,
There's lots of colourful flowers that all look the same.

The birds are chirping and singing a song
I've waited for spring for ever so long.

I've seen lots of frogs jumping around,
Spring has got such a lovely sound.

Hayley Dallow (Age 9)

WWF

Stone cold strides high and wins fights
Kawenti fighting in matches and is scared of heights
Rock is pushing, punching and doing Rock Bottom
Undertaker makes people nice and cotton
Big show gets higher and higher people to fight
Tajari looks like he's knocked out of sight

George Davis (Age 8)

Birthday Poem

I can't believe today is here,
I want to shout and cheer,
The letterbox slams and on the mat,
Birthday cards sat on by my cat.

"Happy birthday, happy birthday" my Mum sings,
I feel so special, just like a king,
Yippee a bike I've got,
The cat wants a ride, but I think not.

Rat a tat tat, Nanny's at the door,
With my present that sits on the floor,
I'm so pleased, I gave my Gran a hug,
Even the cat purrs on his rug.

Abby Delaine (Age 11)

The Tree

The tree is as brown as a chestnut
It is by a river with golden tears.
It's branches stretch over the river
It has squirrels eating nuts on its branches

The leaves are books flapping in the wind.
The branches are like lizards crawling in the air like birds

The tree grew for years like minutes
It makes oxygen like a machine working through the years

Tom Davies (Age 8)

Inside My Wonderful Head

Inside my head
There's a door under my bed
That leads to a flower bed
The flowers smell sweet
I picked a rose and it made a big hole in the ground
And it lead to a graveyard.

Inside my head
There's a creepy graveyard
I saw ghosts in chains
And skeletons lying beside graves
That have been dug up to eat.

Inside my head
There's a nasty place
Where catfish are killing fish and eating them
And fighting jellyfish to see who's the hardest
And the jellyfish are winning
With their poisonous stings that can kill anything they want.

Jade Davies (Age 8)

Questions, Questions And More Questions

Why do bees sting?
Why do door bells ring?
Why do we have a mobile phone?
Why does it have a ring tone?
I don't know what I'm talking about.
Why do people die?
Why did I kill a fly?
"Shut up!" mum tells me,
So I end the poem!
BYE!

Bandi Dikki (Age 10)

Following A Map

Deep are the caverns
Nearby the woods
Over a snake of sparkling blue,
Now we see mountains
Bare are their peaks,
The fairies have not been through
Sprinkling whites, silvers and creams over all the land.

There is a hut as brown as a bear,
As described on the map "We're nearly there".
There is a forest where pumas are,
My destination now is not far,
I see a village quiet and small,
Now to a house tiny but warm,
Where I shall rest through night until dawn.

Blythe de Gruchy (Age 9)

Volcano

The careless volcano
Still tired,
Still and sleepy
In the mountain grassy.

The awakening volcano
Slowly emerges,
Rustling and popping
In the nights whisper.

The vicious volcano
Still going,
Running and jumping
Down the mountainside.

The tired volcano
Slowly cooling,
Tired and sleepy
In the ashy mountain

Lauren England (Age 9)

Red Is...

Red is love and kind
It is like the sunset
Red is blood that flows
Inside of me.
Blood is from scabs that
Fall off your knees.
Red is the colour of
Anger and hate
That people have of others.
Red is a lion roaring mad
It's got scared on it's mind.

Amy Duggan (Age 9)

The Ocean

Waves are curling,
White foam swirling.
Fish swimming,
Mermaids singing.
Ships are sailing,
Water twirling.
Shells whispering,
Seaweed twisting.
Children playing,
Shouting and running.
Waves are curling,
White foam swirling.
In the . . . . . .
    OCEAN

Lucy Ellison (Age 12)

Weather

Where does the morning dew come from?
From the memory of fallen clouds.

Why can't you see through a cloud?
Because they are the earth's elite guards,
Impenetrable to only the strongest forces.

Where is snow when it's not winter?
Called away to the coldest planets
To bring freezing perils to its inhabitants.

Where does the autumn weather go?
It sinks to the core of the earth to be imprisoned in a cage.

What is snow?
Down from a weather beaten penguin's stomach.

Lawrence Daniels (Age 11)

A Harvest Prayer

When the dew lies on the fields,
When the silken webs are in the trees,
Then we have our harvest supper

Acorns falling off the trees,
Conkers in between the leaves
Then we have our harvest supper

Grain is collected and washed,
Apples have been picked from trees
Then we have our harvest supper.

All the animals collect food for winter
Then we have our harvest supper.

Jamie Everard (Age 7)

Queen Victoria

Old Queen Vic
Got quite sick
So they called
For a doctor
Quick, quick, quick!
The doctor came with his
Ointments and pills
And said he would cure
Her for a bill, bill, bill
The Queen shouted
'GET HIM OUT!'
THEN SHE GAVE A SIGH AND SAID
'RIGHT YOU UNGRATEFUL LOT NOW I'M GOING TO DIE'

Mariyha Darfshan (Age 10)

Winter Days

Haiku

Glittering white snow
Gleaming in the moonlit sky
Melting in the sun.

Snowflakes swarm the air
Floating round in the cool breeze
Landing on the snow.

Children fill the paths
Sliding on wooden sledges
Through the city streets.

Craig Emery (Age 12)

Ruby Red Is the Sun

At the crack of dawn.
As the sun woke the earth,
Silently but quickly.

Ruby red was the colour
Gleaming at the sea in a tropical way,
Tropical but scorching

At the stroke of midday.
The sun shone its best, sweltering at the earth,
Sweltering but gleaming.

Patrick Downes (Age 9)

A Girl's Head

In my head there is a chocolate river
Running through my thoughts,
Quickly, rapidly, swiftly.

In my head I'm in the money,
Copper coins, fabulous cash.

In my head I see a dream
That is yet to be discovered, created,
formed.

In my head there is an animal,
Running, hiding, scared.

In my head there is a black cat
Catching a mouse.

In my head there is a mystery
That cannot be solved, cracked, worked out.

Emma Ferguson (Age 11)

Spoilt Brat

"NO, NO NOOO"
I don't want that,
Yes I suppose,
Definitely not,
And "IF I DON'T HAVE
MY WAY I WILL
SCREAM"
Give me this,
Give me that,
That's nice daddy,
"I WANT IT
NOW"
Back at school I'm the best,
My curly locks in plaits, they really go with my eyes,
But that's enough I have to go
TRAMPOLINING!

Sophie Dunster (Age 10)

A Medley Of Sport

The snooker balls are in place
The surfer wears a frown
The gymnast bends to tie a lace
The athlete ducks down

The dartsman takes careful aim
The swimmer prepares to dive
The jockey takes his horses reins
The hockey player, drives

The gun, bangs, cracks
The whistle shrills loudly
The players arch their strong lean backs
The winner stands tall, proudly

Laura Evans (Age 13)

The Coral Reef

The way I see the coral reef.
Is a band of glistening gems.
The fish they sing
The dolphins dance
The whales dive into a world of paradise.

Baby fish are dazzled by the sheer beauty of the reef,
I'd love to be a baby so I could live the fantasy
The baby whales are spellbound by the magical paradise.

The waves look like crystals dancing
On a disco ball that's spinning in the dark
This is what I think of this special paradise.

Maddy Dempster (Age 10)

My Little Kitten

My little kitten plays with his ball
Mylittle kitten gets bunged up in a bit of wool
My little kitten stays up all night
My little kitten he's a sight
He runs up stairs, he runs in the room.
You should have seen him
He runs with dad
He runs with mum
I think he is quite dumb
My mum said he is a crazy cat
Why can't that cat sit on that mat?

Louise Deigan (Age 13)

I Don't Know What To Write

I don't know what to write,
I'm hoping my pen will help me,
By producing a poem and getting it right.

I'm sitting on my chair,
Looking out the window at the sky.
Whilst playing with my hair,
And rubbing my eyes.

I'm trying to use my brain,
Doing my best to think,
But I'm staring at the rain,
Which makes me need a drink.

I got so bored I talked to Dave,
But he carried on writing away,
So I thought of what it's like to live in a cave,
Just for a day.

Gregg Exall (Age 13)

Nothing To Do?

Nothing to do?
Nothing to do?
Put your sister down the loo
Spread some marmite on the ledge
And throw your granny in the hedge.
Chuck some sugar in your hair
Shove the peas in your underwear
Then I'll stick him in the bin.
Take the cat to a cave
On the way I'll give him a shave!
Give your sister a mighty slap
Then it's time to take a nap.

Sam Deville (Age 8)

As Useless As . . . .

A magician without a trick
A footballer without a kick
A board with no pen
A pub with no men.

As useless as . . . .

A volcano with no lava
A man not called father
A moon with no light
An army without a fight

As useless as . . . .

A torch with no light
A man who can't fight
A car with no engine
An Antarctic with no penguin

As useless as . . . .

A boy with no toy
A clown with no joy
A ruler that's not straight
A person who cannot wait

Sean Edwards (Age 11)

The Sounds Of The Seasons

The plopping of snow falling off branches,
The crackling fire burning bright and warm;
The rustling of the Christmas tree,
These all sound like Winter to me.

The gushing of cool, clear water,
The squeak of an awakened mouse;
The buss of a busy bee,
These all sound like Spring to me.

The splashing of kids in a swimming pool,
The chatter of seagulls on a wall;
The crashing of waves way out at sea,
These sound like Summer to me.

The pitter-patter of rain on the ground,
The grunting badger lying down to sleep;
The chugging tractors hurry to bring in the harvest,
These all sound like Autumns best.

Then again we come round to Winter,
The years come and go;
All generations then will
Discover the sounds of the seasons.

Stephen Ellard (Age 12)

Pancakes

Pancakes are sweet
Pancakes are yummy
Pancakes are delicious
Pancakes are jammy
Pancakes are fantastic
Pancakes are sticky
Pancakes are amazing
Pancakes are sugary

Lauren Everard (Age 6)

New Eltham

New Eltham is a homely place,
Where children can have fun.
They play in the park,
And down the streets until the day is done.
The children share lots of good times.
And happy memories too.
They welcome children who don't live there,
And of course they'd welcome you!

Kate Elliott (Age 12)

My House

In my house the bees buzz
Making honey for us
I play with my sister
She plays with her Barbies
My mum does the jobs
My dad watches football

Isaac Ellis (Age 5)

Metaphor Poem - The Moon

The moon is a jaffa cake, small and round
The moon is a white balloon let loose in to the sky
The moon is the North Pole thrown into the night
The moon is a flame burning in the dark
The moon is a golf ball hit into space
The moon is a spirit gliding through the night
The moon is a snowy owl searching for its prey
The moon is candyfloss waiting to be eaten
The moon a baby wrapped up in silk

Sophie Errington (Age 11)

The Popcorn Mountain

Mount Tonu, a menacing geological monster is about to erupt.
Here comes the ominous rumble.
People praying, trees are swaying, the ground is shaking violently
Mount Tonu is firing fire bombs like shooting popcorn.
Slurping lava is now rapidly spewing out of the crater
And flowing like a river towards the panic stricken town.
The sulphurous smell is horrible, it is like millions of rotten eggs.
Furthermore the heat is immense, you can't breathe.
She sprawls more fiery liquid down her humongous body
Like sweat dripping off a boxer.
The lava has hardened . . . . . the village has gone . . . . . the people are dead . . . . .
I lie thinking of this date 1923
It will stay in my mind forever!!!

Ashley Eaves (Age 10)

Come And Dance

With the rappers rapping
And the drummers drumming
The beats start thumping
And you start jumping

The DJ spins his colourful decks
And I wonder what song he will play next
As I jumped up and started to dance
The music sent me into a trance

I saw my friend across the floor
Standing by an exit door
The glitterball spins round and round
In my heart I belonged to the sound

Luke Emery (Age 9)

Weather

What is a hurricane?
A massive twirling spinning top out of control.

What is the sound of a snowflake falling?
The sound of a butterfly's gentle heart beating.

What is fog?
Fog is the ice king's breath, frozen in the air.

What is the sun made of?
It's made from dragon flames from earth.

What is rain?
Tear drops from mars.

Matthew Edgley (Age 11)

Five Things In A Wizard's Pocket

The first thing in a wizard's pocket ,
Is a bucket full of luck.

The second is a magical sculpture
Shaped like a duck.

The third is the gem of light
To shine upon the world.

The fourth is the gem of sight
Your eyes will truly reveal.

The fifth is the greatest of all
The diamond of love, to share with your
Allies chums, companions, mates
And even your friends above.

Chelsey Edmonds (Age 10)

The Wild Outdoors

The wild outdoors is so great and so shiny,
It makes you wonder why the inside is so tiny!
The green grass, the fresh air and the brick floors,
There isn't a care in the wild outdoors.

I sometimes wonder why I did not discover this earlier,
I suppose as I was getting older I was getting a bit girlier -
Indoors there is nothing but slippery floors,
It's nothing like outside in the wild outdoors.

Monkey bars, yellow swings and great blue slides
And the sea is so shiny especially the tides!
I go out all the time and I enjoy myself to heaven,
I probably won't enjoy it as much when I get to eleven.
Inside there is nothing but fancy doors,
There is nothing inside like the wild outdoors!

Tegan Edwards (Age 9)

The Sharks Bite

The sharks red fierce eyes
Watches for it's victim to make the wrong move.
Then it strikes!

It's furious dagger like teeth,
First pierce the skin;
Then tears the victims limbs apart!

The only thing the victim can do to stay alive is:
Swim for their life and scream for help,
And if they are bleeding stay ut of the water!

If you are caught by a shark
Poke your finger in the shark's eye,
And try to swim away from the deadly shark!!!

Beware of the sharks bite!

James Elkin (Age 11)

Evil Of The Earth

Death and violence all around,
Like thunder and lightning hitting the ground,
Your friends are all dead,
There is nothing but danger
The adrenaline rush is seriously major.

Your shaking in your boots, scared of hell,
So many hates in life making it worse,
Nothing to lose, nothing to choose
You are going to be dead without any dread.
Knowing nothing, forgetting everything,
Surely you will have to tell of the evil war,
WAR IS: EVIL OF THE EARTH.

Philip Edwards (Age 17)

Motorbike

Sitting there,
The Kawasaki lives
With engine roaring loudly,
Exhaust pipe smoking violently
And driver in his black leather gear,
On the dark waxed seat.
The green coloured bodywork,
Gleaming with cleanliness.
The components jump into action,
The bike has begun its journey
Speeding along country roads
Accelerating on motorway straights.
Into the distance,
Never to be acknowledged again!!

Callum Essam (Age 12)

The End

The universe,
Cold, dark, chaotic.
Amongst the stars, no peace.
Only war.
Vast armies, many species.
Some for good, some for evil.
All is dark.
Huge machines of death crush all underneath.
Skies of flame, earth lies bleeding.
Emperors finest, scream hatred as they kill.
God's weep, demons laugh.
All is lost.

Flee, but where to run?

Aaron Edwards (Age 12)

Candy Floss

Candy floss is pink
Candy floss is fluffy like a cat
Candy floss looks like pink bubbles stuck together
Candy floss is sticky
Candy floss is a load of pink nail varnish
Candy floss is like hair
Candy floss is like fur
Candy floss stands on a stick
Candy floss is candy floss.

Karina Evemy (Age 7)

School Time

S is for school, we go most days
C is for classroom where we hate to go
H is for hope to run away
O is for onomatoposia we learn
O is for open that door for me
L is for loos, sometimes smelly

T is for time, it always goes slow
I is for irritable noises we make
M is for mean, some people are
E is for education we all need

Tom Eyres (Age 11)

Football Fans

F ootball is the best it's the most popular in the world,
O h, come and play I'm sure you'll have fun,
O ver in the premiership with Man U and Arsenal,
T rying to win the league,
B oys are better than girls well that's what I think,
A rsenal is my favourite team,
L iverpool 0 - Arsenal 1 is my favourite score,

F ootball fans are the best
A nd my dad is going to take me to see Arsenal again
N ever mess with the ref he's the boss
S o in my poem I tell you that football is the best!

Miles Easy (Age 10)

My Best Friend

Ella is my best friend,
We do everything together,
We stay in the park,
Way after dark,
Listen to the radio in my car.

Ella is my best friend
She shares her lunch,
I share my secrets,
We're best friends,
No one can beat us
Even if they try!
Because we're unbeatable!!

Grace Eldridge (Age 10)

Untitled

Begin with an overflowing bowl of boisterous boys
Having a punch up with some ten year olds,
Then crush it up and pour it in to a big bowl of cheeky chidren
Next mix for three minutes and whisk until light,
Then add some giggling girls playing with their hair,
Then beat hard for ten minutes.

After that mix it all together and boil some cheeky girls
And then smother them on the bread and cook it for twenty minutes.
There you go you've got some bread to make a teacher mad.

Philip Evans (Age 9)

Different To You

I like to party
I like to sing
I like to do almost everything.

I like to cycle
I like to walk
But most of all I like to talk

I like pets
I like food
I like people in a good mood.

I don't like fighting
I don't like pies
But most of all I don't like lies.

I don't like spiders
I don't like snakes
I don't like cars without any brakes.

The things I don't like
And the things I do
Are the things that make me
Different to you.

Bronwyn Edwards (Age 10)

My Nan

My Nan is great,
She looks after me,
She's totally brill,
I love her too!

She makes cups of tea,
And she's a chatterbox,
She lives in a flat,
Which is lovely and cosy!

My Nan has got brown hair,
With very fancy clothes,
She wears a lot of make-up,
And pointy high-heels!

Her eyes are brown,
They twinkle like stars,
Her perfume smells like a flower,
But her feet are really smelly!

But of course, I love my Nan!

Charlotte Forbes (Age 10)

The Wind

The wind......
Racing like a horse in a field, chasing like cat and mouse,
Sweeping through the trees like a brush.

The wind......
Bobbing like a duck on the water, humming like a bee flying by,
Fluttering like the leaves on a tree.

The wind......
Booming over the hills like tents, galloping over the waving sea,
Drumming like a big bass drum.

The wind......
Clucking like a chicken on the farm, shaking the house as it goes by,
Creaking like the floor-boards.

The wind......
Screaming like a firework in the air, sweeping up seagulls as they pass,
Whisking through the broken windows.

The wind......
Playing like a dog in the snow,
Brushing against the children's coats, leaping over fences.

Emily Eskriett (Age 10)

White Is . . . .

White is as beautiful as the soft snow,
Swaying and floating on the sea
White is as calm as a woolly cloud
Cool as a whisper in the breeze
White is as pale as Snow White's cheeks,
Resting peacefully on the ground
White is an angel with sparkling wings,
Flying up to heaven.

Gaby Evans (Age 9)

Storm

When there is a *Storm* I hide under the bed
When there is a *Tornado* that has sucked me in I am dead
When there is an *Earthquake* I shake
When there is a *Storm* I hide
When there is an *Eruption*
I am scared and
Dead!

Joseph Edwards (Age 9)

What Is The Weather?

What is a tornado?
The whirl in the bath when some one pulls the plug

What is the wind?
A giant but quiet horn being blown by Mother Nature

What is the sun?
It is a blushing face of the blue sky

What is rain?
It is the baby drops of rain running down from the Heavens to Earth

What is Snow?
It is the ice cream dripping off Angels round cones

Becky Evans (Age 10)

Sidcup

Children play in the parks
On their scooters and on their bikes
They jump skip hop and throw
They run around
And go with the flow.

Children play together in the Glades
And climb up through the trees.
They poke around the conkers and the leaves
Looking for bugs, sometimes they find bees.

They build a dam together in the tiny stream
They hope to catch a Stickleback
But just get in a real old mess
And collect only rubbish and weeds.

Rosie Edney (Age 12)

Toothpaste

A new tube, glistening on the side,
Smooth as smooth, just waiting to be tried.
Suddenly it's in my hand,
Fingers gripping like a rubber band.
A jet of minty goo,
Squelches all over the floor.
I don't think there is anymore!
Gurgle, spit, swallow, choke
It's all down my front, this is no joke!
Froth is up behind my ears.
And I can hear footsteps, coming up the stairs,
Ooops.....

Hannah Edwards (Age 12)

What Is Red?

Red is blood bleeding from inside
Red is a cherry being picked off a tree
Red is the colour of a rose
Red is the colour of a berry
Red is the colour of a strawberry
Red is the colour of a raspberry
Red is the colour of rosy cheeks
Red is the colour of an apple
Red is the colour of lava
Red is the colour of tiles
Red is the colour of a jotter

Joshua Eke (Age 9)

My Day

I get up in the morning,
Then I wake dad up to stop him snoring
Mum gives me some tea in my mug
And there climbing up the window was a hairy bug
At school
I met my friends they're really cool,
After school I'm going to a swimming pool

Kerry Emmerson (Age 9)

A Smooth Stinky Brick

A smooth stinky brick, that's what I am!
A smooth dirty brick!
I'm as tough as quadruple glazing!
And I'm always miserable because
I just get stuffed into a dirty wall

Luke Ebsworth (Age 9)

Guess Who

I have three bags of wool
I gave one to the master
And one to the dame
And one to a little boy who lived down the lane
Who am I?

Maximillian Elliott (Age 9)

The Spring

Spring is the time to blossom
When roses come out,
So it makes it look cosy
But when the bumble bees come out,
It makes me feel lovely
The days get longer so take your time.

Michael Elsom (Age 9)

The Robber Rhino

The revolting robber rhino called Rob
Robbed the rich Rosemary of Rome
With rage!!!!
Rummaging Rome,
Robbing the rich.
Rob ran round and round Rome . . . .
With
RAGE!!!!!!!

Toby Emerson (Age 7)

Night Time

Dewdrops sparkling on the ground like stars in the sky,
Trees swaying to the sound of crickets chirping
Stars wink at the moon
And the old owl flies past like a ghost

Harry Ewing (Age 9)

Christmas Acrostic

C heering children opening presents,
H appy robins singing calmly,
R eindeer floating around in the sky,
I vy and holly making the day prettier,
S nowmen dancing merrily,
T ime for Christmas dinner,
M assive turkey sitting on a plate waiting to be eaten,
A nd the day is full of fun,
S miling faces are everywhere.

Emily Ellis (Age 9)

Wolf

His piercing eyes like bullets,
Follow passers by,
As fast as a firework and powerful like a murderer.
His claws like knives that can run through skin.
The beast of the dark,
The king of the woods,
The leader of moonlight.

Florence England (Age 11)

If I Had Wings

If I had wings
I would touch a feathered flock of birds
And glide over the angry sea

Tirion English (Age 9)

What Makes A Teacher Angry!

Weigh out with some bad language boys,
Sprinkle with some silly name calling,
Whisk round a bowl the weird writing,
Drizzle with dangerous paper notes.

Mix in with pathetic paint flicking,
Cheeky girls whining for their mum,
Combine gradually with the calling out,
Served with a rogues ruler fight for the finishing touch.

Rachel East (Age 9)

On The Bus

I rush to Class two's cloakroom,
Shouting in the playground.

I have to wait for the teacher,
To take me to the bus.

I ask who's in the front,
Definitely not me.

I sit on the very back seat,
My friends shout.

The bus driver tells them off,
But they still scream and shout.

They get dropped off,
Now there's some quiet.

I get dropped off,
And don't know what to do.

Rebecca East (Age 8)

Ruin

Dirty windows
Creaking door
Raven's piercing eye

Broken stones
Finger trees
Buzzard floating by

Blocked up well
Cracking bell
Jackdaw's gleaming hoard

Crumbling walls
Empty halls
Haunt of feathered things

Byron Edwards (Age 10)

Untitled

The
Soft
Gentle
Snow
Glistening
In the light
And the icicles
Hang from the bridges

Mark Friend (Age 8)

In My Dream I Met The Queen At Buckingham Palace

In my dream, I met the Queen, at Buckingham Palace.
I entered into a beautiful big hall with portraits everywhere,
A glittering crystal chandelier hung above my head,
Before my eyes, I could see a huge marble staircase with a royal red carpet.

In my dream, I met the Queen at Buckingham Palace.
Through a door I found myself in a grand throne room,
A gold throne encrusted with diamonds, rubies and emeralds stood before me,
And upon the ruby red cushion sat - the majesty herself, her corgies sat obediently at her feet.

In my dream, I met the Queen, at Buckingham Palace.
She wore a gold crown covered in jewels, like a ring of burning fire on her head,
She wore a royal blue silk gown with diamonds as buttons,
She wore high healed shoes studded with emeralds.

In my dream, I met the Queen at Buckingham Palace.
Out in the gardens I stood on a neatly cut lawn, bright flowers all around and vines high above the ground,
Guards marched up and down just around the corner,
And by a stable full of horses stood a shiny clean white limousine.

In my dream, I met the Queen, at Buckingham Palace.
I saw in the dining room, a table a mile long,
Gold padded velvet chairs set all along, and scrumptious dinners waiting to be eaten.
When in my dream, I met the Queen at Buckingham Palace

Abigail Fairbairn (Age 11)

If My Friends Were

If my friends were an alcoholic drink
They'd be champagne
Lively and bubbly and getting up my nose
Like Willy Wonker's exploding chocolate bars
Making me smile throughout the day.

Emily Fenner (Age 11)

Limerick

There was a young man from Kings Langley
Who's teeth were all loose and jangly
He bit on a sprout
Some teeth fell out
And the rest were left all dangly.

Joe Frewin (Age 12)

Last Day At School

Last day at school I feel happy
Chairs stacked on tables
Ceiling is cracky
The hall is clear
The Headmaster draws a blind
The cook is here to say goodbye
The teacher has something on her mind.
The printer is printing
The last bit of paper
Muddy walls, dirty sinks,
They take out the pins
So the wall's safer
Collect artwork, lunch boxes and PE bags
Dust the corners in the ceiling
Clean the dirty rags.

Christopher Fowler (Age 7)

Cats

Anybody's lap will do,
Fitted in a cardboard box,
In the cupboard with your frocks - anywhere!
They don't care!
Cats sleep anywhere
Cats sleep anywhere
Any table
Any chair
Top of piano,
Window-ledge
In the middle
On the edge
Open drawer
Empty shoe
But
Anybody's lap will do

Clare Freeman (Age 12)

Boys!

I hate boys,
I hate boys,
I hate it when they show off.
And when they're noisy and suspicious,
I hate boys,
They're liars and they're creeps.

I love boys,
I love boys,
I love the way their blue eyes twinkle,
And their blonde hair's in a ruffle
I love boys,
The innocent little boy look you just can't resist.

I hate boys,
I hate boys,
I hate the charm that they never mean,
And their forgetful, stupid minds,
I hate boys,
They're sour losers and they just can't face it!

Anastasia Fawcett (Age 11)

Dear Queen

Dear Queen
You are never mean
You have a golden ring
And you sing
I'm sorry to say
You're Mother and Sister have passed away
You are the best in the West
And in the rest

Mohammed Faheem (Age 10)

Weather

When it is a bright sunny day,
God is happy
When it is a dark cloudy day
God is stroppy
When it is a dark stormy day
God is angry
When it is a wet rainy day
God cries
When it is a cold snowy day
God is cold
When it is a windy day
God is drying his beard with a hairdryer
When it is an earthquake
God is shaking
When it is a freezing frosty day
God is sprinkling sugar on a cake

Samantha Foot (Age 8)

The Milky Way

In the glistening sky,
Are millions of twinkles catching your eye.

Though you can look back in time,
There's always one thing puzzling your mind.

Can you imagine the intensity of brightness,
Blinding flashes making you nauseous.

Yet the stars are revolving round a point,
Where light is being sucked deep down to never return.

Which leaves history all lost,
In wondering where does it all go.

What will happen in the future, who knows,
But we know the Milky Way still glows.

John Frayne (Age 14)

Passenger Floater

I sit tall and proud in the water.
I feel the sticky varnish being painted over me.
My name is on the side I want to show it off.
I am being surrounded by people gazing at me.
I feel proud as if I was a king.
I feel like an elephant at the zoo.
If the public want to see me they have to pay.
People are trusting me.
I feel like I have to keep them safe.
I am sailing swiftly and beautifully away.

Alice Freeman (Age 10)

Dolly, My Sister And I

If I were a car, I'd be a Porsche,
Red and shiny,
Like a ripe cherry,
Fast and furious and a bit of a showoff.

Although, if my sister were a place,
She'd be the moon, calm and tranquil,
Like a glass of plain water,
A person you can't reach easily.

And if Dolly, my hamster, were the weather,
She'd be the sun, bright and beautiful,
Like a sunflower showered in radiant light,
She can brighten up my world any day.

Grace Fieldhouse (Age 12)

The Road To Mordor

Down the road to Mordor
Riding next to Gandalf
Merry and Pippin,
By my side
Nobody strays afar.

Nearing Misty Mountains,
Where Goblins are no more,
There the bones
Of their kings lie
Untouched, ghostly, dead!

Down the road to Mordor
Riding next to Gandalf
Merry and Pippin,
By my side
Nobody strays afar.

Then to the Elvenkings home
Where here
My dear Bilbo came
To rescue and save his dear beloved friends.
But he is no more.

Kathryn Fallaize (Age 10)

Fruit

Fantastically fresh fruit
Odd oval oranges
Oodles of oatcake
Delicious dainty dumplings

Elliot Fenton (Age 8)

The Day I Got My Puppy

I remember Budd,
Curled up, fast asleep in his bed,
Looking nervous,
He wakes up,
So skinny and hungry,
He needed to be fed.

I remember being fast asleep,
Feeling something touch my leg,
A big bang - A yelp,
I saw Budd on the floor,
Crying for help.

I remember him getting run-over,
Feeling tears,
Rolling down my cheeks,
Now still feeling the fears,
I try to think about him,
Not the bad times,
But the good.

Joanne Ford (Age 12)

Beelzebub On The Fields Of War

An evil broth is brewing
The mixture's almost done
A little hint of secrecy
A lie let loose to run

A forked tongue which slithers in
And paints both ears bright red
Conspiracy so neatly planned
For blood so much to shed

They meet upon the field
Armies dressed so bright
And yet they look on nervously
Unsure still why they fight

The leaders speak of bravery
And glorious victory
Whilst each word so strongly said
Comes from the mouth of He

He lurks beside the bodies
To watch the bloody sea
He whispers to his war
And takes each soul in glee

Rosy Fenge (Age 15)

Fog

As the fog rolls on the harbour,
I stand by the rocky cliffs,
The men shout as they labour,
And the noise gently drifts.

And then as if by magic,
The waves twist and turn,
The harbour starts to vanish,
And the mist begins to churn.

Keeley Fairbrass (Age 13)

Distant Friend

I sit and stare across the field,
Searching for her; yearning for her.
But something is blocking her, a shield,
Trapping her in my mind, a dark corner.

She is so far away; she can't reach me,
I stretch towards her, but she's not here.
She's just a faded memory,
A distant friend who whispers in my ear.

But then she leaves me, all alone,
Without her, apart from her.
And now I sit here on my own,
Searching for her, yearning for her.

Kathryn Fowler (Age 11)

Find The Fox

The fox is at home,
With his long bushy tail,
Checking around with his beady eyes,
Hungry and starving looking for food.
He has a little sniff with his wet damp nose,
He smells some food and steps a little further,
As the smell gets stronger and stronger,
He steps closer towards danger.
The farmer is waiting at the top of the hill,
Aiming very carefully at the predator,
The fox is now very near and . . .
BANG the fox is dead.
The next day the farmer's guilt
Has made him think some more,
He's now decided he would make his fences higher still,
For he now thinks hunting is cruel,
And now says it must come to a halt.

James Ferguson (Age 9)

Where I Live

Unlike most I live in a close,
Full of beautiful flowers,
Where people tend their gardens,
Every little hour
There are houses,
There are bungalows,
I wouldn't like to live anywhere else,
Unlike most I live in a close.

Grace Fright (Age 10)

The Magic Box

I will put in my box
A first amazing step.
A sip of water on the hottest day of India,
Seeing a baby open its first tiny eye.

I will put in my box
Four golden glowing wishes,
Three sparkling silver magic spells,
Two glimmering bronze pennies.

The box is shiny
With six gold stars on the lid,
There are four twinkling lights in the corners
It is made of glass,
The hinges are made of skeleton toes from people.

I will swim in my box
On the high waves of the Atlantic Sea,
I will climb in my box
Up the highest mountain in New Zealand,
I will swim to the bottom
Of the water in Portugal.

Chelsea Foster (Age 9)

Safari

Deep in the wildness,
The dusty plains of Africa
Where the animals and creatures
Are waiting, waiting to strike,
Lions crouching and when their
Prey are in their reach they pounce
As quick as lightning.

The elephant thuds across the Savannah.
When it reaches water it jumps!
Muddy water splashes everywhere
Their long trunks wave around.
The elephant is wise
He remembers everything.

Jennifer Farmer (Age 13)

The Forest

Trees are all alone,
Cold and dark, black and gloomy,
The stump of the tree.

Pitch black in the dark,
Flowers grow in the hot sun,
All different flowers.

Molly Fowler (Age 8)

Elephants

Elephants are nice
Elephants squash mice
They are fat and thin
Not a tin
Elephants are keen
Like they have seen
The whole world
They are big and small
They know how to call
Elephants stomp all day
And they are very grey
They live in an unknown place
And they never have a race
Elephants play games
Like they have names
They eat and drink a lot
But not out of a pot
They make a lot of noise
Some are even boys

Craig Freestone (Age 10)

I'm A Frog

You think of me as a bit of fun,
When witches put me in potions and spells
With my slimy skin rotten and gross,
I need a kiss, then I'll turn into a handsome prince
But at the thought you cringe and shudder,
You gaze at me then I hop - you run,
Shrieking and yelping as you go,
As I have big bobbly eyes which stare
And my slimy skin glistens in the sun.
You don't respect me.

You're wrong, I'm not like that,
I'm handsome and special my skin is magnificent.
I am sporty, I swim like an Olympic swimmer gliding through the water,
Pushing it all back like a machine working away,
I am friendly really.

All I want is love and respect
For you to touch me and not pull away in disgust
And for you to know what I really am like.
This is all I want,
Please.

Ellen Fulton (Age 11)

Ghost

I heard a noise I looked around,
I saw a shadow on the wall,
I was terrified I couldn't get to sleep,
I thought I was dreaming
So I went to get a drink from the kitchen
When I got there I saw a ghost, I was terrified
The ghost was see through
It was dressed in my mum's clothes
I was screaming, my mum came in my room
I was dreaming

Kelly Flaherty (Age 10)

School Day Emotions

Monday is like a grain of sand
As it slips away through your fingers,
Tuesday is like a long lecture
Boring, boring and never ending,
Wednesday is like a fun house
Full of nice fun surprises,
Thursday is like a huge maze
Long and endless,
Friday is like a . . . . well relief
The school week is finally over.

Rebecca Frith (Age 11)

A Question And Answer Poem!

What is thunder?
- the beat of a gigantic drum.
What is the sun?
- the face that watches upon us.
What are stars?
- a million twinkling lights in a black cave.
What is snow?
- a giants soft white blanket fallen out of his bed.
What is fog?
- a smoke that never ends.
What is the wind?
- a werewolf's first howl.

Robyn Fletcher (Age 10)

Autumn Days

Autumn has come, everyone is glum,
Leaves are falling, the wind is calling.

Colours of leaves, I'm gonna freeze!
The sky is grey, it's too cold to play.

Wrap up warm, there's gonna be a storm,
Raindrops falling, insects crawling.

Autumn has come, everyone is glum,
Leaves are falling, the wind is calling.
It's the Autumn day warning!

Matthew Fursse (Age 10)

Unknown

Crying,
Give me mercy, all I want is freedom,
Freedom to live, to laugh and dance,
Crying.

I left,
I left my home, the place I was fleeing from,
Sorrow, need and sickness was there,
I left.

Dying,
Rotting bodies, no water or plant life,
The deaths of my good friends kill me,
Dying.

Escape,
That's what I wanted, but this place is far worse,
Locked away, probed and tested,
Escape.

Crying,
Give me mercy, all I want is freedom,
Freedom to live, to laugh and dance,
Crying.

Nicola Fishwick (Age 12)

Dolphins

Dolphins are like shimmering pebbles in the sea,
Being reflected on by the sun.

As their slender bodies glide through the water,
People say,
"They are just like Olympic swimmers!"

As their echoing sound is heard by fish,
Their mouths are showing their pearly white teeth,
Which many other fish would not do.

Chloe Fidler (Age 8)

Cats, Cats, Blooming Cats

Cats cats blooming cats,
Always chase those big fat stinking rats
Who annoy the cats.
I like cats but not rats.
Someday those cats will certainly kill the rats
Then there will be no more of that.

I really do hope those rats will go
So they stop chewing my toes.
And then a cat got stuck in the hosepipe,
He got really mad and started to chase the rats.
A rat ran under a mat by a cat,
The other cat pounced on the mat,
The rat moved so the cat couldn't catch it.

I jumped and slipped and killed a rat,
As well as that I slipped and killed a cat.
Oh well that's that.
No more nonsense, see about that.

Jamie Fletcher (Age 9)

Have You Seen Humpty

Bill and Ben,
Went to the hen,
And said have you seen Humpty?
We've lost him again,
He is a big pain,
But I bet he'll be ok.

Jordan Foden (Age 9)

The Sea

The sea is a prowling tiger,
A race track for white horses.
The sea is a hungry animal,
With the shore as its prey.
The sea is a person with many moods,
When it is angry, the cliffs shake with fear.
The sea is a blanket on an enormous bed.

Caroline Flux (Age 11)

Peaceful River

Peaceful river, the sun reflecting its shimmering beauty,
Gathered round for picnics and games of football,
Children dipping their toes into the cold water,
Old people smiling and watching their grandchildren playing in the river.
Teenage lovers gazing at each other,
People walking their dogs looking up at the sun.
Down at the peaceful river where all your cares and troubles float away . . .

Charlie Fowler (Age 11)

You Used To Be My Everything

You used to be my Romeo, and I was your Juliet.
You used to be my shower, and get me nice and wet.
You used to be my bed at night, and keep me cosy and warm.
You used to be my sewing machine, for whenever things got torn.
You used to be a lot of things,
In and out my house,
Even behind the skirting board,
You were the little mouse.

You used to be my plant, that never ever died.
You used to be my truth machine that never ever lied.
You used to be my goldfish, swimming in a bowl.
You used to be my fire that never needed coal.
You used to be my telephone, on which I had no bill.
You used to be the photos, on my windowsill.

You used to be a lot of things,
In and out my house,
Even behind the skirting board,
You were the little mouse.

Emma Fletcher (Age 13)

My Pencil Case

On the road without a fuss
Penguins going for a ride
Open the zip, ten pens inside
Blue, black, yellow, green
Loveliest multie colours ever seen
Pencils sharp and rulers long
My pencil case is heavy and strong.

Marie Farmer (Age 16)

The Way Things Link

The flower has a,
Petal which rhymes with,
The kettle in the kitchen with,
A sink rhyming with,
The stink let off by,
A germ rhyming with,
The worm that lives in,
The soil rhyming with
Some foil which raps,
A cut of meat, which rhymes with,
A fleet of,
Ten sheep rhyming with,
A high leap which a
Cricket does. This sport is played with
A ball hit with,
A bat, which has
A red handle, belonging to
A kettle rhyming with
A petal coming off,
A flower

Christopher Foster (Age 11)

Mow Mow Black Cow

Mow, mow,
Black cow,
Have you any milk,
Yes sir, yes sir
Three bags fulll,
One for the milk maid,
One for the dame,
And one for the little shop down the lane.

Ben French (Age 10)

Dragon!

Fire breather,
Human eater,
Smoke sneezer,
Land heaver,
Green, brown, black and grey,
Meet one you'll have to pray,
The dragon!
High flyer,
Avoids the wire,
Leather like wings,
Your head will spin,
Teeth like daggers,
Mouth of death,
Pray you're not its next meal.
The dragon!
Scales like stone,
Mountainous body,
Do your best,
You're not a wolly.
THE DRAGON!!!!!

Tammi Ferguson (Age 11)

In The Night

In the night,
There'll always be something,
To give you a fright.

All of a sudden you'll hear a clatter,
Your teeth will start to chatter,
Your hair starts to stand,
And your heart starts beating,
Like a big brass band.

You're glued to the spot,
You're shaking a lot,
And YELP!
You're screaming for help!

Then you realise nothing's the matter,
Your heart doesn't pitter and patter,
You've reached home post,
And you haven't seen a ghost,
BUT BEWARE!
YOU MIGHT BE IN FOR A SCARE!

Bianca Fuentes (Age 10)

Lost Skull

Suddenly I saw
In the corner of my eye
I saw a skull
Nearly covered by the gorse
Laying with loose teeth
And a greeny skull
With bones shining through

Bill Farleigh (Age 8)

I Wonder

I wonder what it's like
You know, being the Queen?
Does she have her en-suite
In her bedroom?
Or her very own limousine?
Or does she keep an elephant
In her royal garden?
Does she have her own servant
To wash up all the dishes?
Does she have a great big pool
And a tank full of fishes?
Does she ever have second thoughts
About being the Queen?
I wonder what it's like
You know, being the Queen?
Is Buckingham Palace
As nice as chocolate
Or just old fashioned?
I wonder what it's like?

Alexandra Gordon-Stuart (Age 10)

No Longer My Concern

I try to help,
but no one cares.
They'd be better off,
if I wasn't there.

I know they hate me,
but care, I do not.
One day they're down,
the next they're not.

I'm so sick of these people,
and the advantages they take.
I really don't care,
this statement I make.

So please refrain from everything,
for it's no longer my concern.
Please refrain from everything,
it's no longer my concern.

Steve Fletcher (Age 14)

The Gorilla Rap

I'm da baddest grilla' in de west side,
I'm da baddest grilla' in de north side,
When I walk in da room,
My face goes boom,
Wiv' all dat swingin' hippin tune,
I'm gonna boogie on down,
Wiv out a frown,
Coz me boys av got me back,
If I get banged down,
So now I'm coming to da end of my rap,
Coz my knuckles are hurtin' wiv all dat,
SMACK!

Thomas Grepne (Age 11)

Crossroads

Once again we stand at the crossroads,
Smothered by the stifling sun.
Beneath our feet
Meet four eternal paths,
Their dusty surfaces shimmering
In the noonday heat.
Seemingly identical, the mute roads
Guard the secret of their destinations.

A faint fresh breath of breeze
Cools the pulsating air
And continues north,
Stirring new life in its wake.
Chaos, colour, danger, joy -
I choose this path.
The journey is just beginning.

Kezia Gaitskell (Age 18)

The Recipe For An Angry Teacher

Weigh out a class of hyper children
Mix a group of giggly girls with a crunch of bad language,
Add a pinch of cusses with a dollop of careless mistakes
Stir a dribble of ruler fights with a dash of whining children.

Add a splash of paper letters with a drizzle of paper aeroplanes,
Mix a knead of girls fiddling with hair with a tea spoon of homework late.
Serve a bake of dancing children in front of an angry teacher.

Joanna Flashman (Age 9)

The Snow

The snow is my favourite weather
It falls so gently and makes a beautiful blanket for the ground
A lovely blanket of soft snow
Getting thicker as it falls without a sound

But when it gets thick it starts to get noisy
Because people go sledging and make a huge roar
Or they will come out to make a snowman standing tall
But when the snow melts they have to wait until next year for it to fall.

Edward Fairbairn (Age 8)

September 11th

Planes soar through the air, carrying their danger.
They soar elegantly over the tall skyscrapers
Sneaking up as quiet as a summer's breeze.
Then mass destruction and mayhem
As they hit the tall building, like thunder
Bringing its immense power to the earth.
Terrorism rules the day.
But good will triumph, terror is evil,
But revenge is sweet.

Philip Fitzpatrick (Age 14)

Swimming

S wimming is fun,
We love swimming very much,
I could jump in the swimming pool
M y sisters take me swimming also as teachers too,
M y habbit is swimming every day,
I t is a great thing to do,
N othing else but swimming every day,
G oing swimming is good!!

Aysha Fiaz (Age 10)

Stars Of Animals In The Sky

When the sun sets darkness falls
The stars appear one by one
Leo the Lion the King of stars
Appears so tall and fierce
The great dog is chasing the hare
So fast he is but still doesn't catch the hare
The great bear pads her way through the dusty dark sky
When the sun rises the stars disappear
When the moon rises they'll be out again.

Dominic Finch (Age 10)

The Tin Mine

I attract tourists.
I am the silhouette on the hill.
I stand tall and straight.
When once I used to work
Now I stand wrecked
I feel forgotten
And yet so many people know me.
I am pure Cornish
And I live on the moor.

Ella Frears-Hogg (Age 10)

Teachers

Teachers are normally bossy,
They tell us what to do.
Teachers say what our homework is,
I hope it isn't Literacy.
Teachers tell us off, if we talk in class,
They tell us to be quiet,
If they catch us talking.
The teacher says "say you're sorry",
When they ask a question,
They wait for an answer,
If we wait too long, they lose their temper,
Then the teacher shouts "I'M WAITING!"
As soon as they stop speaking,
They say "Get to work children",
When the teaching is finished,
I say "I'm glad that's over".

Jack Furnival (Age 9)

A Winter ABC

A ll	**N** ow
B ranches	**O** ccupy
C rystalled	**P** laces
D aintily	**Q** uickened
E ven	**R** aging
F rosty	**S** now
G rass	**T** orrents
H as	**U** nder
I cy	**V** arious
J ewels	**W** ild
K een	**X** citing
L uminous	**Y** ews
M ounds	**Z** ig zagging everywhere

Amy Friend (Age 10)

Colours Of The Rainbow

What is red?
Red is a robin's breast perched on a branch
What is orange?
The sunset is orange glowing in the distance
What is yellow?
The sun is yellow high up in the sky
What is green?
The grass is green swishing in the breeze
What is blue?
The summer sky is blue sitting behind the clouds,
What is indigo?
Sparkly stars are indigo sparkling in space
What is violet?
Bluebells are violet blowing in the field.

Tom Fox (Age 8)

The Wind

The breeze of the wind blows,
The birds sing in the trees,
Now it's getting on,
The gale is approaching,
Now I'm getting scared,
Everything blowing everywhere.
Leaves, pieces of wood,
The wind is getting stronger!
It's turning into a hurricane!
I run inside to watch the hurricane as
It blows in from the sea,
Cars are blowing into fences,
Trees are blowing too.
Now it's dying down,
It's dying down into a gentle breeze.

Zachary Fountain (Age 8)

What Is the Sun?

Where is the sun? Where did it go?
I've looked everywhere, I just don't know.
I open the door, it's snowing outside,
I wonder where the sun is, has it gone to hide?
I put on my coat, into the cold,
There goes Mr. Whiskers he's very old!
Will the sun come out another day?
I look up at the sky, it's really grey!
As I look around icicles drip down my back,
I do up the zip of my extra warm mac!
The freezing snow has stopped coming down,
The golden SUN is shining all around!

Emily Franklin (Age 11)

. . . . ? . . . .

I don't know what to write,
I'm giving my pen a nasty bite,
Now let me stop and think,
Not pencils or ink,
Not rackets or balls,
And definitely not school!

I'm getting very ill,
Because I'm sitting so still,
I don't know what to write,
I'm giving my pen a nasty bite.

Kathrine Foy (Age 11)

Haunted

Welcome to the house of terror,
Where people scream and they shiver,
Boos and scares floating in the air,
Ghosts seem to be everywhere,
Please, help, get me out of here,
I think I'm goikng to die of fear,
Zombies dancing, skeletons smiling,
The atmosphere is rising near,
Help get me out of here,
The end is hopefully getting near,

Jamie Frost (Age 15)

The Playground

So many games to play,
It, football, and rhymes to say.
Kick, bounce, climb and run,
Lots of laughs so much fun.

Chatting, shouting, flirting boys,
Girls squealing, lots of noise
Skipping, jumping, singing a song,
I wish I could do this all day long.

Relax, gossip till the bell rings,
Stand still, then go in.

Rachelle Flaherty (Age 11)

The Sharpest Fang Snake

Snakes slither across the ground, slowly.
Watching you carefully.
You have to be carefull, there is one right behind you.
Creeping up with the sound of rattles and similar to sizzling sausages.
The fierce colours of the snakes scales.
It scares me right to death.
But my mother says htey can't get you.
They are locked away in te cage,
Look behind you you have a fright you can especailly see them in the night.

Leoni Fletcher (Age 9)

Homeless

Feeling lonely walking along the road,
Eating nothing but air,
No-one cares that I have no family, but me,
People's smiling faces running through the street,
I cry sad tears as I think of what I could have had.
My cold bones shake with fear as I think of the stormy night ahead!
For I know what will happen soon.
Because I have no place to go but the next street!

Alison Franklin (Age 10)

Love Is...

Love is looking at the sea going in and out and when the sun shines on it.
Love is the colour of the sun's red, yellow and orange.
Love is the sound of frogs in the bright, blue pond.
Love is hearing the cool DJs on the radio playing "Who Let The Dogs Out?"
Love is the smell of pollen from summer grass.
Love is the smell of properly cooked eggs and sizzling sausages.
Love is the touch of lovely Fat Cat.
Love is the feel of my Mum's cat coat.
Love is the taste of Rice Crispies in the bright morning.
Love is the taste of pie at midnight in the fridge.
Love is the world to make wonderful friends.

Charlie Foster (Age 7)

The 7-Eyed Jelly Monster That Ate Our School

The 7-eyed jelly monster that ate our school
Slithered on a car thinking he was cool,
The 7-eyed jelly monster started to wobble
Ate a man and all you could hear was gobble, gobble, gobble.

The 7-eyed jelly monster started to cough
Listened to Slipknot and turned into a goth
The 7-eyed jelly monster that ate my teacher
Then he started eating the preacher.

The 7-eyed jelly monster that now had a big belly
All the adults thought he was smelly
But all the kids ate him because they like jelly.

Darren Fox (Age 11)

Bats

I woke up, got out the belfry
Oh why does it have to rain?
I was darting garden to garden
Picking up mosquitoes every minute
It started raining really hard
I managed to carry on

I saw the horizon coming up slowly
I flew back to the belfry quickly
I wrapped myself up tightly
Upside down I went to sleep
Suddenly the rain stopped
I hope tomorrow it's not raining

Ben Franks (Age 10)

A Witches Spell

An elephant's eye and toad's toes,
This is the way the spell goes.

Fishes fins and the brain of a bat,
Mixed together with a dead rat.

Boil it burn it with fire and flame,
And with the other ingredients do the same.

Leave it in the pot to bubble and bubble,
And there you have the perfect trouble.

Sadie Forrest(Age 11)

Little Chick

Little chick in the egg
At Easter
Little chick in the pond
At Easter
Splish, splosh, splish, splosh
In the pond
At Easter
Little chick in the rain
At Easter

Rachel Francis (Age 10)

Jumping Frogs

Five green frogs jumping on a lily pad
Five green frogs jumping on a lily pad
And if one frog should accidentally sink
There'd be four green frogs jumping on a lily pad
Four green frogs jumping on a lily pad
And if one frog should accidentally sink
There'd be three green frogs jumping on a lily pad
Three green frogs jumping on a lily pad
And if one frog should accidentally sink
There'd be two green frogs jumping on a lily pad
Two green frogs jumping on a lily pad
And if one frog should accidentally sink
There'd be one green frog jumping on a lily pad
One green frog jumping on a lily pad
And if that one frog should accidentally sink
There'd be no green frogs jumping on a lily pad

Oliver Friend (Age 8)

Rain Poem

Pitter, patter, pitter, patter
The rain is dripping on me.
Pitter, patter, pitter, patter
I see the rain gleaming on lots of cars.
Pitter, patter, pitter, patter
The rain is soaking my clothes.

Swish, swosh, swish, swosh
It's still raining.
Swish, swosh, swish, swosh
The rain is splashing on the street.

Pitter, patter, pitter, patter
It's raining . . . . all day!

Louis Fendt (Age 7)

Recipe For an Angry Teacher

Pour a jug of angry teachers on top of a gang of hot sweaty boys
Gently stir them around with some calling out loud
Whisk in some awful spelling mistakes
Add a hint of jumping on the tables
Top with a squirt of homework in late
Drizzle with a bunch of careless mistakes
Smothered with a gang of giggling girls
And top with one annoyed head teacher

Nicole Fitzsimons (Age 10)

The Sea

A giant monster,
Big teeth viscously tearing up ships
And spitting the wrecked remains away.
Dangerous and angry, it surges and roars,
Chasing me with its sharp, salty claws.
The waves reach up into the sky
As if trying to hold the storm,
And pulls the rain down into its darkest depths.
But when the morning comes, everything is quiet and still.

Emma Friend (Age 10)

My Nanny

My Nanny is very brave,
caring, considerate and funny.
If ever you met her you would
immediately love her.
With the things she does
and the things she says.
I hope my Nan will get better,
or my cheeks will get even wetter.
I love my Nan lots and lots.
Jolly, jiggling Nan.

Natasha Fenn (Age 12)

Black

Black is the black bird flying through the air
Black is a dark nights sky.
Black is a new car tyre
Black is the colour of a blackboard
Black is the colour of all
Black is the colour of a Zebra's stripes
Black is the colour of coal
Black is the colour of a Tazmanian Devil

Tom Fisher (Age 8)

Rain Poem

Splitter splotter splitter splotter
My clothes are damp and wet
Splitter splotter splitter splotter
My hair is soaked and tangled
Splitter splotter splitter splotter
The drain is going slurp, gurgle, slurp
Splitter splotter splitter splotter
I'm wet through
Splitter splotter splitter splotter

Georgia Gilling (Age 6)

Transport

T rains whizzing past stations never stopping
R ockets blasting up high into the cold air of the universe
A eroplanes full of air and speeding, flying in mid air
N auticals under the ocean with the fish saying hello
S ubmarine seeing lots of coloured fish slapping their fins
P arachute falling faster than light and getting faster each second
O ver the sea the ship sails by
R ocks and boulders stop the boat which can't move
T rains flying past blurry towns, shops and people

Laura Fletcher (Age 9)

Angel

I know you're watching day and night
With your halo shining bright
And your wings spread out wide
Through the night sky you glide.

You fill my life with joy
And for every other girl and boy
I can feel when you're near
Now my life has no fear.

Krystina Giles (Age 12)

The Fire

The fire is like a ravenous dragon
Burning trees as it goes across the lit city.
Its blazing eyes like sparks through the night,
And when the flaming fire strikes!
His razor-sharp claws swoop down and flickers blow up!
Its mass jaws spreading the red hot flame.

It shadows its prey ready to pounce and
ROAR!!! It stealthily darts and the chase is on . . . .
Its flailing wings making ash rapidly zoom past!
And at last he catches his prey and
SNAP! SNAP! SNAP!
The prey is dead and the predator rests,
Its snores making mini aftershocks which reach the earth's core.

Paul Farnell (Age 9)

Harvest Poem

Harvest is when conkers and acorns come out
At harvest farmers are binding the fields
Ripe brown, green and yellow leaves
Van full of food for people who have not got anything
Early in the morning blocks of hay come on the road
Sweet lovely food coming into the church
Tall lovely flowers fall down to earth

Danielle Fysh (Age 10)

Weather Poem

Where does the rainbow end?
Beyond the edge of the next world.
What is the sound of thunder?
An angry giant stomping down a concrete staircase.
What is an aurora?
The phosphorescent dust of passing fairies.
How does the wind move?
It cuts through you like an invisible knife.
What is the taste of fog?
Tasteless candyfloss that stings the back of your throat.

Farrel Gray (Age 11)

The Silly Poem

One old ogre opening Oly's wheat
Two tired tortoise tiptoeing to bed
Three thinking troops throwing food
Four fairies flying from Oz
Five fantastic fish frying freshly
Six singing sparkly stars on the stage
Seven seals sinking slowly down to sea

Alyx Gregory (Age 7)

The Cat

The cat slinks round the corner,
And jumps onto the wall,
He prowls and he pounces,
As he goes to caterwaul.

He fights with his enemies,
He scratches with his friends,
He does this all evening long,
Until the night ends.

And when the sun rises,
He runs along the street,
He curls up in his basket,
And pretends he's been asleep.

Philippa Goodall (Age 12)

Twinkle Twinkle Little Star

Twinkle twinkle little star
I really, really like chocolate bars,
But since I've got no money,
I have an empty tummy.

Joshua Goswell (Age 9)

Mea Sonster

There's a mea sonster in the sea,
And it's tickling me.
It ulled me punder,
Punder the sea.
There's a mea sonster
And it's tickling me!

Rebekah Goodwin (Age 11)

A Man Called Bob

There once was a man called Bob
Who desperately wanted a job,
So he looked through the pages,
And searched for ages,
And just ate a corn on the cob.

Michael Glaze (Age 10)

Stonehenge

Enormous stones leaning on each other
Very tall might fall.
Looking up to the heavens
The moon shines bright on the ground
Making shadows on the land

Alastair Garner (Age 7)

Tyrannosauras Rex

The sharp, toothy Tyrannosauras-rex
Called Toras
Was trampling through tracks
When a thud came . . . . . .
He stood tall on his two legs
And "RROOOAAARRREEEDDD"
The forest shook
The noise was deafening to dinosaurs.
Then, there was silence
And the tree laid down dead!

Christian Grimble (Age 7)

Art

Inspiration,
This thing all artists want.
Journeys made all over the world,
Just to find this little something.
Painters, they paint,
Exactly what they see.
The drops of paint form beautiful scenes.
And singers chant their feelings and thoughts.
The poet finds inspiration all round,
Or creates it in her mind,
From nothing.

Agnes Granroth (Age 14)

At The Restaurant

"Bread with mustard, or cream and custard?"
"No, just some chips, please."
"Would you like some meat, it's lovely to eat?"
"No, just some chips, please."
"Don't have the chicken, it's just no good!
Have the turkey, yum, you should!"
"No, just some chips, please."
"Have some ice-cream, it's good (I doubt!)"
"Good grief, I'm going to shout!
Just some chips, please!"
"Sorry, sir, why didn't you say?
'Cos we're outta chips today!"

Leanne Goddard (Age 10)

Jump

The air is rushing past my face
Faster faster, I turn to face the cloud
I am enveloped in a weird white stuff
I try to grab the cloud around me
It disappears in my hand.
Suddenly I can see the ground
Everything is small.
Nothing but the wooshing of
The air around me.
I am roaring towards the ground,
I have to pull the cord

My head is jerked back.
I slow down and suddenly the thrill is over.
All that's left is for me to float
Slowly back to earth.

James Grainge (Age 13)

David Coulthard

Zoom zoom zoom
Driving past the audience in his McLaren
Zoom zoom zoom
Taking over Button now Irvine
Zoom zoom zoom
All the fans cheering him on
Zoom zoom zoom
He's taking a pit stop
Zoom zoom zoom
It's the last lap
Zoom zoom zoom
Irvine and Coulthard are fighting for the lead
Zoom zoom zoom
It's the last corner
Zoom zoom zoom
Coulthard has taken the lead
Zoom zoom zoom
David Coulthard wins the British Grand Prix

Harry Gillham (Age 12)

Last Day At School

It was very early morning and I started to wake
I went to my classroom my books I had to take
Then tidy the classroom sort things out
Out of the door happily I shout, shout, shout.
Take things off the wall
And then go into the hall
Tidying trays
In all sorts of ways
It's time to go home bye bye
I shut the door it's home time

Ellie Graham-Coombes (Age 7)

Two Chris Grahams

People don't understand there are two Chris Grahams:
The one that walks, the one that glides.
The one that shows, the one that hides.
The one that studies really hard.
The one that refuses to even start

Two Chris's: One whose perfect as good as gold.
One who doesn't do as he is told.
One who soars through the sky, one who never tells a lie.
One who dreams through the night.
One whose ready for a fight.

One who calls people names.
One who wins at many games.
One who gets in a mood, one who is never rude.
One who travels over land.
One who gives his command.

People don't understand there are two Chris Grahams.
One who is a free as a bird
One whose seen and always heard.
One whose deep within my soul,
One I hope I can control!

Chris Graham (Age 11)

Smouldering Embers

Smouldering embers
Glowing delicately with
Slight wavers of smoke

Victoria Garbutt (Age 11)

The Prince Awakens

The night was alive,
The rumbling and tumbling of the thunder,
The rattling, rolling of the lightning,
And the rustling of the rain and wind,
Added to the tension of the night

Inside the lab the whirr of the machines,
And the bubbling of the test tubes went on
Whilst on his back the monster was lain
Covered from head to foot with dirty white bandages

A clap of thunder, a violent flash,
The clouds cowering from the storm
The howling the rattling and the shaking of the hatch
Along with the violent gusts of air
It was loud, it was noisy but the servant didn't care,
The button was pressed

The noise went on then, abruptly stopped
The storm abated, silence once more
The table landed with a tinkling thump,
The chains creaking, loud as they could
The monster's eyes flickered open

Sam Gunn (Age 11)

Poppet

Gold like the sun
You are so much fun.
Smooth curly fur
You bark and don't purr.
Run round the house
Like a scurrying mouse.
Gentle, sweetheart
Let's pray we ne'er part.
You'd play with a bead
Like a crow with a seed.
A sweet little nose
You're scented with rose.
You fight with the cat
And you sleep on your mat.
Wagging your tail
You're bold and not frail.
Walks get you soggy
You silly little doggy.

James Gibson (Age 14)

Trees In Winter

The spidery tree
Spiky and strong
With trunks and twigs
All twisted and long

George Goddard (Age 6)

Sister

Always a blue bow
Never any arrows
Rusty scrap
But gold

A new
Badly conditioned
Short story on peace

A cowardly poodle
Sitting nicely, head up
Mouth neatly shut
Not ready to scamper

A still ocean
Trickling, trickling
Tiny waves rolling, rolling
In the sunny sky

A brittle
Thin plant,
Slouching in the still air.
A soft, rough, black rose
Fragrant and sweet

Ian Gossage (Age 12)

The Senses Of Winter

The frosty, bitter air strikes my face and hands,
With the harsh rain spitting at my hair,
While the crisp, crunching blanket of snow beneath my feet softens, and
Weeps as the winter sun rises.

The season for skiing is upon us my friends,
The silky, fresh snow lays on the bare trees,
Snowflakes stroke my cheeks as they fall to the sodden ground, frozen
Lakes gleam as the moonlight touch weakens.

The smell of winter is purified and clean,
I taste the dreary sea of mist, and my
Breath is captured, billowing out in the damp country air, the echoes
Of children rejoicing seem eerily distant, almost unreal.

The snow silence is almost unbearable,
As I return to my cottage a tingling sensation spreads from my feet
Upwards. I remove my bleached, dripping boots and stare at the
Different, delicate winter wonderland.

I know I am protected by my misted window,
From the cold, which touches everything outside,
In a harmless way . . .

Carley Gates (Age 13)

Feelings

When I feel lonely I am as lonely as a wounded soldier
When I feel angry I am as angry as a rhinoceros
When I feel sad I am as sad as a graveyard
When I feel happy I am as happy as a rainbow

Nicholas Georgiou (Age 6)

Sidcup

Young children play in the parks
Teenagers hang around on street corners
From night to night
The elderly stray out of sight

Jade Gillespie (Age 11)

What Are Stars?

The star is a diamond of a wedding ring
Stars are a sun glowing in a pale blue sky
They are sparkling yellow sparklers on firework night.

Jasmine Golding (Age 9)

First Wave

My favourite childhood memory, would probably be,
Something that I like doing, which will involve the Sea,
I remember when I was six, and moved down here to Devon,
And when I got here and looked at the place, I saw that it was heaven.
We immediately drove down to the beach, ladled with all our gear,
Then we jumped in the sea and knew we were finally here!
My dad pushed me onto a wave, and I'm there looking astounded,
And after getting onto my feet, I fell off and got pounded!
I picked myself up, and thought it was really fun,
I shouted to my dad out loud, "look what I have done!"
I smiled at him like I was king, and ruled all of the world,
And commanded what the water did, as it swirled and it swirled and it swirled!
After an hour of total bliss, I eventually got out of the sea,
My mum gave me a cup of soup and I was as happy as can be!

Ben Gatley (Age 13)

Leisure

What is this life if full of care,
I've plenty of time to stop and stare.

Time to walk my dog around the block,
Oh my god now look at the clock.

Time to exercise to keep me fit,
I listen to Gina she's my number one hit.

Time to go swimming and play with my friends,
It is a laugh when they act like hens.

Time to watch TV at 8.00 at night,
I like to watch Eastenders but it's a bit of a fright.

Time to play with my rabbit but I wish he didn't bite.
I have to sort him out even at night.

What is this life if full of care
We have no time to stand and stare.

Rachael Gibson (Age 9)

Autumn

Leaves all fall off trees
Brown leaves I find on the floor
Brown leaves are all dead.

Abigail Gomez (Age 8)

Battle For Peace

A sea of blood, the pain in faces,
Bodies lying in forgotten places,
Men fighting in battle trying to win,
Asking themselves how did this mess begin.

Many young boys not knowing why,
They've been taken from home mostly to die,
Fear on their faces but trying their best,
Knowing as soldiers they're put to the test.

Suddenly it's all quiet, have we won?
Do I chance putting down my gun,
I look across to call my friend,
And realise his life has come to an end.

The tears start to fall but I'm still alive,
I know I must leave him to try and survive.
I kiss him goodbye and I can't look back,
As I hear the enemy start to attack.

I run and run searching for cover,
Praying and hoping I'll soon see my mother.
Then over the hill I see the others,
I know I'm safe now with my brothers.

Lauren Gregory (Age 12)

The Queen

The Queen is our leader and proud to be,
Rich and healthy as we can see,
Those dresses, I wish I could wear,
But I have no chance,
All I do is stare.

I love the crowns that she often wears,
But I'm just ordinary, so who cares?
Her beauty shimmers in the light,
I think she's a beautiful sight!

The Queen is our leader and proud to be,
And now she's celebrating her jubilee,
We should all stand and shout and cheer,
To say our thanks,
In her special year!

Remy Gawne (Age 8)

Teddy

T eddies are nice
E very night I cuddle one
D own in my bed
D addy likes my teddy
Y ou like my teddy

Lea Goddard (Age 5)

Football Team

We want a ball,
And we all call.
Over here,
But you're nowhere near.

He's very tall,
And he makes me fall.
He's the coach you know,
And he does like to throw.

I got up and passed,
And then I put someone in a cast.
The ambulance arrives,
I told a load of lies.

"Hey boy,"
"You're playing like a toy."
I was in defence,
I am as good as a fence.

"Hey Cean,"
"You're on the team."
Oh no the football test
I don't care this is the best.

Nicholas Gowrie (Age 10)

The Ghost Town

There was a town
an empty town,
a town with out any light
a town not so bright.

No people I hear
only lost souls beneath the ground.
people, what I seek is fear
a little whisper far away, a faint sound,
there she lays
on the floor and who I saw?

A girl not moving and
not breathing,
only her spirit I see,
a laugh in the park
the swings moving but the spirit I hear
is laughing on a hill top,
she came and told me
this town is no ordinary town she said.

This place is a Ghost Town!

James Garfield (Age 12)

Winter

Snow falling to the ground
But not making a sound
Snowdrops peeping through the snow
Children playing in the snow
Red roses from the biting wind

Matthew Garrod (Age 11)

Why

Who do leaves fall from trees?
Why don't humans get fleas?
How does gravity keep us down?
Why do muscles let us frown?
How do we blink?
Why don't ships sink?
Why do magnets have poles?
Why are small horses called foals?
Why is wood opaque?
Why isn't metal easy to break?
How do grasshoppers hop?
How do brakes make a car stop?
How does our heart beat?
Why don't worms have feet?
How do birds fly?
Why do you have to ask
WHY?

Jessica Gilbert (Age 11)

In The City (shortened version)

I was a stranger
In the city,
Didn't seem to fit
In the city.
So many things to talk about,
So many things to worry about
Flammable air,
Watch out over there
Smoke flows out of the chimneys above
Fills the atmosphere,
Oh dear
Walking down an alley
Everybody is running
In the opposite direction
Got to go, got to go
Smoke flows out of the chimneys above
Fills the atmosphere
Flamable air
Watch out over there
In the city.

Jack Goodall (Age 10)

Inside My Head

Inside my head
There's a beautiful place
Home to a royal king
And his hard working servants
A place with a pleasant queen
And a nicely dressed princess too
Inside my head
There's an untidy house
With messy rooms and smelly toys

Grace Gardener (Age 7)

Snowflakes

Snowflakes
down
down
down
falling
floating
fluttering
down
down
down
shimmering
shining
smash!
melt I'm dead

Ben Haskins (Age 7)

Why?

How can electricity make things work?
Why do light bulbs turn bright or turn dim?
How can batteries make circuits complete?
What's a buzzer, how do they buzz?
What *is* electricity?
How could I use it?
What are circuit symbols for?
Why does electricity give you a nasty shock?

How do roots keep a flower upright?
What are nutrients?
Why are mosses green and not blue?
Why do leaves fall off trees in Autumn?
What are petals, what are they for?
What are seeds, where do they come from?
Why do cows eat grass?
Why do I keep wondering why?

Samantha Graham (Age 10)

Aliens

Aliens are thick
Aliens are lovely
Aliens are inside
Aliens eat me
Aliens are naughty
Aliens are taking over the world

Jason Green (Age 8)

Ghostly Skies

Upon the silent, silver skies,
Along the stars a pale ghost flys,
Through its monstrous heads o five
No living man is left alive.

On a hill, there is a graveyard,
With pale skeletons, bony and hard,
In the grave, there is a coffin,
Rotting and fading, into nothing.

Upon a tree, some bones lie,
Glowing against the cold, night sky,
The tree is bent and near to nothing
Bending over the dark, black coffin.

The smothered grass all burnt and black,
If you come in here, there's no turning back,
When the thorns are battered and cut,
With a horrible clang, the black gates shut.

Upon the silent silver skies,
Along the stars, a pale ghost flys,
Through its monstrous head o five,
No living man is left alive.

Hannah Green (Age 9)

The Twelve Months In A Year

January brings a glow to your cheeks.
February brings a chill to your toes.
March brings a cleaning frenzy.
April brings more than a shower.
May brings out the buds of spring.
June brings the sun upon us.
July brings the summer altogether.
August brings the barbecue burning
September brings children a new turning
October brings sweets and treats.
November brings Guy Fawkes and fireworks.
December brings a cheer to our hearts.

Ayisha Govindasamy (Age 9)

Animals

Cheetahs are fast, sloths are slow.
Kangaroos jump and ants crawl.
Birds fly and elephants walk.
Fishes swim and frogs hop.
Tigers chase and cats pounce.
Dogs run and mice scamper.
Bulls charge and snakes slither.

Tom Graham (Age 8)

Bishop's Wood Poem

We tasted bread
And ate some cheese
The Saxon lady there said
"No cartons please"

We built a shelter
From bracken and wood
It was raining
So we added a hood

We drove to Bishop's Wood
We got off the coach
Made ourselves comfy
And hammered a brooch

Then we had lunch
And thatched some willow
But then we had to go
I had my coat for a pillow

The coach journey ended
We were back at school
We had lots of fun
And missed assembly in the hall.

Anna Gardner (Age 9)

Nothing Interesting Happened At School Today

Nothing interesting happened at school today,
In the morning we had tiring French,
But the teacher thought it was break and let us play,
And we escaped through an excavated trench.

Then we were caught and had detention,
Writing out line after meaningless line,
But a bird caught the professors attention,
And we escaped, through an underground mine.

Then we were caught and were punished
So we had to clean up after science,
I spilt liquid and the windows vanished,
And we escaped, hoping nobody knew of our absence.

Then we got caught and were given a letter,
To show to our strict mums and dads.
But the teacher started to feel better
He ripped it up and stopped getting mad.

Finally school has ended,
It's the finish to an extremely dull day.
Most days I'm normally exhausted,
Nothing interesting happened at school today.

Catherine Goswell (Age 10)

My Cat

My cat catches bugs and sits on rugs,
My cat is a soggy moggy,
My cat has a froggy moggy face,
Everyone calls him Tase.

Ellie Gowshall (Age 6)

Grass

This is the grass that grows tall and green
And it grows from the ground.
Grass is green, green, green, green,
But always on the ground.

Freddie Goring (Age 8)

A Recipe To Make A Teacher Mad

Begin by weighing out a giant handful of boisterous boys with a bowl of messy ink
Mix it together, then add a pinch of annoying backchat with a sprinkle of feeble excuses.
Melt it together then let it cool down
Later add a fierce ruler fight with a load of scruffy doodling.
Crush it together, then top it with a touch of careless errors.
Then combine it with a pinch of deadly dangerous pencil flicking.
Next add a load of bad language with a hint of calling out
Whisk it together, bake it for five or ten minutes
Serve it in front of a teacher and eureka!! You have an angry teacher

Scott Greenfield (Age 9)

Seasons

In the summer the sun shines bright
Swimming and playing to our delight
The days are long and we stay out late
Our fishing lines are full of bait
Now it starts to get colder!

Leaves are falling very fast
It's even worse than the past
The trees are getting very bare
Warm days are getting very rare
Now the snow is starting to fall!

The ground is very white
The days are getting dark not light
We are getting ready for Santa to come
Leaving out lots of rum
Now the flowers are starting to grow!

The sun has just come out
Lots of children sing and shout
Newborn animals are running around
Where can the Easter bunny be found
NOW IT STARTS ALL OVER AGAIN!!!

Cassie Gruitt (Age 10)

A Days Weather

It's raining today what an awful shame
It's like winter all year long.
Spring is here flowers appear
And birds sing sweet little songs.
Summer's arrived, the sun is hot
We're having a ball.
Oh no a leaf has dropped
Is it the start of fall?
It's raining today what an awful shame
It's like winter all year long.

Chloe Gee (Age 9)

What Pet Shall I Have?

Shall I have a cat, or maybe a rat?
I think I'll have a dog, o wait a frog!
I want a fish, and I'll call it Trish.
I'll have a horse, yes of course!

I could buy a cow, but I don't know how.
I might have a rhino but it will damage the lino.

Maybe a mouse that can sleep in the house.
I could get a snake, but it would have to be fake.

Oh well, I guess I'll never know, if I can get a rat
Or a cat to sit on the mat.
I am getting a bit sleepy now,
So I think I'll sleep tight, but in the morning
I just might . . . . .

Francesca Gallone (Age 8)

A Burning Forest

A burning forest with wild animals scared
The birds fly up high,
The terrified deer squeal and run
The hunters shout for help and run
The tiger roars and is getting mad
But the fire is spreading bad.
A burning forest with animals scared

Alex Ghouri (Age 9)

Holiday Poem

S is for salty sea.
H is for hot holiday.
E is for eating a lolly on the beach.
R is for raining when people get wet.
I is for when I go inside to bed.
N is for not doing what mum says.
G is for going to have dinner.
H is for having tea.
A is for playing with my animals.
M is for mum helping me with my homework.

Simone Gray (Age 10)

Senses

I like to hear the birds singing
And all the people chattering to themselves
I like to smell all the lovely smells
And school dinners that have been made
I like to see children's names on the happy board
And our spotlessly clean carpet
I like to taste all the different kinds of snacks and fruit

Nicola Green (Age 7)

Snowflake Show

Snowflakes dancing calm and gentle,
Flit, flit making gestures,
To and fro singing softly,
Howling to their colleagues,
Windows covered their show must commence,
No need for playscripts,
Lines are learnt by heart,
Gentle, gentle movements glow,
Conducted by a wailing wind,
Snowflakes acting has a successful rythm,
Their winning show,
No better than a white Christmas!

Amberley Gregson (Age 10)

Spring

Spring danced
Through the new born field
Sprinkling its marvellous magic
Waking the flowers
Bringing the colours back to life.

Spring raced
By the rushing river
With laughing children following behind
Putting a smile on the fishes face.

Emma Grocott (Age 12)

Sharks

Sharks are meat-eaters
Sometimes they eat people
Because the people look like seals.
A group of sharks is called a school.

Stephen Harris (Age 12)

The Dance Of Autumnal Leaves

Twisting, turning, forever soaring,
Through gnarled hands to them emploring.
Glinting russet in the glimmer of an eye,
Never to fail, never to die,
Amber, auburn, chocolate brown,
Pirouetting to the ground.
Footsteps rustled, shuffled and scrunched,
Families huddled in the tightest bunch.
Hovering weightless on whispering winds,
Flutter-by, spiral-by on veined honeyed skins.
To be a leaf is heaven you see,
Always to sparkle, spin, stealthily.

Carly Holmes (Age 13)

Options

Options to be chosen
Decisions to be made
Everyone's a winner
Too many subjects saved

Thoughts for the future
Careers on the mind
Things moving forward
Don't leave me behind!

Friends getting busy
Teachers marking books
I've decided on my options,
Let's take another look

Emma Gilbert (Age 13)

Inside My Head

Inside my head
There's a place
Where all the
Beautiful towers
Hang over the large city
And tiny jets swoop
Over the massive town
They pick up
All the people
And fly together

Thomas Guess (Age 7)

Weed

Slowly.
Quietly.
My legs start to grow.
But nobody knows, nobody cares.

Anticipating.
I lie in wait.
I wait for the sun.
But nobody knows, nobody cares.

Ground.
Hard.
Though my piercing head is there.
But nobody knows, nobody cares.

I grow;
The sun, my friend.
I sway with the wind - I am there.
But nobody knows, nobody cares.

Man.
Enemy.
I'm destroyed forever.
But nobody knows, nobody cares.

Caroline Gabbott (Age 11)

Black Queen

Black Queen is very scary
She's black from head to toe
She tries to go sunbathing in the bath
But don't you know you go sunbathing in the sun

You'll be horrified and terrified
Whenever you see her,
You'll yell right out of your shoes.

Your body will quiver and shiver
Now black queen will just stand there
Screaming and shouting so horrifically

Within the tick of the clock there was just silence,
And then black queen just strolled away as quiet as a mouse
Then all of a sudden you could hear the laughing of the Black Queen!

Katie Gregory (Age 8)

Autumn

Season of conkers and fireworks
And mellow fruitfulness
Blackberries along the canal.
White jungles of frost on the window
Acorns falling off trees, leaves changing colour
Ice to slide on in the playground.
Finishing swimming in the half term.
Going to bed quite early.

Lauren Gentry (Age 9)

Swimming

"Swim over there," my mum said,
"Right to the other end of the pool,
Front crawl, face under, and remember,
Don't stop!"
"Fifty metres," I thought to myself.

Everyone else was swimming up and down
As fast as cheetahs racing after their prey.
Everywhere, a flash of bright costumes.

My mum calling to me from what seemed like metres away,
Waves shimmering all around us.

But I stayed still.

I thought of dolphins gliding along in the vast ocean,
And whales cruising the sea.
But I remained lifeless.
Suddenly, I thought, "I can do this!"
Thrusting my arms and legs forward,
I splashed my way down to the end of the pool.
My mum said,
"Well done."

Toby Gilbert (Age 10)

The Queen

I look around,
I don't know how I got here, do you?
I feel like I've just stepped into a church, shadows loom in the corners like animals waiting to pounce.
I creep from room to room, some with wallpaper others painted
I'm in a dream aren't I?

The Queen herself is above me, I look around and see a dead dove in a painting, poor little thing.
This corridor goes on forever! The walls are rich red, while this ceiling is painted with so much care!
The portraits seem to follow me wherever I go, whatever I do.
There are vases from the far East and places like Greece.

But as the morning sun slides above the horizon like a fiery ball,
A bird makes a call like a song in the distance.
I walk into the biggest room yet, with a ceiling as high as the sky!
There is her throne, choked with pillows and fabrics and yes a few diamonds.

What's happening! The ceiling is disappearing
There's a mist
I open my eyes, it was only a dream, I told myself it was only a dream.

Harrier Gordon-Head (Age 10)

What Is Spring?

Spring is when the weather becomes warmer
My Granny's garden is full with birds
They fly around me
The bulbs grow into flowers
Daffodils are bright and beautiful

Winter goes to bed
In the morning when I go to school it is cold
But then the sun rises into the sky and shines like a candle
And it gets warmer and warmer,
In time for my lunch playtime

George E. Goody (Age 6)

I Wish I Lived In A Castle

I wish I lived in a castle,
With the flag flapping way up high,
I could look over the top of the battlements,
And see all the way to Rye,

I'm surrounded by suits of armour,
They glisten in the morning sun,
But when I try one of them on,
It really weighs a ton!

But no, I live in a normal house,
With no armour or no flags,
I sit down and listen to the radio,
And polish it with some rags!

James Green (Age 9)

A Dream About The Palace

Late last night I had a dream,
About going to the palace,
Opening those magic doors,
Suddenly . . . .silence.

Walking right past the winding stairs,
Looking at all the pictures spying on us,
The chandeliers glistening up ahead,
The ornaments lying all around.

There was the Queen, there was the Queen!
Sitting on a chair,
She smiled at me and disappeared
I really wish I lived there.

Amy Goss (Age 10)

You'd Better Beware

Don't come round here you'd better beware,
You would only come round if it was a dare.
I doubt you'd come back fully alive,
So you better start running if you want to survive.
My new pet is strong and mean,
It's the greediest thing you've ever seen.

It's big and green my fighting machine,
His teeth are yellow and he does make a bellow.
Bang that drum beat that bum he's fourteen inches and ten long
He's big and hairy and very scary
So join in with the chorus he's my
Stegasoras!

Amy Gray and Chelsea Melhado (Age 10)

The Future

A tiny corral in a small pink bay
Surrounded by large fish
Swimming in an enormous ocean

A quiet bubbling sound
Listens to the large crackling sound
In the darkness

The new tennis ball rolls around on the grass
And watches the explosion of an atom bomb
Far away in the distant future

The seed in the ground
Sits quietly and wonders
What the future has in store

Robert Hunter (Age 12)

Why Walk Away?

To get up and walk away would be
Too easy.
So stay and stand the ground which is rightfully yours.
For every right there is a wrong
Looming;
So watch your back if you want to stay.
So where do we go from here?
You've never tried to be like me.
You don't know what it is like.
Have you ever tried to be like me?
Have you ever been in my shoes?
If you ever step in my ground

It won't be quite as soft as it seems.

Alex Green (Age 14)

Christmas

Christmas trees all alight,
Holly on the door,
Ruldoph with nose so bright,
Is a sight so sore.
Santa's sack full of toys,
Tinsel all around,
Mary with a baby boy,
A happy time I've found.
So this is my christmas.

Liam Gregory (Age 9)

The Sea

The calm sea is like a turtle dove,
Peaceful and serene,
The lapping waves - are birds pecking at the grain,
The seaweed the trees where the doves sit and coo,
The tiny fish are the buzzing bees,
The rocks the flowers.

The stormy sea is like an angry lion,
The waves his claws as he tries to slash people,
The rocks his pearly white teeth as he tries to snap,
The crash of waves his menacing roar,
The seaweed is his swishing tail,
The rolling of the waves his irritable growl,
The floating debris the rotting remains of his enemies,
The fish his loyal followers.

Madeleine Gripton (Age 11)

Diving!!!

When I dive
I go up and down
wee
wee
wee
I do not drown
I spot a fish
orange and bright
it kills the light
and never says

GOOD NIGHT!!!!!!!

Robert Grimshaw (Age 9)

I Would Like

I would like a big black dog to run around with me
And a ginger and white cat to cuddle up with me.

I would like a white horse to gallop in the fields with me
And a golden hamster to play with me.

I would like an orange fish to swim with me
And a red parrot to chat with me.

I would like a green tortoise to walk slowly with me
And a brown monkey to swing with me

I would like a green frog to jump with me
And a black and white rabbit to bounce with me

Lauren Geraghty (Age 7)

The Flood

The flood is a terrifying thing
Splashing the walls and knocking down trees
It covers the cars and land all around
People are shouting: Get up to higher ground!

The thick black water is climbing up the stairs
It clings to everything, smells lingering in the air
The water's receding: Oh what a relief!
The clean up begins, people cold with chattering teeth.

Puddles of water are left on the ground
Brooms and mops clattering about
Cheers fill the air, people happy it's over
Getting everything back in the right order.

Marie Goodrum (Age 12)

Banana Banana

Banana banana
In a bush
Are you waiting
For a push?
Banana banana
In a tree
Will you come
To tea at the
Sea?
Banana banana
On a plate
Are you waiting
For a mate?

Jamie Gray (Age 7)

The Razor Rainbow Fish

Red racing
Rainbow fish
Races up a ramp
With razor sharp teeth
Flying through the air
Over red rolling
Atomic barrels.

Harry Giles (Age 8)

Hen

Egg layer
Queen strutter
Keen pecker
Chick watcher
Nest maker
Loud clucker
Sunday roast

Emily Gallop (Age 11)

A Day In The Mountains

Fresh white snow on the tall pointing mountains,
A cold breeze rushes through my hair,
My eye travels over the people skiing,
I feel my eyes stinging in the wind that carries the snow blocking my view,
I see the clouds in the faint view that I have,
The sky seems to have swallowed the clouds making the sky a continuous white stream of milk,
I hear the yells of happiness on the mountains as people slide down the hills,
A glimpse of blue is seen behind me where a trickle runs away from the cold so not to freeze,
I see flakes of snow as it sets like icing on a cake,
I feel the excitement run through me like riding a rollercoaster for the very first time.
Pleasure runs through me like an Olympic runner going for gold,
The snow begins to stop, I see a clearer view of the amazing sight,
The view is all around me, no beginning, no end.
As much as I have to leave I can't bring my feet to move.

Rachel Grout (Age 11)

Ghosts

The leaves lie thick upon the ground.
The wind howls in the mists sound
Shuffled, whining, hissing rustles through the leaves left on the bare trees
The wind shivers through the ground and bursts in the air
It whispers through the ground and wails in the woods
Images flow and flutter, flickering in the mist
Groaning scratched voices echo in the air
GHOSTS, ghosts are there to scare
They swish and sway, they whirled and curl,
They fly and flutter, they glance.
Ghosts, ghosts are everywhere
They're never going for they swear
The fair breeze blows
The moon glows
The ghosts have their way to show what they know . . . .

Riya George (Age 11)

When The Moonlight Touches The Lake

As night falls I arise from sleep
I'm the cloak and dagger, with a high-pitched squeak
In the darkness my wings softly beat
I am like a shadow empty and pitch black
I devour the blood red skies, like blood from a victims back
Seizing my prey as wisdom they do lack
In one night I seize much prey
'Till dawn approaches, I soar and hide away
'Till then I wait for the end of the day
But when the moonlight touches the lake
I arise again to warn the dark world I AM AWAKE!

Rachel Gill (Age 12)

The Smiling Shark!

I am a shark,
Lurking, lurking in the shadowy
Depths of the ocean.
I am a great white
The most feared of all.
I lurk in the unexpected
Beneath the weed. There I lurk waiting,
Waiting, waiting in the shadow.
Waiting to pounce.
I have a wise toothy grin.
Light glints on my tooth,
There I await my prey; The unwary.
There I glide silent and deadly,
Waiting for you to swim into my trap.
So beware the shark that grins,
Glides and gloats because once you are in my trap
You will never see the world again.
I laugh to myself for I am the cleverest of my kind.
You are never safe in my world,
I am the master of the ocean.

Jenny Gregson (Age 12)

Bedtime

Bedtime bedtime
Brushing my teeth
Bedtime bedtime
Pillows in a heap
Bedtime Bedtime
Listening to TV
Bedtime bedtime
Cuddling Ted
Bedtime bedtime
Hear mum shout
Bedtime bedtime
Just . . . a . . . sleep . . . zzz

Paris Holden (Age 7)

What Am I?

I have sharp teeth
I eat lots of meat
I run very fast
To catch my prey
I have a long tail
And lots of spots
I'm happy in the wild
What am I?

A Leopard (upside down)

Arran Heath (Age 7)

Guinea Pigs

Sitting in my lap,
Like a fat gentleman,
As still and silent as a deserted house,
As soft as a teddy bear,
But with razor sharp claws,
Digging in my leg.

Staring at me,
With black bead eyes,
That flash red in the dark.
It's mud brown,
Night black,
Snow white hair,
Moulting over my jumper.

Back in its cage,
It starts plodding like an old man,
Squeaks like bicycle brakes,
And falls silent.

Samantha Hole (Age 11)

Weather

What is thunder?
It is beating drums in the sky.

Where does the rainbow end?
At the edge of the universe beyond the stars.

What is the sound of a snowflake falling?
The peaceful beating of a dove's wing.

Where does the wind go?
Back to heaven above the clouds.

What is a hailstone?
The tiniest crystals falling from the sky.

Esme Gray (Age 11)

Pigs

A gentle oinking,
The joy of a newborn pig,
A helpless baby,
Such weakness from the mother,
How will the piglet survive?

The piglet must rest,
Some soft straw helping it sleep,
It's breathing slowly,
The mother watches proudly,
As she eats some golden straw.

Lucy Griffiths (Age 10)

The Coach

The coach of solid gold is pulled through the crowd,
With lovely white horses in pairs at either side.
Inside the golden coach is Queen Elizabeth,
Wearing an embroidered dress,
With emblems all around.

The coach glistens in the sun,
There are soldiers everywhere,
She gives a little wave of her hand and a gentle smile.
The crowd cheers,
Long live Queen Elizabeth!

Eleanor Gill (Age 9)

Jungle Fun

Trees stand like towering giants
Shadows sleep under towering trees.
Coconuts hang on for their lives
The sky is like a floating sea.
Birds bury themselves in trees
Animals bathe in golden sunlight.
Baby animals playing in the warm sun.
Mothers watch their babies play.
Birds sing like opera singers in the tree tops
Lions are on the hunt
Mothers watch out for killers
The unlucky baby may loose his life today.

Mitchell Gray (Age 10)

Autumn

Conkers dropping off the tree

Crackling conkers crunching on the crunchy leaves
Squirrels munching all the acorns.

Crunchy leaves crunching
On the crunchy grass.

The robin's were chirping
Like whistles in the wind.

The fur on my jacket
Keeps me nice and warm.

The fireworks are colourful
In the sky.

Taryn Gerlach (Age 9)

That's What's In My Head

Inside my head.
There's a wizard's castle,
Full of dragons and devils,
Screams and shouts,
Roars and clatters and splatters of blood,
That's what's inside my head.

Inside my head
I'm under the sea
Dolphins and whales swim past me
Fish and coral so pretty
This is the place I would always like to be.

Beth Gould (Age 8)

Imagine My World

Close your eyes say your goodbyes to the old world
Put your heads together and imagine my world.
Hooting in the morning singing at night
The new moon shining bright.
Snowing in the summer sunny in the winter bunnies at Halloween
A hump upon a giraffe a neck upon a camel
A deck on the inside a flat on the outside
Get tied up and imagine my world

Kimberley Garbett (Age 11)

Inside My Head

Inside my head there's a place
Where fishes are dancing to their brides
Shells play music while seals bounce balls
And dolphins show off

Inside my head there's a graveyard
With swinging zombies and laughing ghosts
No-one has been before because you'd be scared to death!

Katie Gibbs (Age 7)

The Witches Spell

Dried newts tongue from the Prince of Wales
And the coming tail of the Atlantic Whale
Some ears from the sleepyhead
And the stinky stuff from my bed
Frogs belly to brain ripped out hearts
Lizards legs from head to toe
Smelly bomb-bombs blowing up
In the wood and in the hut

Ben Gilbert (Age 8)

Ice

Ice is a dagger ready to kill.
Ice is a magic wand doing tricks.
Ice is fear, cutting into hearts.
Ice is a fire burning in a stove.
Ice is a mirror glistening in the dark.
Ice is a lion, ready to pounce.
Ice is a rainbow dancing in the wind.
Ice is a bomber-death in the sky.
Ice is a train rushing through the tunnel.
Ice is evil yet ice is good.
But what, what is ice?

Robert Gray (Age 10)

Sorry!

Miss, sorry I'm late,
I had to kiss, people I hate

Miss, sorry, I was delayed,
My little brother was misbehaved.

Miss, sorry, I was held up,
I stood in muck, yuk!

Miss, sorry I'm late!

Chloe Green (Age 8)

Colours

Red is the sun disappearing.
Blue is the warm sea.
Yellow is the light daffodil.
Orange is the soft smooth orange.
Green is the spiky grass.
Purple are the smooth shiny grapes.

Gregory Huff (Age 6)

Last Day At School

I collect my toys
put the chairs up
go home the girls and boys
the last day of school
we clean the trays
we clean the classroom
lost property is cleaned up
reading folders P.E. bags
shut the door
collect our coats

Daniel Humphries (Age 7)

The Owl And The Pudding Boy

The owl and the pudding boy
Fought for some bread
In the city of Kacaboo
They did fight until dark
Which gave them a mark
And that made them lose a shoe.
They said they were glad
Although they were sad
They screamed that life was not fair
The boy was called Burt
He said he was hurt.
And so he walked back to his lair.

Eleanor Gooch (Age 10)

The Forest's Story

I remember when life was good
The newborn birds were my grandchildren
The existing trees were my bodyguards
My wild flowers made me proud as they sprouted happiness
My wild fowl leapt for joy like prancing daffodils
The sun and moon were my allies
My colours glistened a gleaming rainbow
My night,
My day,
My stars,
My sun,
My forest,
Myself,
My world,
My dear forest friends
Come find me I am your life,
Your forest,
Your world.

Alice Gradwell (Age 9)

Teddy

You're there in the morning when I wake up to the sun,
Together forever in never ending fun.
Shadowing me at breaktime and on the train to school.
Everybody thinks I'm a total utter fool.

Your perfect little features and your squeaky, round tum,
Your little button eyes are all thanks to mum.
But the best part by far is your fantastic fluffy fur,
It remains as soft as ever, year after year after year.

If I didn't have you teddy, I don't know what I'd do,
How could other people possibly live without you.
We've travelled round together, going far and wide,
Whenever I look down I know you'll be by my side.

Laura Haden (Age 12)

The Blue Creature

The blue creature, with a gungey feel,
Eighteen legs with purple spots,
Ugly as can be,

The blue creature,
With no eyes and eightyfive noses,
And two green ears sticking out of his head,
Looks like my mum when she's just got out of bed,

The blue creature,
With lots of friends,
Five arms,
And also spikey.

Francesca Griffiths (Age 10)

Cats

I think cats
Are rather nice

Their tails are long,
Their ears are ginger
They are cuter than a dog

They are cuddly as a teddy
Their noses are pink
They are very good at thinking

They have funny names
And they think about money
And no-one seems to like them much

Megan Harmsworth (Age 7)

Skateboarding

Jumping onto the plain black deck
Pushing off with my right side leg
Riding down a concrete path
Manualing over slabs broken in half
'Ollieing' past the old paper shop,
Kick-flipping over an old broken mop.
Grinding on the step hand rail,
Riding over an Alsations tail!
Heel-flipping over a small blue fence,
Falling off in front of all my friends
Getting on and riding past,
Finally I can boardslide, yes at last.
The sun goes down at the end of the day
It's time to put my board away.

Jamie Harvey (Age 12)

The Forest

Whistling through the dark dark trees
Was the whizzing, winding breeze.
As I gazed upon the sky
Rows of stars caught my eye.

As night approached, stars shone bright,
Animals wandering all night,
How lucky I was to be here
In the forest so near.

As I turned to go home,
I turned and looked back,
To look back at the forest
And follow the right track.

Laurie Higdon (Age 11)

My Fear Is Exams

Exams, Exams are difficult
They make me feel cold inside.
When we start it makes me shiver,
Also they make me quiver

I really hate exams, they're the worst thing on my mind.
They make me have butterflys in my tummy
When I think about my work I just get disturbed
Because of all the people around me.
Exams are terrible as people always say,
Even when I take an attempt I always lose marks
I always hated exams.

Rachael Green (Age 9)

Daniel

Daniel was a nice boy
Who was loads of fun
He always made me laugh
He was like the sun on a happy day

He would come round and say
Are you coming out to play?
For half a day?

I will remember his cheeky smile
All the while
When we're all outside

Rachel Hulin (Age 11)

My Nana

My Nana is 54 years old.
She is as small as a mouse,
As round as a button,
As quick as the wind.
She is in charge of Avon,
Always saying "Do you want a cup of tea?"
When she got stung by a bee she cut off a bit of her finger.
She's always in a happy mood,
Laughs a lot.
She's still in the prime of her life.

Cameron Greenwood (Age 11)

The Dragon

The dragon has come to dance and sing
Its eyes are blazing red staring at our feet
And dancing with its spiky feet
Its scaly tail is swift and quick
Its body - its sparkling body! - blazing red.
It's breathing with its breath.

Rory Haworth-Galt (Age 6)

Pirate Ships Sailing

Six tiny pirate ships, sailing the seven seas; all they had for dinner was a bucket of mouldy peas.
Suddenly the ship stopped, a stingray they see,
Horrid Mister Stingray, don't sting me!

Five sobbing sailing ships, not pirates any more; they think Mister Stingray took the key to the treasure door.
Suddenly the ship stopped, a shark they see,
Horrid Mister Shark, don't bite me!

Four sad sailing ships, sailing here and there; captain has got his telescope, looking everywhere.
Suddenly the ship stopped, a squid they see,
Horrid Mister Squid, don't suck me!

Three cross sailing ships, really fed up now; another one of their crew going down and down and down.
Suddenly the ship stopped, a rainbow fish they see,
Please Mister Rainbow fish, sparkle at me.

Two furious sailing ships, ready to explode; the rainbow fish didn't bother to tell them the code.
Suddenly the ship stopped, an electric eel they see,
Please Mister Electric Eel, don't shock me!

One lonely sailing ship, crying off his head,
Along comes his mother, "You cry baby, go to bed!"

Emily Hosier (Age 7)

Rats! Rats!

Rats! rats! scurrying rats,
They clamber and scramble,
Hither and thither.
With their tails waving,
They squeeze through gaps,
And climb up bars:
Rats are into everything!

Rats! rats! here comes food!
Whiskers twitching, feet scampering,
Following their noses,
Nibbling and gnawing
On bits and pieces:
Rats like eating anything!

Rats! rats! feeling sleepy,
Stretching and yawning.
Then settling down to rest,
And with a final twitch
And a flick of their tails;
Rats like sleeping anywhere!

Sara Hardy (Age 9)

Halloween

Ghosts and Ghouls come out tonight,
Devils and Vampires that hide from the light,
Wizards and Demons with blood red eyes,
Witches and Bats that fill the night skies.

Blood curdling screams that will fill you with dread,
So many creatures lurk under your bed,
Grotesque grinning faces that creep up behind,
Spine chilling stories that will blow your mind.

The house is haunted, the old door creaks,
All is quiet and nobody speaks,
Distant whispering abound in the air,
You turn round to look but there's no-one there.

Cauldrons and curses and bumps in the night,
Black Cats and Werewolves that screech, howl and bite,
Spooky house, Ghosts galore,
Strange figures that knock on your door.

Lauren Hudson (Age 11)

The Mirror

Is that you, you see before your very eyes?
Or is that reflection just a pack of lies?
How can you be positive? How can you be sure?
Maybe you have three legs and covered in fur?
Or seven fingers and twenty toes
And a metre-long, pointy nose?
That famous glass we know and love,
But the question is, is it one we can trust?

Faye Harrison (Age 13)

Rocket

Smoking slow,
Misty fog
Burnt toast, smokey smell.
Multicoloured steam -
Dragon's breath; hot and flaming.
Bird flying, crooked, diving and swooping
Swinging through the stars like a dragon
Screaming and crying
Sparky, spikey lightning, crunching and crackling.

Isobel Holley (Age 8)

You're As Useless

As a chair with no legs
As a washing line with no pegs
As a field with no grass
As a square with no mass

As useless
As a lolly with no lick
As a chewed up stick
As a pencil with no lead
As a book not read

As useless
As a hand with no ring
As a singer who can't sing
As a tele on mute
But you ain't half cute

Charlotte Hulse (Age 11)

Queen's Jubilee

Queen Elizabeth the 2nd
When her father died she became Queen
Elizabeth is her name
Elizabeth is her name
Never disappointed with her country
She is never unhappy with her throne
Jubilee is very special to her
Unique and special
Beautiful Queen
Intelligent
Lovely like a flower
Elizabeth is her name
Elizabeth is her name

Hollie Harrison (Age 9)

What Am I?

I'm a stalker through the air,
I'm as dark as the night.
Little humans beware.
I usually like a bite.

I'm a bug eater.
I hear horses as they lie in their hay.
I stay away from the heater,
And sleep through the day.

Only the best equipment can detect me,
I hang from wooden beams,
I'm more silent than a bee.
I stealthily leave when a piece of wood gleams.

Now I start to go to sleep,
It is always the same.
I hear a noise and have a peep,
Then it is back to the old life again.

Dominic Hughes (Age 10)

The Star

A star is shiny and pretty,
A star glows in the dark,
Golden star, star, star fantastic star,
Wonderful star, pretty star, a star is
Bright golden star, glowing star,
Star is shiny, flashing star.

Chelsea Heron (Age 8)

Moving House, Moving On

Put your childhood in a box,
And tie it up tight,
Make sure that nothing breaks.

Wrap up your love,
To keep it safe and sound
Make sure it gets there safe.

Wave goodbye to your world
With a tear in your eye
Watch memories and friends
Pass you by.

You're not sure what to do
When you leave your home
Everyone is left behind.

But even though I'm young
I'll never forget
Nor regret
Where I came from.

Amy Hancock-Martin (Age 14)

The Day The World Stood Still

America, the untouchable country, so safe so strong,
Now under attack from the invisible enemy.
Staring at my T.V in disbelief,
The images of terror, too much to take in.

September 11th, a day the world will remember,
The skies were blue and the streets were busy.
The two towers reached upwards towards the sky,
Full of knowledge and security.

The aeroplane above so normal and routine,
It must be a terrible accident, "Oh no not again!"
Families devastated and torn apart,
Life so precious ended without reason.

Can life become safe and happy once more?
The world stood still and thought,
Where is the face behind this nightmare?
What next?

Courtney Holbourn (Age 12)

A Snake Slithers

A snake slithers on a sunday shore,
It's tongue hisses as many times as a woman kisses,
It's skin is as dry as a flower on a very hot summers day.

Aidan Hogg (Age 10)

Hobgoblins Beware!

As the stormy lightning-lit night drew in,
The Hobgoblins wake in their underground lair.
The tunnels are muddy, but the Hobgobbies don't care,
They're going to do no good tonight,
So beware, beware, BEWARE!

The fairies are sheltering under their blanket of mushrooms,
Not knowing what tonight will bring.
They eat their banquet and party on,
With no regard to the weather, they still dance and sing.

The Hobgoblins creep into the town,
And down a chimney they go.
Into the bathroom - they know what they want,
Carrying four razor blades, they dart out in a row.

Into the forest they quietly crawl like ants,
But the fairy party continues unaware.
They run out from hiding, chop down all the mushrooms
And dart back to their lair,
With food enough for a feast.

Hobgoblins about...
SO BEWARE, BEWARE, BEWARE!

Tarn Huxford (Age 10)

The Room!

Walls are coloured eggshell
Ceiling's coloured white
Rows of clever students
A teacher not so bright

Talking in the back row
Laughing in the front
Teacher's giving essays
To students who just grunt

The whiteboard all black
The teacher's all confused
That's what it's like in English
A pen is left unused

The bell for lunch has gone
But all are kept behind
Because the teacher isn't happy
At what she cannot find

Half done homeworks hidden
Uncompleted essays scrapped
Teacher giving lectures
To students who are trapped.

Ashley Hooper (Age 15)

Tigers

I'm being hunted down
Like a pack of foxes,
Every day and night
My race is going
I won't be there
To kill your pests
The only way they like me,
Is to have my head on a wall
Or my coat on their back

Lee Henderson (Age 11)

An Undiscovered World

Eyes, peering at me
Mysterious stares from fish
The living urchins
Looking harmless and gentle
Like underwater flowers

As I swim deeper
I come to a coral town
Crowded and busy
Underwater's beautiful
Yet an undiscovered world.

Anna Hamilton (Age 11)

The Angels

I can fly with angels,
I can see their wings.
The blue sky against their white gown,
A special peace begins.

I can hear the angels,
Singing songs of love.
I can think with angels,
From the skies above.

Many people see them,
They see their haloes shining bright.
They take away the darkness from around my bed at night.

They watch the child sleeping,
Peaceful things they see.
Every night the angels wish, that we're happy as can be.

I can fly with angels,
Singing songs of love.
The blue sky against their white gown,
A special peace begins.

Charlotte Hale (Age 11)

A Summer's Morning

Wake up and feel the breeze
The sun shining down like a lightning beam
Open the curtains
See the trees waving like a birds feathered wings
Step out side on the bone dry grass
And feel the heat hitting your heart
The birds tweet like never before
You sit down and wait to hear some more

Mike Hindle (Age 12)

Mornings

Don't you just hate people who sing in the morning?
Don't you just hate people who are cheerful?
What's wrong with being grouchy and bad tempered?
Who wants the curtains open anyway?
If that cockerel crows once more, it will be in the pot on Sunday.

Mum shouts again "Are you nearly ready?"
How I wish I'd packed my bag the night before.
Abandoned trip to the station, forgot my maths book,
Eventually make the train with seconds to spare,
Mornings don't get any better until I've had my bacon roll.

Clare Harlow (Age 14)

The Smell Collector

A stranger called this morning
Dressed all in black and grey
Put every smell into a bag
And carried them away.

The scent of my deodorant,
The scent of all soap,
The scent of all the fresh air,
The scent of my packed lunch.

The scent of all the flowers,
The scent of all my toys,
The scent of all the fish and chips,
And the scent of the boys and girls.

A stranger called this morning
He didn't leave his name
Left us all smell less
Life will never be the same.

Laura Honor (Age 10)

Cats

Small cats,
Tall cats,
Sitting on the wall cats,
Black cats,
Fat cats,
Sitting on the mat cats,
Red cats,
Orange cats
Little tiny, scaredy cats
Sad cats,
Bad cats,
Very, very mad cats.

Katy Hailey (Age 7)

I Had A Little Pony

I had a little pony
Its colour was dapple grey
He rolled about in the grass
And always loved to play

He ran about like crazy
He jumped very well
He trotted over trotting poles
And never ever fell

I cried and cried my eyes out
When I found he'd gone away
I loved my little pony
Especially to this day

Zoë Hall (Age 9)

The Magic Box

I will put in my box
A large swimming pool
The biggest and cleanest football pitch
A nice sandy sunny beach in the Caribbean.

I will put in my box
A sound of a lost whale,
A screech of an eagle that's seen its prey
And a hoot of an owl that is trying to sleep

My box is made from
Gold, glass and bronze,
Its hinges are made from finger joints
And no ends in the corners of hidden walkways

In my box
I will swim the longest distance
I will play the best game of football
After that I will sunbathe in the Caribbean.

Gavin Hansell (Age 9)

My Zoo

In my zoo I've got,
1 elephant with a trunk and a bump
A giraffe with a long neck
A camel with a hump and a bump
A tiger with a roar
7 monkeys that jump tree to tree
A whale with a tail
10 fish that have a wish
An ostrich with grass to run in
A hippopotamus and Tom Katopolus
And those are the things in my zoo
Oh and not forgetting the gift shop.

Nathan Hall (Age 8)

Fruit

Bananas are long, thin and tasty
They have yellow skins
They're full of wonderful delight
They're good for you and me.

Apples are shaped like full moons
They can be red or green
They are crunchy, yummy, tasty fruits
The best that's ever seen!

Oranges are shaped like the world
They are orange, scrummy and sweet
They are juicy fruits to eat
Yum! Yum! Yum!

Emma Hughes (Age 7)

Ghost Teacher

The school is closed, the children gone,
But the ghost of the teacher lingers on,
As the daylight fades, as the daytime ends,
As night draws in the dark descends,
She stands in the classroom, as clear as glass,
And calls the names of her absent class.

The school is shut, the children grown,
But the ghost of a teacher, all alone,
Puts the date on the board and moves about,
As the night draws on and the stars come out,
Between the class, a glow in the gloom,
Calls for quiet in the silent room.

The school is in ruin, the children fled,
But the ghost of a teacher lingers yet,
As the night creeps up to the edge of the day,
She tidies the plasticine away,
Counts the scissors, a shimmer of glass -
And says "Off you go!" to her absent class.

Kirsty Gathercole (Age 9)

A Star

A star is shiny
A star is bright
Shooting in the air
Like a rocket in despair
Is it going anywhere?

Sam Hosier (Age 12)

Last Day At School

It's my last day at school I give a present to my teacher
She does the register
Then we have to do some art
Then it is playtime and people have old toys

The toys at playtime are old
The toilets smell
The children and the teacher
Are waiting for the bell

All of us are going to lunch now
We go outside now
It's line up time now
Now it's home time

When it's home time we all tidy the class up
We take the things off the walls
Then we get our coats, reading folders and P.E. bags
And it's holiday time.

Erin Hunt (Age 6)

Snow

As I rustle through the icy world of white,
My fingers scream for warmth,
The chilling gale, ready for the kill,
The dress of snow, untouched,
Obliterated suddenly by a rabbit's paw prints.

A small robin starts drowning
In a sea of white only to be
Rescued by a caring young girl,
Posts wear white hats and eat
White candy floss while dogs
Come and knock the floss out of their grip.
Snow falls as if the devil's cat
Had got amongst the angels
And had started ripping their feathers out.
SNOW! what a wonderful thing.

Andrew Hamilton (Age 11)

Home

My head is at home,
My head is not here,
The lazy clock moves like a snail.
My head is at home,
My head is not here,
The day's work has left me so pale.
My head is at home,
My head is not here,
Outside the leaves are like rain.
My head is at home,
My head is not here,
The daydreams are playing again.

Ellen Hastings (Age 9)

The People In My Life

If my mum were an item of clothing
she'd be a bright blue/pinky top
slimming and perfect
she'd dazzle like alight
beautiful and everyone could see her!

If my dad were a vegetable
he'd be a swede
he's soft and mushy just like a pea
he's a soft touch here and there
and he makes me smile everywhere!

If my brother were a building
he'd be a music studio
he bops his head like a nodding dog
he's musical and funny
and has the rhythm of a drum!

Sophie Hacking (Age 11)

The Kid

One day a girl, a very hungry girl stepped in the kitchen to get a galor tin
A tin full of cookies to stick in her belly, her mum heard a creak.

She saw her mum staring in the kitchen door,
The girl stood still, then got on the floor
Her mum looked away so she carried on, now she's past the stove oh, oh no.

She saw her mum staring in the kitchen door
The girl stood still, then got on the floor
Her mum looked away so she carried on.

Now she's on the shelf all by herself, now she's got the tin
The big galor tin full of cookies to stick in her belly
So she carried on but she fell off the shelf.

Her mum saw her then sent her to her room.

Natasha Henderson (Age 10)

Night Hunter

I am a sky diver and king of the air,
A phantom - I silently glide through the night,
Weaving in and out of trees.
I spot my prey,
Plunge down,
Then I sweep back up with it clasped in my beak.
I fly swiftly through spiralling winds,
Dive into my barn,
Sharing my gift with all.

Francesca Hanratty (Age 9)

Love

Happines is pink
It smells as sweet as
A red rose
Happiness tastes like
A strawberry cake
It sounds like a
Bird chirping
Happiness feels as
Warm as a kitten
It always lives in a
Heart of a warm person.

Humera Hussain (Age 10)

Peace

The song of blades flying through the air, the red mist rising,
The dance of the warriors evading attack, the devil's face leering.
The artistic arc of cold steel, the attack from behind,
The agonies of ripping flesh, his wound surely fatal.

I chanced upon a warrior, who'd descended to the ground,
His armour, dented, damaged; his body, strangely sound.
"Why is it," I enquired, "That man such as yourself,
Be stricken on the ground, with barely any health?"

"I pray, my fellow, you depart, for these are dangerous places,
Of no respite or mercy, but of sorrow and weeping faces,
Of cleansing souls by torture, from the signs of heresy,
And corruption of the people, in the dead society."

More blood is drawn from this terror war, when will it quench its thirst?
It is like this with any struggle, mankind is surely cursed.
For bickering forms a snowball, which tumbles never to stop.
What is the difference between peace and war?
The answer; not a lot.

Tim Huzar (Age 14)

Anger

Anger turns your face purple,
It makes your knuckles go white,
Sometimes fills you with pleasure,
Sometimes fills you with fright.

It will come one minute,
Then by the next it's gone,
This small bit of anger,
Passes to everyone.

Loud bangs pass through your mind,
It begins to get on your nerves,
Then it makes a silent bang,
But it's the loudest one you've ever heard.

Anger takes many forms,
In language and in movement,
While some feelings can be good,
This one is no improvement.

Anger will come,
Sometimes it will never go,
People might notice,
Then again they might never know.

Elizabeth Hague (Age 9)

I Wonder If . . . . .

I wonder if the Queen is polite,
I wonder what her house is like,
Does she like it a lot,
I wonder if her butler is tall.

I wonder if she was having thirty God children
Will I ever want that many
I wonder if she'll ever want to meet me,
I wonder if I'll ever meet her.

I wonder if she wants to be the best Queen,
I wonder if I'll make a good Queen,
I wonder if she likes being a Queen,
I wonder if she wonders a lot.

I wonder if she's ever fallen off her chair
I wonder if she's had any accidents,
I wonder if she wishes she was normal,
I wonder if she likes her job.

I wonder if she liked school,
I wonder if she passed her 'A' Levels,
I wonder many things,
I wonder if they'll come true!

Freya Hawkins (Age 10)

My Holiday Poem

I went on holiday with my mum and dad,
Nothing in our hotel was bad,
We sat on the Jersey beach,
Eating a sweet juicy peach,
Then we went back to our hotel.

Aimee Hampton (Age 10)

Space

On Pluto it is extraordinary
It is cold and gloomy.
Neptune river of blue
And a clear ring around it.
Uranus is a huge ball of gas
A blue ball with rings around it
Saturn rings of ice and rocks
Jupiter great red spot glows from the rest
Mars is a rusty red it has a deserty look
Venus has a goldeney look
And it looks like a small sun
Mercury is a lonely place to be
We end this poem with the Sun
It is the hottest of them all.

Kelly Hawkins (Age 11)

Stars

Stars
Are as
Bright as
The sun blazing
They are the night light of the world
They are scattered across
The sky blue like little counters
Sometimes you see
Shooting stars
Zooming
By

Naomi Hackett (Age 9)

Fun In The Sun

At the beach there's a very bright sun
And the fun has only just begun
I go and fly my kite
And I see an aeroplane going for a flight
I go in the sea and have a little splash
And go to the pier to spend some cash

Sacha Hughes (Age 7)

Trees In Winter

The branches are long
They look fantastic
They have got so many branches that they overlap each other
They make lots of patterns
The leaves are ever so pointy
They have long roots
They make a big shadow
Their twigs are thin and spiky
The branches look like elephant trunks
In Autumn they start to become bare
The leaves are falling from the trees
The snow lays deeply upon the thick branches
As the branches get longer and thicker they look like fingers
As the bark gets dark brown you can see all of the colours and patterns
The roots are mighty, strong, lacey, twisted and long lasting
You can sit there for ages and draw the outlines of them
The leaves feel feathery and feels like spider webs
When the trees are leafless, they go fan-like
The branches are weaving, interlocking and spreading out
The dainty buds are waiting for spring so they can burst open

Lisa Harrison (Age 10)

Cats

I am a cat I have a mat.
I have a bed in a shed.
I am a boy I have a toy.

I am a cat I'm very fat.
I find it hard to move.
My fur is very smooth.

Thomas Horton (Age 7)

Snow

Watch it fall on Christmas Day,
Look outside and shout "Hooray!"
Stare at the little white stars forming beautiful patterns,
Hear it sprinkling from the sky,
Play in it, make snowmen with it,
Kill people in avalanches with it,
Gaze at it and see it fall softly in your hands,
Throw it at your friends,
Run out to it every morning,
So have some fun,
Now and then,
Until it goes and comes again!

Hermione Hotson (Age 9)

The Door

Go and open the door,
Maybe there will be a fair ground
Maybe there will be a dump.

Go and open the door
Maybe thee will be a steaming waterfall,
Maybe there will be a dirty river.

Go and open the door,
Maybe there will be your dreams, dream,
Maybe there will be your worst nightmare

Go and open the door,
It could just be normal,
Or you could be in outer space.

Ellie Hawkey (Age 9)

Rain Forest

Splashes of colour here and there,
Eyes watching everywhere,
Flowers blooming pink and blue,
Like precious gems, gleaming new.

Colours moving, trees swaying,
Bushes stirring all in motion,
Lizards moving hard to see,
Sitting camouflaged in a tree.

Refreshing waterfall calm and tall,
Flows down never ending,
To seek all,
Embedded with secrets hidden beneath,
Its unbreakable clutches, strong and deep.

Hettie Hickling (Age 12)

Leisure

What is this life if full of care,
I've plenty time to stop and stare.

Time to do work in class,
Geography, science and also maths.

Time to play with a football,
Let's kick it against the wall.

Time to play on my playstation game,
When I have to switch it off it's such a shame.

Time to have a good day at school,
Having to go to the swimming pool.

Time to read my reading book,
Could you help me please I'm stuck?

Time to play with Haider the pest,
When he comes he makes a mess.

A good life I've got, it's full of care.
I'm pleased I've got time to stop and stare.

Qasim Hussain (Age 9)

Dolphins

Dolphins swimming
Through the water.
Listen, listen to the noise.
Does it squeak?
Or does it speak?
I think it's trying to speak.
YES!
It is speaking,
But in a different language.

Emily Hoare (Age 8)

For Sale

1920's Queen.
Had 50 years experience of ruling.
Comes with corgis and Buckingham Palace.
Loves horses,
Owns lots and GAMBLES!!
Can ride.
Large family horribilis.
May need one or two facial repairs,
But otherwise sound.
Will only sell to suitable titled owner,
Or swap for something truly unique.
For more information call 01555-512808.

Hannah Hills (Age 11)

Bramberry Hill

The night was bitter,
My heart was a 'flitter
The wind was harsh and chill.
Who rode that horse
With such tremendous force
As I trudged up Bramberry Hill?

The wind took a form in the moonlight,
The wind was set loose that night,
I heard the crack of the musket,
I heard the crack of the musket,
The cry was loud and shrill -
As I trudged up Bramberry Hill.

I saw the gleaming rider fall,
And then I heard the fatefull call -
Which signified his death?
I heard the hoofbeats, fading slowly,
And I saw the carcass stretched out by the mill,
As I trudged up Bramberry Hill.

Theo Hopkinson (Age 10)

Inside The

Inside the tortoises shell the crinkly skin
Inside the crinkly skin the tortoises blood
Inside the tortoises blood the snow wind
Inside the snow wind the tortoises ear
Inside the tortoises ear the North Star
Inside the North Star the ants cray
Inside the ants cray the tortoises foot
Inside the tortoises foot the rotten toenail
Inside the rotten toenail the tortoises pray
Inside the tortoises pray the heart pumping
Inside the heart pumping the tortoises shell

Thomas Hawkins (Age 11)

I Walked By The Sea Shore

I walked by the sea shore,
Hoping for more,
Only eating ice cream,
When I hear a scream,
Coming from nowhere,
It sounded like a bear,
Enormous and hairy,
And it sounded quite scary,
Big loud roar,
As I walked along the sea shore.
Then out of nowhere I heard footprints coming near,
He spoke and sounded like Alan Shearer!

Apria Hunjan (Age 8)

Seasons

Winter's here, it's time to cheer.
It's nearly Christmas Day.
Get wrapped up warm,
It's cold outside.
I'm going to play.

Winter's passed, it's Spring at last,
A time when flowers grow.
So let's go out to play again
Now we've got rid
Of all the snow.

Hip, Hip, Hooray! It's summer's day,
And time off school is near.
Get on your shorts,
Let's go and play,
'Cos school hols are here.

Autumn gold. It's getting cold.
Back to school again.
Let's go outside
And have some fun.
Oh no! Here comes the rain!

Dean Heaps (Age 9)

Red Is . . . .

Red is like the burning sun
That warms our skin in the summer
Red is the fire that warms us in the cold.
It helps us sleep if we are frozen
Red is as warm as Mars
It will burn your feet if you step on it

Danny Hale (Age 9)

Sir Francis Drake

There was a young sailor called Francis Drake, they thought he was a fake,
The mop and him soon made friends, as he cleaned the Captain's lens.

The Panama they crossed, the men well they got lost
In 1533 this was all going on, it was all taking so long.

They raided Spanish ships, their ships they hitched,
Plymouth they headed for, going back to Plymouth for more.

Queen Elizabeth was there to meet, she said come on and have a seat,
Quick 'cause you will be off to fight a Spanish fleet, would you like a piece of meat.

As he sailed around the world, he met a few ships as well
The waves were rough, and he was tough, he then packed his stuff.

He captured five ships, he thought the sailors were hip,
The ship got stuck, they were not having good luck!

Lisa Hancock (Age 9)

The Magic Box

I will put in the box
The sound of the last dodo
The last stone of the parthenon
The last doctor's medicine

I will put in the box
The last crash of Amelia Earhart
Roald Dahl's first book
A child's first word

I will put in the box
A cold sun and a warm snow
A car which runs on bread crumbs
And snow which never melts

My box is made from gems and shells
Its hinges are made from dogs legs
It seems just a funny shape.

Geert Hellendoorn (Age 8)

Out On Town

Red hot lips,
Hair gelled down,
Skin tight jeans
Out on town.

Fluoro pink cheeks,
Sweet smelling spray,
Cool blue trainers,
All going my way.

Well curled lashes,
Sexy green top,
Glitzy glam bag
Loud cool pop.

Abigail Harland (Age 10)

Jumping January

Autumn has now ended
The ground is layed with white diamonds
White men are being built,
This is Jumping January

Loads of white diamonds are thrown around
Big brown monsters come
People wear fluffy clothes,
This is Jumping January

Wind whistling in my ear
Whitey white diamonds on the ground
Evergreen trees stand up tall
This is JUMPING JANUARY!!!

Sebastian Hart (Age 10)

The Snowy Owl

He glides through the night sky looking for prey,
Scanning the dark forest for mice.
He spots one rustling through the grass.
With white snowy wings outstretched
He swoops down,
Snatches up the creature,
And flies back to his nest.

Jordan Hitchon-Anderson (Age 11)

Spider

I hate the spider
I hate the spider
I hate the way it scuttles and scampers
With colossal legs and beady eyes
I hate the spider

I love the spider
I love the spider
I love its furry coat and twitchy legs
The way it sprawls and crawls
I love the spider

I hate the spider
I hate the spider
I hate its spindly body and gleaming eyes
Or bony legs and crumpled face
I hate the spider

I love the spider
I love the spider
I love the way it fleets and propels
I love the way it crafts its china-like web
I love the spider

Zoë Holroyd (Age 11)

The Bushfire

Flames are leaping across the planes,
Hunters are racing just like rain,
Animals waiting then sprinting away,
The fire has been raging for more than a day,
Leopards and cheetahs have a price to pay,
Is the fire here to stay?

Antelopes and zebras fly like a bird,
The fire has stampeded another herd,
Racing, chasing, the animals were
But then you hear the lion roar.
The noise of thundering feet.
The hunter's heart really beat
It's the fire, here to stay.

Josh Hesmondhalgh (Age 9)

Anger

Anger creeps up on you.
Dressed in heavy leather red and black,
She walks down the street calmly but grimacing,
Her eyes black deep, black swirling.
People around bursting with anger,
With the power to destroy.
Anger begins to bubble and rise.
Anger erupts like a volcano burning, flaming.

Sara Hough (Age 12)

Swimming

Everyone ready here's the ball,
Oh no! Henry's running
He knows he's going to fall.

Henry tries to dive,
Oh look! He does a belly flop.
Oh dear he's a bad number five.

Oh bother! He's made a tidal wave,
Oh look there's his trunks,
Well that isn't a big enough save.

The time has come,
The lesson is over,
Miss, my tummy's numb.

Henry no time to mime,
I don't care if you want to,
It's the end of swimming time!

Charlotte Ham (Age 9)

My Christmas Poem!

Christmas trees are decorated, tinsel on the walls,
Children are havin' loads of fun as the snowflakes start to fall.
Outside it's getting frosty, water turns to ice,
People look in shop windows and say, "Oh that looks nice!"
Shoppers spend a bob or two, buying Christmas gifts,
When people do their shopping they hear the ping of lifts.
When they get home they unpack, sit down by the fire,
People knock on doors, oh how lovely it's the choir!
Carols are then sung again, all throughout the streets,
People hurry past them, hear the pattering feet.
They then all go to bed, the fire's been put out,
Something comes down the chimney and gives a quiet shout.
"Ho ho I'm covered in soot, as dirty as can be,
This jobs wearing me out, why does it have to be me!"
Santa then finishes packing, hops up on his sleigh,
"Come on Rudolph!" he shouts, "go the other way!"
He finishes his job, just as the sun rises,
Children start to wake up, in for big surprises.
And faintly in the distance, they hear something say,
"Ho Ho Merry Christmas, and have a happy day!"

Amy Hope (Age 13)

A White World

A church bell ringing,
Echoing down your street
Carol singers follow
Marching to the beat

They get inside
And Oh! What a treat
A roaring fire
To warm their feet

Children playing in the cold,
Up to their knees in snow
I'm going to follow with my sledge
Bye bye, and off I go

In a room,
There's a glowing light
As the children come in
From their snowball fight!

Tom Hart (Age 11)

The Seven Eyed Jelly Monster

The seven eyed jelly monster that ate our school
Coughed and choked on a science lab stool
The monster was still hungry he even ate Mrs Press
Followed up by the pupils of her seven set four class.
The monster soon met another green jelly mate
Her name was Georgina they started to date
They were happy, joyful as they slithered around
Then they settled down on the ground
The army came to sort them out
All of a sudden you could hear children shout.
The monster was shrinking from the inside
Soon his belly had gone Georgina ran to hide.
Children piled out in a bundle
Then came Mrs Press who was in a grumble

Carl Harvey (Age 11)

Going To Search For Aliens

It is dark and spooky
It is freezing out here
I wish I hadn't come

That is an Alien, "Help!"
"Help! Help!"
"Please come and help"
"Wake up you have bumped your head"
Bumped on the metal
"Ow it hurts"
"It is bleeding, I feel dizzy".

Darian Hedley (Age 8)

Twice Dawn

The following of gold upon the light, misty air,
Enshrouded with dark fogs,
The slow glitter of frost above hard-hearted earth,
The shining of the sun on the ice horizon.
Wisps of clouds are coloured with fire
Like the smouldering of phoenix-feathers.
Fire in the sky and ice on the ground
Are nothing but the contradicting lights
Of air-dawn and earth-dawn.

Elizabeth Hadfield (Age 16)

Mafia Mania

There was something there.
What could it be?
Maybe it was a Mini,
Or maybe it was me.
What was there?
What could it be doing there?
Maybe it was a mafia,
Floating on the sea.
Thanks to god it was only a dream.

Robin Holt (Age 10)

Crocodiles Are The Best

I'm the greatest of all the animals
I am a crocodile
I swim silently through the long
And sparkling River Nile.

I'm a brilliant crocodile
I'm the king of all the water
I bring back all my food
For me and my daughter.

My teeth are sharp as daggers
I have rough, sandpaper scales
I'm the colour of an Autumn leaf
And I've one of the longest tails.

Some people think we're annoying
Some people think we're a pest
But you really have to admit it
Crocodiles are the best!

Sarah Hunter (Age 10)

School Laughter

School laughter can be good
School laughter can be bad
School laughter can be weird
School laughter can be recognised
But of course there is one word
That sums it all up
And that word is
FUNNY

Karl Home (Age 9)

A White World

When you look out of the window at winter
This is what you might see
Snow covered in the garden and fence
Leaves fallen off the tree.

Dewdrops on the silk webs of spiders
Ice cubes nestled in the grass
Lots of snow blanketing the trees nearby
Falling down very fast.

Fluffing snow spreading all over the fields,
Leaves crunching on the ground
Powdered frost surrounding deserted lands
Not a single sound.

Cold winds moving swiftly
Snow falls softly from the sky
It is near Christmas, winter is here
This is a white world, just nearby.

Sophie Hughes (Age 10)

I wonder

I wonder if the Queen looks nice,
While sitting upon her throne?
Of she doesn't get what she wants,
Does she whine and moan?

I wonder if the Queen gets bored,
With what she is shown?
I wonder if she cries at night,
When she's all alone?

I wonder if the palace is clean,
Shining, sparkling and white,
Would I like to live there?
Or is my house just right?

I wonder of the palace is big and wide,
With lovely chandeliers?
I bet she's never seen some mud
In all her fifty years.

Adam Hughes (Age 10)

Fishes

There are fish in the sea and
They are tickling me.
It's making my legs smooth,
Because they were all rough before.
They like it in the sea,
Because its got a quiet shore.

Justin Holt (Age 10)

Late

'Sorry that I'm late Miss
I'm late for my work'
'It's maths boy
It's maths boy
You're late for your maths'
'Sorry that I annoyed the class
I'm late for my picture'
'It's a class picture boy
It's a class picture boy
You're late for your picture'
'Sorry that I'm late Miss
I'm late for my history'
'It's geography boy
It's geography boy
You're late for your geography'
'Sorry I'm late Miss
I'm late for my science'
'It's P.E boy
It's P.E boy
You're late for your P.E'

Sean Hosler (Age 8)

What, Where, Why?

What is snow?
- The fluff from a giant's toy teddy.
Why do clouds float?
- To prevent being attacked by animals.
Where do clouds come from?
- Another place where cotton roams.
Why does it rain?
- The clouds are losing weight.
Where do hailstones come from?
- The planet made from ice.
Where does wind come from?
- An empty cave with gusting walls.
What are hailstones?
- Hard hitting pellets falling from space.
What is lightning?
- The earths firework display.
What is thunder?
- Drums beating loudly.
What is the earth?
- A blue and green gobstopper floating in space.

Rebecca Hood (Age 11)

Red Is...

Red is hot and burning like fire
Red is good colour it makes me feel good
Red is a special colour
Red is a books colour
Red is the colour of the sun goes down
Red is the colour of a drink
Red is the colour of a pen
Red is the colour of a book
Red is the colour of a car
Red is the colour of eyes.

Joshua House (Age 9)

Dentist

Going to the Dentist
Very, very scared.
Buzzing and ouching
Shushing and spitting
Screaming and blubbing
Clicking and nervous
And a little bit dizzy.
Worried and clattering
Moaning and zizzing
Afraid and frightened.
The drill, the drill!
Eeching! Screeching!
Zizzing! Gurgling!
Going back home now
And never going back!

Jim Heath (Age 10)

Leisure

What is my life if full of care,
I have plenty of time to stop and stare.

Time to get into my bed,
And rest my sleepy head.

Time to ride my bike,
Until I get to Wyke.

Time to play with Hannah at home,
Then I'll speak to her on the phone.

Time to go and swim with my mum,
And hope soon DAnielle will come.

Time to go and watch T.V,
And then soon I'll have tea.

Time to go and rest in bubbles,
Then forget about all my troubles.

A good life I've got its full of care,
I have plenty of time to stop and stare.

Gemma Houlston (Age 9)

Red

Red traffic lights beaming on a car
Red roses blowing in the wind
Red flames shooting in the sky
Red strawberries floating in cream

Christopher Hill (Age 8)

Armageddon

Armageddon looms
Upon lurid landscapes

Devastation creeps
While children are asleep

Anarchy reigns
In tempestuous skies

Dissension beats
With frenzied discord

Mortality claims
With a noxious embrace

Corruption intoxicates
Those which are chaste

Amy Hubbard (Age 15)

Happy Golden Jubilee

H aving your two birthdays each year
A great invention called the mobile phone
P eace in England and hoping in all the world
P leasure to have you for a QUEEN!
Y ou cried when Princess Margaret and Princess Diana died.

G oodness in you all the time
O h my goodness when the twin tower CRASHED!
L oving QUEEN! We will always love
D early we love having you as our Queen
E ngland won the world cup
N ature mother is just like you

J ust like a twinkle in the sky you made people glad
U pwards of 50 corgis that you had
B elieving in your heart
I n the time you have been Queen!
L oving your sister Princess Margaret
E njoyable that you travelled the world
E njoy your Golden Jubilee enjoy your Golden Jubilee!

Joanne Hill (Age 9)

Frightened

In a spooky house on a shadowy hill,
My fearful heart started to crack slowly,
It wobbled and shook like a piece of jelly.
I felt like an icicle that is about to melt and disappear.
My eyes are shocked and wide.

Jed Harrison (Age 10

The Forest's Story

I remember when life was good
When my flowers were bright and dancing
And birds were nesting in my elms
When my squirrels ate the nuts off the ancient oak tree
Streams ran along under the wooden bridges
And bushes grew berries as red as blood
Waterfalls were frothy white as they hit the rocks at the bottom
Insects wriggled over the logs and grass
When leaves were crispy and crunchy in Autumn
And my rabbits leaped over sticks and low branches

Children save me or I'll have nothing left
The sound of the birds have gone
And the fire has come and wrecked my home
The wooden bridges have rotted and collapsed
The flowers are dead and ripped
The waterfalls have stopped and are not frothy anymore
My leaves don't dance in the cool breeze
And the squirrels have all run away
I wish everything was like it was

Megan Hailwood (Age 11)

Fox

Chased through the country
Men on horses with guns
Death at every corner
Bloodthirsty dogs, merciless men
I feel hate
This is hate
Hate for the men who murder
Hate.
Chased for sport, chased for fun
Blood at every gateway
Hellish dogs, inhumane men
I feel hate
This is hate
Hate for the men who murder
Hate.
Horror, terror, darkness
They don't think
My life is theirs
FOX

Amy Hirst (Age 12)

Stomping Stamping

Stomping, stamping in the rain
Up the street and back again.
Stomping, stamping in the rain,
Friends are coming out to play.
Stomping, stamping in the rain
I want rain every day!

Aston Hibbert (Age 7)

A Haunted House

Down the road there is a haunted house
You can hear the creak of a stair,
The squeak of a mouse
Go inside
There's a screeeech of the door,
And the CRACK! of the floor.

Hear the pipes going leaky,
And the stairs going creaky

It lies under the night sky
Waiting for people to go by

It listens to the breeze
Rustling through the trees

It watches the flying bats
And listens to the scurrying rats,

And in the morning -
It sleeps . . . . .

Hayley Harrison (Age 10)

Football

Football is a crazy game,
The fans all start to rant and rave,
When there is a riot,
The police will get involved.

My favourite team is Chelsea,
They have the best goalie,
They thrash their opponents,
And win the Premier League,

There is 11 players,
2 linesmen 1 Ref,
A load of subs,
A bunch of screaming fans,

1-0 2-0 3-0
Chelsea win again,
Up the league they go,
Chelsea win again,

I wish I could play football,
As good as those on T.V,
But I can't even,
Can't even get in the school team.

John Hards (Age 13)

Winter

Playing in the snow
Building snowmen in the snow
It is very cold.

Jane Hopcutt (Age 8)

The Car

Running at miles of speed,
Not a chain, lock or lead.
Doesn't stop,
Doesn't have time to knock.
Rubber melting wheels,
It's a monster trying to kill.

Lights leading,
Shining and gleaming.
Sparkling bright,
Leaving you standing out of sight.

Engine roaring and purring,
Fuel moving and stirring.
Bowling around the bends,
As the postman stands and stares.

The colour of blood red,
Just waiting to be fed.
Lights flashing in the night,
Not hard to be out of sight.

Simon Hogben (Age 12)

Golden Jubilee

It's your Golden Jubilee
It's your Golden Jubilee
You have two birthdays every year
It's your Golden Jubilee

It's your Golden Jubilee
It's your Golden Jubilee
Will Young won Pop Idol
It's your Golden Jubilee

It's your Golden Jubilee
It's your Golden Jubilee
Inventions have been made
It's your Golden Jubilee

It's your Golden Jubilee
It's your Golden Jubilee
Princess Margaret and Diana died
It's your Golden Jubilee

It's your Golden Jubilee
It's your Golden Jubilee
You're the best Queen there's ever been
Oh it's your Golden Jubilee.

Elizabeth Hopkinson (Age 9)

Little Miss Cool

Little Miss Cool
Sat on a stool,
Eating some ice-cream,
Along came a fly,
Straight down from the sky,
And made Miss Cool shout and scream.

Philip Hollindrake (Age 7)

The Meat-Eating Horse

I'm a meat-eating horse
I used to eat grass
But that daily routine
Didn't long last.
I ate meat since birth
You probably think I am wild
They said "You don't belong on earth
You really weird child"
I'm a horse
Because of me
My parents divorced
And that's my story
I had to tell
(I think a wicked witch
Cast me under a spell)

Danielle Hook (Age 10)

The Seven Eyed Jelly Monster That Ate Our School . . .

The seven eyed jelly monster
that ate our school . . .
It ripped our books and drank
from the pool

It followed me to the science floor
and slithered sloppily under
the classroom door

It landed on Jordan with a friendly slurp.
chewed him a bit and let
out a burp

It then rolled over to the teacher too
took a large bite and spat
out her shoe

Jordan Healy (Age 11)

A Dream Of Reality

Creation calls
Freedom's prison,
An ugly beauty
Willingly forced.
The pleasure of pain,
The happiness of depression.
A motionless wind
Disturbs my peace,
And I dance to a
Music with no notes.
I am soaked with the
Rain that fell
Tomorrow,
And I see with
Eyes that are
Blind.
Night attacks day
As I await a dream,
A dream of reality.

Siobhan Hodson (Age 17)

Space

I have always wanted to go to space to see if it is interesting,
I have always wanted to blast off in a rocket and see the stars go by
While I'm there I will search for aliens in a space buggy,
My favourite planet is the blue ringed Uranus, I like the colour blue
I can see my shadow reflecting on the moon, big, black and bold.

Chloe Hawkins (Age 9)

The Worm

I love the worm,
I love the worm,
I love its mixture of riggles and wiggles,
The way it descends into the darkness of the earth,
I love the worm,
I love its delicate body

I hate the worm,
I hate the worm,
I hate its pathetic little squirms,
And its slimy, filthy body,
I hate the worm,
I hate its filth and slime

I love the worm,
I love the worm,
I love its innocence and its pinkish colour,
The pattern it makes as it travels,
I love the worm,
I love its wavy body!

Luke Hemsley (Age 11)

My Neighbours

My next door neighbours
Are an absolute pain,
They do weird things
They're really insane

They smoke all day
They smoke all night
They bicker and shout
They always fight

They watch TV
All day long
Blare music out
With oldies songs!

On weekends
They go out late
Then come back
With a different date

Oh how I wish
They'd move away
'Cause I can't stand them
One more day!!!

Natalie Haines (Age 12)

My Mum

My mum has beautiful blue eyes they sparkle too
My mum's hair is brown it sparkles
My mum likes chocolate a lot
My mum loves me
My mum likes birthdays
My mum likes going out
My mum likes flowers
My mum likes people visiting her
My mum likes pretty things
My mum is a beautiful thing

Rhianne Hicks (Age 6)

I Wish

I wish...I wish...I wish...
I was a little, yellow fish.
A fish...a fish...a fish...
Oh, I wish... I wish...I wish...

I live in the deep blue sea.
Come and swim with me.

Oh, I wish...I wish...I wish...
I was a little, yellow fish.

Lauren Holding (Age 9)

The Coronation

The Queen is here,
The horses are trotting,
The golden coach is glistening,
I can see her dress
With embroidered symbols,
It is a stunning sight.
The crowd is cheering
All through the night.

Juliette Horwood (Age 8)

My Best Friend

My best friend is called Katy
She has a face like me,
Her hair is straight and coloured honey blonde.
Her eyes are blue
Just like you
She likes to dance
So that's my friend called Katy

Jenny Hall (Age 10)

Swimming Is Fun

Swimming is cool
Warm and wet in the swimming pool,
I wish my bed was in the swimming pool
Mother's and Father's can join in too.
Me and my friends go after school,
I like going swimming because it's fun
New children go every day.
Going swimming on Sundays,
Cleans your minds for mondays.

Omera Hussain (Age 10)

Seal Birthdays

Monday's seal will help to hoove
Tuesday's seal is sleek and smooth
Wednesday's seal is bright and spotty
Thursday's seal plays ball and shouts "gottie"
Friday's seal drives a big bargain
Saturday's seal makes a great fuss about parkin'
But the seal which is born on the Sabbath day
Is fair and beautiful and willing to play.

Melanie Hargreaves (Age 9)

Harvey Our Lodger!

His whiskers are grey,
He doses in the sun all day.
He looks forward to his walks never knowing whom he might meet.
But not as much as coming to put up his feet.
Harvey's quiet and gentle with bright twinkley eyes,
He sometimes acts daft but I think he's quite wise.
He never does anything he doesn't want to,
Like working or schooling like you and me do.
He's a little old man who lives in our house,
He's my friend Harvey the Whippet.

Allyce Humphreys (Age 12)

Snow

Children gazing,
Out of the frosty window,
At a blanket of snow,
Like Christmas day is here.

Trees shiver in the icy wind,
Children throwing snowballs,
With frost bitten fingers.

By midnight Jack Frost,
Had done his work,
Icy patterns on the windows,
And doors.

Nothing stirs on the icy stillness,
No creak of a door,
Nor a squeak from a mouse,
Only the snow swiftly falling,
Once more.

Jessica Hoyland and Jade Acklam (Age 11)

African Safari

The sun rolls high,
Into the sapphire sky
Over the African plain.
At the watering hole,
Animals drink,
The sun stares down
With light
Which touches everything in sight.

Elephants plod across the plain
While lionesses are on the hunt,
Their mates stand proud,
With golden manes,
And then they'll go to sleep.

The giraffe reaches up
To the big green tree,
Totally unaware,
That we stand and stare,
On this great safari.

David Hall (Age 11)

Senses

I like the sound of children shouting and screaming at their friend.
I like the sound of doors sqeaking and banging.
I like to touch the rough stoney wall and hairey balls.
I like the smell of food in the hall.

Shaun Hutchinson (Age 7)

Guess The Animal??

Sean, the super snapper
Stomped sadly
Some say "stupid stomping Sean go and get stuck and stay!"
So silly Sean
Stomped away
So silly Sean stayed away.

Matthew Hall (Age 7)

Spiders

Spiders make me shiver,
Long hairy black legs,
Spiders make me cold and cringe.
Big ones, small ones fat ones too
It makes me quiver inside.
Spiders are creepy and crawly,
I can't stand the look of them.

Laura Harrison (Age 9)

Water Horses

In the night on the water
In the night on the sea.
What a sight you might see.
Three giant water horses on the night sea.
You might have a fright!
If they catch sight of you that is.

In the morning they're gone like a flash, in the night they come with
CRASH.
They ride on the sand dark as night.
Then go back to the water out of sight.

Daisy Hillyer (Age 9)

What Is The Moon?

It is the welcoming light at the end of a tunnel,
It is a glistening pound coin sparkling in a blue wallet,
It is colossal cat's eye shining on it's big blue face,
It is a glistening milk bottle top in a massive blue background,
It is a giant lolly pop which has lost its stick.

It is a big shining bubble waiting to be burst,
It is a silver plate on a dark blue table cloth,
It is a slice of cheese waiting to be eaten,
It is a white balloon that has floated up into the night sky,
It is a sparkling diamond on a blue velvet dress.

Kit Holmes (Age 10)

My Dog Rover

He is ever so hairy
He has big brown eyes
If anyone was to see him
They would say what a size
He is friendly and loyal
He is handsome and strong
It is hard to be mad with him.
When he has done something wrong.
He is one of the family
One of the gang
His tail is so strong it hits with a BANG!

Amy Harrigan (Age 9)

What Is . . . . A Ghost?

A ghost is the bullying wind flustering about the fragile trees.
It is the humble dark, lying there, waiting to scare you.
It is the morning sky over looking the calmful earth.
It is a gallant unicorn striding through the forest.
It is a castle lumbering on a dampened hill.
A ghost is the bitter wind that goes where it pleases.
It is a goalpost standing still and stern on a cold winter's day.
It is a silky smooth swan flowing on a silent river.

Dale Hart (Age 10)

Twisted

I stormed out,
I stormed out into the dark night,
I stormed out into the dark night and came across a disturbed man,
I stormed out into the dark night and came across a disturbed man who came towards me,
I stormed out into the dark night and came across a disturbed man who came towards me,
With a knife and homicidal tendencies.

We're great friends so much in common.

Charlotte Jordan (Age 16)

The Night Sky

The night sky,
Sparkling of stars,
Spelling silhouettes
As bright as Mars.

The night sky
Dull and dark
A gloomy glow
Up there not a mark

The night sky
Mist and frost
Icy cold
All clouds are lost

Lauren Hammond (Age 9)

Yellow Poem

There is a sun in the sky
Literacy books
There is a sun in the sky
Sandy beach
There is a sun in the sky
Buttercups
There is a sun in the sky
Lemon pancakes
There is a sun in the sky
Daffodils

Lauren Holt (Age 8)

Baby

Smelly baby in the house
Crying all night long,
Nap time is a relief to me,
Talcum powder on the floor,
Dirty nappies in the bin,
Drinking milk all the time,
Tiny hands and feet
Cute and funny,
Being sick,
Making funny faces.
He is starting to walk,
Giggling at me,
Holding my hand,
Lovely!!

Andrew Hamilton (Age 9)

The Game

It galloped through the dense undergrowth,
Its drawn out golden hair bustling in the treacherous wind.
Its long sloped body straightened out,
The power driven legs now at an ordinary pace.
Then out of the stillness came shouts and flames licking around them
The faded body went into a low crouch position,
Its head lifted and the great horn cracked through the breeze,
It took off, smashing mindlessly,
The noises died down,
The lights faded,
The golden prize pushed its gold trimmed head under the foliage.
There the unicorn slept.

Patrick Hall (Age 11)

Journey Poem

Journey through the desert
Boiling in the day
Cold at night
Sand everywhere
There are bones on the ground
Not much life
No buildings not even one house
The sun shines down like a fireball
Only sand spiders and a few other bits of life
No water at all

Thomas Harling (Age 8)

Inside Outside

When I'm outside I play skipping
But when I'm inside I have to do work
When I'm outside I play games
But when I'm inside we do maths
When I'm outside we play the dare game
But when I'm inside we do english
When I'm outside we play 'it'
But when I'm inside we do history
When I'm outside boys chase me
But when I'm inside we do science
When I'm outside we play hide and seek
But when I'm inside we do P.E.
When I'm outside we play hand stands
But when I'm inside we do music
I like being outside!

Mollie Hamblin (Age 8)

Bats

Asleep in the belfry, silently sleeping
The darkness, no light,
The protection and safety.
People outside hustling and bustling,
Shouting and yelling,
But quiet up here.

Gliding through the night, no people near
Mosquitoes buzzing around,
Swiftly I fly in search of insects somewhere.
Rapidly, I go through the sky,
No-one sees me fly,
Back to the belfry we fly.

Asleep again, no disturbing us
Noisy outside,
Quiet up here.

Scott Hayes-Watkins (Age 10)

The Monkey And The Frog

The monkey and the frog went to sea
In a beautiful purple fairy.
They took some drink and a kitchen sink
Wrapped up in a fifty pound dairy.
The frog looked up to the moon above
And sang to a small banjo,
Oh lovely monkey, oh lovely monkey, you are, you are.
What a beautiful monkey you are.
The monkey said to the frog "you elegant hog".
How charmingly sweet you sing
Oh let us be married how long we have carried,
To the land where the bong tree grows,
And there in the mud a piggy wig stood,
With the ring at the end of ear, his ear, his ear.
With a ring at the end of his ear.

Huma Hanif (Age 10)

Blooming Flowers

Spring is a lovely time of year, there are lots of flowers like,
Daffodils are as yellow like, the burning sun
Pansies remind me of a happy face,
Like it was always my way
Tulips are like gates as they open and shut,
Like the sun does to the tulips
Bluebells are as blue as the sky,
On a warm spring day
As the shrubs come out to play
We have got to start watering them
Or else they will die.
Spring is a lovely time of year,
Look all around you, it's nearly here.

Sacha Harden (Age 11)

The Little Unicorn

Trotting through the dark green woods
A silver creature with tender heart
A graceful horn arrow sharp
Unicorns stand up on the skyline
Whinnying to one another
A mad explosion of lightning struck
A burst of power when the unicorn dashes by
Solid hoof nail
Iron foot shaped print on the grass
So gentle to little children
They stand up on the hills
In majestic position.

Laura Haden (Age 9)

A Winter's Night In A Graveyard

The night was still and silent,
On the funny plum shaped hill,
The snow perched on the gravestones,
So sad and yet so still
The wind whistled through the air
Making scary shapes in the cold still air
It was midnight already "Ding Dong, Ding Dong!"
What's that noise?
A shrieking, cold shrieking noise in my ear
I was running, yet I didn't know where
I tripped I fell!
Then the screaming stopped
As the sun came up
It was the beginning of a new day.

Mia Insole (Age 11)

I Danced For The Queen

The doors opened,
She was sitting on her golden throne.
She called me in,
I walked steadily,
"Good morning", I said
And She replied
"Good morning, my sweet darling".
The music started,
She smiled at me as I danced.
Soon she started to hum to the tune.
Then the music finished.
She smiled at me, at me.
I danced for the Queen.

Juliette Ives (Age 9)

The Giraffe

You have never seen a neck like this
A slimy slivering snake
Legs like trembling sticks
With polkadots high and low
Ears with pointy tops
Just like the tip of a mountain
A nose like a splodge of paint
With eyes as fierce as fire.

Natasha Ivens (Age 8)

My Rats

My rats are cute and cuddly,
But they always play fight,
When I try to get to sleep,
They keep me up all night.

Their names are Candy and Sugar,
They really are that sweet,
They scamper around their cage,
On their little tiny feet.

My friends think they're lovely,
They think that they are great,
They're really, really friendly,
Just like my best mate.

They eat their basic rat food,
And sometimes get a treat,
They eat cheese and tomatoes,
And things that are sweet.

Maddy Hughes (Age 9)

My Friend Sarah

My friend Sarah is a beautiful, bottle nosed dolphin.
She swims through the ocean so elegantly.
She has a friend (who is blue whale),
Her name can't be mentioned,
Never mind that!
Once she took me to the bottom of the ocean.
I tried not to be afraid of the great shark,
But it was so dark.
Soft was the sand,
So I picked it up with my hand.
Soon I found some treasure,
What a pleasure!!!

Danielle Herbert (Age 8)

Dragon Dreams

I was asleep in my bed,
I had a strange dream and what a strange dream it was.
The cat went mad,
The dog went bonkers,
And I had a dragon for a pet.
It snapped its teeth,
And had a smirk on its face,
And what a drooling mouth it had.
It went in my room,
And it jumped out of my window,
And I never saw it again.

Matthew Hawkins (Age 8)

My Computer

I like my computer
Turn it on oh no the screen has gone strange
Huh it was just the aerial
Which went out of range.

I'm going online the screen blinked, now it's fine.

Oh no it's gone wrong
Well I haven't been on it for long.

Niall Hughes (Age 9)

My Mum

My Mum looks like a queen in a golden chair.
My Mum sounds like a singing lady.
My Mum smells as good as some perfume and blossom.
My Mum tastes like a bright red strawberry.
My Mum feels as cuddly as a whole packet of feathers.

Katy Jessop (Age 5)

Cinderella

Cinderella had two ugly sisters,
Who were full with spots and blisters.
They made her clean all the plates,
And didn't allow any mates.
There was an invitation at the house,
Cinderella had one friend that was a mouse.
The ugly sisters went to the ball,
Cinderella heard a frightening call.
The call sounded calm,
Cinderella felt like a palm.
Fairy Godmother said you can go to the ball,
Only if you promise not to fall.
You must be back as midnight falls,
Or you shall hear my calls.
The clock struck twelve,
Cinderella heard the bells.

Aneesa Hussain (Age 10)

My Horse

My horse is faster than your horse
Your horse is smaller than <u>mine</u>
My horse can gallop faster than your horse
Your horse can eat more than mine.

Your horse is black
Mine is white
Because they're friends
They won't fight.

My horse can get scared
So they stand together in the night
They might have babies
That are white.

Mine is fluffier
Yours is thinner
But they're both horses
And they get on together

Sophie Harvey (Age 10)

What I Want To Be When I Grow Up!

I want to be a nurse,
Who works on a ward,
I want to be a police lady,
Who fights fraud.
I want to be a teacher,
Who teaches art,
I want to be a fire lady
Who is smart.

Katie Horne (Age 9)

Bullying

The trickle of blood runs down her mournful face.
As her eyes fill up, with a lonely tear,
There is a feeling of hurt and disgrace.

She has to stand up strong, show she's not scared.
Instead, loses her senses of right and wrong.

'Maybe it's my fault I'm big?
No wonder they laugh at me.'
She decides to excuse.

'Look at me; my hair is a mess,
I feel like a pig, I'm hardly any less.'

As the satisfied miscreant runs away,
Leaving her with nothing but pain, silence...
Nothing to say.

The speechless victim left in tears.
Who deserves to feel these fears?

As she falls to the floor, there is nothing to hear;
The feeling of tranquility is all too near.

Nadia Jawad (Age 13)

Trees

I used to live in a rain forest far, far away,
but then along came one day . . . . .

A gang of people with a saw,
my tree came down, I hit the floor.

I tried to run,
but they made fun.

So please, please,
don't cut the trees.

Charlotte Hall (Age 11)

Being A Ruler

Being a ruler is very annoying,
When all the children draw on you
I was made to draw boarders,
And underline titles too.
I hate it when they snap me in half
They would probably just laugh
But I love it when they measure things with me
And make shapes with me too,
I help them with their homework
And underline the date,
You wouldn't like to be a ruler
I'd rather be a rubber.

Jonny Holliday (Age 8)

War On Terrorism

We had: Fear
         Anger
         Hurt
         Upset
         Police
         Fire
         Crying
         Plane
         Crash
         Disappointment
         Terrorism
         War
         Death

We need: Peace
         Happiness
         Friendship
         Joy
         Fun
         Laughter
         Marriage
         Love

Georgia-Mae Holmes (Age 8)

The Sea Eagle

The fisher of the skies
Is watching its prey with its evil eyes.

It senses its food and glides.
Then dives down, down, down
And snatches the fish away.

The black and white king is approaching its nest.
Watching with its eagle eyes.
It's the king of the skies.

Patrick Hunter (Age 8)

Weather

What is the fog that comes in spring?
It's a filthy white curtain that's see-through.

How soft is a summer's cloud?
It's as soft as a queens pillow.

What colour is sheet lightning?
Lightning is the colour of a butterfly's wings.

Why does it gently rain?
It rains because Heaven is a misery.

Why does the sun set at Twilight?
Because the sun has run out of battery power.

Victoria Holder (Age 11)

Green

Green is the rustling woodland garden
Green is the crocodile sitting on the shore
Green is the colour of leaves on the tree
Green is the apple hanging from the tree
Green is the colour of seaweed swaying with the tide
Green is the moss clinging onto the wall
Green is the swamp water rippling away from a stone

Ryan Halls (Age 8)

The Mysterious Stones

Down at the Stonehenge silence falls around,
The stones stand still as can be.
Some are lying very still, some are standing very tall,
They are waiting for time to pass by.
As soon as time passes by they start sinking into the ground,
Their great shadows disappear as the sun starts going down.
It gets so dark that I cannot see,
I started to gaze up at the mysterious stones.

Stephanie Hall (Age 8)

Loudly

LOUDLY he jumped off the stage
LOUDLY he interrupted the teacher
LOUDLY he scraped his nails on the board
LOUDLY the old house creaked
LOUDLY the tide crashed against the cliff
LOUDLY she rummaged through her bag
LOUDLY the motorbike zoomed past us
LOUDLY the class left the room.

Alex Johnson (Age 12)

Sonnet Moon?

So peaceful. Why no language? Why no sound?
The cool moon so relaxed, engaged in thought,
So endless though down on the dusty ground,
Moon men tread. Engulfed by the dark space bin.

These Moon men, what are they like? Silver skinned.
How do they speak? The new talk. Can they eat?
Their home, not Saturn. More life but no rings.
Do they have time? Our time. Do they have feet?

Now the moon, with mind. A different mind.
Does the moon know us? Do we know the moon?
Is the moon good? Can it? The moon is kind.
The rounded shape, perfect. Not like a spoon.

The Moon is so surreal, and so calm,
Like the monks in a church singing noon psalms.

Dominic Jones (Age 12)

My Dream

I woke up one day
Rose from my bed
From the worst dream
Ever said

I was a soldier
In the war
Helping others
Healing sores

The world was in battle
It was a bloody war
There were so many people
Dead on the floor

The blasts and bangs
Destroyed all land
The world was clenched
In deaths cold hand

All was destroyed
To the earths very core
The whole world
Was no more

Alistair Hardy (Age 11)

Death In The Sea

Searching for treasure
What's that, shine the light on it
They are still down there . . .

Searching for treasure
Are they brave or just plain mad?
They did not return . . .

Joshua Jackson (Age 9)

Childhood Memories

Sandy Tunafish Island
Rocks, Yedidalga
But for shells, go to Boaz

A great palace at Vouni
Soli, mosaics
A past yet undiscovered

Bright colourful glade orchids
Singing cicadas
Noisy, yet ever peaceful

Oranges, lemons, grapefruit
Long days in the sun
A recipe for Cyprus

David Jones (Age 13)

The Storm

The sky was like a butterfly
Until a gust of wind pulled and tugged me
As quick as a flash the sky turned into a cloak of black
The trees were swaying side to side
Boats were crashing on the rocks
People dying
Voices calling
Destroyed homes collapsing
I fell to the ground left alone
A light shone bright
I could hear a voice calling my name.

Tara Ingham (Age 9)

Colours Are.......

White are the angels
Singing in heaven.
White is the colour
Of the puffy clouds.
Gold is the colour
Of the sun in the sunset.
Gold is the colour of the archangels.
Silver is the colour of the moon and the stars.
Silver is the colour of God!

Hayley Hollister (Age 9)

My Recipe For An Angry Teacher

To begin with take a whip of cheeky children
And add it to a dash of careless errors

After that boil a bunch of chattering children
Mixed with a lock of swearing.

Then bake a bunch of groaning girls
Stirred with some messing about.

Finally whisk an ounce of screaming girls
Crush them all together and then Bob's your uncle
You have a dose of making teachers angry.

Gavin Ireland (Age 9)

Perilous Ocean

The lapping tide of the lowly ocean
The horses manes are high
What secrets in the depths beneath,
What perils in the sky.

The rusty ships all gone and dead
The octopuses lair
The dreaded sea bed of the deep
And the mermaids with seaweed hair.

The mermen swim over the cobblestones
The whales sing their call
The horses manes flap in the breeze
And onto the sand they fall.

Emily Jenkins (Age 12)

Star Wars

Guns firing, droids clicking along the path,
People dying, destroyer droids rolling,
Gungans fighting for victory.
Light sabers on, bang, crash, boom they go,
The sith jumps Obi-Wankenobi jumps.
The force is strong with this one.
Nabbo starfighters revving up their engines,
Off they go to war!
Droids blowing up all the time,
The light saber kills the sith, fear leads to hate,
Hate leads to suffering,
Suffering leads to the dark side,
The dark side leads to death,
Battle tanks firing,
Gungans fighting for victory!

Oliver Ison (Age 9)

I Love You Because . . .

I love the way you talk to me,
The way you laugh and think,
I feel one day that we could be,
More than a crush or link,

You always smile so sweetly,
And gaze across the room,
Would he like to meet me?
Or does the fear come too soon.

I love the way you play your tricks,
How you make me feel complete,
But most of all I love you for you,
Which no one can compete!

Hayley Jenkins (Age 12)

Pea!

In a land where all around was bare,
Food was scarce no trees anywhere.
Crops have died,
Rivers have dried,
The only water in which they had was dull and dirty.
Their life expectancy less than thirty,
A young man all tattered and dirty,
Tumbled down to the ground.
And in front of him to his delight he found a,
PEA!!!
FOOD!
He shouted, Food, Food!
Had no one heard?
Then to his surprise a forest of people came charging towards him,
Grabbing, twisting, pulling, punching and hurting, screaming,
Ahh!
But where is the pea?
Squashed in the sand,
People started licking it just to get a tiny taste,
Until nothing was left.

Gareth Jones (Age 12)

Love Is...

Love is staring at the stars twinkling in the dark sky.
Love is looking at my Mum and Dad's lovely, beautiful eyes.
Love is hearing people laughing and happy.
Love is listening to the wind blow side to side.
Love is the smell of fresh swirling water in the deep sea.
Love is the smell of cold snow.
Love is the touch of my fluffy, cuddly teddy bear when I cuddle it at night.
Love is the feel of smooth, white paper.
Love is the taste of bubbly chocolate in my mouth.
Love is the taste of a big, round, crumbly chocolate cake.
Love is the world being happier and no wars.

Jessie Judd (Age 7)

The Giver The Receiver And The ANGEL

It came to me walking slowly in the flickering light
Not a being, cloud or shiny gown was in sight.
I was armed with ten thousand spears ready for anything,
I was just a lonely grounds keeper.
It's child like voice said it flew here on my soul!
Comfortable, quick and reliable.
It offered me wings of flight and a crown of gratitude.
As I looked up I could see smiles on joyful angels,
I took the feathery headdress and the wings that
Tickled me and made me giggle, I held them close and
Then I
WAS ONE

Daniel Jones (Age 10)

My Favourite Season

Spring is my favourite season
Children come out to play
I go to my friend's house
Nearly every day

Spring is my favourite season
I like the lovely sun
I like to play with my friends
We have lots of fun.

Spring is my favourite season
I come out to play
With my friends behind me
Every single day

Laura Jeffrey (Age 8)

Alien Species

A bandoned it
L onged for it
I nked all over it
E aten it
N icked it
S igned up for it
P aralised it
E nded it
C aught it
I ndirected it
E dited it
S ent it away

Daniel Jones (Age 9)

Day And Night

The sun rise,
The moon dies,
Day begins,
Stars disappear,
Sun reappears,
Day begins,
Sun falls down,
Moon turns around,
Night begins,
Light disappears,
Dark reappears,
Night begins,

Rebecca Johnston (Age 11)

I Hate Hospital

I hate hospital...
Lying in a bed, doing what your mother said.
Lying there you cannot stare
Because the walls are bare.

I hate hospital...
Being pushed along an aisle
Not a wink nor a smile.

I hate hospital...
I think it's a sin
Mummy's going to throw me in the bin.

I hate hospital...
When you put the gas mask on
Do not sing a little song.
You cannot speak or hear
While you drift along to dreamland.

But five seconds later you are in a bed.
'All finished,' that's what Mummy said.

Alexander Jewell (Age 10)

Stars

A bright shining star
Shines down on me with starlight
Silvery light flows

Sophie Janik (Age 8)

The Highest Diving Board

"I dare you to dive off".
"Go on don't be a scardy cat scardy cat scardy cat".

Off Emelye ran and queued in the line
Off I ran and pushed in front
My turn came beating beating my heart is beating
Came into my head.

I stood at the top toes over edge and slowly
Peered over nearly falling forward
Ready! Steady! Jump!

Down! Down! Down!
Take a breath
Splash! Down! down! Down!
Panic! Panic!
Running out of breath need to swim to the top
Gasp that fresh air

Yes I did it!
Did it!
Going back for more!
Going back for more!
Going back for more!

Jessica Janes (Age 10)

Butterfly

"Butterfly" my swimming teacher said
Suddenly a terrible chill went down my spine
"Now kids get in line"
We all got into place
I'm glad it was not a race
5, 4, 3, 2, 1
Go
Get ready to make a fool of myself!
My heart was pounding
Pounding! Pounding! Pounding!
All the sweat was draining
Draining! Draining! Draining!
My arms went splish
My legs went splash
Splish! Splash! Splish! Splash!
It just wasn't working
So ashamed so embarrassed
I swam back to the side
What a fool
I thought to myself
I shan't be doing that again!

Emelye Janes (Age 10)

Wiggly Worm

My Dad found a huge wiggly worm,
When he showed me, it made me squirm.
It was very long and thin,
He found it under our dustbin.

Connor Jordan (Age 7)

The Spotted Water Snake

My scaly body
Scraped along the
Swampy River.

I slither across the long
Bushy grass
I hunt for my prey.

There's something behind me.
I turn to look.

Nothing there.

I carry on.

I hear it again.
But this time
I don't turn round.

I feel myself
Being ripped in half.
I'm dead.

Faye James (Age 13)

The Wheel

What would we do without it?
We wouldn't drive a car,
Or ride a bike,
Such an important thing the wheel is to us.

No transport,
No big red bus,
No trains or taxi's,
Oh, we would have struggled if the inventor hadn't got it right.

It looks so simple,
A curved edge it has,
Made out of almost anything,
Turning on a small shaft.

It just goes round,
And round,
And round,
Oh what a boring life the poor wheel has.

Stuart Jasnoch (Age 13)

Joys Of Spring

As the sun awakens
On this fresh spring morning
The newly born lambs bound across the meadows,
And the birds sing joyfully in the blossoming trees.

The running streams tickle over the pebbles,
The daffodils nod in the spring breeze,
And there's not a cloud in the clear, blue sky.
Oh, what a perfect spring morning.

Kate Jefferys (Age 14)

Why Do Catz Pounce?

Why do catz pounce?
Why do balls bounce?
Why are planets far away?
Why don't aliens come to stay?
Why do magnets repel each other?
Why do I have a brother?
How do fish get in the sea?
How did God make you and me?
Why does the moon shine so bright?
Why are stars always white?
Why doesn't gravity pull down planes?
Why does it always rain?
Why do snakes slither?
Why do trees wither?

Rachel Jolley (Age 11)

My Brother Is Annoying

My brother is annoying
He thumps down the stairs
He eats all the coco-pops and
He never even shares.

My brother is annoying
I have the remote control
He nips and hits but
He just can't get hold.

My brother is annoying
When mum and I are trying
To speak all he wants is
To listen to the radio so loud
We have to shriek.

My brother is annoying
When I am trying to do my homework
He flicks things at me
And calls me a jerk

Hannah Jelley (Age 9)

The Winner

He stood there strong and tall,
A powerful, muscular horse.
A tough, strapping, mighty animal,
An elegant, athletic type.
He is an intense, vivid black;
And as fast as a steam engine,
An agile and swift sprinter.

Charlie Johnston (Age 11)

What Is Black?

Black is an ant
That walks small
Black is bird
That eats them all
Black is a shadow
That shows yourself
Black is a shadow
That shows on the shelf
Black is the night
That takes you to sleep,
Black is a fly
That jumps on the sheep.

Rowan Jeggo (Age 7)

The Forest's Story

I remember when life was good.
When flowers sang like my choir
When badgers and foxes trotted over the foliage floor
And squirrels gathered my beech nuts
When birds foxtrotted along my leafy branches
And wolves howled my own serenade,
When leaves clustered at my tree trunks,
And my highest branches were star gazers
When my magical waterfalls played through my heart,
And ducks swam leisurely all day long
When swans reached their graceful necks up to my boughs,
And my streams chattered along thoughtfully,

Citizens, come to my remains, for your ancestors once played amongst my trees,
All that is left of my tumbling rivers is a little trickle
They took away all my beauty and wrecked my trees
They stripped me of my respect
Men built factories and polluted my eyes,
Now I cannot see anything but smoke
Everything has gone and
FADED away!

Christel Jones (Age 11)

Stonehenge

Stonehenge glistening in the shadows
Standing tall
People admiring the stones as they go by
Looking up to the heavens
Standing silently as the sun goes down
Shadowy cracks creeping over them
Stonehenge standing in the shadows

Maxine Johnson (Age 7)

Summer

Summer comes people put on sun cream
Summer comes we play on the beach
Summer comes we make sandcastles
Summer comes we have ice cream and ice lollies too.
Summer comes we go on the climbing frame
Now it comes to the end of summer
Getting cold means autumn's coming.

Hannah Jones (Age 7)

Chameleon

I can think sharply
And I can change
To any colour
Say green and beige
I can wag my tail
Just like a dog
Except a lot faster
Unlike a frog.
I can change size so big
That even a ship would capsize,
So there you have it
That's the way of the Chameleon.

Chris Jerromes (Age 11)

Forest Fire

The day they lit
The dancing demons in the woods
Didn't they flicker, didn't they twirl
Didn't they set
Their devilish claws round the burning timber
Didn't they grow wild and escape.

And night and day, night and day
Don't they burn wild out of control
Don't they tear down the forest tree by tree
And burn and burn again

Oh put them out, oh put them out
The dancing demons of the woods

Matthew Jeavons (Age 11)

My New Rabbit

Today I got a rabbit,
Who drives me up the wall,
Earlier on he jumped out of my hands,
And fell in the swimming pool.

But luckily my rabbit lived,
He's alive and well,
My Mum doesn't know yet,
So you'd better not tell.

Because of this incident,
Because my rabbit dashed,
From my arms into the pool,
I'm going to call it 'Splash'

But then something terrible happened,
It stayed in my mind for hours,
When Splash was in the garden,
He ate my Mum's best flowers!

So we bought my rabbit a hutch,
Some hay, a water bottle too,
And no one will ever love him,
As much as I do.

Alitia Jefferies (Age 10)

Sizzler

The hot sun is shining,
Everyone's getting hot,
Children are building sandcastles,
Why, there's a lot.

The hot sun is shining,
The water is glowing afar,
Children are eating ice-creams,
While the adults are at the bar.

The hot sun is shining,
The sizzling sand is soft,
Children are playing,
And the mums are chatting a lot.

The hot sun is shining,
The crabs are pinching your toes,
Children are getting tired,
And the dads say it's time to go.

The hot sun is shining,
Everyone's gone home,
Children are fast asleep
The beach is now alone.

Hollie Jordan (Age 11)

Rat!

I am the fuel,
For your engine,
Of hatred.

I do what I need,
To survive my dank, dark world
Alone

Ryan Jelbert-Luckman (Age 13)

Football

Faster than Owen faster than Ronaldo,
Veron and Keane, Scholes and Rivaldo,
And dribbling like Giggs going down the wing,
All through the match the crowd shout and sing,
All of the sights of the scarves in the stand,
Fly as high as a bird proud and grand,
And ever again in the wink of an eye
Beckham's free kicks whistle by

Ben Jackson (Age 12)

What Is . . . . Colour?

What is red?
- Red is a BT phonebox phoning the rest of the world
What is blue?
- It is the great blue sea running from coast to coast.
What is green?
- Green is a literacy book sitting on the top of the pile peeking around at the world.
What is yellow?
- Yellow is the sun shining over the world
What is the colour orange?
- It is a gleaming fire sprinting through the forest.
What is purple?
- The colour purple is the shiny ink from a gel pen writing a letter.
What is white?
- White is a fluffy cloud drifting across the pale blue sky.
What is brown?
- Brown is the crunch leaves drifting from their lonely branches.

Claire Jermany (Age 10)

I Have Been Adopted By A Cat

I have been adopted by a cat,
Yes you have read this correctly,
My cat chose very carefully,
So what do you think of that.

Perhaps I had to pass a special test,
To stroke her in the right motion,
And hold her like a baby,
It's strange that she thinks my house is best.

I wonder what goes on inside her head,
Maybe she likes her funny new name,
Or the way that I call when I want her to play,
But I think most of all she loves sleeping on my bed.

She could have chosen anyone in my street,
When she found me she looked so sad,
All covered in dirt and with nowhere to live,
I'm GLAD it was me she wanted to meet.

Max Jones (Age 10)

If I Was A Witch

If I was a witch there's things I'd like to do
I'd do wicked things and put a spell on you.

I'd fly on my broomstick
Put on my special hat
I'd check I looked really ugly
And take along my cat.

I'd have black teeth,
Long nails and a long warty nose
I'd cook frogs and spiders in my cauldron
And zap things till they froze.

My name will be Evil Edna
And I'd turn you to a toad
My spell would not be broken
'Till you found the code.

Kia Jason-Ryan (Age 9)

The 7-Eyed Jelly Monster That Ate Our School!

The 7-eyed jelly monster that ate our school,
When he did it he thought he was ever so cool,
In the school slithering and sliding,
Wobbling through the classroom whistling and miming,
In the music room messing with the decks,
Walking through the English corridor and scoffed at Mrs Press,
Bit Miss Grey,
Thinking she was hay,
It all ended (the jelly),
By seeing a big belly.

Emma Jones (Age 11)

Sweet As Sugar

Add some liquorice,
If you're feeling peckish.

Maybe some bubblegum
But not enough to fill your tum.

Do you like candy?
No, Well give them all to Mandy.

Put in some strawberry laces,
As long as a huskies traces.

A couple of chocolate mice,
Make it taste really nice.

Mix in some fruit salad,
When you taste it, you'll sing a ballad.

Just a pinch of sherbert,
But keep it away from herbert.

For the finishing touch,
I'll add two bars of fudge.

Mmmmmmm Yummy!!

Jaymie Jarvis (Age 10)

My Loving Poems

If Sophie were a plant
She'd be a daisy
Looking beautiful at every glance
Kids in the spring gazing
Making daisy chains like our friendship.

If Grandma were a toy
She'd be a teddy
Cuddly and warm like a bundle of wool
To hug she's always ready
She's always there for me.

Tihana Jurcevic (Age 11)

The Shark

Scaring, swimming, catching, killing,
Delving, diving, jumping, bumping,
Crunching, lunching, smashing, mashing,
Ripping, kipping, staring, glaring,
Twisting, turning, eating, beating,
Travelling all around
Scaring all around is the
Shark.

Oliver Jones-Evans (Age 10)

Fluff Stuff

I can explain why I'm late for school,
Because on the way today
I met a fluffy orange thing,
It invited me round its house.

Its house was a fluffy orange dome,
All fluffy and orange inside
We suddenly started taking off,
It said "Come to my planet Fluffomia."

Fluffomia was made from orange fluff,
With orange clouds in the sky,
A fluffy orange poodle,
Being walked by its fluffy orange owner.

I rode on the back of a fluffy orange dolphin,
In the fluffy orange sea,
I played a game of fluffy orange netball,
With fluffy nets and a fluffy ball.

Then I said to the fluffy orange thing,
"I'm sick of fluffy orange stuff!"
It was insulted and sent me down to Earth,
In its fluffy orange spaceship.

Maria Jacques (Age 9)

Lights

The moon has gone behind the cloud.
A wall of darkness
An aeroplane flies over with the
Lights flashing on the wings
A train goes past with the carriages lights on.
I see a car breaking down the road
And I see the red lights
I see the twinkle of the stars
I see the light off the TV.

Alec Jones (Age 9)

Our Queen

On February 6th fifty years ago,
A Princess called Elizabeth was so full of woe.
Her Dad had just died and it meant for you see,
That the beautiful Elizabeth a Queen was to be.

And so now today in year 2002,
Queen Elizabeth still reigns over me and you.
She has always tried her best, for all in the land,
And so fifty years on she deserves a big "hand"!

Jenny Jewell (Age 9)

Not Last Night But The Night Before

Not last night but the night before,
I heard a little knocking on the door,
I went down stairs to let her in,
She said "Hello may I come in?"

"The Queen," I screamed, "The Queen is here!"
"Please please please don't scream my dear.
I've come here to ask a great favour,
But you have to be on your best behaviour.

Can I sleep in your big bed,
To rest my tiny weary head.
I love my palace but its much too big,
And all my servants keep doing a jig".

"Yes you can but do me one favour,
Write your autograph on this piece of paper.
There it's done now go to bed,
And rest your tiny weary head".

David Jarman (Age 11)

The World Cup

For so many years,
There has been too many tears,
Because the England team,
Can't achieve their ultimate dream.

When England are good,
They are truly brilliant,
But when they are bad,
They are dire.

Is England the team to beat?
If they are it would be a great treat,
Not just for me,
But for the whole country.

Reece Kent (Age 11)

The Cheetah

Twinkling his eyes in the darkness,
Creeping around in the shadows,
Investigating every move each animal makes.
The Cheetah
Sprinting to catch its food
Chasing until it catches what it is seeking
Pouncing over, under and on its prey
The Cheetah
Ripping fur and meat from creatures
Killing the innocent victim that he saw
Wrestling with friends and enemies
The Cheetah

Luke Jackson (Age 9)

Night

I can travel but cannot be seen or heard,
Glide through the late hours, stealing light.
Free from trouble, I haunt and scare,
I shape the loneliness of the night.

I can capture the day leaving flakes of fire,
While my black wavy hair weaves a nightmare.
Or hold in the moon with dark rain clouds,
Darkening the calm, cold and frosty air.

My dark and deep, hollowed eyes,
Watch from below and from above.
My mouth is a pit, bottomless and dark,
My cloak is a wave, like the wings of a dove.

I rise from the depths of Hell to the heights of Heaven,
I follow the moon, like a hissing snake.
I control the wind and the rain,
Making the ocean silently shake.

Stephen Jenkins (Age 11)

The Great Stones

Great stones shimmering in the sun
Standing as time goes by
Some are resting on the ground
Some are waiting to be understood
Quiet all around them
As the sun sparkling on them
It's like the world has stopped
No-one moved

Robyn Jones (Age 8)

Fantasy

Castles and strongholds
Are ruled by the king.
Who guards them from the ruthless Trolls.

Alexander Kiker (Age 12)

Weather

Where is lightning when it isn't flashing?
Trapped in the deepest depths of hell.

Where does the rainbow end?
At the furthest edge of the world protecting a pot of gold.

What is a snowflake?
A tiny handcrafted cobweb made by a fairy.

What is a hailstone?
A frozen teardrop from a newborn baby.

What gives the snow its sparkle?
A brush from a graceful swan's wing.

Alice Jary (Age 11)

Trees In Winter

My arms are cold black and bare
Does anyone really care
My coat lies beneath on the ground
Once green and waving clinging on sound.
Now dry and crumpled blowing about
It's winter but not for long
I'm just waiting for Spring to come back to me
To let everyone see
I'm a beautiful tree.

Thomas James (Age 5)

Stonehenge

At Stonehenge rocks were balancing
Leaning and stretching into the sky,
And sparkling in the lovely warm sun
Quietly falling to the ground,
Crumbling, smashing into dust,
Everywhere silence,
Quietly floating in the air like never before
Going up and down from heaven to earth.

Chris Joyce (Age 8)

A Recipe For An Angry Teacher

Drizzle a classroom full of noisy children into a bowl of screaming dinner ladies
Add a group of selfish children being naughty to give it a kick
Pour some incredibly bad language and
Mix slowly with some hypnotising screen savers.

Add a pinch of cheeky children playing on swizzly chairs,
Patiently wait for it to bubble with shouts and crying children.
Pick up a handful of guilty children heading for the head teacher.
Drop a spec of innocent beaten up infants and
Bake to get broken computers and torn up stationery.

Pollyanna Jones (Age 10)

Royal Family

I was just thinking about the Queen's Golden Jubilee,
"Oh what a horrible time it'll be.
I wish I knew how the Queen and her family feel,
I can't believe Queen's Mother passed away for real.
The Queen Mother is the best,
Now her body is at rest.
She's lying there beside her beloved husband she lost,
But she's lying there underground in the frost.
1936 she came to the throne,
But now she's lying there instead of a dog's dusty bone.
You lost your sister now your mother too,
I know how you feel and I already knew.
What about the Queen's Golden Jubilee
Oh what a horrible time it will be.

Aneesah Jan (Age 10)

I Wish

I wish I had a guinea pig.
I wish I had a stick insect that was called stig.
I wish I had a monkey.
I wish I had a dog that likes to eat lots of flowers.

I wish I had a chinchilla.
I wish I had a spider that scared people away.
I wish I had a rabbit.
I wish I had a tortoise that likes to eat grass.

I wish I had a budgie.
I wish I had a hen that likes to sing.
I wish I had a koala.
I wish I had a frog.

Chantelle Jones (Age 10)

The Midnight Caller

The moon was gleaming like a round silver coin
Sending patches of light to the ground,
The voles were scuttling around rustling the leaves
Like footsteps following the wind,
Owls were flying like ghosts, swooping and swerving around
Stars winking like piano keys

Crickets were chirping in night time orchestras,
Ash trees like flags in the wind,
The wind was whistling along like a paperboy,
And that was the sign for the midnight caller.
Awooooooooo.

Sophie Jolliffe (Age 9)

Monsters

At the bottom of my bed.
Monsters!
Creeping round my bedroom
Monsters!

What creeps up on you at night?
Monsters!
What lies at the bottom of your bed
Monsters!

In your bed.
Or in your head
Everybody has. . .
. . . Monsters!

Martin Kimberley (Age 10)

My Special Place

There is this place where I like to sit
Watching the world pass by,
While I'm dreaming away
Time feels like it flies,
There I just sit and wait.

A gentle breeze kisses my face
Surrounded by flowers,
Grass swaying in the wind
Sunshine fills my heart,
There I just sit and wait.

Sitting alone in my special place
I listen to the stream,
In my secret garden
Watching the sunset,
There I just sit and wait.

Emily Kenny (Age 11)

The Queen

The Queen is precious
The Queen is royal
The Queen is rich
The Queen is loyal
The Queen is good
The Queen is grand
The Queen is kind
The Queen owns a lot of land
The Queen is nice
The Queen is clean
The Queen is crowned
The Queen is not mean

Ryan Kelly (Age 9)

Darkness

Darkness hits the land,
As the moon comes up,
The colour dies the darkness comes,
A owl hoots from barn to barn.
The shadows raise from the sun,
The light water turns to the dark blood cells of mine,
The clock ticks minute by minute as the night goes on,
The moon and stars come out at night to give you a tiny bit of light.

Mollie James (Age 8)

My Pet Snail

Playing in the garden, I met a slimy snail,
I found him hiding on my swing, by following his trail.
He'd crawled across the garden, it had taken him all day.
He'd carried his luggage on his back, for his holiday.

There he met a ladybird, crying she was lost.
"I'll help you find your family, come this way through the frost".
She followed him all through the night, by seeing that shiny track,
Till they found the pumpkin field, and her family's welcome back.

Eleanor Jones (Age 7)

Little Girl

A little girl gave me a pearl,
What a lovely present!
All I have to do now is think,
What to give back!
I've thought for a while,
And a cheeky smile has,
Come upon my face!
I think I'll give her,
A money box full of chocolate TEDDIES!

Chloe Philipa Jagger (Age 9)

What's It Like On Jupiter

What's it like on Jupiter
Is it dark? Is it cold?
Is it warm? Is it mould?
Is it red? Is it green?
Is it purple? Is it blue?
Is it normal? Is it big?
Is it small?
Will I like it? I don't know.

Ellis Kent (Age 8)

The Chinese New Year

The Chinese New Year
Has come at last,
People getting ready
With their masks,
Waiting for ages,
Suddenly...Bang!
Here it comes
It's the Chinese dragon,
Now the New Year is in.

Matthew Koziol (Age 7)

My Pet

My pet likes to squeak,
It goes eek, eek, eek,
It nibbles the bars,
It chews them very hard.

It is rather annoying,
But I love her so much,
Can you guess who she is?
SHE'S A GUINEA PIG!

Chloe Kingscote (Age 6)

The Jaguar

Stalking in the long golden grass,
Vaulting towards the devastated enemy,
Lashing with its gleaming claws.

The Jaguar
Ripping out grim blood from the panicking prey,
Digging in his lethal red jaw,
Sneaking away from the scene of the crime

The Jaguar
Slurping the murky water into his snarling mouth,
Curling in the shade of the gloomy jungle,
Lying on his black skin on his blanket of leaves on the shadowy ground

Anthony Johnson (Age 9)

Autumn Riddles

It's like a purple bubble on the bushes
It's like a purple bulb lying on a plant
It looks like a juicy sweety in a shop
It's like a rubber with lots of circles blasting off
It's like a purple ball squirting off
It's like a bouncy ball
It's a very shiny thing
It has lots of round things on it
What is it?

A Blackberry (upside down)

Tom Kotopoulos (Age 8)

My Invisible Friend

My invisible friend,
People don't really think that he is there,
But I know that he is there,
When something breaks I get into trouble,
But I will always say it was not me,
It was, it was my invisible friend,
My Mum or my Dad just say "Yes, what ever!"
But I know that he is there.

Daniel Kent (Age 11)

Harry Potter

H arry Potter is now one of the most famous books in the world,
A nd the Philosophers stone is his new movie.
R on is Harry's friend and also a wizard,
R andolf is the head guard of Gringoots Bank.
Y ears and years Harry Potter is going to be famous!

P rofessor Quirrel defense against the dark arts teacher. And the
O wls name is Snowy
T he Philosophers stone is a huge hit to people,
T hese are Harry Potter books, Harry Potter and Prisoner of Azkaban, the chamber of secrets, the goblet of fire.
E njoy your read and just admire, because J.K
R owling is one of the best authors ever!!

Jamie Kemp (Age 11)

Nearly Christmas

Christmas is near
It's nearly nine
I have a strange feeling
It's nearly time.

It's time its time
It's Christmas time
I'm running down the stairs to see
What Father Christmas has brought for me.

Jamie Johnston (Age 9)

Boys

Boys are mysterious people,
One even tried to climb a church steeple
And then you think you've seen enough,
You may find one who's eating fluff.
Some say boys are natural twits,
That's proven when then show their bits.
But I myself think they're the best,
And they will only rest,
When the are old timers

Byron Jackson (Age 10)

Last Day At School

We all clean up the classroom
We make the carpets clean
We dust the window shelves with a broom
Pull everything down off the big high wall
Getting our things out of our trays when we have done our work
It's time for the summer holidays
Last day at school
We collect our PE bags
We polish the glass and dust the walls with some rags
Children playing in the class they have brought lots of games
Get all the work from off the walls
The teacher shouts the children's names

Alice Jefferies (Age 7)

The Night

The lightning flashed, the thunder roared,
Across the sky the low clouds soared.
The mist was thick, the air was tight,
The moon shone dimly in the deep dark night.

His feathers were fluffed, he was ready to fly,
Down down flew the raven then up to the sky.
To the topmost window, where he made a small nest,
And there he lay down for the whole night to rest.

Test tubes were bubbling, machines rattled on,
The curtains were open but the sunlight had gone.
The hustle and bustle from the lab could be heard,
And slowly but surely awakened the bird.

The button was pushed, the whole room went dark,
There was no more lightning, not even a spark,
The silence was sudden, but didn't last long,
The thunder stopped rumbling but the bird sang it's song.

It sang and it sang but nobody spoke, and slowly but surely the monster awoke.
The lightning flashed, the thunder roared,
Across the sky the low clouds soared.
The mist was thick, the air was tight,
The moon shone dimly in the deep dark night.

Natalie Kerr (Age 12)

The Cake

There was once a cake
And we had it to bake

We jumped in the lake
And we saw a snake

The snake was fake
And saw my friend Blake
Eating a flake!

Hassan Khan (Age 10)

Swimming

Swimming is fun but we can't really run
Wet, wet, wet here and there.
It always soaks through my hair.
Moving in the water fast to slow,
Moving my body head to toe.
In the water it is hot,
Nothing's better than swimming a lot.
Going swimming every day,
It's the best I really do say.

Ambia Khatoon (Age 9)

Animals

Animals are great,
Whether they are big or small.
Each individual
I love them all.
Whether they're fluffy or scruffy
Or tatty and torn
They all look so cute
Even when they are just born.
If they're fat or thin
Or scrawny too
They all look so cute
I don't know where to begin.

Lisa Kendall (Age 12)

The Fairground

I love it at the fairground when you hear...
The popping of the balloons,
The giggle from the children,
The munching from when you eat a hamburger,
The swishing from the slides.
I love it at the fairground when you hear...
The smashing of the dodgems,
The rushing if the children,
The screaming from the children,
When they are on the roller coaster.
I love it at the fairground,
Because it's as fun as it can be!

Kristina Knell (Age 11)

I Would Be

I would be an engineer fixing rally cars.
Being a top engineer cleaning Schumacher's car until it's clean,
I would be paid and use it for my bill.
I would fix anybody's car even an old Ford Fiesta.
I would work at the AA and be their top man,
I would fix Giggs's car.
And even fix a jet.
Even the Japanese will want me.
I would fix Liverpool's bus even though they're rubbish,
Because I will be the best there ever was.
Because I have fixed nearly every car in the world.
I will make the army's tanks and 4 x 4 vehicles.
I can make anything even the mayor's car.

George Kennedy (Age 8)

Ode To The Lesson

Dedicated to the next class I enter.
To fill it full of knowledgeable banter.
To pass viscous rumours, gossipy letters,
To tie round our waist, worn out sweaters.

To gaze upon a boy, who I love truly,
Or just to be naughty and unruly!
To chat away the ticking time,
To conjour up the next rhyme.

To doodle upon all I find,
To wind up the teacher, wind, wind, wind.
To drive Miss or Sir insane,
Throwing little paper planes.

To text your very best mate.
Or ask some guy, on some date.
Ode to the lesson,
I look forward to,
Someday learning in you!

Rosie Kirton (Age 13)

Teenagers

Teenagers age 13,
Hoping to be 16.
Teenagers are 14,
Getting the gift of the gab.
Teenagers are 15,
Hoping for the year to go speeding.
Teenagers 16,
Boogying on down.
Teenagers are 17,
Relieved from the CGCSE's.
Teenagers are 18,
Taking their driving test.
Teenagers are 19,
Starting to transform into an adult.

Aimée Knight (Age 9)

The Elephant

Watch out for the elephant
As immense as a house
Not like a tiny mouse

Watch out for the elephant
It weights a ton
It likes to eat a tasty cream bun

Watch out for the elephant
It's very strong
Its trunk is very long

Watch out for the elephant
It's as grey as a cloud
When it steps it's more than loud

Watch out for the elephant
It likes to roll in the mud
It rolled in mud as much as it could!!

Rudd Kellett (Age 10)

A Place I Loathe

As the mist rolled over the land of death,
It revealed a wall of headstones.
Rows of them longer than the Great Wall of China,

Broken headstones, crumbling
At the constant bombardment
Of the ever falling rain,

A sleek black line slides into place.
Carrying within it a coffin,
Within this coffin there is a person being carried to their final resting place
Where they will never wake.

Lewis Kirkman (Age 13)

My Poem About The Queen

In 1952 when my Nan was three,
Princess Elizabeth became Monarchy,
King George's death shocked the nation,
"God Save The Queen" was the new Proclamation.

In 1977 when my Mum was nine,
Silver Jubilee celebrations was a fantastic time,
Charles, Andrew, Edward and Anne,
Are her children by Phillip, her man.

In 2002 now I am nine,
Celebrating the Golden Jubilee is mine,
"God Save The Queen" we will all call,
"Long may she reign" from one and all.

Claudia Knight (Age 9)

Going To Sleep

Laying in my bed look out the window
Trees howling and smashing at my window
My brain closing down after a hard day
My brother and his friend drinking away
Trees look like monsters scaring me to death
Now I'm going to sleep
My mum shouting that poems cheap
Goodnight

Louis Kennedy (Age 9)

Opposites

Monkeys in a house
People in a zoo
A cow going quack
And a duck going moo

Runners on a pitch
Footballers on a track
A devil blowing kisses
And an angel going SMACK!

A brainbox with a question
A dunce with a brain
A model with bad acne
And a beggar who is vain

An Eskimo in Barbados
A Texan at the Pole
A fairy with a black heart
And a vampire with a soul

A script with tasty recipes
A cookbook of exciting plays
A speech proclaimed in silence
And a poem that lasts for days (hint)

Sarina Kidd (Age 11)

The Penguin

Across the deep white snow
He waddles along, a rusty old man
A small yellow sand like beak
With black cloven feet.

As white as the snow and as black as the night,
He is winter on his own
A soft chair floating in the dark sea
He shouts and screeches like a whistle.

He is a large fish,
With a stuffed coat of feathers
Shoulders hunched like a strong man
He slide into the sea.

Emily Ketchen (Age 11)

My Fear Of Exams

Sometimes exams are very hard
Sats will be worse.
Nothing is worse than tests
The horriblist things in the world.
I always think my mark will be the lowest.
The pages are long and difficult.
I feel like tearing them up.
The working out boxes are too small.
I hate tests!

Jamie Kirby (Age 10)

Bishops Wood Poem

We tasted bread
We ate some cheese
The Saxon lady said
"No crisps please!"

We built a shelter
From bracken and wood
Mr. Henderson said
"Everyone please put up your hood"

We went up a hill
There was no town
Everyone was happy
"Look there's a crown"

We went into a hut
Someone bumped their head
We all had fun
We had bread instead

We went to a bush
We teased some wool
It was a bit dark
The weather was dull

Yasmeen Khalid (Age 9)

Francis Drake

When Francis was very young he went to sea and ate sharks tongue
And quickly pleased most of the crew by instantly pleasing the Captain too.

When the cat flew overboard young Francis Drake was oh so broad
And quickly saved the Captain's cat she landed in an old fur hat.

For Drake's bravery all that day the crew all cheered hip hip hooray.
From now on he is the Captain, but half his crew only spoke Latin.

They sailed to the sunny shores of Spain and had a break without no rain,
But while Drake was at his sleeping the Spaniards began their sneaky thieving

But Francis Drake was quick to hear, and collected his men but got no cheer.
He quickly killed the spanish men, and burnt his ships down all ten.

He sailed back to the shores of Plymouth, and was greeted by Queen elizabeth,
Who seemed oh so keen, to ask Drake where he had been.

When Francis Drake got away, he had a well earned holiday.
And we still remember him today, for his voyage with no delay!

Lucy Sarah King (Age 9)

Loomo The Leopard

Loomo the large leopard with luminous eyes
Leapt upon Laxie the lady Lima
Laxie did a loop in the sky and
Hooked her long tail around a large tree.
Loomo gave a loud roar
Then he saw a lizard that leapt under a log
At the sight of Loomo
The lizard leapt away as fast as his little legs could carry him

Alex Kemp (Age 7)

Love

Love is bright red
Love smells like roses
Love tastes like chocolate
Love sounds like a soft violin
Love is a soft feeling
Somewhere in your heart
Love lives in your heart.

Farzana Khan (Age 10)

Loneliness

There was a poor little boy sitting by a lamp,
Some may say he was a tramp,
Some big boys came over and called him names,
And then went off to play their games,
The little boy asked if he could play,
But the big boys told him to go away,
Then another little boy came into town,
And on his head he wore a crown,
"Can I play?" said the boy by the lamp,
"Yes, you can come see my camp,"
So the boys went off to the new boys camp,
"Oi you scamp,"
A big boy said,
"Can I play?"
"Yes any day,"
Said the two little boys in their camp.

Thomas King (Age 10)

All About Me

I am a girl
Who wants to twirl.

I've got sisters
Who always complain about blisters.

I've got a mum who wants to be fancy
But her name is Nancy.

I've got an auntie
Who wants to eat bounty.

I've got a dad
Who wants to be a lad.

I've got a brother called Adil
Who wants to go to Brazil.

Sadiya Khan (Age 10)

The Night Before My Birthday

I went to bed the night before,
My mum said "goodnight" and closed the door.
I closed my eyes and tried to sleep,
I even tried to count some sheep.
Then I heard the clock downstairs
It was 11 o'clock but then who cares?

"How long will it take?" I said to myself
As I pulled a book down off my shelf.
I flicked through the pages not taking it in
Then I heard it again the clocks ding ding.
It was nearly morning I just couldn't wait
For my big birthday treat and my big slice of cake.

Sam Kirbitson (Age 11)

Death

Death is dark red.
It smells like
Burning fire.
It tastes burnt
And crusty
It sounds like
Two cars crashing together
It feels sharp and crunchy.
Death lives
In a broken down castle.

Mehreen Khan (Age 10)

Remember September

On September the 11th,
Someone was to blame,
It wasn't the people passing by,
But the hijacker on the plane.

It crashed into one twin tower,
Life will never be the same.
As the plane broke through the wall,
The tower burst up into flames.

Tumbling, tumbling, down and down,
Onto the busy street below.
The crowd turned and fled for their lives,
They didn't stand to watch the show.

The incident shocked the world at once,
Earth was crying that day.
It took months to clear up the mess-
Let alone the cost to pay.

Think of how many people died,
Thanks to a group of selfish men.
Stranded at the top of the tower,
Knowing they were all going to die...But when?...

Laura Klette (Age 13)

Pollution

I want to tell you something new,
You should not destroy the trees,
You may be safe now but later you won't.
The pollution is high,
We must stop or we'll die.
The sea is weak
All the animals will die out
The trees are being cut down
The animals are disappearing
Because of you and your stupid town
The pollution is high,
We must stop or we'll die!

Adam Kennerley (Age 11)

Trucks

Trucks are mean,
Trucks are fast,
Trucks are keen,
Trucks are last.

Brakes screech,
Horn beeps,
They are really neat!!
Trucks sometimes carry meat.

Daniel Kidson (Age 10)

The Environment

If you wish to preserve
All the beauties you have seen . . .

Don't throw tin cans
Into the brook,
I saw you drop that bubblegum
You sneaky little crook!

And if you dearly love
The butterflies and bees,
Then keep you plastic carriers
From hanging in the trees.

To keep poor little rodents,
From turning into burgers;
Keep those beer tags off the beach -
You could prevent a murder!

Finally put old automobiles in a skip,
Woods *shouldn't* be a rubbish tip!

If you wish to preserve
All the beauties you have seen . . .
Then be sure to keep
The environment clean!

Becky King (Age 11)

The Stormy Nightmare

The night dark and damp like the inside of a prison cell,
Thunder rumbled like the drone of a distant bee,
Lightning streaked like a flame in the roaring fire.

A drenched raven dragged it's limp body to the top most window,
His fiery eyes searched through the mist,
He peered into the forgotten laboratory,
Rain slashed his ruffled feathers,
Then he hunched back into a raven black slumber.

They stared anxiously at the monster as if his eyes were to open,
Anticipation filled the air, lingering at that nervous time,
Hanna, Frans and Igor stared at each other,
The flickering lightning flashed again.

The empty atmosphere hung mysteriously,
The wind whistled through the cracked windows.

Silence settles like the dawn of a new day,
Emerging from the swirling mist was the strange operating table,
There he was,
The penetrating noises of the storm aborted, gentle rain began to fall.

Corinne Kinvig (Age 12)

Imagine

Imagine we could have no lessons in a week
Imagine there was week of play
Imagine no school for the rest of the year
Imagine you were allowed food fights at lunchtime
Imagine you were allowed to chuck rulers
Imagine there were no teachers
Imagine there were no headteachers
Imagine teachers let us talk
Imagine we could have book authors in every day

James Kinchen (Age 8)

From Stream To Sea

The air rushes through the trees
Answering the waters call,
But when it turns to face it,
No huge cascade of thunderous water.
A trickling stream it finds,
Gently winding its way through the green fields.

But suddenly, it changes
Turning into a fast running river
Moving swiftly like a train
Through fields of grass, corn and flowers

Then, it comes to the coast
Pouring unafraid over the cliff
Now a waterfall, falling into the sea, calm again.

Amy Kenyon (Age 12)

School

School was dark,
Abandoned alone,
The door
Like a ghoul,
Creaking and cracking.

The door crept open,
A shimmering
Shadow appeared,
A breeze
A breath
Of icy air.
Crept down my spine,
With a shiver.

I peered inside,
To see what was there,
That chilly,
Cold shadow,
Was lost.
I was alone out there!

Emma Kehoe (Age 12)

Boomerang

Bound bone snapper
Mad whistler
Whooping spinner
Hovering through the air
A Weapon

Edward Kellett (Age 8)

The Human Body

Bones are my skeleton
They help me stand,
Sometimes they break,
So we need a helping hand.

Veins are blue and red,
They are under your skin,
They run around your body,
And they are as hard as tin.

Muscles are very tense,
You get them if your strong,
Some are very big and
Some are very long.

Skin is all over you
It is pale or tanned,
Some people have freckles,
And it is smoother than sand.

Stefanie King (Age 12)

Tonight At Noon

Pigs will eat bananas,
America will be the capital of France,
Plants will die in spring,
The mice will chase elephants,

    Tonight at noon,
Tony Blair will vote for Japanese people to rule the world,
The most famous sport will be eating jam sandwiches,
Food will change to sweets,
Death will take over lives,
Time will change to 26 hours not 24 hours.
Teenagers will go to clubs in sunlight.

    Tonight at noon
You will be mine.

Lindsey King (Age 10)

Recipe For An Angry Teacher

Pour a menacing gang of boisterous boys
Into a bowl full of pathetic excuses.

Add a few expressive ruler fights
And glaze with some giggling girls fidgeting with each others hair

Mix vigorously with some dangerous pencil flicking.

Top with a pinch of late homework, leave to prove and . . .
Voila! An angry teacher.

Alex Kingsbury (Age 10)

My Noisy Sister

My noisy sisters go cling, clong, clang
When she is dropping things
Whenever my sister goes up the stairs
She sounds like a herd of elephants.

Oliver Killner (Age 6)

My Mother

As thin as a stick,
She sits slurping tea,
Slurp, slurp, slurp.
She sits munching Haribo,
Munch, munch, munch.
"Put the kettle on!" she'll say,
And I'll moan and groan.
She looks like a thin banana.
If she was a piece of furniture she would be a lamp,
Standing big and tall
If she were an animal she would be a purring little cat.

Victoria Keighley (Age 11)

Hilarious Haikus

I will have three kids,
They will ALL be very fat
They'll be called Bob.

My eyes see the world,
My hands touch the soft soil,
What a dirty world!

I say a dead priest,
Impaled on some big spikes,
He was dead holy.

I saw a bad man,
So I hit him on the head,
With a frying pan.

Spring, the flowering,
Of all things under the sun,
For example, me!

I'm not very rich,
So the best price for me,
Is, completely free.

Michael Knight (Age 11)

Waves

Crash, crash!
The waves of the sea
Crash, crash!
I will mash
Crash, crash!
I will break
Crash, crash!
The waves of the sea.

Jonathan Knox (Age 9)

If I Had Wings

If I had wings
I would taste the monstrous
Ice-cream mountains
As cold as wintery ice

Johanna Kingman (Age 9)

Harvest

Harvest is here
Apples are ripe
Rice is given at harvest time
Voles run in the fields
Each grain of corn is separated
Straw is gathered in
Tons of food is given to the poor

Kristian Kendal (Age 10)

Love Is...

Love is looking at my baby brother at night-time when he has a little smile.
Love is night-time when the fireworks explode onto lovely colours.
Love is hearing people singing Christmas carols outdoors at christmas time.
Love is hearing my Mummy and Daddy saying, "Love you"
Love is freshly cooked sausages, bacon and eggs.
Love is to smell deodorant on me on a school night.
Love is to touch animals at the zoo.
Love is to feel Mummy's fur coat.
Love is to taste sticky toffee pudding from the microwave.
Love is to taste cheese on toast with HP sauce.

Christopher Keep (Age 7)

Autumn

Autumn is time for harvest, time for icy walks
You should go and get some shiny scratched conkers
Fruit is fine if you find a filled one
If you're lucky you will find a huge pumpkin,
But not one person is lucky for time in Autumn
(Meaning playing out with your friends)
Squirrels are soft in sight you should stand still so you see them
Autumn is near Christmas that is one good thing about Autumn great!

Danielle Kirk (Age 10)

My Cat

Our class cat is very funny
And he also has a bunny.
In the night he has a fright
Then he does turn white.

Abigail Kromer (Age 5)

Detention For Me

D is for dullness, watching the clock
E xciting! not.
T ormenting to see the children play
E motions tears when my parents discover
N othing, nothing to do
T is for teasing, seeing them play
I 'm reading a book about the art Kung Fu.
O is for it's over, at last I'm out!
N ow I am free without a doubt.

F inally I'm gone out of there forever!
O h no I'm not going back there, never.
R unning around on the playground.

M y mates are cheering because I'm here
E veryone has to go in now.

Mikey Kennedy (Age 10)

Green Is . . . .

Green is happy like the grass
Green is lovely like the big green mountains
The tall trees and the green flowers
And a juicy green apple to eat.

David Knight (Age 8)

Cinderella

Cinderella is cool,
She makes all the boys drool

All the girls wish they were her
But the problem is they all wear fur

She has two ugly sisters
They are mean, nasty and covered in blisters

Her sister would say "clean the walls scrub the floor
And don't forget to polish the door

Cinderella went to the ball
Hearing a beautiful red shawl

At midnight her headsmen will turn into mice,
But after that Cinderella was still very nice

Manjot Kaur (Age 10)

The Wind

The wind slices through the air like a cold sword,
It dances round the clouds teasing them.
Many men may not notice though millions may,
That the wind whistles like a farmer looking for his dog.
It is like a big angry man,
The wind hollers like an angry man again.
Now it is like a boy screaming because he's cut his knee.
The wind can be so kind yet so mad and angry.
The wind opens the door and comes in,
The wind jumps over the wall.
The wind whispers in the runner's ears,
The wind trips him up!

Dariush Kamali (Age 9)

Kindness

Kindness is bright pink,
It smells like perfume,
Kindness tastes like chocolate and sweets,
It sounds like the jingle of bells
It feels as smooth as silk
Kindness lives in the clouds

Adeel Kausar (Age 9)

What Is The Fire?

The fire is an orange and brown flower
The fire is a boiling sun that is orange and yellow.
It is flames taking a man up to the cold and bright moon.
The snakes slithering up the fireplace

Roxanne Kinchlea (Age 9)

India

In India there's very short supply
We've only got one half of an apple pie

It seems like there's no ground to walk upon
The war is going on so long

All the children are crying
People are getting them to sleep or trying

My children are being good
So I cover them up with a woollen hood

In India it is very hot
They have to sit in the shade a lot.

Amy Lawrence (Age 7)

Night

A badger rustles through the night
Feasting alone, out of sight

An owl swoops by to find a meal
A small fish and a slimy eel

A fox crawls out of his den
And creeps towards a chicken pen

People in their cosy beds
Covers pulled up to their heads

Alex Kerfoot (Age 8)

Toaster

Toaster, toaster lovely toaster,
Up and down you go
Ping, pong, ding, dong lovely toaster
Toaster, toaster lovely toaster,
Up and down you go
Ping, pong, ding, dong,
Toaster, toaster lovely toaster.

Jessica Kerry (Age 9)

Love

Love is red,
It smells like a rose
Love tastes like sweet chocolate
It sounds like some twinkling stars
Love feels like a soft cuddly teddy
Love lives in the centre of a heart

Kiran Kausar (Age 9)

Snake

Slimy, slippery, Sam the snake
Woke up from his scaly, sleep
Then slowly . . . . started to
S L I D E to the swamp.
Sam the snake, spat out
Venom at a tree stump.
Sam circled around the swamp,
Sam the snake was . . . .
Sleepy . . . . . .
Then Sam the snake,
Started to sleep again.

Tony Lea (Age 8)

The Prince Awakens

The night was filled with thunder and lightning.
Rattling and crackling, it was frightening.
Black thunder clouds, racing through the night sky.
Like a cat and mouse chasing, hear them cry.

A raven as black as the night.
Swooping down out of sight.
His feathers are soaked through to skin
He is very, very old and very, very thin.

Rain rattling and flashes of lightning
Excitement building, tension tightening.
Followed by a clap of thunder.
Will he wake, everyone wonders.

A huge monster lying so still.
He steams continuously like a grill.
He lays still on a slab of stone.
His muscles twitch he starts to groan.

A silence, that could be cut with a knife
They stand back as he comes to life
Holding their breath, their hearts skips a beat.
As their Prince rises to his feet.

Robert Lally (Age 12)

Lions

Lions run very fast.
Lions have a hard task.
Lions pounce on herbivores,
Lions show their terrible jaws,
Lions use their scary paws.
Lions go and wash their teeth and have a drink
And then their tongue goes all pink.

Jake Lewis (Age 6)

Tiger

"Tiger, Tiger, please can you pounce?"
Said the monkey
When he went near the forest.

Christopher Lambert (Age 5)

School

In the school I get sad
Because I miss my Mummy and Daddy,
When school is finished
I get happy.

Billy Leman (Age 5)

The Poetry Competition

I'm in a competition,
I've had to write a poem,
There are lots of people here,
But I am going to show 'em.

I heard about the competition,
In class one day at school,
Mrs Hackett said "Go on please enter!"
So I did because I think she's cool!

I'm feeling very nervous,
About the poem I have written,
My hair has all been chewed,
And my nails have all been bitten.

I hope the judges like it,
It took a lot of time,
Especially as I tried,
Very hard to make it rhyme.

They are looking at my poem,
They've got a smile on their face,
Look they're announcing the winner,
Have I won first place?

Josie Lee (Age 11)

What A Bore!

I fell on the floor
And got very sore
I had to go to the doctor
To have an insore
The let me have a week at home
I went into the door
And had to go to the doctor again.

Jamie Kirkwood (Age 8)

Our Loyal Queen

A queen's smiling face
Fifty years of fun and joy
A queen's smiling face.

Abbie Lacey (Age 9)

Easter

Easter eggs
An egg is yum
But an Easter egg
Is yum a lot

Robert Knee (Age 5)

How Would You Feel?

How would you feel to live a life of danger?
Watching round bush and tree.
How would you feel with responsibility to protect others?
Especially your family.
How would you feel to be the world's most wanted?
Hiding your precious treasure.
How would you feel about running away?
And living a life with no pleasure.
How would you feel to be hunted and chased?
Always being aware.
How would you feel without a home?
Finding sanctuary nowhere.
Just stop and think how lucky you are
With all life's novelties.
When elephants all over the world,
Are hunted for their ivory.
How would you feel to live a life of danger?
Watching round bush and tree.
How would you feel to be an elephant?
How would you feel to be me?

Anjli Lakhani (Age 14)

Nanny Lay There

As I walked into the damp room,
I saw her face, lifeless,
Lips frozen water.
Trying to see past it she cried a silent tear.
As she lay there, blank faced,
In her mind she watched a clock,
Ticking, ticking,
Slower and slower.
I sat by her side and held her hand,
Skin transparent, she closed her eyes to rest some more.
Her face was now pale; peace rested in her eyes
And tranquility lay in the air.

Jenner Lambert-Hill (Age 12)

The Red And Pink Car

There was a car,
That didn't live far,
It was red and pink too,
The owner smoked fags,
Everyone thought he was an old hag,
Never a fan of the locals,
Whenever he went past,
He always went fast,
Maniac he was,
He was quite often on his phone,
Now his house is called the red and pink zone.

Dan Lees (Age 11)

Sweets

Hard and boiled, chewy sweets,
Chocolate, fruity and toffee treats.
Sweet and sour and normal too,
Luscious for everyone, me and you.
Like Jelly Tots, cola bottles and lollipops,
Chewy and colourful with sugar on top.
Sucking, melting and crunching loud,
Munching happily, smiling proud.
Sticks and tags and wrappers too,
Lots of sweets for me and you.
Strawberry, lime and banana splits,
Bubble gum millions and sugar pips.
Blowing bubbles in the sun,
Popping and bursting with my chewing-gum.
Raspberry, orange and lemon sherbet,
Mints and popcorn for me and Herbert.
Chomps and fudges and chocolate drops,
Fruity gums, hard sucking pear drops.
Wine gums, chewits and all those treats,
All for us are all those sweets!

Hannah Lingley (Age 14)

True Love

Her hair was as gold as the sun,
His eyes were as blue as the sea,
Their hearts were as red as roses,
It was love that's plain to see.

She glided across the floor,
As gracefully as a swan,
His words were sweet and simple,
It was love that will last on.

Standing outside the holy church,
Hand in hand standing proud,
Newly wed for a lifetime of love,
Their smiles shone love all around.

Rebekah Lucas (Age 11)

Adjective Poem

I got a new toy
My grandad is very old.
I am kind.
I was very angry.
Jack is funny.
I have a pretty dress.
I'm glad I don't have to eat my dinner.
It's cold outside.
I'm very busy with my work.
This poem is good.

Kate Luty (Age 9)

The Prince Awakens

Low clouds race across the sky,
Rumbling and tumbling as they passed by.
Rain fell down in the dampened night,
And from the castle came a bluish-white light.

His feathers were fluffed, he was ready to fly,
Down, down flew the raven, then up to the sky,
To the topmost window, where he made me a small nest,
And there he lay down, for the whole night, to rest.

Inside, test tubes were bubbling machines rattled on,
The curtains were open, but the sunlight had gone.
The hustle and bustle of the lab could be heard,
And slowly but surely awakened the bird.

The atmosphere tense, the lightning flashing,
The rain could be heard and the thunder was crashing,
Outside a thunderstorm was brewing up,
Excited Hanna wished the monster good luck.

The button was pressed, then no-one would speak,
Not even the raven dared open his beak,
The rain was now gentle, the storm had calmed down,
An eerie silence lingered all around.

Lois Lancaster (Age 12)

Creation Poem

God made animals such as
Gerbals, octopuses, donkeys, snakes
Rabbits and elephants.
God made countries like
Turkey and continents like Asia,
And he made igloos, oceans and nature
He made everything.

Freddie Leighton (Age 10)

Lead And Roots

Stare with watery eyes
Your path outstretched in front of you,
And feel with every agonised step you tread
A little more of your imagination
Ripped apart
By the all-consuming inevitability of it all.

Leaden legs and rooted mind
Not only lack the energy
But fight against the need
To break from the road.

Escape the path.
Run,
And don't look back.

Michael Lea (Age 17)

What's It Like In The Future

Will it have my friends?
Will I like it?
Will we have strange feet?
And strange arms too?
Will we all live in a zoo?
Will it just be normal?

Joe Laurance (Age 8)

The Underwater Journey

The fishes soft flippers
Brush against me like layers,
I can hear the dolphins splashing
But I can see them moving.
I can taste the salty water
Between my teeth.
The jellyfish can see me right beneath.

The water catches ripples,
The octopus swims by,
His leg tickles.
The waves move swiftly
I can hear them gently.
I can see lots of tail fins move,
I catch and eat what I choose.

Hannah Lewis (Age 9)

Monsters

Monsters scream at me,
Monsters fly away with me,
Monsters go to Mars.

Mark Lawrence (Age 7)

Leisure

What is this life if full of care,
I've plenty time to stop and stare.

Time to go to the swimming baths,
Where I have some very good laughs.

Time to play with my dog,
Where she jumps over a log.

Time to go to Jade's house,
Where her brother acts like a mouse.

Time to lay on my bed,
Dreaming of something in my head.

A good life I've got its full of care,
I'm pleased I've got time to stop and stare.

Danielle Longstaff (Age 9)

Mid Night Creatures

In the night the owl is singing
its mid night song
all night long.

The hedgehog is hurrying,
scurrying and burrowing
to find its home.

The fox is a thief, who watches the leaves,
who looks for his tea in the bins
blown over by the wind.

As the morning is breaking,
the sun is rising
and people are waking.

Animals creep home to their beds
now it's their turn to sleep.

Ben Latimer (Age 8)

Untitled

One old Ogre opening Ogre cereal
Two tickling toes tip toeing to the teacup
Three tied tree houses trying to trick the trees
Four fairies flying from fairytales
Five funkee fish flapping fins.

Hannah Leather (Age 8)

As I Sit On The Hill

As I sit on the green sloping hill looking down on the small city.
The sun shone brightly on the hill like a torch.
The sky was blue like a clear blue sea.
The birds are chirping happily in the leafless trees
And the wind tickled my face like a soft feather. Ah bliss.

A sudden blood shot scream breaks the silence followed by a loud explosion.
Black smoke rises like hells flames rising from the earth.
Men with strange black metal on their heads with weird wood and metal sticks
Spurting fire from their noses the screaming gets worse.

A gigantic metal beast made the beautiful green hill turn to mud in seconds.
The sky was filled with massive birds humming
Humming over the sounds of the birds happy chirpy singing.

One by one houses began to turn to flames and smoke with the touch of a small log.
The birds begin dropping these small logs
And the golden sun disappears in the black smoke and the clouds then nothing

It was all over as I sat on the brown mud filled hill
Looking down on the wrecked city with the screams and car alarms still going.
What was all this for, what have we done wrong.

Tom Law (Age 15)

50 Years

Now there's crop tops,
Funky trousers
Then they had patterned skirts,
Silk red blouses.

Now we've got sandals,
Shoes with flippers
Then they had boots,
Toe holed slippers.

Now we travel by car,
Or fly in the sky
Then they had rusty cars,
Or boats passing by.

Now we have washing powder,
A cool washing machine
Then they had grubby clothes,
Tubs that made clothes clean.

Now there's funky Steps,
S Club 7 too
Then they had Elvis Presley,
Frank Sinatra too.

Emma Lawrence (Age 8)

The Magic Box

I will put in the box

A giggle from a baby
A pot of sand from a hot beach
A very first birthday

I will put in the box

A funny story from my grandad
A pencil from years ago
My brothers favourite toy

I will put in the box
A frog with eight legs
A spider with four legs

It has eagles claws for hinges
And dinosaur pictures on the top
And some toy cars stuck on the side

I will put a jet pack on the back
And fly to the moon.

Chris Lynn (Age 9)

A Fruity Poem

What is green?
An apple is green.
Juicy and crunchy and green.

What is yellow?
A banana is yellow
What is green?
A grape is green
What is orange?
A Peach is orange

Kane Longman (Age 5)

The Dark Cats Of Darkness

There was a cat,
A black stray cat.
His name is at the end.
Throughout his life is to defend.
He doesn't do martial arts,
The art she does is dark.
He wasn't tamed,
But he was named.
He's thin without food,
He's always in a bad mood.
Where he lives is a bin,
Where it was it's Kings Lynn.
He likes his name,
He thinks being tame is lame.
His name isn't thin or fat,
His name is Matt.

Amy Lee (Age 10)

Salamander's Fire

Always terrified of fire, I crawl out of my house,
As grand explosions disturb my sleep, quiet as a mouse.
The Inferno engulfs my shelter, I can't imagine why,
This fire started, how at all, because now I'm going to die

A rain of golden sparks fall slowly from the moon,
As screaming, shouting rockets certainly spell doom.
Bodies holding sticks of sparks are heading over here,
I, Salamander, am not as lucky as the rabbit, or the deer.

After the great bonfire, all is quiet here,
The rabbit has returned, and so has the deer,
And, after the bonfire, with the fury and flashes,
I, tiny little Salamander, crawl slowly from the ashes.

The hot, burning sticks of sparks have all cooled now,
And I have no idea where the devils went, or how.
All the wildlife is back with the rivers cool flow,
Now the peace is back inside the meadow.

Alex Littleboy (Age 11)

Elephant

The sun slowly rose over the sandy hill.
It was beautiful; everything silent and still.
In the heart of Africa's soul
We washed in the water-hole.
All of a sudden the silence was broken.
But, not a word was spoken.
It was like a warm car heating humming,
The door slammed; we all started running.
The hunter then shot his deadly accurate rifle.

We all jumped; stopped.

That was it.

He had got her; she was gone!!!

Kate Ladkin (Age 12)

Submarines

The under water submarine
It torpedoes quick and mean
The periscope its enemy-searcher
Sonar used for the screened alarmed.

The big grey swimmer of the sea
The noisy glider of defense it will
Be the slow riser to show its head
The quick-submerge to hide in the sea bed.

The fire of bombs to damage each other
To defend against harm like one big brother
To make our shores as safe as can be
Our great metal sharks of the sea.

Darren Lake (Age 11)

Frost

I knew I was needed soon.
Autumn shouted my name, disturbing my slumber;
The wind tore down the leaves as the summer slid away.
Old ladies told me by putting on winter scarves;
Young mothers told me by shouting at children not to 'catch cold'.
I settled here and there as I froze the ponds.
I heard the birds shriek, 'Jack Frost is about.'
I froze the dew on the grass, making it white with fear,
I froze the tops of the cars and slipped inside to meddle with the locks.
I caught people's noses and the tops of their ears,
I sneaked inside scarves and winter hats.
I settled on tops of houses and blocked up pipes.
I kept people inside near warm fires. . . .

Until the winter sun came and melted me away.

Alexis Lewis (Age 15)

Searching The Stars

Exploring space as
We don't know it
Always searching for
Something new

A planet, a comet
Or a new race maybe,
Who knows?

Up in space
Through the stars
Passing Venus
Passing Mars

What's that?
A new planet

Nicholas Le Masonry (Age 12)

Jelly Dancer

Watch her ride the waves,
As she swiftly swirls her tentacles,
And she dances on the gentle tide.

She is like a crystal,
With rainbow colours shining through her
And she dances on the gentle tide.

She makes no sound,
Only the water trickling past her,
And she dances on the gentle tide.

She will give you a stinging fright,
If you brush past her waving tentacles,
And she dances on the gentle tide.

Chelsey Leigh Lockhart (Age 11)

Snow

A white blanket
Puts the grass to sleep.
Cuddly white lambs
Jump down from the sky.
A storm of cotton wool.
Sprinkle icing on a cake.
Patterned paper falling from space.
An army of polar bears,
Going into battle.
A choir of angels
Dancing down from heaven.

Emma Lowman (Age 11)

Hope And War

Hope is snowy white,
It smells like a lily in clear water,
Hope tastes sweet and warm,
It sounds like birds singing in the air,
Hope feels soft and loving,
It lives in your bedroom.

War is burning orange,
It smells like red, hot lava,
War tastes like burnt toast,
It sounds like bombs, destroying towns
War feels hard and hot,
It lives in the heart of a volcano.

Jenna Lockett (Age 8)

The Blue Winged Birds

A nice chicken pie
The little birds fly
Down the old oak tree
Their wings were blue
They sang toodle-doo
Till they flew away.

The little fish swam
Over the golden sea
He flung off his hat
To a big fat bat
As the moon went in

Joshua Lekha (Age 9)

Mr. Pritchard-Jenkins, (Teacher)

He slipped around the door and pounced upon the desk
A jaguar on a long winter hunt.
He eyed his nervous pupils,
His eyes settled on a terrified young male,
And he pounced, using his terrifying maths questions.

Spelling was worse . . . .
He eyed his targets as they waited for their terrifying words to come.
They were as hard as rock and twisted their minds.

In English he used metaphors, as a pack of wolves.
They circled the poor, defenseless, young children waiting to pick one out,
And attack viciously with unanswerable questions . . . .

Jamie Lawrenson (Age 10)

At Playtime

You can hear the children playing and shouting,
You can hear the ball whizzing across the field.
You can hear kids crying after they have fallen.
You can hear groups of girls giggling.
You can hear braces of boys bursting balloons.
You can see teachers in the staff room talking and drinking tea.
You can hear and see everyone is full of glee at playtime.

Matthew Lockwood (Age 9)

Bouncer...Bouncer

B ouncer is fast, friendly and fun,
O ver the jump he goes
U nder the midnight sky, his shiney white coat glows,
N ever naughty, never bad,
C urled up in his soft straw bed he dreams of carrots good and bad,
E ven though he's full of bounce he never kicks or bucks about!
R unning and grazing in the field he begins to feel tired and goes to sleep.

Poppy Le Marechal (Age 9)

The Thunder

The thunder is a sneaky cheetah
Fast and furious
He clashes down when you least expect it
With crystal teeth and jaws
Hour upon hour he has cautious fear
He swipes and demands his prey
Scratching madly with his razor claws
Earning his prize fortunately departing with the blood like bones
Through the breath of the air and wind
With the moon shining gold and silver beaming its light at the Earth
He twists and turns howling long and clear

Christopher Lewis (Age 9)

Different Machines

Clang munch crash,
I get lots of cash.
Ping bang bong,
It sings a lovely song.
Bang shoot fire,
The machines a big liar
Wash dry comb,
It's time to go home.

Kate Lindeman (Age 9)

Stonehenge

Bright rocks
Shiny in the moonlight
Rocks as still as time
The great rocks
Are looking up to God
Silence all around
The day has begun

Alistair Long (Age 8)

Aliens

T taught it
H hatched it
E evolved it

A argued over it
L licked it
I incubated it
E electrocuted it
N nicked it
S spat at it

H handled it
A abducted it
V viewed it
E employed it

I insulted it
N nourished it
V made it a villain
A assaulted it
D dimwitted it
E executed it
D dealt with it

Matthew James Lamont (Age 9)

Madness

Madness is a dull grey,
It smells like a rotten apple,
It tastes like squashed strawberries dipped in mud,
And an eyeball getting nailed in wood.

It feels like a rock hitting you on the head,
And a devil sucking your blood,
A vampire eating your flesh.
A mummy tearing your brain apart.

So next time watch out.

Nidha Latif (Age 10)

The All-Purpose Household Job-Doer

It whirrs, it whizzes, it pops and munches,
It zooms, it zaps, it clangs and crunches.
It's the All-Purpose Household Job-Doer!
It does your homework in five seconds flat,
It'll even give the dog a pat!
It clicks, clacks, clunks and chinks,
It bangs, bongs, booms, and bings.
It's the All-Purpose Household Job-Doer!
It's two metres tall and five metres wide,
It'll even get your shoelaces tied!
It whirrs, it whizzes, it pops and munches,
It zooms, it zaps, it pops and crunches.
It's the All-Purpose Household Job-Doer.

Charlie Lockwood (Age 10)

Leisure

What is my life if full of care,
I have plenty of time to stop and stare

Time to go and lay down,
Then tomorrow I can go to town.

Time to go roller blading in the hall,
Let's make sure Robin doesn't fall.

Time to go and play with my friend,
And then I'll give Paris my CD to lend.

Time to go and read my magazines,
Then I'll have toast and beans.

Time to go and listen to my favourite group
Whilst mum is having a hot bowl of soup.

Time to get a hot bath,
Then I'll have a good laugh

A good life I've got it's full of care,
I have plenty of time to stop and stare.

Fern Luciw (Age 9)

The Midnight Darkness

When I wake up in the middle of the night,
What I see is such a terrible sight,
All around me eyes are following,
Spooky shadows are wallowing and wallowing.

All of a sudden, my heart skips a beat,
I hear the sound of padding feet,
Is anyone there?
I must beware!

Sophie Law (Age 11)

A Bee

Have you ever seen a special bee?
I have once it ran after me
It buzzed busily all day long
Until I sang it a super song
I made him so dozy
He felt really cosy
His cheeks went all rosey
And I had a peaceful end of the day.

Katie Lofthouse (Age 8)

Green Poetry

I want to buy a big football
Crocodiles swimming in a swamp
I want to buy a big football
Children climbing trees
I want to buy a big football
And score the winning goal.

Stewart Lucas (Age 9)

Leopard

The leopard stands still waiting, waiting
So still so sleek.
There's a rustle in the bush
An antelope puts its head around the corner
And starts to run, run, run.
The leopard stands still waiting, waiting
So still so sleek.
The leopard pulls the antelope to its bloody death
Its blood dripping, dripping, dripping.
The leopard stands still waiting, waiting
So still so sleek.
It finishes its meal for the day
But its spotted robe is mangled in blood
The blood of the antelope.
The leopard stands still waiting, waiting
So still so sleek.

Laura Lambert (Age 12)

The Forest's Story

I remember when life was good
When my flowing waterfalls splashed
When wild, colourful flowers were dancing
And the birds woke me up with their cheerful song
Horses were jumping and flying over mossy logs
The rope swing hung on my bare branches
My berries were as red as anger and squirrels were squealing under my trees
The bugs and the insects have their own little world under the undergrowth
My leaves were flicking on the trees
Oak trees swaying over pure blue rivers

Children be kind, find me and help me before all the flames hit the top
My pure blue rivers are now red rough rivers
Leaves were crimpling and turning black
The berries were gone and the fire was taking over
Squirrels were scattering up to the top of the tree
And the horses cantering flicking things behind
My waterfalls trying to climb up instead of falling into fire
Deer sprung off popping flames
I can remember when life was good
When my flowing rivers splashed like they should!

Jessica Lander (Age 11)

The Jungle

The tigers awake, as well as the snake
   and so are the monkeys in the tree,
The birds in the sky are just passing by
   wondering what they would see.
The lions just stay while jungle drums play
   and so do the elephants too,
The leopards walk by and stare at the sky
   looking for something to do.

Josh Lee (Age 9)

The Short Trunk

Why do elephants have long trunks?
Why do twins sleep in bunks?
Why do Venus Fly Traps always eat flies?
Why do leprechauns always tell lies?
Why do helium balloons float up into the sky?
Why is investigating put down to a spy?
Why is glass transparent and plastic opaque?
Why do our muscles always ache?
Why are chimps the closest to us?
How come pupils ride in a school bus?
Why do big sisters think they're the boss?
Why does sugar dissolve like candy floss?

Why is the world full of . . . .

WHYS!

Jessica Levett (Age 10)

Stonehenge

The stones sleep in the morning
And wake up in the evening
The stones look for their own spaces
They sink from the sky like a diamond sparkle
While talking to each other in silence
The stones carefully go into the ground
And crumble and fall

Andrew Langford (Age 7)

Little Tiger

Little tiger is wandering
Off into the woods
He doesn't want to go to bed.

Esther Mobbs (Age 4)

Sally Sure

Sally Sure
Sally Sure
Are you sure?
Are you sure about going to the shore?
Sue's mum reassured her about the shore.
So Sally went to the shore more and more.
She found that the shore was a good place
To walk better than her own wooden floor.
After a while her feet got sore and she didn't
Want to walk on the shore any more.

Matthew Lord (Age 10)

The Future

When I gazed into the future, I saw destroyed buildings
When I gazed into the future, I saw a robot doing chores.
When I gazed into the future, I heard the sound of a cane hitting a slave.
When I gazed into the future, I heard the sound of children zooming on their hover scooter.
When I gazed into the future, I smelt the garbage pile that was piled high in the sky.
When I gazed into the future, I smelt the fresh smell of the chocolate factory.
When I gazed into the future, I tasted the cold nights air.
When I gazed into the future, I tasted some freshly made chocolate.
When I gazed into the future, I touched a dead body.
When I gazed into the future, I touched a new born baby.

Daniel Leather (Age 10)

What Is Red?

What is red? A red ant is red crawling up bark on a tree.
What is blue? The sea is blue, where the shadows float through.
What is grey? The deep dark clouds are grey tumbling over the fields.
What is yellow? A buttercup is yellow making my chin glow.
What is black? The top notes of a piano are black making sweet music.
What is green? Fairy liquid is green making frothy bubbles.
What is silver? Glitter is silver sparkling in my hair.
What is colourful? A rainbow is colourful spread across the sky.

Megan Laws (Age 8)

A Solar Swirl

A rip in the deep sky of space
Slow twisting turning mess
Dots of wavey colours
A ball of gas
Mixed with scribbles of green,
White,
And blue.

Sam Lawless (Age 10)

Snow

When snow falls it is like a new life has hit the world.
The soft white blanket covers the ground.
Children playing, joyfully and happily
Throwing snowballs all around
But as the day grows older the sun becomes stronger
And the snow starts to melt
By the end of the day all the snow has gone
Leaving not a trace only puddles of water
Will it come again tomorrow?
Well I do not know
But in my dreams I think of snow racing down
Then when I wake up I realise that the snow isn't there
I pray to God please let the snow come again
Even if, it is next year.

Ricky Marinaro (Age 14)

Creation Poem

God made everything,
Bees and trees and camels,
Night with day,
Sun and moon,
God made everything.

Cats, rats and bats,
Lord god made them all!

Who made dogs frogs and hogs,
God made them all.

Robert Luchford (Age 9)

The Local Walk

Houses with lights on, houses without,
Houses that are quiet, houses that shout
Cars whizzing by, lots of traffic jams as well.
Children watching out, while they're about.
Coloured vans, cars and bikes,
Waiting for red, amber, green lights.
Children talking while they're walking
Then back to school for the working of their local walk.

Maria Lunnon (Age 11)

Dennis The Dog

Dennis the dog
Was dressed up like a clown
He liked to hang upside down

He wore blue trousers
And a black tie
Behind his back, he hid a pie!!

Dominic Loomes (Age 9)

Deep Space

Is there anything more wondrous,
Than the wonders of the world?
That defies time and gravity,
And go on forever, for all infinity.

Since man has understood stars,
Man has ached to experience,
But is so diminutive,
To suppose life that's primitive.

Extra terrestrials are visualised futuristic,
Floating vehicles and bug eyes,
Three fingers and a big head,
With minds as heavy as lead.

The most exciting thing about space,
Must be the super massive black holes,
At the centre of our galaxy,
Travelling to which would be daring.

Space has an extreme existence,
Long before you and I,
But we cannot witness first hand,
But can see from the sea or on land.

Steven Melia-Chamberlain (Age 13)

Jumbo Fire

Blazing fire spreads across the cave,
Getting hotter, bigger
The animals scared, bad tempered leaping out,
Hiding away.
Hunters scared, guilty as well.
The animals confused no way out
Trying to find a safe place to hide.

Bethany Lealman (Age 8)

Haiku

I do like forests
The trees that are so fragrant
Beautiful to me.

Antony McMurdo (Age 12)

Dark Night

The stars were winking and blinking in the sky
And the moon stared like a big silver eye.
The wind fingers stroking my face,
As the shadows dance to the bass
The crickets chirping like a choir of strings
As the nightingale sings to the moon.

Freya Lincoln (Age 9)

What Is?

What is a bird?
An animal with wings,
What is a toy box?
Something that holds things.

When does a cat purr?
When it is happy,
When does a baby cry?
When it needs its nappy.

What makes a tree grow?
Water and soil,
What do you wrap sandwiches up with?
Plastic bags and tin foil.

What are cactus?
Spiky plants,
What are ballerinas?
People that dance.

What is jewellery?
Necklaces and rings,
What is a pop star?
Someone that sings.

Chloe Makin (Age 7)

Art

I like art its really fun
Getting messy using paints
Smudging chalks and drawing saints
Using pencils using pastels
Using crayons copying flowers
But the best thing I must say
Is getting messy - hooray

Jenny Lucas (Age 9)

A Monkey's Tea

It swings on a tree
Eats bananas for dessert
And black bugs for tea

Khalid McMahon (Age 8)

Snow Flakes

From the unlit sky they drift,
They cast frosty, shadowed icy paths,
Pearl white blankets they crate,
Half-heartedly they freeze you,
Shivering icicles drip,
Bright and shiny,
Clear as a crystal.

Stephanie Lampshire (Age 11)

If You Want to See A Tiger

If you want to see a tiger
You must slowly creep into the creepy jungle
I know a tiger who's living down there,
He's very creepy, he jumps out at you quickly
Yes, if you really want to see a tiger
You must slowly creep into the jungle, keep quiet.
Go down into the jungle and say
"You don't scare me, if you want some meat
Go far in the jungle and find some and don't come back to me.
But if you do come back I will give you some meat."

Jessica Lane (Age 8)

Last Night I Had A Dream . . . . . I Met The Queen

Last night I had a dream . . . . I met the Queen
Quietly I walked across the great big hall.
Up and up the very tall stairs I went, I looked really small.
Everything looked so big.
Every step I took echoed through the big palace.
Nearer and nearer I got to the Queen. Then I saw her
She said "hello", I said "hello" back.

That was my dream about meeting the Queen.

Ruby Lewis (Age 8)

That's My Cat!

The cat that prowls around silently, slyly, sluggishly.
That's my cat!
The cat that pricks his ear while listening, looking, lurking.
That's my cat!
The cat that whips his tail hurriedly, hastily, happily.
That's my cat!
The cat that laps up milk quietly, quickly like a queen.
That's my cat!

Siobhan Langley (Age 10)

Night Fall

Silence falls around the stones,
Sounds of stones crumbling
Moonlight shines around me,
Quietly stands while years go by,
Towering high above them,
Slowly sinking into the ground
Staring up to the Gods above them.

Emily Long (Age 8)

Food

Eggs, kipper, sausage and chips,
Doughnuts that make you lick your lips,
Crisps, fruit, chocolate and sweets,
Ice-cream, biscuits and other treats,
Chicken, pizza, pork chops and fish,
Sausage and beans make a good dish,
Orange, apple, banana and pear,
African fruit is very rare,
Sandwich, pasty, roll and bun,
Some have cheese in, so give me one,
Tomato, lettuce and carrots too,
Make a salad that's good for you,
Breakfast, dinner, lunch and tea,
I like food as you can see!

Callum Lytton (Age 8)

Where I Live

I like my home near the sea,
A place that is just right for me,
Built upon the side of a hill,
The air around is far from still.
Try and guess the place I live in,
By using the clues that I have given.
Broadstairs is the name of the place,
Where life moves at a slower pace.

Ben Lavender (Age 10)

Sunrise

Sunrise,
A beam of light shining brightly,
Sunrise,
Warming the earth with its light,
Sunrise,
Flowers, trees and gardens revealed,
For all the world to see,
Sunrise.

Jamie Lakey (Age 10)

My Puppy

She's small
She's cute
She's black and
She's fluffy
She's hurt her paw

Danielle Marchment (Age 7)

Tasty, Crunch, Yummy Fruit

Oranges are round, juicy and sweet.
They look so good to eat.
They look very scrummy and yummy.
First they are picked.
Then washed and dried.
That's why they are shiny on the outside!

Grapes are juicy they are sweet
They are good, so good to eat.
They are yummy they are good.
Eat them! Eat them!
Please, you should.

Strawberries are shaped like an oval.
They're juicy, tasty and sweet
They are good to eat.
Yum! Yum! Yum! in my tum! tum!

Alice Malcolm (Age 7)

Nanny

I can remember a time,
From yester year.
When I sat on your lap,
And never shed a tear.
You gently rocked me to sleep,
At the end of the day.

You'd stroke my hair,
With your soft caress.
Hold me close, in a loving embrace.
I'd close my eyes,
And be in heaven.

One morning I knocked on your door.
I tried to wake you,
But all was in vain.
For from this sleep,
You'll never wake again.
An eternal slumber,
Of peace and serenity.
I love you Nanny.
Always remember me.

Kayleigh McMahon (Age 13)

Tiger

My teeth are sharp
My fur is stripy
I go out hunting in the night
I am a tiger watch out
I like eating monkeys
And antelope and sometimes you!

Joseph Mobbs (Age 7)

Christmas Time

Tinsel on the christmas tree
Presents on the floor
Mistletoe hanging from the ceiling
Holly on the door.

Baubles on the christmas tree
Lights, twinkling merrily
The smell of mince pies baking
To be enjoyed for tea.

Snowflakes falling from the sky
A shiver down my back
Did I see reindeer then
With Santa and his sack

The sound of song,
The carol singers singing of great festive cheer
Reminding us this time of year
That God, beloved, is near

David-Jon Meenaghan (Age 13)

A Baby's Odyssey Of Birth

An explosion of fantastic phlegm
Hurtled me through a winding wormhole
Winding, winding...
Like a yo-yo spinning in the air
Spinning, spinning...
I saw a sad world so that is where I go

Like a fireball scalding the world
I was rolling to the ground
Rolling, rolling...
A sloth's heart blowing up behind me
Rolling, rolling...
Like a sopranos voice in SLOW-MO
I came into the light.

I am a fresh round cabbage
My mouth starts to bubble like lava,
Like a fried egg frying,
An illiterately mad being.
I am a baby now, all through with birth.
Babbling, babbling...
A new beginning

Timothy Morris (Age 12)

Snakes

S limy snakes slithering across the rain forest
N ibbling left overs as it goes
A nd poisonous too
K nocking leaves as it goes
E ating little bugs
S ounding horrid

Louis Moore (Age 7)

A Nightmare

One thing is I don't know why,
My teacher was flying in the sky.
I saw him on a witches broom,
Gliding in my stinky room.

I ran indoors and up the stairs,
And caught him scoffing my eclairs.
I tried to stop this evil beast,
Eating my eclairs for a feast.

He went down stairs to find some toast
I hope he doesn't spot my roast.
But with my luck he ate it all,
And pushed me out into the hall.

I asked him why he had done this deed,
He said he was looking for a feed,
Why did you go in my room?
He said so I can use his broom.

He said he was sorry and said goodbye
But I know my teacher and that's a lie.
In the end he flew by,
Carrying my last pork pie.

Jamie Mountford (Age 12)

Michael Owen

I'm writing a poem
About Michael Owen
The footballer we'd all like to be.

The sound of applause
With the goals that he scores
Makes us happy especially me.

With his red and white kit
Looking so fit
Just what we all want to see.

When I dream in school
About Liverpool
I know exactly who I want to be!

Ben Mills (Age 7)

Our Dads

Dads go to work
Dad plays with me
Dads make dinner
Dads decorate
Dads wash the plates
Dad gives me shoulder rides
We love our dads

Sophie Maude (Age 6)

My Family

My Mum's always great to me,
She lets me make pancakes for tea,
She gives me a cuddle when I'm feeling sad,
She's always around me which makes me glad.

My Dad sometimes acts a fool,
Although I think he's really cool,
He teases me and makes me wild,
It's really great to be his child.

Gemma, well she's my big sister,
When she's not around I really do miss her,
She looks after me when Mum and Dad are out,
She doesn't usually have to shout.

I have another sister called Kerry,
She is always chatty and merry,
She doesn't stop talking to me from morning till night,
To have her around is an absolute delight.

Then there's me, Rebecca Kirsti,
Quite nutty, a loon, that's me,
A bit of a joker when I'm not at home,
I couldn't imagine being alone.

Rebecca Mullett (Age 11)

The Moon Is...

A scoop of vanilla ice cream in a black bowl
Loads of bombs gone off
A lump of cheese in a dark fridge
A luminous smile
Sweetcorn on a black plate
A ghostly face
A child's dream holiday
A torch in a black night
A bitten biscuit
A cricket ball
A massive jewel.

Emma Maxwell (Age 12)

The Queen

In my dream I met the Queen
Riding in a limousine.
I asked how many years she had been on the throne
She replied, fifty years.
She asked me where I lived
I said Aston Abbotts.
The Queen was fading,
It was my mum I was late for school!

Louis Lacovara (Age 7)

The Lone Skier

The lone skier whizzes down the slope,
The cool, fresh air whistling through his hair.
Behind him is a deer,
Looking at him through her long eyelashes.
The lone skier whizzes down the slope.

The lone skier stops to look at the magnificent mountains,
Covered in a white blanket of snow.
In the trees beside him stands a deer,
Gazing at the skier.
The lone skier stops to look at the white mountains.

The lone skier skids to a halt at the bottom,
And sweeps his eyes up the mountain.
He spots the deer looking out at the valley,
With the wind ruffling her fur.
The lone skier has not been alone.

Emma Marsh (Age 14)

Into The Breach

Fleeing from the hunting hounds of hell.
Seeking safe sanctuary 'way the eye of the storm.'
Terror.
Blind to all but an escape route.
Jaws of death snapping, yet tasting.

Reaching home, a hole to hide in.
Barrage of blows, threatening still.
They prey and the predator.
Now it knows its only path.
A path we are all walking.

It does the only thing left to be done.
Set up spiders have strangled it in web.
Another victim.
Nothing is done to help its 'worthless' cause.
It steps outside.

James McIntosh (Age 14)

Orange

Orange is the smell of the stuffy classroom that
Poor pupils have been stuck in all afternoon.

Orange feels like the rough grooves embedded
In the thick treetrunk's bark.

Orange is the sound of the crackle of a Skip crisp
Sizzling and melting in your mouth.

Orange tastes like a lime peel,
It is the sight of a sandy brick stuck to your house.

Orange is this orange poem.

Sarah Mosely (Age 11)

My House

My house is big and bold,
Nearly everything in it is silver or gold,
My bedroom is big,
My brother's is small,
Mine is tidy,
His is dull.

My garden is massive,
Although it seems to be small.
My dad has a shed,
Full of old and new tools.

I am so grateful,
To have a huge house.
I try so hard to look after it,
So it doesn't look like a big rubbish pit.

Katie Manning (Age 9)

It Was Just Black

I'm walking along a road
The lamps are dull not bright,
I start to turn onto a path
And there's still no light.

I turn around a corner
The lake is cold and bare,
I look to where the playground is
But there is nothing there.

I start to walk back home
Back to number ten,
Suddenly I hear a cockerel
And a clucking hen.

I like the sound of the cockerel
It tells me morning is near,
Soon the blackness of the night
Will gradually disappear.

William Madge (Age 8)

Desert Wasp

Hovering, flying
Ready, spying
Comes in for the kill
Spider left, no life, no will.

They burst forth from it's stomach
And eat it's flesh
They destroy it's body
The soul of their créche.

They fly away for another day
To prey upon another victim.

Jamie Minhinnick (Age 11)

An Early Morning Journey

I was so comfy and warm in my own little dreamy world,
Not a sole could get me if I was wrapped up in bed.
The cosy warmth of the room helped my eyes become droopy.
I always used to look forward to it the night before, but not remember
A thing the next morning, my head stuffed with dreamy thoughts.
The memory of my most recent fantasy was rapidly trickling away as I woke.
Clenching the soft duvet in my fists and pulling my arms to my chest I thought, it's too early.

I heard a distant alarm go off, but still in and out of sleep it had no affect.
I snuggled back into my beloved environment.
Suddenly I felt giants hands creep under my relaxed body, startling me at first.
His arms were strong and they slowly lifted me high above my snug bed,
Still wrapped in my cacoon, I could hear distant whispers as I was carried away.

My mind was confused with the contrast. I cracked through my eggshell and stretched my wings.
I was sitting in a cold but stuffy car; the smells of poisonous exhaust smoke assaulted my nose.
I could see dew-wet grass and only silhouettes of the trees against the dawn-toned sky.
The early morning was crisp and pure; the street lamps appeared fuzzy out of the steamy windows.
I gazed at the empty road; it was silent. I heard the whispers again and identified Mum and Dad.
The low drone of the car engine started as my sister spoke my name.
We looked out the back window and waved goodbye to our little house on St. Brannocke Well Close.
'We'll be back soon.'

Ernest Martin (Age 13)

Going Far Away

Going far away,
Where we've
Never been
Before,
It is home time
Now.

Klein Mason (Age 8)

Christmas Jingle

Christmas is coming
Everyone's humming
I'm getting presents
Some people are peasants
There's a Christmas cheer
Every year
Yippee it's here
Will it snow
I don't know
Rudolph's nose glows
So Santa knows where to go
I've got a tree
With a key
Santa's elfs
Fill the shelves
I built a snowman
Called lowman
There's a sledge
On the window ledge.

Daniel Malcolm (Age 9)

Terrible Dream

It was an awful dream,
I dreamt that I was falling off the tallest tower,
My head swirling.
I was screaming out loud,
Falling down and down,
The ground getting closer and closer,
Colours were turning round and round in my head,
Getting worse and worse,
Red, yellow, grey, blue, orange and black,
The ground was so close now it was scary,
The last thing I saw was colours twirling all around,
Then I jerked awake and knew it was only a dream.

Franziska Marcheselli (Age 9)

The Jubilee Celebration

To celebrate the Queen's long reign,
People have come by car, bus and plane.
Great excitement all around.
The air is filled with joyous sound.

It's fifty years that she has ruled.
That allows all children a day off school.
And now they have come to celebrate.
A special day in history they will create.

Soon the Queen appears in a horse drawn carriage,
With all the glamour of a Royal marriage.
The crown jewels glisten in the bright sunlight.
The celebration is set to last all night.

Marcella Mackey (Age 8)

Dragon

Lonesome creature,
Dwells far from others.
Always alone;
Never a friend in the world.

Unveil this awesome creature.
See freedom, strength,
A fearless soul.
But nothing more.

In the air
Swoop and glide.
Never to be captured:
Always free.

But always one thing stays.
The greed, the want for more.
Always more, never less.
The curse that grips like an iron claw.

Flames come forth.
Bright and daunting.
But only cove
For a tormented heart.

Bryony Mather (Age 12)

Forget

I wrote a poem last week
But I forget how it went
So I'm afraid this will have to do.
Sorry!

Kevin McAuley (Age 16)

Inside My Head

Inside my head
There's a house
Full of ghosts
And screams for help

Inside my head
There's a land full
Of sweets and chocolate
Where nobody is ever hungry

Inside my head
There's a place filled
With rides and
People screaming

Inside my head
There's a wonderful place
There's fish and dolphins
Dancing together

Rebecca Melland (Age 8)

Dreams

Listen, in the dark, what can you hear?
Dreams, telling their stories.
Ignore the scientific facts
Dreams are what you want most and cannot have.
They're not what you're thinking of when you go to sleep,
They're your ultimate, innermost desires.
Waiting to show their true colours while you sleep.
Dreams are your sanctuary, from the real world.
Dreams are your wishes, spreading their wings,
Scattering showers of multicoloured light.

Nightmares, on the other hand,
Are evil dreams,
Banished from society.
Sowing wickedness, and polluting your mind,
With acid rain.
They're your phobias your worries, your prejudices.
Waiting and one night they will roam your head,
Dressed all in black, with tattered wings.
Destroying the innocence and purity,
Of your childhood mind.

Zoë Monnier-Hovell (Age 13)

Stonehenge

Stonehenge is standing while time goes by
Looking up to the heavens
Shining in the sun waiting to fall
Resting in the shadows
The moon shines onto the rocks

Joe Mesnard (Age 7)

Skateboarding

I like to skateboard back and forth
I can do good tricks like the Ollie North
I Kickflip, Heelflip and Backflip flare
I do all these tricks when I get big all.

I like to grind on big long rails
But you know there comes a stack and a bail
I get back up and skate some more
It's better than doing the house chores.

I Ollie down big stair sets
I Ollie over puddles without getting wet
I like to stall on big high walls
I hold it there without a fall.

I can Manuel from here to there
I now do this with great care
I like to skateboard all the way
So there you have it my skateboarding day.

Sean Melia (Age 11)

The Outing

We're dreaming sweet dreams, and then awake at dawn,
Travelling in the car is like one big yawn.

The destination's here, the sun's shining bright,
Playing childish games but always end in a fight.

Mothers talking, admiring the lovely day.
We hear the nearing tune, ice creams "Hurray!"

The cold sensation of ice cream lingers.
I make the water ripple with my fingers,

When I'm lying in the boat, soaking up the sun.
Mum's rowing hard kids have all the fun!

We settle down and get out the lovely food,
Tasty sandwiches and cakes put us in the right mood.

We pack away our picnics and head for the rocks,
Way down below kids are laughing on the docks.

We're fighting and climbing hoping not to fall,
People are bustling around like a busy shopping mall.

I scramble down the rocks to feed the ducks bread,
I feel so much happier now that they are fed.

I'm tired now, it's dark, and I can see the moon
I'm going home now, don't worry I'll be back again soon.

Jenny Marley (Age 14)

My Mum . . .

My mum is the one who has golden brown hair,
My mum is the one who looks after me,
My mum s the one who tucks me into bed,
My mum is the one who reads me stories each night,
My mum is the one who takes me to places at the weekend,
My mum does all these things.

Beth Mortimer (Age 6)

Ghost Poem

In the dark of the night I'm walking home,
Turning, twisting, terrified and alone.
The wind is howling, swaying, moaning.
Every noise sends my stomach churning.
Realisation occurs, the wind is still,
I'm not alone, the air is filled,
With ghoulish, grotesque bodies around,
No human elements to be found,
Screeching, shrieking, slicing through the air
No-one to help me, no-one to care.
I hear the screaming inside my head,
The noise now is mine-please don't let me be dead!

Laura Murphy (Age 12)

Holiday

I remember the sea
Rough and getting black near the shore
Pushing me back and splashing me
Rocking the pedal boat
Rocking, falling.

I remember the pedal boat
Taking us too far out
Scratching me after I jumped in
The bright sea,
Hurt me.

I remember the sand
Roaring hot and black
Dirtying my feet
Black,
Dirty.

I remember the people
A friendly old lady, helping us
A small girl, asking to be my friend
A kind man, looking after our shoes
Friends are good to have.

Stacey McLeod (Age 11)

Sidcup!!!

The children play down the park
Kicking the football.
Skipping
Trees to climb
Lots more games to play
Only dodging the cars from
Road to park from park to road
Down out side my house.

Lauren Merrell (Age 12)

Wasp

His skin is yellow fury
Eyes are made of fire
He wants a lot of food
He is in desire

His body is a gold mine
Because his stripes are gold
He gives a sting like a needle
And he is very bold.

He flies around the sky,
And as a bird of terror
He flies around the sky
And is light as a feather.

Noel Martin (Age 9)

Scaly Dragon, Christian Knight

Upon a hilltop late one night,
Scaly dragon, Christian Knight,
Claws and jaws and sword and shield,
Stood face to face on Battle Field.

The sequin spangled overcoat,
The teeth of gleaming pearl,
The claws of ice that shatter night,
And tail with mocking curl.

The mail in the silver light,
The blade of moonlight great,
The visor which enhances sight,
And shield with crest of saint.

The toss of head,
Blood chilling roar,
The swish of tail,
The widening jaw.

They circled the black hilltop,
The canvas wings set sail,
The sword flashed in the dim light,
Which power did prevail?

Natasha Moakes (Age 11)

Mary's Ball

Mary's ball as light as a feather
Mary's ball all different colours
Mary's ball flew over the wall
Mary's ball never came back
Mary's ball came back again
Mary threw it back over again
She threw it too hard she couldn't catch it

Ella Montgomery (Age 8)

Mothers

You only have one mother
Treasure her with love
For one day she will join
The angels up above.

Up above where it is magic
And no-one cares who you are
Maybe she belongs up there
To be treated like a star

But at the moment she is with you
Love her and she will love you
You only have one mother
Treasure her with love
For one day she will join
The angels up above.

Kayleigh Muir (Age 13)

The Sight Collector

A stranger called this morning
Dressed all in black and grey
Put every sight into a bag
And carried them away

The smile of my sister
The red glowing sun
The colour of my bedroom
The icing on a bun

The prettiness of the flowers
The writing in my book
The darkness of my shadow
The brilliant meals I cook

The shape of my hair clips
The colour of shirt sleeves
The refreshing colour of a rainbow
The crispy autumn leaves

A stranger called this morning
He didn't leave his name
He left us truly sightless
Life will never be the same

Sarah Maude (Age 9)

The Red Sun

The red sun
The red sun is boiling hot
The red sun is fiery
The red sun is like the planet Venus
The red sun is bigger than the planet Venus
The red sun is a big ball of fire
The red sun can burn if you go too near

Molly McGowan (Age 7)

Who Is She?

She visits many countries
To see if they are interesting

Shakes people's hands
Looks around schools

Rides in a carriage
Rides on a horse

Watches people work
Wears a golden crown

She is very kind
She makes people happy

Emma Marriott (Age 8)

Mosquito

Sticking to the wall,
I warm up my wings and patiently watch Adolf Hitler.
I smell his warm, sweet, tasty blood.

Dusk creeping in swallowing the pink and grey sky.
I bend my thin knees then leap like a spring of the wall.

I buzz. I buzz in Adolf Hitler's ears. It irritates him.
I dodge his hands which try to hit me and sting me on the nose.
I hear his shouts; it makes me laugh.

I flee to tell my friends what I have done.
They inspect me carefully.
Soon it will be midnight: feeding time.

Midnight dawns on us.
Our bulgy eyes look in all directions then we all leap at the same time.

We prepare ourselves for an invasion.

We swarm the houses looking and smelling for blood.
We insert our noses into their necks we hear their immense pain
We sting drawing the blood of "powerful" leaders,
Of famous people and of Kings and Queens.

The invasion is over! We have won the war.
Back to the underground.

Kemo Marriott (Age 13)

My Mum

My mum looks like a flower with blue petals.
My mum sounds as good as Hollywood 7.
My mum smells as good as a flower that smells like perfume.
My mum tastes like a wedding cake.
My mum feels like a silk cushion.

Lydia McMillan (Age 5)

The Magic Box

I will put in the box - A tiny star from the midnight sky
Some soft notes from a music box, a silk picture of a purple flower

I will put in the box - A blade of the greenest grass
A spine of the smallest porcupine, a fragment of the biggest leaf

I will put in the box - The loudest cry of a baby
The biggest wish of a scots man, the smallest step on a beach

I will put in the box - The sun on a rainbow
A zombie on a flying rug, a horse on a man

My box is made of the finest wood
Silver moons and gold stars, on the lid are tiny waves.

I shall swim with the dolphins
Ride free with wild horses and cure animals from diseases.

Janine Masters (Age 12)

Bright Kite

Bright
Kite in the
Night up at
Height in the night
Shine light on
The night held
Tight in the
Night
With
All
My
M
i
g
h
t
.
.
.
.
.

Stacey Mayo (Age 10)

Rain

Rain is like an invasion,
With lots of drops of rain,
Every day you go out in it,
You will feel the pain.

Rain makes big puddles
Which us children play in.
Rain falls on the window,
Which makes a big din.

Rain makes things wet,
Apart from waterproofs,
My house has leaks,
From the roof.

Samuel Marker (Age 8)

The Ocean Is...

A salty fish bowl,
A huge puddle,
A dolphin's playground,
A huge collection of shells,
A ton of water,
A shark's heaven,
A fishes nightmare,
A whale's world,
A road of sand,
A polluted puddle,
A million ton of rocks,
A lobster's home,
A seal's destiny,
A crab's castle.

Kate McNichol (Age 11)

Change

The summer
Still brings
Beach and castles
With children playing
Like it did last year

The autumn
Still hangs
Green and brown trees
Like it did last year

The winter
Still comes
Snow and fog
With frost all around
Like it did last year

The spring
Still rain
Littered showers mornings
With sunlight
Like it did last year

Kerry Munnings (Age 9)

What Is The Moon?

The moon is a white cloud
It is a white sheepskin

Kayley Marshall (Age 8)

Journey Downstairs

As I tiptoe down the stairs
Cowardly at two o'clock
On christmas day
Trying to rush
But also to be slow
Trying to be very very quiet
Frantically I crawl into the front room
But there it is
There's the feeling
I can just smell the mince pie now
Just taste the jam tarts now
Just feel the icy snow now
Just eat the pud and cream now
But there it was
There it was
There was my very own
Christmas present
Gleaming with light
But then, then, then
Mother.

Kelly McDowall (Age 9)

Daffodil

Scratching slowly through the soil,
Quietly solemnly
My nose, legs and arms appear,
Sniffing the earthy soil.

Voicelessly swaying in the wind,
By night my mate appears beside me,
When morning comes, a little pool of us
Orange, yellow, white.

By night a pool becomes a sea,
In the morning we have our daily diet
Of water and sun.

Dewdrops on our petals,
Trickling quietly,
Making us soft and silky.

We multiply by night,
And stand as an army by day.

Lisa Machen (Age 11)

Rain

Drip drop splish splash
We're jumping in the muddy puddle
Drip drop splish splash
Pitter patter in the streets
Drip drop splish, splash
Up the streets and back again
Drip drop splish splash

Ian Marriott (Age 7)

The Sun

Bright golden disk
Shimmering in the sky
A yellow sun flower
Smiling down at me

A rich orange glow
Warming up the sky
A hot ball of fire
Just watch it glow

A glimmering CD
Dancing above our heads
Makes me happy
When I'm feeling blue

Then at dusk
It changes the sky
All filled with magic
And beautiful colours

Kirsty Mackellar (Age 10)

Why???

Why do plants photosynthesise?
Why do animals have a different size?
Is there intelligence in the universe?
How did we learn to converse?
Why doesn't the moon fall from the sky?
Why do scientists always ask why?

Why does the sun burn in the sky?
How can some animals fly?
Why do some animals have tails?
Why are slugs with shells called snails?
Why did the big bang happen?
Why does science bore most children?

Robert May (Age 11)

Queen Elizabeth

Q uite a remarkable lady.
U sually with Prince Phillip.
E legant.
E ach day another visit.
N ever goes anywhere alone.

E verybody wants to meet her.
L ovely jewellery.
I s very elegant.
Z oom lenses take her pictures.
A lways the Ambassador.
B uckingham Palace is her London home.
E xtremely busy.
T ime to congratulate her Golden Jubilee.
H appy Birthday your majesty!

Chloe Malin (Age 9)

Ready For September

From summer skirts, shorts and stuff
To itchy trousers and scratchy shirts
A week before school
Your hair gets cut shiny and new
(Not like it used to)
As new and shiny as your new new shoes

Bethan Morris (Age 9)

Spiral Galaxy

Bright splodges of paint exploding.
Early Christmas lights.
Crystals smashed - flown into space
The middle's like a second sun
A loose spiral in the sky

James Martin (Age 10)

Feelings

My anger is sometimes indescribable
It lashes out, like a sword
Slicing through hearts of steel.

My happiness is like a blast
Of laughter, joy, and song
Feeding the world.

My rage sears through the emptiness
Of my forgotten realm
My rage makes aggression, seem like a lamb.

My loneliness rings through my mind
Tearing through my head
With the pain of reality, the torture of souls.

My peace is like a river
Trickling over the ground
Fish darting, hoping for success.

My regret has disappeared
Gone to the wind
Like a grain of sand on a beach

Ross Ian McDowall (Age 10)

The Day I Dream I See The Queen

I dream, I dream,
I see the Queen,
Tall and smart, in her palace,
Chandeliers, bright red rubies,
Shining diamonds, glittering emeralds

I dream, I dream,
I see the Queen,
Eating dinner, watching TV,
Mile long dresses, bright black shoes,
Crown on her head, sitting on her throne.

I dream, I dream,
I see the Queen
Lying in bed
Taking off her crown, putting on her pyjamas
Drifting off to sleep

Out the big strong doors,
Home I go looking at
The bright gold carriage
Time for my bed
I dream, I dream

Gary McGinn (Age 10)

The Elves And The Shoemaker

A man in a business with shoes
Gave customers boots for their toes
But one day, he got a shock,
His money had run out like sheep in a stock
He said without further ado,
"Oh dear, I need more kinds of shoe!"
But something ripped up his despair
A light showed up in the air.
The light turned into an elf,
And he said "Hello my name is Nelf!"
The elf said he could help,
About the money disappearing off his shelf.
His plan was to make shoes of new kinds.
But they would have to try lots of times.
After lots of hard working weeks
The shop was so big, there was no chance of leaks.
The shoemaker said "Thank you Nelf!"
"You really put life back on my shelves!"

Callum McMillan (Age 9)

Red

Red is the colour of my handwriting pen
Red is the tomato being munched by my brother
Red is the colour of my girlfriend's lips
Red is the colour of Luke's rosy cheeks
Red is the colour of my writing in my book
Red is the colour of my scruffy jotter
Red is the colour of my literacy folder and book

Thomas Mason (Age 8)

The Playground

Silent, mouselike
Like a mouth waiting to be fed
The thunder rumbling like an empty stomach
The wind howling like ghost children
Desolate, a tense silence
Trees wave their gnarled fingers
Bidding the last moments of peace farewell
Suddenly the doors burst open,
A stream of red and grey flows out
A crowd of obstreperous children
Running, walking
Whispering, shouting
Until the clamour of the bell
The clouds stare down upon bare tarmac
Fallen leaves jump across the ground
Benches sigh with joy,
As the only thing that climbs on them are the raindrops
The wind caresses the tree tops
Harmony returns

Rachel McGoff (Age 11)

Bad Weather

When I hear thunder,
Oh how I wonder,
When will it decide to stop.

Lightning so high,
Cracking the sky,
Making sounds, crack, sizzle, pop.

And when I see rain,
It drives me insane,
Hearing sounds pitter, patter, plop.

Hear the wind blow,
Ever so low,
Slowly...Slowly...STOP!

Daniel Muldoon (Age 10)

The Eye

Eye eye, squishy eye
In my big head
Made of jelly with a big black hole
Swimming in a pool of tears.

Blinking in the hot sun
Eye-lashes stop the dirty stuff from . . .
Getting in!

Seeing things coming towards me
Get out if you can.

Jessie Mainor (Age 8)

Sports Day!

Sports is really fun,
Pace you need in a race.
Obstical courses are really tough,
Running I'm good at,
Training is needed,
Sweating likely.

Delight when you've finished,
Air drives you through the hurdles
Year, it happens every year.

Sports day beats work,
It's a bit tough,
Someone at the end might go in a huff
There's always fun for all.

You scurry off in the 100 metre race,
To win it you need a bit of pace,
To do the hurdles you need to jump,
To cool you off you need a water pump.

Luke Murphy (Age 10)

Snowscape

A soft downy chick wonders which of these awkward black-on-white blurs is its mother
One hundred thousand shrill calls arise; each one a unique blend of trills and subtle crescendos
But one voice raises above the rest, calling guidance, and the plump chick answers;
A tiny, high voice, barely audible above the crash of waves and squeak of penguin
Yet it is recognised, and one blur waddles nearer, until the minute specks of black are visible on its sleek chest,
The odds are against this chick though. Newly born it is defenceless, buffeted by high gales, the piercing cold.
The Leopard Seals wait until the mother grows weary, then home in for the kill.
The chick is lucky, this time.
One year later . . . .
A soft downy chick wonders which of these awkward black-on-white blurs is its mother
One hundred thousand shrill calls arise; each one a unique blend of trills and subtle crescendos
The mother hears the chick's pleading, wavering, high voice
And suddenly senses the presence of Leopard Seals.
Remembering her own close encounter as a chick
She instinctively runs to protect her unguarded baby.
The chick is lucky, this time.

Patrick McEntee (Age 13)

Spring

Daffodils bursting into life, tulips and blue bells,
And oh such sweet smell
All rejoicing in the shining sun,
It makes me wake up no longer glum.

We like to play in the shining light,
All our faced beaming bright
Fun, fun, fun in the shining sun,
Fun to be had by everyone.

Evening comes
And the sun goes to bed
We all lay down our sleepy heads.

Chloe Murray (Age 8)

Ocean Deep

In the depths deep, deep down,
Under the sea there's another town.
A water world this place would be,
Down there, under the sea.

Fish swim in schools watch out for the net!
Down in the deep, it's very wet.
There's a rotting shipwreck down there in the sea,
Full of treasure, for you and me.

Dolphins swim in this wonderful world,
Shells lay scattered we are told.
Divers swim down to take a peep,
At this world, when sharks sleep.

Sea weed grows on the sand,
Rocks with mussels a world that's grand.

Rose Mortimer (Age 8)

Spring Is Awake Again

A stir of flower petals
A crack of an egg,
A pour of fresh water,
A handful of spring air.
Whisk a handful of leaves.
A pinch of some daffodil pollen,
Sieve some spring blossom
Spread some strips of grass.
Roll the spring colours,
Sweeten the spring daisies
Whip the spring lambs
Beat the spring smell.

Sian Morgan (Age 9)

The Queen

I have seen the Queen.
She's not tall,
but small.
It's her golden Jubilee,
you see.
She wore her crown,
whilst visiting our town.
We had a party in our street,
with lots of lovely food to eat.
It was a huge celebration,
to remember the Queen's coronation.
I was given a souvenir spoon,
and I was totally over the moon.
We had such fun,
in the warm summer sun.
And we toasted the Queen.
But how I did scream.
When Mum came and said,
"Now come on Olivia it's time for your bed!"

Olivia Moor (Age 8)

The Cat

The cat wiggled through a crack in the thick, brick wall, and jumped up onto an apple tree's branch. The cat then looked down upon the great, green grass and noticed a little round robin, pecking at a crusty crumb of bread. The cat leapt and sped away, after the pecking bird. The bird looked up and gazed lazily at the cat and with one final look, the bird flew away. The cat groaned with disappointment, and crawled under an emerald, green bush to wait for its next prey. The cat's eyes began to droop and he looked at the wild garden before him, and fell asleep.

One eye popped open, and then the other. It was pitch black and only the moon above lit the garden and its adventures lurking in the depths. The Cat's eyes sparkled and he strutted around the garden, swinging his tail high in the air. His ears pricked up and his eyes grew wild. A mouse was scurrying across the grass. The cat sprawled across the grass and pounced on the small creature and slashed his claws against the mouse's neck, the mouse fell helplessly to the ground. The cat, proud of its capture, carried the mouse back to his den and lay it on the doorstep of his loyal companion. He pattered one soft paw on the door, and made a high pitched, pleading call. Footsteps were coming from behind the door.

Rachel Moden (Age 13)

Clear Round

The horse gracefully went into a trot,
The prancing round quite a lot.
As she flew over the first fence-
The crowd went all silent and tense.
Next was greatest of all, the hedge,
After that the plunge onto the water's ledge.
Cantering around she was faced with the wall,
Over they flew no problem at all.
At last the final fence appeared,
This was the one she most feared.
None of the poles came clattering to the ground,
Yes, they had done it, a CLEAR ROUND!

Kirsty Marren (Age 11)

The Moon

The moon is as glittery as a star
It is beautiful as can be.

It looks like an eye spying at you.
It is a football in the sky.

As soft as cotton.
It looks like a plate
And it can't go down.

I like the moon very much.
The moon is good.

Emily Morrison (Age 5)

The Bed Monster

There's something under my bed.
His tummy's rummbling like it's never been fed
And it smells like my dad's feet
And like Grandma's old meat

It's now crawling up my covers
And jumping on me like my brothers
It's dribbling on my leg
Like a yellow rotten egg

It's now licking my face
At a fairly quick pace
It's a monster no it's not ..
It's my fluffy dog Spot

Joseph Morgan (Age 9)

Trick Or Treat

Trick or treat trick or treat
If you don't, smell our feet.
On Halloween go trick or treating,
Leave when the full moon is gleaming.

Trick or treat trick or treat,
If you don't, smell our feet,

Witches and ghouls will arise,
So better go in disguise.

Trick or treat trick or treat
If you don't, smell our feet. . . .

Ahh! a ghost has spotted me!!!

Jessica Mancoo (Age 8)

Goodbye For I Must Go

Goodbye for I must go to Seatown near the sea.
With pebbles which may warm on beaches
And sun and sea shining
On the beaches of Golden Cap.

Even in winter it's like a frozen lake,
For the waves are frosty hands,
And the wind is Jack Frost breath.
And I can see enormous waves
Thrashing and crashing in war.
I'm watching from an Inn with chips in front.

In the summer Seatown is a flower
And the hills look like gold
And seas are lapping like cats.
I'm listening from a canvas tent
With a cool, chocolate milkshake.
I should be very content.

Goodbye for I must go, and though the journey sickens,
I must say goodbye to the country
And to the town of sea,
For now and evermore.

Cressida Mason-Fayle (Age 10)

Football

Kicking
Up from the ground
Passed the midfield players.
Tackled the defenders and shot
A goal!

Connor Mattimore (Age 8)

Foxes

Foxes foxes,
Don't kill foxes
For they have a right live.

Though they're a pest to farmers,
And kill chickens all the time,
For fixes have a right to live.

Don't chase the foxes, just for a sport,
With dogs chasing them day and night,
For foxes have a right live.

Protect the foxes, don't kill the foxes,
And ban the hunting games,
For foxes have a right to live.

Foxes Foxes,
Don't kill foxes,
For they have a right to live!

Lee Marriott (Age 10)

The Sea World

A girl is lying on a rock -
Dazed, as the ripples move around her.
And yet, it looks as if she is floating
On top of the ocean's light fingers.
The wind beats the girl, but yet,
She still stays dazed
As if hypnotised
By the beauty of the horizon.

Still she stays on her tiny universe of rock.
The breeze creeps past with gentle tread,
Brushing her hair back,
Picking her up as if she were a feather.
As the seas' sweet touch splashes her face,
She opens her eyes and smiles.

I hide quickly behind a tree.
She walks away and yet,
Not a sound comes from her shoes.
Her hair whispers behind her like magic thread.
I creep down to my own home
And close my eyes and dream of the sea.

Maud Morrish (Age 8)

In the Jungle

Roar roar roar tiger roaring in a jungle
Roar roar roar tiger can you see a jumble

Roar roar roar tiger roaring in the jungle
Roar roar roar tiger roaring in a flood.

Roar roar roar roaring against the flood
Roar roar roar tiger roaring on a flood.

Jerome Mason (Age 6)

My Best Friend

Andy is my friend
He's really really 'good'
But sometimes he can
Drive me round the bend.

At maths he works out every sum
He's really really good
But if he's stuck on a question
He will look ever so glum.

He's always always answering
He can usually get four right
If he gets it wrong
He goes deadly white.

Conner Matthews (Age 8)

Francis Drake Poem

There was a boy called Francis Drake, he went on a journey that he could make,
Francis rode on a brown wooden boat, and he went with his lucky yellow coat.

They stopped for a break at the friendly spanish, he slept in a hut what looked like a palace.
When night time came the Spanish attacked, Francis threw them off with their bags unpacked.

He left the Spanish and sailed back to Plymouth, and saw the lovely Queen Elizabeth,
She thanked him and gave a hand, but he had to leave to the next American land.

He decided to sail back to the Spanish, his crew did not see him because he went in a vanish,
The journey was long and cold, but they stole silver and gold.

When Francis and the crew got back home, everybody thought they're not alone,
He threw his sweaty clothes in the bin, while Queen Elizabeth crowned him.

While the party was going for him, Queen Elizabeth opened a bottle of gin,
He said all this sailing made me thin, and threw the healthy stuff in the bin.

Abigail Louise Moyes (Age 9)

Colour

What is red?
- It is blood racing down a stinging cut knee
What is green?
- It is the summer leaves swaying in the breeze
What is blue?
- It is the cloudy sky looking down on us
What is orange?
- It is a cute cat's ginger fur pouncing on birds
What is purple?
- It is a bunch of grapes on a crowded market stall
What is white?
- It is a falling snowflakes outside, landing on the soft snow

Jessica Mills (Age 10)

The Sniffing Contest

Today was the day it was time to begin
As the Mothers sit round sipping their gin.
The children lined up all in a row
As the mothers shouted "What ever you do don't blow your nose".

Then the Judge with a yelp straightened his back
Put on his glasses and hung up his mac.
He inspected the children and announced with a grin
"Let's get this contest started let the sniffing begin".

The kids were all sizes, some short and some tall
It was very hard to tell who sniffed best of all.
On the end of the row stood a sweet little girl,
Her hair brushed and shiny and hanging in curls.

This little girl's sniff was as loud as could be
It even shook birds out of their trees,
She was the clear winner and that was for sure,
She won two boxes of tissues and a round of applause.

Charlotte Morley (Age 9)

Place To Place

Place to place
Place to place
How do I get there?
A running race

Bus to train,
Train to plane,
How do I get there?
It's a pain.

Scooter to bike
Bike to car
How do I get there?
I'm going to Par

Robert McClelland (Age 9)

Seasons

When Autumn comes
The leaves do fall
They cover the ground
For us to clear.
When winter comes
Rain does fall
It makes us wet
But not for long
When spring comes
Temperature does rise
But not too hot
As that's to come
When summer comes
Sun does shine
It gives us a tan
Oh give me mine.

Terri McBeth (Age 12)

How Things Have Changed

There used to be no TV, now the world is full of them,
You used to have to walk everywhere, no cars to drive you there,
I wonder how you lived with no TV or cars?

No high heels, instead low flat boots,
No crop tops to go out in,
I wonder how you lived with no high heels or crop tops?

No noisy washing machines, back then the tubs,
The grubby clothes instead of funky ones,
I wonder how you lived with no washing machines and having grubby clothes?

No Elvis Presley or the Beatles,
Instead S Club 7 and Hearsay,
I wonder how you lived with no S Club 7 or Hearsay?

Your life was very different not having these things,
But instead you had others,
That we will never have.

Roma Macphail (Age 8)

Dreams

Dreams are like invisible friends,
They re-create memory's,
They tell you stories that never end.

Dreams are like movies,
But each time you watch them,
They're never quite the same.

Dreams are like ghosts,
Once you get interested,

They Disappear!!

Victoria McLennan-Wiggin (Age 10)

There's something In the Freezer

There's something in the freezer,
It's eaten all the food,
It's smelly and it's not in a very good mood.
There's something in the freezer
It smells a bit like cheese,
I hope it stays there so it will freeze.
There's something in the freezer
It's smelly and it's not in a very good mood
There's something in the freezer
It's face is black and white
It does not come out in day time,
But it comes out at night.
There's something in the freezer,
It came into my room,
So I hit it on the head
With a kitchen broom.

Lauren Mott (Age 8)

Pancakes

Mix the bowl
It goes in the pan
It goes sizzle sizzle
Toss it in the air
It spirals
It lands in the pan
I catch it
I eat it
Yummy!

Kate Marks (Age 5)

Fire

Flames burning red and hot
An electrifying flame
Uncontrollable fire leaping in the air
Unbeatable fire burning
Blazing flames

Deer racing but flames too hot
Animals sprint and confused
Alarmed and frightened
Are the animals

Kristofer McLaren (Age 8)

The Sun

The flaming sun,
Brings all sorts of fun,
As it showers down its golden beams,
On earth there is a glistening gleam,

They make our planet very bright,
As we look up at its amazing height,
When we see it sitting in the sky,
We also wish we could fly,

When the sky is ruby red,
It's time for the sun to go to bed,
As it hides behind the distant hills,
It darkens houses and grey mills.

When it awakes in the morning time,
It shines on silvery snail slime.

Vicky Morriss (Age 9)

I Have A Hamster

I have a hamster, her name is Claws,
When she does tricks she gets a round of applause.

But...
Over the bed, squeeze through the funnel round her wheel
WATCH OUT FOR THAT TUNNEL!

I have a hamster she's golden and white
She is very friendly but cheeky at night

And then...
Over her bed, squeeze through the funnel round her wheel
WATCH OUT FOR THAT TUNNEL!

I have a hamster be careful she may bite
But only a nibble 'cos she's hungry at night.

So...
Over her bed, squeeze through the funnel round in her wheel
zzzzzzZZZZZZ! Shhhh
She's asleep in her tunnel

Bethany Miller (Age 10)

Weather

It's really good when the rain is about.
We can jump in puddles, scream and shout.
But come and shine burning sun.
When you come out we can all have fun.
In winter we might see the snow.
The children might think the rain is low!
Then we might have hail stones.
If you're unlucky these could break your bones.
Then we've got the ice.
Slippy, slippy, CRACK a slice!

Emma Managan (Age 9)

Green

My homework folder is green,
My pencil case is green,
Coloured pencils are green,
Felt tips are green,
Fresh leaves on the tree lovely and green,
Green grass on the field,
Green soap on the side of the bath,
Limes are green in the fruit bowl,
Green nail varnish, very dark.
On the side of the bath there's a bottle of green handcream
Sometimes the sea looks green.
I put some bubble bath in my bath that was green.
Green is a lizard,
Green is a snake twirled round a branch,
Green is a lime jelly wobbling on a plate.

Rebecca May (Age 8)

Why

Why do lions run?
Why do plants lean towards the sun?
Why are bushbabies eyes so big?
Why do only some people like the fig?
Why do rabbits hop?
Why do bugs destroy the crop?
Why don't the planets fall from the sky?

Why do plants grow?
Why can't we fly like the crow?
Why do cows make milk?
Why do only some worms make silk?
Why do we have to eat?
Why does honey taste so sweet?
Why are some animals as small as mice?
Why at weddings do people throw rice?
Why can't we touch the sky?
Why do kids always ask why?

Mark McDonald-Leslie (Age 11)

Dogs

I don't like dogs,
Dogs have sharp jagged jaws,
They make me go all cold and shivery,
I nearly fall and faint on the floor.

My Mum and Dad say,
Look at that dog over there,
But I think that's a dog, it's not,
It's a dinosaur,
With sharp, pointed, jagged,
Bony teeth,
And gooey gums inside.

When they prowl and look very big and smart,
They jump and bite, and eat *YOU ALL UP!*

Jordan Mitchell (Age 10)

I Hate Maths

I HATE maths!
I don't know what it's for.
Some people think it's good
But I think it's a bore.

All that adding,
All those sums.
When I need a calculator
I just borrow my mum's.

Decimal points and fractions
I just don't understand.
I really hate maths.
It's the worst subject in the land!

Rebecca McKeown (Age 9)

The Wind

The wind...
Humming like a bee looking for pollen,
Soaring through the air like a bird,
Hovering like a kestrel spying on its prey.

The wind...
Whistling as it blows through the grass,
Whooshing round the trees like a scared mouse,
Cracking and crunching as it breaks branches from the trees.

The wind...
Howling like a wolf calling for its mate,
Plucking leaves from branches as it flies by,
Soaring through the air as it zooms past birds.

The wind...
Swirling past children like a tornado,
Jolting over the water like a torpedo on the move,
Shattering boats against the rocks.

The wind...
Sailing like a boat on the lake,
Dropping apples from trees,
Leaping over walls.

Sam Mathers (Age 11)

The Old Teddy

The cuddly teddy bear who really likes hugs,
He is light brown and fluffy
He is as worn and faded as my school jumper
Which has been in the wash too many times,
I am ancient and dull or that's what it feels like.

Katie-Anne McCarthy (Age 10)

Football

My fave sport is football,
Running around.
If you were famous you would hear the cheers,
That sort of sound!
Kicking, shooting, it's all too good.
If you haven't tried it, you should, YOU SHOULD!!
Being tripped up, all those fouls,
Penalties, yelling,
Oh! the terrible howls!
Strikers, midfield, and up front,
And that referee can be a spoilt old runt!
So if you have my style of laughter
And some not so great,
Go to football training, and don't be late!

Susan Miller (Age 10)

Stars

Baubles
hanging
in the sky

Beams of light
nowhere
to go

Mini balls
of fire
clinging
in the air

Heavenly Bodies
decorating
the black
night sky

Sun arising
as angels
close
their windows
over dawn

Anna Miles (Age 10)

Rain Poem

Splish! Splosh! Splish!
Splosh! Splosh! Splosh!

Play in the rain.
Splosh! Splosh! Splosh!

I love the rain.
Splosh! Splosh! Splosh!

I am soaking, bottom to top!
Splosh! Splosh! Splosh!

Oscar Maynard (Age 7)

Mice

I like mice they're very nice
They eat your cheese
Mice have sharp claws
And long tails
And they sneak around
Mice are tiny
You get them at night
You get them brown black and white
Mice dig holes
They dig with their sharp teeth

Chloe Miller (Age 9)

Did You See It, Did You Hear it, Did You Feel It?

Did you hear the parrots talking,
I heard it,
Did you see the hippo smoking,
I saw it,
Did you feel the sun go down,
I felt it,
Yow, I went to de forest too,
Did you feel the cheetah run passed you,
I felt it and saw it,
Did you hear the laughing monkey,
I heard it,
Lets end our rap like this,
Did you hear it,
I heard it,
Did you see it,
I saw it,
Did you feel it,
I felt it.

Tom Matthews (Age 13)

Questions

Why can leopards run faster than humans?
Why do waves climb up so high?
How do birds fly through the sky?
How do plants grow from seeds?
Why does gravity pull us down?
How do human brains work?
How do animals evolve?
Why doesn't the sun burn up the sky?
Why are clouds up so high?
Why do snails leave silver trails?
Why does a question always want to be answered?
Why do children always ask. . .
WHY?

Kathryn Miller (Age 10)

Dogs

If fear of dogs,
I don't know why,
Their long, sharp claws,
And fearsome bark,
They make a shiver climb up my spine.

Their long, slimy tongue,
That hangs out of their sharp, jagged jaws,
That makes me shiver and quiver until I drop.

Natalie Meegan (Age 9)

The Dancer

She moved lightly on her feet,
To the rhythm of the beat.

Her body felt light and free,
She was as happy as could be.

The audience faces lit up with light,
As they saw her dance with sheer delight.

Oh, how she loved to dance . . . . .

Abigail Marsh (Age 10)

Summer Sizzler

Summer heat, so good to meet
Today's a summer sizzler
On the sunbed take a seat
Meet my grizzling sister

Roses blooming everywhere like a sheet of silk
'Cause today's the day we have a summer sizzler
Crazy Daisie's in my way
In the summer sizzler
In the summer sizzler

In the class exam I don't pass
Because it's a summer sizzler
Drinking a cold drink
Because it's a summer sizzler
Because it's a summer sizzler

Daisie Mearing (Age 11)

The Storm Ravens

The day they sent,
The groups of ravens into the sky,
Didn't they screech and flash their beaks,
Didn't they set the river banks,
Bursting with their claws,
Didn't their diving lightning rip and tear!

And, through the storm, through the storm,
Don't their weapons scare,
Don't they burn and bite the trees,
And soot and foul the air.

Oh quieten down, quieten down,
To soften the sky after the storm.

Duncan McKenna (Age 11)

Old Friend

How have you been old friend? I haven't seen you in a while,
You look happy with your dancing eyes and beaming smile,
How are you old friend? It's been far too long,
The way that fate parted us was harsh and wrong,
Do you miss me old friend? Think of me at all?
Its un-nerving how only silence and space catch me when I fall,
Can you hear me old friend? Why don't you say?
Are you thinking back, back to our day,
How is the new place old friend? You don't need me,
You told me that this new world moves ever so strangely,
Do you care old friend? That I'm not there,
What about all the thrill, the excitement, the dare?
What do you think old friend? Tell me how you feel,
Do you feel like me? That this world isn't real,
Why so quiet old friend? All is not said and done,
Old friend?
Old friend don't leave me alone.

Frankie Murray (Age 13)

Sunshine

S unshine sparkles everywhere while children play their games.
U nder the tree people rest and sleep
N ow it's time for lunch, children having picnics
S andwhich, crisps, apple and cold drinks are ready
H ow birds sing flying in the sky
I will never forget this day! People lying there
N ew bathing suits, now it's the
E nd of the day!

Tommy Miles (Age 10)

Wa-Wa

I'd like to tell you about my Grandpa,
My cousins and I all call him 'Wa-Wa',
But there is something more unusual,
He always pours orange juice on his cereal!

His hair is short and silver-grey,
Like an elephant's hide in the sun of the day,
His hearing is failing, his eyes are still blue
Through steel-rimmed glasses they twinkle at you.

He comes from Yorkshire, but lives mostly in Spain,
I think it's because he hates the rain!
You wouldn't believe how funny he looks,
In his black scuba suit reading his books!

He loves the sea and to stay afloat,
He climbs aboard his sailing boat.
As for his grandkids, he adores all nine,
I love my Wa-Wa, because he's mine.

Holly Moseley (Age 10)

My Robot Zink

My robot Zink
His body parts go clink
He zooms around and
Makes toy towns.

He talks really funny
It goes like this
Zib zab lib lab
But sometimes he does sign language

His head is red
His legs are yellow
His eyes are jelly
Just like his belly
That's my robot Zink.

Jennifer McMillan (Age 9)

Red

Arsenal are at the top of the table
A bright red door
Arsenal are at the top of the table
It's Poppy Day
Arsenal are at the top of the table
Bright red blood
Arsenal are at the top of the table
Blazing red traffic lights

George Mearing (Age 8)

The Night Sky

The night sky
Still black
Cloudy and cold
In the misty moonlight.

The night sky
Still dark
Thundering and lightning
In the cold stormy night.

The night sky
Still shines
Gold and colourful
In the starry sky.

The night sky
Still bright
Space shuttles and satelites
In the bright light.

Ashley Miller (Age 9)

The Jam

The big eye starring, never blinking,
The rusty spokes like blood shot eyes,
In the traffic jam it waits,
Wedged together like pieces of lego.

Out of the corner of his eye,
He spies a crystal cobweb, gleaming after the night's rain,
A diamond drop of dew falls to the ground.
Smashing into hundreds of pieces, still stays the web of silk.

A never ending sound of hooting escapes the cars,
A multi coloured road brightens the street,
A bicycle wheel day dreaming,
Standing still, it's like being stuck in strawberry jam.

Reece Millar (Age 10)

Bertie The Hamster

Every sunday I clean Berties cage,
I tip his bedding into the bin,
I give his food to the birds,
I pour his water down the sink.

But today there is no Bertie to put back.
Dad says that he had a good life and two is very old for a hamster.
I look into his empty cage.
And remember his soft nose.
His warm,
And his tiny body sitting on my hand.

Shona Maclean (Age 8)

Just Kids

Just kids, just kids they like to do the candle.
Just kids, just kids they like to be gentle.
Just kids, just kids they love to know their prayers.
Just kids, just kids they love to play dares.
Just kids, just kids.

Josie Mitchell (Age 8)

My Best Friend

Lucy Kidd is my best friend,
But sometimes she drives me round the bend.
We always share our food at lunch,
Me, Lucy and our friends make the perfect bunch.
Lucy is a very fast runner,
Especially on the field in summer.
When we're older we'll go on double dates,
Because forever and ever we'll always be best mates!

Anna Moore (Age 10)

Exams

There I was sitting all alone
With my impossible exam paper,
I'm in my worst fear ever,
Will I fail or will I pass,
I'll find out sooner or later,
Will I find an answer to the question.

I know I'll get through, I have to,
No I'm going to fail!
My mind's racing around and around,
I'm getting dizzy,
I'm going to faint,
"Please put down your pens!"

Luke Thomas Milner (Age 10)

A Bees Life

Bees are buzzing in the sky
Near the blazing sun up high
Shining on you
They wizz around every flower
Collecting pollen by the hour
Honey for you
They fly so fast, they're really busy
The speed they go makes me dizzy
Working for you.
Heat rising from the ground
I can only hear one sound
Buzzing for you.

Douglas Matthews (Age 9)

The Toucan

T all and beaky
O ld and well known
U gly and parched
C anoeing around in the air
A bsailing down trees.
N eeding room to breeze.

Ollie Martin (Age 8)

Blue Is

Blue is bright and very light
It's very dark at night
The river is dark you can hear a bark
Blue is cool and very cold
Blue is the sky in the late afternoon,
Blue is water that turns into ice.

Scott Matthews (Age 9)

The War!

R emember the war, chaos, blood, gore,
E veryone crying, dying and planes flying
M others wailing for their soldier sons,
E xplosion, sacrifice, NIGHTMARES!
M oaning while bullets rush through the air,
B ombs whistled through the country,
E nemies in their tanks with guns, and bombs,
R unning from the gun fire,
A eroplanes crashing to the ground
N eeeeeeeeeeee boom, more bombs,
C rying is non stop like a clock never stops ticking,
E veryone is scared of the war.

Gabriella Macis (Age 10)

Best Friends

Best friends are cool
Best friends are great
Best friends are the best mates
They'll never let you down
Best friends are the best friends to have
Best friends look after you
Even when you're ill
They'll play anywhere even on a hill
They'll play and play every day
And they'll never go away
But my friend is different
Because she is not a friend
She is my best friend ever.

Amber Metcalfe (Age 9)

Rain

A good and bad thing to life.
The stinging salt in your eyes.
Fiercely the king of the clouds opens his eyes.
Drizzle appears from the sky.
An enemy to historic humans.
A great wetness to life.
A life saver for the world.
A disastrous life stopper.
The crash bang snap sound creates the world.
A black scenery of rain to watch.
Plants and trees pray to the rain for giving life to them.
A disturbance to the animals for some a life threaten to life.
A great gift from God to us.
A scary night make to the world.

Sophie Maynard (Age 10)

Guinea Pigs

I have two guinea pigs
They're cute, soft and cuddly,
Snuggling in fresh hay,
Runs in their cage
Likes to keep warm,
Talks to each other,
Gentle and warm,
Munches on apples and celery,
Fight with each other,
Plays with each other,
Crawls up your shirt,
Claws your skin,
Plays in your hair,
Guinea pigs are wonderful

Katie McIlveen (Age 8)

Snowdrops

Silky snow white petals,
Smooth as the snow,
Sways in the breeze,
Sparkles in the sky,
Like a gem,
Soft as a baby's arm,
White as the clouds,
Delicate as a paper,
Pure as the sky,
Icy soft,
The crystal white paint in a crystal white box,
Glowing in the night,
It falls slow like a turtle swimming underwater,
Hanging like a bit of paper swaying.
It swoops and dives like an eagle getting some food,
Growing through the ground.

David Margrie (Age 9)

It's Not Fair Miss

It's not fair Miss
It wasn't me
I didn't chuck the food Miss
Don't blame it all on me

It's not fair Miss
They were ganging up on me,
I didn't punch her in the face Miss
They did it to me

It's not fair Miss
They were talking to me
That's why I only got 3 lines done Miss
Don't be cross with me

Kim Moody (Age 9)

Rain

Oh, no not the rain	(splish)
Oh, please not again	(splash)
It is such a pain	(splish)
I just hate the rain	(splosh)
Oh, no not the rain	(splish)
Oh, please not again	(splash)
It's driving me insane	(splish)
I just hate the rain	(splosh)
Oh, no not the rain	(splish)
Oh, please not again	(splash)
Crashing on the window pane	(splish)
I just hate the rain	(splosh)
Oh, no not the rain	(splish)
Oh, please not again	(splash)
Always whooshing down the lane	(splish)
OH JUST GO AWAY!!!	

Hannah Monk (Age 10)

Flowers Smell

Flowers smell like me,
Like a honey bee.
Flowers grow in mud and manure.
They smell like me for sure!
Flowers are short.
Flowers are tall
But my favourite flowers of all
Are the ones that are yellow, pink or blue,
And the ones that are sent from me to you.

Jessica Marsden (Age 8)

Homework

Have to have it
Do just a bit
Mum says "Come on Kelly!"
I just want to watch the telly

Work, work, work,
Mustn't shirk
Poems today and they've got to rhyme
Goodness me, is that the time!

Dad comes in
Says "What's that din?"
"Can't do homework with music on" mum shouts,
Dad yells, "The cat's had enough and now she's gone!"

Kelly Mutch (Age 11)

The Cat

Inside the cat's eye a solar eclipse,
Inside the solar eclipse the cat's black fur,
Inside the cat's fur the heart of a lion,
Inside the heart of a lion a streamline set of bones,
Inside the streamline set of bones the cat's mouth,
Inside the cat's mouth a lonely forest,
Inside the lonely forest the bird screaming the death call,
Inside the bird screaming the death call blood dripping,
Inside the blood dripping the cat's tooth,
Inside the cat's tooth a mountain of decay,
Inside the mountain of decay the cat's nose,
Inside the cat's nose the meowing of the wind,
Inside the meowing of the wind the cat's eye.

Thomas Moran (Age 11)

Untitled

If I had wings,
I would touch the gleaming golden sun,
And glide over the calm blue sea.

Wayd Meikle-Braes (Age 9)

The Owl

The owl emerges from his dark damp ditch
Eyes glinting like gold.
He slowly spread his wings,
And glides to the next oak tree
He almost disappeared
As he camouflages into the tree branches.
Then spotting the perfect meal for his young,
Whoosh! He swoops to catch his prey.
Quick as a flash he grabs the mouse
And carries it back to his fledglings.

Ben Mikkelsen (Age 11)

Ghost Hunter

Shining light glitters in the air
A black shadow moves in the light

Ghosts watch in horror and run in fear
Her sniff, sniffs like never before
She lurks in every corner
And sniffs in every crack

Nearly sunrise
She swishes around and runs in fear
And never returns
Until the next sundown of the year

Huxley Mann (Age 10)

The Thunder

The thunder is a mysterious panther
Magnificent and black
He rumbles and groans in the sky
With his blade sharp teeth and terrifying roars
Hour upon hour he snaps his jaws
The crashing, smashing clouds
And "rain, rain, rain, rain, rain!"
The vast panther prowls
Striking with his paws.

Sarah McCarthy (Age 8)

Inside The Cats Eye

Inside the cat's eye, a mountain of dust,
Inside the mountain of dust, the cats fur,
Inside the cat's fur, a moving junction,
Inside the moving junction, the cats feet,
Inside the cat's feet, a bumpy horizon,
Inside the bumpy horizon, the cats claws,
Inside the cat's claws, the voles cry,
Inside the voles cry, the frozen tears,
Inside the frozen tears, the cats teeth,
Inside the cat's teeth, the cold wind,
Inside the cold wind, the icy lake,
Inside the icy lake, the cats eye.

Anna Moyne (Age 10)

Hill Trail

Patter of the rain as it trickles down the trees,
Snapping of the branches underfoot,
Whistling of the wind as it travels through the hills,
Crackling of the leaves by my feet,
Voices of the children fussing as they walk,
Bleating of the sheep in the field,
These are the sounds of the
Hill Trail

Louise Mathewson (Age 10)

Joy

Joy is yellow,
It smells like a sweet banana,
Joy tastes like the hot burning sun,
It sounds like a telephone ringing
Joy feels like a soft baby,
Joy lives in the sweet green grass.

Sian Mistry (Age 10)

Leisure

What is this life if full of care,
I've plenty time to stop and stare.

Time to go swimming and splash around,
When I came out I found one pound.

Time to play football and score lots of goals,
When I turned around I saw one mole.

Time to go on the computer and play lots of games,
As many games as I may.

Time to go to the Valley Parade,
And watch Bradford City play.

Time to play on my guitar and learn lots of songs,
Sometimes right and sometimes wrong.

Time to draw with my friends,
Sometimes with pencils and sometimes with pens.

A good life I've got, it's full of care,
I'm pleased I've got time to stop and stare.

Lucy Mawson (Age 9)

Leisure

What is this life if full of care,
I've plenty of time to stop and stare.

Time to take my rottweiler black and brown,
Out for a walk but never to town.

Time to spend time with my family,
Mother, father granny and me.

Time to read a book,
Sometimes written by a cook.

Time to read a book,
Sometimes written by a cook.

Time to draw and paint I do like painting,
But never of something fainting.

Time to play games with friends of mine,
The games we play are very fine.

Time to play with people on my scooter and bike,
If we go to the park it is much of a hike.

A good life I've got, it's full of care,
I'm pleased I've got time to stop and stare.

Charlotte Newby (Age 9)

Autumn

The road is lined with seas of leaves,
Yellow, orange and red.
Whilst animals gather to get food, then rest their sleepy head.

Conkers falling from the trees,
Children playing kicking leaves.
Sometimes rainy; summer's gone
Getting colder as days go on.

Days are shorter, sunlight fading
Shining weakly on the forest floor,
Winters coming, Natures ready,
For the cold winds at our door.

Alison Marsh (Age 11)

Angels

Angels are made purely from heart,
They are the very pictures of art,
Their halos are as silver as stone,
But all Angels never moan.
They have wings that make them take flight,
They make them shine a golden light,
Most Angels are very wise,
But when you see one you won't believe your eyes.
Angels are here, Angels are there,
Angels are everywhere.
I know, my Grandad is out there.

Arthur Moore (Age 11)

Ghosts

Light ghosts are scary
Light shadowy, see-through ghosts are even scarier
They are noisy when the want to be,
If you be quiet they won't go woooo,
They will float through walls, only if you see them,
They will go invisible when you shout aaaah,
They scare me when I see the dark shadows floating on the wall,
That's the time when I shout aaaah.

Ben Paul Manley (Age 9)

Ghastly

G rabbing your hair with terror,
H earing the noises you thought you would never hear,
A lone, alarmed and alert,
S wallowing hard,
T rying to escape
L ost in this spine-chilling place
Y our life is over

Jade McElligott (Age 11)

One Wicked Withered Witch

1 wicked withered witch
2 tiny troublesome turkeys
3 thick threatening thorns
4 furry funny fossils
5 friendly frozen fridges
6 silly school scissors
7 slow scientific snails
8 early electronic eagles
9 nice neat newts
10 tame tennis tadpoles

Georgia McCarthy (Age 8)

Blue Is

Blue is cold, damp and wet
When it is raining you will not sweat

The sky is big bigger than me
And it is blue bluer than the sea

Blue is some tears running down a face
When you see blue you don't have faith

Blue is sad it makes you feel bad
But when you cry people get mad

Aaron Morris (Age 9)

Rain

Drip, drop, drip, drop,
Falling down the window pane.

Drip, drop, drip, drop,
Will the sun come out again?

Drip, drop, drip, drop,
Wet, wet, wet, do you like the rain?

Ellie Muhairez (Age 11)

Happiness

Happiness is the sound of birds singing
And when we are winning.
Happiness looks like a dream
Eating a cake with fresh cream.
Happiness is a bird flying free
Happiness brings out the best in me.

Nicola Malaney (Age 9)

Sir Francis Drake

When Francis Drake was only ten he sailed around on the Pelican
He always knew what to do, he had a nice moustache too.

Francis Drake was very bold and he hardly ever passed out cold
When he came back from the sea the Queen offered him a cup of tea.

The Queen said "Give this ship your own name" in a very narrow London Lane
"OK" old Drakey quickly said, then he went straight to bed.

He called his ship the Golden Hind and he set out to find
A very jungley land but he found lots of sand.

He quickly went back to England and said "I've discovered Finland"
The Queen let him have a nice long break, he had lots of fun by a lake.

But then out of the blue a note came with all the Spanish men to blame
It was hurriedly scribbled, our big castle has been nibbled.

The Spanish had really big ships and they got kissed by cannon ball lips
So Francis became royal and the Queen made him very loyal.

Philip Mosscrop (Age 9)

Sinister

S pine-chilling noises
I nvestigating footprints
N ervously looking,
I n dark places
S pectacular floorboards creak
T hreatening hounds
E vidence is found
R ound the corner is sinister

Rebecca Nicholls (Age 11)

The Moon Is Being Attacked

The moon is getting wet dew drops in the month of May,
Skunks are making a smell they want the moon to go away,
The creatures are moving chip chip chipping away,
The trees are acting like a vibra slap wanting to bounce to the moon,
The twigs are snapping wanting to kill the moon.

Adam Nelson (Age 8)

Dancing In France

I like to sing
I like to dance
Why don't I
Go to France?

Joss Neale (Age 9)

Taste Collector

A stranger called this morning dressed all in black and grey
Put every taste into a bag and carried them away

The sweetness of the jam the chewiness of toffee
The pink juicy lamb and the cream in your coffee

The hot crunchy bread the smooth tasty cheese
The soft and herby spread the mushy green peas

The squidgy cream cake the hot Sunday roast
The scrummy chocolate flake and the hot buttered toast

The fat red cherry the hot greasy chips
The shiny black berry and the hot spicy dips

A stranger called this morning he did not leave his name
Left us only tasteless life will never be the same

Jonathan Norris (Age 11)

It's TV Time

I get home from school,
It's TV time.
I rush in first, cos
The remote's mine.

I have my tea
And scoff it down,
Then on go the cartoons
They make my dad frown.

There is Tucker, Hey Arnold and Sabrina,
Sister Sister, Rugrats and Taina.
"It's bedtime for you"
Said my mum.
So off I go to bed
To suck my thumb.

Stephanie Monks (Age 10)

Red

Red is bright,
That wears you out.
Drinks to drink,
Ice pops to lick,
Cherryade fizzing on my tongue.
Smarties, strawberries in a bowl.
At school spelling books are bound
On a piece of paper red crayon written all over.
Lipstick on my lips.

Lisa Mendham (Age 9)

Happiness

Happiness is orange,
It smells like delicious flowers,
Happiness tastes like a yummy chocolate
It sounds like a bell ringing in a church,
It feels soft and comfortable,
Happiness lives in a bright colourful house.

Sonia Maryam (Age 9)

School Days

Every school morning
We have, maths on the board
And then have assembly
And we sing
Mrs Genner's group go to the craft room
In the afternoon
We go on RM maths.

Jack Maddison (Age 8)

A Summer's Day

Welcome to my world
The birds and the bees are singing
The trees and my knees are trembling
I suppose this is what I was expecting
I suppose this was what I was rejecting
The time I was inflicting
Now in my prime I am trying
To rhyme about my sad time
I stand alone in a field
Where are my birds and bees?
Alone in the world
I suppose what I am trying to say
Is that I am an acorn
But where is my shell,
Or my tree?

Zara Newfield (Age 12)

So Like Your Grandad

Running down the street
People say "You're so like your Grandad"
At school my teacher says
"You're so like your Grandad"
He's a good joker, he's loveable,
He's kind, he's tall, he wears hats
Good to be with, fun to play with, he's special to me
But most of all HE'S MY SUPERMAN!!!

Craig Marchment (Age 8)

Wonder Car

A blood red sports car with a fiery revving engine,
Roaring like a lion, ready to go.
It's sleek, slender shape is totally awesome.
Fumes billowing out from the glowing exhaust pipe,
Like a dragon's breath.
The driver's excitement goes off the scale . . . and it's
GO! GO! GO!

Christopher Modak (Age 9)

Fireworks

Everybody cheered as the fireworks began
With a crash and a bang
It was like sparkling glitter in the sky like a star
They were banging and booming
As the fireworks shattered very slowly
The sky is perfect and delicate
The sky twinkles as the moonlight shines

Natalie Marshall (Age 8)

Days Of The Week

I like Monday schools has begun,
I'm going to have a week of fun.
I like tuesday we will bake,
A nice round sponge cake.
I like Wednesday I go to the swimming baths,
And I have a good laugh.
I like Thursday I ride my bike
And a boy walked past called Mike.
I like Friday I can doze,
After I have a snooze.
On Saturday I play out all day
Especially in May.
On Sunday I read books,
And help cook.

Kate Netherwood (Age 7)

Night

In the deep arcane night
The wintry cool breeze licks over
The moon arises
Radiating a luminous light.
As a rabble of stars
Pours over the sky,
Shimmering like tears of happiness,
Then the glistening tide bruises in
Gradually like a hatching egg,
Then deeper through the night,
Not a sound to be heard
Everything is motionless as can be,
Then, as the night drowns,
The stars go to sleep,
And the moon tucks into bed,
The sun yawns,
Bursting its beam of light,
Shattering the dusky night.

Eric Ng (Age 12)

Red Is . . .

Red is loving and kind
It makes me feel happy
Red is lovely and warm
Roses are as red as the sun
Red is joyful times
Like Christmas with shining lights
Red gleams with excitement
Like a bright red star
Red is anger and hate
Like me feeling sad.

Meg Mossemenear (Age 8)

My Best Friend

My best friend is a nice young lad,
He plays with me and talks to me.
He never drives me mad,
That's my best friend.

My best friend is as kind as can be.
He takes me to the cinema,
Or plays on the P.C.
That's my friend.

My best friend isn't always kind,
We fight and fall out.
He drives me out of my mind.
That's my friend.

My best friend comes and says he's sorry,
We make up and go out or play at footy,
My sadness goes and I'm happy again.
I like my friend.

Jack Nowell (Age 10)

Last Day At School

Last day at school
When we tidy up
Carpets are as neat as me
Collect up all the cups
Pull everything off the walls
Take it home to mummy.

Close the windows tightly
Walls as neat as paper
Collect all our things
Then we go home for summer holidays

But before we go home
We say goodbye to our friends
Then the teachers close the doors
And go home.

Alexandra New (Age 6)

A Food Poem

A pricots are dry and sweet
B ananas are yellow and good to eat
C akes are yummy in my tummy
D o you like being funny
E ggs are runny and scrummy
F lour is soft and white
G rapes are all right
H oney makes me feel light and bright
I ce cream is cold and tickles my throat
J elly is wobbly on my plate

Jessica McNamara (Age 8)

Strange, But Normal!

The cobweb glistens in the sun,
The diamonds of dew run down each single thread,
The cobweb is left alone,
The spider is dead.

The marble rolls across the floor.
Inside the marble is a blurred sky blue,
Orange, red,
And purple too.

Buttons are really tiny eyes,
Sewn upon our clothes.
The eyes are all different colours,
Orange green and mauve.

All these things seem unusual,
And they might well be,
But they're actually quite normal
So don't believe everything you see!

May Newland (Age 10)

Stripple The Cat

Stripple the Cat, had some kittens, dressed them up in socks and mittens,
Everyday, she fed them milk and made their new bed out of silk.
Every time she groomed their fur, the kittens always seemed to purr,
And when the kittens started to grow, Stripple screeched, and made them go!

Now poor Stripple was all alone, with her kittens up and grown.
She started to cry each night and day, and wished she hadn't scared them away.
Her ears drooped, and tail low, and she was all unhappy, so . . .
She went and lived with her long, lost boy, and now was filled with laughter and joy.

They invited all the kittens round, but then, one of the kittens found:
A dead and stinky, dirty mouse, in the long lost boyfriend's house.
Unfortunately, Stripple hissed, and scared her long lost boy to bits!
He ran away, and 'til this day, her long, lost boy lives far away . . .

Naomi Northcott (Age 10)

The Forest's Story

I remember when life was good
When the animals were enjoying their amusements
And when the streams were rushing down the rocks and stones
When the light was beaming into my eyes
And my tree branches covered with nests
When the flowers were dancing in the sunlight
And the chirpings of the birds gave me a comfy feeling
But now everything's gone, all gone.
I miss the river,
I miss the nests on my strong, outstanding branches
I miss everything It is all . . . . . Gone
My magnificent life is over
All there is now is fire, smoke and

```
A       S       H
A       S       H
A       S       H
A       S       H
 A       S       H
 A       S       H
  A       S       H
```

Thomas Norman (Age 11)

Spring

Daffodils dancing,
Through the breeze of the wind,
Like ballet dancers.

Trees bursting,
With new leaves,
Appear to be smiling,
And laughing joyfully.

Sunny golden chicks,
Hatch out of their eggs,
Song thrush singing in the oak tree.

Jamie Moore (Age 9)

The Dentist

I went to the Dentist
Felt
The noises - buzzing sound.
The chair - up and down.
The Dentist was humming and clicking.
The drill was *buzzing* and *sizzing*
I don't like the dentist.
Feel nervous
The Dentist reading.
The Dentist helping me up.

Ben McDonnell (Age 10)

Hurry Up Christmas

They said my name in the room next door,
I know I shouldn't, but I wanted to hear more.
I walked a little closer and put my ear to the wall,
The murmuring became clear not just muttering along the hall.
They mentioned Christmas presents, I jumped for joy,
Wondering if I was getting clothes or a toy.
I strained to listen, but the dishwasher clanged,
The kettle whistled, the taps dripped,
Is my hearing being tricked?
So many sounds inside my head,
Although I did hear a few words they said,
Mobile phone, gift vouchers, those shoes I nearly bought.
But I must get away before I am caught.
Quietly I crept away,
Now knowing I was in for a merry christmas day.

Emma Nottingham (Age 11)

September 11th

Standing were twin towers,
Now only rubble,
So many lives lost,
Families drown with sorrow,
The world know the terrorists.

Americans will remember it as war
He hides away in the mountains of Afghanistan
Troops search for the terrorist,
His name,
Osama Bin Laden.

Alexandra Noel-Johnson (Age 10)

A White World

I can't think why outside is white
Yesterday it was green, this can't be right
Mum says it's snow
What that is I do not know.

I have to investigate the wood,
If that is white it should look good,
I can make a snowman with dad,
I won't complain this isn't bad.

All this whiteness, why is it here?
Most of my family are all near,
All of my cousins, aunties, uncles and family
Everyone making a fuss of me.

I know this time, it's when Santa comes
When I get presents from dad and mum,
Sorry, got to go
Got to go and play with the snow.

Rebecca Newbury (Age 11)

Swimming

I like swimming
In a swimming pool
I think it's wicked
And I think it's cool

You can splash around
You can swim under water
You can start to shout
And say where is my daughter

When it's time to get out
The swimming pool
Always remember
It's COOL!!

Banisha Nayyar (Age 10)

Bully Gang

As I turn the corner of my street.
I see a gang of boys,
Each one with a baseball bat
And the biggest one is Roy.
Shall I carry on walking?
Or shall I go straight home,
Are they going to batter me?
As I am alone.
They've turned to the corner shop
Who's it gonna be?
I'm walking the other way
Oh no, they're running towards me.

Shamraiz Najib (Age 9)

I Hate Wasps

Sometimes spiders are creepy,
But wasps are definitely creepy,
They sting you when you disturb them,
Not like spiders,
All they do is walk around and eat flies.

I hate bees and wasps,
When you eat an apple,
They eat it too,
I hate the way they look,
They make you cringe and shiver.

I hate the way they buzz,
It sounds like an alarm went off,
I hate the look of their hive,
The honey looks like it went off,
Not like spiders.

Paul Norton (Age 9)

The Mouse And The Giraffe

The mouse and the giraffe went to the ocean
And found a dark pink potion
The mouse took some drinks and plenty of sink,
Wrapped in a toilet roll
The giraffe looked up and found a bowl
And found a person fall
The mouse and the giraffe looked and frowned
And saw a leaf that was brown
The giraffe sung
And found a ring
And put it on his wife
And she only had a little life
She cried on and on
The mouse ate a yogurt by a lovely spoon
And saw a lovely cocoon
The mouse and the giraffe looked and frowned
And saw a leaf that was brown

Saman Niazi (Age 10)

Snow Storm

The snow is a fluffy white blanket
That gently covers the ground,
The snow is a sequinned dress
That twists and twirls around.

But the snow is a dangerous beast
As it takes on a different form,
The snow is a ghostly galleon
Adrift in the raging storm.

The snow is an icy sheet of glass
Where children love to play,
The snow is a silky path of white
But it only lasts one day.

Amy O'Brien (Age 10)

The Solar System

Why is the moon so shiny and bright?
How does it stay up all night?
Why is Mars not made of chocolate?

Why can't you drink the milky way?
Is the moon made of cheese?
If it is can I have some please?
Why are the stars so far away?
Why is the sun so fiery and hot?
Why is the moon white?
Why are the planets all in a line?
Why does the sun shine?

Lee Nobbs (Age 11)

Alphabet Poem

A is for Alice who breaks all her toys
B is for Bonnie who beats up boys
C is for Charlotte who goes to ballet
D is for Daniel who drinks off a tray
E is for Emmy who makes everyone sad
F is for Freddy who is very bad
G is for Gina who thinks she's the best
H is for Harly who wears a big vest
I is for Illy who runs after Billy
J is for Julie who is very silly
K is for Katie who likes netball
L is for Louise who is very tall

Lucy Nicholas (Age 8)

Nature

What is green?
Holly is green, as prickly as a hedgehog.
What is violet?
Grapes are violet, shiny on a plate.
What is yellow?
Corn is yellow, blowing in the breeze.
What is orange?
Lava is orange, pouring down a hill
What is blue?
A waterfall is blue with water rushing through a stream.
What is brown?
Wood is brown, with bark protecting it.
What is grey?
A squirrel is grey, dashing up a tree.

Alex Neale (Age 8)

Flowers

Flowers are so bright.
They grow to such a height!
There's different kinds, like . . .
Roses,
Daises,
Daffodils,
And tulips.

Flowers make you happy,
Brighten up your day.
Then along came a wind and blew them all away!
You feel really sad.
You have a bad pain.
You'll have to gather all the flowers
And start all over again!

Danielle Ogle (Age 10)

Dylan The Cautious Dog

Dylan's a cautious dog he is everyone's delight
For he likes to check things out without a single bite.
For he's the king of the park, helping dogs in plight
For when they eventually catch up with Dill he never gets into fights.

Dillboy, Dillboy there's nobody like Dillboy
He's broken every doggie law but still such a joy.
He's always very kind and make that friendly too!
But sometimes when he's feeling blue he likes to say BOO!

Dylan is a crossbred dog he's very slender and sly
But I tell you once again he'll never say goodbye.
His coat is nice and shiny his chest has lots of curls
He prances round here and there especially for the girls.

Dillboy, Dillboy there's no-one like Dillboy
For sometimes he stands quiet and still he's like a cuddly toy.
You may meet him in his home or one day on a walk
Just remember this that he's the Napoleon of Pork!!!!

Jordan O'Hara (Age 11)

If My Sister Were A Car!

If my sister were a car
She'd be a fast, flashy Ferrari
A shade of sparkly silver
She speeds round corners like
A lightning bolt
Showing off to her friends

Martha Norley (Age 12)

Friends

Friends are always there for you
They leap and sing in all you do
Playing together at school
Playing games we think are cool
We always do things together
We've always hated rainy weather

Bethany Nash (Age 8)

Homework

Homework is boring
When I read it to my mum she started snoring
I think I'm going to be sick
Ow, my brother gave me a kick
My sister said "That must hurt".
Oh really that homework
HONESTLY!

Zainab Nawaz (Age 10)

Teacher Terror!!
(In the style of Hiawatha)

Give me of your brains O children
Of your clever minds O children.
Dozing in the stuffy classroom,
Gazing out the misty window.

Writing out so many letters.
All the time we're working, working.
Like a busy business worker.
Like a busy story writer.

Rachel Nagy (Age 11)

What Is Red?

Red is a rose which is sprouting in the spring
Red is a sweety paper which shines like a ring
Red is my literacy book that sits on my desk

George O'Brien (Age 6)

The Snowy Owl

Searching for its prey,
Camouflaged in the snow, waiting.
A mouse appears below.
The owl hovers over the ground,
And then swoops.
He stabs his claws into the mouse,
Snatches him up in his beak,
And flies back to his nest.

Ashleigh McCarthy (Age 10)

The Fox

Eyes green,
As big as golf balls.

Scrounging around for scraps
Rubbish in his mangy fur.

Knocking down bins,
Running through streets
Jumping at the slightest bit of light.

Deep in the dark forest,
The scavenging creature roams
In and out of tall dark trees
Limping as he goes.

The sun starts rising
Up into the sky.

The mangy
Red furred creature
Runs into his small hole in the ground
And
Waits for the sun to lie low . . .

Lauren Obertelli-Leahy (Age 13)

The Life Of Water

Water starts its life as a stream
Young and carefree,
Dancing down hills and in and out of rocks
As it joins other water, it matures;
Slows down,
Life is no longer a game,
Every day another struggle to reach the ocean.
Along the way it meets challenges
Pollution, litter and dead animals,
Until one day, it achieves its goal.
FREEDOM

Hannah Nutting (Age 11)

My Pony

My pony is brown,
My pony is soft,
When I brush his mane and tail quite a lot,
I give him lots of bedding night and day,
He always eats all the hay,
His tack needs to be cleaned!
He waits for me by the gate,
When I get there he goes quite mad,
Flicking his head and tail all around.
He can be quite naughty but never lets me down.
I LOVE MY PONY HE IS THE BEST!

Emma Nobbs (Age 8)

Queen...

Do you ever get bored,
Sitting on your throne?
Do you ever get lonely,
All on your own?

Do you get bored with life,
Do you think it's unfair?
Do the servants ask you,
"Do you want a pear?"

Is the palace pretty,
Are the servants nice?
Do they give you cream cakes,
Or do they think twice?

Do you like the guards,
Standing at the gates?
Are they ever friendly,
Are they ever late?

What are you like in the morning?
Are you, "Should I wear black or blue?"
Do the maids come and say,
"It's really up to YOU!"

Philippa Oliver (Age 9)

The Queen's Table

Munch, munch, munch!
I went to lunch
At the Queen's table
I got a label
On it was my name,
But, "What a shame!"
My friends went
As they lent
Over to see me

Eleanor Newell (Age 8)

It's A

It has two lights,
    It has a wonderful sight,
It has black leather seats,
    It's always neat,
It is red as blood
    Almost covered in mud
It's got a bumper
    As soft as a jumper
Drives far
    It's a . . .

Amraiz Najib (Age 10)

Why?

Who do only some metals conduct electricity?
Why do chickens lay eggs?
Why do magnets attract and repel?
Why do frogs have frogspawn?
How come the lights work when only switched on?
What makes cats have fur,
What makes them purr?
Why do you need a battery to light a bulb?
Why do humans have skin?
Why do you need a battery in a circuit to make a bulb light up?
Why are bees attracted to flowers?
Why do we get an electric shock?
Why do dogs chase after sticks?
What makes electricity work?
What keeps a flower upright?
I ask all these questions, but who is going to tell me the answers?

Jessica Overland (Age 11)

Goodbye And Good Luck To My Best Friend

Good luck for the future,
I hope that your dreams come true,
Good luck for the hard times,
I'm sure you'll see them through.
Just remember I'll always be there,
Always in your head to love and care,
I'll always be in your mind,
Even if I'm not always kind.
I will be there no matter if your happy or sad,
But always remember,
Never forget,
That together we are completely *MAD*!

Komal Odedra (Age 12)

Space

Space is a mystery place,
Mercury is as hot as lava,
Venus' volcanoes are as big as mountains,
Earth's oceans are as deep as outer space,
Mars is red like shiny rubies,
Jupiter's colour is like a rainbow,
Saturn's rings are protective like a suit of armour,
Uranus is as cold as icicle droplets,
Neptune's colour is as pale as the sea,
Pluto's size is as small as can be,
Next to that we do not know,
Space is a mystery place,

James O'Keefe (Age 12)

Orpington

As night time falls
You notice it more.
The noise that is
Caused by the balls,
Up against the walls
Or maybe the door.
"Please don't do that anymore"
The children shout louder
And cars screech longer
But still the children play in the street,
Looking for friends they would like to meet.

Jo-Anna O'Connor (Age 13)

The Tiger's Roar

Inside the tiger's roar , is an echoing cave.
Inside the echoing cave, is the tiger's eye.
Inside the tiger's eye, is the scorching sun.
Inside the scorching sun, is the tiger's fur.
Inside the tiger's fur, is the black volcano.
Inside the black volcano, is the deer's dark cry.
Inside the deer's dark cry, is the misty mountains.
Inside the misty mountains, is the tiger's teeth.
Inside the tiger's teeth, is the night's sky.
Inside the night's sky, is the tiger's whisker.
Inside the tiger's whisker, is the silver hill.
Inside the silver hill, is the tiger's claw.
Inside the tiger's claw, is the icy glacier.
Inside the icy glacier, is the tiger's roar.

Rachel O'Leary (Age 11)

A Hooker For England

The place where I would love to be,
Is at Twickenham playing rugby,
A hooker, for England that's what I'd be, with all of my family watching me.
Our studs sound like thunder, the crowd roars like a lion,
The grass is as green as the valley as I come charging like a bull,
For my first match for England.

The place where I would love to be,
Is at Twickenham playing rugby,
The ball breaks loose the passes fly, and I score yet another try.
I run like the wind, with my team galloping like horses behind me.
I'm gripping the ball as tight as a vice, another try now would be really nice.

The place where I would love to be,
Is at Twickenham playing rugby,
My heart beats like a drum I'm over the line
We have beaten the enemy the score's twenty six - nine

I'm here in the place where I'd love to be,
I'm at Twickenham playing rugby,
A hooker for England that's what I am,
My dad's in the crowd, he is my biggest fan.

Joshua Owen (Age 9)

Schools Out

The bell goes for home time.
Everyone shouting
"See you Monday"
Teachers saying
"Phew I'm glad the week-end's here"
Boys and girls meeting down the town
Kissing cuddling each other.

Katie O'Shea (Age 9)

My House

My house is perfect,
Night is like coal, very dark,
Where playful dogs bark and children play,
Where trains run up and down the railway,
People stay on the gold, sandy, hot beach all day,
Where the road twists and winds,
Swimming, bowling and busy shops, everything
That's my fantastic home.

Laura Oliver (Age 9)

My Friend Melissa

My friend Melissa
Is really funny
She has hair the colour of honey
She has got lots of money
She is the best on RM maths in the school
She is very cool
She has got a rabbit called Thumper
Who she loves very much
Melissa is my best Friend.

Carina Nea (Age 8)

What Am I?

I am:
    The devil of the house,
    The thief,
    A genius at tormenting,
    A vacuum cleaner collecting fun.

I take pride in being a grade A* at annoyance.

I like asking irritating questions about others private lives
Calling people big, rude names.

What am I?

A younger brother (printed upside-down)

David Osment (Age 11)

The King

This ball of soft, yellow cotton wool floats majestically through space,
All alone but for nine underlings, as nothing more than a tiny spot on the foot of a giant spider.

However he is king of his small area, the head puppeteer pulling the strings
Of everything in the solar system and ensuring everything goes as it should.

Everyone obeys this king; when he is happy and shining
Everyone else does likewise and goes outside to enjoy his radiance, but when he is sad, so are his courtiers.

This tired old man is fascinated to watch out of his window as everything goes round
Like his servants always moving around the palace and peasants entering or leaving his kingdom.

His is a keen astronomer even though to his advisers his is the subject of their astronomy.
To him these blind fools can see nothing compared to the billions of things he knows exist.

There is a family quarrel in his kingdom.
It makes him sad to see one part, third closest to him, unaware that it is tearing itself to pieces.

But he is happy to see we small stupid humans getting on with life,
Just like we watch very small children getting on with theirs.

He wishes that he could grow into a super nova and control the galaxy
But he knows it will never happen and that he will stay a small lonely king for the rest of his life.

The sun, just a tired and lonely old man.

Christopher Petheram (Age 12)

Whale

Grey-white
Enormous fish
You remind me of the sea
You swim in the sea
Very very big

Peter Osborn (Age 7)

My Dream Car

It is shiny red with black seats
And I love it heaps.
The engine rumbles as
Along the road it tumbles.
If I see my friend I'll give a toot.
Vicky can sit in the front,
And Mark and Mrs Preston in the boot.

Dan O'Brien (Age 12)

What Is The Moon?

The moon is a rocky wasteland
               waiting to be civilised
It is a metallic silver spot
               on a black AC Cobra
The moon is a forty watt bulb
               in a prison cell
It is the last polo
               in the almost empty pack
The moon is a silver bullet
               shot through the gloomy WW2 skies

Dwayne Officer (Age 12)

Animals poem

Hey everybody what's up whats'up yeah,
Going to tell you about animals everywhere,
There's bats and bees and birds and bears,
And spiders, which live under the stairs.

These animals are just like you,
Don't you know they have feelings too?
Some people kill animals just for fun,
Which isn't nice for anyone.

Rebecca O'Shea (Age 13)

Barley Field In August

Field of barley, waving and swaying in the gentle breeze
Tall and slender, sun-kissed, calling us to play
Splashes of scarlet poppies, fragile like tissue
Inviting sight to a young child's gaze.

Red Admiral flitting, fluttering, floating on the wind
Swallows swoop and soar, dive and dip!
Timid harvest mouse so busy, scuttling and scurrying
Sharp-eyed hawk looms silently overhead!

Shrieking with laughter, our adventures have begun
We are soldiers in battle, explorers, pixie folk who hide and seek
Long golden stems scratching at bare legs,
Not a care in the world as we fall and collapse in a heap!

Lying flat amongst the rustling ears
No other sound invades my secret thoughts.
Forming shapes and pictures from marsh - mallow clouds
Ball of fire penetrates my summer haze as crimson sky unfolds.

Closing my eyes, I bask in the sun's warm glow
Capture the moment and wish it would never end
Though evening fades and dies such beauty still lives on
And memories stay forever in my melancholy heart.

Alice Parkin (Age 14)

Playstation

A musical box with hiding voices inside.
A great entertainer of the computerised world.
A secret worker that's always ready for action.
A clever machine that hums gently when it's thinking.

Sam Pearce (Age 10)

The Amazing Match

I was walking on the pitch
When I fell into a ditch
And all the crowd jeered.
I was just about to score
When I heard a massive roar
And all my team mates cheered!

I wondered why they were cheering
They must have been hearing
Some strange and funny sounds.
Overhead, above the ground,
We all saw something quite profound.
It was a bird flying way out of bounds!

The game was finally underway,
Though it should have been played yesterday,
But the pitch was too wet and muddy.
There were twelve minutes remaining
As it started raining,
And I scored the winning goal, "Oh goody!"

Jamie Proctor (Age 9)

Useless

You're as useless

As a ship without a crew
As a buckle without a shoe,
As a key without a lock
As a shoe without a sock.

You're as useless

As a pocket without a hole
As a mine without some coal.
As calm as an ox
As thick as a box.

You're as useless

As a horse without a neigh
As Santa without his sleigh,
As a horse without a stable
As a book without a label.

Your're nearly as useless as
ME!

Danica Parker (Age 11)

Bedtime

Evie it is time for bed,
Time to rest your sleepy head.
See you in the morning light,
Bright and breezy, a delight.

Anna Pritchard (Age 8)

The Night Sky

The night sky
Pitch black
Thunder and lightning
In the violent sky

The night sky
Sparkling stars
Shooting and shining
In the frosty sky

The night sky
Shining moon
Bright and shining
In the beautiful sky

The night sky
Big rockets
Shooting and blasting
In the cold sky

Kelly-Marie Pearce (Age 9)

Oranges,
The Developed Consciousness Of

Our native country,
The Caribbean,
When mentioned, brings hot,

Sweet tears to our eyes.
Evil people come take us away
From our homes

In the lush green trees.
Squash us together in darkness for days.

On arrival, feeling queasy
After the long haul, we are
Separated. And taken away to

The land of Somerfield.
Hustle-bustle. Noise. Ignorant people.

They grab us. Then try to kill us.
They attempt to peel off our skin.
So we spit in their dirty
Faces - our spit is very acidic.

One day we will get revenge!
We will take over the world.
Peel off THEIR skin!

Jonathan Preston (Age 12)

The Pure Green Light!

One night I was in my room,
I looked out through the gloom
I sat up in my bed,
But then I banged my head.
A pure green light
Flew out of sight
This pure green light was there
Swooshing through the air.

Rachel Price (Age 10)

The Song Of The Whales

The song of the sea
Whistles and sings,
As time goes by

The waves lap against the shore
Making a gentle sound
As time goes by

As the sea makes a gentle noise
Another sound is heard
The song of the whales.

Rebecca Porter (Age 9)

What Am I?

I am the Lord of the ocean,
I am the King of the sea,
Waves are lapping in rhythm,
Flowing and breaking for me.

I am strong and agile,
I am graceful and light,
Snapping at the fishes,
From morning until night.

I am in smooth, grey armour,
I am a bright crescent moon,
On moonlit ripples at night
Down in the depths at noon.

I have a fiery eye,
I have a squeaky voice,
Searching sea-bottom ship-wrecks,
Finding human toys.

I have a very long nose,
I have a permanent smile,
And finally at last,
You'll find me on a bathroom tile

What am I?

Dolphin, Ocean King

Sophie Quantrell (Age 11)

The Tigers

The tigers were pouncing
On their prey
And suddenly there was
A Bang!

Evie Pritchard (Age 6)

I Love Cats!

I love cats!
Big cats, little cats,
Siamese and fat cats!
My Mum had cats,
Called Rusty, Ollie and Hoppy.
But they all died,
And Mum cried,
I patted her on the back.
A few years later
Lucy died.
We all cried
And I patted Dad on the back!
I miss our
Cats.

Jessica Phillips (Age 9)

Trooping The Colours

In the crowd I stood, excitedly,
Waiting, waiting,
The bands began to play,
So skilfully blending,
Playing 'God save the Queen.'

Then the army marched in procession,
Amazing, amazing,
Elegant horses prancing, snorting softly,
Their coats gleaming in the sunlight,
Marching around the courtyard,
Pulling shining cannons.

Then the amazing arrival,
Fascinating, fascinating,
The Queen glorious in her garments,
Stepping gracefully out of her dainty carriage,
Gleaming white, drawn by a horse so beautiful,
Such an exciting moment,
Rows of soldiers upright and still saluting their Queen.

Congratulations to our Queen!

Isobel Petersen (Age 9)

The Snowy Owl

He emerges from the darkness of his lair,
And files to the top of a great oak tree.
He searches for his prey,
His eyes shine like two golden balls.
Looking closely, he spots a water rat.
He swoops, wings outstretched, to pursue his victim.
He grabs it with sharp talons,
The returns to his nest to devour it.

James Pemberton (Age 11)

My Way Through The Woods

Down a leafy path,
Through the shady trees.
I heard a cuckoo laugh,
Caught sight through the leaves.

I continued on my way,
I saw a rabbit, vole and rat.
Three deer, two hares and a jay,
And a very lost looking cat.

It joined me on the way,
My house I could almost see.
My sister came to say,
Come along it's time for tea.

James Palmer (Age 11)

The Night Sky

The night sky
Still dark
Cold and meteorites falling
In the shiny moonlight

The night sky
Still pitch black
Thundering and lightning
In the stormy night.

The night sky
Still laying there
Cloudy and stars falling
In the bright sky.

The night sky
Still windy
The moon still bright and birds migrating
In the misty moonlight.

Hayden Palmer (Age 9)

Easter

Easter eggs yum yum
Most of them will fill my tum.
Some up high some down low
I shrink and shrink and grow and grow.
I eat the ones high and low.
Easter hunts are my best.
Other people eat the rest.
Yum yum Easter eggs
Make me feel like a pile of eggs or pegs.

Megan Pardoe (Age 6)

The Sea

Young yet old,
With ever changing moods,
She's a best friend
And enemy to a sailor.

Carefree yet angry,
Brimming with life,
She thunders and crashes
Upon the shore.

Unpredictable and independent,
Her depths guard the greatest secrets,
Calmly resting on her sandy floor,
Watching, waiting, wondering . . .

Sophie Papa (Age 12)

The Magic Box

I will put in my box
Lots of red sand.
And lovely yellow stars
And a white cat.

I will put in my box
A dog with a black mark
And a red sun.
And a blue star.

My box is made of wood.
It has red and yellow stars in the top.
Down the side it has got a picture of a dog.

I will fly to a little star in my box
It looks like a planet.
And the planet is red and blue.

Jimmy Phelippeau (Age 9)

Lessons

Some are boring,
Some are fun
Some are interesting
Some are silly,
Some are tiring,
Some are too much for me,
Some are short,
Some are long,
Some are easy,
Some are hard,
Some just aren't my type,
Some I just can't understand,
But I like them all.

Jamie Parsons (Age 8)

Bat Talk

Hi, I am a bat,
My species is a pippistrelle,
I hunt every night for my favourite food,
Delicious insects all night long.
I eat nearly 3000 bugs,
Day or night to keep me alive.
I'm flying through a forest,
It is peaceful and quiet,
Silent and calm.
I can hear owls,
Hooting at one another,
I darted to some insects I saw.

The day is coming, I need to sleep.
So I hang upside down and drift off.
I wrap myself up in my wings,
I am all cosy in the cave, in the dark,
I am safe from my preditors,
Good night.

Grace Powell (Age 10)

What Should I Write?

I have no idea what to write
No idea at all
I'm looking around to see what I can write about
Nothing
Hoping that my brain will think of an amazing idea
Nothing at all
Come on pen write something
Just stood still

I've got something yes that will work
But what am I going to write about it
Forget it
Yes that will definitely work
I can also write about it
I can't believe it
My pen is actually moving
Mucked it up
That's another piece of paper in the bin

I think I'll stop now even though I haven't started
I'll put my pen away now and I'll try again tomorrow
If I have enough time

David Powell (Age 12)

The Feel Of Things

I like the frosty crunchy snow
I like to feel the cold sparkling snow,
I like the glowing light in the moon
I like to feel my soft pillow,
I like the sun shining like light,
I like the feel of my bed because it's mine

Zara Peck (Age 7)

Our English Teachers

Have you heard of Mrs Green?
She's really kind, and very clean.
She always seems to have us in mind,
Like I said she's very kind.
Everyone likes her every bit,
She's quite funny too, I must admit!
She checks our work up to date,
And excuses you if it's sometimes late.
To please her you just have to smile,
'Cause that'll keep her happy for a while!

There's also Mrs Windsor
Who's always ready to help,
But when it comes to stories
You'll have to do it yourself!
Right now we're doing a play with her
It's called Cinderella,
It's about a pretty girl
And a very handsome fella!

Krupal Patel (Age 12)

Nature

I like the smell of flowers,
I could look at them for days,
I could stare at them for hours,
In all their different ways.

Insects are crawling,
All around,
The frogs could be calling,
A little sound.

Trees have leaves,
Falling off,
If they were alive,
They could have a cough.

Next is the pond,
Cold and wet,
I could go fishing,
If I had a net.

Ending with the wood,
Dark and creepy,
It's very wet,
I can get weepy.

Emma Pearce (Age 8)

The Moon

The moon is round,
A ball, a bauble,
A fairy, as white as a face.
An eye, a wheel, it's glittery!
As white as an igloo,
As silver as a candle,
A yo-yo bouncing!

Megan Parker (Age 6)

Grapefruit, Grapefruit

Grapefruit, grapefruit,
Hanging on a bush,
Grapefruit, grapefruit,
I think you need a push,
Grapefruit, grapefruit,
Sitting on the floor,
Grapefruit, Grapefruit,
I'll see if you are sore,
Grapefruit, grapefruit,
Lying in a tree,
Grapefruit, grapefruit,
Are you sitting in a garden?
Grapefruit, grapefruit,
I think you said pardon!

Jay Perkins (Age 6)

Why Oh Why

Why does Jupiter have rings around it?
Why are most plants green?
Why are shadows cooler than sunlight?
Why are big cats mean?

Why do flamingos stand on one leg
Why do stars shine?
Where do floods come from why does it rain?
Why do puppies whine?

Why are animals kept in zoos?
Why is the sun hot?
Why do we have to eat the right things?
Why do we cook in a pot?

Why is Mercury closest to the sun?
Why is Pluto blue?
Why do planets grow tall and straight up?
How do we make glue?

All these things, I've been wondering why?
Like how far up is the sky?
Why do cats walk head first?
I think my brain is going to burst!

Emily-Rose Penman (Age 10)

Celebrations

Friendly families come to celebrate
I am so happy you are our Queen
Folk adore you royal Queen
Time has gone by so quickly
You are our loving and loyal Queen
You have been queen for so very long
Everybody should really like you
Always people will love you
Respecting people will never forget you.

Alex Perrey (Age 9)

Horses

Munching on the grass all day,
Sniffing at the golden hay,
Nibbling on the fresh white oats,
Licking on my tasty salt float.

Rolling on the muddy ground,
Making a noisy neighing sound,
Galloping freely on the grass,
Shouting joyfully "I'm free at last"

But how I love my warm stable,
The hay and straw welcoming me,
A lovely quiet place to be.

Jessie Phippen (Age 11)

Dreams

In a state of sub-consciousness,
You float in your thoughts,
A world of your own,
Nothing can harm you.

Images fill your mind,
And then one swallows you,
You can see, smell, feel, hear, taste,
It all seems so real.

Then the scene changes,
You're running,
This is no dream,
It's a nightmare.

You're falling,
Falling and there's nothing you can do,
You try to escape,
Pull yourself out.

But it's a dream,
There's no way out. . . .

Makeeta Pooley (Age 14)

The...

The kids!
The house!
A constant mess!
I come to work so I can rest

Morne Prinsloo (Age 10)

The Dwarfs

Snorted every dwarf
When they caught him gulping
Came towards him gobbling
Jumping, bouncing, growling
Huffing and puffing
Barking, bouncing blowing
Plucking and pushing
Sweeping and washing
Full of moans and groans
Pulling monster faces
Fragile but wiry
Gorilla like - tiger like
Snake and lizard like
Slug paced in a worry
Cat voiced in a blower.
Shelter pelter, hurry curry.
Whistling like people
Flapping like birds
Pouncing like panthers!

Gemma Powell (Age 11)

A Childhood Memory

Running, skipping, charging down the hill,
Dandelions sway like delicate fairies,
While brightly coloured buttercups
Are blown away by the slight breeze.

I turn to see all the people watching me,
I stop and stare, then run
The excitement is so thrilling out here
My heart is thudding like a drum.

Down the hill, I run and run
To find the end is near
My feet seem to keep on going
This was my greatest fear.

I meet the people once more,
As I begin to walk to the top.
They see me look all hot and sticky
As I mount the hill, all hot

Running, skipping, charging down the hill,
Facing what lies ahead.
I begin to fear what I have chosen
And decide to depart instead.

Kirsten Pugsley (Age 14)

What Is Red?

The Queen's chair is red that she sits in
A balloon is red that bubbles in the air
A cage is red that hooks up for you

Robyn Parry (Age 7)

The Venom Cobra

The venom cobra has very sharp teeth;
Never ever call it a thief.
The venom cobra has a very long body;
Sometimes you may call him soggy.
The venom cobra has a very long tongue;
It helps him hiss just like a song.
The venom cobra spits out poison;
When it's prey makes any sudden movements.
The venom cobra has bog soft scales;
When his venom hits its prey it will never fail.
The venom cobra eventually grows out of its skin,
So it might as well throw it in the bin.
The venom cobra is a dangerous foe,
But also it moves very, very slow.
The venom cobra is as silky as a worm,
But when he gets up he still stands quite firm.
The venom cobra slithers in to bed
Because he has been well enough fed.
The venom cobra is very slick,
But if he gets caught he might get quite sick.

Christopher Poulton (Age 11)

September 11th, 2001

"Boom!" and bloody "Boom!" again,
The sound raged out across the scene.
The sight of the rampaging revolt, relentlessly running,
Made your stomach turn and your face go green.

A Twin departing the world,
For the first time leaving a friend.
For the fault of a gravity defying air caresses,
Determined to pursue, right through to the end.

Shelter where you can, God's innocent folk,
In Cafes, subways or under vans,
For the death cloud of dust descends into deadening darkness,
But the Bible does not promote man killing man.

An hour, a week, the world had stopped spinning,
Evils indefinite dent made in history.
The U.S. of A vowed to respond in the way,
Of fighting on land, in air, and at sea.

Americans are left to pick up the pieces,
The death toll's high and rising,
Other nations leave, with the sense not to grieve,
And a hate bred of fear and despising.

Thomas Payne (Age 14)

The Night Forest

Rustle, go the leaves, as if sharing a secret,
And the oak trees sway, like hammocks in the breeze.
Tne full moon sparkles like huge shimmering diamonds,
And crows squawk loudly, as they flutter by,
Animals are wide awake, sniffing and prowling,
The owl is hunting, the wolves are howling.
I can feel the wet grass under my feet,
And I'm the only one that's not asleep.

Helen Payne (Age 9)

Inside The . . . .

Inside the tiger's eye, the forest's blazing fire,
Inside the forest's blazing fire, the tiger's paw,
Inside the tiger's paw, the hills of extinction,
Inside the hills of extinction, the tiger's tail,
Inside the tiger's tail, the journey of life,
Inside the journey of life, the tiger's fangs,
Inside the tiger's fangs, the last cry of a helpless deer,
Inside the last cry of a helpless deer, a river of tears,
Inside the river of tears, the tiger's blood,
Inside the tiger's blood, the stream of exhaustion,
Inside the stream of exhaustion, the tiger's breath,
Inside the tiger's breath, a flame of fear,
Inside the flame of fear, the tiger's eye.

Rebecca Phillips (Age 11)

Last Day At School

My classroom was very messy
We have to tidy up
We have to clear the tray
And teachers coffee cup

We have to put chairs up
And clean the floor
Collect my PE bag
And go out the door

We have to clear out work
Collect toys or games
Check the lost property
Things with our names

Turn the lights off
Close the door
And say goodbye
Won't see you any more.

Jake Pockett (Age 6)

There Was A Cat

There was a cat,
Who wore a hat
Who ate a bat
That saw a rat,
The rat saw me,
But I can't run away,
I have to stay,
But it was O.K
When the cat came back,
It saw a rat
But the cat was too fat.

Max Patrick (Age 8)

The Magic Box

I will put in the box
The wild sun in Tenerife
The first time I score a goal
I will put a playground to play on

I will put in the box
A dog pulling a person
And a football playing with a player
And a car driving a person

My box will look as shiny
As gold metal

I will fly in my box
A football match
And invite some friends
To play with

James Poulton (Age 7)

The Queen's Jubilee

The Queen who took this magnificent job,
She has a strong heart,
She always smiles.
Her silky clean clothes are always smart.
The Queen who took this magnificent job

The Queen's special celebration
Is a very good creation
To bring happiness to all the nation.

The Queen has worn the crown for fifty years
And has never burst into tears.
I wonder if she has any fears,
The Queen has worn the crown for fifty years.

Alice Penn (Age 7)

Shape Poem

With beady eyes and curly tails
Munching food from an old tin pale
Wet round snouts, rough coats of pink,
Pigs are lovely, but they don't arf stink!!!

Holly Pegg (Age 11)

My Birthday Comes

My birthday comes with early waking
My birthday comes with our family arriving
My birthday comes with people cheering
My birthday comes with giving out presents
My birthday comes with us lot playing
My birthday comes with me opening presents
My birthday ends with everybody leaving

Felix Poole (Age 7)

The Owl

The owl sits in a tree,
Looking for prey with large glittering eyes.
Waiting for a mouse to come along,
Almost invisible with his camouflage,
His beak is ready to rip the flesh from a vole,
His talons are ready to snatch up a creature.
Feathers fly as he snatches one up
And flies back to his branch to eat his prey

Katie Parker (Age 10)

The Forest's Story

I remember when life was good
The children sliding down slides
Creating rope swings
I remember when the stream flowed
Water speeding from a waterfall
My trees were high;
Oaks, conifers, evergreens, birches, elms
When the wildlife ran around as free as a bird . . . .

But now they're gone
Left with fear of being killed by hunters
The stream is now just a huge dirty puddle
Now there are no more trees just roads and huts
Just the mud that once lived in the forest

Sean Pitman (Age 11)

Gold

Gold is the colour of the sun's rays.
Gold is the colour of a child's gaze.
Gold is the colour of sand on the beach.
Gold is the colour of a growing peach.
Gold is the colour of falling leaves.
Gold is the colour of the wind on the trees.

Jack Phelan (Age 8)

Francis Drake

When Francis Drake was 10,
He went to sea with three fat men,
And Drake returned to America with 29 ships,
By winning wars with salty lips.

When he shaved with a knife,
He had to save the cats life,
And destroyed the Spanish king,
By burning the kings beard of string.

When Francis Drake sailed to Plymouth,
He met Queen Elizabeth,
And Queen Elizabeth had asked where he had been,
To Spain with my incredible team.

When Queen Elizabeth said "Let's celebrate,"
He said "But I'm in a state!"
And he got some decent clothes,
By the way he's got to blow his nose.

He wanted to sail seven seas,
But, he almost caught the fleas,
There was mice on the floor but the bacon was raw,
The crew was thirsty but they couldn't have a cup of tea.

Yasmine Phipps (Age 9)

Matt The Rat And His Purple Hat

There was a fat rat whose name was Matt,
He lived in the first floor penthouse flat
And always wore the most splendid purple hat.
He would wear it to the theatre, he would wear it to his club
He would wear it when he was shopping he would wear it in the bathtub.
Matt's hat was very flamboyant, Matt's hat was very flash,
It was made of purple velvet and cost a lot of cash.
He would wear it to do his garden and even to clean his car,
His friends could not believe it they thought he was quite bizarre!
He would wear it when he went to work and even when he went bed.
Matt would not take off his hat off no matter what anyone said.
Matt's hat was his crowning glory.
He just would not take it off.
And that is the end of his story.
Matt the rat was such a toff.

Elizabeth Parry (Age 9)

Why Me?

When I was young, my life was fun
But now it's toil and trouble
I go to school each day to learn
But still get in a muddle
The teachers they are there to help us
If we need them to, but do I raise my hand and ask,
"Please Miss I need some help."
No 'course I don't the kids'll laugh and make the teacher yelp
You noisy lot now quieten down or I will keep you in.
It's time for us to read out loud,
So Sammy will you begin.
Oh no why me it isn't fair,
This seemed to make her mad.
Detention for you my girl she said.
What for I haven't done anything bad.
That night I walked out of the gate
Knowing that I'm half hour late.
What do I tell my mum and dad.

Samantha Paige (Age 11)

Spring

Spring is here,
Our favourite time of year.
Pink blossoms covering the bushes,
Trees in the background sweetly swaying in the air,
Bees humming, people coming.
The wind is blowing, the rivers are flowing.
Brand new bulbs stretching up to the fresh breeze.
But don't forget, pollen might make you sneeze!
Baby ducklings swimming around,
While spring is here to stay!!!

Harriet Phippen (Age 8)

Bunnie Rabbits?

You can get them from vets,
And make them your pets.
If you love them,
They'll love you.
Feed them every day, and play.
Don't ever be apart,
Give them a space in your heart.
They love to play in the sun,
With them the adventure has just begun.
Help it if it is in danger,
To you it's no stranger.
For a treat I'll give it a bun,
We'll have lots of fun.

Aalia Parveen (Age 10)

Before The Concert

Clapping audience,
Still me,
Velvet curtains,
Warm me,
Smooth notes,
Calm me,
Guiding music,
Light my way through the tune.
As my shaking fingers hit the strings,
So may I become calm.
As my music comes to an end,
So may I be first to hear applause.
Velvet curtains hear me,
Smiling audience still my shaking hands,
I will play the violin.

Alice Pickworth (Age 8)

There Was An Old Lady From Looe

There was an old lady from Looe
Who drank inky tea from a shoe,
Though it tasted quite nice,
She added some rice and it turned the old lady blue.

A few days later
An old man mate her
Under some mistletoe
Even though, she had already loved an old man called Moe.

He wanted to marry
But he can't even carry
So that's what is really stupid,
And guess what, he has even got his own cat called Cupid.

Charlotte Penny (Age 10)

Metaphor Poem

A book is a secret, written.
A dream ready to be unlocked;
It is an emotional guide.
A time stopper, for everything around you;
It is another life being told for us.
It is a magic key, another world.
It is a boat trip of adventure,
A dull black to a whizzing white.
It's a secret voice in your ear,
It's excitement, it's life, it's finished.

Kizzie Peters (Age 10)

Untitled

The seed has been in the muddy ground,
The seed can't be weathered until it's been found,

The silver water is waiting to be use by the
Man, to the mud where the seed was buried.

The seed has been waiting for this very day,
It has been pushing and struggling to get through the gray.

It is red, pink and grey, shiny and smooth
By the light of the sun, and the dark of the moon.

The weed is growing and the flower is proud

The rain has been falling from the sky
The flower has been falling from the sky
The flower has grown an inch taller than its normal size.

The roses life was pretty and calm
Now it is the end of the precious life it had to enjoy.

Kym Peacock (Age 9)

Up In The Spidery Attic

Up in the spidery attic!
Ancient vampire coffins,
Dusty werewolf fur,
A crinkly fire breathing
Dragon scale,
Bloody spiders
A cracked skull and
Blood stained dead rats.
Down in the creepy cellar!
Tattooed zombies,
Slimed stained mummified mums,
Bloody vampire teeth,
Dead hug up bats,
Dripping fresh blood on the floor and,
Hung up humans heads!
Dripping green blood!

Arron Ploszynski (Age 10)

Message From The Sea

"Whoosh!" goes the rough sea,
Spitting at the sand!
"Brrhh" what a cold day,
Look at my hands.
First is a big wave,
Then there is a small
Last there's a medium
And that was all.
I think it said
Please leave me
The ocean goes down with peace!

Samantha Patterson (Age 9)

The Sea

The sea is...

A sharks restaurant,
A sheet of blue,
A fishes home,
A death trap,
A dolphins water bowl,
A whales swimming pool,
A bed for ship wrecks,
Cold,
Blue and green,
A pound for boots,
Work for fisherman,
A colourful piece of land,
A corner of the sky,
A fishes fin,
A swimming pool for us.

Ellis Prior (Age 10)

Dreaming About The Queen

I fish a dream from my mind,
And leave all the others behind,
About the Queen,
Who is healthy and clean,
With all her glossy things,
And her shiny gold rings.

When I knocked on her door,
I fell flat on the floor,
As there was the biggest room I had ever seen before,
It was packed full of beautiful things,
The huge mirrors, the giant doors,
Just that stair made my mouth water.

She had famous items on display,
Which meant I would have an interesting day,
The Queens jubilee,
Is very special to me!

Edward Pugh (Age 10)

Whole

The bit of me which controls my health
(I don't know - it's probably shaped like a pickled gherkin)
This bit's completely tied up to
(for example) the bit that controls my happiness
(which is pink and wafts out strawberry).
I don't just mean I'm sad when I'm sick.
Everybody feels that. But I work
As a whole. When I'm disappointed,
Upset, irate, I puke, I sweat,
I work as a whole. And I cannot fake
A passion which isn't there.

Harry Perrin (Age 18)

Summer

The sun shone brightly
As it jumped lightly
Twinkling down on the sand
On a seaside bay
On a summer's day

It softly shimmered
While on the sea it glimmered
And made all the seagulls squawk.

When all were gone the red sun peered up
Night time was coming.

Laura Phillips (Age 9)

Dolphin

Blue or turquoise not amber or green
A dolphin soars under the sea
Not a bunny or a cat
Not a dog or a bat
I may be shy but wait and see
How friendly I can be.
Swimming smoothly on my back
Don't leave,
Don't pack,
Don't stay in and watch TV
Come in the water and play with me.

Abbie Pegler (Age 9

When I Gazed Into The Future

When I gazed into the future,
I saw the world being destroyed in front of me.
When I gazed into the future,
I heard the horrifying sound of screams in the air.
When I gazed into the future,
I smelt the disgusting smell of pollution around me.
When I gazed into the future,
I saw the schools completely empty - dead silence.
When I gazed into the future,
I heard the buzzing of flying police cars on the chase.
When I gazed into the future,
I touched the stone walls stopping people from getting out.
When I gazed into the future,
I tasted the terrible food in which they were being given.
When I gazed into the future,
I smelt the horrible smell of toxic waste being dumped on the fields.
When I gazed into the future,
I touched the only thing left in our world that was good, the last tree.

Rosie Pitfield (Age 11)

To A Rose

Breathtaking elegance,
A Queen standing tall over her emerald subjects.
The reddest wine,
Sipped from the dawn's rising sun.
A red ruby,
Supported on a green statue.
Dew drops rest upon you,
Like tears on a silken pillow.
It's heart warming,
Like love's first kiss.
Charming - magnificent - radiant.
A picturesque sunset
Over a pea green sea,
Beauty beyond imagination.

Victoria Palmer (Age 9)

The Wind

The wind was as gentle as a new born baby
The wind was as quiet as a mouse
The wind tickled the girl's hair
The wind silently swayed us sideways
The wind was as cold as an iceberg
The wind wildly whizzed round the farm
The wind was as loud as an elephant's trumpet
The wind was as fast as a cheetah
The wind was as strong as a boulder
The wind crept into the ladies room
The wind howled like a wolf
The wind waved wickedly,
As it said goodbye.

Frederica Poznansky (Age 9)

Spring

In the leaves the hedgehog lay
Like a spiky football
Slowly it unravels like a scroll

There the bat hangs with a mouth
As dry as a dessert
And a belly that rumbles like a volcano

The spring weather looks like a brown world in the rain
And the crispy leaves cover the world waiting for a spring breeze

The daffodils as yellow as the sun
The tulips as blue as the sky
And snowdrops as white as the clouds

And the world begins to blossom again.

Adam Patrick (Age 11)

Weather

What is the touch of a snowflake falling?
A tiny cold pinprick on your cheek.
What is the taste of the summer breeze?
The charcoal taste of the back garden barbecue.
What is the sound of the rain falling?
The constant drumming of a million feet running
What is the touch of the sun's blazing rays?
A thousand shots of electricity.

Ellyn Richardson (Age 11)

Stonehenge

Gigantic stone standing in the sunset
Falling on top of each other
Standing there as time goes by
Sinking into the ground
Shimmering in the sunlight
Some are tall
And some are small
Some are smooth
And some are bumpy

Katie Padfield (Age 8)

Little Tiger

Little Tiger went into the forest
He saw all of his friends

Charlotte Poole (Age 4)

Snow

Snow I love snow
Lets have a snow ball fight
"Get down!
Lets make a base
"Never"
Strike on, hit
"Get down again"
Oh NO grown ups
Don't knock them out
Let's stop
I'm cold
I'm going to have a shower.

Lawrence Poole (Age 9)

Francis Drake

When Francis Drake was only ten, he gathered together a group of men.
They went out to sea on a trip, and travelled along in his wooden ship.

When he came to see the Spanish, all of a sudden they decided to vanish.
He went to sleep for a long time, when Francis woke up they said that gold's mine.

He went to Plymouth for some tea, Elizabeth said would you do something for me.
He sailed back to the sea for some treasure, on a map he had to measure.

They named the ship the Golden Hind, when they got there they said look behind.
They sailed in and saw a big cave, they sailed in wave after wave.

Francis had some silver and gold, lots of coins that the ship had to hold.
Francis turned around his ship, before the waves started to dip.

Elizabeth he went to see, what presents have you bought me.
I have bought you silver and gold, now I must go back on the road.

Brendon Parr (Age 9)

Blackie My Rabbit

Blackie is a lovable rabbit.
She is like a round ball of fluff.
When we see if she wants to come out in the run
She jumps up onto the wooden box.
Blackie doesn't really eat rabbit food but enjoys vegetables.
She is very precious to me.

Georgina Phipps (Age 6)

My Favourite Colours

Red is the sun at the end of the day.
Yellow is the fine sand at the sea.
Orange is the bonfire burning slowly.
Green is the really soft grass.
Blue is the shining sky.
Purple is the night coming nigh.

Catriona Phillips (Age 6)

The Fisherman

I went to the pier and saw a boat
I saw the fish flapping in the ocean
The fishermen waited for their catch below the waves
Which bounced up and down almost hitting the clouds
I stayed until the fish were caught
And watched as the gulls cried for their dinner
We went home at sunset it was as beautiful as magic
We went home and snuggled in bed and slept like angels.

Ellé Poole (Age 6)

Where I Live

Where I live is a fantastic place,
It's a quiet and little street.
We're closer to France than to London,
A Dickens place to be!
In summer wow! A dragon plays on the sand,
And children feed him money.
In winter waves crash where people swam
I'LL NEVER MOVE FROM HERE!!!

Nicola Parker (Age 10)

My Birthday Comes

My birthday comes with early waking
My birthday comes with the door opening
My birthday comes with papers flying
My birthday comes with people visiting
My birthday comes with me getting presents
My birthday comes with people singing "Happy Birthday"
My birthday comes with everyone going

Elliot Poole (Age 7)

Our Mums

Mums polish
Mums clean up
Mums take us to bed
Mums iron a lot
Mums make our beds
Mums bake
We love our mums

Jake Petty (Age 6)

The Forest Story

I remember when life was good
When the creatures were my offspring
And the undergrowth was my carpet
The lullaby of my birds
The whistling of the bracken in the breeze
The fracture of the conkers as they cracked on my floor
My long fingers protected my creatures from the pelt of the rain
The feel of the brambles stabbing my skin
Then there was the hymn of my wild flowers, I'll never forget that

Look well and hard you'll find me, my children still live inside you

Now you can only smell oil and smoke
The carpets are burnt with factories
My children are vanished along with new species
The flowers don't sing their harmony any more because they're lifeless
And now I'm killed. I'll never live again.
But I still remember when life was good.

Hanna Preece (Age 9)

Last Night I Had A Dream....I Met The Queen

Q ueen Elizabeth became queen in 1952,
U sually she lives in Buckingham Palace,
E lizabeth likes to ride horses and race,
El izabeth has six grandchildren two are called
                                William and Harry,
N ormally the Queen has six corgis.

E lizabeth is a strong-minded woman,
L ots of people go to see the Queen,
I think the Queen is very pretty,
Z ara is one of the Queen's grandchildren,
A nne is her only daughter,
B eing a Queen is a wonderful thing,
E lizabeth has 11 dogs,
T he Queen likes her Corgis best,
H er reign has been fifty long years.

Laura Prentice (Age 8)

What The Teachers Always Say

"Please Miss can I go now?" I ask
But the reply is always the same
"Eat your peas!"
"Please Miss can I go to the toilet?" I ask
But the reply is always the same
"Finish your work first!"
"Please Miss can I go and get a drink?"
But the reply is always the same
"Tidy the classroom first!"
"Please Miss can I go and get a tissue?" I ask
But the reply is always,
"It doesn't look as though you need one!"
That's the way it always is!

Lydia Preece (Age 9)

Purple

Purple is the glitter that comes out of your pen
Purple are the grapes growing generally
Purple is the costume that Boo wears in the movie,
Purple is the colour of my literacy folder
Purple are the curtains hanging in my room
Purple is a felt tip colour
Purple is the teacher's white board pen

Nikola Quinn (Age 9)

The Snowy Owl

Trying to find its prey in the forest,
Waiting for his moment to attack.
His eyes burn like hot flames.
His feathers open like big arms,
His beak is a sharp knife.
He spies a mouse in the grass
Then swoops down to catch his prey.
Killing it with his talons.

Jessica Page (Age 11)

The House On The Hill

The darkness smothered the waxing moon
And the wind like hounds howled and scratched at the rusting locks
The flaking white paint of the house was illuminated by the sudden crack of lightning
And the needle rain plummeted to earth, piercing anything in its path
The clock in the hall slowly ceased to tick
And the eyes in the murky portraits stared into the gloom
As the waves and sea grass crashed and rolled against the cliff
        The front door slammed
And the man in his room arose, gripped with cold fear.
He edged down the rough, winding staircase and when the next bolt of lightening shone
His eyes rested on the twisted padlocks on the basement door - twisted in pain and broken.
As the darkness was punctured with the first rays of sunlight and the hounds yelped away with their dark masters.
He saw with new horror the hands on the clock pointing to the rotting door.
Wet footprints reached down the gravel to a filthy mass of wood and twine.
This was the outside door to the basement where no human lurked.

Ailsa Raw (Age 13)

The Dark

A plague of what is to come
In endless sleep shunting
Past the unworthy stars
A dark lords dungeon under the command of a boy
A giant sheet covering where light doesn't show
A black war under the stars
A granted demons face looking nervously past the dawn
A sack filled with coal that had the eyes of evil
The unknown fear scolding towards a depth of pitch black stars

Jack Peto (Age 9)

My Sister

Chrissy's hands are as soft as silk
And as fine as can be.
She has wild blond hair,
That blows in the wind.
With her cheeky smile
That is willing to tell
All the secrets that she knows!

Emma Price (Age 9)

The Mystery Of The Night

I saw stars winking as if sharing an unknown secret and
Dewdrops gathering on the floor like drops on the sink
While the moon shines as if sharing jewels
And birds pecking like a vibra slap
I feel scared as well as pleased
That I saw the moment at night.
I'll tell them but they won't believe me but I know it's true.

Hannah Pye (Age 9)

The Snake

Red snake
Rattles and shakes
Looking pretty scary
In the very big, hot desert
He strikes

Matthew Ploszynski (Age 8)

Creation Poem

Cats and rats and bats, he made all of those
Rivers and lakes, he made to go with the seaside
Elephants stomp across the lands, God made them too
Ants that scurry along leaves, God made them too
Tigers that roar at you.
India, England, America, God made the world
Oranges, pears, apples, bananas, God made them
Night and day, stars, moon and sun, God made those things too.

Alissa Plumb (Age 9)

Blown Away!

Rustles in the wind
Long refreshing breaths of air
Calm voices travel
Frozen long season
Leaves blown from ancient, bare trees
With clean air whirling.

Emma Polak (Age 12)

Winter

When winter comes,
The world freezes over.
Breath hangs in the air
Like fog over the fields.

The frost on the lawn
Crunches beneath my feet
And Jack Frost has painted
All the trees white.

When the snow arrives
Over excited children
Throw snowballs and
Make snowmen in the park.

Every morning I awake
To the sound of cars
Being cleared of ice
Or engines unable to start.

When the temperature drops
I like to stay warm inside
With a blazing log fire
And watch winter games on the tv.

Sarah Riley (Age 11)

My Mouse

My pet is a mouse,
It lives in a house
It always fights,
Every night
He plays poker,
He's never a joker
His little mice,
Play with the dice
His mouth is so big,
You can fit in a pig.

Pryanka Patel (Age 9)

Blue

Feeling . . . blue
The sky . . . not blue
Your face . . blue.

The accident . . . a blur of blue
The pain . . . . blue
The tears . . . . blue

The grief . . . . blue
The sadness . . blue
The fear . . . . . blue

A new life, no life . . . blue

Emily Reed (Age 12)

The Clock

The clock is ticking all night long
Tick Tock, Tick Tock, Tick Tock
Oh why won't the clock stop?

It's like a race against time
Like you're running away from your scariest dream
Like having no family, you're all alone in the world.

The clock is ticking all night long
Tick Tock, Tick Tock, Tick Tock
Oh why won't the clock stop?

It hunts you down like a prowling tiger
It pulls you into a pit of snakes
It seeps through you like scorpions venom.

The clock is ticking all night long
Tick Tock, Tick Tock, Tick Tock
Oh why won't it stop . . . at last it has stopped
I knew it would in the end, but heaven will be great,
Without my disease called AIDS
Aids has killed me, brought me to the end.

Carrie Anne Reeves (Age 11)

The Snake Poem

They are slithery and small and big and humongous
Their eyes move from side to side.
Their backs are the colours of the flowers.
Their teeth are small but sharp like arrows.
Their tongues are split as a broken tree bark.

Ajay Patel (Age 9)

Sun

Sun always shined in the summer
In the morning it shined to brightly
At lunch time the sun shined like normal
At night it is not shining it has gone.

Katie Potton (Age 10)

The Planets

The planets are wonderful things all sizes all colours.
There's cratered dusty Mercury right next to the sun,
Then there's Venus hottest of all,
Next it's Earth the only life support of them all,
Cold dusty Mars cratered like the moon,
Giant Jupiter with it's red spot watching down on,
Saturn with it's rings like outer platforms all around the planet,
Greeny silver Uranus with it's magnetic force,
Beautiful Neptune stormy cold windy,
Then last of all there's little Pluto the coldest loneliest of them all.

Alex Polding (Age 10)

At The Dead Of Night

At the dead of night
All the foxes come into sight
They are cunning and sly
You'll probably only see them through the corner of your eye

At the dead of night
They will start a vicious fight
They are private and unspoken
They have vanished by the time you have been woken

At the dead of night
They scavenge for food with all their might
They are sprinty and quick
They can be there and gone in just one click

So next time you are awake long after nine
Look out the window and check the time
If you're lucky you might just see a fox, cunning and sly
Out of the corner of your eye!

Emma Ryle (Age 12)

The Enormous Storm

The enormous storm started when it got really windy
Whirlwinds started blowing all over the town
Gusts of wind were blowing leaves about
Freezing cold weather freezes your hand
Hurricanes blow down trees on beaches
Cyclones are ripping up the sea twisting and turning
Finally the storm moves on to a different place

Daniel Rixson (Age 8)

Three Senses

The essence of book before it is read,
Tension's odour before an evil thing is said.
These I have smelt.

On a violin a sad ballad is played,
With a cheerful jig merriment is made.
The sound of silence is a treasured matter.
The ringing noise after a biting blow.
The squeaking croak of a throaty crow,
The singing water of a bubbling stream.
Dripping noise of the pearliest cream.
These I have heard.

The cool water flowing down my throat.
The creamiest milk from the purest of goats.
The salty taste of crispy sizzling bacon
Gingerbread's interesting attractive flavour
Marzipan's tanginess a taste I savour.
Newly baked cookies still steaming and mild,
And the passion fruit has a taste that is fantastic and wild,
These I have tasted.

Sarah Robinson (Age 12)

Tornado Nearing

Wind howling,
Floor boards creaking,
Doors slamming,
Windows breaking,
Trees falling,
Houses swaying,
Tornado nearing.

People crying,
People running,
People dying,
People falling,
People crawling,
Houses swaying,
Tornado nearing.

Lawrence Roots (Age 11)

Horse

As fast as lightning
Galloping through the field fast.
Slow down, pretty face.

Susie Pollard (Age 8)

Kittens

Damp nose, soft purring,
Fast asleep, not one stirring.
Silky fur, freshly groomed,
Tiny kittens, tails plumed.

Rosie Richardson (Age 11)

The Bats Are Back

Bats are black
Bats are brown
They fly so high
They hang upside down

Bats are big
Bats are small
They have long ears
Some are so small

They fly at night
They sleep at day
They fly so fast
To catch their prey

Their prey are bugs
So sweet for they
Eat three thousand
Every day

Jake Rose (Age 10)

The Prince Awakens

The night was damp,
The low clouds racing across the midnight sky,
Scaring all the passers by
The rain falling from upon high

The soaking wet raven with ice cold feet,
Fluffing out his feathers,
Came and sat within the sleet,
Upon the open hatches

The necessary repairs that needed to take place
Then waiting for another three days
Until the right weather came
The whirring, whirring of the machines.

Thunder whistled like violent whirlwinds
Then DANGER, DANGER.
A great silence descended
After the great explosion,
The storm abated.
And the table came wafting from above
And the whimper, whimper of the monster.

Natalie Roughsedge (Age 11)

It's A . . .

It's a Trouble maker,
         Clothes taker,
         Mother annoyer,
         Mood swinger,
         Food lover,
         Pukes over cover.

         It's a   Teenage sister!

Charlotte Robertson (Age 10)

Looking At The Wind

Whirling around,
Seizing anything in my path
Howling like an angry child,
Sending a shiver down your spine.

I can be gentle,
A breeze on a summer's day,
Dancing, fluttering your hair.

I can be bitter,
A storm on a winter's day,
Growling and bellowing,
My icy teeth biting into you.

I whirl around

Helena Rogers (Age 11)

Public Warning And Remonstrance!

Remonstrance to all citizens!
Please guard your daughters and sons.
There are bullies about;
Big, medium and little ones!

Doctors amazingly can
Behave worse than infants,
For bullies can wear suits
And speak with nice accents.

Public servants, alas!
Are prone to be menaces.
Keep on guard, citizens!
Beware of their devices.

You wouldn't believe it but
Judges and academics
Can grow into bullies!
Statesmen can! And clerics!

Perhaps, it's a disease?
Perhaps, you can catch it
From proximity to one?
All citizens should watch it!

Candice Robinson (Age 14)

I'm A Mouse

I'm a mouse, I only come out at night,
I'm a mouse, I don't want a fight,
I'm a mouse who goes squeak,
I make people go eek!
All I want is a home,
So leave me alone.

Emily Ruscoe (Age 11)

Why The Weather?

Why the weather?
Why the bother?
Why the weather?

When it's sunny
It feels like heaven
The sun is as bright as honey.
It's not dark to seven.

When it's cloudy
The sky's so light
It makes you feel so drowsy
Clouds so fluffy and white

Why the weather?
Why the bother?
Why the weather?

Sophie Richards (Age 11)

The Scent Collector

A stranger called this morning
Dressed all in black and grey
Put every smell into a bag
And carried them all away

He took the scent of bacon
Sausages an' all
He took the smell of beans
And beer brew as well

He took the smell of soup
Cheese and sweetcorn cool
He took the smell of mustard
And burning rubber too

The smell of Diesel went boom
The smell of the Dog went out the window
The scent of custard died
The smells probably went to **_SHINZO_**

Sam Robinson (Age 9)

The Draught Of Living Death

This is a powerful potion,
People believe it is magical
Some even think it is evil.
Only you can decide!

The potion is a sleeping potion so powerful
Only those with utter strength
And with the strongest will to live
Can awake and survive the ever-lasting sleep.

So will you sleep forever?
That is my question!
And what dreams will you dream?
Will they be peaceful?

I advise you do not take my potion.
No dreams may it give, only strange hallucinations
Be warned for my little bottle of potion is known as
THE DRAUGHT OF LIVING DEATH!

Rebecca Rankin (Age 11)

Yellow Poem

Yellow buttercups blowing in the wind
Sandy beach
Yellow buttercups blowing in the wind
Lemony lemons
Yellow buttercups blowing in the wind
Sun sunny
Yellow buttercups blowing in the wind
Yellow tea cup
Yellow buttercups blowing in the wind

Ellè Richards (Age 8)

Summer

I like it when it's summer
You get to hang around with your friends
And make daisy chains
You go to the beach
And have ice-creams and cold lollies
I like it when it's summer
I see all the birds singing
And the bunnies hopping up and down
The smell of flowers
And the stripy bumble bees fly through the air
I really like it when it's summer!

Harriet Russell (Age 9)

A Class Three Pie

To make a class three pie you need;
Tia's feet, smelly and bony
Joseph's brain, big and useful
Naomi's ears, flapping like mad
Laura's skull, guarding her brain
You need,
Niall's hair, brown and short
Charlotte's kidneys, cleaning blood
Katie's lungs, help her breathe
Saskia's liver cleaning her blood
Ella's tonsils, in her throat
Mayumi's small intestine,
Shelley's large intestine,
And mine and Joss' muscles
That's how you make a class three pie
There is one problem no-one wants to eat it!

Jack Race (Age 9)

Queen For Sale!!!

1920's Queen for sale! Very fragile
If dropped; will break instantly
A few cracks; easily fixed
Rusty around the limbs, needs oiling
A few grey hairs, but nothing a respray can't fix.
Almost 50 years on the throne! Highly experienced
Needs a big home but a cosy one.

Comes with large, troublesome family
Who may need some attention
Must be handled with care
Wrapped up warm when being
Transported in carriages.
A low price of £50!!
(*Servants may be required!!!*)

Christopher Rowlands (Age 11)

Warzone 1

Bang - Bang the lights went out
Oh no what a shout!

The Germans are here!
They have flooded the pier!

Everyone in the bomb shelter.
Everyone in? Good it's helter skelter.

People are dead:
Others are sick and ill in bed.

Hooray we win!
We flooded them,
Let's celebrate with a gin.

Kenny Rowe (Age 10)

My Dog Scruffy

My dog Scruffy
Is the scruffiest dog you will ever meet
He is so fluffy
And has such tiny feet.
He thinks he's cool
Because he can swim
In my friends swimming pool!

When my dog goes for a walk
He chases the ducks who don't even want to talk
He gets so angry, when the ducks won't play
Because when my Dad, pulls him away,
All the ducks want to play!

Brittany Ramsbottom (Age 9)

ME!

I used to think it was great fun
Watching them pick on her being so bitchy
It must have really hurt
It used to be quite funny
Until I looked to see
That it wasn't her they were picking on
But this time it was me
I wished I hadn't laughed now
Because it aches inside
The trouble that they caused me
Was far too much to hide
Now I know what it feels like
Being picked on time after time
I now know not to laugh at them
And that bullying is a crime

Emma Redfearn (Age 14)

The Monster In My Cupboard

Last night when I jumped into my cosy bed,
I layed and looked at the ceiling,
But when I peered down at my cupboard,
I got the strangest feeling.

His googly eyes, his wrinkly skin,
I really don't know where to begin,
His snotty nose, his smelly feet,
His nails were certainly not neat.

His shadow peered across the room,
His roaring I ignored,
I swear I saw him yesterday,
The monster in my cupboard.

Nia Root (Age 11)

Freezing

The freezing cold snow,
The slippy frosty ice,
Which stops the rivers flow,
Some people find it nice.

Freezing but refreshing,
Having snowball fights,
It's freezing out here,
I tell you! It's freezing!

Now I'll go in,
To warm my feet by the fire,
The winter is here,
And it's freezing!

Samantha Robinson (Age 11)

Up In Space To Planet Saturn

Jupiter and Saturn are
The largest planets in the solar system.
The planet is full of so much wisdom.

The colours are orange and white it stays together tight,
It is a grand to be near, to has a myriad of patterns.

Saturn is full of gas.
I looked out of the spaceship window that was made of glass.
Saw Saturn as we passed.

Hannah Raddy (Age 11)

The Search For Water

Lost in the desert,
On camel back,
Rides a thin man.
The search for water.

Golden sand lies everywhere,
Like a sleeping cat,
The sun is burning,
The search for water.

Lizard lies on the rock,
Runs at the sound,
It's only camel snorting,
The search for water.

Man jumps off,
Shouts in the air,
I've found it!
He's found the water!

Josie Rylands (Age 8)

Inside My Head

Inside my head
There's a classroom
With cream colour lockers
And light brown desks.
Teachers teaching useless children
Some children being naughty
Some being kind and gentle
The automatic bell rings!
Out run all the children

Elliott Riley (Age 7)

Who Do We Appreciate!!!

2, 4, 6, 8,
Who do we appreciate
Not the King, not the Queen
But St Mary's netball team

2, 4, 6, 8,
Get a move on, we'll be late
Don't go the office way
If you pass you'll have to pay

2, 4, 6, 8,
I can see the school gates
Let's go in don't make a sound
St Mary's school must be proud

2, 4, 6, 8,
Who do we appreciate!!!

Louise Frances Roberts (Age 9)

Feelings

My hatred is for someone who hurts people's feelings,
Crushing their courage and making them feel empty inside.

My love is for someone who is kind and helpful,
Caring for people who, feel unwanted.

My jealousy is for someone who has what I want,
Not being able to have it makes me envy that person.

My sadness is for anyone or anything that is ill or sick,
It's like a drooping flower dying.

My excitement makes me feel happy inside
Feeling as though I'm riding on a rollercoaster.

My happiness is for someone who enjoys life
For life is not worth living, unless you're happy!

Abigail Rowley (Age 11)

Purple Silence

Through these waves,
Deep, inside every distorted message
Cries relentless screaming.
Polluting my sullen dreams,
Weeping for far off warmth,
Long since shrouded in purple silence.
Waiting, to crawl inside your heart,
Flashing past me, these constant questions
Escape mist covered truth.
And all the while I wonder; Who is talking?
Chords of familiar echoes, lost
In the tangle of my mind.
No light shall penetrate these bad dreams.
It's me,
And I am talking to myself.

Helen Richardson (Age 13)

Someone In Our School Today

Two girls sitting there playing with each others hair
A bunch of sensible boys doing their work

The year two's sitting nervously for their test
A tough gang of year six playing a game of rugby

A group of teachers relaxing in the staff room eating
Our grumpy old caretaker sweeping the hall floor

Our jolly headmaster letting us out to play
The year five standing up saying their time-tables

The deputy head standing up shouting and screaming
The bell rings loudly out of their classroom to their parents

Selina Russel (Age 10)

What Is The . . . . Moon?

It is a bowl of porridge that's been thrown into the sky
It is a satellite dish circling the world
It's a mouldy orange been swallowed by the hungry sky
It is a huge mirror reflecting the golden sun
It is a silver boomerang been punched up to heaven
It's a pancake that's been tossed into the solar system
It is a wheel zooming around the world's atmosphere
It is a grey button that was flicked into the clouds
It is a 10p coin that was flipped too high
It is a round ball kicked high into the dull sky
It is a shiny balloon that floated up to heaven
It is a white paint lid that exploded from the tin
It is a pizza base that was lobbed by an angry Italian chef
It is a custard pie that missed the funny clowns face
It is a discus thrown by a famous Greek athlete
It is the top of a cake blown away by the strong wind
It is a sparkling catherine wheel spinning into space

Elliott Reed (Age 11)

Down Behind The Dustbin

Down behind the dustbin
I met a dog called Pat
"What are you doing down here" I said,
"I'm looking for my hat".

Down behind the dustbin
I met a dog called Steve
"What are you doing down here" I said,
"Nothing, I'm just about to leave".

Down behind the dustbin
I met a dog called Dick
"Can I have one of your sweets" I said,
"Yes just take your pick".

Amy Rendell (Age 12)

If You Want To See A Tiger

If you want to see a tiger you must go into the jungle calmly and softly
I know a tiger who's living down there, he's a mean one who eats you all up and jumps up at you.
Yes, if you really want to see a tiger, you must be silent otherwise he will eat you . . .gobble!
Go down carefully and say "You nice tiger, you nice one".
Then he won't eat you but if you say something nasty he will
And you'll be all gone but you might be lucky and someone might save you.

Brooke Richards (Age 7)

Francis Drake

When Francis Drake thought he was king, he liked to dance and also sing.
'Till one day he had a letter, saying "You have to sail to Fransetter".

At that time he was only ten, but he got lots of mighty men.
He liked to sail across the sea, on board he had a friend called Lee.

Sir Francis Drake he had no fear, till one day he saw an island near,
He quickly got his guns all ready, then he gave the orders ready steady . . .

He had a battle with them lot, he burned their ships to make them hot,
At last he won against those people, he said "watch out I am lethal".

He carried on sailing across the sea, he lost his little friend called Lee,
When Lee died Drake got mad and he was also very sad.

He sailed back home in one day, "Congratulations" the Queen would always say,
When he arrived everyone cheered, he saw a man with a very long beard.

He sailed for three years, him and his crew they had no fears,
They travelled around the world, every week the ship curled.

Then he sailed back home one week, when he got there his boat had a leek,
To tell the Queen what he had seen, as she asked him where he'd been.

Tiffany Radmore (Age 10)

The Dolphin

A bottle nosed dolphin with silver smooth skin,
Sharp white teeth along with a pink tongue,
Sunshine beating down on a silver back.
Here comes a tidal wave pushing the dolphin,
A fin peeping from the deep blue sea,
Also a flipper going up and down,
Diving down beneath the waves,
Sea foam around its blowhole.
The dolphin is friends with everyone.
Feeding fish into the mouth of a dolphin.
A teardrop shape while diving,
No stripes or spots has a dolphin,
But they can have freckles,
Diving under the night sky,
Goodnight little dolphin.

Laura Ruthnum (Age 8)

A White World

As snow starts to fall,
A throwing of a ball,
Reminds me that Christmas is near.

As the winter sales start,
I'm there like a dart,
Of buying kids clothes I've no fear.
When the couples start to skate,
I realise I am late,
And my warm cup of soup should be ready.

Shmeika Richards (Age 10)

Questions

Do teachers get tired of talking?
Do dogs get tired of walking?
Do Dads get tired of working?
Do babies get tired of burping?
Do singers get tired of singing?
Does the Hunch Back get tired of ringing?
Does Einstein get tired of knowing?
Does the wind get tired of blowing?
Do you know the answers?
I'll ask you all one day
'Cause I'm getting tired of reading
And I've had enough today.

Pietro Rinaldi (Age 12)

Butterfly

Butterfly with beautiful wings
Some colours are like diamond rings

Some are like a patchwork quilt
But some are like a sea of felt

Butterfly is like the best rainbow
The sparkly chrystals in the fluffiest snow

A shimmery fish deep in the sea
A cluster of stars shining on me

Others are like a bed of flowers
But butterfly hides when it showers

Tara Emily Ramsey (Age 11)

The Forest's Story

I remember when life was good, the friendly animals would have a conversation with me
My friends were all around,
The gushing waterfall would flow rapidly and birds would hum sweet melodies
The winding paths would twist and turn throughout me
And flourishing flowers looked very attractive standing straight
I watched the lively children laughing and playing merrily
And contentedly watched the squirrels collect food for the winter
I was sad to see the badgers hibernate, but they'd be back soon
I was delighted to look upon the school boys having snowball fights
But felt embarrassed when I became bare in the winter
But what a fantastic feeling it was when I got my brand new leaves in spring
People help me I am yours to look after, so save me from this terrible nightmare
Find my wreckage and rebuild me. One day some humans came and removed my fellow trees
They built a motorway right next to me, frightened all my friends away,
Now I stand tall, but all alone.
The flowers who I once admired, have been flattened or killed
The badgers left and went to another forest.
My friends the squirrels, who I loved to observe in the freezing winters
Have gone to collect their nuts elsewhere
I miss my ancestors, but now you can help me! help me! help me!

Olivia Rylance (Age 11)

I Wonder . . .

I wonder what would happen if scissors forgot to cut,
If scissors never cut again I wonder what would happen.
I wonder what would happen if glue forgot to stick,
If it never ever stuck again I wonder what would happen.
I wonder what would happen if candles forgot to light,
If they never ever lit again I wonder what would happen.
I wonder what would happen if the grass forgot to grow,
If it never ever grew again I wonder what would happen.
I wonder what would happen if the sun forgot to shine,
If it never ever shone again I wonder what would happen.
I wonder what would happen if pens forgot to write,
If they never ever wrote again I wonder what would happen.
I wonder what would happen if I forgot to wonder,
If I never ever wondered again I wonder what would happen.

Jane Robertson (Age 12)

A Message For Life

I sat on my beach waiting to hear a sound or call
To see a large, strong sailing ship mast hung strong and tall
And then I see a bottle lying in the sand
I pick it up I see inside I hold it in my hand
I think to myself that poor old man but then I think of me
For I must use this paper now if I am not to see the sea
I am back home now but still I think of him
Washed up on a beach somewhere all because of me.

Sarah Robinson (Age 9)

Vacuum Cleaners

Thumping and creaking like a great roaring monster,
Devouring dust and dirt.
A big plastic monster with wires galore
That sucks all the dirt off the kitchen floor
And leaves the tiles all sparkling white
And sucks up my toys with a great big bite!

Matilda Rossetti (Age 10)

Metal Gear Rex

M ade of the strongest metal
E nding all civil wars
T errorists control this walking battle tank
A ll together the countries fight
L asting forever the war against this monstrous machine

G etting stronger every year
E ating away at all the land
A rmed with nuclear missiles, a rail gun and lasers
R ex is the weapon of death

R uining all the land
E lecting new battle zones every month
X -raying the different countries for battle

Paul Reynolds (Age 12)

A Snowball War

We're in the snow
It's a snowball, get low!
Let's make a base
Mind your face!
This means war
Let's attack some more!

The parents are about
Don't knock them out!
We've stopped the battle
And the hassle!
We're going home
Cold to the bone.

Jack Ryan (Age 9)

Elephants

Elephants come out to play
Kicking balls
Scoring goals
Elephant rides
For you and me
Going in to have a rest
Going to the lake to have a bath
Coming out to play tennis
Home at last Goodnight!

Catherine Roberts (Age 9)

Waves

Waves splash
Upon the shore
Children swim in the sea
They play all day
And they say hurray
Waves crash

Claire Rogers (Age 8)

The Leaping Leopard

The leaping leopard
Still leaps in the light,
Lashing and laying
Under warm summer sun.

The leaping leopard
Still jumps up and down,
Dropping and drinking
On cold autumn days.

The leaping leopard
Still hunts for food,
Frite and fish
In the spring time forest.

Paige Ramsay (Age 9)

My Ambition

I don't know what I should be when I grow up.
I could be a policewoman,
To try and make the world a safer place.
I could be an Olympic runner,
And win every race.
I could be a chef,
If I learnt how to cook.
I could be a fisherwoman,
And catch small fishes on my hook.
I could be a teacher,
To teach the smaller kids.
I could be a waitress,
To bring your platters with very big lids.
I still don't know what I should be, but I'm only ten,
So I'll go to College and I think I'll choose then.

Clare Rich (Age 10)

Trees In Winter

A tree branches heavy with snow,
Snow everywhere too,
Icicles hanging as stiff as a tree,
Twigs so bear snow just lands on them,
Branches so thin they snap,
Trunks about three feet wide and twenty-four feet tall
Trees so dull because there is no leaves,
Snow all over you can't see any grey and brown,
Birds don't build nests in trees because it has no leaves,
Snow falls off all the time but more comes down.

Stacey Richardson (Age 8)

Leisure

What is life if full of care,
I've plenty time to stop and stare.

Time to go for communion bread and wine,
At Bradford Cathedral most of the time.

Time to do S.A.S it's really fun,
After school it's so much cool.

Time to play out, after school,
I am always good, never a fool.

Time to watch a video or two,
But who just who?

Time to play on my dreamcast after school,
My brother is such a big fool.

A good life I've got, it's full of care.
I'm pleased I've got some time to stop and stare.

Timothy Ruthven (Age 9)

The Lonely Soldier

Down in the trenches a soldier does lie,
Fighting a battle but he doesn't know why,
He's cold, damp and wet right through,
If only the people back home really knew.

Our foreheads are dirty, grazes and frail,
The food that we eat is mouldy and stale,
My bed is of stones, gravel and dirt,
I have only one Jacket, Trousers and shirt.

At last the command comes to go over and fight,
But i am determined to fight to the end,
Not for myself but just for my friends.

Kayleigh Ronnay (Age 10)

Terms

When Spring is here,
I can smell flowers near.

When Summer draws near,
All the leaves start to appear.

When Autumn comes,
All the people eat plums.

When Winter is around,
I can't stand flat on the ground.

Cassie Rimmer (Age 9)

I Want To Be...

I want to be an astronaut,
And fly up to the moon,
To look out of the window and see stars,
That will be my dream.

I want to be a pop star,
And win the Brit Awards,
To be number one in the charts,
That will be my dream.

I want to be a millionaire,
And buy a Jumbo Jet,
To live my life in luxury,
That will be my dream.

I realise I'm in reality,
I've woken from my dream,
I'll only be a builder,
That will be my dream.

Harry Rutledge (Age 11)

If You Ever See a Goblin

If you ever see a goblin this is what you do,
Shout and scream because I haven't got a clue.

But I know some things about goblins that might come in handy,
I'll start with things they hate, it's things that are wet or sandy.

It is rather simple everyone knows,
That they have twelve fat fingers, twelve fat toes, two tiny eyes and one very long nose.

But if you ever see a goblin this is what to do,
Shout and scream because I haven't got a clue.

It doesn't stop there, I have some other things as well,
Like they don't have normal heads, they're shaped like a bell.

If you want to know something about their belly,
I will tell you this but only once, it's like a big wobbly jelly.

If you ever see a goblin this is what you do,
Shout and scream because I haven't got a clue.

But if you ever see a goblin and he asks you to play,
Take my advice run right away.

Chloe Richards (Age 9)

Rainy Poem

I'm dancing through the lovely rain
Driperty droperty drip
Jumping in the muddy puddles
Driperty Droperty Drip
Running through the deep flood
Driperty droperty drip

Lily Robinson (Age 6)

Trees In Winter

In the trees little insects are hurting me,
Because they want to make a hole in my trunk
Hey you!
I wiggle my trunk
And they did not get off
I was sad

Glen Restell-Lewis (Age 8)

Little Red Riding Hood

Little red riding hood
So nice and good.
Was on her way to her grandmas
As she heard a wolf saying ha ha.
The wolf eat red riding hood
And sucked all the blood.
The wood cutter heard this
And held a tremendous fist.
The Wolf was killed
With his blood all spilled.
They went to the hospital to help her
All they did was open his fur.
Little red riding hood
So nice and good
Was saved
And there the wolf laid.
Little red riding hood
Never went alone in the woods

Nafisa Rehman (Age 10)

The Forest's Story

I remember when life was good
When the wildfowl ran free
And when the bracken ruled the land.
I was always gossiping with the stream
And the trees gave me shelter
The hollow trees were home to owls
And the birds sang to their hearts content
Children made rope swings from oak tree branches
Annoying moles went straight through me
    Oh happy days!
Children, can you find me now?
Beneath your factories and houses
Big monsters came and savaged my shelter
Tore up my skin,
Sliced up my nails
And ripped up my scalp
    Oh monstrous days!

Thomas Roach (Age 10)

Happy Golden Jubilee

H arry Potter books came out
A truly great loving queen
P rincess Margaret sadly died (we are sorry)
P oor twin towers, Osama is mean
Y did they have to crash into them?

G areth Gates got No.1
O h the years have gone so quick
L uckily you were queen
D oh if you were not queen i'd hit and quick
E ngland won that wonderful cup
N aughty people in the world.

J oy in England 50 years ago and still joy, too
U p to heaven we very sadly will go in a couple of years
B ungee jumpers very brave
I 'd be sick if you weren't queen
L uckily your mum's still alive and so are you
E nd of hope so very sadly
E xcellent inventions over the last 50 years.

Luke Rowlands (Age 8)

Tomlix

There is a cat named Tomlix and he is very strange.
He wears his long leather boots upon his tiny arms.
He wears his coat round the wrong way.
He puts bright red lipstick on his eyelids.
He also puts pale green eye shadow on his lips.
He dyed his hair bright red and orange.
He spiked it, gelled it, waxed it.
And then one night he went out to dinner.
He saw an attractive young cat.
He asked her out, they were going out for six months.
Then they got married and his wife was just as strange.

Hannah Risk (Age 9)

Exams!

Exams they really make me hot and flustered,
You should see me in my chair,
Shivering like mad,
My brain cannot think straight,
And I know I'm going to fail,
And when the results are back in class,
A headache is popping up to life,
When the paper is on the table,
I say to my friend,
"Go fetch me the paper,
It is time"
I open it very slowly, I lick my fingers to unfold the test,
I look at my results and I sat...
Yes I passed!

Olivia Riley (Age 9)

Angel

Angels floating in the air
With their long golden hair
Gleaming happily in the sky
As high as they can possibly fly
They glow like sun-light
Fighting the day into the night
Their souls as happy as Christmas Day
Angels will never go away.
Smiling happily in the sky
Feeling glad that they will never die.
Wings fluttering up to heaven above
With their sweet hearts that love
Beautiful silk dresses they wear
Flying past without a care
Halos sparkling above their head
I love being an angel they all said
As they fly through the air as happy as can be
And they all say goodbye to you and me.

Charleigh Ratty (Age 10)

My Imaginary Elephant

My imaginary elephant
Listens to me with his big ears
He is kind to me and never forgets
He gives rides to me on his enormous back
His skin is tough and grey with wrinkles on
He has small eyes full of happiness
He is clumsy but very strong
If only he was real.

Eloise Robinson (Age 9)

The Guitarist

I wish I could play the guitar
As well as Jimmy Hendrix
But once I gave it a go
I practised for a year
But never got near
Because Jimmy was the king.

His fingers moved so fast
You would of thought they were battery-powered
Up and down they went
Side to side they went
Moving like a machine
Up down, up down, up

Laurence Ralph (Age 10)

The Magic Box

I will put in the box

A blue massive pilot whale
A trimarine from Greece
A topless teenager from Tenerife.

I will put in the box

A laugh from Luton
Ten tiny tigers from Turkey
A joke from a Jaguar.

I will put in the box

A pure gold fleece from a winter lamb
A beep from a flying bus
And a sock from Saturn.

My box is covered in hair from a bear
And the hinges are crocodile claws
The lid shines like an angry cats eyes.

Kerry Ramsbotham (Age 9)

Inside My Head

Inside my head
There is a beautiful castle
Made from all your favourite dreams.
There is chocolate, ice-cream,
Sweets, money and drinks.

Inside my head
Is a fairy castle on the soft clouds.
Fairies watching children on the TV.
Fairies sing while they sleep.

Lucy Robinson (Age 7)

Farmyard Noises

The horse goes neigh neigh
And the cat goes meow meow
And the cow goes moo moo
And the farmer goes Zzzzzz
And the farmer's wife goes sh! sh! sh!

Samantha Rogers (Age 6½)

Little Cute Calfs

Spotty cute calfs
Dribbling after they've drank.
Happy munching grass.

James Reed (Age 9)

If

If I were Ben
I'd say
Give me my pen!

If I were Jake
I'd say
I'd make a cake

If I were Sam
I'd say
Give me that ham!

If I were Mrs Fry
I'd say
Look at my lovely pie!

If I were Lizzie
I'd say
I'm too busy!

Lavana Raza (Age 6)

Snake

I am the lord of the grassland.
I am the king of the plain.1
Winding my way through the bushes,
Twisting, twining, coiling, knotting
Like silken thread I weave.
I flash my white fangs,
Imagine my meal.
Helpless rabbit on its own
I stalk it silently,
It is mine!

Hannah Rolph (Age 9)

The Storm

Wind in the gables
Suck out all the hatches,
Rattling the rattlers
Shed the houses thatches,
Whistle through windows
Rapping as the wind blows,
Shaking all the door frames
Breaking out the glass panes,
Holler down the hallways
Chimney stack and walls quake
Roof tiles and gutter break,
I am stuck inside all day long,
All because of the terrible wet storm

Leanna Robinson (Age 9)

The Quest To The Enemy

Three gold Demons, flying in the sky,
Signal the start of a Quest, in the truth
To Fire, To Water, To Air so high
To end the reign of those Demons aloof
Masterful power, ruling magic flies
Through two mighty kings of leafy roof
Water to call them, wind to bring them
Fire to bind them, and all to break them
Warriors are found, and the Quest brought unto them

Matthew Rushworth (Age 15)

My Birthday

My birthday's on Monday.
I'll be six years old.
I'll have a big cake
With letters of gold.
The letters will say
"Happy birthday to you!"
My friends will all eat it
And my teacher will too.

Alex Rossetti (Age 6)

The Nightmare

One old Oxford organised octopus ordering oysters
Two talented T-Rexes trashing the town
Three tigers trampling tight ropes
Four flying flibberts flying from Finland
Five fat fishes flying from France
Six successful submarines submerging and sinking
Seven snake serpents serving slaves
Eight Egyptian elephants eliminating eighty earths
Nine newts nibbling nets
Ten terrified tornadoes trampling Tomville

Michael Rowden (Age 8)

Horses

Horses are cute
They live in a stable
They gallop around,
But never eat at the table.

In the stable they sit and stare,
Just eat, eat, eat, without a care.
They lay around day after day
Eating lots and lots of hay.

Jeannie Richardson (Age 7)

Grapes! Grapes!

When I take a bunch of grapes from my pocket
And bite one off the bunch,
I feel the grapes dissolving down my throat
It feels like a waterfall
And when they're in my mouth
And when I crunch
It feels like balloons popping in my mouth.

Louis Royden (Age 9)

Easter

Happy
Holidays
Chocolate
Off school
Guinea pigs
Bunnies

George Raymer-Fleming (Age 6)

Green

Green is the colour of the trees in my garden
Green is the colour of the grass in the woods
Green is the frog which jumps on the lily pad in the pond
Green is the colour of moss on the house
Green is the colour of leaves sitting on the tree
Green is the colour of a bush
Green is the stalk of a plant

Stanley Roffe (Age 8)

Red

Red is the sun setting over the ocean,
Red is an apple hanging on a tree.
Red is blood dripping from a cut.
Red is the colour of a red pen.
Red is a real gel pen.
Red is the colour of a sticker.

Jonathan Russell (Age 9)

Recipe For An Angry Teacher

Weigh a handful of pencil flicking boys
Pour a cupful of pathetic excuses
Sprinkle a hint of arguing girls to give it a kick
And stir in a spoonful of doodling boys

Boil a bowlful of swearing boys
Pour a cupful of noisy calling out year 5's
Stir in a pinch of guilty homework in late year 4's
Finally spread a handful of hypnotising computer screen-savers
And wallah!! an angry teacher.

Jessica Ruston (Age 9)

Noel, Noel

C arol singing
H appily
R ound the firelight
I nstruments
S ounding the start of noel
T oddlers and children getting excited when
M aking hats, decorations and cards
A llowing them to stay up late, so hopefully catching a glimpse of
S anta and his sleigh

Stephanie Reed (Age 11)

Transport

T rains speeding past blurred people
R acing cars going viciously past the river of treacle
A n enormous horse trotting past
N autikus goes up and down rapidly on its mission
S hips coming into the crowded port
P ilot flying through the sky rapidly
'O t air balloons floating in the air
R oller skates rolling all over the land
T ransport is very important

Siobhan Raine (Age 8)

The Sea

The sea was a rippling deep blue blanket
The moon, reflected in the blanket, was a ghostly galleon sailing silently
White horses galloped into the bay
But unseen hands pulled them back to the inky desert

As the sun rose, a giant Catherine Wheel,
Its rays changed the blue blanket to a shining sheet of silk.

Danielle Rose (Age 11)

Shoes

Fast shoes,
Slow shoes,
Red and yellow glow shoes.

High shoes,
Low shoes,
Sticky out big toe shoes.

Disco shoes,
Party shoes,
Green and blue arty shoes.

Heavy shoes,
Light shoes,
Purple and pink tight shoes.

Alice Rumbelow (Age 11)

Words

Words mean so much
The only way
To mean anything
They can
Hurt
Offend
Threaten
Yet soothe
Comfort
Slip out
And mean nothing at all

Ruth Snowden (Age 13)

Fly

Fly see saucer
Fly fly down
Me see fly, fly
Fly walk round.
Fly take sip
Me take spoon
Fly look wrong way
Spoon go boom
Cup go wobble
Tea go splat
Fly get big fright
Fly get flat
Fly not fly now
Fly not sip
Fly - just flied on
Final trip!

Joss Reed (Age 10)

Baby

When I was young I always used to scribble,
When I was young I always used to dribble,
I crawled under the mat
I played with my cat
They called me
Madam
Diddle!

Jordan Rough (Age 10)

Summer

The sun is shining
The sea is warm
The children are splashing and splashing
Ladies sunbathing on the warm sand
Teenager's jet skiing and surfing
It is fantastic

Michael Rodriguez (Age 11)

Happy

I'm happy,
I tingle and glow.
I light up,
I twinkle with excitement.
I sparkle in the sun,
Feeling warm.
I float in the air like a bird.
A happy smiling face,
A grin.
I'm very jolly.
I'm cheerful,
Like a squirrel with all the nuts in the world!

Amy Rhodes (Age 10)

Ten Things Found In An Undersea Kingdom

A mermaid brushing her long hair,
Trying to find what to wear.

A king eating his dinner,
Having chips that make him thinner.

Eight pirates finding lots of treasure,
Surely giving them loads of pleasure.

Georgina Riches (Age 8)

Dinner Time

I love dinner time
When the clock hits 12,
We go and wash our hands
I can smell that lovely dinner
I go yum! yum! yum!
Then rush up
And get first
I love my school dinner

Naomi Rowe (Age 8)

Inside My Head

Inside my head
There's a graveyard
With skeletons ringing bells
Blue spiders crawling over grave stones
And bones as church confetti.

Thomas Rank (Age 8)

If

If I were tall
I'd say
Go and play!

If I were Jake
I'd say
Give me a snake?

If I were Lizzie
I'd say
Your very busy!

If I were Ben
I'd say
Give me that pen!

If I were Sam
I'd say
Give me that ham!

Craig Spicer (Age 7)

Haiku

imagination
endless possibilities
wisps of wishful thoughts

nightmarish nothing
little waif upon the rocks
parted blue lips, cold

Rachael Sigee (Age 13)

Kyle The Crocodile

Kyle lunges on the football pitch with that great canine smile,
When the other team see him they are sure to run a mile.
His attack with the ball is very mean,
But it keeps his opponents rather keen.
Once he has marked his selection,
He's always through on goal because they've run in the opposite direction.
He never gets booked by the referee,
Just incase he becomes his tea.
Kyle the crocodile will never lose,
Because there is eleven players for him to choose.
Kyle comes off to take a break,
While the other players just stand and shake.
As the second half is on its way,
Kyle decides today is his lucky day.
As he runs through the defense like a wild boar,
There's one thing you will know he's bound to score.
As he comes off the opposite team boo,
So Kyle replies my next supper will be you.
Kyle has gone for his catch,
So why does he get man of the match?

Jason Smith (Age 12)

The Flood

The rain it keeps on falling
All the night and day
The water it is rising
It just won't go away

The river banks have burst
The roads are two feet under
The flashing of the lightning
The crashing of the thunder

Furniture is floating
I'm afraid it must be said
If this water keeps on rising
I'll have a water bed

I'm trying to get to sleep now
But it isn't easy
It's wet and cold and damp out here
And I'm starting to feel quite queasy

Jamie Smith (Age 11)

Murderer In Your Mind

Crouching in the corner of his cell,
His eyes are unfathomable wells.
He glowers when you pass his way,
He's killing you when his mind's at play.
His anger bubbles in his imagination
He despises you and your nation
He spits at anything he can reach.
He clings onto your fear like a leech
He smiles when the key clicks home,
He killed a man with a comb
The light of day stings his skin,
His scream makes your ears ring.
He knows he's going to pay
He hates you every day
He suffers but what he did
Will haunt you until you're dead

Eleanore Schäfer (Age 12)

About Ice-Cream

Inside my head,
There's an ice-cream castle with wafer towers.
White cream monsters,
People and iced bull dogs,
Play in a pool of ice-cream.

Zach Rathbone (Age 8)

Friends

My best friend was once Joe Beavin
He was so cool he could freeze heaven
He was good at most sports
We were never caught
Without our friends all seven

Daniel Scotcher (Age 14)

Black And Proud

I have no intention in keeping my love.
I'm sure you'll understand if you had a peculiar appetite.
My favourite colours are midnight black and blood red,
My favourite music is black rap.
My favourite materials are silk and velvet,
My favourite times are lunchtime and midnight.

My favourite book is "Wuthering Heights" by Emily Bronte.
My house is made of silver silk that looks just darling in the rain.
My hobbies are eating, reading murder mysteries knitting and weaving.
My friends? there are none.

But I am charming, secretive, attractive and smart.
My favourite activities are sitting in my house
With a nice cup of flesh.

What am I?

Black Widow Spider (upside down)

Kate Stocker-Wright (Age 12)

The River

The winding river makes it's peaceful journey
Down the quiet, sloping valley.
The rushing water cascades over the waterfalls
Into the deep, murky depths of it's
Rugged bottom.
The river's loopy meanders twist and carve
Their way down the inclining valley.
The river's water is coming to the end of it's course,
The sea engulfs the river.
The river enters the twinkling, blue water.
The river has come to the end of it's journey.

Paul Smith (Age 12)

I Saw

I saw a baby jumping through a hoop,
I saw a puppy flying loop the loop,
I saw a blackbird cooking christmas tea,
I saw a mother planting a new tree,
I saw a gardener learning how to skate,
I saw a toddler jumping on a gate,
I saw a kitten shooting in the sky,
I saw a soldier trying not to cry,
I saw a hurt child slide down a drain,
I saw a river shaking with pain,
I saw an ill man blowing a kiss,
I saw the woman who saw all this.

Eleanor Symonds-Tayler (Age 14)

The Writer Of this Poem

The writer of this poem is
Smarter than a piggy
Taller than a tree
Fast as a penalty kick
Thinner than a candle wick

The writer of this poem is a professional football player

But by night a **very good vampire slayer!**
The writer of this poem
Is one in a **Million**
          Billion
                    Trillion
(or so the poet says)
He's called William!!!

William Savage (Age 10)

Rain

Trickling down your window
Making a beautiful sound,
Tapping on your shoulder,
Pattering on the ground.
Creeping through the gaps
That hang above your head,
Or staining a colourful rainbow,
Or even a flower instead.

That trickling down your window,
That making a beautiful sound,
That tapping on your shoulder
Is the best thing all year round.

Michelle Severs (Age 11)

Whitney: The Stubborn Cat!

Whitney is a stubborn cat; she won't do what she's told,
She hates it when she goes outside, especially when it's cold.
She waits until my dad gets up then sits in his chair,
When she is asleep she looks like a ball of hair.
She loves eating ham but it must be cut up small,
If the chunks are too large then she won't eat them at all,
Everybody thinks when she hides on my bed,
That she is a hat that they can wear on their head.
She's normally hungry, and always begs for food,
She can be rather grouchy, but mostly she's in a good mood.
When she's picked up or moved off a chair,
She yowls and meows until her cries fill the air.
She's very soft and cuddly, but scratches when she's mad,
And when you're on the phone she can be very bad.
If she jumps on your trousers, then you'd better help her up,
Or she'll fall off your lap, and give your clothes a pluck.

Amy Steward (Age 12)

Live Your Life

Long and hard it may seem but **live it**,
Sometimes it's easy and laid back so **love it**,
It may seem like a hard dragging time but **live it**,
It can be a long and exciting adventure so **love it**,
Can it be a black hole going on and on **live it**,
Can it be a spring flower just coming into bloom **love it**,
It can make you feel low but **live it**,
It can make you feel high so **love it**,
It can be easy,
It can be hard,
Live it,
Love it,
<u>**It's your life.**</u>

Emily Steed (Age 11)

The Day I Lost My Dog

On a cold winter's day
I went into my house,
And my dog called Kizzy
Lay as quiet as a mouse.

But something is wrong
She looks ill just now
We don't know what to do
Me and my sister have a really big row.

After a while we took her to the Vets
When they told me she had to go I began to cry
On the way home I sat clutching her collar
I thought it wouldn't be the day for my dog to die.

Jodie Simpson (Age 11)

Angels

Angels come from heaven above,
They are full of kindness and love.

Gloria blessed at purified best.

The fiery love
As pure as a dove.

Shimmering heart, never apart
Ghostly, shining, glittery gay.

When he stood in front of me
Glittering as a beautiful key

Coming from the realms above
Comfy cosy as a glove.

Jake Skinner (Age 11)

My Lion

My pet Lion
Likes to iron

He is as tough
As a piece of metal

He always fights
Every night

His mane is furry like
A fluffy toy

His cubs
Pays the subs

He always hunts
But he always grunts

Roxanne Simmonds (Age 9)

A Homeless Child!

Rejected, timid, alone
Nowhere to go, no home
Silent and still
The soft night time drill
The howl of a dog with no bone!

Silent, restless, ignored
Slumped by a shop and bored
I see the dawn ray
For another gloomy day
Another long day alone!

Anna Strand (Age 10)

The Bridesmaid

Camera's are flashing, smiles all around,
I feel like a princess in my pink and white gown.
Everyone's faces light up when they see white,
The beautiful bride slowly strides along the aisle.

Following behind I feel so special,
All eyes are on me as we gracefully parade.
And there the groom stands, looking proud as punch,
With the biggest, proudest grin any man could hold.

As the Vicar begins, sobs can be heard,
From proud Mums and happy family members.
Gold bands of eternity are exchanged,
I feel the prickle of tears of joy behind my eyes.

The well practiced vows are nervously vowed,
"I now pronounce you man and wife," echoes in the church.
With joyous smiles the couple kiss,
Leaving in showers of confetti, I wonder if that will be me.

Claire Slade (Age 14)

Street Noises

Cars go boom and vans go whoosh.
Lorrys go whurr,
And people on the street go chat chat chat.
The checkouts go ting
And the trees go whistle
And the stones grumble grumble grumble
The fire engine goes nee nor nee nor and then!
Boom Boom Whoosh Whoosh
Whurr Whurr Chat Chat.

Joe Smart (Age 7)

The Warming Planet

It started off all nice and green,
Until scientists came on the scene.
Those brainy men, those science guys,
Began to pollute our deep blue skies.
And now the craze goes without end,
Whizzing round every bend,
Throwing litter everywhere,
Recycling, they do not care.
As our planet grows slowly hot
Destroying everything that we've got.
We all know the time will come,
When we have no place to run.
Our planet becomes a ball of heat,
A Venus end it comes to meet.
And whom shall stand there, head down in shame
After all we know who to blame.
So let us react, let us stand.
Restore the green into our land.
Restore the blue into our skies,
To save mother Earth . . . from suicide.

Daniel Smedley (Age 12)

At The Haunted Cave

At the haunted cave
Where no one goes
Lay slimy bones
A monster had his tea,
Without pity for me
At the haunted cave

At the haunted cave
Where no one goes
Lay a brave knight
Who fought in a fight?
Face to face
God gave him grace

Blood on the floor
A torn up door
Monsters roar
As the bats soar
People to save
At the haunted cave.

Pierce Shand (Age 9)

Hiss Hiss Hiss Snake

Hiss hiss hiss snake,
Hissing in the shed,
Hiss hiss hiss snake
Laughing on the bed.

Neigh neigh neigh horse,
Neighing on the farm
Neigh neigh neigh horse
Coming to no harm.

Scott Scully (Age 7)

Drugs

S earching for money
A ching to stop
Y ou cannot leave

N o money left
O ver the edge

T o the limit
O ut of reach

D raining your energy
R uining your life
U nder your skin
G ame's over
S leep at last

Be at peace
Just say **NO!**

Amber Summerfield (Age 13)

My Tongue Twister

Ouch, ouch, scratch, scratch!
Crack, crack, jiggle, jiggle!
Squirt, squirt, rip, rip!
Scratch, scratch, scatter, scatter!
Roar, roar, crawl, crawl!
Dash, dash, crush, crush!
Crash, crash, twist, twist!
Clap, clap, drop, drop!
Shoot, shoot, rush, rush!
Slip, slip, creep, creep!
Shuffle, shuffle, steak, steak!
Gallop, gallop, zoom, zoom!
Juggle, juggle, wave, wave!
Spin, spin, toss, toss!
Blush, blush, twirl, twirl!
Shake, shake, twitch, twitch!
Treble, treble, tingle, tingle!
Trotter, trotter, creep, creep!
Climb, climb, mount, mount!
Attack, attack, swash, swash!
Sink, sink, swamp, swamp!

Daniel Storton (Age 7)

The Dragon

As tall as a sky-scraper
As green as the grass,
As fierce as a tiger,
As quiet as a mouse.

The dragon moves up the stairs.
Turns off the landing light,
If he finds out where your bedroom is
You might just have a fight.

His glowing red eyes,
His smokey breath,
His sparkling teeth,
His liking for a death.

Beware, beware all you out there,
The dragon; is coming.

Leigh Scott (Age 9)

Feelings

When I feel lonely
I feel as lonely as a little seed.
When I feel sad
I feel as sad as a dead tree.
When I feel happy,
I feel as happy as an easter egg
When I feel angry,
I feel like a hurricane.

Phillippa Spencer (Age 7)

Dreams

They are funny things
All soft and fluffy
Or mean and stuffy
That's what my dreams are like!

They are funny things
They come and go
They're quick and slow
That's what my dreams are like!

They are funny things
They can be good or bad
Happy or sad
That's what my dreams are like!

They are funny things
They can be long or short
But never be caught
That's what my dreams are like!

They are funny things
They can be helpful but sometimes not
So remember you need them a lot.
That's what my dreams are like!

Emily Smith (Age 11)

The 'Thinker'

Why?
That strange, grey, squirmy
'Thing'
Inside your head,
That 'thinks'.

Why?

Today
I saw a picture
Of a person's
'Thinker'
In school.
We had to write about it
In our 'Busy Books'

Sir called it Brian,
I 'think' I'll call mine
Fred.

Sam Sweeney (Age 12)

Chocolate

Dark brown
All shapes
Different sizes
You remind me of mud
You are nothing
You are all

Conor Shields (Age 6)

Changing Seasons

Spring's warm breezes and cooling showers;
The arching, gentle bridge of flowers.
Delicate petals made from silk,
As sweet as honey, as smooth as milk.

Lazy days and clear blue skies;
Humming bees and butterflies:
Flowers bloom in colourful arrays -
On a peaceful summer's day.

Autumn's season begins to unfold,
With oranges, yellows, browns and golds;
Leaves fall softly from the trees -
Caught up in the swirling breeze.

Winter is here, the frosty winds blow;
The clouds drift slowly, laden with snow.
All colours have faded; they cannot remain
Until spring starts the seasons again.

Emily Sinclair (Age 11)

The 7-Eyed Jelly Monster That Ate Our School

The 7-eyed pupil who I thought was really cool,
Turned into a jelly monster and ate our school.
First went the tables, then went the chairs,
Then went the children who always stared.

From his mouth, the biggest burp was burped,
From his bum, the biggest ever smell lurked.
From his very own dribbly drool,
He gave the children an extra swimming pool.

He took our headmaster as hostage and ate his wife,
The headmaster kept crying "He's ruined my life".
As he licked with his slimy slurps,
He changed all the children with his man eating burps.

The 7-eyed jelly monster turned into the head,
And 250 jelly monsters were taught instead.
After an hour the slimy jelly monster was dead,
Then they found in the cupboard the shaken up head.

Kirsty Shelton (Age 11)

Nosh, Sports And Other Tosh

A rugby ball is oval shaped,
A skateboard is griptaped.
Ice-cream has flakes -
They taste darn good too!
Chocy shakes and chocolate flakes,
They'll fill you up to the brim.
It takes a lot of nosh to squash
A boarder's and scorer's appetite in.
Rub a dub dub thanks for the grub,
Once you've played for a club
You'll need a scrub-a-dub in the tub!

Tom Summers (Age 11)

Pegasus

He stood tall and smart,
Like a man at an interview.
You could just imagine a thoughtful heart.
His bearded chin rose with powerful grace.
His dead straight wings,
Reached to the clouds.
His flowing mane,
Glowed in the rain.
His cascading tail,
White as snow.
His coat, a shiny mirror.
For all we know,
These legends could be lies.

Tasha Sear (Age 11)

It

It's a   lightning striker
Faster than   a biker
Tail   lasher
Fang   flasher
Scaly   swimmer
Battle   winner
Icy   glarer
Fixed   starer
Body   wrapper
Tongue   slapper
Long   coiler
Anger   boiler
No   fake
It's a   snake

Chris Scott (Age 11)

Inside The...

Inside the Cheetah's eye, the pale moon.
Inside the pale moon, the Cheetah's gleaming teeth.
Inside the Cheetah's gleaming teeth, the ragged forest.
Inside the ragged forest, the Cheetah's foot.
Inside the Cheetah's foot, the fast flowing river.
Inside the fast flowing river, the Cheetah's prey.
Inside the Cheetah's prey, the Deer's cry.
Inside the Deer's cry, the Cheetah's tongue.
Inside the Cheetah's tongue, the rough rocky horizon.
Inside the rough rocky horizon, the Cheetah's spots.
Inside the Cheetah's spots, the black sky.
Inside the black sky, the Cheetah's gleaming teeth.
Inside the black sky, the Cheetah's eye.

Danielle Sargeant (Age 10)

George's School Days

Monday's fun day
Today it's school
Which I enjoy...
............as a rule
English book guzzler
Maths puzzler
Mountains of geography
Ages of history
That's how the day goes on.

Friday's good
Getting stuck
Into technology
Living with biology
Understanding French
Doing P.E. on the bench
Fingers on the keys in ICT
More maths 123
Oh what fun I have at school!

George Shires (Age 9)

White Rabbit

Rabbit
In a big hutch
Eating all it's carrots
Munching on lots of greenery
Greedy

Lucy Sanders (Age 8)

The Thrill Seeker

What were you thinking of,
You fool, you liar?
Was it bravado?
An ultimate desire?
To seek to find,
The everlasting thrill,
And hear earth's screams,
High and shrill.

Through endless cloud,
And crispy air,
You cut through the sky,
Without a care.

What seems the truth,
Is all but lies,
You fall, you yell,
Commander of the skies.
The ground gets closer,
The end is near,
You shout, you scream,
Your motive's clear,
What were you thinking?

Emma Sharrock (Age 14)

Acid Rain

I speak of those who were not born to rise,
Those lesser spotted superiors of self-appointed virtue,
If the sun could keep secrets,
Then the sky could too.
Spilling moments of hatred and disgust,
Scattering, like petals thrown at a black wedding,
Down, down, down.
Acid Rain.

Acid Rain on our parade, the corrosion has already begun,
But nobody can save us from what we are,
Nobody cares enough to untangle us from this web.
As I desire, the smallest star,
Or the sound of daylight to enchant my heart.
But soon what is will cease to be,
Soon everything natural will meet its Maker,
There's no more green.

Acid Rain

Stephanie Simpson (Age 14)

The Queen Is Coming

The gleaming carriage is shining bright,
As it pushes its way through the crowd,
The horses are white like snow on the ground,
They toss and shake their heads like falling snowflakes,
The Queen sits regally in her velvet cloak,
She smiles kindly and waves her gloved hand,
The jostling crowd push and strain against the barriers,
They are eager to see their Queen.

Harriet Schrire (Age 9)

Center Parcs

One day when I was five or so,
We set off for Elveden Forest,
Mum, Dad, Helen, Nigel, Jodie, Matt, Bec and me,
It took ages to get there, so we stopped on the way,
When we got a room for the night,
The adults went for dinner,
As they left us upstairs,
Jodie, Matt and me waited,
Then we grabbed a pillow each
We had a big pillow fight,
When they arrived back from dinner,
Matt and I hid in the bathroom but . . . .
We couldn't get back out!
When we finally managed it,
We went to bed and fell asleep.
In the morning it was really cold,
It took at least another two hours,
Just as we arrived there, a first flake of snow fell,
All I remember about it,
Is the snow, snowmen and snowballs . . . .

Emma Simpson (Age 13)

It Really Puzzles Us

It really puzzles me
how goldfish can swim round and round without getting dizzy.
Because when you
are out and about doing the shopping and being rather busy,
All they do is
swim round and round going at a speed that is very whizzy!!

It really puzzles me
how babies can scream so loud and never lose their voice,
Because when you
turn your back when you think you've got a bit of time to make a choice
All they do is
wake up and start that hullabaloo all over again and when they stop, rejoice!

It really puzzles me
how the world actually began (all the tales make it impossible to tell)
Because when you
ask people who like different Gods you always get confused and, well
All they do is
spin you different stories of big bangs and Adam and Eve and the gazelle.

It really puzzles us
that the world is such an amazing thing with so many secrets still to uncover.

Becky Smith (Age 11)

Teacher

A teacher is an unexploded bomb
That could go off any minute.
Sparks fly from its fiery eyes,
And when it gets angry you'd better say your prayers.
It is a bull in an arena that has just been shown a red cloth,
A seething volcano spouting bubbling lava,
A deadly tiger making you cower in terror.
It is charging rhinoceros and you should treat it the same way-
When you see one coming, climb up the nearest tree!

Luci Sinclair-Brown (Age 11)

Fireworks

Crashing like drums
Glittering, flittering down
Fireworks all around the town,
Loads of sparks explode above,
Just like a little white dove,
Shooting stars go passing by,
Flying very very high,
Zooming through the misty sky
And then all of a sudden...
BOOM!!

Lucy Storm (Age 6)

The Sea

There's a bump in the deep blue sea,
There's a frog on the bump in the deep blue sea.

There's a shell on the frog,
The frog on the bump in the deep blue sea.

There's a cat on the shell,
There's the shell on the frog, on the bump in the deep blue sea.

There's a girl in the sea,
And it's ME!

Gemma Sharpe (Age 6)

If

If I were a teacher at school
I'd say
Go to the hall

If I were a football
I'd say
I've hit a wall

But as a child in school
I'd say school
Is cool.

Joseph Stevens (Age 7)

Little Monsters

He lurks beneath the floorboards,
He surprises anyone who dares to come in.
He's your very own bog monster,
And he jumps out from the seat.
He squelches round the house,
When you are all asleep.
And comes into your room to meet up with Fred,
Who lives under your bed.
They go all sorts of places,
Parties, raves and rants.
There they meet Jim, Francis and Burt,
All bog monsters from your neighbour's loos.
They go round in a gang,
They call themselves little monsters.
They range from 7"To 22".
They scare the wits out of human creatures,
And are wanted by the CLM (capture of little monsters)
Make sure they don't come after YOU!!!

Lydia Shillaker (Age 12)

Coronation

I am standing in the crowd, waiting for the queen,
The crowd moves as one,
Edging closer to the street.

See the queen riding in her golden coach
White horses pulling closer, louder, trotting
The crowd cheering.

The red velvet carpet, she walks down the aisle
The organ playing, her long velvet cape behind,
People cheering.

Whitney Schwalm (Age 8)

My Cat

His eyes are amber traffic lights,
His nose twitching like a leopard,
His face like golden sand,
His fur nice and chequered,
His teeth like white ice-cream.

His purr loud and confident,
He wriggles round your feet,
Looking for a sweet and juicy treat,
Sometimes he is moody, but sometimes he is fun.

He's scavenging for food, where ever he can,
He walks up and down,
Thinking it's a concrete jungle,
Jumping, springing, pouncing with a slight little tumble.

    My cat "Ginger"

Chlóe Sharpe (Age 12)

How Long Next Time!!!

Leaving my family to look for food,
I wander over freshly cut fields,
Stop!! I hear gun shots and barking
The horses are galloping
The predators have found me
The horses gallop faster,
The hounds are barking louder
And the horns are being blown.
My family!! I rush back, No!!
Why me why my family
I'm hoping the predators won't find me, I run
My family were gone in seconds
I look back and tears roll down my face
Why can't they leave us to live our own lives
Now I have to create another family
But how long will they live for

Jodie Swannick (Age 12)

A Typical School Desk

Pencil cases half full,
Holding stuff used for school.
Jotters old and battered,
Rulers, pencils messily scattered.
Paper toys all screwed up,
One kid has a water cup.
Children trading stickers,
Tables scattered with football flickers
The tables are only clean,
When the school day has been.

Gemma Stadden (Age 9)

Winter Wonderland

I woke up one morning and all was well,
Until I stood up and looked out of the window.
The only story that I would tell,
Was about a huge blanket of snow.

At the bottom of the garden the hedgehog lay,
In the silence the cat creeps to its prey.
The hedgehog wakes up at midday,
To find its fate just metres away.

Screaming children throwing snowballs,
One hits Matt and down he falls.
The snowman stands tall and proud,
Up above there is a black cloud.

The sun is out, the snowman's gone,
The grass now makes a green floor.
Now you can hear the robins song,
The white world is no more.

James Simpson (Age 11)

Under The Ocean

Under the blue ocean in the misty sea,
There is something there,
What could it be?
It's purple and big as a cloud,
What could it be?

Maybe a spider,
Maybe it's just the sea.
Is it scary?
Is it calm?
Maybe it is
Maybe it's not.

Here is a submarine.
Maybe it's just the sea
There's the monster,
Oh no will it eat me.

I'm not in the sea?
I am in my bedroom,
How could that be,
I was in the sea.
Thank God it was only a dream.

Jack Stephens (Age 11)

Dentist

I don't like the dentist
Very noisy!
The noise of the drill
The clicking of the chair
So annoying!
The shushing of the sleep gas
The ouching of the people!
The rattling of the
I feel dizzy

Zac Snape (Age 10)

Dinner Time

Dinner time is full of noise,
Spilling drinks and naughty boys.

Some people happy, some are sad,
Some are good and some are bad.

Mrs. Barker will shout and scream,
"Naughty boy you've dropped your cream!"

Then Mrs Proser will jump and shout,
"Now it's wet playtime don't run about!"

Jane Stevens (Age 9)

Francis Drake

There was once a boy called francis Drake,
A very big journey he did make,
Drake went to look for silver and gold,
Gold and silver was given and sold

When he arrived from San Francisco,
He held a great big disco,
Some ships were sunk, some sailors were drunk,
But Sir Francis didn't do this though.

One day the ship had a trip,
And Francis looked really hip,
The crew, they worked all night and day,
Then they used to get their pay!

Francis Drake was thirsty,
And he met a girl called Kirsty,
So off he went to Plymouth,
Then went to lovely Teignmouth

Back he went to Plymouth,
But he missed Teignmouth,
And that is the story of a man,
Who never ever changed his plan.

Natalie Stone (Age 10)

From The Depth Of The Jungle

Faster than lions, faster than woodlouse,
Cheetah and zebra, tiger and dormouse,
And zooming around like a waiter with dishes,
All through the jungle the horses and fishes,
All the sights of the hippo and bee,
Fly as high as high can be,
And ever again in the wink of an eye,
A huge stampede hurtle by.

Ben Such (Age 12)

Storm

People in danger,
Blinding white, lights up the sky,
Peoples life at stake.

Lightning spear thrown straight,
Masks of cloud keep safe the face,
Fists sumo fighting.

Lightning duelling down,
Jabbing in the heart of earth,
Clashing swords light up the sky.

Crashing cars lit up,
Lightning duelling with your fears,
Breaking and smashing.

Josh Stedman (Age 10)

Goodbye And Hello

Goodbye, goodbye to dark winter skies,
To wind and rain, sleet and snow,
To trees stripped of their Autumn glow,
To long dark nights and white frosty mornings,
Goodbye, goodbye to dark winter skies.

Hello, hello to Spring come Summer,
To sunshine and showers, and a soft gentle breeze,
To trees once again covered with emerald green leaves,
To endless sunny evenings and bright fresh mornings,
Hello, hello to Spring come Summer.

Lauren Smith (Age 11)

Black

Black is my jogging bottoms
When I am running around,
Black is thick smoke
From a big burning fire,
The joy stick is black
Like the gear stick in my car.
James Bond wears a black suit
Just like my friend David.
Black is the feeling of things going wrong,
Feelings of sadness,
And of enemies nearby.
Black is the sound of music going wrong.

Thomas Sutton (Age 9)

It Was Then . . . . .

It was then in a hotel in a tree,
The sad news came to me
That my father had died,
With my sadness I cried.

It was then in a hotel in a tree,
The happy news came to me
It was now for me to be Queen!

I had been distraught
But then I thought,
I should be happy
With what I shall be!

Lydia Swift (Age 9)

Spring's Alive Again

Spring's alive again,
The sky is as white as snow,
Spring's alive again,
The leaves are as colourful as a butterfly,
Spring's alive again,
The rain goes down as fast as a shower,
Spring's alive again,
It is freezing like the North Pole
Spring's alive again,
I wish it was Summer.

Mary Smart (Age 9)

The Forest's Story

I remember when life was good
The children swinging on my oaky twisting branches
The flowing stream flew past waving as it passed
Animals laughed and joked while squirrels collected acorns from all my friends.

Singing nightingales nestled in my bark
Massive boulders nest amongst the cemented bramble floor.
Twisting paths ran through the forest
Miniature bridges climbed over the glistening waterfall
Wild flowers thrived in the Autumn sun

The flaking leaves gossiped to me as they overlooked the meadows
While the moist grass whispered happenings beneath
The twittering birds gracefully danced in the cosy sunset.

Children, come, come and find my remains
No more can you hear the gushing water or the rustling flaking leaves
The laughing and playing have fallen . . . . . silence
I miss my friends the ones who I muttered with they told me secrets that I have never told
The giant men came, chopped down and built up, they built as high as my ancestors.
Now I stand lurched in the darkness of the bare forest
All by myself I have nobody to look after me

Children, come, come and find my remains!

Lauren Stewart (Age 11)

The School Trip

We're going on a school trip
I don't know where we're going
I have trembling lips but who cares
We're going to have some fun
Let's hope the weather's fine
I say the sun

We're going on a school trip
I hope I don't slip or fall
I have very little lunch
I also have an apple to munch

We're going on a school trip
Into the unknown
My friend says it's OK
But I'd rather stay at home.

We're going on a school trip
Into the mountains
Let's hope it's sunny for our school trip.

Daniel Sweeney (Age 10)

Dentist

There I was at the scary dentist,
My fear going through my thin body.
Shaking my boney bones to and fro.
The drill oh no, I got to go,
Stuck in the chair, fear getting worse
Some bad news more to go.
Yeh time to go, free at last,
Jumping out of the dentist door,
Skipping with my hands in the air,
Pleased to go Alleluiah!

Sammi Smith (Age 9)

The Dark At Night

Black velvet in the sky,
Big meetings say goodbye,
Darkness is dark,
No people in the park.

Sunshine gives a lovely day,
Moonlight gives a milky way,
Dark darkness gives us stars,
Big bright lights coming from cars.

Darkness makes us scared,
Dream of monsters having glared,
Darkness makes us rest our head,
Everyone go to bed.

Lauren Stevens (Age 9)

The Forest's Story

I remember when life was good
When the birds gossiped on my branches
When sunbeams shone through my leaves
My berries ripened day by day
The stream is my best friend
The children swing on my vines
The marigolds swayed at my feet
My friends bathed in the river
When rabbits young hopped out of their burrows
And owls' eyes glowed like jewels in the night sky
Come and find me under your factories
Come and set me free
I am your dream
I am your world come and find me
Your factories have killed me
My birds, my foxes, my trees,
My best friend, my swaying marigolds
My young rabbit
Your town has killed it all
I am nothing without them.

Grace Stewart (Age 9)

A White Winter

It was a lovely winter's day,
So I went outside and started to play.

I went on the ice which was very thin,
But then I found myself falling right in.

I got out my sledge and climbed up the hill,
I came tobogganing down with such a thrill.

I had a snowball fight which of course I won,
Playing in the snow is lots of fun.

Matt Sowerby (Age 11)

Waiting For The Queen

Standing, waiting for the Queen to arrive,
The sound of horses hooves
Tip tapping on the concrete road,
I felt a tingling inside my stomach,
The sound of the carriage wheels
Becoming louder.

I closed my eyes to make a picture
Of what the Queen looked like,
The crowd is excited with joy on their faces.

The Queen wears a beautiful cloak
Which rests upon her shoulders.
Her gown is velvety and silky.
I watch the Queen glide down the royal red carpet,
I just stood and admired.

Genevieve Stamp (Age 9)

The Magic Box

I will put in the box
A special stone sparkling in the sunshine,
A bat flying past my face like a gust of wind,
A fluttering butterfly flying in the summer breeze.

I will put in the box
A photo of the waving waves,
I will jump in the curling cool computer,
A blue twisting turning tree.

My box is made out of skeleton's funny bones
A chocolate flavour inside
A sparkling sunset caught on the top of the lid.

In my box
I'll become an author
And be a better story maker
Than Roald Dahl

Katie Stevenson (Age 8)

Fairies

The fairies humming wings,
Quickly fly around like butterflies overhead,
Fluttering amongst the heather
Silver wings in the sunlight,
Like new dew on a spider's web
Only those who believe can see the beauty,
As they flit from flower to tree,
They live amidst the woodland glade,
And guide from you and me.

Melodie Stone (Age 11)

The Crowning Of The Queen

Suddenly everyone fell quiet,
All that was heard was the clattering of hooves,
Then the Queen appears in her beautiful coach.

There's not a sound,
It's totally silent,
For the Queen has arrived,
In her beautiful gown.

She walks down the aisle,
Her train behind her,
Everyone still and silent.

She sits on her throne,
The Bishop places the crown on her head,
Everyone cheers
"Long live the Queen!"

Dominique Stavrou (Age 9)

The Stars

The stars are in the sky
They shine so bright.
They only come out at night.
They glow
Like sparkling snow
I'd like to fly
Up very high
To see the stars so very much
And wish I could touch
Them into my hand
As they twinkle over the land.

Emily Stewart-Hanley (Age 11)

Sir Francis Drake

Francis Drake brave and bold, the crew soon did what they were told.
Away they sailed for miles and miles, food was stacked in piles and piles!

Sir Francis Drake made Captain, but before he'd got a slapin',
Francis felt really proud, he ordered people around, quite loud.

Francis Drake discovers gold! Now Francis is quite old.
He still has been brave and bold, he never did feel really cold.

Francis invaded Spain! They really were a big pain!
He got this gold, about which he was told.

Francis Drake found some friends, their native road went round in bends,
They were native Indians! They lived close to Chileans.

Francis sailed around the world when suddenly the boat curled.
Francis Drake enjoyed his journey, he came home one morning very early.

Francis Drake returns home, with all his things including bones.
They all celebrated with a pint of beer, he liked being back home here.

Ben Stribley (Age 10)

How Lucky Is The Queen?

How lucky is the Queen?
Was my dream last night, which gave me such a fright.

How lucky is the Queen?
Red carpets, chandeliers, was the subject of my dream.

How lucky is the Queen?
Tables, mirrors (only the finest) was the subject of my dream.

How lucky is the Queen?
Stairs and four poster beds, was the subject of my dream.

How lucky is the Queen?
Money, gardens, was the subject of my dream.

How lucky is the Queen?
Presents, jewellery, was the subject of my dream.

How lucky is the Queen?
Dresses, services, was the subject of my dream.

How lucky is the Queen?
Meetings, presentations, was the subject of my dream.

How lucky is the Queen?
All those decisions to make, was the subject of my dream.

How unlucky is the Queen?
Jeers and boos, was the subject of my dream.

Jake Stanmore (Age 11)

Save The Elephant

Elephant, elephant
Large, heavy elephant
Protect the elephants and their calves
White long tusks get chopped off,
The elephant will be safe if we do not kill them,
Then tourists will be able to see them in the wild.

Emily Stickler (Age 10)

Big Blue Man

He falls from the sky through the clouds so grey,
And lands on the mountains at the dawn of day.
At the start of the journey from raindrop to sea
To trickle down the mountains with happiness and glee.

Gathering speed as he meets his old friends
Twisting and turning through windy tight bends.
Under the trees he glides and slithers
Longer and wider he turns into a river.

Onwards but slower now nearing the end
What surprise is in stall around the next bend?
It's the mouth of the river and happy to be
Meeting more friends joining the sea.

Vicky Smith (Age 11)

The Touch Collector

A stranger called this morning
Dressed all in black and grey
Put every touch into a bag
And carried the touch away

The whistling of the kettle
The turning of the lock
The purring of the kitten
The ticking of the clock

The popping of the toaster
The crunching of the flakes
When you spread the marmalade
The scraping noise it makes

The touch of the rain drops
On the window pane
When you do the washing up
The popping bubbles wane

A stranger called this morning
He did not leave his name
Left us without any touch
Life will never be the same.

Harriet Smith (Age 10)

Rain And Sun

Rain rain go away
Come back another day
Sun sun come to me
Because I want sun on me

Jasmin Streater (Age 8)

I Love Maths

I love maths!
It's my one desire,
I love maths!
And always will!

I love maths!
Like it's last on earth,
I love maths!
Like it's flavoured candy!

I love maths!
A x and +,
I love maths!
- ÷ ing!

I love maths!
I enjoy it so,
I love maths!
And thaaaat's final!

Luke Stone (Age 9)

The Magic Box

I will put in the box

A bounce from a kangaroo
A wooden gondola from Italy
A marble temple from Greece.

I will put in the box

A joke from a laughing monkey
A glittering dolphin from Florida
And nine naughty numbats.

I will put in the box

A pure golden wing from a flying lamb
A silver fleece from a hungry bird
A buzz from a black and blue bear.

My box is bright pink
With purple lines through it
The lid has lots of rare flowers
And the hinges are daisy stems.

Vicky Sweeney (Age 9)

My Best Friend

My best friend has big blue eyes,
A cheesy grin
And honey blonde hair,
She is very tall,
I like her a lot,
My best friend is Jenny.

Katy Spiby (Age 10)

A Dark November Day

It was a dark November's day,
Storms ruthless throughout the land.
You could hear the cries of the trees,
And the WHIP! of the wind struck sand.

Lightning strung his electric guitar,
And thunder played his drum.
The rain pulled her golden harp strings,
And the wind started to hum.

It already looked like night,
But it was just the blackness of the cloud.
The goose bumps on my body,
Looked like the heads of a protesting crowd.

As I went to bed,
I wished it would go away,
And in the morning my wish had come true,
For now it was a December's day.

Zach Stafford (Age 11)

My Day Out

I woke up this morning
Breakfast on the table
I wonder what it is
Let's look on the label

Getting into the car,
Going to the Bowling Alley
"I'm going to beat you" said Mum
"No you're not!" said Sally.

We'll have two games
"Please sign here then"
"Okey dokey sir, that's fine"
"Can you please bowl on lane 10".

We put down our coats
Mum picked up her ball.
She posed for her balance
Acting the fool.

"I told you I'd beat you," said Sally
"Let's go in the arcade", said Dad.
"I'll play you on a game," said Mum.
"OK, said Dad "I am the best on a joypad".

Rhys Stewart (Age 9)

The Crab

Its legs are like owls claws
Its shell is like a bullet-proof shield
It scuttles around like a flaming hot fire
The middle of its shell is like a burnt burger

Philip St. Clair-Burke (Age 9)

A Journey To The Fair

As I was going to the fair,
I was feeling very happy,
I was talking to my parents excitedly,
I wanted to see the fireworks.
As I was going to the fair,
I was travelling in a car,
I just thought for a moment
About the sweet taste of candy floss
Being in my mouth.
As I was going to the fair
I could almost feel myself
Being on the big wheel,
The wind was blowing my hair,
After that I imagined the ride stopping,
It had finished.
Then at last I got to the fair.
I did all those things I imagined
On my journey to the fair.

Francesca Strappelli (Age 8)

Leisure

What is this life if full of care,
I've plenty time to stop and stare.

Time to walk my dog is fun,
I let him walk, play and run.

Time to play on my computer,
I have a game that has a shooter.

Time to visit my grandma at home,
But when I got there she'd bought me a comb.

Time to play with my friends,
One of my friends has some hens.

Time to feed my fish with cornflakes,
They haven't eaten them for God sakes

Time to go and have a splash,
I'm under water in a flash.

A good life I've got, it's full of care.
I'm pleased I've got time to stop and stare.

Hannah Spencer (Age 9)

Summer

Bright, shiny,
Playing, shouting, moving,
Flowers, blossom - ice, snow,
Snowing, throwing hitting,
Cold, white,

Winter

Francesca Slay (Age 9)

Night

Every evening I see a face,
Pallid, shadowy and gaunt.
It speaks no words but makes me feel,
Anxious and insecure.

Intimidated by this figure,
Dressed in a jet black cape.
He has unkempt hair, shoulder length,
A sou'wester half covers his face.

Moving stealthily and silently,
Enveloping me in his darkness.
Emerging from his deep, dark cave,
I realise he is harmless.

Every evening I see his face,
Pallid, shadowy and gaunt.
He speaks no words but makes me feel,
Anxious and insecure.

Catherine Spence (Age 11)

A Poem For Mothers Day

If I could be anything I'd be a slug
I'd splodge up Mum's body
To give her a big hug.
For Mothers Day.

If I were a Mother I'd love
Mothers Day
Mothers Day
Mothers Day
What a glorious day.

If I could be anything I'd be a snake,
I'd slither up Mum's body
And go hiss hiss hiss
And when I got to her face
I'd give her a great big kiss.

If I was a Mother I'd love
Mothers Day
Mothers Day
Mothers Day
What a glorious day.

Joanna Smith (Age 9)

Bananas

Search for bananas
The rubbery skin peels off
Ready for eating
The cheeky monkey's hungry
As he munches the soft flesh.

Lucy Steward (Age 11)

The One Ring

The one ring that contains the Dark Lord,
One ring to rule them all,
One ring that brings darkness,
The lands of Mordor where shadows lie.

Bilbo's birthday one hundred and eleven,
Disappears with a bang,
Frodo left with task,
Travels across middle-earth to crack of doom.

A tree captures friends,
Frodo lights fire,
Tree squeezes!
On the quest for the one ring . . .

The one ring to rule them all,
Joins Frodo on mission,
A battle takes place,
Trollmen fight for Sauron . . .

Over the one ring that rules them all!

Danny Smith (Age 10)

Drake's Life

Drake became a sailor at ten, and on the boat were grown-up men.
He used to feed the Captain's pet, that was not something to regret.

The cat one day fell overboard, and Drake got out his body-board.
He dived into the water deep and soon after he fell asleep.

And in 1566, the crew thought he really kicks!
Became a Captain the next year, to celebrate they had some beer.

His ship was called the Golden Hind, he could find his way as if he were blind.
He fought the Spanish in a battle, he also killed all their cattle.

He met the Queen in the harbour, but he had to dash to the barber.
One day while playing his favourite game, he had to fight the Spanish again.

He sunk their ships and killed the crew, they didn't know what to do.
He won the fight and returned home, to celebrate they built a dome!!

Patrick Stapleton (Age 10)

The Dragon

The dragons body is long and slender,
Don't get me wrong he's a champion bender.
He knows so many places he doesn't know where to go.
One hundred years is a difficult bend
But slowly his life just comes to an end.

Jenny Stevens-Lock (Age 9)

Emperor

Scholars   [shi]   teach
Farmers   [nong]   grow
Craftsmen [gong]   make
Merchants [shang]   sell
Knights   [armor]   fight
Kings   [crown]   rule
Queen   [jewels]   sparkling
Children   [playing] happily

Jack Smiles (Age 8)

The Boat

Flying over the water spinning through the sun
Quicker than light shooting water behind it
Spraying people swimming in the water
Destroying fish in the sea having fun
Spinning around running hitting the boat, clit a clat!
Captain goes "Land ahoy, land ahoy!"

Luke Sturgeon (Age 9)

My Dolphin

I've got a dolphin,
And his owner is Dolwin
Mine's called Snowy,
And she's so flowy,
She likes fish
In a great big dish
She is white green and gold,
And she swims in the deep so cold.

Carrie-Ann Stafford (Age 9)

As I Look Out My Window!

As I look out my window I see a rich blue sky,
It's always like that where I live so it's really nice,
I love to play out with my friends in the beautiful Larkwood Close,
Just behind my grand marvellous house there's a spectacular playing field,
But when it rains it gets all muddy so I go to Amy's instead,
I have a favourite tree which I always go and climb,
And when it's a nice day I grab my scooter and go out and play,
As I look out my window I see Larkwood Close.

Natasha Subramaniam (Age 10)

Weathers

What is a hail stone?
A frozen tear drop from the crying eye of heaven?

Where does the cloud go?
Into oblivion beyond the furthest horizon.

What colour is lightning?
All the colours of the rainbow showered in a burst of fire.

What is thunder?
A howling dog chained to the entrance of hell.

What is the Sunlight?
A brilliant rip in the fabric of the sky.

Rory Sparks (Age 11)

Valentine's Poem

His eyes are like blue raindrops falling from the sky.
His hair is like a prickly hedgehog.
His skin is like a silk cloth.
His ears are like scrunched up leaves.
His lips are like the waves in sea.
His teeth are like pearls.
It's my dad alright.

Courtney Swift (Age 8)

Save The Dolphins

In the beautiful Atlantic ocean
Are dolphins swimming the oceans waves
Go down, deeper, deeper
Until they reach the oceans coral.

In comes a fisherman's boat,
Throwing their nets into the sea
I think they've caught more than expected,
Quick get a knife, set the dolphin free.

People come on holiday
Paddling in the sea
They throw litter in it
What about the dolphins?

Along comes a shark
Looking for some prey
A dolphin passes by
Crunch, what had the shark just done?

It's dangerous out there
For a dolphin
THINK
Help to save the dolphins!

Sian Smith (Age 10)

Me

A monkey is me,
Leaping all over the house,
A monkey is me.

A monkey is me,
Breaking everything I see,
A monkey is me.

A monkey is me,
Sleeping all over the house,
A monkey is me.

Adam Stubbing (Age 9)

At The Zoo

You walk in the entrance door,
Come in and we'll explore.
Look what the animals eat,
Some eat vegetables, some eat meat.
Workmen clearing up,
Cleaning cages with a mop,
Kangaroos jump and hop,
Fluffy bunnies ears flop.
Hear the mighty lions roar,
Some people run to the exit door.
See the dolphins swim and jump,
Look at the camel's hump.
Watch the silly penguin's flippers flap,
Watch the sleepy tigers take a nap.

Adam Sumnall (Age 9)

On The Road to Morder

On the road to Morder
Where the shadows lie.

On the road to Morder
Where all mortals die.

On the road to Morder
Past Shellob's lair.

On the road to Morder
Eating boiled hare.

On the road to Morder
Past Riverdell we go.

On the road to Morder
Threw the sleet and snow.

On the road to Morder
With your famous band.

On the road to Morder
In the Shadow Land.

Laurence Stancombe (Age 11)

The Sunset

The sun is setting in the sky,
I sit there eating apple pie,
All bright colours, pink, purple and blue,
You're missing a lot, this could be you.

The sun is setting in the sky,
I definitely don't want to say goodbye,
I'll have to go in, it's getting late,
Tomorrow I'll watch again with a mate.

I walk down the path to my house,
I open the door as quiet as a mouse,
I say goodnight to my mum,
I get my last glimpse of the golden sun.

Kiera Stanton (Age 10)

Clowns

Clowns are scary spooky and frightening,
They make me cringe and shiver,
Their noises are spooky and so are their faces.

When I see a clown I jump six feet off the floor
My hair sticks up and my hands go over my mouth.

Jonathan William Spencer (Age 9)

Night Prowlers

Stalking the night
Silently I glide looking for food
Now
I go for the kill
Helplessly the ensnared animal tries to break free
But fails
Or sometimes
I prefer to eat slimy worms
I protect my land by warding off any other of my kin

What am I?

Dominic Sturt (Age 10)

The Fire Poem

I am the fire,
The most destructive thing on the planet.
Whilst I'm burning I can hear screams of horror and sirens coming to put me out.
When I've gone I leave a trail of mess and a smell of ash.
I am as bright as a star and as hot as the sun.
I am a deep red colour, as red as a juicy tomato.
Where I tread I leave a trail of ruins.
You never know, I might be in your living room one day . . .

Jade Stones (Age 8)

A White World

All we could see was white white white,
So I picked up a snowball and started a fight,
All the fish underneath the iced up pond,
So I put on my ice-skates and pretended I was Bond.

I made a tall snowman with a carrot as his nose,
But then he came alive and I asked him to pose,
Snow flakes kept falling thick and fast,
I looked up to the sky and hoped it would last.

Icicles glistening long and white,
They look so beautiful what a sight,
Soft, white, fluffy and wet,
It covers the ground like a blanket.

Tom Spillman (Age 9)

I Said To The Queen

"I said to the Queen as I sipped at my tea.
Does being the Queen fill you with glee?"
"I like to meet people and travel over seas.
I like having people to look after me.
If I wasn't the Queen then what could I be?"
"I really don't know your majesty!"

Dominic Senior (Age 11)

Cinderella

Cinderella was really poor,
She could never have a bit more,
Every day shell do the plates,
And never allowed any mates.
A letter came to the sisters,
You know the ones with the blisters,
It said "My beautiful ladies,
Don't act like that cruel Haides.
Come to my ball,
And act as tall,
As you have ever been.
You'll meet some people who you have never seen."

Sofia Shoaib (Age 10)

Seasons

Summer Summer hot pretty and dry,
Don't we love the shining sun glistening in the sky.
No rain or snow like all the other seasons,
Summer you need shorts and hats for obvious reasons!

Autumn Autumn its reds, golds and browns,
Lots of beautiful colours falling to the ground.
Conkers of Horse - Chestnut trees,
No sign of wasps, only one or two bees.

Winter Winter cold, short days and gloves,
It is the season all children love.
Santa Clause up in the north,
Waiting for December 24th.

Spring Spring new born animals and flowers,
Big plants growing, hanging over us like towers.
Smell the scent of daffodils, you might even smell honey,
This is a great season so you'd better make it funny!!!

All those great seasons passing ever so fast,
I don't think the snow or sun will ever last!
Crunching leaves to growing flowers,
One of these is a favourite of ours.

Sophie Sissons (Age 10)

Clouds

I like the clouds.
They are soft and white like a sheep skin rug.
But best thing is they remind me of my pillow...
Yawn...ZZzzzzzzzzzzzzzzz

Victoria Sharrock (Age 10)

Bugs

I love bugs,
They crawl in my mugs.
I give them lots to eat,
They sleep on my bed sheet!

Bugs bugs bugs
And fat slimy slugs.
I have lots of them in a jar,
They do crawl very far!

I make them sleep on my furry mats,
And then they chase the rats.
I take them to the fair,
And buy them a fluffy bear!

I love bugs, they swim in my pool,
To stay nice and cool.
I give them a rest,
They are simply the best!

Huma Shafique (Age 9)

Dad

He's a big strong man,
As he is a builder,
And how much has he built?
I'll never know.

He's the king of the T.V.
(And also his job)
The screen goes 'flick, flick'
As he turns it over.

The humorous Dad he is,
As he makes us laugh,
Although he changes,
When he comes home.

He's a big fan of food,
He's always first to finish,
He has a great big mountain,
But still he gulps it down.

This person in my Dad,
He is the best,
I couldn't find another Dad,
The same as him.

Jade Seabrook (Age 11)

Tree

tall and Twisted
ivy wRapped
crackEd
dEad

Tom Stanley (Age 13)

The Mysterious World

In the middle of the forest
There is a hexagon of diamonds,
Glowing in the sun like crystals,
As the spider makes his home.

Turning round and round,
In each corner,
Feeling very dizzy,
As the spider makes his home.

A rainbow of colours,
As mysterious as magic,
A big blob of it,
Inside a marble.

Running away,
Rolling away,
The bicycle wheel rolls,
Goodbye bicycle wheel,
As the bicycle wheel goes.

Donna Shoat (Age 10)

Spiders

I like spiders, they are the very best,
They walk 100 million miles,
I like their very cute smiles.

I like spiders they are the very best,
I feed them chocolate-bars,
They crawl upon my daddy's cars.

I like spiders they are the very best,
I like the big fat furry ones,
They eat so many crumbs.

I like spiders they are the very best,
I keep them in jam-jars,
They always nibble chocolate bars.

Spiders are the very best,
Spiders are the very best,
Spiders are the very best,
I like them very much.

Samera Shafique (Age 9)

Sun

Yellowy-redy
Gold circle
You remind me of gold buttons
You are beautiful in the sky
You come out in the day time.

Chelsea Spence (Age 7)

The Magic Box

I will take out of my box a...
Devils tail spike that's burning
A mechanical talking robot
And a diamond shining blue and bright.

I will put in the box a...
Furry frightened fox
A bluish black bubbling beluga
And a black blunt bat.

I will take out of my box a...
Football alive falling faint
An ocean that's green
And octopus orange.

My box is blue
With green gems on it too
On the top it's bright
In the corners there's light
The hinges are like foxes claws.

Chris Shults (Age 9)

In The Deep Blue Sea

In the deep blue sea
At the bottom is a key,
With a big fat fish
Swimming in a dish.

In the deep blue sea,
There's a log sinking in the sea,
On the log there's a dish,
On the dish there's a fish,
On the fish there's a key.

In the deep blue sea,
A frog is hopping in the sea,
There's a sinking log,
There's a fish on the dish,
On the fish there's a key.

In the deep blue sea,
A floating treasure box.
The frog is sitting on the log,
On the log there's the fish on the dish,
On the fish there's a key.
At the bottom of the sea.

Jessica Sharpe (Age 9)

Magic

What is magic for all we know it could be an animal.
A cat a dog or any mammal,
It might be made of socks or it might be made of clocks
But all I know is that I'm glad that I'm not made of magic.

Alasdair Smith (Age 10)

Oh No Poetry!

Writing a poem is really hard,
I couldn't ever be a Bard.
The words won't come, I cannot think,
I'll go and make myself a drink.

The words I know they will not rhyme,
I really haven't got the time.
To write a poem would take me hours,
I've really lost my rhyming powers.

Wait a minute I've had a thought,
Where is that poetry book I bought.
Maybe it will help me out,
Mum's thrown it out, I hear her shout.

Well here I am, not a word will come,
I'm going to go and ask my mum.
Get on she says, you can do it,
You could become a famous poet!!!

Catherine Spedding (Age 10)

A Sun Day In Summer!

The sun awakes
And spreads its light.
The countryside
Is warm and bright.

The meadows whisper,
In the gentle breeze,
And the birds are singing
In the tallest trees.

Flowers nod,
Trees, gently sway,
"We want more sun!"
They seem to say.

The sound of water
Is heard nearby.
The day gets warmer
As time flies by.

The sky's now crimson,
Pink and red.
Evening's coming,
It's time for bed!

Hannah Summers (Age 13)

The Angels

I will always be there,
With our royal love,
Don't be in despair,
I will be back,
When the time is right
Don't ever stop believing,
I will be back.

Susie Smith (Age 12)

Darkness

Darkness is frightening,
With shining lightening,
An eclipse tonight,
Outside not very bright.

Shadows roaming earth,
Figures in the turf,
The gloomy lights scare,
Shadows grow new hair.

The midnight moon shines,
The ghost's scream out loud,
When wolves squal at night.
Please let there be light.

Adam Scarratt (Age 9)

My Mum

She cleans my boots
She makes my bed
She gives me a tablet
If I've got a bad head

She takes me to bed
She kisses night night
She comes back in
If I've had a fright

She reads my books
She irons my clothes
She gives me a tissue
If I've got a runny nose

She makes me nice food
She plays with my toys
She says we're her
Bestest boys

She has funny hair
It isn't curled
My mum is
The best in the world

Ryan Smith (Age 8)

Snowy The White Bunny

Snowy the white playful bunny,
Makes everyone laugh because she's so funny,
With her powerful ears when I'm sad she wipes my tears.
She won't let anyone be sad,
Her magic kiss makes everyone glad.

Sara Shortland (Age 8)

Barney

Barney is my baby boy
He gives me lots of love and joy,
He takes our dirty socks to mum
So she can put them in the washing drum,
Barney's a very clever lad
But sometimes he can be very bad,
He sits beside our chairs at night
Then barks at nothing and gives us a fright,
When we go to bed at night
He always comes in to say nite nite,
In the morning he's much more fun
To wake us up he jumps on our tum,
It doesn't matter if he's good or bad
He'll always be my beautiful cheeky little lad.

Nicola Stolworthy (Age 11)

The Colour Song

What is red ? Roses are red all over the flower bed.
What is green? The grass is green all over the park.
What is blue? Water is blue round the statue.
What is white? Swans are white swimming in the pond.
What is pink? People are pink having lots of fun.
What is violet? Clouds are violet flying in the sky.
What is grey? Stones are grey all over the grass.
What is black? Ants are black looking for food.
What is brown? Dogs are brown eating bones.
What is colourful? A rainbow is colourful all over the world.
What is gold? A sunflower is gold growing in the shining sun.
What is bright? The sky is bright flying with the clouds.
What is silver? The moon is silver floating in outer space.
What is big? The school is big where the children learn all day.
What is flat? Paper is flat on which children draw or work on.
What is small? A mouse is small looking for some big cheese.

Sam Stevens (Age 9)

God's Special Messengers

Wherever you are, I will be,
Near or far you will see me.
The special peace within you,
Is given from above.
I hold within the palm of my hand,
The heaven's special love.

When you were a baby you had such feathery wings
Now that you are grown up, you live like Kings and Queens.
The wisdom and the beauty and all the other special things,
Are in you for ever,
And ever to be seen.

Alexandra Stobie (Age 11)

View Of Chip

Bin emptier
Fat lump
Naughty boy
Thick pillow
Long jump
Better eater
Water drinker
Dribbling mouth
Good listener
Excellent friend
Loving pet!

Igraine Scott (Age 11)

Bookboy

"I don't love you"
That's what you're thinking
Isn't it?
I can read you
As I can read a book
You are just a book
Yet I yearn for you

I bleed for you
I weep for you

All this for a book?

My heart screams
My soul dies

I bleed
I weep
I scream
I die

For what?

A boy?

A book?

Pippa Shaw (Age 15)

Love Is...

Love is looking at my Mum when she is sleeping.
Love is staring at all of my Year 3 maths groups working hard.
Love is hearing the lovely birds in the morning.
Love is hearing the chattering people at school.
Love is listening to the horses when they go neigh in the stables.
Love is when I smell my lovely coffee on a school morning.
Love is the touch of a smooth stone.
Love is the feel of wet bark when it is wet with rain.
Love is the taste if crumble chocolate cake.
Love is the taste of melt-in-your-mouth ice cream.
Love is the whole world having no fighting and having a smile on their face.

Leo Strange (Age 7)

Our Queen

Our Queen was crowned in 1952.
She has been a good Queen and a noble ruler.

Our Queen was crowned in 1952.
She has visited many places and done many good things.

Our Queen was crowned in 1952.
She has had a happy and joyous reign.

Our Queen was crowned in 1952.
She has seen many things, happy and sad.

Our Queen was crowned in 1952.
She will have her golden jubilee this year.

Our Queen was crowned in 1952.
She will be a good, kind and noble ruler for the rest of her life.

Leah Schoenfeld (Age 10)

Leaving

New friends, old friends they're all the same,
First a place in Germany now Green Lane,
New friends, old friends skinny friends tall friends,
Mini friends, small friends go to different places and the fun never ends.

Adrian Sharples (Age 8)

Easter

Its Easter time the chicks come out,
All the people are walking about.
Being dragged by the chocolate eggs,
Now they're plumpy with short legs.

Its Easter time seagulls go funny,
Whilst they're eating chocolate money with hot honey.
They get so plump that they go flump on the sandy beach.

Later on the misty beach
A girl picks up an odd looking peach and then you hear a
    Squawk!

Kathryn Seymour (Age 9)

Transport

T rains trotting on the railway tracks,
R ats! I forgot my scooter lets go back.
A eroplanes glide as the wind blows.
N autilus a famous submarine glows.
S nakes slither under and over the burning desert.
P arachutes fall, they're scared because of the waving trees.
O h no the police are chasing me.
R ocks and boulders roll in front.
T ransport is important it might save your life one day.

Megan Sampson (Age 8)

The Last Man

Every night there's a silent street,
No cars, no people, nothing!
Then . . . at sunrise . . . heavy lorries,
Red cars, blue cars, white cars, green cars,
Black cars, limo colour light,
Then . . . at sundown . . . all is gone,
Except for one man who's
Nearly got his shopping done,
Except for one man who's
Nearly got his shopping done.

Bethany Smith (Age 8)

A Message In A Bottle

I wrote a letter and put in a bottle,
I put it in the sea,
And it went to a small island.

A pirate in a boat got it and read it,
He put another letter in it,
And he got it and threw it away.

Sarah Spiller (Age 8)

The Snowy Owl

The Snowy Owl hides away in a secret hole.
He swoops from tree to tree.
His eyes glint like flames in a fire.
His feathers cover his body like leaves covering a tree.
He swoops on his prey,
Then flies back to his nest.

Kathryn Speck (Age 10)

The Squirrels

Sammy and Sally squirrel scampered.
They stopped and began to suck strawberries.
Suck, suck
"Stop!!" said Billy Badger
"Stop sucking stupid strawberries"
So Sally spat at him.
"Split nuts instead of sucking strawberries"
Sammy and Sally both skidded off
"But sweet strawberries are nice to suck" said Sally to Sammy.

Oliver Stevenson (Age 8)

Primulas

P retty appealing petals
R ed little lines as red as blood
I ncredible colours standing proudly in the sun
M ini petals nice and orange
U nbelievable leaves, leaves are made of velvet
L ovely little golden star in the middle
A s inside where you can't see beautiful buds
S mell so exotic

Tara Smith (Age 8)

The Snowy Owl

The owl leaves her nest.
Her chicks are as round and fluffy as balls of wool.
She hears rustling on the floor.
She spreads her groomed wings.
She flies into the dark night sky.
She hovers over the rustling leaves.
Her eyes glisten like cats' eyes in the headlights of a car.
She fades into the blackness of the sky
And plans her attack.
She swoops to the ground and grabs her prey.
She kills with razor-sharp talons like pit-bulls' teeth.
She returns to her dark nest to feed her young.

Gareth Smith (Age 11)

Trees In Winter

Trees are small
Trees are tall
Trees are dark
Trees have bark
Trees are singing
The kites in the trees are hanging

Sian Suddes (Age 10)

Inside My Head

Inside my head
There's a place
Where owls hoot
And hedgehogs rustle the leaves.

Inside my head
There's a place
Where black and white
Balls go everywhere and
Score a goal every time.

Ben Scragg (Age 7)

Animals

Animals make good pets,
Nobody likes them getting wet.
In my house,
Mice run about.
Animals are furry,
Love them all you can.
So CARE FOR YOUR PET!

Becki Saunders (Age 9)

In The Woods

Dew drops lay in the open woods
Children use their houses as hoods

Foxes huddle up close in the grass
Waiting for the sun to come out at last.

The trail leads to a secret cove
A bird flys free, blue and mauve

The wind swirls free, a twist of rain

Inside the woods there is NO PAIN

Hayley Sharrad (Age 10)

Me

Football	-	Kicker
Go-kart	-	Racer
Plane	-	Flyer
Hockey	-	Player
Basketball	-	Shooter
Fast	-	Sprinter
Chip	-	Scoffer
Cricket	-	Bowler
Model	-	Maker
Den	-	Builder
Sun	-	Basker
Chess	-	Player
Lego	-	Smasher
Mat	-	Walker
Pony	-	Rider
Book	-	Reader
Pussy	-	Stroker
Brick	-	Layer
Poem	-	Writer

This is me

George Stanford (Age 10)

Darkness

At night the moon comes out
As bright as it can get,
Darkness makes the stars shine

Darkness darkness everywhere
Darkness darkness way up there

Black sky sprinkled with golden dots
Stars are rushing everywhere
Darkness makes us say our prayers
There's a big star over there

Darkness darkness everywhere
Darkness darkness way up there . . . . .
But where is it now? Oh it's morning
    NOW!

Jordan Szmidt (Age 9)

Summer Sun

In the summer sun,
They grow tall,
And high in the sun,
Feel the hot summer sun,
Beautiful breeze in the summer sun!

Lydia Stuart (Age 8)

Monsters

On monster land,
There's a big rocky path.
Through the big rocky path,
Is a big stony cave.
In the cave is a group of monsters!

Some are blue,
Some are green,
Some have spiky hair
Like me!

On monster land,
There's a big slimy ditch,
In the big slimy ditch,
There's a group of monsters!

Some are blue,
Some are green,
Some have spiky hair,
Like me!

AAGGGHHHH!!!!!!!!!!!!!!!!!!!

Leo Simikel (Age 8)

Solar System

Why is Mars red?
Why is Neptune blue?
Why is the sun hot?
And how does the moon move?

How did the Milky Way get in space?
Why is Pluto the least hot?
Is there really a man in the moon?
Why does Jupiter have a big coloured spot?

Why does the government send ships into space?
Where does the universe end?
How did Saturn come to have rings?
Why doesn't the sun's light bend?

Joel Sport (Age 10)

Spring's Colourful

Yes it's spring, spring's come again
come on little girl let's play a game.

It's fabulous, fantastic, fresh and new
the spring has come just for you.

I have seen a frog jumping round
I have seen a dog running on the ground.

Roses are red violets are blue
they're all the colours just for you.

Shelley Stacey (Age 9)

Alphabet Poem

A is for Annie
Whose got long hair.

B is for Barney
Whose book has a tear.

C is for Caroline
Who rides a big horse.

D is for Daniel
Who plans to join the Air Force.

E is for Erick
Whose got a spotty face.

F is for Freddy
Who has a speedy pace.

Hannah Sheppard (Age 9)

Ten Things Found In A Space Mans Suitcase

A pair of cocky cool sunglasses
Two blurry blue airtanks
A hyper heavy space helmet
A super silky space jacket
A pair of small slide on space gloves
And three rockety red jet packs.

Adam Shambrook (Age 7)

Daydream

A dull and dreary classroom,
Another boring day,
Suddenly I'm floating,
Very far away.

Another planet,
Another world,
A strange new colour,
A pinky-gold.

A traditional alien,
Green with three eyes,
He takes me to his leader,
Honest, I tell no lies.

Then I'm back again,
Taken to the head,
A premonition was my dream,
I wish I'd had it in bed!

Allan Skellett (Age 10)

Wellington Is Silly

Wellington is silly
As silly as a shoe
He jumps about the class
And shouts out, "boo hoo."

Mark Skipper (Age 8)

Sir Francis Drake

Sir Francis Drake was brave and bold, and was after spanish gold,
Sir Francis Drake had no fear, til night time what did he hear.

Then Elizabeth saying sail away, then I will double your pay,
To £50 and a chunk of meat, Francis Drake gathered his fleet.

Sir Francis Drake, and his crew, honestly didn't have a clue,
Sir Francis Drake was on the look, when he saw Captain Hook.

Sir Francis Drake had a fight, until he was tied up tight,
Drake and his crew got away, then went to Elizabeth to get his pay.

"Well done Drake you done me proud" the crowd were shouting very loud,
Thankyou Drake go to Spain, to fight those Spaniards once again.

Drake gathered up his finest crew, this time they knew what to do,
Blow up the castle! Blow up the king! Get all the gold and get a ring.

I've discovered the earth is curled, and I've sailed around the world,
Now I've sailed the seven seas, were returning with an ease.

"Well done Drake for this prize, Now please Drake may I advise,
Take a nice well earned rest," For Sir Francis Drake is the BEST!

Jack Sampson (Age 9)

My Pets

I love cats but I love dogs more
Cats sit on your lap
And dogs lay on the floor

My dog can do tricks
He can catch a ball
My cat is boring
She just sleeps in the hall

My dog I can take out for a walk
But my cat stays at home
My dog's fur I have to brush
But on my cat I use a comb

They are very different
My dog and my cat
I love them both
So let's give them a pat.

Rossy Shimmen (Age 9)

Creation Poem

God made trees
God made bees
God made rats
God made bats
God made birds
God made friends

Kieron Simpson (Age 9)

Hamster, Hamster

Hamster, hamster
Chews on bars
Hamster, hamster
Come from mars.

Hamster, hamster
very small,
Hamster, hamster
Very cool.

Hamster, hamster
Eats my tea
Hamster, hamster
Pays his fee.

Hamster, hamster
Plays all day,
Hamster, hamster
Sleeps in May

Hannah Sewell (Age 11)

Untitled

Lets go under the floorboard, down down.
Come on and look around,
I have a mouse,
Who lives in my house
He likes to go rolling on the ground,
Where you can hear a tractor sound
I have a prowling cat
Who sits on the mat
Fancy that!
He said to the cat.
"P-urrrlease ss-ir I mean no harm"
"I just want to go to the barn" Gobble!
We had a dog...

Nicola Sewell (Age 9)

St David's Day

Springtimes here, St David's Day grows near.
Flowers stand to attention like soldiers on parade
As small animals stir in the shade.
Daffodils trumpet the warming days.
The sun yawns in the morning haze.
The birds return like a boomerang,
And sing their sweet, charming song,
Like the Welsh on their Saint's Day,
As rabbits hop in midday play,
The green carpet of grass stretches over the land.
March the first is soon at hand.

David Sims (Age 10)

Christmas Poem

The night before christmas you cannot sleep
You sister or brother says lets have a peek
In the morning you rush down the stairs
Mum says bring your teddy bears
My sister and me wander why
um calls to Dad and says get the apple pie
My sister says wait till it defrosts
Dad says I've lost my socks
My sister found them under the chair
I found them under there
My sister wants to build a snowman
Dad says NO WAY MAN!
Mum says get on with that apple pie
Dad says why do I...
A few minutes later
Mum gets out the pen and paper
Dad hands the presents out one by one
Until they are completely gone!
Dad hands the first one to me
I open it, hold it up so everyone can see

Amy Shore (Age 8)

Anger

Anger, raging, anger.
Dressed in a black cloak covering his body.
He begins to ram his horns into buildings showing his anger.
His piercing red eyes glowing above a green scarf covering his mouth.
With a deep screeching shrill voice.
People around disperse, screaming with fear.
With the power to smash through walls.
Anger begins to fly, smashing through the upmost windows of skyscrapers.
Anger erupts and falls to the ground, sobbing into his hands.

Adam Sharkey (Age 12)

The Oyster

The oyster's shell looks like a wave,
But sounds like the gentle sea,
It feels like sand running through my fingers;
On the inside it feels like water.
It's heavenly, the oyster.
So soothing, it's like you're in another world,
God of the sea, he, the oyster.
If you venture to see him your labours will be rewarded with beauty.

James Shinnie (Age 8)

As The Ripples Smooth

As the ripples smooth,
Fallen as we move through the shadows of yesterday.

Gone forever are the good things we have done,
Forever immortalised in overview and memories.
But the sad longings of retrospect can bring it all back in a second.

Baggage are the bad times,
Like a suitcase full of bitterness and regret.
But the happiness of the recent past can help erase grey moments, with time.

As the ripples widen,
Risen as we tentatively venture into the brighter void that is tomorrow.

Oliver Seaman (Age 15)

Westbay!

As I sit upon the rocks,
I see the seagulls as they flock,
Crashing waves against the boats,
The fisherman fight them as their boat rocks.

Looking for their catch of the day,
The people watch in dismay,
For they risk their lives for us each day,
So we can have the freshest, healthiest seafood,
Crab, lobster, prawns and much more,
The list is endless for all to adore.

Lance Samways (Age 11)

My Poem

O ur cat Ruffles.
U sually outside.
R odents beware!

K ate loves to groom her.
I n the rain she is as feeble as a mouse.
T reasure for people not for mice!
T aking care of the left-over milk.
E aten all the cheese you say.
N o bad cat.

Lucy Sanger (Age 9)

The Old Praise Song Of The Jaguar

The Jaguar is the invader of the plains
The camoflauged one of the plains,
The great, great on lying on the sand
It is the plain Lord, the Jaguar,
The biter I go seeking on sand
Off he bounds hunting,
He digs his razor sharp teeth into the gazzel he chose
Back to his layer jamming his teeth in the gazzel's neck
But hunters are coming
Through the plains they come but when they see the Jaguar they flee
The Jaguar roars in anger
Every animal runs for cover
He is the one who can kill Msjita the drought God
He shall rule forever never to die
Cruel one, mean one,
The Jaguar is the killing machine.

Harry Shankar (Age 8)

It's A

It's a deep river
It's a quick arriver
It's a fierce animal
It's a living creature under sea
It's a big creature
It's a big fish
It's a smooth glider
It's a good slider

    IT'S A... SHARK

Tarranveer Singh (Age 10)

Happiness

Happiness is a bright blue,
It smells like fresh air,
Happiness tastes like a soft voice.
It fells like gentle wind blowing.
Happiness lives in a purple violet.

Hardeep Singh (Age 9)

My Dad

My Dad's cool
He's not a fool
He's tough he's strong
He tells me off when I do wrong.

My Dad likes a laugh
But he never wears a scarf
He just loves walking
But he's excellent at talking.

He really likes climbing
When the sun is shining.
He was a dangerous boy
Who had a great toy.

It was a go-kart
Which he smashed apart.

But most of all I love my Dad
He's the best, Dad Dad Dad!

Ciaran Scannell (Age 10)

The Deer

The Deer, the Deer,
The mighty Deer.

The ears that twitch,
The elegant legs,
The slim body,
The small tail.

The Deer, the Deer,
The mighty Deer.

The Stag, the Stag
The mighty Stag.

The ears that twitch,
The elegant legs,
The bony antlers,
The small tail.

The Stag, the Stag,
The mighty Stag.

Rosie Simikel (Age 10)

My Brother

He is a teenager,
Happy . . . but grumpy on Tuesdays.
He cracked his head open tripping over a stone . . .
I'll never forget it.
He is as small as a mouse,
As loud as a lion,
He likes to play on his gameboy.
He likes to say "Make us a sandwich!"
He is very annoying.

Patrick Swailes (Age 11)

What Would Happen If There Was No TV?

What would happen if there was no TV?
    What would happen to me?
No-one would have heard of Dr Who
    Oh what can we do?
No-one would have heard of the Sweeney
    And not even the Tweenies
There would not even be Bugs Bunny
    This is not funny?
What would happen if there was no TV?
    There would be nothing for me to see.

Bill Smith (Age 10)

Lake District Waterfall

Old age water comes tumbling down
Spinning and turning no clear water frown
Down it goes into the glass-clear pool
This old age water comes right down now

Dense, long the plants around
The dreaming - life water when it comes tumbling down
Songbird - whispering the luscious green trees
Around the sprinkling, life-making waterfall

Matthew Sharp (Age 12)

My Cat

My cat is really really funny.
She plays a little bunny game.
She jumps around and plays with my blanket
I say, "Don't! Don't! Don't!
But she still does it.
My cat goes meow, meowwww.
My cat is furry, cuddly, black and light brown.
My cat's name is Rosie because she likes to pick roses.

Tristan Taylor (Age 7)

Stonehenge

Stones as silver as the moon, shimmering bright,
Standing tall as time goes by.
Sinking into the ground waiting to fall.
There are cracks all over the stones.
One of the stones wobbles and then falls!!!

Abigail Scott (Age 8)

Elephants

E lephants are big, elephants are small,
L ovely long trunks, and very tall.
E ars very big, and they are cool,
P ounding everywhere, playing with a ball
H aving a drink because they're out of puff,
A nd they're very big and very tough.
N othing to do, well not enough,
T hey're very nice, and love a hug.

Helena Sampson (Age 9)

Our Mums

Mums make dinner for us
Mums take us to bed
Mums make breakfast for us
Mums read stories to us
Mums run the bath for us
Mums wash our hair for us
Mums pick us up from school
Mums take us to the park
Mums buy us sweets
We love our mums

Leanne Thirling (Age 7)

Wiggly Worm

Wiggly, wiggly, wiggly worm wiggles all
Day and night.
Wiggly, wiggly, wiggly worm
Never turns
Off the light.

Naomi Simpson (Age 8)

A Bad School Day

Mum shouts "Get up, you're late..."
"Grab your pencil case, go to school"
Bossy teacher bellows "No excuse, get to assembly!"
Headmasters talking about boring Jesus.
At playtime bullies bully me, make me cry
I go to first aid and get better.
In the classroom my teacher makes me listen to boring subjects.
At lunchtime dinner ladies make me eat my lunch.
Back in the classroom I learn stupid maths.
Finally at home...
I watch telly, then go to bed
Because tomorrow's another
School day!

Megan Scott (Age 9)

Finding A Goat Horn

Sudden crack of a bone by my thin, long, legs,
Like some smashing pottery but it was this instead.

I had a look down and saw it was old, brown and quite long too,
Then I took a closer look and it was a goats horn.

It was rough and quite cold,
And I ran home to study the old, brown goat horn.

Daniel Snowdon (Age 9)

The Golden Day

The golden coach appears along the road
Stunning white horses, heads held high
Lead it towards the abbey.
Many people waited, waited for the Queen.
Waving flags high in the air, children cheering loud.
Suddenly silence fell over the crowd
The Queen descended elegantly.
Jumping up and down I tried to see the Queen and her wonderful gown.
Her crown glistened in the sparkling sunlight
As she disappeared into the depths of the Abbey.

Lauren Sebley (Age 9)

My Mum

My mum is as intelligent as a dolphin.
As beautiful as a rose.
She looks after my brothers and my sister.
"Get upstairs and get changed."
She is happy and hums along to songs that she doesn't know.
Fit, healthy and alive.
Middle-aged.
As bright as an orange.

Vicky Thorp (Age 11)

I Am A Ruler

I am a ruler
Short and thin
I like to measure
Everything.
My numbers
Go up to 15
Everybody likes
To draw on me.
I am used to
Underline titles
The teacher thinks
It is vital!

Mitchell Thomas (Age 9)

Feelings

When I am angry
I am as angry as a tiger
When I am lonely
I am as lonely as a seed
When I am happy
I am as happy as a butterfly
When I am sad
I am as sad as a garden shed

Max Trueman (Age 6)

My Goldfish

My pet goldfish
Swimming all day
Its shining scales
Shine as armour.
Its gills go in and out
Like a clockwork toy.
Its fins wobble all day swimming.
The colour is a gold coin.

Chris Tanner (Age 10)

Mummy Is A Dummy

My mummy is a dummy,
The babies think she is yummy,
She doesn't like the mouth
Because she heads south,
A dummy she would be
She didn't want to be yummy.

Hannah Tubbs (Age 7)

Rainforest Island

In the depth of a small green island
With palm trees covering the undergrowth
Monkeys chattering, very excited
Berries being eaten by a placid sloth

Near the brook a leopard prowling
Stalking its pray which is hiding there
Darkness falling, hyena howling
Head up to the moon, revealing his lair.

The taunting cries of a wolf cub sounded,
Then dawn breaks with the sun in the sky
The trees reach up but are steadily grounded
Watching the fluffy clouds go by.

Birds are singing their morning chorus
Animals awake to the melody,
They think "as the flowers open before us
The world is at peace with me".

Emily Turner (Age 11)

Robin Hood Left Nottingham

There was a man from Nottingham
Who tried to cross the river.
Oh what a joke
He tripped on a rope now look at him shiver.

Jamie Sims (Age 9)

My Riding Class

When ready for my riding class,
To the stable I will race
Then bring my horse in from the grass
And tie him in his place.

My horse I brush from tail to nose
And when I fetch his tack,
Upon his head the bridle goes,
The saddle on his back.

I lead him out across the yard
To where I take my seat.
Then tug the reins, but not too hard,
And nudge him with my feet.

We join the rest within the school,
Who canter, trot or walk.
Sometimes we jump, and as a rule,
We're not allowed to talk.

Now he is back here, in his stall,
And I've untacked my steed
I hang his manger on the wall,
For he has earned his feed.

Louise Tossell (Age 14)

Survivor

I shed silent tears,
For my companions and peers.
Now that only stands is a silent cross,
To mark their terrible loss.

I knew them from the battlefield,
But now in the ground they're sealed.
They were the ones,
That knew the shot and guns.

I saw my friends go down,
As we stormed the town.
Don't pity me, as I stand alone,
For my heart has hardened to stone.

The mud, guns, death have gone,
Leaving the survivors torn.
It has left a wound,
Which won't heal soon.

The sun has set,
My eyes are wet.
To the lost I call,
But the grief, I just stall.

Christopher Truscott (Age 12)

Fireworks

Fireworks go up and down,
Fireworks make different sounds,
Fireworks make a light in the sky,
Fireworks come in different colours,
Fireworks glow in the sky,
Fireworks colour sparks,
Fireworks sparkle in the sky,
Fireworks light up the dark black night sky,
Fireworks bang,
Fireworks crackle.

Charlotte Thomas (Age 11)

Epitaph to Humanity

Here lies Humanity,
(From date unknown until
Four horsemen ride),
Beloved husband, wife and child all,
Through sad and sorrowful,
(Accident, murder or hand of God),
Rest in what peace you find,
If any.
We commit thy
(Soul, spirit or essence),
To (Fill space as religion dictates)
That you may,
(Live on, re-live,
Or suffer for your wrong).

Emanwel Josef Turnbull (Age 15)

A Mid-Winters Day

It was a cold frosty morning,
Leaves so crisp and white.
Hair blowing in the soft breeze,
So cold you could get frost bite.

Snow is scattered on the ground,
Grass crunching by your feet.
Gleaming cobwebs all around,
Spiders sheltering from the sleet.

Pond frozen over by ice,
Squirrels running from tree to tree.
Everyone's staying inside all day,
That's what mid-winter is to me.

Hayley Toll (Age 11)

Nothing

No one to see, no one in sight,
No one to talk to on this
Dark winters night.

No one is there to walk away,
No one is there to stand and stay.

No one is there to gossip and lie,
No one is there to make you cry.

No one is there to be happy or sad,
No one is there to make you feel glad,

No one is there to offer you a goal,
No one is there not even my soul.

My mind is no more, why am I here,
All I can feel is my wet crying tear.

Oliver Tulett (Age 13)

Cats

Cats are big,
Cats are small,
Cats are fat.
They make a mess with their string ball.

Cats are mean,
Cats are nice.
Cats are cruel
Because they eat mice.

Grace Titmarsh (Age 7)

The Cat

Its back arched, its front paws poised
Slowly, stealthy and silent, it makes no noise
Eyes green and glinting, its fur sleek and black
Ready for the catch.

Determined and deadly, its enemy in sight
Claws stretched out to prepare for the fight
Nose twitching, smelling the fear
Ready for the catch.

Suddenly it darts and pounces in attack
Playfully tossing the mouse on its back
Shivering with terror, the battle near its end
Ready for the next catch.

Hannah Taylor (Age 10)

Mr Nobody

I know a person who you can't see,
His name is Mr Nobody.
He is tall and thin and very wise,
And has big blue wide eyes.

He always eats two pies each day,
And does a little dance or play.
Then he wanders through the park,
Waiting until, it gets dark.

When everyone has gone,
He goes and wanders on and on.
And sees if he can find a place
Where he can rest until he wakes.

Now even though you can't see,
You know a person Mr Nobody.

Emily Thomas (Age 9)

Our Mums

Mums iron
Mums take us to the park
Mums read with us
Mums take us to school
Mums get us dressed
Mums get your shoes
Mums brush our hair
Mums take you to swimming
Mums take us to parties
Mums make tea
Mums make cakes
Mums write with you
Mums take us to bed
We love our mums

Natasha Taylor (Age 6)

Sir Francis Drake

Francis Drake was only a boy, he went to sea with a big old toy,
He started his journey round the world, when he found some very valuable pears.

They sailed to a land, where British were banned,
The Spaniards were there, the place was quite bare.

He sailed on the rough and bumpy seas, to Plymouth for a cup of tea,
Elizabeth was there, she gave him cream and pears.

"Go and kill King P for me?" she said, I was in a deep sleep in my bed,
He said he would take my land as his, "Of course my dear it will be a wiz".

It was a stormy ride he lied to King P, he lied!
A lot was learned, two ships were burned, so their journey is over.

He went to lovely Plymouth then went to rest at Teignmouth
A letter came, and it said,

The Spanish Armada are here, you'd better get your self into gear,
There's the gate, don't dare be late, the Spanish Armada are here!!!

There were bangs and booms, there's going to be load of tombs,
It was all shields and swords, oh praise the lord!

The men were dead, it was quite a dread,
But Drakes men stood till the end.

The Spanish had gone, there was no pong,
All thanks to one man he'll never be banned he is Francis Drake.

Daniel Taylor (Age 10)

Sunshine

It burns me up
Ice-cream's melt in the sun
Hurray hurray the people say every Sunday

Megan Thatcher (Age 7)

A River

A random, rushing, crazy labyrinth
Of slithery, rushing, mechanical eels.
A squadron of mental, motley platoons,
Forbidden beyond the bank.
Nettles, green and forbidding;
Concoctions of reeds with sabres;
Silver birches proud and bony;
Willows sobbing sorrowfully.
Crickets skulking at our feet;
Spiders making footprints, small but plentiful;
Frogs withdrawing beneath the stillness
Creating rings that multiply.
They creep across the surface,
Whipping blockades like an army of stormtroopers,
Disturbing the ceiling of glass suspended
Above the carpet of pebbles.

Michael Tyler (Age 10)

Apples

Apples taste as good as chocolate
My apple looks like a sunshine
My apple feels as smooth as mum's skin
My apple smells as nice as a flavour
My apple is as good as mums
I love apples

Dana Taylor (Age 6)

The Queen's Golden Jubilee - Rap Version!

The queen sits all day on her throne,
And calls all men on her mobile phone.
"Oh come to party fever man,
Come on and bring roast pork and ham."
"Why oh Queeny Queeny Queen?"
"Because it's my Golden Jubilee!"
"In 50 years and all you've done,
I think that this will be most fun!"
"Even when I travelled all around the world?"
"Well yes, of course and that's my word!"
"I'll go shopping, but what to get!"
"Well hats and glitter, and place some bets"
"Why, you're mad! Let's get more money!
Go. Don't be bad it's always sunny!"

Sara Tryon (Age 8)

The Park

Children play all day,
From long summers nights to cold winters eve's,
Children sitting by the stream,
Happily licking their ice creams,
Laughing and joking they count up to five,
In the stream who is going to dive?
Holding hands as they skip around,
Then all falling to the ground,
The big kids play on their bikes,
While the little kids bicker and fight.
The parents sit chatting all day,
Shouting at the kids who are trying to play.
The teenage girls fuss over their broken nails,
While the teenage boys talk to their pals.
As children start to leave the park,
It begins to get dark.
As the sun goes down,
The caretaker sweeps the ground,
And all that is left is one little sound, the creak of
The swing that blows to and fro,
The sun is now becoming very low.

Lauren Garrett and Rebecca Tume (Age 12)

What My Guinea Pig Gets Up To

My guinea pig runs around, chewing the cabbage.
She lays about talking to her friend.
She's getting fatter every second.
She drinks her water right down,
Then has another run around.
She lays down falling asleep but bang,
She's at it again.

Leah Thompson (Age 9)

Owls

Owls don't sleep at night
They come out at night
Make sure they don't bite.

I can't promise or guarantee
But I can say one thing
Try and avoid coming out at night,
Trust me, I am an owl!!

But do not hesitate I'll be nice
As long as you fetch, fetch my breakfast!

I've been waiting for ages, watching the moon
Disappear as the sun comes in the early morning.

And now it's time for me to go and sleep.
But don't forget I come out at night,
And I might just hurt you meek weak mouse!!

Roshni Thakar (Age 12)

Untitled

I looked out through iron cage bars,
I saw wonder, beauty, stars.
I saw delicate flowers in bloom,
I saw silence in a whitewashed room.
I saw ripples in a still grey lake,
I saw snowflakes gracefully make
A blanket of snow hiding the place,
I saw laughter lines in an old woman's face.
I saw the great bright sun at noon,
I saw boldness in the blue corn moon.
I saw the sparkling of a turquoise sea,
I saw how wonderful people could be.
There was no sorrow, depression or pain,
There was no miserable November rain.
There were no poor hungry mouths to feed,
People weren't judged by their colour or creed.
Then a reality when I woke from my dream,
Of how blissfully beautiful a mirage can seem.

Yasmin Taylor (Age 13)

Peace and Conflict

War, conflict, bloodshed, death!
Is this what we want for our world?
Two countries argue and neither back down,
So war begins.
Dreams are shattered,
Lives destroyed,
Fears come true,
All anyone wants is peace and tranquillity.
Where all kinds of races, old and young,
Can get on with enjoying life not fearing tomorrow.
Will there ever be a time,
When we all get on?

Gary Tough (Age 15)

The Storm

Crashing, bashing, clashing, lashing,
Spreading near and far.
Caught up inside its own misery,
Beating down on the rest of the world.

Thunder booms like a beating drum,
Barking out its mournful song.
Lightning stabs at unaware prey,
Like a caged up lion that wants to play.

The rain pours down,
Melancholy and begone.
Ending lifeless like a deflated balloon.

The storm still raged on way into the night,
Crashing, bashing clashing, lashing.
Until the break of daylight.

Abby Tymon (Age 11)

Questions Poem!

How do planes fly?
Why can't gravity be seen?
How do cars move?
Why can't humans fly?
Why do things die?
Why is the snail slow?
Why do bats like darkness?
Why do cats have to bite?
Why is the Universe so big?
Why do humans fight?
How does the heart keep itself pumping?
Why did Dinosaurs die out?
How can sharks swim so fast?
Why is grass green?
Who invented the subject science?
Why are humans scared?
How do people breathe while they're asleep?
Why aren't ghosts real?
Why is electricity dangerous?
Why are people allergic?

David Taylor (Age 11)

My Mum

My mum is the best in the world.
She is as pretty as a rose/
She always shouts...."Put the kettle on will you?"
My mum is as happy as can be.
Her favourite drink is white wine.
She always lollops on the sofa, she never moves!
She is as silent as a mouse.
I love her because she's perfect.

Sarah Taylor (Age 11)

Teachers

Flick to the page number seventy two,
There the instructions explain what to do,
Don't chat to your friends or send notes round the class,
If you've got a question, put your hand up and ask.

Stay in your seat and don't wander around.
Please work in silence, no one make a sound.
If you're not careful, you'll be back here at break,
This isn't funny, your lunchtime's at stake.

No eating in lessons, put your gum in the bin.
Give me your planner and wipe off that grin.
Detentions for you two, go and sit on your own.
Stop throwing that rubber and switch off your phone.

Stop fighting at the back, this is a lesson don't you know?
Hurry up and finish because the bell's about to go.
These are the rules that you have to obey.
Don't argue with me, now just do what I say!

Jenny Tregoning (Age 15)

The Deer

Grazing silently in the glen,
Pulling up tufts of grass,
Frolicking in the meadow of daisies,
Drinking from a lake of shining glass.

Nuzzling fawns in soft sunlight,
Snoozing as the day goes on,
Watching stags clatter their antlers,
Soon the daylight will be gone.

Now as the moon shines down
A gunshot fills the air
And the deer falls into the bracken
Into eternal sleep

Rachael Thomson (Age 11)

Winter Days

Dripping and dropping
Claps of thunder and lightning
Rain lashing the earth.

Will Trenholme (Age 12)

Blue Is . . . . .

Blue is calm, resting
Like the ocean waving slowly
Blue is as bright as the burning sun
It is a beautiful, lovely colour
Blue is the colour of the blue sky.

Emily Thomas (Age 9)

God

God is a wonderful person
He loves each and every one
He helps and cures sick people
And he might live near the sun

In a church we worship him
By praying and singing
We pray to him when we're at home
And inside he's listening

God might be eating his tea right now
He might know my future
He might be talking to Mary
Or shouting or whispering to her

God might be counting his angels
Or telling them to go to bed
God might be going himself
With his pillow under his head

Heidi Thomas (Age 9)

The Monster of Albere

The monster of Albere,
Sits in his mother's armchair,
He is green and slimy, has no hair,
With yellow feet and purple shoes,
He stomps around whilst reading the news.

With ears as big as stepping stones,
Eyes as large as the sea,
He hears everything that's going on,
And sees everything there is to see,
His mouth is as large as an apple tree.

Seven, nine, eight and two,
Are the sizes of his shoes,
His tongue's as scabby as can be,
He's not a pretty sight to see,
But he's very special to me.

He jumps around and plays with me,
He especially loves a cup of tea,
I love to sit on all his knees,
Because he doesn't frighten me,
AFTER ALL HE'S ONLY MY DAD.

Lewis Tillett (Age 11)

My Dog

My dog is such a gentle soul
Although she's small it's true
She brings the cookies in her mouth
And brings the packet too

My dog is such a bad girl
She really knows it too
She still eats all the cookies
And doesn't even chew

Jess Tytheridge (Age 11)

Fisherman

There once was a fisherman called Jow
Who lived in a cabin with Mow
They were up early and bright
They fished until night
And set off again in the morning

They caught fish
They caught boats
They caught trees
And sometimes even peoples coats
They laughed
They cried
But in the end they both died.

Gary Twigg (Age 12)

The Seasons

The autumn is a bird,
As brown, crispy leaves float through the air
Squirrels collect their nuts for their hibernation
The days are getting shorter the nights are getting darker.

The winter is a werewolf,
Its breath smells like a roast dinner.
Its fur is like a crispy tree trunk,
Its breath blows like a hairdryer on full blast

The spring is the world coming to life,
As new baby animals are born.
It's a time to celebrate Easter,
And flowers open to the sun.

The summer is the smiling sun,
As children play on the beaches.
They are cooled by splashing sea waves.

Amy Turner (Age 10)

Desert Island

The Desert Island is like a mother cradling me
She is as peaceful as a new born lamb
She welcomes me like a friend with open arms
She is a baby sleeping
The Desert Island is like a happy ever after story
The sand curls around me like cuddly toys
She is as caring as a cat with its new born kittens
And when I leave she waves me sadly goodbye

Megan Thompson (Age 11)

This Is Our Summer Place

But the trees are bare
And all the leaves are crisp
And the river that we paddled in is slow

Naomi Thompson (Age 8)

Snow

Slowly the snowflakes start to fall,
Twisting and turning as they float down.
Making a blanket over the world,
Rubbing out the dark smudges.

The ice is like a gleaming mirror,
But is as thin as glass.
Now the sun is warming up,
And the snow is starting to fade.
Slowly and steadily the world reappears,
The bad coming back.
The brown bits uncovered,
The snow at an end.

Hannah Thomas (Age 10)

Football

Football, football,
The nation's favourite game,
Football, football,
Football is it's name.

Football, football,
All across the land.
Football, football,
Worth a million grand.

Football, football,
Lots of different teams.
Football, football,
Four separate leagues.

Football, football,
Attracts many large crowds.
Football, football,
Hundreds of grounds.

Football, football,
Is the sport I love.
Football, football,
Sent from above.

Robert Taylor (Age 13)

Water Snake

Sneaking
Slithering
Swimming
Spitting
Shedding their skin
They're sly.
Sammy the sneaky snake
Slurping strawberries
Sssssuper!!!
He will get you!!!

Daniel Turrell (Age 7)

Quack Quack Quack Duck

Quack quack quack duck,
Quacking in the pond
Quack quack quack duck
You are not that blonde!

Honk honk honk goose,
Honking on the hill
Honk honk honk goose
Are you feeling ill?

Baa baa baa sheep,
Baaing in the shed
Baa baa baa sheep
Are you with your head?

Gemma Thomas (Age 7)

Mum

As kind as a loving dog,
As tender as a heart,
This is about my mum,
And we will never part.

Sometimes as mean as a wild dog,
As hatred as a rat,
A hand as hard as a steel rod,
But as smooth as a cat.

Her hair as fair as mild brown pine,
And as soft as cotton wall,
Her heart as bright as a loving couple,
But never will it be dull.

Her eyes as blue as a clear summers day,
And as big as the full moon,
Her nose as pointy as a sharpened spike,
But as small as a head of a spoon.

No body is like my mum,
Well in my my world they aren't,
Even if the were cloned,
I would tell their personality apart!

Andrew Todd (Age 12)

Yellow

Yellow is the colour is custard on warm pies
Yellow is a lightning bolting down on me
Yellow is a daffodil on a summer morning
Yellow is my sandpit all day in summer
Yellow is a ripe banana from the shop
Yellow is a lemon sweet or sour
Yellow is the sun hot and bright

Kerry Tatnell (Age 9)

Mice

They have eyes like black beads
Sewn onto a surface of white cotton.
Little dustcarts
Sucking up everything in their path
And then destroying it
With their teeth as sharp as pointy stones.

They scuttle along like spiders
Wrapped up in their silky, spider web fur
Every now and again
Having to dart out of the way of towering humans
Who shriek with fear and fright.

They live in small, black caves of darkness
Where they roam around like ghosts
Looking for scraps of food
But they are often trapped and killed.

Sophie Thomas (Age 11)

My Best Friend

My best friend is always there,
There when I'm feeling sad.
He always makes me feel glad,
That I have a best friend.

Together we've been through thick and thin,
We're always there for each other.
He is just like a brother,
I know him better than his mum and dad.

He enjoys playing football,
He's up for a dare,
As I've already said,
He's always there.

He's my best friend,
And he's one of a kind.

Phillip Thomas (Age 11)

The Frogs

There was a frog who lived in a wood
But he wasn't very good
He moaned to wear a hood.
And his friends didn't like food.
He always smashed in prickles.
But he never made wobbles.
He always gets in muddles.
He never has muddles.
He loves going on trains.
He travels around in prams.
All his friends were the same.
He always climbs lamps.
He always walks on ramps.
He makes lots of camps.
He goes on lots of boats
He goes home on floats.

Joseph Tindall (Age 7)

It Wasn't Me

It wasn't me!
It wasn't me who kicked the ball.
It wasn't me who kicked the ball that smashed the window.
It wasn't me who kicked the ball that smashed the window that woke the baby.
It wasn't me who kicked the ball that smashed the window that woke the bay who threw a tantrum.
It wasn't me.
I didn't wake her.
Honest, I was in the garden playing football!

Alex Thomas (Age 10)

Leisure

What is this life if full of care,
I have plenty of time to stop and stare.

Time to play football in the park,
My mum gets mad when it gets dark.

Time to read it is such fun,
As I'm tired I lie on my tum.

Time to lie on my comfy bed,
I'm so still you'd think I was dead!

Time to go to Chris' house,
Where his Sega is as quiet as a mouse.

Time to go with my dad golfing,
Stop for dinner at the Blue Dolphin.

Time to play cricket with Matt,
Hit the ball for a six and hit a rat.

A good life I've got it's full of care,
I have plenty of time to stop and stare.

James Taylor (Age 9)

The Graveyard

You walk in
It feels creepy,
You see
Tall stones near
Small stones,
With plenty of dates,
Some were just fate,
The church has a tower,
People come to put down flowers,
Pretty angels and
Inscriptions are
On the stones
Some have reserved places,
For other loved ones.
Coffins in the aisle of the church,
Waiting for their ceremonies
The Father
The Son
And
The Holy Spirit

Melody Tomlin (Age 14)

School

School can be fun, school can be boring.
You get some geeks, you get some freaks.

School can be fun, school can be boring.
Every lesson one hour long!, after PE some people pong!

School can be fun, school can be boring.
We go to school every weekday, you should give us more breaks HAY!

School can be fun, school can be boring.
The teachers are great, but I am not going to be late!

School can be fun, school can be boring.
We don't get the cane, so we miss out on all the pain (Good job!)

School can be fun, school can be boring,
That's school for you, it can be fun and it can be boring.

Freya Taylor (Age 11)

Red Is . . . .

Red reminds me of the best football team
Red is the mysterious devil symbol of the football team and the team is Man United
Red is flowers that gleam in the sun, they are as beautiful as a butterfly in the breeze
Red is my favourite colour that makes me want to shout out.

Robert Turner (Age 9)

Blue Is . . . .

Blue is cool like sky on a frosty, cold winters day
Blue is fun like a bouncing beach ball that we play with all day
Blue berries are wonderful and good to eat

Emily Townsend (Age 9)

City Pigeons

Pigeons live in towns so they can eat scraps,
Chips, crisps and greasy wrappers,
Most people don't like them,
Though I do,
They fly away if they see you.

You usually find them near,
The chip shop, food shop, cake shop and the bakery,
Pigeons are scavengers and act like dustbins.

They are usually black and white,
But they can be brown and pink.
People think they are pests.

Stephen Taylor (Age 9)

Autumn

Leaves dive off the branches into a pool of colour,
Surrounding the trees,
One after the other.

The forest covered in a fiery floor,
Soggy brown leaves,
Float along the wet moor.

Ready for winter,
The leaves are rotten,
Although the magic of autumn, is never forgotten!

Joseph Thorpe (Age 10)

Leisure

What is this life if full of care,
I've plenty of time to stand and stare.

Time to play rugby with my best friend Ash
We give the ball a really good bash.

Time to watch my brother run
And play with his toy gun.

Time to visit grandma mar
I like going it's not far.

Time to look after my little sis
Make sure she gets a goodnight kiss.

Time to go swimming and make a big splash
I stayed so long I had to dash.

Time to leave home for school
School is really cool.

A good life I've got it's full of care
I'm pleased I've got time to stand and stare.

Brogan Trueman (Age 9)

Your Hands

Have you got?
Big hands, little hands
Dirty hands, clean hands
Wet hands, dry hands
Naughty hands, kind hands.
Which hands are yours?

Christina Thompson (Age 11)

Leisure

What is this life if full of care,
I have plenty time to stand and stare.

Time to get all our photographs,
Looking at them brings lots of laughs.

Time to watch TV,
Having popcorn before my tea.

Time to lie in my cosy bed,
Sleeping next to my big ted.

Time to play out,
To scream and shout.

A poor life this if full of care,
I have plenty time to stand and stare.

Anna Taylor (Age 9)

Sea! Sea! Sea!

The waves super sonic
Fiercesome sharks
Over reefs and rocks
In the Indian Ocean.

The sea charges
Over penguins
Piranhas waving banners
In the Atlantic Ocean.

The tidal wave
Erodes the cliffs
Crashing and smashing
On a stormy, thundery night.

Jake Tiffen (Age 9)

Red

Arsenal are winning the FA Cup
A juicy apple
Arsenal are winning the FA Cup
A smelly red pen
Arsenal are winning the FA Cup again
Arsenal are great
Arsenal are winning the FA Cup
Their home kit is red
Arsenal are winning the FA Cup again.

Matthew Thompson (Age 8)

Two Girls

Two girls out and before,
Chasers didn't even know,
For before September.
It's over now but still every show sparkles.
Make it sparkle.
Two girls out and before.
Pressure, spotlight. Chasers knew it wasn't right.
Inspiration shine girls, shine!
Forget all troubles for awaited apprentices.
Two girls out and before should learn to forget.
Chasers tapped upon wooden floors:
Dance girls shine!
Shivers down the spine
But chasers didn't understand,
It was just two girls
      Out and before
      Out and before.

Holly Tarn (Age 13)

Moon Juice

The moon is like a flying fruit
In the sky spilling its juice,
On the ground the mice drink this wonderful taste
And you hear the call of the mighty moose.
The stars create the star dust
That flutter into your house,
They flutter in your eyes and make you go to sleep
And you hear the quiet scratch, scratch of the little white mouse.
The space pips fly from the moon
Into freshly dug soil,
There they will stay all night long
And in the ground they toil.
Sprouting roots until dawn breaks
And joining altogether,
As they form a moon tree
Bad turns the weather.
They flee towards space never to return
And the cogs of the moon turn,
As it flies away.

Ben Taub (Age 10)

In My Head

In my head
There is a shop, full of all my hopes and dreams
And a piece of homework
All loaded up in my mind bag.

In my head
There is a thought of hatred, towards my Mum and Dad
Because they say "No" to everything I want to do
Go out with my friends, play on the computer and watch TV.

In my head
I'm thinking of what's for lunch, burger, chips and chocolate
I wish I was someone else
A pop star, an actress or a vet.

In my head
Are so many things and feelings I don't know what to do with.

Rebecca Toseland (Age 10)

Hector's Like Me

Hector's like me,
The pick of the bunch,
Because after breakfast,
Nothing matters but lunch,
During pudding,
And our lunch break,
We start to think,
Of our dinner plate,
We're both the same,
He's so like me,
After lunch,
Nothing matters but tea.

Emily Taylor (Age 9)

My Bedroom

M essy
Y ummy

B eautiful
E xciting
D og - free
R omantic
O pen to cats
O ften used
M INE!

Ebony Tomkinson (Age 7)

The Warning

It's here
The avalanche
It's come to eat you up
The thick white snow ploughs
Down the hill
BEWARE!

Bertie Thompson (Age 9)

Love Is . . . .

Love is watching the orange sun going down peacefully.
Love is staring at the twinkling, shiny stars.
Love is listening to the sea when the waves crash and the blue sea is shining in the sun.
Love is listening to the birds whistling and tweeting.
Love is the smell of the air on a Saturday in the afternoon.
Love is the smell of toffee ice cream on a Sunday morning at home.
Love is touching my furry dog called Cuddles.
Love is to feel my Mummy's smooth skin.
Love is to taste ice cream, gooey ice-cream.
Love is the taste of chocolate milk shake.
Love is to have no wars or fights.

Sophie Tye (Age 7)

The Cat

He sleeps all day and then at night he wakes up with a yawn,
He stretches once, his claws come out, he's ready for the hunt,
He steals out into the black of night then jumps onto the wall,
He ducks down low avoids the light and waits until the time is right,
When the moon falls down and the sun starts to rise he finally stands up and stretches twice,
It's time to retreat to base,
He starts the race to find his prey sitting in the dish that lay by his bed that misty morning,
He lapped the milk with his slender tongue,
He had a feast that wouldn't last long,
He shook his glossy mound of fur and lay down to snooze once more.

Josie Townsend (Age 11)

The Fir Tree On The Mountain

As the children run down the mountain
Birds fly over their heads whistling their calming tune
The goats hair flashes at the golden sun
Flowers give a sweet scent to whoever passes
The church bells ring while a line of chatting people build up outside
The fir trees play with the children
Swaying their branches to and fro
But one lonely fir tree stands in the corner still covered in a white sheet of snow
From the winter that should have passed long ago
Strong gusts of wind push the small lonely fir tree as far as it will bend
No one will play with it or sit on its branches
Or comfort or support it again.

Eve Taschimowitz (Age 8)

Two Thousand Years Ago

It never snows at Christmas in this dry and dusty land,
Instead of freezing blizzards there are palms and drifting sands.
Years ago a stable and the most unusual star,
Three wise men who followed by camel not by car.
While sleepy on the quiet hills a shepherd gave a cry,
He'd seen a crowd of angels in the silent starlit sky.
In the stables ox and ass stood still and calm,
Gazed upon the baby safe and snug in Mary's arms.
Joseph lost in shadows, face lit by an oil lamps glow,
Stood wondering that first Christmas Day two thousand years ago.

Vikki Todd (Age 13)

Humpty Dumpty On The Moon

Humpty Dumpty sat on a spoon
And sailed to Earth or Moon that noon.
He landed on Moon and saw a baboon
So he jumped on Earth with some cars
He didn't like it because there was some doors.
So that is the end of his trip
And next he will be in a great big drip.

Chloe Thompson (Age 9)

The Rain

The rain drizzles down the windows
The rain pours down from the sky like arrows
It splashes on the pavements all around
The rain trickles down the black gutters
The rain spits down into the small cracks in the road
The rain drops down on car windscreens

Harry Tregartha (Age 8)

Violence And Beauty

V iolence is rage,
I t spreads like running water,
O nce there was no violence in the world and there was peace,
L ove had never been seen before properly,
E veryone was happy until violence started,
N evertheless people liked violence,
"**C** ome peace" cried the people,
   E verlasting cries came until beauty was in sight.
                  It came like thunder!
B eauty had made its point, it had just become Queen,
E veryone was pleased and fought violence,
A ttracts everyone to comply to the rules,
U gly faces are turned to beautiful,
T ime is never wasted,
Y ou can be beauty and not violence.
                    Violence is gone!

Anna Tindall (Age 10)

Old Praise Song Of The Rattle Snake

Here comes the rattle snake, invoker of the grass.
The slimy one.
The slimy one slithering in the grass.
I go out spitting for my prey,
The hunters follow closely,
They are competing for my prey,
So I bite them through and through.
Then I go round the corner laughing like mad.
I eat my prey and say watch out the rattle snake is about,
While the rest of the hunters shiver!

Alastair Tyzack (Age 8)

Trees

Trees are swaying all day long
They do not break because they're strong
It is fun to climb them
If you get high you can make a den
If you fall you'll break your arm
But if you do try to be calm
If you have none in your street
Then plant one in your garden if you have one
And it will make shade from the sun

Scott Thompson (Age 9)

Wizard

Under my bed I keep a box
With seven locks,
And all the things I have to hide
Are safe inside,
My rings, my wand, my hat, my shells
My book of spells,
I could fit a mountain into a shoe
If I wanted to,
I could change a cushion into a bird
With a magic word
Or turn December into Spring
Or make stones sing
I could clap my hands and watch the noon
Like a big white balloon
Come floating to my window sill
One day I will . . . . .

Alexander Tinsley (Age 11)

Home Time

When we are all going to get our things on,
I rush and get my bag,
Because I love home time,
I run home as fast as I can.

When I get home I quickly,
Change my clothes,
And wash my hands,
Then I go to play with my cars.

George Talbot (Age 8)

Geography

The atlas makes the world go round,
It takes us off to foreign ground,
Malta, France, Italy too,
Are a few of the Countries we pass through.
On our way back to Spain,
Down to Gibraltar and back to Bahrain.
Fridays are the days
To be day dreaming in
Geography!

Kayleigh Tonna (Age 11)

Food

F ood is yummy in my tummy.
O ranges are juicy said Lucy.
O lives are green, also black, I don't like them Yuck, Yuck, Yuck.
D inner is ready and we have dates, Mum said "Hurry don't be late."

Jessica Tadros (Age 8)

A Playground Bully

Black cloud threatens sunny sky.

Venomous skipping rope snakes around;
Slices through the air like a dagger.

Smacking legs in its circular path,
Whipping ground on its deadly patrol

Dresses flap as it skids right past,
Lunch boxes rattle as they clatter open,
Sports bags shuffle rolling on their backs.

The rickety bench creeks in defiance,
Tips up on one leg and kills the rhythm -
The rope's stopped in its tracks -
As the dustbin lid leaps up in the air.

The whistle has blown,
Time to coil up.
Hissing and spitting at the bottom of the box.
The playground is safe from the viper's evil glare,
Locked up neatly behind a secure iron padlock.
The notches on the key glisten as the sun reappears.

The menace has been caged for today.

Kay Upcott (Age 11)

Monsters

Monsters, monsters they are so scary,
Some are big and some are hairy.
Some are big and some are small,
And some are very very tall.
Some are nice and some are bad,
And some are very very mad.
Some can run, some can walk.
And best of all some can talk!!!
You can find them in all sorts of places,
Some have very funny faces.
Some are slim some are fat.
Once I saw one eat a cat.

Christopher Turner (Age 9)

Boredom

Boredom is doing your homework
Boredom is your mum nagging you
Boredom is being told something a million times
Boredom is tidying your room
Boredom is doing the same thing all over again
Boredom is going to school
Boredom is doing nothing
Boredom is looking stupid
Boredom is looking at the ceiling
Boredom is horrible

Simon Teasdale (Age 9)

The Night Sky

The night sky
Still shines
Mystical and misty
In the swirling clouds

The night sky
Still gloomy
Dull and dingy
In the damp air

The night sky
Still blue
Twinkling and twittering
In the sparkling stars

The night sky
Still shows
Mars and mercury
In the solar system

Rory Vigus (Age 9)

School

Some people are clever
Some people are dumb
Some people are lazy
And always suck their thumb

Some people are scruffy
Some people are smart
Some people are shabby
And get dirty in art

The subjects that I do
I hate in every way
But when school is finished
I feel merry, bright and gay!

Alex Titmarsh (Age 9)

My Butterfly

Small eggs
Short legs
Munch munch
Time for lunch
Build a cocoon
Open at noon
Out it comes
Beautiful wings
Will it fly
Up so high?
My butterfly

Olivia Taylor (Age 9)

QE2 - 2002

"Lilibet" has become Queen
Joyous Coronation the world has seen
2002 - The Jubilee is here
Gold, not silver, to mark fifty years

Concerts at the Palace,
Opening the gates
Crowds in the gardens
They all can't wait

Swiftly followed by Commonwealth games,
Started in London by famous names
The baton has left, it is on its way
Calling Commonwealth athletes to the UK

Holidays from school and parties in the street
Children excitedly waiting to greet -
Balloons and bunting in red, white and blue.
The Nation is calling "Happy Jubilee to You!"

Catriona Vickers-Claesens (Age 8)

My Mum, Dad And Dog

If my mum were a t-shirt she'd be big and multicoloured
Like a rainbow
The edges would be frayed stained and creased
No longer would she be new but old like she is.

If my dog were the weather he'd be the wind
He'd be there ever present like the weather
I'd listen to the howls and calls
As I'd walk down the street
I'd feel his presence as the wind.

If my dad were a vegetable he'd be a courgette
Small, mean and bitter
Like a raw winter's wind
But warm tender and yummy
When cooked with love and care.

Ella Verrier (Age 11)

My Candle

When I light my candle it lights with a flick
It waves and moves and
Lights up so quick

When I light my candle it lights with a boom
It flickers and dances
And lights up my room

When I light my candle it lights so quick
It shivers and quivers
And has a gentle flick

It lights so bright
It lights so light
That's why my candle is such a pretty sight

Shannon Villa (Age 10)

My Love

Shining nicely across the room
She's lead her life without any gloom
She brightens my day with just a smile
I have liked her for quite a while
But to ask her would take nerves
I have never been good at handling words
But I want her so much
She's perfect to last touch
How can I get her I ask
That is a difficult task
How will I get her to like me
I could go beg and plead
That would be so lame
I should just die of shame

Nathan Wallace (Age 14)

The Chinese Dragon

There's a chinese dragon on the street
Dancing on its Chinese feet
With colours like a paradise rainbow
You may be scared
'Cause it might be said
His eyes are a blazing hot red
And his skin is as rough as lead
While thick grey smoke plunges out of that ugly head.
I do not like this fearsome dragon.
There's a Chinese dragon on the street.

George Verrall (Age 7)

Siberian Tiger

The Siberian tiger it is very quiet,
And it does not dare cause a riot,
It's awake in the night to catch its prey,
And its sleeping most of the day.

Do not dare to wake it when it's asleep,
Or it will grab you with a big leap,
You will have no chance to run away,
Because you will be its daily prey.

Joseph Ward (Age 9)

World Of Nothing

Snowy maned horses toss their mighty heads,
In crystal seas where the clouds ripple,
And sparkled drops rise,
Thrown up by the greens and blues of the deep,
In the sea where nothing moves.

Golden sand under departing footsteps,
Never seen by eyes which cannot be,
Seeing all from their vantage pointed emptiness,
Deepened prints in water-soaked crystals.
But the feet could not be there,
Where only the memory survives,
Of the island where nothing grows.

This is where dreams and hopes hide,
Bathed in the shadows,
Where possibility rules,
And all that you wish for mocks you,
Just out of reach as you sleep,
Seeing things which cannot be.

This is where all that could be, becomes flesh,
In the world where nothing breathes.

Stephanie Wilson (Age 16)

A Recipe For An Angry Teacher

First get yourself a class of wild children,
Add three giggling girls and five angry hot football boys.
A handful of feeble excuses sprinkled with weird faces
And empty homework books
Smothered over with a whining child.

Mix gradually adding hypnotising screen savers
And careless mistakes.
Pour in a bunch of ruler nights and messy work.
Serve this in a plastic bowl for the teachers.

Hayley Waugh (Age 10)

I'm A Boy

I'm a boy
Who has a map
A weird, wonderful strange map
It has a cross in the middle of the desert
But I do not care about some gold
For I have some gold in my heart
Which never rests
I go to sleep and dream of gold
In my heart it is full of gold

Dimitris Vachaviolos (Age 8)

The Castle Way

Close your eyes and go back in time
Travel through your mind,
The castle way as it used to be,
Knights in shining armour,
Arrows shooting through the trees,
Jesters making funny jokes.

The castle . . .
Hard and stoney,
Dark and gloomy,
Creaking doors,
Rattling chains,
Kings and Queens in dining,
Prisoners moaning, "I want some"
Fairytale dreams,
Rapunzel in her turret,
The dragon's fiery flames,
But wake up it's just a dream,
Only some of this used to be.

Gemma A. Ward (Age 8)

Princess

Princess Princess in a tower
Saved by a Prince with wonderful power
With smelly feet and sleepy eyes
He brought her a MacDonald's with large fries
Then handed her a coke
And said is this a joke
They got on a horse and off they rode
On their way they met a toad
That told them about a land of gold

Rachel Victory (Age 9)

The Ocean

The ocean is a sparkling blue,
If we didn't have it,
I don't know what we would do!

Dolphins dive up and down,
While fishes swim round and round,
And eels slither across the ground!

Nobody's giving you a magic potion,
To force you inside the ocean,
So just think before you step in,
Out could come a great grey fin!

Shark's teeth are very sharp!

Gemma Wilson (Age 9)

That Day

That day was strange we both wondered what to do,
All I knew was I wanted to kiss you,
We left it awhile, we talked for a bit,
I jumped on your back that's when our flame lit,
We were inseparable, I stayed by your side,
It was through heaven I just seemed to glide,
When our lips touched my thoughts went away,
I hated leaving you again for another day,
My passion for you grew stronger and stronger,
I couldn't wait for you a moment longer,
When our bodies meet my heart goes wild,
Just like it used to when I was nothing but a child,
We talk every day and every night
I love you with all my heart, my soul, my might,
I close my eyes to see you standing there
I want to tell you just how much I care
I'm writing this for only you to see
Then maybe you will know how much you mean to me.

Rebecca Ward (Age 13)

My Mum

My mum looks like a princess with a golden crown
My mum sounds as good as a pop star
My mum smells like some strawberries
My mum tastes as good as a chocolate bar
My mum feels like a cosy quilt in bed

Ellis Vernon (Age 6)

My Mum

My mum has blue shiny eyes
My mum has got long shiny hair
My mum kisses me goodnight on my head
My mum kisses me and puts a plaster on my knee when I am hurt
My mum loves me all the time until I am dead
My mum likes chocolate and shares it too
My mum plays with me
My mum is the one that tucks me into bed

David Welham (Age 6)

You're As Useless . . . . .

You're as useless . . . .
As a ring with out a gem,
As a dress without a hem,
As a fire with no coal,
As a shoe with no sole.

You're as useless . . . .
As a hair with no style,
As a wedding with no aisle,
As a shopping centre with no mall,
As a garden with no wall.

You're as useless. . . .
As a coffee with no mug,
As a kiss with no hug,
But hey everybody's useless at something.

Melissa Wardle (Age 12)

Gruesome Food

Amelia Thin had lizard skin
Professor Sharp ate a pig's heart!
Mr Rye had potato skin pie
Mr Spice ate lice

George Votsikas (Age 8)

Squig Squog Splat

Jogging in the lovely weather
Drippity drippity drop,
And cart wheeling in the rain
Pitter patter rain drops
Skipping in the beautiful rain
Squidgy squodgy splat.

Maria Vallance (Age 7)

Rainbow

Rainbow rainbow why do you have so many colours
Rainbow rainbow why are you so colourful
Rainbow rainbow you have more colours than three colourful men
Rainbow rainbow will you be there forever

Charley Villa (Age 9)

About The Way It Used To Be . . . .

I've had enough of it,
trying to write this song.
The melody doesn't fit,
and the words all come out wrong.

I am trying to write a song,
about the way we were.
How I tried to make you love me,
how I tried to make you care.
About how I tried to make you feel a depth of emotion,
that just . . . was never there.

I am trying to write a song,
about how I had to make you see,
that paradise and heaven and all that's in between,
were made for you and me.

I've had enough of it,
trying to write this song.
The melody doesn't fit,
and the words all come out wrong.

So I'll write a poem instead.

Katy Winter (Age 14)

The Dark Poem

Dark is the wild panther running to its scared prey
Dark are threatening clouds at the end of a long gloomy day
Dark are the shadows that lurk round the corner waiting to get you
But darkest of all are the haunted woods which the ghosts run through
Dark is the graveyard that is haunted at night
Dark are the devils that disappear from sight
Dark are the owls flying through the night sky
But darkest of all are the underground tunnels where dead people lie.

Emma Whiteside (Age 11)

Stages

Old people, young people
Black people, white people
Grandmas and Grandads
Mothers and fathers
Children to adults so quickly they grow
From children who dream
To kids that wear jeans
From the daring testing teenagers
To the sensible over eighteens
From responsible adulthood
To wrinkly old grannies
Above are the stages of a humans life
It's an everlasting cycle so long this can hardly explain
From a baby to a granny and I'm not going through it again.

Rachael Williams (Age 9)

The Magic Box

I will put in the box
A photo of my family
A secret message
A picture of me when I was young

I will put in the box
An ancient TV
A great old stereo
An old teddy

I will put in the box
A theme park
A swimming pool
A football stadium

It has eyes like a dinosaur
And ears like Mike
It is a funny box
It is red wood

In my box
I will go to the theme park
Go swimming
Run the marathon
And swim with dolphins

Ross Whitmore (Age 7)

Gladiator

G ashes of blood,
L ong silver pikes,
A renas of Death,
D estruction at heart,
I gnorant to fear,
A rmours of Gold,
T aking of souls,
O n going terror,
R ing of his Love.

James Trumper (Age 11)

School Assembly

School assembly,
Where you're all so quiet,
Except the ones behind you,
Whispering to you.

If you want to talk in assembly,
When you know you shouldn't
You have to save it,
Until playtime of course.

Daniel Wheatley (Age 9)

The Ferret King

Ferrets live simple lives or so you may think,
If you stroke their silky fur they will always give a wink,
But there is one, who rules them though he is a lazy thing,
He rules them with a Iron paw for he's The Ferret King.

The ferret king is very rich he owns the most food,
When the ferret peasants whine he gets in a terrible mood,
So the ferret peasants make offerings and ring the ferret bell with a ting,
He smiles lazily and forgives them for he's The Ferret King.

The ferret kings name is Chalkie he loves to get his sleep,
So when he takes his royal nap be sure never to make a peep.
The young throne pretender Sir Polo loves to dance and sing,
But this is useless when trying to beat The Ferret King!

King Chalkie is part of a royal family that goes back far in time,
All albinos with pure ferret blood who would never commit a crime,
The king has soft white fur and glistening ruby red eyes,
When the moon is full the ferret king cries:

"I am wise, I am old and I have a surprise for you all,
We will have a great grand Ferret Ball!"
So by the light of the silver moon the ferrets dance hand in hand in a ring,
Round and round they merrily sing, "We love our great Ferret King!"

Ian Whitehead (Age 12)

Piranhas

I think piranhas are rather cool
Their teeth are sharp
Their eyes are big
They don't wear a scale wig
They're small
Their jaws are big
They can even bite through a wig
They're nice and big
They can nibble your fingers
And no-one seems to like them much.

Matthew Watson (Age 7)

My Rabbit

My rabbit is called Flopsy
She has floppy ears
She is fluffy and silky
I like to stroke her fur
She eats chocolate and vegetables
She thinks they are really yummy
She likes to play
She runs down the stairs
She sleeps in lots of hay in her small warm bed

Emily Woodley (Age 7)

Dance Of The Dragon

A ferocious dragon in the street
A furious dance skipping and twirling
A fiery walk through on its feet
A lovely colour to see whirling
Burst of paradise colours and smell
Maybe really he wants to eat you!!
Bulging eyes fiery blazing red
Don't go to sleep in a cosy bed
It's so much fun dancing

CHINESE NEW YEAR IS IN!!

Elizabeth Wilson (Age 7)

The Putrid Poltergeist

The Putrid Poltergeist, shivering, quivering,
In the grotting graveyard,
Hissing horror and shattering screams,
Wailing in the withered wilderness.

The Putrid Poltergeist shuddering shuffling
In the wailing wind,
Ghostly ghouls and shivering shadows,
Quiver in the slithering slime,
The Putrid Poltergeist
The Putrid Poltergeist

Nadia Walford (Age 12)

Bleeding

I'm bleeding on the outside,
Waiting at the corner after school;
"Are you ready?", you say.

Staggering home, aching;
A cut above my eye.
Bruises and bandages;
I told mum I fell over.
Only you and I know what really happened.

I'm bleeding on the inside.
I want to talk, to speak out,
But I know you will only beat me more.
Sometimes the pain is so bad I think I will burst.
I cry myself to sleep every night;
You've turned everyone against me.
I feel like there is no point to my life anymore.

That's why I decided to end it all.
I hope you're pleased now,
After all;
If I didn't end my life,
You would.

Hannah Wray (Age 11)

Winter

It is very cold,
Children have snowball battles,
All in winter time

Siobhan Wittwer (Age 8)

Mates

My mates are the best,
They're really, really cool.
They're better than the rest,
Alice, Charlotte and Jess.

Alice is really funny,
And she is my closest friend.
She is a bit annoying,
And she drives me round the bend.

Charlotte is normally quiet,
But when she gets between,
Henry and his lunch,
She causes a great big riot.

Jess is really funny,
She always makes me laugh,
So I get a stitch in my tummy.
My mates are the best (sometimes)

Zoe White (Age 11)

Bullies

WHY is life quite so cruel?
Why are people picked on?
Looking different,
Speaking different,
Acting different
WHAT'S the crime,
"Because it's not quite the same as mine."
That's what they all say,
The bullies,
The ones that cause all the pain,
But really the bullies are the ones that are stupid,
Cowardly, lame.
If it isn't that it is something else,
Which isn't actually a reason,
"It was fun, I wanted to."
"They deserved it, they were new."
They don't know how much it hurts,
To be pushed around,
Picked on
And treated like dirt.
They're horrible, the bullies.

Jade Woodhouse (Age 12)

Trees In Winter

Out of my window I can see,
Standing there a little tree,
No leaves or buds for me to see,
All bare and brown as can be,
Straight and tall but looking sad,
Waiting for spring to make it glad.

Sophie Weston (Age 8)

Anger On The Pitch

'Please score a goal' the little boy cried
'Please score a goal' as eleven players tried

Standing in the cold facing the degradation
Of supporting a team doomed to relegation

But dear oh dear whatever could it be
His team has nil the other team has three!

The losing team full of frustration
After an unfair tackle decide on retaliation

Pushes and punches for all to see
'Stop it, stop it!' shouts the referee

What a fiasco! What a shame!
After all, let's face it, it's only a game!

Corina Watts (Age 13)

Spring

Daffodils are as bright as the sun
Bunched together like lemons

Snowdrops are as white as the clouds
Swaying gracefully in the breeze

Grass growing like our hair
It's time for it to be cut

Trees are blossoming pink and white
Like wedding confetti it falls

Lambs are bouncing up and down
Like a handful of springs

The early morning dew lay
Like a blanket on the ground,
Waiting for the red hot bouncy ball
To throw the blanket off.

The twittering sound of a hundred girls
Were waking up, saying good morning
To everyone on the ground.

Dark nights are no longer
The sun stays up
Like a bunch of daffodils

Byron Watkins (Age 10)

Lovely Colours

Red, yellow, orange, brown, golden
The trees are getting older,
The leaves are falling off,
They're all changing colours,
The weather is getting colder,
The colours are getting bolder,
And the days are getting shorter.

Sophie Wilson (Age 10)

The Weather

Rain rain I hate its horrible sound
Rain rain rain I hate it when it's pouring down.
Rain rain I hate it when it saturates me.
I hate the sound when the welly boot hits the puddle.
Rain rain rain I hate the horrible stuff!

Sun sun I love its Shiny Rays.
Sun sun I love the way it keeps you warm.
I love it when there are clear skies
Sun sun I love the bright colours it makes.
Sun sun I love the hot weather it gives you.
Sun sun I love the stuff!

Sam West (Age 9)

Leisure

What is this life if full of care,
I've plenty time to stop and stare.

Time to go to Woodlands club,
To practice cricket and go to the pub.

Time to go to S.A.S.,
To play football that's the best.

Time to play on my bike,
Something I like.

Time to watch Bradford City play,
I scream and shout and say "hurray"!

Time to go to my room to do something bad,
To tidy my room I think it's sad.

Time to watch Ci*TV*,
On my TV it's channel three.

A good life I've got, it's full of care,
I'm pleased I've got time to stop and stare.

Christopher Walker (Age 9)

Amazing Things

Did you know
That flowers came from little seeds
All they need is showers
And protecting from the weeds

Isn't it amazing
Builders are so strong
That churches are always praising
And dustbins really pong

Hannah Wauchope (Age 8)

A Leopard

He gets his prey in the night
He is a patient cat
Waiting for that very moment
Then he can leap to kill

He runs around in his vivid stripes
With his eyes as dark as oil pools
His tail is as furry as a kittens back
And his teeth are like spears

All the birds must think themselves lucky
That they can fly
So they can hide from the leopard

Jack Wheatland (Age 8)

My Poem

I'm not who I appear to be
I'm not that person at all.

Don't judge me by my hoodlum face
I hide beneath it to keep me warm.

Don't judge me by my facial expression
I ned to learn them all.

Don't judge me by my quick sharp tongue
I think God gave me the wrong one.

I know this because it moves before I ask it to
And have to bite it to keep it still.

My crime is not my fault I did not ask to be a teenager
I was happy as a boy.

I am not who I appear to be
I am not that person at all

I will soon escape from this cocoon
And prove it to you all.

Nick Wilson (Age 14)

Changes

Your heart's beating around the clock,
Time ticking away, it doesn't stop,
All these changes are taking place,
The world's rotating and changing every day,
Anything you think of with a name,
There isn't anything in life that ever stays the same,
So you have to watch your time,
Watch your time,
All the time.

Kate Wilson (Age 10)

Beauty Of The Shells

Look at a shell, and it will wash away all your sin,
Thank the sea for washing them in,
Some have whirls,
Some have curls,
It doesn't matter, smooth or rough
The beauty of shells is QUITE ENOUGH!

Shells are more beautiful than all the world,
Ugly and horrible things are to be hurled,
Make way for the beauty of shelldom come,
Watch out! Pirates overhead are drinking rum,
Little shell, all bright and shiny,

So make way for the beauty of shells, OH MIGHTY!

Charlie Walsh (Age 8)

You're As Useless.....

You're as useless . . . .

as a piece of paper without a pen
as a none egg laying hen,
as a teacher without a brain
as a long winter without any rain

You're as useless . . . .

as a back without a spine
as a dinner without some wine
as a bottle of Gin without its G
as a nest without a bee

You're as useless . . . .

as a wig without some hair
as a ghost without its scare
as a bubble without its pop
as a car that doesn't stop

Samantha Williams (Age 12)

Easter

Easter eggs
Bunny
Yum yum yum
Church
Chicks
Pandas
Mini
I like monkeys
Zebras

Layla Wingate (Age 5)

The Sea

The sea is a handful of salt,
And a bucket of sea creatures,
A teaspoon of treasure,
And a spade full of shells.

It s a bag full of happiness,
And a jar full of danger,
A bowl full of trouble,
And a handful of joy.

It is a tablespoon full of boats,
And a cup full of people,
A jug full of seaweed,
And a pool full of water.

Sophie Wright (Age 11)

The Prince Awakens

The night was damp, dark and misty with flashing
Lightning rumbling
Lightning lighting up the sky like a switch
The claps of thunder tumbling, rumbling and mumbling.

A raven rolled in to a dark shadow of a window
Its feathers tucked in to its warm black body
The Raven's tramping, shuffling up and down on his ice cold feet can be heard
The Raven is old, tired and cold, he turns his back into a raven black slumber

In the lab everyone's preparing rustling and rattling!
Cluttering and clattering!
The lights are flickering on and off . . . . .
Waiting for the thunder to come.

Thunder lightning the rain rattling
Violent whirlwinds spun round and round with lightning overhead!
The engine humming, rusty hatches screeching, and long crackling test tubes bubbling.

Silence . . . . . ., silence as they wait,
A whimpering sound comes from the monster
As he slowly opens his eyes,
"Good morning your highness"

Danielle Welsh (Age 12)

The Rock

Rocky the rhino
Ripping trees down
Running through the jungle
Running into rocks
Killing all the animals
By charging into them
Rocks rolling at you!

Conor Ward (Age 7)

My Magic Flower

My magic flower commands my wishes,
Helps you, looks after you and cares for you.
When you are lost in the woods, a maze, in traffic and in trouble
It will love you.

Hanah Wicks (Age 7)

What Is Lilac

Lilac is a flower
Dropping down below
Lilac is a pile of cotton
    d
   a
  n
 g
l
 i
  n
   g
Lilac is a colour
On Joseph's coat
Lilac is a peg
That dries my clothes

Elizabeth Wright (Age 6)

Remember

Remember all those people who gave their lives in vain,
Those people who died for freedom,
Who died fighting but always in pain,
People who will never see the light of day again.

Remember all those people who you knew and loved,
Whose souls float above and smile down on us,
People who are still alive
In our hearts and dearly beloved.

Remember all those people who you ever knew,
Those prisoners, soldiers and many more
Who died without a name,
Remember those families who lost someone.
Remember, remember, remember . . . .

David Wrightson (Age 13)

The Scythe

Sharp, beak like shaped blade,
On a wooden pole of splinters,

Crouching in a foot of a dead elephant,
The view is very blank, one singular colour black,

Next to me an umbrella?
What a useless machine.

I get picked up more often than it does.
The same place I get placed over and over again.

I am used for two jobs,
Farming and killing!

My owner comes for the second time today,
He picks me up, then puts me in a leather holder.

His horse rumbles across the sky,
We land inside a grand palace.

One swipe and the king is dead,
My owner chuckles for no reason.

Back I go into the foot at home,
Until the next journey.

Andrew Walker (Age 11)

Colours

Red is the bright yellow sun at the end of the day
Blue is the warm water and clear sky in summer
Yellow is the bright beautiful daffodil that grows
Green is the fresh grass on the hill
Brown are the roofs of the houses

Beth Wren (Age 6)

Cats!

Feet patter over rooftops looking for trouble,
The body is sleek and thin
Claws are sharp like a butcher's knife,
Ready to slash through anything in its path
Their eyes are the glowing traffic lights in the city,
Watching over us, you and me!
Teeth are fangs,
Torturing their pray!

They walk through the street having no care in the world,
High and proud they are,
Curl up against a blazing fire and
Dream, Dream, and Dream!

Kerrie-Marie Wilson (Age 11)

Homework!!!

Why when the sun is shining,
Should I have to stay in and study!
I want to play with my dog outside
And both get fabulously muddy.

Oh! what is the point of homework
When we still go to school?
All this science, maths and english
Makes me look soooo uncool.

I see no point in homework
It gets me in a stress,
But when others try and help me
It turns out in a mess.

I'd rather be on the internet
Chatting to all of my friends.
But oh this stupid homework
It never seems to end.

My excuses are great while they last
But I know they'll run out someday.
But then when I get to school
What will my teacher say?

Jess Warren (Age 11)

The Bad Bad Night

One bad bad bad night
I will shiver with fright
There is something I will know
In the cold cold air
I will sway in lots of flare

Duval Wallace-Clarke (Age 7)

The Shiny Thing

What is it?
It's shiny,
It's bright,
Its rays are strong,
Sometimes they're long
It doesn't look cool.

It's big and round
It doesn't make a sound,
It's fierce sunrays are blinding.

The shiny think is up in the sky
It makes me hot and sticky,
I think I know what it is,
I don't really know,
After all I am only a baby!

Nick Wilson (Age 11)

My Blue Lady Flowing Free

On the mountain I walk alone, where I go I shall not know,
With my blue silk gown and my golden hair,
I listen, watch and silently stare,
Now on a journey I shall face,
Keeping clear my tear streaked face,
The kingfishers are my eyes with colour we share,
Off I go with my dazzling stare.

The bulrushes are my storytellers they whisper their tale,
As above me the blue birds do sail,
Faster now I quickly pace, round in circles I begin to race,
Now I dive down the rocks with my hair flying behind me,
I grumble as I tumble down into space,
Crash I hit the ground in complete disgrace.

Ahead I see a dancing of blue maidens,
With there pretty white petticoats bubbling up on the shore,
My golden hair has now turned white with the coral oh so bright,
Now its done the end of my journey I have met,
The seagulls welcome me as my silver wings,
I'm flying free, free as I shall ever be,
And I shall no longer walk alone.

Emma Webb (Age 10)

What Is Yellow?

Yellow is the sunset at night.
Yellow is my cuddly teddy bear,
Yellow is a sparkling earring
And the spots on a leopard,
Yellow is the sun in the summer sky,
Yellow is a sparkling daffodil in the sun,
But the best thing that is yellow is my wishing star

Natalie Williams (Age 8)

Chase

Thump, thump, thump.
Alone at last.
Lost them!
Just me and my pounding heart.
Cold ice runs down my back
And trickles on the side of my burning face.
Voices echo in my head;
Taunting grunts that tremor around my weary brain.
My bramble-torn skin oozes blood,
Staining my displaced uniform with fear.
Here they come!
Fear stabs like a blunt dagger in the pit of my stomach.
I run.
The familiar scenery smears either side of me
As I sprint to my front door.
Unlock; slam; collapse;
Alone again.

Ruth Waters (Age 13)

The Big Match

Shuttlecock,
in the air,
opponent moving,
in despair.

Knees bent,
on toes,
hit it hard,
over it goes.

Whack the feathers,
over the net,
grip my racquet,
play a let.

Wrist flick,
feet leap,
feeling sick,
also weak.

A point to go,
take a smash,
hits the floor,
WON THE MATCH!

Pernille Woods (Age 12)

Apples

My apple tastes like gold
My apple smells like silver coins
My apple looks like a plum
My apple feels like smooth glass
My apple is good as gold

Paul Wright (Age 7)

I Am

Drawing's my talent,
It's what I do best,
It comes to me naturally,
I'm like a bird in a nest.

I fly to an island,
Where I drift away,
Drawing's what I concentrate on,
Every single day.

I make bright happy pictures,
To brighten up the day
But when I'm sad and unhappy,
They soon fade away.

The other thing I love,
Is playing my guitar,
I am who I am,
And I'm doing ok so far.

Madeleine West (Age 11)

The Colour Of Everything

Orange is the setting sun
Disappearing below the distant horizon

Pink is angel delight,
Slithering down your throat like a snake

Green is a lawn of waving grass
Swaying softly in the warm breeze

Blue is the sky
When it is over the Atlantic Ocean

Red is the traffic light
When it uses all its power to turn to amber then to green

Yellow is the amber light
When it flashes bright

White is the face of a clown
When she is laughing and joking

Hannah Watts (Age 10)

Blue

Blue is the salty sea splashing on the rocks
Blue is the water running from the taps
Blue is the rainbow spreading over the houses
Blue is the food colouring you put in to cakes
Blue is the sky up so high
Blue is the blueberries all sweet and juicy
Blue is the colour of my school jumper
Blue is the bluebirds singing in the spring

Carrie Warnes (Age 9)

Anything Pie

First add 19 cockroaches crunchy like crisps
Secondly add 18 pizzas
17 live snakes with smooth slippery scales
16 worms
15 spoonsfull of ice-cream to cool it down
14 piranha jaws
13 vampire bat wings too tasty to share
12 grilled rats tails
11 trap door spider's legs some just too small
10 elephant trunks
9 anteater noses
8 frog heads not slimy enough
7 electric eel eyes
6 metres of jaguar fur
5 wasps wings
4 humming bird beaks
3 preying mantis
2 lily pads just like lettuce
1 alien to eat the perfect pie

Alex Wringe (Age 9)

Leisure

What is this life if full of care,
I've plenty time to stop and stare

Time to start to run and play,
Playing football every day

Time to go see city play,
But we lost last night what a shame

Time to go play my computer,
Going on ClarisWorks it's superduper

Time to watch videos TV too,
Shreks my favourite my friend like it too.

Time to play golf my favourite game
No game is quite the same

A good life I've got, it's full of care
I'm pleased I've got time to stand and stare

Matthew Wilson (Age 9)

Dentists!

I do not like my dentist
It is my greatest fear
When I go to the dentist
I always get a tear

Have you seen the sharp pins and needles
That go through your gum
That is why I do not like the dentist
I never have done

Bobbie Whitmore (Age 10)

The Sunset

Beneath the sunset,
Two people bond,
Hand to hand, eye to eye,
As if being forced by a magical wand.

He bending down on his left knee,
Hoping for his dreams to come true,
She imagining what he will say,
Hoping it will be more than I love you.

He still thinking of how to say it,
And still on his left knee,
She is nervous
"Will you marry me?"

Katy Wickings (Age 11)

Questions For The Queen

What's it like on the throne?
What was it like without a phone?

What was it like in September?
Will you always remember?

What was it like at the end of the war?
What is it like being on a world tour?

What is it like being the Queen?
Are people in your family mean?

Thank you for helping those in need
You are their saviour indeed

What is it like wearing your royal clothes?
Did you put on Princess Diana's grave a rose?

What was it like on V.E. Day?
Is it like our holiday?

Have you been happy for 50 years?
I hope you've not had too many tears.

Chloe Wootton (Age 8)

Spring

Pony giving birth
New life is coming
Bird flying high
New life is coming
Tree blossoming on
New life is coming
People are happy
New life is coming

Nicole Whiting (Age 9)

What Is Red?

Red is the hot lava
Red is a star
Red is a persons hair
Red makes me feel hot.
Red means stop!
Red is your anger upon your face

Red is bolognaise
Red is when you're nervous
Red is a rose with a lovely smell.
Red is the sun
Red is a warning
Red is a love heart
Red is a sunrise
Autumn leaves can turn red
Red is wonderful colour
Red is a sunset it's time to go to bed.

Rebecca Wilson (Age 8)

I Wonder What Buckingham Palace Looks Like?

I wonder how big Buckingham Palace really is,
Is it small or is it big,
Is it quiet or is it loud,
Is the Queen really proud,
Oh will someone please tell me what it's like.

Does it have stairs that wind in and out like a snake,
Does it have chandeliers that glitter in the light,
Does it have a swimming pool,
Do the servants have some fights.

Does it have gold four poster beds,
Where the Queen lays her sleepy head,
I wonder how many servants she has one or more,
Oh will someone please tell me what it's like.

I wonder what the Golden Jubilee is going to be like,
Is it going to be celebrated a lot or not,
Will there be a party or just an ordinary day,
Will you have to pay.

Danny Wright (Age 11)

Elephant Rap

I'm a big elephant with flappy ears,
Don't cry when you see me, no need for tears.
I'm an enormous clumsy great walker,
And a gigantic chatty, nutty talker,
I'm the best at the elephant dance,
So come and join me, yeah, dance and prance
For that's what we do at the elephant dance.

Hannah Whitbread (Age 11)

The Forest's Story

I remember when life was good
My old trees would waft in the cool breeze
My streams drifted happily
My creatures leapt with delight
My branches covered in birds nests
My sounds were bright and beautiful
Now things have changed terribly
The poachers are here
My trees don't waft in the breeze
My streams don't drift happily
My creatures don't leap with delight
My branches aren't covered with nests
My sounds aren't bright and beautiful
My forest friends are gone
Where will they find me?
Behind the factories?
Beneath the roads?
Under the rubbish?

Brittanee Winstanley (Age 11)

Black and White

The mighty Zebra roams
The wild plains of Africa
A firm leg, a firm hoof
There is determination in his stride.
A steady beat
A rhythm that would inspire
Drummers to keep that pulse alive.
He moves…Apparently unseen
Yet unwary of the predators
That lurk nearby.
Suddenly….A scattering of black yet snowy flanks
A stab of shocked pain
As he is brought down.
Oh! How his patterned camouflage did not save him
His gallant attempts to escape
Appeared fruitless
He reared his head for one last time
The King that once rode so finely
Over those dusty plains
Fell…Never to rise again.

Rebecca Watson (Age 11)

War

War is the colour of blood,
War is fire left behind after the bombs,
War is the sight of death,
War is money wasted on expensive things,
War is two countries hating each other,
War is guns flying,
War is houses getting ruined and buried,
War is people winning and getting shot down,
War is people hiding behind barbed wire,
War is the sight of death,
War is bricks flying at the tank.

Adam Warlow (Age 9)

Henry V111

Henry V111 had six lovely wives,
Some lost their cherished lives.
A lot were hated a few adored,
He would call to his lord.
For a son to be king,
He would spread out his wing.
He would shoot like a rife,
And look for his perfect wife.
At first he got two lovely girls,
Who loved to wear silky pearls.
Then after that a boy was born,
He was king by dawn.
They all became kings and queens
Their paintings done from different scenes.

Danielle Wilkinson (Age 11)

The Unicorn

Such a beautiful sight
You never did see,
On a twinkling night
She came across me.
How long there we stood
I do not remember,
In that mystical wood
In icy December.

Her face as fair as any flower,
Her tail as soft as silver silk,
Her horn as tall as any tower
And coat as white as milk.
I stared at her hard,
I stared at her long,
And with a swish of her silky-soft tail -
She was gone.

Rachel Winfield (Age 9)

Snow

Snow is a rubber that rubs out bad,
Lightens up the children sad.
Happiness is wild and free,
Covering up this lifeless tree.

A protective team of snow
Covers the hedgehog lying low.
The evil smile of the bright sun
Comes and spoils all the fun.

Christopher Williams (Age 10)

My Piano

I always play my piano
But not always right
I play it in the morning
And I play it in the night

Playing piano is easy
You just press the keys
There are pieces all over the world
Including the seven seas

When you finish a piece
You feel really proud
And you accept claps
From the vast crowd

Sam Wise (Age 11)

The Magic Box

I will put in the box
A golden dress blowing in the cold air
A silver bear glistening in the dark
And sparkling water

I will put in the box
A colourful butterfly
Flying in winding air
A friendly dog barking as loud as it can
A clock ticking and giving me a headache

I will put in the box
A black silver bird
Walking on the ground
A spider flying in mid air

My box is made from
Delicate glass and fragile ice
My box is a secret box
And very unusual

I will go to Mars
To see if aliens are real
And go to the Caribbean and chill out

Sarah Wright (Age 8)

The Peacock

It's rainbow feathers,
The beauty of it,
And the way it's colourful tail,
Springs out like a fan,
The tear shapes on the,
Beautiful rainbow feathers,
The swift movement,
The way it watches you,
Like a tigers pray,
It's face looks lonely,
As if it needs a friend
I can see it's tiny little eyes,
It's waiting for something.

Kayleigh Warner (Age 10)

Inside my Head

Inside my head
There's a place
Where palm trees
Bow down low at my feet
As I walk by
The clashing waves curtsy
As I walk by
Oh there's a throne made of fruit
It tingles in my eye.

Louise White (Age 8)

Leisure

What is this life if full of care
I've plenty of time to stop and stare

Time to get ready for the match
The goalie caught a good catch

Time to run around the pond with ducks
While my mum cooks

Time to get my favourite book
While my dog rolls in the muck

Time to watch TV and videos all day long
When my sister is singing a song

Time to put on my cd's
While I watch my dvd's.

Time to pot a ball
When it rolls in to the hall

A good life I've got if full of care
I'm pleased I've got time to stop and stare

Daniel Wright (Age 9)

Dolphins

They are blue
Live in the sea
Nose as long as a bottle

The eyes are shiny
The skin is reflected
Their tongue as slimy as a slug

Their skin is blue
Their skin is soft
As a delicate as a vase.

Paige Wilson (Age 10)

The Crowd

The crowd is shouting and waving around,
They suddenly go quiet, and there is no sound.
As the coach goes by with the Queen inside,
The people cheer, their hearts filled with pride.

The coach was golden, its horses white
A wonderful picture, one of real delight.
The Queen smiled with pleasure.
For fifty years her people had been her treasure.
'God Bless Your Majesty', someone cried.
The crowd took up the cry far and wide.

Julia Waldron (Age 8)

The Smell Collector

A stranger called this morning dressed all in black and grey
Put every smell into a bag and took them all away.

The smell of sizzling bacon the frying of an egg
The grilling of tomatoes the frying of the bread.

The pollen in the flowers the scent of a rose
Diesel at the garage the smell of my dad's toes.

My dog's breath in the morning the buzzing of a bee
The smell of my toothpaste my morning cup of tea.

The smell of chip fat McDonalds too
Sausage in the morning my dogs pooh.

The smell of Sunday dinner the scent of burning toast
The cooking of the barbecue the smell of the south coast.

The whiff of vinegar the stench of rotting cheese
The scent of fish and chips the smell of a million teas.

The scent of soap of hair gel
The smells with which we can't cope the smell of fresh bread baking.
A stranger called this morning he didn't leave his name
Left us all senseless life will never be the same.

Robert Wilson (Age 10)

Nature

What is green, holly is green as prickly as a hedgehog.
What is yellow, corn is yellow swaying in the breeze.
What is orange, fire is orange with steaming hot flames.
What is blue, a waterfall is blue as powerful as a rushing river.
What is grey, squirrels are grey climbing up a tree with speed like a car.
What is red, cheeks are red shining with guilt.
What is violet, rain is violet making everything in its path wet.
What is gold, the sun is gold lighting up the world.

Stephen Williams (Age 8)

Just Imagine

What is the touch of a winter's wind?
The icy finger of the snow.

What is the taste of fog?
Flavourless candyfloss erupting from a grey leaden funnel.

Where does the rainbow end?
At the furthest edge of the world, guarding buried treasure.

What is an aurora?
An exploding rainbow of breathtaking colours, that becomes an entrance to another world.

Where is lightning when it isn't flashing?
Imprisoned in a cage at the core of the earth.

Chris Wilkes (Age 11)

The Queen

Clip, clop
The carriage is here
It's gold and rich with jewels
And look who's inside
Amazing, Amazing.

Her gown trailing
As up the isle she walked
To the throne
Where she was crowned
Amazing, amazing.

With courage she led
Those fifty years
The nation has been proud
So there's one thing for sure, it's
Amazing, amazing.

Carolina Watters (Age 9)

Whirlpool

Spiralling mouth,
Water whirler,
As cold as ice,
Twizzling turner,
Whirlpool

Whizzing wonder,
Sea spinner,
As deadly as a dragon
Person eater
Whirlpool

Swirling stomach
Colossal consumer
As enchanting as magic
Super swallower
Whirlpool

Evil devourer
Human hunter
As spectacular as a volcanic eruption,
And whoosh you've fallen in

Whirlpool….whirlpool…….whirlpool…..whirlpool….whirlpool

Kathryn Williams (Age 11)

Space

Neptune is light blue with white little spots
It doesn't have a shiny ring
Neptune has eight pure moons
Shining and spinning around
The moon is white it comes out at night
Its light and very bright in the night sky
In space its black spooky and dark
Shooting stars are beautiful in the cold night sky
Neptune is light blue like the beautiful Uranus

Leanne Willcocks (Age 8)

The Wind Is Burning

Wind is one invisible ice cube
Wind is a cold hand closed over you
Wind is like your mum telling you to go to bed
Wind is like one big bad mood
Wind is like a sad film
Wind is like being in a fridge with a fan
Wind is like a spirit let loose
Wind is like a big nightmare
Wind is like a worrying wasp,
Wind is like a rush of lava from the centre of the earth,
Wind is like being dead.

Harry Williams (Age 10)

Hello Big Chello

Hello big chello
You're as soft as a mellow
On a summer's day

Hello chubby bellow
On a white marshmellow
On a winter's day

Hello spring yellow
You're a very nice fellow
And so is your little brother.

Trudy Wan (Age 8)

Sun Rise

Hot as an oven
Coming slowly, slowly up
Shining very bright

Esme Williams (Age 9)

Stonehenge

Heavy stones standing tall
Cracks glistening in the shadows
Shining sun shining on the cracks
Stones looking up to the heavens
Some lying down and some balancing
Rocks pleasantly slanting for centuries
Still as a mountain
Towering high above me

Megan Woodley (Age 8)

Bishops Wood Poem

We tasted bread
And we ate some cheese
The Saxon lady said no
Fizzy pop please.

We built a shelter
From bracken and wood
It was raining we needed a hood.

They showed us how to make a broach
Matthew made a diamond
While we waited for the coach
What a lot we had learned.

Kieron Wheeler (Age 8)

Bats

One afternoon I went out silently, quietly, smoothly
Went swooping at insects especially mosquitoes
Calmly, creeping slowly behind the insects
Then ate insects, alright they were yummy!

The sunlight was shining in the sky
So I went swooping back to my bat box
Where my family were safe and a fast asleep
Went to my bat box straight away.

I'm back at my bat box now I can go back to sleep
Just how I was a few hours ago straight away
So I was ready to close my eyes and go to sleep
Peacefully silently goodnight.

Bianca Walford (Age 10)

Mum

Did you do well at school today?
Yes, mum
And what did the teacher say?
Good, mum
You look kind of down
Yes, mum
No-ones pushing you around?
No, mum
Did you like your lunch?
Yes, mum
Do you want something to munch?
No, mum
Do you have any homework?
Yes, mum
What have you got?
Nothing I can't handle
That wasn't the question . . .

Annabelle Whittall (Age 12)

Night

Trees squabble over who gets the moon for lunch.
Mud squelches me into the ground
Crickets chirping in little bunches
Owls stare at me eyes big and round
Sounds spook me inside
Trees carry me to the land of nod
I can hear the ghost that's just died
The brightness is like little rods
Smells so clear I can see them

Kingsley White (Age 8)

The Owl

He glides through the midnight sky,
As still as a statue
He lands on a roof and gazes up at the stars
Like an astronomer
As he spots his prey, his wings spread
Like a tree branch.
He swoops down.

Nicole Wilkinson (Age 10)

Inside The Lion's Teeth

Inside the lion's teeth, rocky caves
Inside the rocky caves, the lion's whiskers
Inside the lion's whiskers, pointy arrows
Inside the pointy arrows, the lion's eye
Inside the lion's eye, fire of hell
Inside the fire of hell, the lion's claw
Inside the lion's claw, the deer's blood
Inside the deer's blood, the lion's tail
Inside the lion's tail, a never ending forest
Inside the never ending forest, the lion's heart
Inside the lion's heart, a dark swamp
Inside the dark swamp, the lion's teeth

Josh Wells (Age 11)

Halloween

Who goes there?
Stopping at my door,
Waiting for it to open.
Who goes there?
Banging on my door
Standing there some more.
Who goes there?
Getting impatient
Walking outside my window
Who goes there?
Who is it?
Who is it that's outside my door?

Sam Wright (Age 10)

Inside The Kangaroo

Inside the kangaroo's paw,
A layer of fur trees,

Inside the layer fur trees,
The kangaroo's fur,

Inside the kangaroo's fur,
The hard forest floors,

Inside the kangaroo's teeth,
The deers antlers,

Inside the deers antler,
The sorrowful look,

Inside the sorrowful look,
The kangaroos eyes,

Inside the kangaroo's eyes,
The frozen tears,

Inside the frozen tears,
The reflection of the deer's blood,

Inside the reflection of the deer's blood,
The kangaroo's paw.

Rebecca Wheeler (Age 10)

Snake Rap

Der waz a snake called Jake,
Who bought a flake,
Den he put it on his birthday cake,
The cake fell down,
Which gave him a frown
Dat was the end of Jake's cake.

Daniel Williams (Age 10)

Name Poem

Hi Jake
What's the game

Hi Jo
What you know

Later Jo
Gotta go

Hi Eve
Gotta leave

Hi Amatiaz
Is your brother called Shamatiaz

Blake Whitaker (Age 10)

Autumn Days

Autumn days and bare trees,
Jumping in piles of crunch leaves,
So many ways of fun and laughter,
This is autumn after and after.

Autumn days with frost bitten cars,
Leaning over the school bars,
Leaves turn brown and fall from the trees,
We put them in piles up to our knees.

Autumn days the grass stops growing,
And bad weather, rain is coming,
When the leaves fall to the ground,
They make a rustling sound.

Autumn days are nearly gone,
It is that time when birds sing their song,
The buds start to bloom,
It'll be spring time soon.

Billie Louise Ward (Age 11)

Bad Luck

First of June
A luck of prunes
In July
They had to fly
In good August
There were tourers
In September
They met a new member
In October
They used the mower
They didn't remember
The fifth of November
In December
They had all this to remember!

Jake Winearls (Age 7)

Homework

Homework this homework that,
We never get a break,
Normally we have to make a story,
About someone's glory.

If only I could get away,
Just for a day,
Many people say,
On this horrible day.

My friend who I don't like,
But he likes me,
He likes homework,
But do I, I don't think so.

Luke Watkin (Age 11)

Dreams

Dreams to most
Are the images in their sleep
But dreams to me are like stars
That are far beyond my reach.
They sparkle so brightly
Against the dark night sky
They seem so near
But yet so out of sight.
Their light so bright
Shining the colour of blue
But yet so dim
Because they may never come true.
Dreams are just like my wishes
Containing my deepest desire
They're not just my visions
Which I can only fascinate over.
I know that they can come true
Depending on how hard I try
And if I carry on hoping
They won't ever say goodbye.

Jenny Zhang (Age 13)

The Dragon's Dance

The dragons are dancing around town
I wonder if they're real.
A glittering head, a golden tail,
A beautiful patterned body,
Flaming hot smoke coming out.
But don't worry
This is a friendly dragon.
He speaks Chinese.

Jennifer Welsh (Age 6)

I Am The Sun

I am the sun,
I start at sunrise,
I yawn a big yawn
And open my eyes.

I am the sun,
My beams shine bright,
I'm cheerful and happy,
As I move into night.

At sundown I rest,
As the moon starts to rise,
I rest my sleepy head,
And close my eyes.

Hannah Young (Age 9)

My Garden

Sitting on the swing I can see the trees
Swaying in the wind and rabbits hopping about
I can hear the birds singing from inside the porch.

I can see farmers rounding up their sheep
With their dogs in the field beyond
The weather vane is spinning around on the roof of the shed
Like the world spinning on its axis.

In the past men would be out with their guns
Hunting pheasants for tea.
The maids would be busy in the house
And the gardener would be pruning the apple trees for winter.

And today in the garden, in the breeze, the birds, the flowers.
As I walk something flies past me and screeches as it passes.
Then the garden is still.

Paula Yeadon (Age 10)

My Dream Bike

If I had my own bike it would have to be
A shiny green frame
But no-ones would be the same
And black spokes to match the seat,
And silver peddles where to place my feet.
With this I would roam free,
Doing jumps up ramps and pulling wheelies.
I would be like a bird flying, in the air,
With no-one bothering me I wouldn't have a care.

James Williamson (Age 12)

Nanny's Flat

We were in the car and on our way
At nanny's flat we were gonna stay
Where the sky would be blue and the sun would shine
We'd play on the beach right until our bedtime
We'd walk through the market and toy town
Arriving home just before sundown
In the evening to Merry England we'd go
Unless at the pavilion there was a show
Next day early morning we would wake
Eager to play at the boating lake
At the end of the week we'd be homeward bound
We'd be silently sleeping not making a sound!

Tiffany Williams (Age 13)

The Ballad Of Maryling And Christian

Maryling was thirteen and Christian was fourteen
They were very much in love but now they're up above

Their rows were like thunder but now they're eight foot under
They were very much in love but now they're up above

They jumped into the river so they could be with each other
They were very much in love but now they're up above

They jumped into the sea instead of eating their tea
They were very much in love but now they're up above

A note was left on her gown to say that she was going to drown
They were very much in love but now they're up above

They found a note before tea to say that they were going to the sea
They were very much in love but now they're up above

Tomasz Zaremba (Age 11)

Whales

His fins are as big as a mat
They're like a big black bat

His voice is as sweet as the waves
It echoes in the underwater caves

His skin is as rough as a rock
It's scaly and bumpy and I like him a lot!

Melissa Woods (Age 9)

The Smell Collector

A stranger called this morning dressed all in black and grey
Put every smell into a bag and carried them away

The smell of sizzling bacon the smell of bubbling beans
The smell of crackling egg the smell of bleach when mum cleans

The smell of juicy ham the smell of slimy butter
The smell of dew on the bright green grass the smell of the dirty gutters

The smell of thick white porridge the smell of frosted flakes
The smell of burning toast the smell of white iced cakes

The smell of creamy milk the smell of thick sliced cheese
The smell of a warm cup of tea the smell of a plate full of peas

The smell of milky chocolate the smell of sugary sweets
The smell of thick fruity yogurt the smell of tough mouth watering meat

A stranger called this morning he didn't leave his name
Left us only objects (no smell) life will never be the same

Carrie-Jane Walker (Age 10)

Save The Tigers!

Tigers are endangered,
Men hunt them for their fur.

I really want to help them,
But I just don't know how.

Maybe you could make fake fur,
Or even make a tiger reserve.

Anything for these tigers,
They really need our help.

Stop the hunters killing them,
It would make me smile.

Hunters hunters go away,
And don't come back another day.

Melissa Young (Age 10)

Aliens

Big fat aliens,
Come down from,
Space with their,
X-ray guns.
They've got six,
Arms, twelve legs,
And sixteen eyes,
Very ugly and,
Spotty and red.

Calum Wellings (Age 8)

Chocolate

C ocoa
H ate it
O n top
C reep around
O n the outside
L ove it
A dored it
T alk about it
E at it!

Abigail Williams (Age 9)

Inside My Head

Inside my head
there's a house
Where magic people
Wave their thin wands
I can see things disappear
And come back into the room

Nicola Weston (Age 7)

The Wind

The wind hurls down the road quick as a flash
Knocking over trees and gates
With people shouting "Help! OH NO!"
The wind whooshing past your windows
Wind curls round corners bent as a brolly
And knocks the dustbins over quick as a trolley
All the cars getting knocked over
Fish getting swept out to sea
Pushing babies out of their prams
And taking grannies flying high
Cows mooing in the field
People screaming "Hold me down"

Danny Wingate (Age 11)

Embarrassment

Embarrassment is when you wet your self
Embarrassment is when your mum shows up
Embarrassment is when your trousers fall down
Embarrassment is when you get things wrong
Embarrassment is when you get told off
Embarrassment is when you get your sums wrong
Embarrassment is when you fall over
Embarrassment is when you lose all your money
Embarrassment is when you say the wrong thing
Embarrassment is when you feel stupid

Lucy Wilde (Age 10)

Tigers

Tigers are orange, black and white
This is the colour of their stripes.
Tigers are furry cats with pointed ears
With pinkish noses and thin white whiskers.
They are meat eaters with their sharp claws
And showing off their spikey teeth
When they roar.
They sunbathe in the long grass
Playful cubs playing in the long grass.
And when they get some prey
They camouflage away.
Some are cute, some are ugly
But deep inside he's very cuddly.

Thomas Watson (Age 8)

Aliens in the Playground

People scream people shout,
Away with the aliens as they run about.

When the bell rings they put us down
We shout yippee and run down town.

Rebekah Ward (Age 8)

Football

Fans playing drums to the beat of the chanting,
Floodlights shining over the roof of the stadium,
Player doing superb tricks,
Players shooting, goalkeepers saving,
The atmosphere is building . . . WHAT A GOAL!
Fans cheering, scarves waving in the air,
Goals flying in from all angles,
Dreadful fouls causing injuries,
Yellow cards, red cards, what next?
The final whistle goes 5 - 0 to Norwich!

Matthew Whiting (Age 9)

The Barn Owl

As he leaps out of his hollowed out secret den,
His white wings outstretched
He flew round the field
Looking for his prey.
He sees a vole with eyes like ice balls,
His claws sharp like the tip of a spear.
He dives claws first,
He picks up the vole.
Tearing it apart with his mighty claws
He takes it back to his nest.

Joseph Ward (Age 10)

Cloudy Day

A cloudy day is dismal and black,
With a storm on the way that looks quite grey.
It's starting to rain with lightning and thunder,
Must shelter before I get soaked.
Birds tucked away in their nice cosy nests,
Everyone run for home
And get their fires roaring,
Get some hot chocolate to warm you up,
Keep the pets inside the house.
See the thick wispy clouds pass on by,
And then its gone.

Elliot Walton (Age 9)

Queen Elizabeth

Queen Elizabeth, Queen Elizabeth
Where have you been?
I have been to my sister's funeral
And I cried.

Jack Wheatley (Age 7)

The Sea

Sea
Foamy waters
Dolphins playing games
Water washing onto pebbles
Salty water beating up intruders
The swirling undercurrent battling with boats
Cliffs with seagulls feeding their starving chicks
The enormous, colourful and beautiful coral reef gardens
Those secretive mermaids from tales of sailors
Orangey coloured sunsets on the horizon
Vibrant creatures, enormous and petite
Sparkling water emerald green
Slimy seaweed drifting
Not explored
Sea

Jonathan Webb (Age 11)

Juster And Waiter

My mum had nicknames for me and my brother
One of us she called waiter
And the other she called juster.
It started like this:
She'd say,
"Lend me a hand with the washing up will you, you two?"
And I'd say, "Just a minute, mum"
And my brother'd say
"Wait a minute, mum"
"There you go again she'd say,
"Juster and Waiter!"

Natalie Wheeler (Age 10)

I Wonder

I wonder what the end of the Universe looks like?
I wonder what it feels like to be dead?
I wonder how the earth was created?
I wonder if there is a place called heaven or hell?
I wonder what dinosaurs looked like?
I wonder who the first artist was?
I wonder what the answers to all the questions are?
 I wonder, I wonder

Matthew Willis (Age 10)

The Worn-Out Teddy

A fluffy old teddybear hugged by many people
The colour of its fur fading lighter and lighter
As soft as a feather
The children's thoughts "I'll keep you forever and ever".

Melissa Walter (Age 9)

Scary Seas

Ice cold waves attack sandy shores
Wind swirls around jagged rocks.
Waiting like a lion to pounce
Grey stormy sky glaring at sea
Horses gallop to shore
Barnacles gasp for air
When sea floods them.
Screaming winds scare salty seas.
Spiriting seas spray still rocks.
Blow wind blow a faint voice cried.

Scott Winestein (Age 11)

Primulas

P icturesque perfect
R adiant red
I rresistible
M agnificent shades
U nusual colours
L uxurious leaves
A lluring
S oft and silky

Maddie Webb (Age 7)

The Lion

He has claws as sharp as blades,
Teeth as shiny as diamonds
He has hair tatty and tangled,
He eats animals,
Scary to humans,
Strong and protective,
He is the king of the jungle,
He is the Lion.

James Witterick (Age 12)

TV.!

TV!: The biggest distraction!
TV! Really annoys my Mum!
TV! Stops me doing my homework!
 But then again,
 It's already done!

Gemma Wheeler (Age 9)

Formula 1

Faster than Irvine, faster than Zonta,
Fans all cheer for Ferrari and Honda.
And charging along like horses stampeding,
The engines roaring, the hero is leading,
Figures of eight, the finish line awaits,
Bends and curves, chicanes and straights.
As quick as a flash painted cars whistle by,
The race is over, crowds all sigh.

Peter Wheller (Age 12)

Yellow

Flaming sun overhead
Juicy lemons
Flaming sun overhead
Happy faces
Flaming sun overhead
Taste bananas
Flaming Sun overhead

Mark Wright (Age 9)

So Quiet

It was so quiet....
I could hear clouds racing by.
It was so quiet....
I could hear a feather falling.
It was so quiet....
I could hear a dandelion seed floating away.
It was so quiet....
I could hear cheese going mouldy.
It was so quiet....
I could hear a star twinkling.
It was so quiet....
I could hear God talking.

Jack Wetherill (Age 8)

Fireworks

Sparklers spark
All in the dark
Rockets boom
To their own doom
Katherine wheels spin
On a sharp pin
Pets are scared
Sparklers are shared
Wood is getting black
Guy Fawkes may come back!
BOOM! The sound of a rocket goes
Makes you squinch up your toes.

Ben Welthy (Age 9)

Lightning

I was walking down the scary dark road alone at eight o'clock in the night.
It was thundering, I didn't know it would be lightning
Because lightning is my worst fear
But it did so I just ran home
I stopped because in front of me a tree was falling
But I was still dying to get home
So I just ran and jumped over the wrecked tree
I got home, slammed the door shut
Locked the door and stayed inside

Chelsea Webb (Age 10)

Somewhere In A Zoo Today....

A troupe of cheeky monkeys is frantically fighting over a mouldy banana
Two lazy hippos are sleepily bathing in a muddy river
Three snapping crocodiles are excitedly trying to pull the poor zoo keeper into the water full of fish
Four white tigers are happily playing a gentle game of tiger football
A colony of termites are busy for a late breakfast

Greg Walsh (Age 9)

The First Fire

Sparks flying everywhere,
The fire's uncontrollable,
Because it's the first fire.

Orange, red, arches of flame,
The animals and hunters feel the pain.
Because it's the first fire.

These animals are petrified and galloping away,
Running and trying to escape
Because it's the first fire.

Amy Williams (Age 9)

Fire

Fire blazing in the sky
I can see the colours fly,
Red, yellow, orange, brown,
Emerged animals trying to escape

Animals ran and galloped
Nasty roars of terror came
I wonder how they feel
Men trying not to get caught
Also men went purple with the noise
Lights came shooting from nowhere
Safely they were OK

Toniann Young (Age 9)

Friends

F riends if they are proper friends then
R ight now they have friend fever
I s it true we are friends?
E very day the bill gets higher
N ever knowing what to say
D o you know who pays the bill?
S o! who cares, just as long as we are friends!

Joanna Webber (Age 11)

Down My Road

Down my road
It's a very long road
Down my road
It's a very quiet road
Down my road
It's a pond
And in my pond
Is a fish

Ryan Young (Age 6)

Last Day At School

I have to collect my art work and clean my tray
Get my PE bag then go out to play
Get the lost property box to see if anything is mine
Put the chairs up we are doing fine
Tidy up the classroom and collect my toys
I can't wait to go home and get away from the noise.
I am very excited about the summer holiday
I need my lunch box, time to go home and play

Olivia Yeomans (Age 6)

Homework!

Homework, homework every day
Oh no I can't stay
More hard work and boring
Each time I come home roaring
Watch out, the teachers say come
back on Monday
Or finish the homework today
This is a nightmare!
It's not fair

Smeeya Yaseen (Age 10)

Yellow

Yellow is the banana growing on a tree that you pick
Yellow is a baby duckling swimming along in a pond
Yellow is a gel pen that I write with
Yellow is a lightning bolt down at me in town on a rainy day
Yellow is the beak of an owl that looks at you in the night
Yellow is the sunshine that goes down and comes up

Jessica Walker (Age 9)

The Sea

Imagine roaring,
Blue sea whistling the sound
Feel the wind, the waves

Sea lapping the shore
Glittering in the sunlight
A wonderful dream

Rose Walsh (Age 8)

Pink

Pink is the colour of flamingos sticking its head in the water
Pink is the colour of a crab crawling along with a pink star fish
Pink is the colour of the inside of a water melon
Pink is the colour of candyfloss sticking to my face
Pink is the colour of bubblegum chewing, chewing, chewing.

Robert Williamson (Age 8)

A Day In The Life Of My Hamster Oats

Wakey, Wakey the light has gone
The dark is here
So run along
I pick you up for your daily run
So come along let's have fun.

As I go down the stairs
You fidget and fidget until you're down
You're out of sight back up the stairs.

You're in your cage have a midnight nibble
Then off to bed you sleepy head.

"Goodnight Oats!"

April Young (Age 11)

The Clock

Tick, tock, tick, tock,
Ever ticking tocking,
Never ricking rocking,
Never stipping stopping,
When old man shopping.

David Wright (Age 9)

Black Is . . . .

Black is pitch black
And as spooky as a leopard in the room with you
Black is sooty,
Means death and blood
Black is a dark not very nice colour which is night.

Jack Williams (Age 9)

The Stallion

The water was a ripple of moonlight, lapping at the shore,
The night was a darkening blanket, over the windy moor,
The sun was a big tornado chasing away the night,
And the stallion came a charging -
    Charging - charging
The stallion came a charging, on towards the light

Louise Walker (Age 10)

Chocolate

Chocolate cheers me up when I am blue
But chocolate isn't good for you!
Chocolate biscuits are a treat
Nice and crunchy and oh so sweet!
Milk is in chocolate and that's good for you
So I'll carry on munching my favourite food!

Jessica Waller (Age 8)

Red

As red as a strawberry and poisonous berries
As red as my literacy book that I write in
As red as my work book with words in
As red as a lovely juicy tomato that I eat
As red as tomato ketchup
As red as Autumn leaves

Katie Willmott (Age 8)

The Dancing Sea

Swaying and shimmering, mermaids
Curling round blue glowing fishes.
Red crabs scuttling and plucking
Silver clams opening, drumming.

Jack Whitefield (Age 10)

The Toys

When I go to bed at night
I hear a voice
It is a magic thing
A little whisper
Who could it be
It certainly is not me
My Barbie dolls are walking about
With me - myself in the sky flying about
What am I doing
With my teddy in my arms
Wait a minute!
I am back in bed
With my pillow over my head
I wonder what's happened
Maybe it was true
I wonder if it was just a dream
I wonder, do
YOU?

Holly Whitbread (Age 9)

BIOGRAPHIES OF POETS

ABEL, RORY WILLIAM: [b] 27/04/90, Gorleston; [home] Belton, Norfolk; [sisters] Kirsten Jane (10), Jenna Maria (5); [school] Breydon Middle; [fav sub] Science; [hobbies] Swimming, Football, Scouts, Models; [pets] Dog (Ebony), Rabbit (Carrot); [ambition] To be a Forensic Scientist;

ADAMS, NATALIE: [b] 22/12/91 Harlow; [home] Epping, Essex; [p] Lee & Karen; [brother] Dominic; [school] Epping Junior; [fav sub] Literacy & Art; [hobbies] Dancing, Drama & Singing; [pets] Gold Fish, Two Cats; [ambition] To be a Dancer or something connected with Theatre Arts;

AHMED, NAEEM: [b] 19/05/92, Bradford; [home] Bradford, W. Yorks.; [p] Sheena Kosar, Amir Aheer; [sister] Maaria Aheer; [fav sub] Numeracy, Maths; [hobbies] Playing football; [ambitions] To be a Doctor or a Policeman;

AKERS, LAUREN: [b] 29/10/94, Swindon; [home] Thornhill, Wilts; [p] Pippa & Edward; [sister] Emma; [school] Broad Hinton; [fav sub] Maths & Art; [hobbies] Showjumping; [pets] Rolo & Rosie (Ponies), Ronnie (Guinea Pig), Flower (Dog); [ambition] To be a Pop Singer;

ALBERIO, AMIE: 09/04/87, Bury St Edmunds; [home] Bury St Edmunds, Suffolk; [p] Sharon; [sister] Michaela; [school] County Upper; [fav sub] English & Art; [hobbies] Reading, Drawing, Computer, Karate, Rap Music; [pets] Riley (Boxer dog), Sky & Sherbert (Budgies), Ronnie (African Land Snail); [ambition] To be famous Writer, Actress or to work with animals;

ALEXANDER, JAY: [b] 08/09/90, Chelmsford; [home] Chelmsford, Essex; [p] David & Anne; [brother] Jack; [sister] Abigail; [school] St Michaels Junior; [fav sub] Maths & Art; [hobbies] Football; [pets] Cairn Terrier (Lottie); [ambition] To play professional football;

ALLAN, DOMINIC: [b] 28/01/93, Harlow; [home] Epping, Essex; [p] Carole & Peter; [brother] Christopher; [sister] Emma; [school] Epping Junior; [fav sub] Maths; [hobbies] Karate, Computer games; [pets] Dog (Jodie) & Tropical fish; [ambition] To be famous;

ALLEN, AMBER: [b] 13/12/88, Kent; [home] Chislehurst, Kent; [p] Deborah & Laurence; [sister] Paige; [school] Babington House; [fav sub] English; [hobbies] Horse riding & Dog agility; [pets] Rebel (Dog), Romeo & Juliet (Budgies), Sky (Hamster); [ambition] To conquer the world!

ALLEN, CONNOR, MILESON: [b] 09/01/94, Oxford; [p] Wendy & Robert; [sister] Ceara; [school] Bratton Primary; [fav sub] Art; [hobbies] Karate, Drawing & Reading; [pets] Matty (Fish); [ambition] To be an Archaeologist or Marine Biologist;

ALLEN, LAURA: [b] 29/07/93, Derby; [home] Sawmills, Derbyshire; [p] Bridget & Ian; [sisters] Emma & Samantha; [school] Fritchley Primary; [fav sub] Maths; [hobbies] Swimming & Skating; [pets]Dog (Meg) & Horse; [ambition] To be a Vet;

AMISSAH, JOHN: [b] 14/01/92, Blackpool; [home] Fleetwood, Lancs; [p] Gregory & Joyce; [brothers] Stephen & Jason; [sister] Kelly; [school] St Marys RC Primary; [fav sub] Maths; [hobbies] Rugby Union & Football; [pets] Patch (Dog), 3 goldfish; [ambition] To be a Footballer;

ANDERS, THOMAS: [b] 12/09/91 Guildford; [home] Guildford, Surrey; [p] Julie & Martin; [sister] Eloise; [school] Worplesdon Primary; [fav sub] Science; [hobbies] Diving, Reading, Cycling; [pets] Cat; [ambition] To be a Vet & visit Africa;

ANDERSON, JESSIE: [b] 09/10/90, Swindon; [home] Thornwood, Essex; [p] Denis & Julia; [school] Epping Junior; [fav sub] English; [hobbies] Football & Golf; [pets] 2 Guinea Pigs (Rosie & Daisy); [ambition] To play football for the Ladies First Team at Arsenal F.C;

ANTONA, MICHAEL: 20/06/91, Leamington Spa; [home] Kenilworth, Warks; [p] Andreas & Alison; [sisters] Laura, Lisa, Sofia; [school] Abbotsford; [fav sub] History & PE; [hobbies] Golf, Football & Electric Guitar; [ambition] To be a professional golfer;

APPLEYARD, ALICE: [b] 07/12/90, Watford; [home] Watford, Herts; [p] Rosemary & Philip; [sister] Hannah; [school] Knutsford JMI; [fav sub] Art; [hobbies] Drama, Reading, TV; [pets] Dog & Hamtser; [ambition] I am not yet sure;

ARIS, JUDD, MARCOS: [b] 13/12/94, Banbury; [home] Middle Barton, Oxon; [p] Malcolm; [sister] Paige; [school] Middle Barton; [fav sub] Writing; [hobbies] Cycling; [pets] Wallace & Gromet (Twin girl rabbits); [ambition] To drive a Lorry or a Bus;

ASHTON, GRAHAM: [b] 12/03/91, Bethlehem, S. Africa; [home] Farnham Common, Bucks; [p] David & Wendy; [brother] Richard; [sisters] Megan & Caitlin; [fav sub] History; [hobbies] Gaming, Reading & Climbing; [pets] 2 Cats, 1 Dog; [ambition] To own a Collectors Comic Shop;

BAILEY, ALEX: [b] 03/09/94, Southampton; [home] Bishopstoke, Hants; [p] Julie & Wes; [brothers] Connor & David; [sister] Emma; [school] Stoke Park Infant; [fav sub] Reading; [hobbies] Swimming, Dancing; [pets] 3 Cats (Andi, Benny & Sophie); [ambition] To be a Vet & to train Horses;

BAKER, ELLEN: [b] 27/05/91 Reading; [home] Reading, Berks; [p] Nigel Baker & Lesley Lord; [brothers] Alastair & Robert; [sister] Jennifer; [school] Loddon Junior; [fav sub] Art; [hobbies] Tennis; [pets] Cat;

BAKER, LAUREN, ELIZABETH: [b] 05/03/92, Keighley; [home] Keighley, W. Yorks; [p] David & Amanda; [brother] Christopher; [sister] Nicola; [school] Ingrow Primary; [fav sub] English; [hobbies] Listening to music; [pets] Emma (Dog); [ambition] To be a Doctor or Nurse;

BALDWIN, BRYONY: [b] 31/03/90 Sidcup; [home] Sidcup, Kent; [p] Elaine & Mark; [brother] Daniel; [school] Beaverwood; [fav sub] Technology; [hobbies] Gymnastics; [ambition] To be a veterinary Nurse;

BALI, RADHIKA: [b] 22/04/94, Windsor; [home] Beaconsfield, Bucks; [p] Mr & Mrs A.M. Bali; [brother] Arjuni; [school] High March; [fav sub] Maths; [hobbies] Playing the Violin & Dancing; [ambition] To become a Teacher;

BALL, NICOLE: [b] 18/11/95, Basildon; [home] Worlingworth, Suffolk; [p] Linda & Steven; [school] Bedfield V.C.P.; [fav sub] Art; [pets] 2 Rabbits (Spotty & Dotty); [ambition] To be an Artist or a Dance Teacher;

BALL, VICTORIA: [b] 20/11/89 Cambridge; [home] Freckenham, Suffolk; [p] David & Jackie; [sisters] Joanna & Heidi; [school] Perse School for Girls; [fav sub] French; [hobbies] Tennis & Drama; [pets] Black Labrador (Maceley); [ambition] To live in France, to teach English or be a Foreign Diplomat;

BAND, ANGELA: [b] 03/04/90, Canberra, Australia; [home] Orpington, Kent; [p] David & Kim; [brother] Jamie; [school] Babington House; [fav sub] English, Geography & Textiles; [hobbies] Swimming, Acting & Shopping; [pets] 37 Goldfish; [ambition] To be an Actress, Dancer, Singer or Drama Teacher;

BARFORD, DANIELLE, LEAH: [b] 03/10/90, Harlow; [home] Epping, Essex; [p] Natasha & Michael; [brothers] Samuel & Piers; [school] Epping Junior; [fav sub] Science; [hobbies] Swimming, Cycling, Pop Music; [pets] 2 Dogs, 5 Cats, 2 Hamsters, 1 Parrot; [ambition] To become a Vet;

BARING, LAUREN: [b] 16/11/89, Orpington; [home] Orpington, Kent; [p] Alyson & Tommy; [school] Beaverwood School for Girls; [fav sub] English; [hobbies] Singing & Dancing; [pets] Dog (Jazz); [ambition] To be famous!

BARKER, JASMINE, LEA: 29/08/95, Exeter; [home] Exeter, Devon; [p] Shaun Barker & Karen Antrobus; [brothers] James & Jordan; [sister] Lindsay; [school] Montgomery; [fav sub] Reading & Writing; [hobbies] Dancing; [pets] Rat (Lily Savage); [ambition] To be famous;

BARRETT, LUCY: [b] 23/05/93, London; [home] Epping, Essex; [p] Sarah & Gary; [sister] Chloe; [school] Epping Junior; [fav sub] Maths; [hobbies] Tennis, Dancing, Writing Poetry; [pets] Dog (Jake); (ambition) To be a Vet;

BARRON, HENRY: [b] 10/09/90, Yeovil; [home] Quarr, Dorset; [p] Anthony & Julia; [brother] Joshua; [school] Horsington CE Primary; [hobbies] Rugby; [pets] Springer Spaniel (Jenny);

BATES, HANNAH, ROSE: [b] 23/06/93, Northallerton; [home] Thirsk, N. Yorks; [p] Brian & Julie; [sisters] Catherine, Heidi & Lucie; [school] Thirsk Community Primary; [fav sub] English; [hobbies] Playing 'Teachers' & looking after animals; [pets] King Charles Spaniel (Sally); [ambition] To be a Primary School Teacher;

BATES, THOMAS: [b] 03/06/92, Guildford; [home] Guildford, Surrey; [p] Clive & Jacqui; [brother] Matthew; [school] Worplesdon C.P.; [fav sub] Science; [hobbies] Singing, Bowling & Water Skiing; [pets] Guinea Pig (Taylor); [ambition] To work for MI5;

BATESON, ALEC: [b] 20/04/93, Northallerton; [home] Thirsk, N. Yorks; [p] George & Rosie; [brothers] Twins-Harry & John; [school] Thirsk Community Primary; [fav sub] Science; [hobbies] Drawing, Reading & Tennis; [ambition] To be Tennis Player or a Scientist;

BATTY, DANIEL MARTIN: [b] 15/06/91,Northallerton; [home] Hebden, N. Yorks; [p] Paul & Siân; [sister] Catherine Marie; [school] Threshfield Primary; [fav sub] Mathematics; [hobbies] Tap Dancing; [ambition] To be a Scientist;

BAWDEN, FLORENCE EMILY: [b] 20/09/89, Kingston Upon Thames; [home] Bradworthy, Devon; [p] Jenny Bawden & Oliver Dean; [sisters] Libby & Abigail; [school] Holsworthy Community College; [fav sub] Art; [hobbies] Art, Poetry, Frogs & Toads; [pets] Chickens, Guinea Pigs, Gerbils & Dogs; [ambition] To dive in the Great Barrier Reef and to Bungee jump in the Grand Canyon;

BEARNE, JACK: [b] 17/04/95, Eastbourne; [home] Eastbourne, E. Sussex; [p] Kriss & Chris; [sister] Aimée; [school] Roselands County Infants [fav sub] Art & Drama; [hobbies] Drawing, Making things, Cycling, Swimming, Playing with friends & Parties; [pets] 2 Guinea Pigs (Bubble & Squeak), 1 Rabbit (Casper); [ambition] To be an Actor or Artist;

BEAUMONT, DANIEL: [b] 16/11/94, Eastbourne; [home] Eastbourne, E. Sussex; [school] Roselands Infant; [fave sub] Writing stories & Art; [hobbies] Model making;

BEAUMONT, JAMES SEBASTIAN: [b] 27/01/92, Watford; [home] Watford, Herts; [p] Nicola & Graham; [brothers] Oliver (8) & Alexander (3); [school] Knutsford JMI; [fav sub] PE & Athletics; [hobbies] Athletics, Trumpet & Piano; [pets] Greyhound (Portia) & 3 Guinea Pigs; [ambition] To go Quad Biking, Jet Skiing and to become a Movie star and own an Aston Martin DB7;

BEAVEN, GREGORY: [b] 30/04/92, Guildford; [home] Guildford, Surrey; [p] Tracy & Gordon; [sister] Carly; [school] Worplesdon County;[fav sub] PE & IT; [hobbies] Football, Judo & Cubs; [pets] Guinea Pig (Ginger); [ambition] To write like R.L. Steine or play football like Michael Owen;

BECKLEY, LAUREN: [b] 31/01/91, Canterbury; [home] Herne Bay, Kent; [p] Lisa, Martin & Clive (Step Dad); [brother] Jonathon; [school] Herne CE Junior; [fav sub] English; [hobbies] Sports, Reading & Writing; [pets] 2 Kittens (McGonagall & Hagrid); [ambition] To be an Author or Pop Star;

BEECH, KATIE: [b] 29/10/85, Chelmsford; [home] Chelmsford, Essex; [p] John & Catherine; [school] The Hayward School; [fav sub] Art; [hobbies] Horse Riding; [ambition] To work with animals;

BELSMAN, LEONI SARA: [b] 07/05/91, Edgware; [home] Radlett, Herts; [p] Loraine & Paul; [sisters] Claudia, Suzy & Nicole; [school] Newberries Primary; [fav sub] Art; [hobbies] Art & Crafts, Reading; [pets] Goldfish (Fishface);[ambition] To be a Fashion Designer;

BENT, FRANKIE: [b] 13/11/93, Worcester; [home] Kempsey, Worcs; [p] Roger & Della; [school] Kempsey Primary; [fav sub] History & PE; [hobbies] Guitar, Skateboarding, PS2 [pets] Dog (Huckleberry Finn); [ambition] To be a Rock Star (Lead guitarist);

BERESFORD, KATIE: [b] 26/03/91, Crewe; [home] Worthwich, Cheshire; [p] Sandra & Keith; [sister] Lisa; [school] St. Wilfrid; [fav sub] English; [hobbies] Dancing, Acting & Singing; [pets] Molly & Josie; [ambition] To be an Actress;

BHOGAL, DAYSHEEN K.: [b] 13/09/91, Hounslow; [home] Staines, Middx; [p] Harbinder & Bhagwant; [sisters] Harkiran & Nitisha; [school] Kingscroft; [fav sub] English; [hobbies] Reading & Singing; [pets] Cat (Tibby) + 3 Kittens; [ambition] To be a Doctor and see real Penguins in Antartica;

BINGE, JACK WILLIAM: [b] 08/07/93, Stevenage; [home] Buckland, Herts; [p] Kathleen & Robin; [brother] Stuart; [school] Therfield First; [fav sub] Science, English & History; [pets] Boxer & German Shephard; [ambition] To be a Sportsman;

BINNINGTON-BARRETT, VICTORIA MORGAN: [b] 03/09/89, Ipswich; [home] Ipswich, Suffolk; [p] Sharon & Kevin; [school] Stoke High; [fav sub] English & Technology; [hobbies] Music, Karate & Sport; [pets] Rabbit, Hamster & Goldfish; [ambition] To be an Author,

Artist or Pop Star;

BIRCH, KATIE: [b] 05/01/92, Broadstairs; [home] Broadstairs, Kent; [p] Lynne & Trevor; [brother] Martin; [school] Upton Junior; [fav sub] Art; [hobbies] Dancing, Brownies & Gymnastics; [pets] 2 Dogs; [ambition] To be an Actress;

BIRD, LAURA: [b] 16/10/90; [home] North Weald, Essex; [p] Ann & Paul; [brother] Michael; [school] Epping Junior; [fav sub] Maths; [hobbies] Swimming; [pets] Guinea Pig, Rabbit, Dog & Fish; [ambition] To be a Vet;

BIRD, SIMON: [b] 23/05/90, Bristol; [home] Bicknoller, Somerset; [p] Sarah & Paul; [sister] Georgina; [school] Danesfield; [fav sub] Science; [hobbies] Kendo, Saxophone & Magic; [pets] Rat (Scabbers) & Guinea Pig (Sparky); [ambition] To be a Cartoonist;

BOLTON, KATE: [b] 06/08/91, Bristol; [home] Watchet, Somerset; [p] Julie & Philip; [brothers] Joe & Mark; [school] Danesfield; [hobbies] Gymnastics, Netball, Drawing & Writing; [pets] Guinea Pig (Mimo); [ambition] To work with animals;

BOORER, STEPHANIE: [b] 12/12/90, Babury; [home] Banbury, Oxon; [p] Julie & Kevin; [brothers] Simon & Matthew; [sister] Nicola; [school] Hortnton Primary; [fav sub] Art; [hobbies] Martial Arts-Yellow belt; [pets] Dog (Holly); [ambition] To go to College;

BOSE, KANEESHA: [b] 05/05/91, Bradford; [home] Bradford, W. Yorks; [p] Janice; [brother] Aston; [school] Wellington Primary; [fav sub] Maths; [hobbies] Dancing & Reading; [pets] Rabbit; [ambition] To make loads of money!

BOWEN, SIÂN: [b] 11/04/91, Redditch; [home] Catshill, Worcs; [brother] Liam; [school] Catshill Middle; [fav sub] Maths; [hobbies] Swimming & Reading; [pets] Dog & Rabbit; [ambition] To swim with Dolphins;

BOYALL, RACHEL: [b] 09/06/93, King's Lynn; [home] North Wootton, Norfolk; [p] Kay & Keith; [brother] Robert; [school] North Wootton Community; [fav sub] Numeracy; [hobbies] Horse Riding & Skipping; [pets] 2 Rabbits (Rosie & Polly); [ambition] To be a Vet;

BOYCE, EMMA TIFFANY: [b] 31/12/92 Great Yarmouth; [home[Carlton Colville, Suffolk; [p] Martin & Debbie; [school] Whitton Green Primary; [fav sub] ICT, PE & Art; [hobbies] Recorder, Keyboard & Swimming; [pets] 5 Goldfish, best one is Rose; [ambition] Keyboard grade 1, Recorder, Flute;

BRADFORD, BEN: [b] 03/10/95, Epping; [home] Theydon Bois, Essex; [sisters] Francesca & Lottie; [school] Theydon Bois Primary;

BRADY, MELISSA J: [b] 19/11/92, Gt. Yarmouth; [home] Lowestoft, Suffolk; [p] Beverley & Peter; [school] Whitton Green Primary; [fav sub] PE & ICT; [hobbies] Playing football & tennis; [pets] Guinea Pig (Scruff), Rabbit (Sweep); [ambition] To be a Mechanic or Professional Footballer;

BRAZIER, CHRISTOPHER: [b] 12/03/92, Enfield; [home] Goffs Oak, Herts; [p] Nadine & Ian; [sister] Hannah; [school] Woodside Primary; [fav sub] Science; [hobbies] Swimming, Karate & Football; [pets] Cats, Hamsters & Fish; [ambition] To be a Palaeontologist (Fossil Expert);

BRIMSON, JOSH: [b] 10/11/90, Canterbury; [home] Canterbury, Kent; [p] Rupert & Debbie; [school] St Peter's Methodist; [fav sub] Literacy; [hobbies] Archaeology; [pets] 2 Cats (Cassie & Heidi); [ambition] To be a famous Archaeologist;

BRITTON, ANDREW: [b] 25/11/82, King's Lynn; [home] King's Lynn, Norfolk; [p] Lorraine & Neale; [brother] Mark; [sister] Nicola; [school] South Wootton Junior; [fav sub] Art, Design & Technology; [hobbies] Cubs & Computer Games; [ambition] To be famous;

BROOK, HOLLY ANN: [b] 02/01/94, Exeter; [home] Exeter, Devon; [p] Paul & Susan; [brothers] Samuel & Ashton; [school] Montgomery Combined; [fav sub] Art; [hobbies] Reading, Drawing; [pets] 2 Cats; [ambition] To be an Artist;

BROOKS, BEN: [b] 07/10/91, Kingston; [home] Long Ditton, Surrey; [p] Jackie; [school] Thames Ditton Junior; [fav sub] English; [hobbies] Football; [ambition] To become a Footballer or Scientist;

BROUGH, JOSEPH: [b] 17/07/92, Barking; [home] Theydon Bois, Essex; [p] Trevor & Suzanne; [brother] James; [sister] Louise; [school] Theydon Bois Primary; [fav sub] Maths; [hobbies] Football, Tennis, Piano & Guitar; [pets] Cat (Puddkins); [ambition] To be a Professional Footballer;

BROUGH, LOUISE: [b] 26/11/93, Goodmayes; [home] Theydon Bois, Essex; [p] Trevor & Suzzanne; [brothers] James & Joseph; [school] Theydon Bois Primary; [fav sub] History; [hobbies] Dancing; [pets] Cat (Puddkins); [ambition] To become a Teacher;

BRUNDLE, HARRIET ROBYN: [b] 01/05/91, King's Lynn; [home] King's Lynn, Norfolk; [p] Joanna & Robin; [sister] Chlóé; [school] South Wootton Junior; [fav sub] English; [hobbies] Tap & Ballet, Jazz, Reading; [pets] Dog (Molly), Guinea Pigs (Bubble, Squeak, Magic & Minstral); [ambition] To have a novel published and become a Vet;

BRUNNING, EMMA: [b] 01/10/89, Gorleston; [home] Belton, Norfolk; [p] Wayne & Tina; [brother] Kurt; [school] Breydon Middle; [fav sub] Maths & Music; [hobbies] Playing Piano & Football; [pets] Hamster (Henry), Goldfish (Tiny); [ambition] To play the piano on Cruise Ships & travel the world;

BULLOCK, CHLOE: [b] 30/09/94, Macclesfield; [home] Macclesfield, Cheshire; [p] Diane & Glyn; [brother] Liam; [school] Prestbury CE Primary; [fav sub] Art; [hobbies] Swimming; [pets] Goldfish (Isobel); [ambition] To become a Vet;

BURT, HOLLIE: [b] 11/12/92, Maldon; [home] Goldhanger, Essex; [p] Teresa & Terry; [sisters] Jade, Lauren, Aimee; [school] Tollshunt D'Arcy CE Primary; [fav sub] Art; [hobbies] Swimming, Horse Riding; [pets] Dog (Benson); [ambition] To be a Designer or Hairdresser;

BURT, LUCY: [b] 03/02/95, [home] Salisbury; Wilts; [p] Richard & Linda; [sister] Megan; [school] Wyndham Park Infants; [fav sub] Art; [hobbies] Swimming, Dancing & Brownies; [pets] Cat (Topsy), Guinea Pig (Mooney); [ambition] To become a Teacher;

BURTON, ROBERT: [b] 20/11/89, Chatham; [home] Sittingbourne, Kent; [p] John & Sheila; [brother] John; [school] Borden Grammar; [fav sub] Maths; [hobbies] Fossils, Bridge & Scouts; [pets] 2 Dogs; [ambition] To get good A Levels and become a Policeman;

BUTTLE, STEPHANIE: [b] 11/11/89 Horsham St. Faiths; [home] Horsham St Faiths, Norfolk; [p] Mr & Mrs V. Buttle; [brother] Steven Kett; [sisters] Katie Wells & Emma Buttle; [school] Horsford All Saints VC Middle; [fav sub] Art, Creative Writing; [hobbies] Badminton & Art; [pets] Dog & Fish; [ambition] To write and illustrate my own book & become a successful Designer;

BYGRAVE, MIMI: [b] 09/09/92, Bristol; [home] Mudgley & Ashcott, Somerset; [p] Sarah & Max; [brother]

Alexei; [sister] Bertie; [school] Wedmore First; [fav sub] Art, Poetry & writing stories; [hobbies] Drama, Caving & Abseiling; [pets] Cat (Tigger), Rat (Ronny); [ambition] To become a Writer & Poet, also an Artist or Sculptor;

CACKETT, BECKY: [b] 12/10/93 Epsom; [home] Epsom, Surrey; [p] Linda & Roy; [school] Stamford Green; [fav sub] Science; [hobbies] Anilmals, Gymnastics, Dancing & Swimming; [pets] Dog & Hamster; [ambition] To become a Vet;

CAHILL, NATASHA: [b] 16/04/91 Utrecht, Holland; [home] Grassington, N. Yorks.; [p] Imogen & Gavin; [brother] Conor; [school] Threshfield; [fav sub] Art; [hobbies] Horse Riding; [pets] Lurcher dog (Homes), Rabbit (Sooty); [ambition] To become a Vet;

CANFOR-DUMAS, EMILY: [b] 08/02/91, Watford; [home] Bushey, Herts; [p] Coralyn & Edward; [brother] Alexander; [school] Newberries Primary; [fav sub] English; [hobbies] Drama, Dance & Sports; [pets] Cat (Monty), 3 Goldfish; [ambition] To be a Criminal Barrister;

CANNING, STEPHEN: [b] 11/01/93, Braintree; [home] Braintree, Essex; [p] Sandra & Michael; [brothers] Richard, David & Adam; [sister] Sarah; [school] Great Bradfords Junior; [fav sub] English & History; [hobbies] Reading, Writing, Cubs, Walking Swimming & Computers; [pets] Cat, Hamster, Fish; [ambition] To go to University and become an Author and Teacher;

CANTY, SOPHIE: [b] 05/09/92, Walthamstow; [home] London; [p] Lorraine & Anthony; [brother] Timothy; [school] Leverton Junior; [fav sub] English; [hobbies] Dancing; [pets] Cat; [ambition] To become a Teacher;

CAPORN, PETER: [b] 08/07/92 Macclesfield; [home] Alderley Edge, Cheshire; [p] Catherine & Simon; [sisters] Alice & Hannah; [school] Alderley Edge Community Primary;[fav sub] Maths; [hobbies] Cycling, Gameboy; [ambition] To be an Archaeologist;

CAPEWELL, THOMAS: [b] 26/09/91 Harlow; [home] Epping, Essex; [p] Julie & Gary; [brothers] Jack & Harry; [school] Epping Junior; [hobbies] Football; [pets] Dog (Keaton);

CARTMELL, LAURA: [b] 24/07/91 Macclesfield; [home] Over Alderley, Cheshire; [p] Alison & John; [brother] Joe (Joseph); [school] Prestbury Primary; [fav sub] Art, Technology; [hobbies] Walking, Reading, Playing the Violin & Piano; [pets] Cat (Candy); [ambition] To reach grade 8 on the piano;

CARTWRIGHT, JORDAN LOUISA: [b] 06/02/93 Hastings; [home] Hastings, East Sussex; [p] Nicki & Craig; [brother] Mathew; [sister] Stacey; [school] Hollington Primary; [fav sub] English & Maths; [hobbies] Skating, Cycling; [pets] 3 Cats (Pepsi, Ellie & Bailey);

CERASALE, HANNAH: [b] 10/10/90 Watford; [home] Watford, Herts; [p] John & Tracey; [brother] Harry; [school] Knutsford; [fav sub] Maths; [hobbies] Drama & Shopping; [pets] Hamster & a Fish; [ambition] To be an Actress;

CHADHA, KOMAL: [b] 1988 London; [home] London; [p] Deepak & Sangeeta; [brother] Vikas; [school] Wallington High School for Girls; [fav sub] Maths & English; [hobbies] Music & Reading; [pets] Fish & Newts; [ambition] Finding a cure for terminal diseases & creating world peace;

CHEASMAN, REECE DAVID: [b] 27/11/92 Harlow; [home] Waltham Abbey, Essex; [p] Elizabeth & Geoffrey; [brother] Daniel Ross; [school] Leverton Juniors; [fav sub] Science; [hobbies] Cycling, Football; [pets] I haven't got any but love my friends dogs Tess & Pepsi; [ambition] To be a good Mechanic;

CHEESEMAN, SAMANTHA: [b] 21/01/92 Dover; [home] Deal, Kent; [p] Helen & Andy; [brother] Barry; [school] Sandown County Primary; [fav sub] Art & Science; [hobbies] Horse Riding & Swimming; [pets] Dog, Cat, Budgies, Hamster, Fish, Sea Monkeys & 6 African Land Snails; [ambition] To be a Vet or a Veterinary Nurse;

CHERRINGTON, NATHAN: [b] 29/05/91 Rutland; [home] Catshill, Worcs; [p] Paul & Elizabeth; [brother] Saul; [school] Catshill Middle; [fav sub] Maths; [hobbies] Football, Tennis; [ambition] To be a Professional Footballer;

CHIMA, JAHY SINGH [b] 04/01/91 King's Lynn; [home] North Wootton, Norfolk; [p] Jas & Jinder; [sister] Sukhey Kaur; [school] North Wootton Community; [hobbies] English; [hobbies] Football, Rugby, Cricket, Tennis & Golf; [ambition] To be a Vet;

CHISMON, BETHANY JANE: [b] 18/07/96, Maidstone; [home] Maidstone, Kent; [p] Paul & Jackie; [sister] Zoe Alice; [school] Molehill Copse; [fav sub] Maths; [hobbies] Swimming, Reading; [pets] Cat (Tibby), Rabbit (Snow Drop); [ambition] To be a Policewoman;

CHRISTIAN, ROCHELLE MARIE: [b] 23/02/92 Rush Green, Essex; [home] Holmes Chapel, Cheshire; [p] Debra & Stephen, Paul & Jo; [brothers] Conor, Adam & James; [school] Holmes Chapel Primary; [fav sub] Mathematics & Art; [hobbies] Keyboard Piano, Cycling; [ambition] To be a Teacher or to be famous!

CLAGUE, JORDAN EUAN: [b] 15/09/92 Ashford, Kent; [home] Deal, Kent; [p] Graham & Katie; [sisters] Erin Bethany & Stephanie Mae; [school] Sandown CP; [fav sub] Science; [hobbies] Football & Eating!; [ambition] To be a Scientist, be in Computing or play football for Liverpool;

CLARK, ASHLEIGH DELANEY: [b] 26/03/92 Reading; [home] Reading, Berks; [p] Kerry Clark & Adrian Francis; [school] Park Lane Primary; [fav sub] PE & Maths; [hobbies] Swimming, Singing; [ambition] To be a Singer;

CLARKE, ROBERT: [b] 20/10/90 King's Lynn; [home] South Wootton, Norfolk; [p] Roslyn & Robert; [brother] Harvey; [school] South Wootton Junior; [fav sub] Games; [hobbies] Skate Boarding; [pets] Dog; [ambition] To be successful;

CLAXTON, MATTHEW: [b] 08/10/85 Miami; [home] Felixstowe, Suffolk; [p] Alison Pitcher; [brother] Ryan Pitcher; [school] Westbridge; [fav sub] Art; [hobbies] Basketball; [ambition] To go to America;

CLEGG, MELANIE CARA: [b] 08/10/88 Bradford; [home] Shipley, W. Yorks.; [school] Bingley Grammar; [fav sub] Art & English; [hobbies] Internet, Reading, Drawing & Creative Writing; [pets] 2 Cats, Lizard & Tortoise; [ambition] To be happy;

CLOSE, LUKE: [b] 14/10/92 Epping; [home] Epping, Essex; [p] Karen; [brother] Stephen; [school] Epping Junior; [fav sub] Literacy & Maths; [hobbies] Football; [pets] Polecat, Cat, Finches & Fish; [ambition] To play football for West Ham United;

COLE, SOPHIE: [b] 31/03/93 Reading; [home] Caversham, Berks; [p] Jane & Les; [brother] Luke; [sister] Ellie; [school] Micklands Primary; [fav sub] PE; [hobbies] Freestyle Dancing; [pets] Cat (Holly), Rabbit (Robbie); [ambition] To be a Dancer;

COLLISON, CORAL AMBER: [b] 27/10/92 [home] King's Lynn, Norfolk; [p] Mr & Mrs Collison; [brother] Jesse Lee; [sister] Jade Sharee; [school] South Wootton Junior; [fav sub] Maths; [hobbies] Dancing, Singing; [pets] Dogs;

[ambition] To be a Pop Star;

CONNOLLY, EOGHAN PRIOR: [b] 08/06/92 Newcastle upon Tyne; [home] Ashford, Middx; [p] Malcolm Prior & Pauline Connolly; [sister] Catherine Connolly; [school] Kingscroft Junior; [fav sub] Art; [hobbies] Playing computer games; [ambition] To be a Teacher;

COOKE, DAISY: [b] 18/12/92 Coventry; [home] Ivybridge, Devon; [p] Spencer & Sarah; [sister] Millicent; [school] Stowford Primary; [fav sub] Maths; [hobbies] Singing; [pets] Dog (Travis), Gerbil (Salt); [ambition] To be a Teacher;

COOKSON, AMY-LOU: [b] 26/12/88 Preston; [home] Clayton Brook, Lancs; [p] Diane; [school] St. Michael's High; [fav sub] English; [hobbies] Sport, WWF, Music; [pets] 3 Dogs, 2 Cats, 1 Rabbit; [ambition] To be part of WWF or a Singer;

COOPER, JADE: [b] 16/02/94 Macclesfield; [home] Macclesfield, Cheshire; [p] Karen & Bob; [sisters] Amber, Paige; [school] Prestbury Primary; [fav sub] Poetry; [hobbies] Swimming & Gymnastics; [pets] Guinea Pig, Cat & Fish; [ambition] To be a Doctor, Poet, Writer, or Nurse;

COOPER, KATHERINE: [b] 18/01/89 Stevenage; [home] Hitchin, Herts; [p] Peter & Alison; [brothers] Ben & Sam Atkinson -Step Brothers; [sisters] Kimberley & Helen + Lucy Atkinson-Step Sister; [school] Hitchin Girls; [fav sub] Art; [hobbies] Running & Reading; [pets] Black Labradors (Molly & Tess), Hamster (Colin); [ambition] To become a Sports Teacher;

COOPER, SASKIA: [b] 21/08/93 King's Lynn; [home] King's Lynn, Norfolk; [p] Michael & Susan; [sisters] Francesca & Eden; [school] South Wootton Junior; [fav sub] Art; [hobbies] Ballet, Piano, Swimming; [ambition] To become a Teacher;

COOTE, LAURA A.: [b] 07/11/93 Colchester; [home] Lt. Oakley, Essex; [p] Michael & Lynette; [brother] Christopher; [school] St. Joseph's R.C.; [fav sub] Art & PE; [hobbies] Swimming & Dancing; [pets] Cat (Jessica); [ambition] To nurse and look after animals;

CORCORAN, MATTHEW: [b] 04/06/90 Crewe; [home] Winsford, Cheshire; [p] Steve & Denise; [brothers] Marcus & Steven; [sister] Tracy; [school] Verdin High; [fav sub] English; [hobbies] Football & Hockey; [pets[Dogs; [ambition] To be a Footballer;

COSSEY, DEAN: [b] 22/04/93 Epping; [home] Epping, Essex; [p] Caroline Preston; [sister] Siobhan; [school] St. John's Junior;

COSTIN, ANDREW: [b] 30/12/93 Reading; [home] Caversham, Berks; [p] Melanie & the late David Costin, Step Father Simon; [brother] Joseph; [school] Micklands Primary; [fav sub] History; [hobbies] Chess, Pets & Football; [pets] 4 Hamsters, 2 Fish, Rabbit & Guinea Pig; [ambition] To learn Angling & become a Vet;

COWBURN, JAMES: [b] 01/12/90 Maidstone, Kent; [home] Holmes Chapel, Cheshire; [p] Terry & Carolyn; [brothers] Ian (16) & Terry (13); [sister] Lisa (26); [school] Holmes Chapel Primary; [fav sub] Maths; [hobbies] Swimming, Football, Athletics; [pets] Cat (Alfie), Hamster (Jedi); [ambition] To get an Olympic Gold at Swimming & become a Professional Footballer. Have County & District selection for swimming - made the National Swimming Championships August 2002;

CRADOCK, ASHLEY LUKE: [b] 16/01/92 Bath; [home] Hilperton, Wilts; [p] Joanne & Ian; [brother] Benjamin; [sister] Nicola; [school] Hilperton Primary; [fav sub] Art; [hobbies] Swimming & Cycling; [pets] Dog (Solomon); [ambition] To drive a Steam Train & Pilot an Areoplane;

CRANDON, GEORGIA: [b] 29/11/95; [home] Loughton, Essex; [p] Ivor & Angela; [brother] Alexander; [school] Theydon Bois Primary; [fav sub] Art; [hobbies] Playing & Drawing; [pets] Dog (Megan); [ambition] To be an Artist and a Mummy!;

CROUCH, TOBIAS: [b] 22/08/93 Dover; [home] Deal, Kent; [p] Terence & Suzanne; [school] Sandown Primary; [fav sub] Maths; [hobbies] Football & Gameboy; [pets] Dog (Hagar), Bird (Blissy), 2 Fish; [ambition] To be an RAF Pilot;

CROZIER, VICTORIA ABIGAIL: [b] 22/12/93 Harrogate; [p] Ian & Joy; [brother] James Samuel; [school] Roecliffe C.E; [fav sub] English; [hobbies] Brownies, Swimming, Flute & Recorder; [pets] Cat (Oscar), Rabbit (Gizmo);

CUNNINGHAM, MEGAN: [b] 28/03/92 Plymouth; [home] Bere Alston, Devon; [p] Margaret & Rob; [brothers] Gary, Martin & Matthew; [school] Bere Alston Primary; [fav sub] Art; [hobbies] Reading; [pets] Dog (Dougal), Budgie (Bobby); [ambition] To become a Holiday Rep. or Air Hostess;

CUPIT, SAM: [b] 13/10/92 Aylesbury; [home] Soulbury, Bucks; [p] Suzy Cupit & Chris Dowell; [brother] Ben Dowell; [school] Overstone Combined; [fav sub] Science; [hobbies] Searching for Fossils; [pets] 3 Cats; [ambition] To be a famous Palaeontologist;

CURETON, LINZI:[b] 23/08/89 Stafford; [home] Poulton, Lancs; [p] Geoff & Lynda; [school] Baines School; [fav sub] English; [hobbies] Dancing & Reading; [pets] Hamster (Poppy), Rabbit (Flopsy), Cat (Frankie); [ambition] To become a Teacher;

DANIELS, KELLY: [b] 05/06/91 Reading; [home] Reading, Berks; [p] Linda & Graham; [brothers] Stuart & Darren; [sister] Nicky; [school] Micklands Primary; [fav sub] Numeracy; [hobbies] Creating things; [pets] Rabbit, Spider; [ambition] To work with disabled children;

DAVIES, ROAN: [b] 10/11/92 Abergavenny; [home] Abergavenny, Monmouthshire; [p] Anita & Charles; [brothers] Luke & Jack; [school] Our Lady & St. Michael's; [fav sub] Maths; [hobbies] Playing Violin & Swimming; [pets] Goldfish (Prince); [ambition] To be a Surgeon or Violin Teacher;

DAYMOND, LISA: [b] 24/11/90 Plymouth; [home] Bere Alston, Devon; [p] Ian & Diane; [brothers] Christopher & Stephen; [sister] Karen; [school] Bere Alston Primary; [fav sub] Art; [hobbies] Swimming & Listening to music; [pets] Lots; [ambition] To be a Hairdresser;

DEARSLY, HARRY: [b] 15/06/91 Exmouth; [home] Lympstone, Devon; [p] Tim & Judy; [brother] Barney; [sisters] Polly & Abi; [school] Lympstone C.E.; [fav sub] English; [hobbies] Sailing; [pets] Dog, 2 rats; [ambition] To be a Professional Cricketer & Footballer;

DEBENHAM, ANNABEL ROSE ELIZABETH: [b] 12/06/93 Barking; [home] Theydon Bois, Essex; [p] Lisa & Peter; [sister] Charlotte; [school] Theydon Bois Primary; [fav sub] Maths; [hobbies] Swimming, Reading & Girls Brigade; [pets] 2 Cats; [ambition] To be a Maths Teacher and a Mum!;

DEBENHAM, CHARLOTTE ALEXANDRA: [b] 16/07/93 Barking; [home] Theydon Bois, Essex; [p] Lisa & Peter; [sister] Annabel; [school] Theydon Bois Primary; [fav sub] English, Art, Pottery; [hobbies] Swimming, Reading & Harry Potter Books; [pets] 2 Cats; [ambition] To have a good job and be a Mum!;

DEVILLE, SAM: [b] 25/12/93 Cambridge; [home] Westmill, Herts; [p]

Alan & Sue; [school] Therfield First; [fav sub] PE; [hobbies] Football; [pets] Labradors (Rosie & Sophie); [ambition] To be a Footballer;

DEVONSHIRE, LAUREN: [b] 28/01/91 Slough; [home] Hedgerley, Bucks; [p] Nick & Ita; [sister] Emma; [school] Farnham Common Junior; [fav sub] Mathematics; [hobbies] Football, Ballet, Drama; [pets] Rabbit (Whiskers); [ambition] To be a Scientist;

DEWEY, LORNA: [b] 21/01/91 Gloucester; [home] Uley, Glos; [p] Jim & Shirley; [brothers] Adam & Jack; [school] Uley C.E. Primary; [fav sub] Art; [hobbies] Tennis, Jazz Dance, Piano, Violin, Photography; [pets] Allergic to most!; [ambition] To be a Doctor;

DICKIE, MARK: [b] 22/10/88 Cambridge; [home] Graveley, Cambs; [p] Robert & Catherine; [brothers] Peter & Tom; [sister] Helen; [school] St Bede's Inter Church Comp; [fav sub] PE; [hobbies] Football, Computer Games, Films; [pets] Patterdale Terrier (Robbie), Jack Russell Terrier (Anna); [ambition] To be a Professional Footballer;

DICKINSON, LAURA-JAYNE: [b] 19/09/90 Bradford; [home] Bradford, W. Yorks; [p] Alison & Mark; [sister] Georgia; [school] Wellington Primary; [fav sub] English; [hobbies] Reading, Dancing; [pets] 2 Golden Labradors (Ellie & Jess), Cat (Brontie); [ambition] To write books for children;

DISHMAN, MATTHEW: [b] 25/10/87 Basildon; [home] Basildon, Essex; [p] Angela & James; [brother] Ryan; [school] Woodlands; [fav sub] PE; [hobbies] Rugby, Tennis & Football; [ambition] To play Rugby for England;

DOUGLAS, VANESSA GEMMA MARY: [b] 01/01/91 Reading; [home] Reading, Berks; [p] Leonard & Jessica; [school] All Saints Infant; [fav sub] Poetry; [hobbies] Swimming, Cycling; [pets] Kittens; [ambition] To become a Poet;

DOUGLASS, ANDREW: [b] 29/06/91 Colchester; [home] King's Lynn, Norfolk; [brother] Christopher; [school] South Wootton Junior; [fav sub] Art; [hobbies] Football, Judo & Cricket; [pets] Goldfish;

DOWDS, JAMES: [b] 30/01/94 High Wycombe; [home] Gerrards Cross, Bucks; [p] Stephen Dowds & Dympna McDonnell; [brother] Conor; [sister] Sarah; [school] Gayhurst; [fav sub] Maths & Music; [hobbies] Travel, Watching Cartoons, Playing Games; [pets] Cat (Fluffy) & Goldfish; [ambition] To become a Policeman;

DOWNING, ALISHA: [b] 15/11/90 Chertsey; [home] Byfleet, Surrey; [p] Liz & Luke; [school] St Mary's C.E. Primary; [fav sub] English; [hobbies] Art, Karate, Music; [pets] 2 Cats (Fabian & Dandy); [ambition] To travel the world & be a top Clothes Designer;

DOYLE, MADDY: [b] 13/06/91 Crewe; [home] Northwich, Cheshire; [p] John & Helen; [school] St Wilfrid's RC Primary; [fav sub] Art; [hobbies] Horse Riding & Dancing; [pets] Dog; [ambition] To become an Actress;

DRANN KIERAN: [b] 15/08/95 Southend; [home] Bere Alston, Devon; [p] Lorna Drann & Sean Mahon; [brother] Finlay Mahon; [school] Bere Alston Primary; [fav sub] Science; [hobbies] Skate Boarding, Football; [pets] 3 Fish; [ambition] To be a Vet;

DYER, JORDAN: [b] 23/03/92 King's Lynn; [home] South Wootton, Norfolk; [p] Trevor & Beverly; [brothers] Nathan & Callum; [school] South Wootton Junior; [fav sub] History; [hobbies] Boxing, Tennis, Karate; [pets] Dog, Cat, 2 Rabbits, Fish; [ambition] To be a Professional Boxer;

DYSTER, ADAM: [b] 07/12/93 Colchester; [home] Tolleshunt D'Arcy, Essex; [p] Jane & Martin; [school] St. Nicholas; [fav sub] English; [hobbies] Reading & Computer; [pets] Cat, Rabbits, Guinea Pigs; [ambition] To work with animals;

EAST, RACHEL: [b] 02/05/92 Guildford; [home] Guildford, Surrey; [p] Andrew & Kerry; [brother] Adam; [school] Worplesdon Primary; [fav sub] Art; [hobbies] Swimming, Ballet & Tap Dancing; [ambition] To represent England in the Olympic Games;

EAVES, ASHLEY: [b] 02/07/91 Leamington Spa; [home] Kenilworth, Warks; [p] Colin & Renée; [brother] Joseph; [school] Abbotsford; [fav sub] PE; [hobbies] Computer Games & BMX; [ambition] To become an Astronaut;

EBSWORTH, LUKE: [b] 29/08/02 Ashford; [home] Ashford, Middx; [p] Michele & Mark; [sister] Aimee; [school] Springfield Primary; [fav sub] Literacy; [hobbies] Football (playing & watching), Reading; [pets] 2 Guinea Pigs (Whoopi & Snowball); [ambition] To become a Professional Footballer and play for Manchester United

EDGLEY, MATTHEW ALEC: [b] 11/10/90 King's Lynn; [home] Leziate, Norfolk; [p] Glenda; [sisters] Anouska & Hayley; [school] North Wootton Community; [fav sub] Art; [hobbies] All Sports; [pets] Lizard, Fish, 2 Cats, Dog; [ambition] To be a Professional Footballer;

EDSER, CALUM: [b] 29/03/92 Kingston; [home] Hinchley Wood, Surrey; [p] Christine & Mark; [brothers] Duncan & Ross; [sister] Catriona; [school] Thames Ditton Junior; [fav sub] PE; [hobbies] Football, Tennis, Hockey, Swimming, Cycling; [ambition] To be a Footballer or Tennis Player;

EDWARDS, BRONWYN: [b] 14/09/91 Chatham; [home] Sittingbourne, Kent; [p] Mark & Deborah; [sisters] Megan & Briony; [school] Murston Juniors; [fav sub] English & History; [hobbies] Netball, Kick-boxing, Girl Guides; [pets] Dog (Gizzy), Guinea Pig (Fluffy); [ambition] To do my best at school;

EDWARDS, MEGAN: [b] 14/09/91 Chatham; [home] Sittingbourne, Kent; [p] Mark & Deborah; [sisters] Bronwyn & Briony; [school] Murston Juniors; [fav sub] English & History; [hobbies] Netball, Dancing, Kick-boxing, Girl Guides; [pets] Dog (Gizzy); [ambition] To do well at school;

ELLARD, STEPHEN: [b] 25/06/89 Southampton; [home] Braunton, Devon; [p] Martin & Elaine; [sisters] Sara & Rachel; [school] Braunton School & Community College; [fav sub] Information Technology; [hobbies] Swimming, Cycling, Reading; [ambition] To be an Architect;

ELLIOTT, KATE: [b] 13/12/89 London; [home] New Eltham, London; [p] Martin & Lesley; [school] Beaverwood; [fav sub] Technology; [hobbies] Singing & Acting; [pets] Hamster (Missy), Cats (Phoebe & Tabatha); [ambition] To be a famous Singer or Actress;

ELLIS, ISAAC: [b] 29/10/95 W. Mids; [home] Farnham, Surrey; [p] Johanne & Simon; [sister] Daisy; [school] St Peters CE Primary; [fav sub] Maths; [hobbies] Swimming & Reading stories; [ambition] To design toys, computer games and a Robot & help Mum with jobs;

ELLISON, LUCY: [b] 22/04/90; [home] Bingley, W. Yorks; [school] Bingley Grammar; [fav sub] French; [pets] Cat;

EMERSON TOBY: [b] 13/07/94 High Wycombe; [home] Chalfont St Peter, Bucks; [p] Janice & Guy; [sister] Bethany; [school] Gayhurst School; [fav sub] Art; [hobbies] Swimming;

ENGLISH, TIRION: [b] 18/09/92 Pontypridd; [home] West Ewell, Surrey; [p] Peter & Dora; [brothers] Arkady & Sebastian; [school] Stamford Green; [fav sub] PSHE; [hobbies] Horse Riding; [pets] Sea Monkeys; [ambition] To meet Mary Kate & Ashley and get a Dog;

ERRINGTON, SOPHIE MARIE: [b] 04/09/90 Chertsey; [home] Byfleet, Surrey; [p] Mandy & Mark Scholz-Conway; [brother] Harry; [school] St Marys CE Primary; [fav sub] PE; [hobbies] Horse Riding & Swimming; [pets] Hamster, Fish; [ambition] To become an Actress;

EXALL, GREGG: [b] 14/12/88 Worcester; [home] Worcester, Worcs; [p] Brian & Melanie; [brother] Gavin; [school] Nunnery Wood High; [fav sub] PE; [hobbies] Golf, Football, Skateboarding; [pets] Dog (Molly); [ambition] To visit Egypt and study Egyptology;

FAIRBRASS, KEELEY M.: [b] 23/09/88 Calgary, Canada; [home] Wilsden, W. Yorks; [p] Mark & Margaret; [sisters] Lizzie & Sally; [school] Bingley Grammar; [fav sub] Art; [hobbies] Horse Riding, Trampolining & Cricket;

FARMER, MARIE: [b] 16/09/85 Chelmsford; [home] Witham, Essex; [p] Linda & Joe; [brothers] Peter & Christopher; [school] Hayward School; [fav sub] Music & Theatre; [hobbies] Dance & Music; [pets] Fish, Bird, Rabbit;

FENNER, EMILY: [b] 04/08/90 Lewisham; [home] Bromley, Kent; [p] Julie & Martyn; [brothers] Alexander & Nicolas; [school] Babington House; [fav sub] English & Drama; [hobbies] Swimming; [pets] 2 Dogs (Dotty & Chester); [ambition] To work with Dogs;

FIDLER, CHLOE: [b] 28/08/93 Lowestoft; [home] Lowestoft, Suffolk; [p] Andy & Ros; [brother] Toby; [school] Whitton Green CP; [fav sub] Literacy; [hobbies] Playing outside & Swimming; [pets] 2 Cats (Daisy & Clyde); [ambition] To be a Pop Star or Fashion Designer;

FIELDHOUSE, GRACE: [b] 30/12/89 Bromley; [home] Bromley, Kent; [p] Linda & Stuart; [brother] Tom; [sister] Katy; [school] Babington House; [fav sub] Drama & English; [hobbies] Acting & Rounders; [pets] Seth, Wills, Pepys, Portia, Adrian, Phoenix & Dolly; [ambition] To become an Actress;

FISHER, THOMAS: [b] 06/07/93 King's Lynn; [home] King's Lynn, Norfolk; [school] South Wootton Junior; [fav sub] Technology; [hobbies] Collecting Dinosaurs & Book; [pets] Dog & Rabbits; [ambition] To be a Vet , I love animals;

FITZSIMONS, NICOLE LOUISE: [b] 03/10/91 Guildford; [p] Jackie & Tony; [sister] Michelle; [school] Worplesdon Primary; [fav sub] History; [hobbies] Dancing; [pets] Cat (Lucy), Rabbit (Blue Bell); [ambition] To become a Dancer;

FLETCHER, LAURA: [b] 01/11/92 Peterborough; [home] Bromsgrove, Worcs.; [p] Andrew & Sally; [sister] Kerry; [school] Charford First; [fav sub] Art, DT & Poetry; [hobbies] Swimming, Ice-Skating, Scootering; [pets] 2 Cats (Simba & Smudge); [ambition] To get more poems published;

FLETCHER, STEVEN: [b] 14/11/87 Chatham; [home] Milton Regis, Kent; [p] Shayne & Jackie; [sister] Amber; [school] Borden Grammar; [fav sub] Science; [hobbies] Rugby & Collecting Frogs; [pets] Dog (Benny);

FOOT, SAMANTHA: [b] 09/04/93 Aylesbury; [home] Burcott, Beds; [p] Sally & Mick; [brothers] John & Greg; [sister] Vicky; [school] Overstone; [fav sub] Science; [hobbies] Horse Riding; [pets] 3 Ponies & 4 Frogs; [ambition] To become a Vet;

FOUNTAIN, ZACHARY JORDAN: [b] 050893 King's Lynn; [home] King's Lynn, Norfolk; [p] Kevin & Catherine; [sisters] Scarlett Morgan & Martha Brogan; [school] South Wootton Junior; [fav sub] Maths; [hobbies] All Sports & Collecting things; [ambition] To become a Professional Footballer & play for England;

FOWLER, MOLLY CLAIR: [b] 11/01/94 Reading; [home] Caversham, Berks; [p] Helen & Noel; [school] Micklands Primary; [fav sub] History; [hobbies] Art, Rollerblading & Shopping; [pets] 5 Cats & 4 Kittens; [ambition] To become a Singer & Actress

FOX, DARREN: [b] 23/01/90 Crewe; [home] Winsford, Cheshire; [p] Martin & Deana; [brother] Daniel; [sister] Leanne; [school] Verdin High; [fav sub] Science; [hobbies] Watching Everton, Squash, Tennis & Playing football, [pets] Black Labrador (Campbell); [ambition] To be a Footballer and to be a Vet or work with animals;

FREESTONE, CRAIG: [b] 11/10/91 Barking; [home] Theydon Bois, Essex; [p] Susan & Andrew; [brothers] Stephen & James; [school] Theydon Bois CP; [fav sub] PE; [hobbies] Reading & Watching TV; [pets] 2 Dogs (Rover & Lady); [ambition] To be an Actor;

FREWIN, JOE WILLIAM: [b] 31/10/89 Watford; [home] Chipperfield, Herts; [p] Lynne & Tony; [brothers] Dominic & Gerard; [school] Kings Langley; [hobbies] Rugby; [ambition] To play Rugby for England;

FRITH, REBECCA: [b] 07/08/90 Gt. Yarmouth; [home] Belton, Norfolk; [p] Jamie & Philip; [brother] Alex; [school] Breydon Middle; [fav sub] PE, Art, Literacy; [hobbies] Football, Basketball, Dancing; [pets] Hamsters; [ambition] To become a member of the RSPCA Professionals;

FUENTES, BIANCA SOPHIA: [b] 03/03/92 Watford; [home] Watford, Herts; [p] Katy & Paul; [brother] Alex; [school] Knutsford JMI; [fav sub] History; [hobbies] Reading; [pets] Cat (Bueno), 2 Dogs (Jasper & Toby); [ambition] To become a Cartoonist;

FULTON, ELLEN: [b] 17/12/90 Watford; [home] Radlett, Herts; [p] Roger & Ros; [brother] Sean; [sister] Shelley; [school] Newberries Primary; [fav sub] Drama, PE & English; [hobbies] Singing, Dancing, Acting, Netball & Shopping; [pets] Cat (Caramel); [ambition] Not sure yet;

GALLOP, EMILY: [b] 21/10/90, Reading; [home] Theale, Berkshire; [p] Simon & Jackie; [brother] Thomas; [school] Park Lane Primary; [fav sub] English & Art; [hobbies] Swimming & Martial Arts; [pets] 2 Chinchillas;

GARBUTT, VICTORIA: [b] 08/04/90 Northallerton; [home] Boroughbridge, N. Yorks; [p] Brian & Saundra; [brother] John (21); [sister] Sara (23); [school] Ripon Grammar; [fav sub] Technology; [hobbies] Interior Desidn, Playing Piano, Gardening, Shopping, Pets & collecting dolls house miniatures; [pets] Hamster (Milly), Guinea Pig (Gin) & Rabbit (Thumper); [ambition] To be a Vet or Interior Designer;

GATES, CARLY: [b] 31/08/88 Maidstone; [home] Maidstone, Kent; [p] Tracey & Paul; [brother] Phillip; [school] Maidstone Girls Grammar; [fav sub] Science, Art & English; [hobbies] Drama, Dance, Swimming, Tennis & participating in the Duke of Edinburgh's Award Scheme; [pets] Hamster (Sparkie); [ambition] To go to Medical School and become a Paediatrician or become a children's writer;

GEORGE, RIYA: [b] 16/04/90 India; [p] Dr & Mrs George; [brother] Reuben; [school] Babington House; [fav sub] History, French & R.E.; [hobbies] Reading & Sports; [pets] Cat; [ambition] To be a Teacher or Doctor;

GILBERT, JESSICA: [b] 19/09/90 King's Lynn; [home] South Wootton, Norfolk; [p] Amanda & Tim; [brother] Charlie; [sister] Lucy; [school] South Wootton Junior; [fav sub] Art & Music; [hobbies] Playing Cornet & Football; [pets] Cat (Daisy), Dogs (Ben & Bailey); [ambition] To work with young children;

GILES, KRYSTINA: [b] 05/10/89 Worcester; [home] Worcester, Worcs; [p] Ashley & Heather; [brother] James; [sisters] Clare & Patricia; [school] Nunnery Wood High; [fav sub] Design,

Technology & Art; [hobbies] Dancing & Guides; [pets] Dog (Megan); [ambition] To become a Lawyer;

GILLING, GEORGINA RAINE: [b] 02/05/95 Deal; [home] Deal, Kent; [p] Cheryl Joann & Giles Richard; [sister] Emilia Faye; [school] Sandown Primary; [fav sub] Writing Stories; [hobbies] Reading & Cycling; [pets] Pond Fish, but I love dogs, cats & collecting insects; [ambition] To be an Archaeologist;

GODDARD, GEORGE: [b] 12/04/96 Maidstone; [home] Maidstone, Kent; [p] Samantha & Glen; [brothers] Charlie & Harry; [school] Molehill Copse Primary; [fav sub] Literacy & Reading; [hobbies] Swimming & writing stories; [pets] Dog (Gemma); [ambition] To be a Train Driver or Policeman;

GODDARD, LEA: [b] 15/05/96 Hastings; [home] Hastings, E. Sussex; [p] Tina & David; [sister] Maya; [school] Hollington Primary; [fav sub] English; [hobbies] Ballet & Tap; [pets] Cat (Mitzie); [ambition] To become a Ballerina;

GOMEZ, ABIGAIL: [b] 16/12/93 Ashford, Middx; [home] Powick, Worcs; [p] Rachael & Benson; [brothers] Ross, John; [school] Kempsey Primary; [fav sub] Art; [hobbies] Swimming; [pets] Cat (Tuna); [ambition] To become a Vet;

GOOCH, ELEANOR: [b] 18/10/91 Harlow; [home] Theydon Bois, Essex; [p] Peter & Lynn; [brothers] James, Peter, Robert; [school] Theydon Bois Primary; [fav sub] PE; [hobbies] Badminton & Netball; [pets] 3 Rabbits, 2 Fish, 1 Mouse & a Hamster; [ambition] To be a well known runner or gymnast;

GOODY, GEORGE E.: [b] 30/06/95 Exeter; [home] Exeter, Devon; [p] Dawn; [school] Montgomery Combined; [fav sub] Butterflies; [hobbies] Swimming & Skating; [pets] Rabbit (Ruby);

GOSS, AMY: [b] 18/09/91 Aylesbury; [home] Wing, Beds; [p] Janet & Trevor; [sister] Hayley; [school] Overstone Combined; [fav sub] Games; [hobbies] Tennis & Swimming; [pets] Hamsters; [ambition] To be a Tennis Player or an Author;

GRAHAM-COOMBES, ELEANOR: [b] 03/11/94 Oxford; [home] Middle Barton, Oxon; [p] Lynden & Zoe; [brother] Charles; [sister] Olivia; [school] Middle Barton Primary; [fav sub] Art; [hobbies] Drawing & Painting; [pets] Goldfish; [ambition] To swim with Dolphins and be a successful Hairdresser;

GRAINGE, JAMES RICHARD: [b] 10/06/88 Northallerton; [home] Well, N. Yorks; [p] Kathy & David; [brother] Philip; [school] Ripon Grammar; [fav sub] English; [hobbies] Acting & Reading; [pets] Greyhounds; [ambition] To be an Actor, Commentator or Writer;

GRAY, JAMIE: [b] 25/09/94 Reading; [home] Reading, Berks; [p] Abigail & Matthew; [brother] Sam; [school] Micklands Primary; [fav sub] Science; [hobbies] Computer & Cycling; [pets] 2 Kittens & 2 Hamsters; [ambition] To become a Policeman;

GREGORY, ALYX: [b] 08/06/94 Reading; [home] Earley, Berks; [p] John & Terri; [brothers] Jack & Callum; [school] Loddon Junior; [fav sub] Art & Literacy; [hobbies] Drama, Singing & Dancing; [ambition] To be a Pop Star or Author;

GREPNE, THOMAS: [b] 26/10/90 Reading; [home] Reading, Berks; [p] Sarah & Marcus; [sister] Rachael; [school] Micklands Primary; [fav sub] Literacy; [hobbies] Football, Cars & Bikes; [pets] Cockatiels & Fish; [ambition] To become a Footballer;

GRIFFITHS, LUCY: [b] 02/05/91 Reading; [home] Reading, Berks; [p] Melanie & David; [brother] Jack; [school] Park Lane Primary; [fav sub] Science; [hobbies] Reading & playing music; [pets] Dog, Guinea Pigs, Hamsters, Budgies & Fish; [ambition] To become a good musician at grade 8;

GROUT, RACHEL: [b] 23/07/90 Norwich; [home] Cromer, Norfolk; [p] Stella & Billy; [brother] Sam; [school] Cromer High; [fav sub] PE; [hobbies] Athletics & Reading; [pets] Dog (Flossie) & Guinea Pig (Crumble); [ambition] To be an Author;

HACKING, SOPHIE: [b] 17/06/90 Beckenham; [home] Beckenham, Kent; [p] Deborah & Mark; [brother] William; [school] Babington House; [fav sub] German, English, Drama; [hobbies] Dance, Drama & Singing; [ambition] To be an Actress, Dancer or Waitress;

HADEN, LAURA: [b] 01/08/92 Banbury; [home] Shottswell, Oxon; [p] Julie & Mykee; [brother] James; [school] Hornton Primary; [fav sub] English & Art; [hobbies] Horse Riding; [pets] Ponies (Toby & Messy Jessie; [ambition] To be in the Olympic Riding Team;

HAGUE, ELIZABETH: [b] 16/09/92 Sheffield; [home] Darley Dale, Derbyshire; [p] Sarah & Stephen; [sister] Charlotte; [school] Darley Dale Primary; [fav sub] English; [hobbies] Playing the flute & dancing - Ballet, Tap & Modern; [pets] 2 Cats (Treacle & Pudding); [ambition] To be a Lawyer and Writer;

HAILEY, KATY: [b] 04/08/94 Dover; [home] Walmer, Kent; [p] Sal & Perry; [sister] Lizzie; [school] Sandown CP; [fav sub] Maths; [hobbies] Swimming & Cricket; [ambition] To be an Author or Maths Teacher;

HAILWOOD, MEGAN ROSE: [b] 09/09/90 Ormskirk; [home] Mawdesley, Lancs; [brothers] Josh & Jake; [school] Richard Durnings Endowed; [fav sub] Art & Gym; [hobbies] Member of Wigan Harriers Athletic Club; [pets] 2 Cats (Sugar & Spice); [ambition] To be a Vet & to swim with Dolphins;

HAINES, NATALIE: [b] 07/03/90 Sidcup; [home] Bexley, Kent; [p] Mark & Debbie; [sister] Michelle; [school] Beaverwood School for Girls; [fav sub] Art; [hobbies] Drawing & Dancing; [pets] Dog (Milly), Cat (Josie); [ambition] To work in Sea World or be a Vet;

HALL, NATHAN: [b] 13/08/93 Frome; [home] Frome, Somerset; [p] Jane & Chris; [brother] Rory; [school] Mells First; [fav sub] History; [hobbies] Golf & Cubs; [pets] Jaws the Fish; [ambition] To become a Golfer;

HAM, CHARLOTTE: [b] 14/04/92 Yeovil; [home] Horsington, Somerset; [p] Judith & Andrew; [sisters] Emily & Isabelle; [school] Horsington Primary; [fav sub] Art; [hobbies] Netball & Gymnastics; [pets] Dog (Ruby); [ambition] To be a Pop Star!!

HAMMOND, LAUREN: [b] 03/02/93 Lowestoft; [home] Lowestoft, Suffolk; [p] Mark & Julie; [brother] Philip; [sister] Amy; [school] Whitton Green Primary; [fav sub] Art; [hobbies] Reading; [pets] Dog & Hamster; [ambition] To be a Journalist;

HARDEN, SACHA: [b] 19/05/91 Staines; [home] Egham, Surrey; [p] Peter; [brother] Kerry; [sister] Siân; [school] Kingscroft Junior; [fav sub] Maths; [hobbies] Karate & Music; [ambition] To become a Journalist;

HARLAND, ABIGAIL: [b] 11/05/92 Chatham; [home] Sittingbourne, Kent; [p] Linsey & Andrew; [brother] Ashley; [school] Murston Junior; [fav sub] Maths; [hobbies] Netball & Dancing; [ambition] To excel in all that I do;

HARLOW, CLARE: [b] 31/07/88 Harlow; [home] Saffron Walden, Essex; [p] Lorraine & Jon; [brothers] Owen & Joseph; [school] The Perse School for Girls; [fav sub] Biology, History & Games; [hobbies] Cycling, Walking, Cinema; [pets] Guinea Pigs (Frizzy, Lizzie & Fanta), Bernese Mountain Dog (Tess); [ambition] To live and teach in Scotland;

HARRISON, LISA MARIE: [b] 12/09/92 Maidstone; [home] Maidstone, Kent; [p] Malcolm & Janet; [brother] Anthony; [school] Molehill Copse CP; [fav sub] Mathematics; [hobbies] Sport; [pets] Boxer Dog (Bruno); [ambition] To become an Actress or Teacher;

HART, SEBASTIAN: [b] 08/01/92 Walthamstow; [home] Epping, Essex; [p] Dawn & Owen; [brother] Christian; [school] Epping Junior; [fav sub] PE; [hobbies] Cubs, Playing Golf & Football; [pets] Woody, Mice, Bird & Fish; [ambition] To become an Astronaut and travel to Mars;

HARVEY, CARL: [b] 07/10/89 Winsford; [home] Winsford, Cheshire; [p] Raymond & Jasmine; [brother] Ben; [school] Verdin High; [fav sub] PE; [hobbies] Football; [pets] Cat (Fabia) & Rabbit (Harry); [ambition] To be a Professional Footballer;

HARVEY, LUCY: [b] 06/03/92 Orsett; [home] Nazeing, Essex; [p] Colin & Teresa; [brothers] Charlie & Alfie; [sister] Kelly; [school] Epping Junior; [fav sub] PE & Maths; [hobbies] Swimming; [pets] 3 Dogs; [ambition] To do well at School;

HAWKINS, THOMAS: [b] 11/01/91 Canterbury; [home] Herne, Kent; [p] Patrick & Anne; [school] Herne Junior; [fav sub] Art, Games, D.T., English; [hobbies] Playing Roller Hockey, Rugby, Cricket & Golf, Skateboarding & Skating; [pets] 2 Rabbits (Snowy & Floppy); [ambition] To play Roller Hockey for England or be the next Tiger Woods;

HAYES-WATKINS, SCOTT: [home] Deal, Kent; [school] Sandown CP; [fav sub] History; [hobbies] Karate, Cubs, Reading & Rugby; [pets] Dog, Cat & Hamster;

HEAPS, DEAN: [b] 16/06/92 Preston; [home] Preston, Lancs; [p] Steven & Jacky; [sister] Emma; [school] Holy Family RC Primary; [fav sub] English; [hobbies] Swimming, Ju-Jitsu, Keyboard; [ambition] To swim in the Olympic Games;

HENDERSON, NATASHA: [b] 11/10/91 Plymouth; [home] Bere Alston, Devon; [p] Linda & Mark; [school] Bere Alston CP; [fav sub] PE; [hobbies] Computer & Dancing; [pets] Dog (Penny), Rabbit (Benjamin); [ambition] To become an Actress;

HICKLING, HETTIE: [b] 18/02/90 Sidcup; [home] Chislehurst, Kent; [p] Nicola & Sam; [brother] Alexander; [sister] Eleanor; [school] Bromley High; [fav sub] Art & Drama; [hobbies] Horse Riding & Art; [pets] Rabbit (Flopsy); [ambition] To be an Interior Designer;

HICKS, RHIANNE: [b] 19/09/95 Epping; [home] Theydon Bois, Essex; [p] Vicky & Mike; [sister] Josie; [school] Theydon Bois Primary; [fav sub] Art; [hobbies] Dancing, Rainbows; [ambition] To go Scuba Diving, be a Lifeguard and be a Fashion Designer/Artist;

HIGDON, LAURIE S.: [b] 21/03/90 Stockport; [home] Barnstaple, N. Devon; [p] Christine & Malcolm; [sister] Bryony; [school] Braunton School; [fav sub] Music & Art; [hobbies] Shopping & Dancing; [pets] 2 Dogs; [ambition] To be a Musician or Lawyer

HILL, CHRISTOPHER: [b] 13/09/93 Epping; [home] Epping, Essex; [p] Keith & Vivienne; [sister] Jenny; [school] Epping Junior; [fav sub] Art; [hobbies] Rugby, Swimming, Cubs, Guitar; [pets] Black Labrador (Tumble) & 5 Goldfish; [ambition] To be a Scientist or a Builder;

HOLLISTER, HAYLEY: [b] 09/03/93 Abergavenny; [home] Llanfoist, Monmouthshire; [p] Helen & Lee; [sister] Cerys; [school] Our Lady & St Michael's RC Primary; [fav sub] Art; [hobbies] Swimming, Dancing, Brownies; [ambition] To design book covers & write poems;

HOLMES, CARLY: [b] 18/12/87 Harrow; [home] Coulsdon, Surrey; [p] Sue & Des; [brother] Lee; [school] Wallington High School for Girls; [fav sub] History; [hobbies] Horse Riding, Reading; [pets] Dog (Holly); [ambition] To become a Veterinary Surgeon;

HOLMES, GEORGIA MAE: [b] 26/07/93 Bradford; [home] Bradford, W. Yorks.; [p] Neil & Bev Holmes; [brother] James Kendall; [sisters] Laura Upton & Grace Holmes; [school] Wellington Primary; [fav sub] Art & DT; [hobbies] Playing with pets; [pets] Rabbits, Cat, Fish & Hamster; [ambition] To be a Vet;

HOOD, REBECCA: [b] 18/10/90 Reading; [home] Tilehurst, Berks; [p] Tony & Caroline; [brother] Ryan; [school] Park Lane Primary; [fav sub] Art; [hobbies] Art & Sport; [pets] Budgie (Charlie); [ambition] To become a Cartoon Animator;

HOPE, AMY LOUISE: [b] 07/09/88 Worcester; [home] Worcester, Worcs.; [p] Andrew & Jude; [sister] Sophie Kate; [school] Bishop Perowne High; [fav sub] Drama; [hobbies] Football & Reading; [pets] Cat (Blod); [ambition] To be a TV Presenter;

HOPKINSON, THEO: [b] 25/10/91 Hammersmith; [home] Esher, Surrey; [p] Jo & Frank; [brother] Isaac; [sister] Hetty; [school] Thames Ditton Juniors; [fav sub] Literacy; [hobbies] Warhammer, Rugby, Football, Reading; [ambition] To become a Writer or Rugby Player;

HORWOOD, JULIETTE: [b] 01/07/93 High Wycombe; [home] Little Chalfont, Bucks; [p] Paul & Helen; [sister] Victoria; [school] High March; [fav sub] Art & Maths; [hobbies] Horse Riding, Gymnastics; [pets] Dog & 2 Fish; [ambition] To be a Three Day Eventer & a Vet;

HUFF, GREGORY MARTIN: [b] 09/06/95 Theydon Bois; [home] Theydon Bois, Essex; [p] Martin & Julie; [brother] Jonathan (9); [sister] Hannah (3); [school] Theydon Bois Primary; [fav sub] Maths; [hobbies] Football & Chess; [ambition] To be a Headteacher and make up all the rules!

HUGHES, MADDY: [b] 08/01/93 Blackpool; [home] Fleetwood, Lancs; [p] Elizabeth & David; [brothers] Elliot & David; [school] St Mary's RC Primary; [fav sub] Mathematics; [hobbies] Keyboard, Swimming & Brownies; [pets] Rats (Sugar & Candy); [ambition] To be a Vet;

HUGHES, SOPHIE KAY: [b] 01/10/91; [home] Nazeing, Essex; [p] Sharon & Dennis; [school] Epping Junior; [fav sub] ICT, PE & Art; [hobbies] Gameboy & Drawing; [pets] Dog (Amber), Guinea Pig (Dusty) [ambition] To be an Author;

HUNJAN, APRIA: [b] 08/04/93 Croydon; [home] Reading, Berks; [p] Salinder & Paramjeet; [brother] Hartaj; [school] Loddon Junior; [fav sub] Design & Technology; [hobbies] Singing, Dancing & Swimming; [ambition] To be a Singer, Writer or Poet;

HULIN, RACHEL: [b] 1990 Trowbridge; [home] Melksham, Wilts; [p] Jane & Rob; [school] Corsham School; [fav sub] Drama & Art; [hobbies] Running; [pets] Hamster & 2 Fish; [ambition] To be a Nanny or a Runner;

HUZAR, TIM: [b] 07/02/87 Ash; [home] Ash, Surrey; [p] Paul & Jacky; [brother] Lois; [sister] Bryony; [school] Ash Manor; [fav sub] English; [hobbies] Writing & Skating; [pets] 3 Cats; [ambition] To become an Author;

INGHAM, TARA LOUISE: [b] 11/10/92 Ipswich; [home] Ipswich, Suffolk; [p] Mark & Wendy; [brother] Luke; [school] Downing Primary; [fav sub] Maths; [hobbies] Swimming & Football; [ambition] To become a Vet;

ISON, OLIVER: [b] 25/10/92 Peterborough; [home] South Wootton, Norfolk; [p] Nick & Fiona; [brother] Jonathan; [school] South Wootton Junior; [fav sub] Art & Technology; [hobbies] Rugby, Football, Skiing; [pets] Guinea Pig (Munchie); [ambition] To play football for Liverpool;

JACKSON, LUKE: [b] 26/11/92 Harrogate; [home] Boroughbridge, N. Yorks.; [p] John & Lesley; [brothers] Lee, Anthony, Scott & Lewis; [sister] Vicky; [school] Roecliffe CE Primary; [fav sub] Maths; [hobbies] Football, Gameboy & Playstation; [pets] Chocolate Labrador (Max); [ambition] To enjoy life;

JAMES, THOMAS: [b] 16/07/96 Maidstone; [home] Maidstone, Kent; [p]

David & Suzanne; [sisters] Millie & Ellie; [school] Molehill Copse Primary; [fav sub] English; [hobbies] Cycling & Puzzles; [ambition] To work with Computers;

JANES, EMELYE SIAN: [b] 13.05/92 Reading; [home] Tilehurst, Berks; [p] Lee & Elaine; [brothers] Joshua & Ciaran; [sisters] Charlotte & Jessica; [school] Park Lane Primary; [fav sub] English; [hobbies] Swimming, Walking & Music; [pets] Budgies, Tortoise & Fish; [ambition] To be a Marine Biologist and to see Tigers in the wild;

JANES, JESSICA AMY: [b] [b] 13/05/92 Reading; [home] Tilehurst, Berks; [p] Lee & Elaine; [brothers] Joshua & Ciaran; [sisters] Charlotte & Emelye; [school] Park Lane Primary; [fav sub] English; [hobbies] Swimming, Flute & Violin; [pets] Budgies, Tortoise & Fish; [ambition] To live in Africa and to see Pandas in the wild;

JANIK, SOPHIE: [b] 31/08/93 Gloucester; [home] Uley, Glos; [p] Delia; [sister] Eleanor; [school] Uley CE Primary; [fav sub] Art & DT; [hobbies] Horse Riding & Drawing; [pets] Black Cat (Milo); [ambition] To be a Vet or a house sitter for animals, or a Dancer & Pop Star!

JEFFERIES, ALITIA: [b] 08/02/92 Stevenage; [home] Stevenage, Herts; [p] Leigh & Lauraine; [brother] Shane; [school] Woolenwick Junior; [fav sub] Art, PE & History; [hobbies] Swimming, Running, Skipping & Basketball; [pets] 2 Rats (Monica & Phoebe); [ambition] To be a Model & to swim with Dolphins;

JEFFERYS, KATE: [b] 11/02/88 Maidstone; [home] West Malling, Kent; [p] Robert & Beverley; [brother] Christian; [school] Maidstone Girls Grammar; [fav sub] History; [hobbies] Cinema & Reading; [pets] Hamster (Russel); [ambition] To be a Teacher;

JENKINS, EMILY: [b] 18/10/89 Cromer; [home] Cromer, Norfolk; [p] Carol & Andrew; [sister] Laura; [school] Cromer High; [fav sub] English & Science; [hobbies] Dancing; [pets] Hamster; [ambition] To become a Doctor or an Architect;

JENKINS, HAYLEY: [b] 22/05/89 Worcester; [home] Worcester, Worcs; [p] Sharon & Neil; [brother] Daniel; [sister] Kelly; [school] Nunnery Wood High; [fav sub] English; [hobbies] Voluntary work at a Reptilian Pet Shop & Music; [pets] Tortoise (Shelly), 2 Bearded Dragons, 2 Giant Millipedes, and a Casked Head frog; [ambition] To work with animals possibly as a Veternary Nurse or similar;

JERROMES, CHRISTIAN: [b] 29/01/91 Redditch; [home] Catshill, Worcs; [p] Andrea & David; [school] Catshill Middle; [fav sub] Maths; [hobbies] Playing the Drums; [ambition] To be a world class drummer;

JESSOP, KATY: [b] 03/01/96 Eastbourne; [home] Eastbourne, E. Sussex; [p] Jacqui & Mark; [brother] Isaac; [school] Roselands C.I.; [fav sub] Writing, Literacy; [hobbies] Dancing, Swimming & Drawing; [pets] Cat (Cleo); [ambition] To own a Dog, go to Disneyland and to be a Dog Catcher;

JEWELL, JENNIFER ELIZABETH: [b] 28/01/93 Aylesbury; [home] Wing, Beds; [p] Malcolm & Margaret Elizabeth; [sister] Deborah Charlotte; [school] Overstone Combined; [fav sub] English; [hobbies] Swimming & Gymnastics; [pets] Tabby cat (Wally) & Black cat (Tramp); [ambition] To be a Policewoman;

JOHNSON, ALEXANDER: [b] 26/06/90 Watford; [home] Kings Langley, Herts; [p] Pieter & Jane; [brother] Anthony; [school] Kings Langley; [fav sub] ICT; [hobbies] Football; [pets] Dog (Star); [ambition] To be a Professional Footballer (in goal);

JOLLEY, RACHEL ANNE: [b] 12/10/90 King's Lynn; [home] King's Lynn, Norfolk; [p] Nicole & Anthony; [brother] Simon; [school] South Wootton Junior; [fav sub] Science; [hobbies] Netball, Tennis, Football, Table Tennis, Gymnastics, Badminton; [pets] Dogs (Lucy & De-De), Cats (Blacky, Amy, Katy & Zak); [ambition] To be a Veterinary Nurse;

JONES, DAVID: [b] 23/05/02 Brighton; [home] Braunton, N. Devon; [p] Tim & Liz; [brothers] Stevie & Mikey; [school] Braunton Comprehensive; [ambition] To be a Marine Biologist;

JONES, GARETH: [b] 26/03/89 Aldershot; [home] Ash, Surrey; [p] Andrew & Lorraine; [sisters] Eleanor & Laura; [school] Ash Manor; [fav sub] Drama; [hobbies] Swimming; [ambition] To be in a Band;

JONES, HANNAH: [b] 09/06/02 Bury St Edmunds; [home] Dovercourt, Essex; [p] Debbie & Ian; [sister] Meredith; [school] St Joseph's RC Primary; [fav sub] PE; [hobbies] Swimming, Dancing (Ballet, Tap & Modern); [pets] Dog (Wizzywig);

JONES, POLLYANNA: [b] 31/01/92 Guildford; [home] Guildford, Surrey; [p] Graham & Chriss; [brothers] Alfie & Isaac; [school] Worplesdon Primary; [fav sub] French; [hobbies] Horse Riding, Art & Writing; [pets] Cat (Ivana), Hamster (Boo); [ambition] To become a Vet;

KEEP, CHRISTOPHER: [b] 08/01/94 Reading; [home] Reading, Berks; [p] Alison & Michael; [brothers] Ashley, Jamie & Nathan; [school] Park Lane Primary; [fav sub] Maths & English; [hobbies] Football; [pets] Cat, Hamster; [ambition] To become a Chef;

KENDALL, LISA: [b] 19/04/89 Preston; [home] Hoghton, Lancs; [p] Carl & Sandra; [sister] Nicola; [school] St Michael's CE High; [fav sub] English; [hobbies] Playing with pets & Trampoline; [pets] 2 Dogs (Spike & Bobby), 1 Rabbit & 2 Guinea Pigs; [ambition] To work with animals maybe as a Vet;

KENNERLEY, ADAM STUART: [b] 12/09/90 Stockport; [home] New Mills, High Peak; [p] Andrew & Antoinette; [brother] Jack; [fav sub] Design & Technology; [hobbies] Football, Tennis, Animals; [ambition] To become a Marine Biologist;

KETCHEN, EMILY: [b] 16/05/90 Taunton; [home] Watchet, Somerset; [p] Barbara & John (Deceased); [brothers] David & Martyn; [sister] Laura; [school] Danesfield Middle; [fav sub] Design & Technology; [hobbies] Hockey & Tennis; [pets] Cat, Bird, Fish; [ambition] To become a Policewoman;

KINVIG, CORINNE: [b] 17/03/90 Crewe; [home] Winsford, Cheshire; [p] Valerie & David; [brothers] Craig, Liam & Kieran; [school] Verdin High; [fav sub] PE; [hobbies] Running & Swimming; [ambition] To be an Athlete;

KIRKMAN, LEWIS VINCENT: [b] 26/02/88 Basildon; [home] Basildon, Essex; [p] Hilary & Paul; [brother] David Thomas; [school] Woodlands Secondary; [fav sub] History; [hobbies] Juggling, Unicycle & modelling Balloons; [pets] 2 rescued Cats; [ambition] To become a Pharmacist;

KIRTON, ROSIE: [b] 04/08/88 Hitchin; [home] Hitchin, Herts; [p] Sarah; [sisters] Chloe & Florence; [school] Hitchin Girls'; [fav sub] English & Art; [hobbies] Writing stories & poems; Drama, Drawing & listening to Nu-Metal Music; [ambition] To become a successful Writer, Artist or Actress;

KNIGHT, DAVID: [b] 02/07/93 Abergavenny; [home] Abergavenny, Monmouthshire; [p] Gareth & Cheryl; [school] Our Lady & St Michaels RC Primary; [fav sub] Mathematics; [hobbies] Football, Rugby & Judo; [ambition] To be a Footballer;

KNIGHT, MICHAEL: [b] 28/05/90 Leighton; [home] Moulton, Cheshire; [p] Anne & Chris; [brother] Alexander; [sister] Stephanie; [school] The County High; [fav sub] Maths; [hobbies] Playing Chess; [pets] Dog (Pippa);

KOTOPOULOS, THOMAS: [b] 10/11/93 Greece; [home] Cranmore,

Somerset; [p] Dean & Susan; [brother] Nik; [school] Mells First; [fav sub] Maths; [hobbies] Rounders; [pets] Dog (Kipper); [ambition] To invent playstation games;

LACOVARA, LOUIS: [b] 04/05/94 London; [home] Aston Abbotts, Bucks; [p] Lisa & Matthew; [sister] Ria; [school] Overstone Combined; [fav sub] Maths; [hobbies] Horse Riding; [pets] Pony (Harry), Dogs (Missy & Tom); [ambition] To become a Jockey;

LAKE, DARREN PETER: [b] 28/06/91 Plymouth; [home] Bere Alston, Devon; [p] Andrew & Nicola; [brother] Steven; [school] Bere Alston CP; [fav sub] Maths; [hobbies] Playstation & Football; [ambition] To join the Parachute Regiment;

LAKEY, JAMIE ROBYN: [b] 07/12/90 Plymouth; [home] Pensilva, Cornwall; [p] Julie & Paul; [brother] Gareth James; [school] Pensilva Primary; [fav sub] English; [hobbies] Swimming & Music; [pets] 2 Cats (Muska & Pepsi); [ambition] To be a Make Up Artist;

LAKHANI, ANJLI: [b] 24/09/87 Cambridge; [home] Impington, Cambridge; [p] Suil & Bindu; [sisters] Anisha & Ashna; [school] Perse School for Girls; [fav sub] Chemistry; [hobbies] Singing & Dancing; [ambition] To become a Lawyer;

LAMBERT, CHRISTOPHER: [b] 12/07/96 Colchester; [home] Monk Soham, Suffolk; [p] Jacqueline & Mark; [school] Bedfield Primary; [fav sub] All subjects; [hobbies] Tractors, Farming & Animals; [pets] Chickens, Guinea Pigs, Cat, Horse; [ambition] To be a Farmer;

LANDER, JESSICA: [b] 26/11/90 Ormskirk; [home] Parbold, Lancs; [p] Ann-Marie & Jim; [brother] Tom; [sisters] Marie Therese, Sarah & Katie; [school] Richard Durnings; [fav sub] Art & Technology; [hobbies] Gymnastics & Dancing; [pets] Rabbit (Max); [ambition] To be an Actress or Dancer;

LANGFORD, SALLY: [b] 23/05/87 Tiverton; [home] Bideford, Devon; [p] Shirley & Dave; [brothers] Tom, Jack & Sam; [sister] Sarah; [school] Bideford College; [fav sub] Drama; [hobbies] Sport; [pets] Cats (Zippy & Lucy); [ambition] To play Tennis for my County;

LATIMER, BEN: [b] 02/11/93 Aylesbury; [home] Stewkley, Bucks; [brother] Daniel; [school] Overstone Combined; [fav sub] Sport; [hobbies] Football, Rugby, Cycling; [pets] Guinea Pig (Lightning);

LEE, JOSH: [b] 18/12/91 Harlow; [home] Theydon Bois, Essex; [p] Donna & Steven; [brothers] Jamie, Jake & Jordan; [school] Theydon Bois Primary; [fav sub] Art; [hobbies] Painting Warhammer Models; [ambition] To do well in all subjects at school;

LEIGHTON, FREDDIE: [b] 10/03/92 Harlow; [home] Epping, Essex; [p] Caroline & Mark; [brothers] Sam & Archie; [school] Epping Junior; [fav sub] Science; [hobbies] Collecting James Bond material; [ambition] To be a Film Star;

LEMAN, BILLY: [b] 01/11/95 Frimley; [home] Farnham, Surrey; [p] Bill & Claire; [brother] Bradley; [sister] Alice; [school] St Peter's Primary; [fav sub] Art; [hobbies] Drawing & Football; [pets] Hamster (Herman) & Parrot (Zulu); [ambition] To become a Fireman;

LEWIS, CHRISTOPHER R.: [b] 14/03/93 Braintree; [home] Braintree, Essex; [p] Malcolm & Jacqueline; [brother] Daniel; [sister] Jessica; [school] Great Bradfords Junior; [fav sub] Design Technology; [hobbies] Football, Tennis, Swimming; [pets] Rabbits (Bubble & Dusty), Gerbil (Jonathan); [ambition] To invent computer games;

LEWIS, HANNAH AMELIA: [b] 21/11/92 Cambridge; [home] Cambridge, Cambs; [p] Annabelle & Steve; [brother] Charlie (4); [school] Queen Edith Community Primary; [fav sub] PE & Maths; [hobbies] Sports & Reading; [pets] Golden Retriever (Gemma-11), Collie Cross (Tiggy-14); [ambition] To be a Vet and to travel the World and have a pet dog;

LEWIS, RUBY: [b] 02/07/93 Hemel Hempstead; [home] Wing, Beds; [p] John & Kay; [sister] Maya; [school] Overstone Combined; [fav sub] Art; [hobbies] Writing, Dancing & Singing; [pets] Hamster (Spike); [ambition] To be a famous Actress or Artist;

LINGLEY, HANNAH RIANE: [b] 25/11/87 Stevenage; [home] Stevenage, Herts; [p] Richard & Karen; [sisters] Emma & Sarah; [school] Hitchin Girls School; [fav sub] Art; [hobbies] Dancing & Drawing; [pets] Fish, Dog & Guinea Pig; [ambition] To become an Artist;

LOCKHART, CHELSEY-LEIGH: [b] 05/11/90 Plymouth; [home] Bere Alston, Devon; [p] Steve & Amanda; [sister] Paris-Jade; [school] Bere Alston Primary; [fav sub] IT; [hobbies] Horse Riding, Youth Club & Clothes shopping; [pets] 3 Dogs, 2 Cats, 2 Guinea Pigs, 1 parrot, 1 Snake & Horse (Tia) [ambition] To be a Vet, go to Australia & own my own stables and horses;

LORD, MATTHEW: [b] 05/08/91 London; [home] Theydon Bois, Essex; [school] Theydon Bois Primary; [fav sub] PE & Maths; [hobbies] All Sports; [ambition] To become a Professional Golfer;

LOWMAN, EMMA: [b] 03/12/90 Chertsey; [home] Byfleet, Surrey; [p] Steve & Debbie; [sisters] Sarah & Laura; [school] St Mary's CE Primary; [fav sub] Drama; [hobbies] Singing & dancing to Gareth Gates; [pets] Hamster, Cat; [ambition] To be famous and meet Gareth Gates;

LUCAS, JENNY: [b] 21/07/02 London; [home] Theydon Bois, Essex; [p] Glenn & Kathy; [twin brother] James; [school] Theydon Bois Primary; [fav sub] Art & English; [hobbies] Drawing & Dancing; [pets] Silver Tabby Cat (Charky); [ambition] To be a Pop Star, Writer or Artist;

LUCAS, REBEKAH: [b] 16/06/90 Barnstaple; [home] Braunton, Devon; [p] Neil & Jo; [brother] Michael; [school] Braunton; [fav sub] Drama & English; [hobbies] Singing, Dancing & Drama; [pets] 2 Cats (Rosa & Garfield); [ambition] To be an Actress in Musicals;

LUTY, KATE: [b] 30/04/93; [home] Threshfield, N. Yorks.; [p] Nicholas & Anne; [sister] Ruth; [school] Threshfield Primary; [fav sub] Maths; [hobbies] Horse Riding;

MACKEY, MARCELLA: [b] 11/04/93 Harrow; [home] Chalfont St Peter, Bucks; [p] George & Ellen; [brother] Myles; [sister] Claudia; [school] High March; [fav sub] Art; [hobbies] Drawing, Sewing, Line Dancing; [pets] Dog (Thunder), Rabbit (Dusty); [ambition] to become a Fashion Designer;

MADDISON, JACK: [b] 11/12/93 Colchester; [home] Dovercourt, Essex; [p] Don & Margaret; [sisters] Kirsty, Joanna & Louise; [school] St Josephs RC Primary; [fav sub] Maths; [hobbies] Computer Games; [pets] Dog (Bouncer); [ambition] To be a computer expert;

MADGE, WILLIAM: [b] 09/03/93 Plymouth; [home] Ivybridge, Devon; [p] David & Janet; [school] Stowford Primary; [fav sub] History; [hobbies] Rugby, Football, Golf, Playing the piano & clarinet; [pets] Cat, Stick Insects & Fish; [ambition] To become a Poet!

MAKIN, CHLOE: [b] 13/03/95 Croydon; [home] Sanderstead, Surrey; [p] Nicki Makin & Paul Sullivan; [sister] Alicia Makin; [school] Hamsey Green Infants; [fav sub] Art; [hobbies] Dancing, Reading & Writing; [pets] Hamster (Snowball); [ambition] To be a Poet or Dancer (Ballerina);

MARINARO, RICKY: [b] 20/10/87 Milton Keynes; [home] Braunton, N. Devon; [p] Wendy & Pasquale; [brother] Joshua; [school] Braunton School; [fav sub] PE; [hobbies] Football; [ambition] To do well in life;

MARKER, SAMUEL: [b] 08/06/93 Blackburn; [home] Ivybridge, Devon; [p] Nick & Liz; [sister] Gemma; [school] Stowford Primary; [fav sub] Maths; [hobbies] Football & Cubs; [pets] Kitten (Socks); [ambition] To be a professional Footballer;

MARSDEN, JESSICA-PAIGE: [b] 03/03/93 Preston; [home] Preston, Lancs; [p] Karen & Peter; [brother] Jake (12); [sisters] Hannah, Adelle (12), Vicky (13), Nicola (15), Leanne (18); [school] Holy Family Primary; [fav sub] Maths & PE; [hobbies] Dancing & Swimming; [pets] Cat (Molly); [ambition] To be happy forever!;

MARTIN, NOEL: [b] 25/12/92 Hastings; [home] Hastings, E. Sussex; [p] Meseret; [sister] Natalie; [school] Hollington Primary; [fav sub] Maths; [hobbies] Football; [ambition] To be a Footballer;

MARTIN, OLLIE: [b] 22/05/92 Bristol; [home] Mells, Somerset; [p] John & Sophie; [brother] Bàl; [sister] Minty; [school] Mell First; [fav sub] ICT; [hobbies] Sport & Woodwork; [pets] Cats, Goats & Dogs; [ambition] To be a Motorsport Engineer;

MASON-FAYLE, CRESSIDA RUTH: [b] 17/09/91 Stroud; [home] Uley, Glos; [p] Patrick Fayle & Tracy Mason-Fayle; [brothers] Benjamin Jack & Alfred Bartholomew; [sister] Rosie Baxendale; [school] Uley CE Primary; [fav sub] English; [hobbies] Reading, Drama & Dance; [pets] Rabbit (Nora); [ambition] To be a Writer or Actress;

MATHERS, SAM: [b] 30/03/91 Bradford; [home] Shipley, N. Yorks.; [p] Andrew & Julie; [brother] Joseph; [school] High Craggs Primary; [fav sub] Science; [hobbies] Playing on computer; [pets] 3 Dogs; [ambition] To join the Army or Police Force;

MATHEWSON, LOUISE: [b] 11/01/91 Reading; [home] Reading, Berks; [p] Sharon & Graham; [school] Micklands Primary; [fav sub] Maths; [hobbies] Football & Reading; [pets] Goldfish; [ambition] To join the RAF;

MATTHEWS, TOM: [b] 17/11/88 Canterbury; [home] Herne Bay, Kent; [p] Linda Benge; [brothers] Nick & Leigh; [school] Hornbeam High; [fav sub] Drama; [hobbies] Football, Tennis & Sports; [pets] Dog, Parrot, Guinea Pigs & Budgies; [ambition] To be an RAF Pilot;

MAYNARD, OSCAR: [b] 30/12/94 Dover; [home] Deal, Kent; [p] Paul & Nicky; [brother] Due 23/06/02; [school] Sandown CP; [fav sub] Science; [hobbies] Drawing & Lego; [pets] Dog (Blossom); [ambition] To be a Fireman;

MAYO, STACEY: [b] 23/05/91 Birmingham; [home] Bromsgrove, Worcs; [p] Toni Persarlcis & John Mayo; [sister] Chloe; [school] Catshill Middle; [fav sub] Art & Literacy; [hobbies] Judo, Swimming & Cycling; [pets] Fish; [ambition] To be an English Teacher;

McBETH, TERRI: [b] 28/05/90 St Albans; [home] Bovingdon, Herts; [p] Debbie & Alex; [brother] Mark; [sisters] Bethany & Holli; [school] Kings Langley; [fav sub] Music; [hobbies] Drama & Dance; [ambition] To be an Actress;

McCARTHY, SARAH: [b] 16/05/93 Braintree; [home] Braintree, Essex; [p] David & Sylvia; [brother] Shane; [sisters] Kerry & Ashley; [school] Great Bradfords Junior; [fav sub] Literacy; [hobbies] Dancing, Running & Reading; [pets] Hamster, Parrot, Terrappins & Fish; [ambition] To work with animals and write poetry;

McDONNELL, BEN: [b] 14/05/92 Dover; [home] Deal, Kent; [p] Nicki & Mac; [school] Sandown CP; [fav sub] Maths; [hobbies] Football; [pets] Cockatiel (Popeye); [ambition] To be a Footballer;

McILVEEN, KATIE: [b] 02/07/93 King's Lynn; [home] King's Lynn, Norfolk; [p] Gill & Rob; [brother] William; [school] South Wootton Junior; [fav sub] Art; [hobbies] Piano, Dancing & Reading; [pets] Guinea Pig, Cat, Dog, Horse; [ambition] To be a Vet and to swim with Dolphins;

McKENNA, DUNCAN: [b] 05/09/90 Liverpool; [home] Holmes Chapel, Cheshire; [p] Judith & Robert; [brother] Sean; [school] Holmes Chapel Primary; [fav sub] Design & Technology & Maths; [hobbies] Football, Computers & Reading; [pets] Rabbit (Toast); [ambition] To become a F1 Racing Driver;

McLAREN, KRISTOFER RYAN: [b] 19/10/93 Northallerton; [home] Thirsk, N. Yorks.; [p] Ruth & Colin; [brother] Jordan; [school] Thirsk Community Primary; [fav sub] History; [hobbies] Football; [pets] Rossi, Saffy & Cleo; [ambition] To be a Lawyer or a Footballer;

McMAHON, KAYLEIGH: [b] 06/07/88 Maidstone; [home] Larkfield, Kent; [p] Jackie, Chris (divorced); [brothers] Andrew & Michael; [sister] Lisa; [school] Maidstone Girls Grammar; [fav sub] History; [hobbies] Reading & Cinema; [pets] Ziggy; [ambition] To be an Archaeologist or Historian;

McMAHON, KHALID: [b] 07/07/93 Abu Dhabi, U.A.E.; [home] King's Lynn, Norfolk; [p] Maria; [school] North Wootton Primary; [fav sub] History; [hobbies] Drama, Reading & Making up stories; [pets] Cat (Molly), Rabbit (Snowy); [ambition] To be an Actor or Writer;

McMILLAN, LYDIA: [b] 31/12/95 Hamilton NZ; [home] Eastbourne, E. Sussex; [p] Jonathan & Sarah; [sister] Samantha; [school] Roselands Infants; [fav sub] PE; [hobbies] Swimming & Cycling; [pets] 2 Cats; [ambition] To be a Vet;

MEENAGHAN, DAVID-JON: [b] 03/09/88 Worcester; [home] Worcester, Worcs; [p] Trish; [sister] Joanna; [school] Bishop Perowne High; [fav sub] Physical Education; [hobbies] Rugby & Football; [pets] Dog, Cat, Fish; [ambition] To become a Vet or a Policeman;

MEIKLE-BRAES, WAYD: [b] 09/10/92 South Africa; [home] Ashstead, Surrey; [p] Craig & Haley; [sisters] Tyla & Amba; [school] Stamford Green CP; [fav sub] Science; [hobbies] Football & Computer Games; [pets] Would love a Dog; [ambition] To be goalkeepr for England;

MILLER, ASHLEY: [b] 12/09/92; [home] Lowestoft, Suffolk; [p] Dawn & Jon; [sister] Sian; [school] Whitton Green Primary; [fav sub] Maths; [hobbies] Football, Skateboarding & BMX.ing; [pets] 2 Cats; [ambition] To be a professional Footballer;

MILLER, CHLOE: [b] 02/03/92 Ashford; [home] Staines, Middx; [p] Jacqueline & John; [sisters] Sadie & Sophie; [school] Kingscroft Junior; [fav sub] English & PE; [hobbies] Football & Squash; [pets] Dog & Guinea Pigs; [ambition] To work with animals;

MITCHELL, JORDAN: [b] 02/02/92 Keighley; [home] Keighley, W. Yorks; [p] Glenn Mitchell & Nicola Hull; [brother] Adam; [school] Ingrow Primary; [fav sub] Art; [hobbies] Listening to Music; [ambition] To be an Artist;

MONNIER-HOWELL, ZOË: [b] 08/10/88 Cambridge; [home] Cambridge, Cambs; [p] Marianne Monnier; [sister] Danielle Monnier; [school] Perse School for Girls; [fav sub] Biology; [hobbies] Japanese Anime, Music, Computing; [pets] One fat arthritic cat (Kitty), The tail-less wonder cat (Katy); [ambition] To be a Vet or Doctor;

MOOR, OLIVIA: [b] 05/01/93 London; [home] Beaconsfield, Bucks;[p] Sara & Jonathan; [sisters] Sophia & Serena; [school] High March; [fav sub] Art & Drama; [hobbies] Art: painting & drawing, Brownies; [pets] Goldfish (Goldie); [ambition] To become a Hairdresser & own a Dog;

MOORE, ANNA: [b] 09/04/92 London; [home] Thames Ditton, Surrey; [p] Sara & Fred; [sister] Olivia; [school] Thames Ditton Juniors; [fav sub] PE & English; [hobbies] Running, Writing & Swimming; [pets] 8 Fish in pond; [ambition] To be an Actress in 'Eastenders';

MORAN, THOMAS: [b] 11/09/90 Eastbourne; [home] Herne Bay, Kent; [p] Gillian & John; [sisters] Becky & Amy; [school] Herne CE Junior; [fav sub] History; [hobbies] Computers & Football; [pets] George, Poppy & Galaxy; [ambition] To become a Pilot;

MORGAN, SHENTON: [b] 12/10/94 Eastbourne; [home] Eastbourne, E. Sussex; [p] Chloe; [brother] Joshua; [sisters] Kimberley & Jasmine; [school] Roselands Infant; [fav sub] Maths; [hobbies] Art & Swimming;

MORLEY, CHARLOTTE: [b] 06/03/92 Watford; [home] Radlett, Herts; [p] Sharon & Maurice; [brother] Paul; [sisters] Tina & Eleanor; [school] Newberries Primary; [fav sub] Art; [hobbies] Brownies, Piano, Playing & Reading; [pets] Cat (Nessie); [ambition] To be a Fashion Designer;

MORRIS, TIMOTHY: [b] 04/06/89 Leicestershire; [home] Loughborough, Leics; [p] Roger & Shelagh; [sister] Jemima; [school] Loughborough Grammar; [fav sub] Art; [hobbies] Cycling; [pets] 2 Cats;

MORRISH, MAUD: [b] 10/08/93 London; [home] Chiselborough, Somerset; [p] Claire Morrish & Simon Laycock; [school] Norton Sub Hamdon Primary; [fav sub] English; [hobbies] Writing & Drawing; [pets] Dog (Norah), Cat (Mrs Lewis); [ambition] To write plays and be an Actress;

MORRISON, EMILY FERN: [b] 05/05/96 Dover; [home] Deal, Kent; [p] Michelle & Tony; [sister] Ruby; [school] Sandown CP; [fav sub] Reading; [hobbies] Drawing, Dancing & Reading; [ambition] To be a Dancer & Artist;

MOSELEY, HOLLY: [b] 25/10/91 High Wycombe; [home] Beaconsfield, Bucks; [p] James & Julie; [brother] Max; [sister] Lucy & Francesca; [school] High March; [fav sub] English; [hobbies] Reading & Karting; [pets] Dog; [ambition] To become a Lawyer;

MOTT, LAUREN: [b] 14/09/93 Norwich; [home] Eccles on Sea, Norfolk; [p] Paul & Andrea; [brother] Adam; [sister] Sophie & Eleanor; [school] Happisburgh First; [fav sub] Art & English; [hobbies] Collecting Rocks & Fossils and China Dolls, Reading, Drama, Gymnastics & Music; [pets] Dog (Brisk), Guinea Pig (Sooty); [ambition] To be a Pop Star of famous Artist;

MULDOON, DANIEL: [b] 26/10/91 Glasgow; [home] Preston, Lancs; [p] Paul & Hilary; [brother] Joesph; [sister] Ann; [school] St Mary's & St Benedicts; [fav sub] Art; [hobbies] Reading, Sleeping & TV; [ambition] To become a famous Hairdresser;

MULLETT, REBECCA: [b] 20/01/91 Bromsgrove; [home] Catshill, Worcs; [p] Sean & Julie; [sisters] Gemma (19) & Kerry (12); [school] Catshill Middle; [fav sub] Maths & English; [hobbies] Swimming (competitive); [pets] 3 Cats, 1 Dog; [ambition] To become a Vet;

MURPHY, LAURA: [b] 03/11/89 Sidcup; [home] Sidcup, Kent; [p] Dolores & Michael; [sister] Aisling; [school] Babington House; [fav sub] English; [hobbies] Reading & Netball; [pets] Rabbit (Marmalade); [ambition] To become a Lawyer or Author;

MURPHY, LUKE: [b] 26/05/91 Upton, Wirral; [home] Kingsmead, Cheshire; [p] Kim & Chris; [brother] Ben; [school] St Wilfrids Catholic Primary; [fav sub] Maths & Science; [hobbies] Football, Rollerblades & Playstation; [pets] Several Goldfish named after Everton players; [ambition] To play football for Everton;

MURRAY, CHLOE: [b] 29/06/93 Greenscombe Farm; [home] Bruton, Somerset; [p] Jacqueline & Steve; [brothers] Luke & Oliver; [school] Bruton Primary; [fav sub] Art; [hobbies] Swimming & Cycling; [pets] Cat (Pod); [ambition] To work in a Hospital;

MURRAY, FRANCESCA: [b] 21/02/88 Enfield; [home] Barrow, Suffolk; [p] Lance & Brigitte; [brother] Sean; [sister] Dani; [school] County Upper; [fav sub] English; [hobbies] Writing, Reading & Listening to Music; [pets] 4 Cats (Quizzy, Slugger, Minx & Kookie); [ambition] For people to read what I have written, or be reading about me

NELSON, ADAM: [b] 23/07/93 Norwich; [home] Hempnall, Norfolk; [p] Lesley & Ian; [brother] Zachary; [school] Saxlingham Nethergate; [fav sub] Maths; [hobbies] Reading, Weather & Tennis; [pets] Cat (William); [ambition] To have more work published and to become a Policeman;

NEWLAND, MAY: [b] 25/03/92 [home] Epping, Essex; [p] Cathy & Terry; [brother] Eddie; [school] Epping Junior; [fav sub] PE; [hobbies] Football, Running & Piano; [pets] Cat (Tiger);

NORMAN, THOMAS DANIEL: [b] 25/09/90 Ormskirk; [home] Hilldale, Lancs; [p] John & Caroline [brother] Patrick John; [sister] Annelise; [school] Richard Durnings Endowed; [fav sub] Art; [hobbies] Football & Cricket; [pets] Cat (Suki); [ambition] To be a professional Footballer or design computer games;

NORTHCOTT, NAOMI: [b] 25/10/91 Exeter; [home] Lympstone, Devon; [p] Brian & Alison; [brother] Richard; [school] Lympstone Primary; [fav sub] Art & Drama; [hobbies] Dance, Singing & Sports; [pets] Guinea Pig; [ambition] To be a famous Pop Star!

NOTTINGHAM, EMMA: [b] 28/12/88 Stevenage; [home] Hitchin, Herts; [p] Gillian & Clive; [sister] Lucy; [school] Hitchin Girls'; [fav sub] Art; [hobbies] Drawing, Dancing & Playing the Flute & Piano; [ambition] To be a Cartoonist;

NOWELL, JACK: [b] 13/03/91 Preston; [home] Lostock Hall, Lancs; [p] Peter & Helen; [brothers] Ernie & Jeff; [sister] Lisa; [school] St Marys & St Benedicts RC Primary; [fav sub] Maths; [hobbies] Playing Violin, Football & Swimming; [ambition] To teach Violin;

NUTTING, HANNAH: [b] 08/04/90 Northallerton; [home] Bingley, W. Yorks; [p] Jonathan & Kathrine; [brothers] Matthew, Joshua & Asher; [school] Bingley Grammar; [fav sub] Art & Music; [hobbies] Dancing & Flute; [pets] Guinea Pigs; [ambition] To be a Lawyer;

O'CONNOR, JO-ANNA: [b] 23/11/89 Orpington; [home] Orpington, Kent; [p] Jeannette; [brothers] Paul, Simon & Robert; [school] Beaverwood School for Girls; [fav sub] English; [hobbies] Dancing; [pets] 2 Dogs;

O'KEEFE, JAMES MICHAEL: [b] 17/07/89 Canterbury; [home] Herne Bay, Kent; [p] Tina O'Keefe & Stephen Reeves; [brother] Dean Mark; [school] Herne Bay High; [fav sub] Science; [hobbies] I.T. Club, Music & Fishing; [pets] Cat (Frankie); [ambition] To become an Architecural Designer or a Musician;

OLIVER, LAURA: [b] 05/05/92 Margate; [school] Upton Junior; [fav sub] History; [hobbies] Singing, Dancing & Acting; [pets] Dog, Hamster & 4 Cats; [ambition] To be a Singer, Actress Dancer or Vet;

OLIVER, PHILLIPA: [b] 31/12/92 Aylesbury; [home] Wing, Bucks; [p] Liz & Les; [sister] Lisa; [school] Overstone Combined; [fav sub] English; [hobbies] Clarinet, Horse Riding, Athletics & Gymnastics; [pets] Rabbit (Ruffles); [ambition] To be a Hurdler;

OSBORN, PETER: [b] 25/01/95 Crawley; [home] Eastbourne, E. Sussex; [p] Mark & Jayne; [sisters] Olivia & Hannah; [school] Roselands Infants; [fav sub] Sports & PE; [hobbies] Football & Fishing; [pets] Dog & Goldfish; [ambition] To be a Footballer;

PALMER, HAYDEN: [b] 27/01/93 Lowestoft; [home] Carlton Colville, Suffolk; [p] Nigel & Paula; [brothers] Nathan & Chris; [sister] Louise; [school] Whitton Green Primary; [fav sub] Maths; [hobbies] Football, Swimming; [pets] Cats (Tilly & Tigger); [ambition] To work in a Bank or be a Footballer;

PARKER, KATIE: [b] 16/08/91 Shipley; [home] Shipley, W. Yorks; [p] Elaine & Michael; [sister] Sarah; [school] High Crags Primary; [fav sub] Art; [hobbies] Drawing & Bowling; [pets] 4 Dogs; [ambition] To be a Dog Groomer;

PARR, BRENDON: [b] 27/06/92 Tiverton; [home] Tiverton, Devon; [p] Christine & Andrew; [brother] Jason; [school] Tidcombe Primary; [fav sub] Art & Maths; [hobbies] Cricket & Football; [pets] Dog (Dandy), Rabbit (Bubbles); [ambition] To be a Moto-Cross Rider or play Cricket for England;

PARSONS, JAMIE: [b] 09/07/93 Oxford; [home] Grove, Oxon; [p] Gail & Andy; [brother] Luke; [sister] Carrie; [school] Millbrook CP; [fav sub] Maths; [hobbies] Football & Collecting;

PATRICK, ADAM: [b] 01/01/91 Surrey; [home] Staines, Middx; [p] Coralie & Mark; [brother] Nathan; [school] Kingscroft Junior; [fav sub] Science; [hobbies] Football; [ambition] To be an Animal Trainer;

PERKINS, JAY: [b] 31/03/95 Canterbury; [home] Woodley, Berks; [p] Miranda & Neil; [sister] Hope; [school] Micklands Primary; [fav sub] Science; [hobbies] Drawing & Dancing; [ambition] To be an Artist and sell my pictures in a Gallery;

PERRIN, HARRY: [b] 08/02/84 Welwyn Garden City; [home] Welwyn Garden City, Hertsfordshire; [school] St Albans; [ambition] To be heard;

PETTY, JAKE: [b] 02/04/95 Northallerton; [home] Thirsk, N. Yorks; [p] Barry & Debbie; [sisters] Rochelle & Nichola; [school] Thirsk Community Primary; [fav sub] English; [hobbies] Cricket & Football; [pets] Cat (Whitney); [ambition] To play cricket for Yorkshire;

PLOSZYNSKI, ARRON: [b] 20/06/91 Reading; [home] Woodcote, Oxon; [p] Alison & Julian; [brothers] Matthew & Jack; [school] Woodcote CP; [fav sub] Art; [hobbies] Football & Scouts; [pets] 4 Goldfish; [ambition] To be a top-class Chef;

PLOSZYNSKI, MATTHEW: [b] 11/05/93 Reading; [home] Woodcote, Oxon; [p] Alison & Julian; [brothers] Arron & Jack; [school] Woodcote CP; [fav sub] Science; [hobbies] Football & Cubs; [pets] Goldfish; [ambition] To travel around the World;

POOLEY, MAKEETA: [b] 11/11/87 Bangor; [home] Tholthorpe, N. Yorks; [p] Fiona & Andrew; [sister] Danielle; [school] Ripon Grammar; [fav sub] History; [hobbies] Reading & Singing; [ambition] To travel the World and to work with Children;

POULTON, CHRISTOPHER: [b] 15/12/90 Preston; [home] Hoghton, Lancs; [p] John & Anne; [school] St Mary's & St Benedicts RC Primary; [fav sub] History & Science; [hobbies] Karate & Tennis; [pets] 2 Goldfish (Fish & Chips); [ambition] To be an Actor or a Scientist;

PREECE, LYDIA: [b] 27/01/93 Wigan; [home] Grove, Oxon; [p] Cathy & Andrew; [brother] Edward; [sister] Abigail; [school] Millbrook CP; [fav sub] Literacy & Art; [hobbies] Painting & Swimming; [pets] Cat (Silvie); [ambition] To be a Vet and spend lots of time with animals;

PRENTICE, LAURA MAY: [b] 31/08/93 Aylesbury; [home] Wingrave, Bucks; [p] Tracy & Jon; [brother] Kieran; [sister] Hannah; [school] Overstone Combined; [fav sub] Maths; [hobbies] Cycling; [pets] Cats; [ambition] To become a Teacher;

PRINSLOO, MORNÉ: [b] 20/03/92 Rustenburg, S.Africa; [home] Epping, Essex; [p] Connie & Elize; [sister] Mandi; [school] Epping Junior; [fav sub] PE & Science; [hobbies] Magic Tricks; [pets] Dog (Jessica); [ambition] To be an Army Trainer;

PRIOR, ELLIS LUCY JAYNE: [b] 31/01/92 Guildford; [home] Worplesdon, Surrey; [p] Lesley & Barry; [sister] Georgina; [school] Worplesdon Primary; [fav sub] PE & History; [hobbies] Dancing, Football & Tennis; [pets] Chickens, Ducks & Fish; [ambition] To be a Dancer;

RACE, JACK: [b] 24/11/92 Harwich; [home] Harwich, Essex; [p] Kelly & Andy; [sister] Siän; [school] St Josephs RC Primary; [fav sub] PE & Maths; [hobbies] Football, Tennis & Wrestling; [pets] Cats & Fish; [ambition] To become a famous Footballer;

RADMORE, TIFFANY: [b] 16/10/91 Tiverton; [home] Tiverton, Devon; [p] Nadine Hutchings; [brother] Jack; [school] Tidcombe Primary; [fav sub] Literacy & Art; [hobbies] Reading & Socialising; [pets] Cat; [ambition] To Be an Actor;

RAMSBOTTOM, BRITTANY-ROSE: [b] 08/07/92 Blackpool; [home] Cleveleys, Lancs; [p] Shirley & Paul; [brothers] Kurt, Jordan & Elliot; [school] St Mary's RC Primary; [fav sub] Maths; [hobbies] Dancing & Acro; [pets] Dog (Scruffy) & Guinea Pig (Free-Way); [ambition] To be a Ballerina or Teacher;

RANKIN, REBECCA: [b] 07/09/90 Hastings; [home] East Farleigh, Kent; [p] Andrew & Judith; [sisters] Amanda & Louisa; [school] Sutton Valance Primary; [fav sub] English; [hobbies] Trampolining & Reading; [pets] Cat (Tyger) & Rabbit (Sooty); [ambition] To be a Writer or a Vet;

RATTY, CHARLEIGH JAYNE: [b] 18/05/91 Harlow; [home] Waltham Abbey, Essex; [p] Lorraine & Peter; [school] Leverton Junior; [fav sub] Science; [hobbies] Skating & Horse Riding; [pets] Dog, Fish & Bird; [ambition] To be a Hairdresser;

RAW, AILSA RACHEL: [b] 14/09/88 Stevenage; [home] Hitchin, Herts; [p] Michael & Sarah; [brother] Aaron; [cousins] Hannah & Andrew West; [school] Hitchin Girls'; [fav sub] History; [hobbies] Reading & Singing; [pets] Rabbit (Peter), Guinea Pig (Charlotte); [ambition] To become a Teacher or Historian;

REED, ELLIOTT: [b] 06/02/91 King's Lynn; [home] North Wootton, Norfolk; [p] Sarah & Roger; [sister] Megan; [school] North Wootton Primary; [fav sub] Maths; [hobbies] Computer & Playstation; [pets] Hamster, Rat & Dog; [ambition] To be in a James Bond Film!

RESTELL-LEWIS, GLEN: [b] 27/07/94 Chatham; [home] Maidstone, Kent; [p] Mary & Dylan; [school] Molehill Copse; [fav sub] History; [hobbies] Tennis & Swimming; [pets] Cat (Darcy); [ambition] To be a Racing Driver;

RICH, CLARE: [b] 08/01/92 Sutton; [home] Hinchley Wood, Surrey; [p] Tammy & Danny; [brothers] Tom & Joe; [sister] Emma; [school] Thames Ditton Junior; [fav sub] Art & English; [hobbies] Music, Reading & Cycling;

RICHARDS, BROOKE: [b] 26/07/94

Reading; [home] Reading, Berks; [p] Dave & Julia; [brother] James; [sister] Georgia; [school] Loddon Junior; [fav sub] Art; [hobbies] Swimming & Bowling; [ambition] To be a Teacher;

RICHARDS, CHLOE: [b] 30/05/92 Exeter; [home] Exeter, Devon; [p] Debra & Steven; [sister] Devon; [school] Montgomery Combined; [fav sub] I.C.T. (Computers); [hobbies] Gymnastics & Swimming; [pets] Dog (Poppy), Cat (Levi) & Hamster (Misty); [ambition] To be an Archaeologist or Scientist;

RICHARDSON, HELEN TESS: [b] 06/01/89 Cambridge; [home] Royston, Herts; [p] Mary & Ian; [brother] Mark; [school] Perse Senior School for Girls; [fav sub] Music; [hobbies] Writing, Drawing, Piano, Flute, Guitar, Seeing Friends, Reading & Eating; [ambition] To become a Journalist;

RICHES, GEORGINA: [b] 21/08/93 Chelmsford; [home] Great Notley, Essex; [p] George & Hannah; [brother] Scott; [school] White Court Primary; [fav sub] English; [hobbies] Reading, Drama, Dance & Singing; [pets] Dog (Pepe), Cat (Albert); [ambition] To work with children and to act in my spare time;

RISK, HANNAH E.: [b] 04/07/92 Falkirk; [home] Wrecclesham, Surrey; [school] St Peter's CE Primary; [fav sub] Art; [hobbies] Horse Riding & Brownies; [pets] Rabbit (Murphy);

RIXSON, DANIEL: [b] 19/05/93 Aylesbury; [home] Wing, Bucks; [p] Anne & Martyn; [sisters] Amy & Katherine; [school] Overstone Combined; [fav sub] Maths; [hobbies] Playing Football; [ambition] To be a Footballer;

ROACH, THOMAS DAVID: [b] 23/04/91 Liverpool; [home] Parbold, Lancs; [p] Nick & Julie; [brother] James; [sister] Charlotte; [school] Richard Durnings Endowed Primary; [fav sub] Art; [hobbies] Cricket, Rowing & Cycling; [pets] Springer Spaniel (Charlie) & Hamster (Ron); [ambition] To be a Rally Driver;

ROBINSON, CANDICE: [b] 25/09/87 Basildon; [home] Basildon, Essex; [p] Marie Moores & Lee Robinson; [school] Woodlands; [fav sub] Art & ICT; [hobbies] Poetry & the male gender!; [pets] Fish; [ambition] To be smart, rich and happy;

ROBINSON, ELOISE: [b] 12/07/92 Harrogate; [home] Ripon, Yorks.; [brother & sister]] 1 older brother & 1 younger sister; [school] Fountains CE Primary; [fav sub] 'Elephants'; [hobbies] Craft of all kinds; [pets] Border Terrier; [ambition] To see Elephants in the wild;

ROBINSON, SARAH: [b] 14/12/89 London; [home] London; [p] Camilla & Alan; [sister] Hannah; [school] Wallington High; [fav sub] Graphics; [hobbies] Reading & Gymnastics; [ambition] To get good results in my summer exams;

ROBINSON, SARAH: [b] 02/10/92 Plymouth; [home] Ivybridge, Devon; [p] Graham & Angela; [brother] Matt; [sister] Claire; [school] Stowford Primary; [fav sub] History; [hobbies] Tennis, Keyboard & Dance; [pets] Cat (Patch); [ambition] To be a Poet or Singer;

RODRIGUEZ, MICHAEL: [b] 13/08/90; [home] Felthorpe, Norfolk; [p] Paul & Fiona (Stepmum); [brothers] Sibs & Russell; [sisters] Katie & Zoe; [school] Horsford Middle; [hobbies] Go-Karting; [pets] Dog, 2 Cats, 2 Rabbits & Fish;

ROSE, DANIELLE: [b] 06/12/90 Chertsey; [home] Byfleet, Surrey; [p] Gillian & John (Dad died when I was 5); [brother] Nicholas; [school] St Mary's CE Primary; [fav sub] P.S.E.; [hobbies] Dancing; [pets] Cat, 2 Dogs, 3 Rabbits, 2 Mice & 1 Hamster; [ambition] To be a Psychiatrist & to be happy;

ROSSETTI, ALEXANDER: [b] 19/10/96; [home] Theydon Bois, Essex; [p] Gillea & Dominic; [brother] Hugo; [sisters] Matilda & Gabriella; [school] Theydon Bois Primary; [fav sub] Maths; [hobbies] Football, Beavers & Tennis; [pets] Rabbit; [ambition] To play football for England;

ROSSETTI, MATILDA: [b] 20/01/92 London; [home] Theydon Bois, Essex; [p] Gillea & Dominic; [brothers] Alexander & Hugo; [sister] Gabriella; [school] Theydon Bois Primary; [fav sub] English; [hobbies] Dancing, Music, Brownies & Tennis; [pets] Rabbit; [ambition] To be a Vet and to write books;

ROUGH, JORDAN LUCY: [b] 06/09/91 Ashford, Middx; [home] Staines, Middx; [p] Bob & Samantha; [school] Kingscroft Junior; [fav sub] Art & PE; [hobbies] Dancing; [pets] Rabbit (Thumper);

ROWE, KENNY: [b] 19/10/91 Liskeard; [home] Tavistock, Devon; [p] Toni & Ian; [school] Bere Alston CP; [fav sub] Maths; [hobbies] Lorries; [ambition] To be a Lorry Driver;

ROWLANDS, CHRISTOPHER: [b] 19/04/91 Macclesfield; [home] Prestbury, Cheshire; [p] Alison & Gordon; [brother] Matthew; [school] Prestbury CE Primary; [fav sub] Science; [hobbies] Tennis, Squash & Violin; [pets] Rabbit (Snowball); [ambition] To be a Civil Engineer or Architect;

ROWLEY, ABIGAIL ALEXANDRA: [b] 31/10/90 Cambridge; [home] Cherry Hinton; [p] Martin & Joanna; [brother] Dominic; [sister] Chloé; [school] Queen Edith Primary; [fav sub] English; [hobbies] Swimming, Reading, Horse Riding & Music; [pets] Cat (Meekoo); [ambition] To become a Vet;

RUSCOE, EMILY: [b] 04/01/91 Wexham; [home] Farnham Common, Bucks; [p] Brie & Tim; [brother] Giles; [twin sister] Harriet; [school] Farnham Common Junior; [fav sub] Science; [hobbies] Reading, Writing Poetry & Animals; [pets] Guinea Pig, Dog, Rabbit; [ambition] To be a Vet;

SAMPSON, HELENA: [b] 03/05/92 Barking; [home] Theydon Bois, Essex; [p] Deborah & Martin; [brother] Guy; [school] Theydon Bois Primary; [fav sub] Design; [hobbies] Painting, Drawing & playing Piano; [pets] Cat (Kuki) & Tropical Fish; [ambition] To be a Designer;

SAUNDERS, BECKI: [b] 13/04/92; [home] Epping, Essex; [p] Mark & Pav; [sister] Rachel; [school] Epping Junior; [fav sub] Art; [hobbies] Dancing, Swimming, Piano & Clarinet; [pets] Dog;

SCANNELL, CIARAN: [b] 26/10/91 Bucks; [home] Grantley, N. Yorks; [p] Linda & John; [brother] Aidan; [sister] Mhairi; [school] Fountains CE Primary; [fav sub] Maths; [hobbies] Football, Cricket & Climbing; [pets] Chickens; [ambition] To be the best walker and climber and to climb Mount Everest;

SCOTT, IGRAINE: [b] 04/12/90 London; [home] Kent; [school] Sutton Valence Primary; [fav sub] English & Science; [hobbies] Roller Blading & Reading; [pets] 3 Border Collies; [ambition] To be a Detective Inspector in the Metropolitan Police Force;

SEAR, TASHA: [b] 18/03/90 Taunton; [home] West Quantoxhead, Somerset; [p] Marion & Russell; [brother] Toby; [school] Danesfield; [fav sub] Science & PE; [hobbies] Riding, Hockey & Atheltics; [pets] Ponies (T.P., Otty & Bubbles), Hamster (Smudge), Dog (Fern) & Cat (Toggi); [ambition] To be a Vet and to win Badminton 3 .D. E.

SENIOR, DOMINIC MICAHAEL: [b] 18/12/90 Skipton; [home] Cowling, N. Yorks.; [p] Michael & Eileen; [school] Threshfield Primary; [fav sub] Science; [hobbies] Sports, Football & New Metal Music; [pets] Cat & 3 Dogs; [ambition] To be rich & famous;

SEWELL, NICOLA: [b] 24/12/91 Ashford, Middx; [home] Staines,

Middx; [p] Timothy & Annette; [brothers] Luke, Matthew & Adam; [sisters] Rebecca & Rachel; [school] Kingscroft County Junior; [fav sub] Art; [hobbies] Tennis, Art & Sewing; [pets] 2 Cats (Tabitha & Jasper); [ambition] To become an Actress;

SHAMBROOK, ADAM: [b] 12/03/94 Oxford; [home] Braintree, Essex; [p] Chris & Sara; [brother] Ben; [sister] Amy; [school] White Court; [fav sub] Maths; [hobbies] I belong to a Football Club & Swimming Club;

SHAND, PIERCE: [b] 17/09 92 Gorleston-on-Sea; [home] Lowestoft, Suffolk; [school] Whitton Green Primary; [fav sub] Maths; [hobbies] Football & Tennis;

SHARRAD, HALEY JO: [b] 19/08/91 Maidstone; [home] Kingswood, Kent; [p] Jo; [brothers] Jem Sharrad, Aaron & Jason Collins; [sister] Kerry-Ann Sharrad; [school] Sutton Valence Primary; [fav sub] Art; [hobbies] Art, Pets & Music; [pets] Pomeranian Dog (Elly), Hamster (Widget); [ambition] To be an Artist;

SHARROCK, VICTORIA: [b] 21/11/91 Keighley, W. Yorks; [home] Preston, Lancs; [p] Richard & Ann; [brother] Daniel; [school] Holy Family RC Primary; [fav sub] Maths; [hobbies] Scuba Diving; [pets] Goldfish; [ambition] To write poetry and stories;

SHORT, DONNA MARIE: [b] 13/03/91 Harlow; [home] Epping, Essex; [p] Hazel & Paul; [sisters] Trina & Anita (Twin); [school] Epping Junior; [fav sub] PE; [hobbies] Tennis & Rounders; [ambition] To be a Singer;

SHORTLAND, SARA: [b] 30/06/93 Derby; [home] Crich, Derbys.; [p] Martin & Dawn; [brother] Steven; [sister] Suzi; [school] Fritchley CE Primary; [fav sub] PE; [hobbies] Vaulting; [pets] Cats & Rabbit; [ambition] To Vault for England;

SIGEE, RACHAEL: [b] 16/03/88; [home] Warlingham, Surrey; [p] Andrew & Lesley; [brother] Joseph; [school] Wallington High School for Girls; [fav sub] English, Spanish & History; [hobbies] Reading, Shopping & Chatting; [ambition] To go to University, to succeed in life and be happy;

SIMMONDS, ROXANNE: [b] 13/07/92 Ashford; [home] Staines, Middx; [p] Alison & Steve; [brother] Leon; [sister] Chlöe; [school] Kingscroft Junior; [fav sub] PE; [hobbies] Playing Football; [pets] Hamster (Poppy); [ambition] To become a professional Footballer;

SIMPSON, JAMES: [b] 05/11/90 Enfield; [home] Epping, Essex; [p] Michele & Stuart; [brother] Daniel; [sister] Charlotte; [school] Epping Junior; [fav sub] Maths; [hobbies] Football; [pets] Dog, Cat & Fish; [ambition] To be a Footballer;

SIMPSON, NAOMI: [b] 30/06/93 King's Lynn; [home] North Wootton, Norfolk; [p] Stephen & Sarah; [brother] James (3); [sister] Samantha (10); [school] North Wootton Community; [fav sub] RE; [hobbies] Dancing & Brownies; [pets] Hamster (Dominoe) & Cat (Spotty); [ambition] To be a Doctor or Policewoman;

SINCLAIR, EMILY: [b] 24/07/90 Bromley; [home] Beckenham, Kent; [p] Garry & Arlene; [brother] Anthony; [sisters] Emma, Harriet, Katherine & Jessica; [school] Bromley High; [fav sub] Maths, Art & Music; [hobbies] Singing, Ballet & Art; [pets] 3 Cats (Sugar, Spice & Katie); [ambition] To be successful in all that I do;

SISSONS, SOPHIE MEGAN: [b] 19/10/91 Bristol; [home] Abingdon, Oxon; [p] Amanda & Lez; [brother] Josh; [sister] Ella; [school] Dunmore Junior; [fav sub] Drama, PE & Music; [hobbies] All Sports; [ambition] To be a Teacher;

SMART, MARY: [b] 13/02/93 Bromsgrove; [home] Bromsgrove, Worcs; [p] Stella & Graham; [brother] Harvey; [sisters] Florence, Emily & Helen; [school] Charford First; [fav sub] Maths; [hobbies] Disco Dancing Competitions; [pets] Jack Russell (Buffy) & 2 Cats (Poppy & Bullet); [ambition] To be a professional Dancer;

SMITH, BECKY: [b] 30/05/90 Bath; [home] Corsham, Wilts; [p] David & Janet; [brother] Alexander; [school] The Corsham School; [fav sub] Drama & PE; [hobbies] Horse Riding & Sports; [pets] 2 Cats (Mog & Molly), Hamster (Jake); [ambition] To become a Vet;

SMITH, BILL ROGER: [b] 30/04/91 Bramhall; [home] Catshill, Worcs; [p] Roger & Shirley; [brother] Jack; [school] Catshill Middle; [fav sub] History; [hobbies] Drama & Drawing; [pets] 4 Goldfish; [ambition] To be an Historian, Author or D.J.;

SMITH, GARETH ADAM: [b] 29/09/90 Bradford; [home] Shipley, W. Yorks; [p] Sharon & Carl; [school] High Crags Primary; [fav sub] IT; [hobbies] Football; [pets] Dog, Cat, Gerbil & Tortoise; [ambition] To travel around the World;

SMITH, JAMIE: [b] 02/04/90 Harrow; [home] Grt. Yarmouth, Norfolk; [p] Mark & Mandy; [brother] Adam; [sisters] Kelly-Marie & Shannon; [school] North Denes Middle; [fav sub] Science; [hobbies] Drama Club, Cycling; [pets] German Shepherd (Max) & 2 Gerbils; [ambition] To be a Policeman;

SMITH, LAUREN: [b] 13/09/90 Exeter; [home] Exeter, Devon; [p] Graeme & Linda; [brothers] Todd & Jake; [school] Montgomery Combined; [fav sub] Art; [hobbies] Karate, Guides, Playing the Flute;

SMITH, VICTORIA KATHRYN: [b] 07/12/90 Leamington Spa; [home] Radford Semele, Warks; [p] David & Kathryn; [brother] Andrew David; [school] Abbotsford School; [fav sub] Games; [hobbies] Horse Riding & Golf; [pets] Labrador (Kipper), Hamster (Chester); [ambition] To be a Vet and own lots of Labradors and Horses;

SPENCE, CATHY: [b] 25/12/90 Stockport; [home] Holmes Chapel, Cheshire; [p] Sheryl & Michael; [brother] David; [school] Holmes Chapel Primary; [fav sub] English; [hobbies] Horse Riding & Dancing; [pets] 2 Rabbits, 1 Fish; [ambition] To become an Interior Designer and a professional Showjumper

SPENCE, CHELSEA GRACE: [b] 16/02/95 Eastbourne; [home] Eastbourne, Sussex; [p] Wendy & Stephen; [school] Roselands County Infants; [fav sub] Music & History; [hobbies] Music & Dancing; [pets] 2 Dogs, Rabbit, Guinea Pig & Hamster; [ambition] To be a professional Pianist;

SPICER, CRAIG: [b] 01/12/94 Truro; [home] Reading, Berks; [p] Donna & Jon; [brother] Stefan; [school] Micklands Primary; [fav sub] Maths; [hobbies] Computers; [pets] Cat, Rabbit, Guinea Pig & 2 Fish;

SPORT, JOEL: [b] 18/07/91 London; [home] King's Lynn, Norfolk; [p] Rosie & James (Dad died 3 years ago); [brother] Jamie; [school] South Wootton Junior; [fav sub] Computers (IT); [hobbies] Computer Games; [pets] Fish (Can't have a cat as I am allergic); [ambition] To be an Actor and to grow out of cat allergy!

STAVROU, DOMINIQUE: [b] 09/08/92 Wexham; [home] Chalfont St. Peter, Bucks; [p] Rob & Heather; [sister] Sofia; [school] High March; [fav sub] Science & Art; [hobbies] Sport & TV; [pets] 3 Cats, 1 Fish , 1 Dog & 2 Horses; [ambition] To be a Marine Biologist;

STEDMAN, JOSHUA: [b] 07/08/91 Woking; [home] Canterbury, Kent; [p] David & Cyra; [brother] Kieran (5); [sister] Hannah (8); [school] St Peters Methodist; [fav sub] PE; [hobbies] Football & playing Drums; [ambition] To be the first player ever to score 5 goals for England against Germany!

STEED, EMILY: [b] 12/11/90 Ripon; [home] Ripon, N. Yorks.; [p] Mrs & Mrs J. Steed; [sister] Angharad; [school] Ripon Grammar; [fav sub] English; [hobbies] Horse Riding and Animals, Animals, Animals!; [pets] 4 Chickens, 2 Rabbits, 2 Guinea Pigs, 2 Fish; [ambition[To be a Vet;

STEVENS, LAUREN: [b] 06/02/93 Reading; [home] Caversham, Berks; [p] Sally & Mark; [sister] Charlotte; [school] Micklands Primary; [fav sub] Handwriting; [hobbies] Brownies, Art & Swimming; [pets] Dog (Ellie) & 3 Fish; [ambition] To be a Pop Star or famous Poet;

STEWART, RHYS: [b] 03/07/96 Stevenage; [home] Stevenage, Herts; [p] Sharon & Sean; [sister] Chloe; [school] Woolenwick Junior; [fav sub] Sport; [hobbies] Playing Football & Rugby; [pets] Goldfish; [ambition] To meet the Liverpool Squad;

STICKLER, EMILY LILLIAN: [b] 26/11/91 Dover/Deal; [home] Deal, Kent; [p] Geoffrey & Carol; [brother] James (3/1/96); (school] Sandown Primary; [fav sub] Maths & Science; [hobbies] Gardening, Sport & Swimming; [pets] Cat (Ebernizer); [ambition] To explore the World & get into Grammar School;

STORM, LUCY: [b] 21/11/94 Reading; [home] Salisbury, Wilts; [p] Valerie & John; [brother] Thomas; [sister] Anna; [school] Wyndham Park Infants; [fav sub] Art; [hobbies] Ballroom Dancing, Swimming, Brownies, Drawing & Writing; [ambition] To be a Catoonist;

STORTON, DANIEL: [b] 13/08/94 Keighley; [home] Utley, W. Yorks; [p] Mick & Janet; [school] Laycock Primary; [fav sub] Design Technology; [hobbies] Judo, Football & Trains; [pets] 4 Rabbits; [ambition] To drive a Bullet Train in Japan;

STRAND, ANNA C.: [b] 08/11/92 Oxford; [home] Didcot, Oxon; [p] Keith & Yadz; [brothers] Russell & Adam; [sister] Lydia; [school] Northbourne Primary; [fav sub] English; [hobbies] Reading, Writing, Drawing, Cycling; [pets] Cats (Timmy & Smuggles), Guinea Pig (Hero); [ambition] To become a Vet or Writer;

STRAPPELI, FRANCESCA: [b] 17/06/93 cambridge; [p] Anna & Mario; [brother] Giuseppe; [sisters] Caterina & Paolina; [school] Queen Ediths Community Primary; [fav sub] English & Art; [hobbies] Dancing; [ambition] To become a Teacher;

SUBRAMANIAM, NATASHA: [b] 28/12/91 Brentwood; [home] Broadstairs, Kent; [p] Rags & Vanessa; [brother] Joshua; [school] Upton Junior;

[fav sub] English; [hobbies] Dancing; [pets] Fish; [ambition] To be a professional Dancer;

SWANNICK, JODIE: [b] 18/09/89 Chester; [home] Exeter, Devon; [p] Jean Swannick & Malcolm Lee; [sister] Laura; [school] Montgomery Combined; [fav sub] English; [hobbies] Swimming & Socialising; [ambition] To be a Vet or Drama Student;

SWEENEY, DANIEL: [b] 26/07/91 Chester; [home] Little Budworth, Cheshire; [brother] Thomas; [sister] Caroline; [school] St Wilfrid's Catholic Primary; [fav sub] History; [hobbies] Moto Cross, Motor Cycling & Football; [pets] 1 Boxer Dog & 2 Cats; [ambition] To be a Pilot or Moto Cross Rider;

TASCHIMOWITZ, EVE: [b] 02/05/93 Bristol; [home] Loxton, N. Somerset; [p] Peter & Liz; [brothers] Joseph & Isaac; [sister] Naomi; [school] Weare First; [fav sub] PE; [hobbies] Sport, Music & English; [pets] Goldfish [ambition] To be a Musician, Poet, Author, Footballer or Basketball Player;

TAYLOR, JAMES: [b] 02/05/92 Bradford; [home] Bradford, W. Yorks; [p] Linda & Richard; [brother] Matthew; [school] Westwood Park Primary; [fav sub] Science; [hobbies] Football & Cricket; [ambition] To join the Navy or become a Footballer;

TAYLOR, ROBERT JAMES: [b] 07/05/89 Chorley; [home] Chorley, Lancs; [p] Christopher & Karen; [brothers] Jonathan & Thomas; [school] St Michaels CE High; [fav sub] Maths & French; [hobbies] Football, Reading & Squash; [pets] Tropical Fish, Cat & Rabbit; [ambition] To own a Ferrari and earn pots of dosh!!;

TAYLOR, STEPHEN JAMES: [b] 10/02/93 Crewe; [home] King's Lynn, Norfolk; [p] David & Paula; [brother] David; [sisters] Anna & Emily; [school] South Wootton Junior; [fav sub] Maths & I.T.; [hobbies] Computing; [pets] Dog (Sweep) & the Gerbills; [ambition] To be a Computer Programmer and part time Rugby Player;

THOMAS, EMILY LOUISE: [b] 04/05/92 Beverley; [home] Chalfont St Giles, Bucks; [p] Michael & Lisa; [brother] Matthew; [school] High March; [fav sub] Maths & Art; [hobbies] Golf and listening to music; [pets] Cat (Mystophyus); [ambition] To be successful;

THOMAS, HEIDI: [school] St Wenn School; [fav sub] Art; [hobbies] Line Dancing;

THOMPSON, BERTIE: [b] 27/07/92 Truro; [home] Zennor, Cornwall; [p]

Tamsin & Pete; [brothers] Tim & Greg; [school] Nancledra CP; [fav sub] Maths; [hobbies] Surfing & Football; [pets] 2 Dogs, 3 Cats & 2 Fish;

THOMPSON, LEAH TRACY: [b] 09/09/92 Leeds; [home] Keighley, W. Yorks; [p] Nikki & Andrew; [brother] Jake (football mad); [sister] Ella Grace (pets mad); [school] Laycock Primary; [fav sub] Literacy; [hobbies] Drawing pictures; [pets] 2 Guinea Pigs (Sooty & Sweep), 1 Hamster (Roddy the Rodent); [ambition] To become an Artist or Pop Singer;

THOMPSON, MEGAN: [b] 11/01/91 Deal; [home] Deal, Kent; [p] Barbara & Stephen; [brothers] Gary & Mark; [sister] Beth; [school] Sandown CP; [fav sub] History; [hobbies] Cricket, Recorder & Guides; [pets] 1 Cat, 3 Goldfish, 2 Tortoises, 1 Giant African Snail; [ambition] To play for England Ladies Cricket Team;

THOMSON, RACHAEL MEGAN: [b] 30/06/90 Scotland; [home] North Stainley, N. Yorks; [brother] Jack; [school] Ripon Grammar; [fav sub] English; [hobbies] Reading, Writing & Karate; [pets] Dog (Abby); [ambition] To be an Archaeologist or Author;

TILLETT, LEWIS: [b] 12/10/90 Harlow; [home] Epping, Essex; [sister] Alison; [school] Epping Junior; [fav sub] Science; [hobbies] Swimming, Rugby; [pets] Dog & Fish;

TODD, VIKKI: [b] 20/01/89 Hereford; [home] Worcester, Worcs; [p] Jane & Nigel; [school] Bishop Perowne High; [fav sub] Art; [hobbies] Dancing, Athletics & Rounders; [pets] Dog (Spike); [ambition] To be a professional Dancer;

TOMKINSON, EBONY: [b] 26/08/94 Harlow; [home] Harlow, Essex; [p] Pam Hallesy & Ken Tomkinson; [school] William Martin Junior; [fav sub] Creative Writing; [hobbies] Swimming, Writing, Cycling, Performing; [pets] Rabbit (Hunny), Cat (Lucky) & 2 Koi Carp; [ambition] To be an Ice Cream Lady;

TOUGH, GARY: [b] 30/07/86 Aldershot; [home] Ash, Hants; [school] Ash Manor; [fav sub] Music; [hobbies] Drumming & Sport; [ambition] To be a successful Drummer;

TUBBS, HANNAH: [b] 03/07/94 Chelmsford; [home] Galleywood, Essex; [p] Glen & Erica; [brother] Antony; [sister] Lauren; [school] St Michael's CE Junior; [fav sub] Art; [hobbies] Reading;

TUME, REBECCA: [b] 30/03/90 Sidcup; [home] Orpington, Kent; [p] Jo; [sister] Alexandra; [school]

Beaverwood School for Girls; [fav sub] Art, Technology & English; [hobbies] Swimming & Dancing; [pets] Dog (Daisy); [ambition] To have a happy and healthy life;

TWIGG, GARY JOHN: [b] 27/10/89 Crewe; [home] Winsford, Cheshire; [p] Nigel & Christine; [brothers] David & Christopher; [school] Verdin High; [fav sub] Maths; [hobbies] Fishing, Coin collecting & Football; [pets] Yorkshire Terrier (Ben);

UPCOTT, KAY: [b] 12/09/90 Guildford; [home] West Horsley, Surrey; [p] Esme & Dave; [brother] Ian; [school] The Raleigh; [fav sub] English; [hobbies] Drama & Dancing; [pets] Cat (Lucy); [ambition] To be an Actress or a Journalist;

UPTON, KATE: [b] 08/02/90 Bideford; [home] Bideford, Devon; [p] Jan & Mike; [sisters] Amy & Lucy; [school] Bideford College; [fav sub] Music; [hobbies] Trampolining, Music & Friends; [pets] 3 Cats (Scampy, Crystal & Lily; [ambition] To be an Author and Primary School Teacher;

VERNON, ELLIS: [b] 05/12/95 Brighton; [home] Eastbourne, E. Sussex; [p] Mandy & Jeff; [brother] Lloyd; [school] Roselands Infant; [fav sub] Maths; [hobbies] Karate & Football; [pets] Dog (Gizmo); [ambition] To be a Fireman or Policeman;

VERRIER, ELLA: [b] 07/05/90 London; [home] London; [p] Jenny Verrier & David McSpirit; [school] Babington House; [fav sub] Textiles & English; [hobbies] Piano & Motorcycles; [pets] 2 Rats & a Dog; [ambition] To become a Vet;

VICTORY, RACHEL: [b] 24/01/93 Chelmsford; [home] Chelmsford, Essex; [p] Anne-Louise; [brother] Ryan; [school] St Michaels CE Junior; [fav sub] Science; [hobbies] Cycling, Reading & Roller Blading; [pets] Rabbit (Snuffles); [ambition] To become a Vet;

VOTSIKAS, GEORGE: [b] 20/02/93 Whitehaven; [home] Threshfield, N. Yorks; [p] Ann & Dimitris; [brother] Matthew; [sister] Jenny; [school] Threshfield Primary; [fav sub] History; [hobbies] Computers & Watching videos; [pets] 2 Goldfish; [ambition] To be a Palaeontologist or a Pilot;

WALDRON, JULIA M.: [b] 26/03/93 Windsor; [home] Beaconsfield, Bucks; [p] Christopher & Helen; [brother] Ross Deering; [sister] Claire Deering; [school] High March; [fav sub] Art; [hobbies] Violin, Dancing, Drama & Swimming; [pets] 2 Rabbits; [ambition] To be a Vet or a Singer;

WALKER, LOUISE: [b] 26/03/91 Bath; [home] Hilperton, Wilts; [p] Kathi & Paul; [sister] Natasha; [school] Hilperton CE Primary; [fav sub] Art; [hobbies] Trampolining, Dancing & Flute playing; [pets] Ginger Cat (Honey); [ambition] To be a 'Blue Peter' Presenter;

WALLACE-CLARKE: [b] 30/05/94 Reading; [home] Berks; [p] Karen & Colin; [brothers] Lemar & Liam; [school] Micklands Primary; [fav sub] Science; [hobbies] Football & Quad Biking; [ambition] To be a Scientist and Footballer;

WALTER, MELISSA: [b] 25/10/91 Chertsey; [home] Shepperton, Middx; [p] Gillian & James; [brother] Matthew; [sister] Rachel; [school] Springfield; [fav sub] Sport; [hobbies] Swimming & Art; [pets] Hamster (Misty); [ambition] To be an Artist;

WARD, BILLIE: [b] 14/09/90 Enfield; [home] Epping, Essex; [p] Jane & Tony; [sister] Toni-Jayne; [school] Epping Junior; [fav sub] Maths; [hobbies] Dance & Gymnastics; [pets] Cat (Sam); [ambition] To be an Interpreter for B.S.L. (British Sign Language);

WARD, CONOR: [b] 19/06/94 Gerrards Cross; [home] Gerrards Cross, Bucks; [p] Linda & Charlie; [sister] Aishling; [school] Gayhurst; [fav sub] Art; [hobbies] Playing football & basketball; [pets] Dog (Luckie); [ambition] To be a Footballer;

WARD, GEMMA: [b] 24/02/93 Slough; [home] Farnham Common, Bucks; [p] Karen & Keith; [school] Farnham Common Junior; [fav sub] PE & Music; [hobbies] Dancing & Swimming; [pets] 2 Cats, 1 Fish & 1 Bird; [ambition] To be a Writer;

WARD, REBECCA: [b] 08/01/89 Maidstone; [home] Maidstone, Kent; [p] John & Denise; [sister] Philippa; [school] Maidstone Girls Grammar; [fav sub] English; [hobbies] Swimming; [ambition] To be a Hairdresser & Model;

WARDLE, MELISSA: [b] 27/11/89 Winsford; [home] Winsford, Cheshire; [p] Andrew Wardle; [brothers] Michael & James Hine, Robert Wardle; [school] Verdin High; [fav sub] Food, Drama & History; [hobbies] Netball, Rounders & Football; [pets] Dog (Smokey) & Bird (Cocky); [ambition] I would like a career in Business, I would also like to see all of my poems published;

WARNER, KAYLEIGH: [b] 01/11/91 Harlow; [home] Theydon Bois, Essex; [p] John & Jill; [sisters] Nicola & Lisa; [school] Theydon Bois Primary; [fav sub] Art; [hobbies] Netball & Tag Rugby; [pets] Dogs (Scamp & Lucky), Cat (Tiggy), Rabbit (Toffee); [ambition] To become a Vet;

WARREN, JESS: [b] 28/02/90 Chelsfield; [home] Cundall, N. Yorks.; [p] Chris & Blue; [school] Ripon Grammar; [fav sub] English; [hobbies] Drama, Boys & PE; [pets] Dog (Star), Cat (William); [ambition] To be a Marine Biologist;

WATTS, CORINA: [b] 04/06/88 Hammersmith; [home] Grayshott, Surrey; [p] Hazel & Paul; [sister] Kimberley; [school] Bohunt; [fav sub] Food Technology & Drama; [hobbies] Drama & Swimming; [pets] Hamster & Dog; [ambition] To travel the World and to attend Acting School;

WAUGH, HAYLEY: [b] 20/09/91 Guildford; [home] Guildford, Surrey; [p] Jenny & Garry; [brother] Bradley; [sister] Katy; [school] Worplesdon First; [fav sub] English; [hobbies] Reading & Dancing; [pets] Dog (Sonzi); [ambition] To be a Writer;

WEBB, JONATHAN MICHAEL: [b] 13/11/90 Oxford; [home] Abingdon, Oxon; [p] Steven & Gail; [brother] Richard Steven; [school] Dunmore Junior; [fav sub] English; [hobbies] Judo, Reading & Swimming; [pets] Cat (Simba); [ambition] To become a Black Belt in Judo and become an Author;

WEST, MADELEINE LOUISE: [b] 16/08/90 Canterbury; [home] Herne Bay, Kent; [p] Jan & Phil; [sister] Jennifer; [school] Herne Bay High; [fav sub] Art & Music; [hobbies] Football, Guitar & Art; [pets] Hamster (Daisy); [ambition] To be a famous Artist and to be in a Rock & Roll Band;

WEST, SAM: [b] 27/10/92 Birmingham; [home] Wing, Bucks; [p] Paul & Nicola; [brother] Ryan; [sister] Tara; [school] Overstone Combined; [fav sub] Maths; [hobbies] Football, Tennis, Swimming & Reading; [pets] Goldfish; [ambition] To play professional Football and beat my Dad at Tennis;

WHEATLEY, DANIEL: [b] 29/09/92 Norwich; [home] Grove, Oxon; [p] Nicholas & Lisa; [sister] Laura; [school] Millbrook Primary; [fav sub] Maths; [hobbies] Cubs & playing my Drums, Gameboy & Golf; [pets] Dog (Josie); [ambition] To become a Vet;

WHEATLEY, JACK: [b] 19/07/94 Guildford; [home] Farnham, Surrey; [p] Clare & Tim; [sister] Mollie; [school] St Peters CE Primary; [fav sub] Art & History; [hobbies] Judo, Chess & Football; [pets] 2 Cats (Pippin & Peru); [ambition] To be a Stuntman;

WHEELER, NATALIE: [b] 20/10/91 Reading; [home] Tilehurst, Berks; [brothers] Andrew & Thomas; [sister] Lauren; [school] Park Lane Primary;

[fav sub] Art & English; [hobbies] Netball & Writing; [ambition] To become famous;

WHITEFIELD, JACK: [b] 22/05/91 Cornwall; [home] St Ives, Cornwall; [school] Nancledra; [fav sub] Art; [hobbies] Skate Boarding, Surfing & Tennis; [pets] Cat (Marli); [ambition] To become a Chef;

WICKINGS, KATY BETH: [b] 29/09/90 Canterbury; [home] Chestfield, Kent; [p] Linda & John; [brother] Mark; [school] Swalecliffe CP; [fav sub] PE & English; [hobbies] Art, Swimming, Sports; [pets] Hamster (Peanut), Dog (Gem); [ambition] To be a Pop Star;

WILDE, LUCY: [b] 12/10/91 Redditch; [home] Bromsgrove, Worcs; [p] Carol & Greg; [school] Catshill Middle; [fav sub] Maths; [hobbies] Trampolining; [pets] 2 Dogs; [ambition] To become a Vet;

WILKES, CHRIS: [b] 26/09/90 Warrington; [home] King's Lynn, Norfolk; [p] Steve & Louise; [sister] Laura; [school] North Wootton; [fav sub] Science; [hobbies] Computer Games & Playing Guitar; [pets] Dog (Tessa), Hamster (Hex); Cat (Gizmo); ambition] To become a Pilot;

WLIKINSON, DANIELLE ANNE: [b] 16/09/91 Ashington; [home] Blyth, Northumberland; [p] Lisa Cresswell & Paul Edward; [school] Delaval County Middle; [fav sub] Art; [hobbies] Dancing-Tap, Ballet & Modern; [pets] 2 Cats (Comfy & Zowie); ambition] To dance on a big stage and be an Artist;

WILLIAMS, CHRISTOPHER: [b] 30/05/91 Bradford; [home] Bradford, W. Yorks; [sister] Emma Dobson; [school] Westwood Park Primary; [fav sub] Maths; [hobbies] Karate & Playstation; [pets] Cat (Scamp);

WILLIAMS, HARRY: [b] 11/09/91 Truro; [p] Sara & Nick; [sister] Katie; [school] Nancledra; [fav sub] DT & IT; [hobbies] Scouting, Piano & Animals; [pets] Cat, Snake, Crow, Lizard, Guinea Pigs & Newt; [ambition] To be a Herpetologist;

WILLIAMSON, ROBERT: [b] 11/08/93 King's Lynn; [home] King's Lynn, Norfolk; [p] Michele; [sister] Isobella; [school] South Wootton Junior; [fav sub] History; [hobbies] Football & Gymnastics; [pets] Dog (Meg); [ambition] To be a Footballer;

WILSON, PAIGE: [b] 11/10/92 South London; [home] Macclesfield, Cheshire; [p] Cheryl & Kevin; [brother] Austin; [school] Prestbury Primary; [fav sub] Art, Drama, Games, Violin; [hobbies] Acting, Sports, Arts & Crafts, Pets; [pets] Dog (Belle); Guinea Pig (Fudge); [ambition] To be an Actor, Writer or Artist;

WILSON, ROBERT: [b] 15/07/91 Northallerton; [home] Thirsk, N. Yorks; [school] Thirsk Community Primary; [fav sub] Maths; [hobbies] Football; [pets] Dog (Lucy);

WINTER, KATY: [b] 03/01/88 London; [home] Great Gransden, Nr. Cambridge; [p] Liz & Rob; [sister] Lottie; [school] Perse School for Girls; [fav sub] English & Drama; [hobbies] Acting & Music; [pets] American Cocker Spaniels (Fred & Punch); [ambition] To be a Singer;

WISE, SAM: [b] 02/08/90 Canterbury; [home] Herne Bay, Kent; [p] Barbara & Chris; [brother] Michael; [school] Herne Bay High; [fav sub] Music; [hobbies] Skateboarding, Basketball & playing Piano; [pets] Dog (Sweep); [ambition] To be an Actor or Musician;

WOODLEY, EMILY RONNIE: [b] 03/03/95 Hackney [p] Jaqueline & Stephen; [brothers] Eddie & Bradley; [sister] Ellee Belle; [school] Theydon Bois Primary; [fav sub] Art, Writing, Science & English; [hobbies] Dance, Gym & Writing Poems; [pets] Goldfish in garden sink; [ambition] To be an Artist;

WOOTTON, CHLOÉ MICHELLE: [b] 21/07/93 Leeds; [home] Bradford, W. Yorks; [p] Sarah Beaumont & Robert Wootton; [brother] Luke A.; [sister] Jessica L. & Rebekah V.; [school] Wellington Primary; [fav sub] Art; [hobbies] Swimming, Singing, Reading; [pets] 2 Hamsters (Lucky & Patch) & 11 Fish; [ambition] To be a Singer;

WREN, BETH MARIE: [b] 28/10/95 Goodmayes; [home] Theydon Bois, Essex; [p] Brian & Frances; [brother] Jake; [sister] Emma; [school] Theydon Bois Primary; [fav sub] PE; [hobbies] Rainbows; [pets] 2 Dogs and a Rat; [ambition] To be a Pop Star;

WRIGHT, DANIEL: [b] 17/01/92 Bradford; [home] Bradford, W. Yorks; [p] Carole & John (Step dad); [sisters] Gemma Wright & Bethany Adamson Wright; [school] Westwood Park Primary; [fav sub] Maths; [hobbies] Football; [pets] 2 Cats; [ambition] To be a Footballer or a Policeman;

WRIGHT, PAUL LIAM: [b] 22/10/94 Keighley; [home] Bradford, W. Yorks; [p] Deborah & Graham Broadbent (step dad), Tony Wright (dad); [brother] Jason Wright; [school] Westwood Park Primary; [fav sub] Art; [hobbies] Table Tennis; [pets] 3 Cats (Cougar, Snowball & Jigsaw); [ambition] To become a Policeman;

YEOMANS, OLIVIA: [b] 28/07/95 Oxford; [home] Middle Barton, Oxon; [p] David & Jo; [brother] Charlie; [sister] Annabel; [school] Middle Barton Primary; [fav sub] English; [hobbies] Swimming & Riding; [ambition] To be a Teacher;

YOUNG, TONI'ANN ELLEN: [b] 02/11/92 Northallerton; [home] Thirsk, N. Yorks;[p] Sally & Jamie; [brothers] JJ Joshua & Danny; [school] Thirsk Community Primary; [fav sub] English; [hobbies] Reading, Writing & Singing; [pets] Dogs (Gromitt & Cassie); [ambition] To become a Teacher;

INDEX OF POETS

A

Abbott-Garner, Philip 17
Abel, Rory 20
Abel, Samantha 21
Abrams, Ben 23
Acklam, Jade 158
Acock, Dakota 18
Adams, Emily 24
Adams, Jessica 56
Adams, Kate 17
Adams, Katrina 27
Adams, Lucy 27
Adams, Natalie 23
Ager, Teresa 19
Ahern, Harvey 24
Ahmed, Naeem 26
Ainsworth, Philippa 18
Akers, Lauren 18
Akhtar, Mubeen 19
Alberio, Amie 20
Albright, Joshua 38
Alexander, Jay 20
Ali, Shahnaz 25
Alison, Tom 27
Allan, Dominic 15
Allen, Amber 26
Allen, Bryony 25
Allen, Connor 21
Allen, Jeni 25
Allen, Laura 22
Allen, Molly 22
Allison, Hollie 22
Almond, Reese 19
Altaf, Henna 25
Amissah, John 27
Amphlett, Melissa 23
Anders, Thomas 23
Anderson, James 26
Anderson, Jessie 26
Anderson, Luke 19
Anderson, Sarah 24
Andrews, Grace 23
Antell, Elizabeth 19
Antona, Michael 27
Appleton, Sarah 25
Appleyard, Alice 17
Apps, Laura 17
Archer, Aliena 26
Aris, Judd 17
Armento, Katie 23
Armstrong, Robynne 20
Arrow, Peter 26
Ashman, Laura-Jayne 22
Ashton, Graham 24
Ashworth, Luke 25
Askew, Gary 25
Asmat, Ifrah 18
Astill, Richard 18
Atcheler, Rebecca 24
Atkins, Joanne 22
Atkinson, Gabrielle 18

Austin, Jamie 25
Austin, William 26
Avis, Lauren 19
Axon, Victoria 21
Axten, Jessica 21
Ayling, Ross 27

B

Baggaley, Harriet 39
Bagnall, Katharine 44
Bagnall, Roly 39
Bailey, Alex 31
Bailey, Ashley 40
Bainbridge, Maia T. 48
Baker, Amelia 45
Baker, Clarissa 57
Baker, Ellen 44
Baker, Henry 62
Baker, Lauren 48
Balaratnam, Indra 34
Baldwin, Bryony 56
Baldwin, Hannah 48
Baldwin, Katie 51
Bali, Radhika 29
Ball, Elliott 47
Ball, Nicole 49
Ball, Victoria 43
Bamgboye, Yvonne 45
Band, Angela 32
Bannister, Marie 49
Bardsley Hannah 56
Bardsley, Elizabeth 60
Barford, Danielle 38
Barham, Robert 42
Baring, Lauren 45
Barker, Charlie 54
Barker, Jasmine 29
Barker, Melissa 52
Barker, Nate 29
Barker, Rebekah 33
Barlow Griffin, Poppy 41
Barnard, Martin 28
Barnham, Fergus 50
Barnham, Finlay 48
Barral, Heather 55
Barrett, Emma 56
Barrett, Lucy 52
Barron, Henry 49
Barron, Katherine 11
Barton, Aaron 61
Barton, Jessica 42
Barton, Kate 32
Bass, Ryan 28
Bate, Matthew 60
Bates, Ellen 54
Bates, Hannah 53
Bates, Thomas 60
Bates, Victoria 40
Bateson, Alexander 54
Batten, Jennie 38
Batty, Daniel 40

Bawden, Florence 39
Baxendale, Ashley 46
Baxendale, Michael 35
Baxtor, Rebecca 32
Bayfield, Hannah 50
Bayton, William 56
Beagley, Benjamin 59
Bean, Lauren 59
Bearne, Jack 35
Beattie, Robert 46
Beaumont, Daniel 37
Beaumont, James 38
Beaven, Gregory 32
Beavis, Hannah 35
Beazer, Jessica 54
Beckley, Lauren 42
Bedford, Elliot 34
Beech, Katie 57
Begum, Yasmin 33
Beilby, Annabel 49
Bektas, Umut 46
Bell, Vicki-Lea 37
Bellamy, Emma 61
Bellamy, Melissa 29
Belsman, Leoni 53
Bennellick, Mitchell 33
Bennett, Katie 53
Bennett, Lily 29
Bennett, Rose 47
Bennett, Tom 55
Bent, Frankie 35
Bentley, Aaron 51
Bentley, Lee 51
Beresford, Katie 28
Beresford, Rebecca 15
Berney, Harriet 41
Berry, Aron 31
Beswick, Jack 33
Betts, Harry 34
Betts, Kimberley 31
Bhatti, Maria 52
Bhogal, Daysheen 55
Bibi, Juwaria 49
Bibi, Sameena 41
Biggin, Jonathan 50
Bignell, Charlotte 29
Binfield, Georgia 44
Binge, Jack 42
Binnington-Barrett, Victoria .31
Binns, Sarah 54
Birch, Katie 60
Bird, Beth 55
Bird, Laura 48
Bird, Simon 40
Bird, Thomas 34
Bishop, Adam 51
Bishop, Jack 58
Bishop, Rebecca 34
Black, Kerrie 61
Black, Laura 59
Blackford, Alex 57

Blackmoor, Mayumi 61	Budd, Louis 47	Chismon, Bethany 60
Blandamer, James 58	Budd, Mica 60	Choudhry, Saba 82
Blower, George 55	Buisson, Robyn 43	Chown, Rhiannon 73
Blower, Ulia 42	Buller, Imogen 52	Christian, Rochelle 72
Blunt, Anna 13	Bullinger, Edward 55	Christie, Nina 81
Boddy, Sophie 30	Bullock, Chloe 35	Christoforou, Anna 68
Bolding, Josh 56	Bullough, Harry 38	Chui, Zoe 75
Bolt, Jacob 28	Bulpin, James 37	Chung, Samson 81
Bolton, Amy 48	Bunce, Kieran 50	Church, Chantelle 76
Bolton, Jade 60	Buncombe, Katie 35	Ciechanowicz, Heni 62
Bolton, Kate 43	Bunting, Tim 38	Clague, Jordan 66
Bolton, Matthew 45	Burfoot, Dennis 58	Clare, Hannah 67
Boorer, Stephanie 49	Burgess, Emma-Louise 39	Clark, Ashleigh 66
Booth, Rosanna 42	Burke, Chloe 30	Clark, Bethan 76
Boroughs, Tom 50	Burns, Hannah 55	Clark, Charlotte 67
Bose, Kaneesha 50	Burns, Jonathan 28	Clark, Nathaniel 64
Bowden, Laura 47	Burrell, Abigail 39	Clark, Thomas 79
Bowe, Emma 36	Burrows, Tom 61	Clarke, Alice 75
Bowen, Siân 36	Burt, Hollie 48	Clarke, Emily 83
Boweren, Rebecca 46	Burt, Lucy 43	Clarke, Nicholas 76
Bowes, Jemma 60	Burton, Robert 14	Clarke, Robert 81
Bowler, Rosie 59	Busby, Jessica 48	Claxton, Matthew 79
Bowles, Ben 40	Butcher, Jack 57	Clayton, Jake 65
Bowmer, Tiffany 40	Butler, Rebecca 31	Clegg, Melanie 64
Boxall, Georgina 59	Butler, Stephanie 10	Clements, Jamie 54
Boxall, Laura 53	Buttle, Stephanie 41	Clements, Sarah 62
Boxall, Laura 61	Button, Rebecca 57	Clifton, Rachel 80
Boyall, Rachel 58	Bygrave, Mimi 32	Clink, Emily 68
Boyce, Emma 43	Byrne, Sian 41	Cloake, Sam 62
Bradford, Ben 44	Byrom, Chris 37	Close, Luke 77
Bradshaw, Amy 56		Coates, Virginia 65
Bradshaw, Jack 57	**C**	Cockburn, Nicola 71
Bradshaw, Scott 36	Cackett, Becky 74	Cole, Sophie 68
Brady, Melissa 36	Cahill, Natasha 76	Coleman, Jade 78
Brady, Natasha 47	Caley, Lauren 69	Coles, Lawrence 73
Branch, Loui 37	Campbell, Crysta 69	Coles, Lindsay 83
Bransom, Jade 36	Candler, Kimberley 71	Collingwood, Natalie 63
Brazier, Christopher 32	Caney, Mark 70	Collins, Ben 79
Brennan, Ellis 52	Canfor-Dumas, Emily 75	Collins, Robert 70
Brent, Elizabeth 30	Canning, Stephen 77	Collison, Coral 76
Brenton, Lilian 46	Canty, Sophie Louise 75	Collyer, Ellie 69
Brierley, Emily 51	Capewell, Thomas 83	Conium, Mark 78
Brimson, Josh 43	Caporn, Peter 75	Connolly, Charlie 80
Brindle, Ashleigh 52	Carson, Eve 72	Connor, Brandon 84
Britton, Andrew 58	Carter, Ben 76	Connolly, Eoghan 83
Britton, Nicola 55	Carter, Leon 64	Conway, Hannah 64
Brook Kent, Joseph 51	Carter, Scott 82	Cook, Alex 75
Brook, Holly 39	Cartmell, Laura 82	Cook, Alice 70
Brook, Shaun 47	Cartwright, Jordan 64	Cook, Alice 82
Brookes, Anna 49	Carver, Jacob 77	Cook, Amy 81
Brookes, Harry 59	Cass, Andrew 71	Cook, James 70
Brooks, Ben 36	Cattermole, Aaron 72	Cook, Joshua 83
Brooks, Stephanie 51	Cattermole, Robyn 85	Cook, Michael 81
Brough, Joseph 53	Cave, Emma 69	Cooke, Daisy 82
Brough, Louise 33	Cerasale, Hannah 74	Cooke, Lisa 74
Brown, Amy 44	Chadha, Komal 72	Cookson, Amy-Lou 68
Brown, Benjamin 34	Chalstrey, Alexander 68	Coombes, Amber 81
Brown, Emma Louise 45	Chaney-Williams, Matthew 69	Coombs, Gemma 65
Brown, Emma 37	Chapman, Alfie 82	Cooney, Stacey 84
Brown, Matthew 45	Chapman, Ben 65	Cooper, Jade 73
Brown, Sam 56	Charge, Zoe 71	Cooper, Jamie 74
Browning, Fraser 57	Charlton, Chelsie 68	Cooper, Katherine 72
Brundell, Ciara 30	Chave, Elishia 7	Cooper, Samantha 80
Brundle, Harriet 58	Cheasman, Reece 83	Cooper, Saskia 78
Brunning, Emma 51	Cheese, Emelia 72	Coote, Laura 71
Brunsdon, Amy 30	Cheeseman, Alice 73	Corcoran, Matthew 73
Bryant, Claire 53	Cheeseman, Samantha 76	Corfield, Stephanie 78
Bual, Karina 28	Cherrington, Nathan 66	Corley, Joseph 62
Buckingham, Chelsea 59	Chima, Jahy 79	Cornwell, Robert 80
Buckley, Michael 46	Chisholm, Tess 71	Cossey, Dean 82

Costin, Andrew 62	De La Warr, Michael 86	Edmonds, Chelsey 103
Cove, Emma 82	De Maria, Eleanor 94	Edney, Rosie 107
Cove, Nikki 80	de Mora, Stephen 97	Edser, Calum 94
Coveney, Ben 67	De Smet, Emily 92	Edwards, Aaron 104
Coverdale, Daniel 65	Deacon, Sam 95	Edwards, Bronwyn 105
Cowan, Leah 62	Dean, Bethan 92	Edwards, Byron 108
Cowburn, James 67	Dean, John 96	Edwards, Hannah 107
Cox, Millie 69	Dearsly, Harry 90	Edwards, Joseph 106
Cox, Penny 70	Debenham, Annabel 80	Edwards, Megan 97
Cox, Simon 78	Debenham, Charlotte 93	Edwards, Philip 104
Cox, Victoria 85	Deeks, Joe 87	Edwards, Sean 102
Cozens, Joseph 68	Deigan, Louise 101	Edwards, Tegan 103
Cozens, Liam 68	Dela Fuente, Max 85	Eke, Joshua 107
Crabb, Connor 77	Delaine, Abby 98	Eldridge, Grace 105
Crabb, Lana 83	Dempster, Maddy 101	Elkin, James 104
Cradock, Ashley 76	Dennis, Rose 86	Ellard, Stephen 102
Craig, David 63	Denton, Oliver 91	Elliott, Kate 102
Craig, Scott 74	Deol, Kayleigh 87	Elliott, Maximillian 107
Cramer, Robert 70	Desai, Fatima 88	Ellis, Emily 108
Crandon, Georgia 85	Desai, Hava 95	Ellis, Isaac 102
Crawford, Callum 71	Deville, Sam 101	Ellison, Lucy 99
Creasey, Leanne 67	Devonshire, Lauren 97	Elsom, Michael 107
Crees, Cameron 73	Dewey, Lorna J. 95	Emerson, Toby 107
Creese, Laura 61	Dickie, Mark 84	Emery, Craig 100
Cressey, Nick 66	Dickinson, Laura 86	Emery, Liam 98
Crocker, Kerry 81	Dignum, Emily 96	Emery, Luke 103
Crocker, Luke 66	Dikki, Bandi 99	Emmerson, Kerry 107
Croft, Bethany 77	Dishman, Matthew 86	England, Florence 108
Croft, Harry 70	Dive, Amy 89	England, Lauren 99
Cross, Abigail 62	Divito, Hannah 90	English, Tirion 108
Crouch, Toby 81	Dixon, Alex 88	Errington, Sophie 102
Crozier, Victoria 74	Dixon, Jessica 92	Eskriett, Emily 106
Cummings, Callum 67	Dodd, Hannah 94	Essam, Callum 104
Cunningham, Megan 79	Donnelly, Shane 93	Evans, Becky 106
Cupit, Sam 78	Douglas, Margot 89	Evans, Gaby 106
Cureton, Linzi 63	Douglas, Vanessa 85	Evans, Laura 101
Curley, Lois 63	Douglass, Andrew 93	Evans, Philip 105
Currigan, Vicky 63	Dowds, James 95	Evemy, Karina 104
Curtis, Ryan 83	Down, Jessica 86	Everard, Jamie 100
	Downes, Patrick 100	Everard, Lauren 102
D	Downing, Alisha 94	Ewing, Harry 108
D'Averc, Rhiannon 96	Downing, Lisa 98	Exall, Gregg 101
Dallow, Hayley 98	Dowzell, Charlie 93	Eyres, Tom 104
Dance, Rebecca 88	Doyle, Elliot 96	
Daniel, Charlotte 88	Doyle, Maddy 89	**F**
Daniels, Kelly 89	Doyle, Peter 87	Faheem, Mohammed 110
Daniels, Lawrence 100	Drann, Kieran 87	Fairbairn, Abigail, ...109
Danis, Olivia 97	Drew, Suzanne 90	Fairbairn, Edward 117
Darfshan, Mariyha 100	Drewitt, Caroline 84	Fairbrass, Keeley 111
Davidson, Joshua 90	Drewitt, Deborah-Louise 92	Fallaize, Kathryn 111
Davies, Emily 92	Drinkwater, Hannah 91	Farleigh, Bill 116
Davies, Jade, ...99	Driver, Richard 90	Farmer, Jennifer 112
Davies, Jake 85	Drummee, William 94	Farmer, Marie 115
Davies, Lucy 84	Dubois, Charlotte 96	Farnell, Paul 122
Davies, Matthew 95	Duff, Olivia 88	Fawcett, Anastasia 110
Davies, Roan 98	Duggan, Amy 99	Fendt, Louis 120
Davies, Thomas 95	Dunbar, Paul 87	Fenge, Rosy 111
Davies, Tom 98	Duncumb, Jenni 89	Fenn, Natasha 121
Davies, Zak 91	Dungate, Chloe 87	Fenner, Emily 109
Davies, Zak 95	Dunster, Sophie 101	Fenton, Elliot 111
Davis, George 98	Dyer, Jordan 91	Ferguson, Emma 100
Davis, Katie 85	Dyster, Adam 93	Ferguson, James 112
Davis, Megan 94		Ferguson, Tammi 115
Davison, Bryony 90	**E**	Fiaz, Aysha 117
Davison, Graham 86	East, Rachel 108	Fidler, Chloe 114
Dawes, Katie 87	East, Rebecca 108	Fieldhouse, Grace 110
Dawson, Hannah 92	Easy, Miles 105	Finch, Dominic 117
Day, Alicia 97	Eaves, Ashley 103	Fisher, Tom 121
Daymond, Lisa 77	Ebsworth, Luke 107	Fishwick, Nicola 114
de Gruchy, Blythe 99	Edgley, Matthew 103	Fitzpatrick, Philip 117

Fitzsimons, Nicole 121
Flaherty, Kelly 113
Flaherty, Rachelle 119
Flashman, Joanna 117
Fletcher, Emma 115
Fletcher, Jamie 114
Fletcher, Laura 121
Fletcher, Leoni 119
Fletcher, Robyn 113
Fletcher, Steve 116
Flux, Caroline 114
Flynn, James 14
Foden, Jordan 114
Foot, Samantha 110
Forbes, Charlotte 105
Ford, Joanne 111
Forrest, Sadie 120
Foster, Charlie 119
Foster, Chelsea 112
Foster, Christopher 115
Fountain, Zachary 118
Fowler, Charlie 114
Fowler, Christopher 109
Fowler, Kathryn 111
Fowler, Molly 112
Fox, Darren 120
Fox, Tom 119
Foy, Kathrine 118
Francis, Rachel 120
Franklin, Alison 119
Franklin, Emily 118
Franks, Ben 120
Frayne, John 110
Frears-Hogg, Ella 117
Freeman, Alice 110
Freeman, Clare 109
Freestone, Craig 112
French, Ben 115
Frewin, Joe 109
Friend, Amy 118
Friend, Emma 121
Friend, Mark 108
Friend, Oliver 120
Fright, Grace 112
Frith, Rebecca 113
Frost, Jamie 119
Fuentes, Bianca 116
Fulton, Ellen 113
Furnival, Jack 118
Fursse, Matthew 113
Fysh, Danielle 122

G
Gabbott, Caroline 131
Gaitskell, Kezia 116
Gallone, Francesca 130
Gallop, Emily 134
Gambrill, Jade 8
Garbett, Kimberley 137
Garbutt, Victoria 124
Gardener, Grace 127
Gardner, Anna 128
Garfield, James 127
Garner, Alastair 123
Garrett, Lauren 300
Garrod, Matthew 127
Gates, Carley 125
Gathercole, Kirsty 144
Gatley, Ben 125
Gawne, Remy 126

Gee, Chloe 129
Gentry, Lauren 131
George, Riya 135
Georgiou, Nicholas 125
Geraghty, Lauren 134
Gerlach, Taryn 136
Geron, Chelsea 141
Ghouri, Alex 130
Gibbs, Katie 137
Gibson, James 124
Gibson, Rachael 126
Gilbert, Ben 137
Gilbert, Emma 131
Gilbert, Jessica 127
Gilbert, Toby 131
Giles, Harry 134
Giles, Krystina 121
Gill, Rachel 135
Gill, Eleanor 136
Gillespie, Jade 125
Gillham, Harry 123
Gilling, Georgia 121
Glaze, Michael 122
Goddard, George 124
Goddard, Lea 126
Goddard, Leanne 123
Golding, Jasmine 125
Gomez, Abigail 126
Gooch, Eleanor 137
Goodall, Jack 127
Goodall, Philippa 122
Goodrum, Marie 134
Goodwin, Rebekah 122
Goody, George E. 132
Gordon-Head, Harrier 132
Gordon-Stuart, Alexandra 116
Goring, Freddie 129
Goss, Amy 132
Gossage, Ian 124
Goswell, Catherine 129
Goswell, Joshua 122
Gould, Beth 136
Govindasamy, Ayisha 128
Gowrie, Nicholas 126
Gowshall, Ellie 129
Gradwell, Alice 138
Graham, Chris 124
Graham, Samantha 128
Graham, Tom 128
Graham-Coombes, Ellie 123
Grainge, James 123
Granroth, Agnes 123
Gray, Amy 133
Gray, Esme 136
Gray, Farrel 122
Gray, Jamie 134
Gray, Mitchell 136
Gray, Robert 137
Gray, Simone 130
Green, Alex 133
Green, Chloe 137
Green, Hannah 128
Green, James 132
Green, Jason 128
Green, Nicola 130
Green, Rachael 139
Greenfield, Scott 129
Greenwood, Cameron 139
Gregory, Alyx 122
Gregory, Katie 131

Gregory, Lauren 126
Gregory, Liam 133
Gregson, Amberley 130
Gregson, Jenny 135
Grepne, Thomas 116
Griffiths, Francesca 138
Griffiths, Lucy 136
Grimble, Christian 123
Grimshaw, Robert 133
Gripton, Madeleine 133
Grocott, Emma 130
Grout, Rachel 134
Gruitt, Cassie 129
Guess, Thomas 131
Gunn, Sam 124

H
Hackett, Naomi 146
Hacking, Sophie 144
Haden, Laura 138
Haden, Laura 161
Hadfield, Elizabeth 151
Hague, Elizabeth 146
Hailey, Katy 143
Hailwood, Megan 154
Haines, Natalie 156
Hale, Charlotte 142
Hale, Danny 149
Hall, Charlotte 163
Hall, David 158
Hall, Jenny 157
Hall, Matthew 158
Hall, Nathan 143
Hall, Patrick 160
Hall, Stephanie 164
Hall, Stephen 16
Hall, Zoë 143
Halls, Ryan 164
Ham, Charlotte 150
Hamblin, Mollie 160
Hamilton, Andrew 144
Hamilton, Andrew 159
Hamilton, Anna 142
Hammond, Lauren 159
Hampton, Aimee 146
Hancock, Lisa 149
Hancock-Martin, Amy 141
Hanif, Huma 160
Hanratty, Francesca 145
Hansell, Gavin 143
Harden, Sacha 161
Hards, John 155
Hardy, Alistair 164
Hardy, Sara 140
Hargreaves, Melanie 157
Harland, Abigail 149
Harling, Thomas 160
Harlow, Clare 142
Harmsworth, Megan 138
Harrigan, Amy 159
Harris, Stephen 130
Harrison, Faye 140
Harrison, Hayley 154
Harrison, Hollie 140
Harrison, Jed 154
Harrison, Katy 7
Harrison, Laura 158
Harrison, Lisa 147
Hart, Dale 159
Hart, Sebastian 150

Hart, Tom 151	Hosier, Emily 139	Jelbert-Luckman, Ryan 170
Harvey, Carl 151	Hosier, Sam 144	Jelley, Hannah 168
Harvey, Jamie 138	Hosler, Sean 152	Jenkins, Emily 165
Harvey, Sophie 162	Hotson, Hermione 147	Jenkins, Hayley 165
Haskins, Ben 127	Hough, Sara 150	Jenkins, Stephen 173
Hastings, Ellen 144	Houlston, Gemma 153	Jermany, Claire 170
Hawkey, Ellie 147	House, Joshua 153	Jerromes, Chris 169
Hawkins, Chloe 156	Hoyland, Jessica 158	Jessop, Katy 162
Hawkins, Freya 146	Hubbard, Amy 153	Jewell, Alexander 167
Hawkins, Kelly 146	Hudson, Lauren 140	Jewell, Jenny 172
Hawkins, Matthew 162	Huff, Gregory 137	Johnson, Alex 164
Hawkins, Thomas 148	Hughes, Adam 152	Johnson, Anthony 175
Haworth-Galt, Rory 139	Hughes, Dominic 141	Johnson, Maxine 169
Hayes-Watkins, Scott 160	Hughes, Emma 143	Johnston, Charlie 168
Healy, Jordan 156	Hughes, Maddy 161	Johnston, Jamie 176
Heaps, Dean 149	Hughes, Niall 162	Johnston, Rebecca 166
Heath, Arran 135	Hughes, Sacha 146	Joliffe, Sophie 174
Heath, Jim 153	Hughes, Sophie 152	Jolley, Rachel 168
Hedley, Darian 151	Hulin, Rachel 139	Jones, Alec 172
Hellendoorn, Geert 149	Hulse, Charlotte 140	Jones, Chantelle 174
Hemsley, Luke 156	Humphrey, Stephen 11	Jones, Christel 169
Henderson, Lee 142	Humphreys, Allyce 157	Jones, Daniel 166
Henderson, Natasha 144	Humphries, Daniel 137	Jones, Daniel 166
Herbert, Danielle 162	Hunjan, Apria 148	Jones, David 164
Hesmondhalgh, Josh 150	Hunt, Erin 144	Jones, Dominic 164
Hibbert, Aston 154	Hunter, Patrick 163	Jones, Eleanor 175
Hickling, Hettie 147	Hunter, Robert 133	Jones, Emma 171
Hicks, Rhianne 157	Hunter, Sarah 152	Jones, Gareth 166
Higdon, Laurie 138	Hussain, Aneesa 162	Jones, Hannah 169
Hill, Christopher 153	Hussain, Humera 145	Jones, Max 171
Hill, Joanne 154	Hussain, Omera 157	Jones, Pollyanna 173
Hills, Hannah 148	Hussain, Qasim 148	Jones, Robyn 173
Hillyer, Daisy 158	Hutchinson, Shaun 158	Jones-Evans, Oliver 171
Hindle, Mike 142	Huxford, Tarn 141	Jordan, Charlotte 159
Hirst, Amy 154	Huzar, Tim 145	Jordan, Connor 167
Hitchon-Anderson, Jordan 150		Jordan, Hollie 170
Hoare, Emily 148	**I**	Joyce, Chris 173
Hocking, Jessica 16	Ingham, Tara 165	Judd, Jessie 166
Hodgson, Rebecca 13	Insole, Mia 161	Jurcevic, Tihana 171
Hodson, Siobhan 156	Ireland, Gavin 165	
Hogben, Simon 155	Ison, Oliver 165	**K**
Hogg, Aidan 141	Ivens, Natasha 161	Kamali, Dariush 185
Holbourn, Courtney 141	Ives, Juliette 161	Kaur, Manjot 184
Holden, Paris 135		Kausar, Adeel 185
Holder, Victoria 163	**J**	Kausar, Kiran 185
Holding, Lauren 157	Jackson, Ben 170	Keep, Christopher 184
Hole, Samantha 135	Jackson, Byron 176	Kehoe, Emma 182
Holley, Isobel 140	Jackson, Joshua 164	Keighley, Victoria 183
Holliday, Jonny 163	Jackson, Luke 172	Kellett, Edward 182
Hollindrake, Philip 155	Jacques, Maria 172	Kellett, Rudd 178
Hollister, Hayley 165	Jagger, Chloe Philipa 175	Kelly, Ryan 174
Holmes, Carly 130	James, Faye 167	Kemp, Alex 180
Holmes, Georgia-Mae 163	James, Mollie 175	Kemp, Jamie 176
Holmes, Kit 159	James, Thomas 173	Kendal, Kristian 183
Holroyd, Zoë 150	Jan, Aneesah, ...174	Kendall, Lisa 177
Holt, Justin 152	Janes, Emelye 167	Kennedy, George 178
Holt, Lauren 159	Janes, Jessica 167	Kennedy, Louis 179
Holt, Robin 151	Janik, Sophie 167	Kennedy, Mikey 184
Home, Karl 152	Jarman, David 172	Kennerley, Adam 181
Honor, Laura 143	Jarvis, Jaymie 171	Kenny, Emily 174
Hood, Rebecca 153	Jary, Alice 173	Kent, Daniel 176
Hook, Danielle 155	Jasnoch, Stuart 168	Kent, Ellis 175
Hooper, Ashley 142	Jason-Ran, Kia 171	Kent, Reece 172
Hopcutt, Jane 155	Jawad, Nadia 163	Kenyon, Amy 182
Hope, Amy 151	Jeavons, Matthew 169	Kerfoot, Alex 185
Hopkinson, Elizabeth 155	Jefferies, Alice 176	Kerr, Natalie 177
Hopkinson, Theo 148	Jefferies, Alitia 170	Kerry, Jessica 185
Horne, Katie 162	Jeffrey, Laura 166	Ketchen, Emily 179
Horton, Thomas 147	Jeffreys, Kate 168	Khalid, Yasmeen 179
Horwood, Juliette 157	Jeggo, Rowan 168	Khan, Farzana 180

Khan, Hassan 177
Khan, Mehreen 181
Khan, Sadiya 180
Khatoon, Ambia 177
Kidd, Sarina 179
Kidson, Daniel 181
Kiker, Alexander 173
Killner, Oliver 183
Kinchen, James 182
Kinchlea, Roxanne 185
King, Becky 181
King, Lindsey 183
King, Lucy Sarah 180
King, Stefanie 182
King, Thomas 180
Kingman, Johanna 183
Kingsbury, Alex 183
Kingscote, Chloe 175
Kinvig, Corinne 182
Kirbitson, Sam 181
Kirby, Jamie 179
Kirk, Danielle 184
Kirkman, Lewis 178
Kirkwood, Jamie 186
Kirton, Rosie 178
Klette, Laura 181
Knee, Robert 186
Knell, Kristina 177
Knight, Aimée 178
Knight, Claudia 179
Knight, David 184
Knight, Michael 183
Knox, Jonathan 183
Kotopoulos, Tom 176
Koziol, Matthew 175
Kromer, Abigail 184

L

Lacey, Abbie 186
Lacovara, Louis 199
Ladkin, Kate 190
Lake, Darren 190
Lakey, Jamie 197
Lakhani, Anjli 187
Lally, Robert 186
Lambert, Christopher 186
Lambert, Laura 193
Lambert-Hill 187
Lamont, Matthew James 192
Lampshire, Stephanie 196
Lancaster, Lois 188
Lander, Jessica 194
Landon, Sophia 10
Lane, Jessica 197
Langford, Andrew 194
Langford, Sally 13
Langley, Siobhan 197
Latif, Nidha 193
Latimer, Ben 189
Laurance, Joe 188
Lavender, Ben 197
Law, Sophie 193
Law, Tom 189
Lawless, Sam 195
Lawrence, Amy 185
Lawrence, Emma 189
Lawrence, Mark 188
Lawrenson, Jamie 192
Laws, Megan 195
Le Marechal, Poppy 192

Le Masonry, Nicholas 191
Lea, Michael 188
Lea, Tony 185
Lealman, Bethany 196
Leather, Daniel 195
Leather, Hannah 189
Lee, Amy 190
Lee, Josh 194
Lee, Josie 186
Lees, Dan 187
Leighton, Freddie 188
Lekha, Joshua 191
Leman, Billy 186
Levett, Jessica 194
Lewis, Alexis 190
Lewis, Christopher 192
Lewis, Hannah 188
Lewis, Jake 186
Lewis, Ruby 197
Lincoln, Freya 196
Lindeman, Kate 192
Lingley, Hannah 187
Littleboy, Alex 190
Llewellyn, Carly 12
Lockett, Jenna 191
Lockhart, Chelsey Leigh 191
Lockwood, Charlie 193
Lockwood, Matthew 192
Lofthouse, Katie 193
Long, Alistair 192
Long, Emily 197
Longman, Kane 190
Longstaff, Danielle 188
Loomes, Dominic 195
Lord, Matthew 194
Lowman, Emma 191
Lucas, Jenny 196
Lucas, Rebekah 187
Lucas, Stewart 193
Luchford, Robert 195
Luciw, Fern 193
Lunnon, Maria 195
Luty, Kate 187
Lynn, Chris 190
Lytton, Callum 197

M

Machen, Lisa 206
Macis, Gabriella 219
Mackellar, Kirsty 206
Mackey, Marcella 201
Maclean, Shona 218
Macphail, Roma 213
Maddison, Jack 224
Madge, William 200
Mainor, Jessie 208
Makin, Chloe 196
Malaney, Nicola 222
Malcolm, Alice 198
Malcolm, Daniel 201
Malin, Chloe 207
Managan, Emma 214
Mancoo, Jessica 210
Manley, Ben Paul 222
Mann, Huxley 220
Manning, Katie 200
Marcheselli, Franziska 201
Marchment, Craig 224
Marchment, Danielle 197
Margrie, David 219

Marinaro, Ricky 195
Marker, Samuel 205
Marks, Kate 213
Marley, Jenny 203
Marren, Kirsty 210
Marriott, Emma 204
Marriott, Ian 206
Marriott, Kemo 205
Marriott, Lee 211
Marsden, Jessica 220
Marsh, Abigail 216
Marsh, Alison 222
Marsh, Emma 200
Marshall, Kayley 206
Marshall, Natalie 224
Martin, Ernest 201
Martin, James 207
Martin, Noel 203
Martin, Ollie 218
Martinm Kimberley 174
Maryam, Sonia 224
Mason, Jerome 211
Mason, Klein 201
Mason, Thomas 208
Mason-Fayle, Cressida 211
Masters, Janine 205
Mather, Bryony 202
Mathers, Sam 215
Mathewson, Louise 221
Matthews, Conner 211
Matthews, Douglas 218
Matthews, Scott 218
Matthews, Tom 216
Mattimore, Connor 211
Maude, Sarah 204
Maude, Sophie 199
Mawson, Lucy 221
Maxwell, Emma 199
May, Rebecca 214
May, Robert 207
Mayard, Sophie 219
Maynard, Oscar 215
Mayo, Stacey 205
McAuley, Kevin 202
McBeth, Terri 212
McCarthy, Ashleigh 229
McCarthy, Georgia 222
McCarthy, Katie-Anne 215
McCarthy, Sarah 221
McClelland, Robert 212
McDonald-Leslie, Mark 214
McDonnell, Ben 226
McDowall, Kelly 206
McDowall, Ross Ian 207
McElligott, Jade 222
McEntee, Patrick 209
McGinn, Gary 207
McGoff, Rachel 208
McGowan, Molly 204
McIlveen, Katie 219
McIntosh, James 200
McKenna, Duncan 216
McKeown, Rebecca 214
McLaren, Kristofer 213
McLennan-Wiggin, Victoria 213
McLeod, Stacey 203
McMahon, Kayleigh 198
McMahon, Khalid 196
McMillan, Callum 208
McMillan, Jennifer 217

McMillan, Lydia 205
McMurdo, Antony 196
McNamara, Jessica 225
McNichol, Kate 205
Mearing, Daisie 216
Mearing, George 217
Meegan, Natalie 216
Meenaghan, David-Jon 198
Meikle-Braes, Wayd 220
Melhado, Chelsea 133
Melia, Sean 202
Melia-Chamberlain, Steven 196
Melland, Rebecca 202
Mendham, Lisa 224
Merrell, Lauren 203
Mesnard, Joe 202
Metcalfe, Amber 219
Mikkelsen, Ben 220
Miles, Anna 215
Miles, Tommy 217
Millar, Reece 218
Miller, Ashley 217
Miller, Bethany 214
Miller, Chloe 215
Miller, Kathryn 216
Miller, Susan 215
Mills, Ben 199
Mills, Jessica 212
Milner, Luke Thomas 218
Minhinnick, Jamie 200
Mistry, Sian 221
Mitchell, Jordan 214
Mitchell, Josie 218
Moakes, Natasha 204
Mobbs, Esther 194
Mobbs, Joseph 198
Modak, Christopher 224
Moden, Rachel 210
Monk, Hannah 220
Monks, Stephanie 223
Monnier-Hovell, Zoë 202
Montgomery, Ella 204
Moody, Kim 219
Moor, Olivia 209
Moore, Anna 218
Moore, Arthur 222
Moore, Jamie 226
Moore, Louis 198
Moran, Thomas 220
Morgan, Joseph 210
Morgan, Shenton 16
Morgan, Sian 209
Morley, Charlotte 212
Morris, Aaron 222
Morris, Bethan 207
Morris, Timothy 198
Morrish, Maud 211
Morrison, Emily 210
Morriss, Vicky 213
Mortimer, Beth 203
Mortimer, Rose 209
Moseley, Holly 217
Mosely, Sarah 200
Mosscrop, Philip 223
Mossemenear, Meg 225
Mott, Lauren 213
Mountford, Jamie 199
Moyes, Abigail Louise 212
Moyne, Anna 221
Muhairez, Ellie 222

Muir, Kayleigh 204
Muldoon, Daniel 208
Mullett, Rebecca 199
Munnings, Kerry 206
Murphy, Laura 203
Murphy, Luke 208
Murray, Chloe 209
Murray, Frankie 217
Mutch, Kelly 220

N
Nagy, Rachel 229
Najib, Amraiz 230
Najib, Shamraiz 227
Nash, Bethany 229
Nawaz, Zainab 229
Nayyar, Banisha 227
Nea, Carina 232
Neale, Alex 228
Neale, Joss 223
Nelson, Adam 223
Netherwood, Kate 224
New, Alexandra 225
Newbury, Rebecca 227
Newby, Charlotte 221
Newell, Eleanor 230
Newfield, Zara 224
Newland, May 225
Ng, Eric 225
Niazi, Saman 228
Nicholas, Lucy 228
Nicholls, Rebecca 223
Nicolaides, Zoe 9
Nobbs, Emma 230
Nobbs, Lee 228
Noel-Johnson, Alexandra 227
Norley, Martha 229
Norman, Thomas 226
Norris, Jonathan 223
Northcott, Naomi 226
Norton, Paul 227
Nottingham, Emma 227
Nowell, Jak 225
Nutting, Hannah 230

O
O'Brien, Amy 228
O'Brien, Dan 232
O'Brien, George 229
O'Connor, Jo-Anna 231
O'Hara, Jordan 229
O'Keefe, James 231
O'Leary, Rachel 231
O'Shea, Katie 232
O'Shea, Rebecca 232
Obertelli-Leahy, Lauren 230
Odedra, Komal 231
Officer, Dwayne 232
Ogle, Danielle 228
Oliver, Laura 232
Oliver, Philippa 230
Osborn, Peter 232
Osment, David 232
Overland, Jessica 231
Owen, Joshua 232

P
Padfield, Katie 245
Page, Jessica 247
Paige, Samantha 242

Palmer, Hayden 236
Palmer, James 236
Palmer, Victoria 245
Papa, Sophie 236
Pardoe, Megan 236
Parker, Danica 234
Parker, Katie 241
Parker, Megan 238
Parker, Nicola 246
Parkin, Alice 234
Parr, Brendon 246
Parry, Elizabeth 242
Parry, Robyn 239
Parsons, Jamie 237
Parveen, Aalia 242
Patel, Ajay 249
Patel, Krupal 237
Patel, Pryanka 249
Patrick, Adam 245
Patrick, Max 240
Patterson, Samantha 243
Payne, Helen 240
Payne, Thomas 240
Peacock, Kym 242
Pearce, Emma 238
Pearce, Kelly-Marie 234
Pearce, Sam 234
Peck, Zara 237
Pegg, Holly 241
Pegler, Abbie 244
Pemberton, James 236
Penman, Emily-Rose 238
Penn, Alice 241
Penny, Charlotte 243
Perkins, Jay 238
Perrey, Alex 238
Perrin, Harry 244
Peters, Kizzie 243
Petersen, Isobel 236
Petheram, Christopher 232
Peto, Jack 248
Petty, Jake 246
Phelan, Jack 241
Phelippeau, Jimmy 237
Phillips, Catriona 246
Phillips, Jessica 235
Phillips, Laura 244
Phillips, Rebecca 240
Phippen, Harriet 242
Phippen, Jessie 238
Phipps, Georgina 246
Phipps, Yasmin 241
Pickworth, Alice 242
Pitfield, Rosie 244
Pitman, Sean 241
Ploszynski, Arron 243
Ploszynski, Matthew 248
Plumb, Alissa 248
Pockett, Jake 240
Polak, Emma 248
Polding, Alex 249
Pollard, Susie 250
Poole, Charlotte 245
Poole, Ellé 246
Poole, Elliot 246
Poole, Felix 241
Poole, Lawrence 245
Pooley, Makeeta 239
Porter, Rebecca 235
Potton, Katie 249

Poulton, Christopher 239
Poulton, James 240
Powell, David 237
Powell, Gemma 239
Powell, Grace 237
Poznansky, Frederica 245
Preece, Hanna 247
Preece, Lydia 247
Prentice, Laura 247
Preston, Jonathan 235
Price, Emma 248
Price, Rachel 235
Prinsloo, Morne 239
Prior, Ellis 243
Pritchard, Anna 234
Pritchard, Evie 235
Proctor, Jamie 234
Pugh, Edward 244
Pugsley, Kirsten 239
Pye, Hannah 248

Q
Quantrell, Sophie 235
Quinn, Nikola 247

R
Race, Jack 252
Raddy, Hannah 253
Radmore, Tiffany 255
Raine, Siobhan 263
Ralph, Laurence 260
Ramsay, Paige 257
Ramsbotham, Kerry 261
Ramsbottom, Brittany 253
Ramsey, Tara Emily 256
Rank, Thomas 264
Rankin, Rebecca 252
Rathbone, Zach 265
Ratty, Charleigh 260
Raw, Ailsa 248
Raymer-Fleming, George 262
Raza, Lavana 261
Redfearn, Emma 253
Reed, Elliott 255
Reed, Emily 249
Reed, James 261
Reed, Joss 263
Reed, Stephanie 263
Reeves, Carrie Anne 249
Reggler, Katherine 16
Rehman, Nafisa 259
Rendell, Amy 255
Restell-Lewis, Glen 259
Reynolds, Natalie 9
Reynolds, Paul 257
Rhodes, Amy 264
Rich, Clare 258
Richards, Brooke 255
Richards, Chloe 259
Richards, Ellé 252
Richards, Shmeika 256
Richards, Sophie 251
Richardson, Ellyn 245
Richardson, Helen 254
Richardson, Jeannie 262
Richardson, Rosie 250
Richardson, Stacey 258
Riches, Georgina 264
Riley, Elliott 254
Riley, Lauryn 12

Riley, Olivia 260
Riley, Sarah 249
Rimmer, Cassie 258
Rinaldi, Pietro 256
Risk, Hannah 260
Rixson, Daniel 250
Roach, Thomas 259
Roberts, Catherine 257
Roberts, Louise Frances 254
Robertson, Charlotte 251
Robertson, Jane 257
Robinson, Candice 251
Robinson, Eloise 260
Robinson, Leanna 261
Robinson, Lily 259
Robinson, Lucy 261
Robinson, Sam 251
Robinson, Samantha 253
Robinson, Sarah 250
Robinson, Sarah 257
Rodriguez, Michael 264
Roffe, Stanley 262
Rogers, Claire 257
Rogers, Helena 251
Rogers, Samantha 261
Rolph, Hannah 261
Ronnay, Kayleigh 258
Root, Nia 253
Roots, Lawrence 250
Rose, Danielle 263
Rose, Jake 250
Rossetti, Alex 262
Rossetti, Matilda 257
Rough, Jordan 263
Roughsedge, Natalie 251
Rowden, Michael 262
Rowe, Kenny 253
Rowe, Naomi 264
Rowlands, Christopher 252
Rowlands, Luke 260
Rowley, Abigail 253
Royden, Louis 262
Rumbelow, Alice 263
Ruscoe, Emily 251
Rushworth, Matthew 262
Russel, Selina 254
Russell, Harriet 252
Russell, Jonathan 262
Ruston, Jessica 263
Ruthnum, Laura 256
Ruthven, Timothy 258
Rutledge, Harry 258
Ryan, Jack 257
Rylance, Olivia 256
Rylands, Josie 253
Ryle, Emma 250

S
Sampson, Helena 295
Sampson, Jack 291
Sampson, Megan 288
Samways, Lance 293
Sanders, Lucy 271
Sanger, Lucy 293
Sargeant, Danielle 270
Saunders, Becki 289
Savage, William 266
Scannell, Ciaran 294
Scarratt, Adam 286
Schäfer, Eleanore 265

Schoenfeld, Leah 288
Schrire, Harriet 271
Schwalm, Whitney 273
Scotcher, Daniel 265
Scott, Abigail 295
Scott, Chris 270
Scott, Igraine 287
Scott, Leigh 269
Scott, Megan 296
Scragg, Ben 289
Scully, Scott 268
Seabrook, Jade 284
Seaman, Oliver 293
Sear, Tasha 270
Sebley, Lauren 296
Senior, Dominic 283
Severs, Michelle 266
Sewell, Hannah 292
Sewell, Nicola 292
Seymour, Kathryn 288
Shafique, Huma 284
Shafique, Samera 285
Shambrook, Adam 291
Shand, Pierce 268
Shankar, Harry 294
Sharkey, Adam 293
Sharp, Matthew 295
Sharpe, Chlóe 273
Sharpe, Gemma 272
Sharpe, Jessica 285
Sharples, Adrian 288
Sharrad, Hayley 289
Sharrock, Emma 271
Sharrock, Victoria 284
Shaw, Pippa 287
Shelton, Kirsty 270
Sheppard, Hannah 291
Shields, Conor 269
Shillaker, Lydia 273
Shimmen, Rossy 292
Shinnie, James 293
Shires, George 271
Shoaib, Sofia 283
Shoat, Donna 284
Shore, Amy 292
Shortland, Sara 286
Shults, Chris 285
Sigee, Rachael 264
Simikel, Leo 290
Simikel, Rosie 294
Simmonds, Roxanne 267
Simpson, Emma 271
Simpson, James 273
Simpson, Jodie 267
Simpson, Kieron 292
Simpson, Naomi 295
Simpson, Stephanie 271
Sims, David 292
Sims, Jamie 297
Sinclair, Emily 270
Sinclair-Brown, Luci 272
Singh, Hardeep 294
Singh, Tarranveer 294
Sissons, Sophie 284
Skellett, Allan 291
Skelley, Nathan 15
Skinner, Jake 267
Skipper, Mark 291
Slade, Claire 268
Slay, Francesca 280

Smart, Joe	268	
Smart, Mary	275	
Smedley, Daniel	268	
Smiles, Jack	281	
Smith, Alasdair	285	
Smith, Becky	272	
Smith, Bethany	288	
Smith, Bill	295	
Smith, Danny	280	
Smith, Emily	269	
Smith, Gareth	289	
Smith, Harriet	278	
Smith, Jamie	265	
Smith, Jason	265	
Smith, Joanna	280	
Smith, Lauren	275	
Smith, Paul	266	
Smith, Ryan	286	
Smith, Sammi	276	
Smith, Sian	282	
Smith, Susie	286	
Smith, Tara	289	
Smith, Vicky	278	
Snape, Zac	274	
Snowden, Ruth	263	
Snowdon, Daniel	296	
Sowerby, Matt	276	
Sparks, Rory	282	
Speck, Kathryn	289	
Spedding, Catherine	285	
Spence, Catherine	280	
Spence, Chelsea	285	
Spencer, Hannah	280	
Spencer, Jonathan William	283	
Spencer, Phillippa	269	
Spiby, Katy	279	
Spicer, Craig	264	
Spiller, Sarah	288	
Spillman, Tom	283	
Sport, Joel	290	
St. Clair-Burke, Philip	279	
Stacey, Shelley	290	
Stadden, Gemma	273	
Stafford, Carrie-Ann	281	
Stafford, Zach	279	
Stamp, Genevieve	276	
Stancombe, Laurence	282	
Stanford, George	290	
Stanley, Tom	284	
Stanmore, Jake	278	
Stanton, Kiera	283	
Stapleton, Patrick	281	
Stavrou, Dominique	277	
Stedman, Josh	274	
Steed, Emily	267	
Stephens, Jack	273	
Stevens, Jane	274	
Stevens, Joseph	272	
Stevens, Lauren	276	
Stevens, Sam	287	
Stevens-Lock, Jenny	281	
Stevenson, Katie	277	
Stevenson, Oliver	289	
Steward, Amy	267	
Steward, Lucy	280	
Stewart, Grace	276	
Stewart, Lauren	275	
Stewart, Rhys	279	
Stewart-Hanley, Emily	277	
Stickler, Emily	278	
Stobie, Alexandra	287	
Stocker-Wright, Kate	266	
Stolworthy, Nicola	286	
Stone, Luke	278	
Stone, Melodie	277	
Stone, Natalie	274	
Stones, Jade	283	
Storm, Lucy	272	
Storton, Daniel	269	
Strand, Anna	267	
Strange, Leo	287	
Strappelli, Francesca	279	
Streater, Jasmin	278	
Stribley, Ben	277	
Stuart, Lydia	290	
Stubbing, Adam	282	
Sturgeon, Luke	281	
Sturt, Dominic	283	
Subramaniam, Natasha	281	
Such, Ben	274	
Suddes, Sian	289	
Summerfield, Amber	268	
Summers, Hannah	286	
Summers, Tom	270	
Sumnall, Adam	282	
Sutton, Thomas	275	
Swailes, Patrick	295	
Swannick, Jodie	273	
Sweeney, Daniel	276	
Sweeney, Sam	269	
Sweeney, Vicky	279	
Swift, Courtney	282	
Swift, Lydia	275	
Symonds-Tayler, Eleanor	266	
Szmidt, Jordan	290	

T

Tadros, Jessica	309	
Talbot, George	309	
Tanner, Chris	296	
Tarmey, Luke	14	
Tarn, Holly	306	
Taschimowitz, Eva	308	
Tatnell, Kerry	303	
Taub, Ben	307	
Taylor, Anna	306	
Taylor, Dana	299	
Taylor, Daniel	299	
Taylor, David	301	
Taylor, Emily	307	
Taylor, Freya	305	
Taylor, Hannah	298	
Taylor, James	304	
Taylor, Natasha	298	
Taylor, Olivia	310	
Taylor, Robert	303	
Taylor, Sarah	301	
Taylor, Stephen	305	
Taylor, Tristan	295	
Taylor, Yasmin	300	
Teasdale, Simon	310	
Thakar, Roshni	300	
Thatcher, Megan	299	
Thirling, Leanne	295	
Thomas, Alex	304	
Thomas, Charlotte	297	
Thomas, Emily	298	
Thomas, Emily	301	
Thomas, Gemma	303	
Thomas, Hannah	302	

Thomas, Heidi	301	
Thomas, Mitchell	296	
Thomas, Phillip	304	
Thomas, Sophie	303	
Thompson, Bertie	307	
Thompson, Chloe	308	
Thompson, Christina	306	
Thompson, Leah	300	
Thompson, Matthew	306	
Thompson, Megan	302	
Thompson, Naomi	302	
Thompson, Scott	309	
Thomson, Rachael	301	
Thorp, Vicky	296	
Thorpe, Joseph	305	
Tiffen, Jake	306	
Tillett, Lewis	302	
Tindall, Anna	309	
Tindall, Joseph	304	
Tinsley, Alexander	309	
Titmarsh, Alex	310	
Titmarsh, Grace	298	
Todd, Andrew	303	
Todd, Vikki	308	
Toll, Hayley	298	
Tomkinson, Ebony	307	
Tomlin, Melody	304	
Tonna, Kayleigh	309	
Toseland, Rebecca	307	
Tossell, Louise	297	
Tough, Gary	300	
Townsend, Emily	305	
Townsend, Josie	308	
Tregartha, Harry	308	
Tregoning, Jenny	301	
Trenholme, Will	301	
Trueman, Brogan	306	
Trueman, Max	296	
Trumper, James	314	
Truscott, Christopher	297	
Tryon, Sara	299	
Tubbs, Hannah	296	
Tulett, Oliver	298	
Tume, Rebecca	300	
Turnbull, Emanwel Josef	297	
Turner, Amy	302	
Turner, Christopher	310	
Turner, Emily	297	
Turner, Robert	305	
Turrell, Daniel	303	
Twigg, Gary	302	
Tye, Sophie	307	
Tyler, Michael	299	
Tymon, Abby	300	
Tytheridge, Jess	302	
Tyzack, Alastair	309	

U

Upcott, Kay	310	
Upton, Katie	14	

V

Vachaviolos, Dimitris	312	
Vallance, Maria	313	
Vernon, Ellis	313	
Verrall, George	311	
Verrier, Ella	311	
Vickers-Claesens, Catriona	311	
Victory, Rachel	312	
Vigus, Rory	310	

Villa, Charley 313
Villa, Shannon 311
Votsikas, George 313

W

Waldron, Julia 325
Walford, Bianca 328
Walford, Nadia 315
Walker, Andrew 320
Walker, Carrie-Jane 331
Walker, Chirstopher 317
Walker, Jessica 335
Walker, Louise 336
Wallace, Nathan 311
Wallace-Clarke, Duval 320
Waller, Jessica 336
Walsh, Charlie 318
Walsh, Greg 334
Walsh, Rose 335
Walter, Melissa 333
Walton, Elliot 332
Wan, Trudy 327
Ward, Billie Louise 329
Ward, Conor 319
Ward, Gemma A. 312
Ward, Joseph 311
Ward, Joseph 332
Ward, Rebecca 313
Ward, Rebekah 332
Wardle, Melissa 313
Warlow, Adam 324
Warner, Kayleigh 325
Warnes, Carrie 322
Warren, Jess 320
Waters, Ruth 321
Watkin, Luke 329
Watkins, Byron 317
Watson, Matthew 315
Watson, Rebecca 324
Watson, Thomas 332
Watters, Carolina 326
Watts, Corina 316
Watts, Hannah 322
Wauchope, Hannah 317
Waugh, Hayley 312
Webb, Chelsea 334
Webb, Emma 321
Webb, Jonathan 333
Webb, Maddie 333
Webber, Joanna 335
Welham, David 313
Wellings, Calum 331
Wells, Josh 328
Welsh, Danielle 319
Welsh, Jennifer 330

Welthy, Ben 334
West, Madeleine 321
West, Sam 317
Weston, Nicola 331
Weston, Sophie 316
Wetherill, Jack 334
Wheatland, Jack 317
Wheatley, Daniel 314
Wheatley, Jack 332
Wheeler, Gemma 333
Wheeler, Kieron 327
Wheeler, Natalie 333
Wheeler, Rebecca 329
Wheller, Peter 334
Whitaker, Blake 329
Whitbread, Hannah 323
Whitbread, Holly 336
White, Jake 8
White, Kingsley 328
White, Louise 325
White, Zoe 316
Whitefield, Jack 336
Whitehead, Ian 315
Whiteside, Emma 314
Whiting, Matthew 332
Whiting, Nicole 323
Whitmore, Bobbie 322
Whitmore, Ross 314
Whittall, Annabelle 328
Wickings, Katy 322
Wicks, Hanah 319
Wilde, Lucy 332
Wilkes, Chris 326
Wilkinson, Danielle 324
Wilkinson, Nicole 328
Willcocks, Leanne 327
Williams, Abigail 331
Williams, Amy 335
Williams, Christopher 324
Williams, Daniel 329
Williams, Esme 327
Williams, Harry 327
Williams, Jack 336
Williams, Kathryn 327
Williams, Natalie 321
Williams, Rachael 314
Williams, Samantha 318
Williams, Stephen 326
Williams, Tiffany 330
Williamson, James 330
Williamson, Robert 336
Willis, Matthew 333
Willmott, Katie 336
Wilson, Elizabeth 315
Wilson, Gemma 312

Wilson, Kate 318
Wilson, Kerrie-Marie 320
Wilson, Matthew 322
Wilson, Nick 318
Wilson, Nick 320
Wilson, Paige 325
Wilson, Rebecca 323
Wilson, Robert 326
Wilson, Sophie 317
Wilson, Stephanie 312
Winearls, Jake 329
Winestein, Scott 333
Winfield, Rachel 324
Wingate, Danny 332
Wingate, Layla 318
Winstanley, Brittanee 323
Winter, Katy 314
Wise, Sam 324
Witterick, James 333
Wittwer, Siobhan 316
Woodhouse, Jade 316
Woodley, Emily 315
Woodley, Megan 327
Woods, Melissa 331
Woods, Pernille 321
Woodworth, Rosie 12
Wootton, Chloe 323
Wray, Hannah 316
Wren, Beth 320
Wright, Daniel 325
Wright, Danny 323
Wright, David 336
Wright, Elizabeth 319
Wright, Kirsty 15
Wright, Mark 334
Wright, Paul 321
Wright, Sam 328
Wright, Sarah 325
Wright, Sophie 318
Wrightson, David 319
Wringe, Alex 322

Y

Yaseen, Smeeya 335
Yeadon, Paula 330
Yeomans, Olivia 335
Young, April 336
Young, Hannah 330
Young, Melissa 331
Young, Ryan 335
Young, Toniann 335

Z

Zaremba, Tomasz 331
Zhang, Jenny 330

366